Child Development

Early Stages Through Age 12

Seventh Edition

Dr. Celia A. Decker

Professor of Family and
Consumer Sciences, retired

Northwestern State University
of Louisiana

Natchitoches, Louisiana

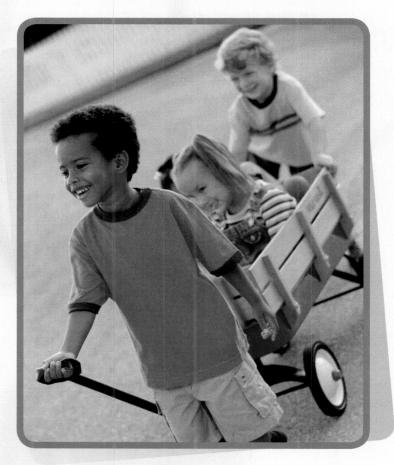

Publisher
The Goodheart-Willcox Company, Inc.
Tinley Park, Illinois
www.g-w.com

The Goodheart-Willcox Company, Inc. Brand Disclaimer: Brand names, company names, and illustrations for products and services included in this text are provided for educational purposes only and do not represent or imply endorsement or recommendation by the author or the publisher.

The Goodheart-Willcox Company, Inc. Safety Notice: The reader is expressly advised to carefully read, understand, and apply all safety precautions and warnings described in this book or that might also be indicated in undertaking the activities and exercises described herein to minimize risk of personal injury or injury to others. Common sense and good judgment should also be exercised and applied to help avoid all potential hazards. The reader should always refer to the appropriate manufacturer's technical information, directions, and recommendations; then proceed with care to follow specific equipment operating instructions. The reader should understand these notices and cautions are not exhaustive.

The publisher makes no warranty or representation whatsoever, either expressed or implied, including but not limited to equipment, procedures, and applications described or referred to herein, their quality, performance, merchantability, or fitness for a particular purpose. The publisher assumes no responsibility for any changes, errors, or omissions in this book. The publisher specifically disclaims any liability whatsoever, including any direct, indirect, incidental, consequential, special, or exemplary damages resulting, in whole or in part, from the reader's use or reliance upon the information, instructions, procedures, warnings, cautions, applications, or other matter contained in this book. The publisher assumes no responsibility for the activities of the reader.

Library of Congress Cataloging-in-Publication Data

Decker, Celia Anita.
  Child development : early stages through age 12 / Celia A. Decker. -- 7th ed.
  p. cm.
  Includes index.
  ISBN 978-1-60525-293-3
  1. Child development. 2. Child psychology. I. Title.
HQ767.9D43 2011
305.231--dc22

                                                    2010001417

Cover Image: Copyright Masterfile Corporation (RF)

Child Development: Early Stages Through Age 12 will help you understand how to work with and care for children as they grow. It explains how children develop physically, intellectually, socially, and emotionally. *Child Development: Early Stages Through Age 12* will also help you apply what you have learned to meet children's needs in the best possible ways.

Children are different from adults. You need to know how children grow and develop in order to work with them effectively. This text begins by explaining the study of children. It helps you understand why studying child development is important—whether you become a parent, work in a child-related field, or just spend time with children.

The text also discusses the choices and preparation involved in becoming a parent.

This text takes you from the prenatal stage through the child's school-age stage of development. The text presents the facts and theories about the child's development. Many examples are provided to help you apply this information when working with children of all ages.

Child Development: Early Stages Through Age 12 helps you explore how family situations affect children. It explores the special needs and concerns of children with special needs. You will also learn about ways to care for children, including play activities, ways to keep children healthy and safe, group programs, and child-related careers.

Welcome to *Child Development:*
Early Stages Through Age 12

This text focuses on understanding and meeting the developmental needs of children from the prenatal period through age 12. Key features include

★ physical, intellectual, and social-emotional development information for each stage

★ practical guidance on meeting children's developmental needs at each stage

★ colorful charts, boxed features, and chapter activities designed to enhance and extend your learning

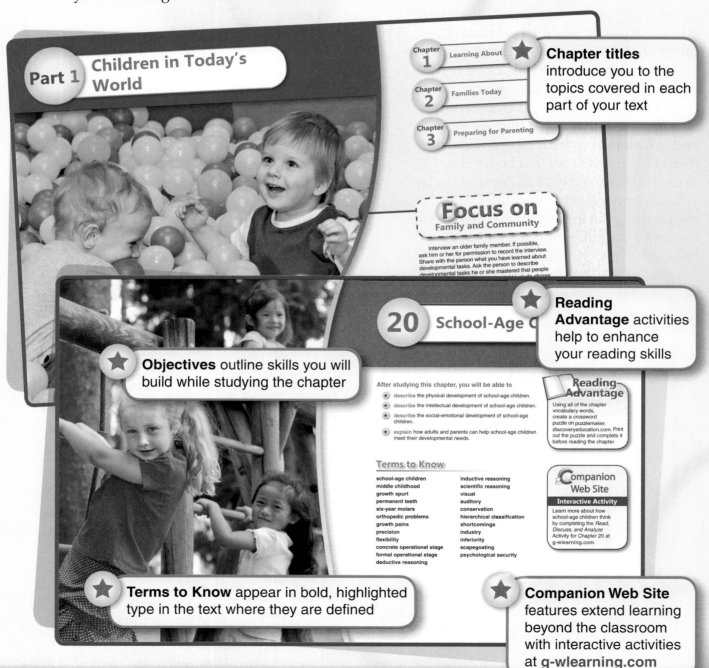

Part 1 Children in Today's World

Chapter **1** Learning About

Chapter **2** Families Today

Chapter **3** Preparing for Parenting

★ **Chapter titles** introduce you to the topics covered in each part of your text

Focus on Family and Community

Interview an older family member. If possible, ask him or her for permission to record the interview. Share with the person what you have learned about developmental tasks. Ask the person to describe developmental tasks he or she mastered that people

20 School-Age C

★ **Objectives** outline skills you will build while studying the chapter

★ **Reading Advantage** activities help to enhance your reading skills

After studying this chapter, you will be able to

★ describe the physical development of school-age children.

★ describe the intellectual development of school-age children.

★ describe the social-emotional development of school-age children.

★ explain how adults and parents can help school-age children meet their developmental needs.

Reading Advantage

Using all of the chapter vocabulary words, create a crossword puzzle on puzzlemaker. discoveryeducation.com. Print out the puzzle and complete it before reading the chapter.

Terms to Know

school-age children	inductive reasoning
middle childhood	scientific reasoning
growth spurt	visual
permanent teeth	auditory
six-year molars	conservation
orthopedic problems	hierarchical classification
growth pains	shortcomings
precision	industry
flexibility	inferiority
concrete operational stage	scapegoating
formal operational stage	psychological security
deductive reasoning	

Companion Web Site

Interactive Activity

Learn more about how school-age children think by completing the *Read, Discuss, and Analyze* Activity for Chapter 20 at g-wlearning.com.

★ **Terms to Know** appear in bold, highlighted type in the text where they are defined

★ **Companion Web Site** features extend learning beyond the classroom with interactive activities at **g-wlearning.com**

Depth Perception

Depth perception is the ability to tell how far away something is. It requires the development of binocular vision. Depth perception is needed for safety purposes. It keeps a person from stepping off an object far from the ground. People also use this skill to judge how far something is so they can reach it. Depth perception is rather well developed by seven to nine months of age. However, children are not safe from falls for many years.

Language: Brain Development Research

Language is closely related to mental development. Brain development research shows language wiring begins at birth,

if not before, 9-8. The first wiring has to do with the sounds of language, for these are needed to understand speech and to speak. The wiring follows this sequence:

★ During the first half-year, babies distinguish small differences in sounds. They are prepared to learn any language.

★ Because there are so many connections, pruning begins at six months of age. Babies come to notice only major differences in sounds in the languages they hear from caring adults. (Brain development research says they ignore language from the radio or television.) Even in adults, the brain detects small differences in sound through context clues; that is, through hearing the entire word or the word used in a phrase. For this reason, spelling words are often pronounced and then used in sentences.

★ By 12 months of age, babies complete the auditory maps needed for their own language. Learning to speak another language without "an accent" becomes much more difficult as the wiring for the sounds of other languages begins to be pruned away.

Not only does wiring for language sounds begin early, between 9 and 12 months, the brain's speech center begins the wiring process.

Language relates to mental growth in other ways, too. As people understand more concepts, their vocabularies tend to grow. A person's **vocabulary** consists of the words he or she understands and uses.

Focus on Science
Object Permanence

Try an object permanence experiment on babies who are four, six, and eight months old. To do the experiment, follow these steps:

★ *Step 1:* Place a toy in front of the baby. Let the baby play with the object.

★ *Step 2:* Take the toy and use a small baby blanket or towel to partly cover the toy.

★ *Step 3:* Take the toy and completely cover it with a blanket or towel.

★ *Step 4:* Take the toy and cover it with a box.

★ *Step 5:* Take the toy, place it in a small box, and place that box in a large box.

At any step, if the baby cannot find the toy, stop the experiment. Note the age of each baby and how many steps he or she could do. Share your findings with the class.

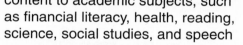

Focus On... relates child development content to academic subjects, such as financial literacy, health, reading, science, social studies, and speech

---

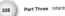

Social-emotional development is an important type of development. It has three main parts. The first part is a person's **disposition** or mood. Some people have a more cheerful disposition, and others are more moody. The second part is learning to interact with people and social groups. These may include family members, schools, and clubs. The third part includes the ways people show feelings through emotions of love, fear, anxiety, and anger.

Emotions are thoughts that lead to feelings and cause changes in the body. For example, if you are upset at someone or something (a thought), you may become angry (a feeling). Your anger may increase your heart rate (change in your body).

Social-emotional development happens as quickly during the first year as physical and intellectual development. A baby enters the world with some unique traits. These traits are the root of the child's later personality. By the end of the first year, personality traits show even more. As a baby's social world expands the infant forms ideas about whether the world is a friendly place. The baby begins to express feelings with different emotions.

Temperamental Differences in Infants

Temperament is the tendency to react in a certain way, such as being cheerful or grumpy. Sometimes the word *disposition* also defines the ways people react. Experts think temperament is partly inherited. They also think a person's temperament may be due to prenatal conditions and ease of birth. These

Learn More About...
Characteristics of a Baby's Temperament

Some experts rate characteristics of a baby's temperament. These ratings place most babies in one of the following three groups:

★ Easy—Easy babies have regular habits, such as eating and sleeping. They respond quickly to a new situation. They are cheerful.

★ Slow to warm up—These babies take more time to adapt to new situations.

★ Difficult—Difficult babies are irregular in their habits. They often withdraw or protest—even scream—when facing new situations.

Researchers found that 4 in 10 babies are easy. One in 10 babies are slow to warm up, and 1 in 10 are difficult. A few babies cannot be grouped because their temperaments vary from day to day.

Easy babies usually get off to a good start with their parents. Difficult babies often have a rough start, which may cause parents to have increased feelings of anxiety. If the parents are stressed, this may cause increased stress in the child. Good, consistent care of difficult babies may make them happier. This supportive care includes extra holding, cuddling, and soothing. Easing these babies into new situations and alerting them to upcoming changes is also helpful.

Learn More About... motivates you to seek further information related to chapter content

---

Preschoolers' Gross-Motor Skill Development

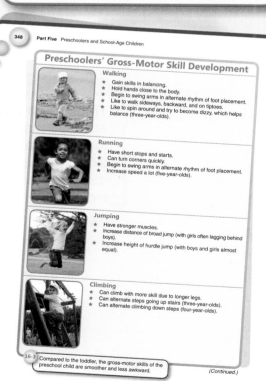

Walking
★ Gain skills in balancing.
★ Hold hands close to the body.
★ Begin to swing arms in alternate rhythm of foot placement.
★ Like to walk sideways, backward, and on tiptoes.
★ Like to spin around and try to become dizzy, which helps balance (three-year-olds).

Running
★ Have short stops and starts.
★ Can turn corners quickly.
★ Begin to swing arms in alternate rhythm of foot placement.
★ Increase speed a lot (five-year-olds).

Jumping
★ Have stronger muscles.
★ Increase distance of broad jump (with girls often lagging behind boys).
★ Increase height of hurdle jump (with boys and girls almost equal).

Climbing
★ Can climb with more skill due to longer legs.
★ Can alternate steps going up stairs (three-year-olds).
★ Can alternate climbing down steps (four-year-olds).

16-3 Compared to the toddler, the gross-motor skills of the preschool child are smoother and less awkward.

(Continued.)

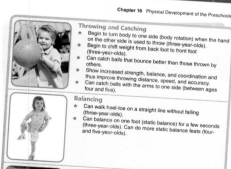

Throwing and Catching
★ Begin to turn body to one side (body rotation) when the hand on the other side is used to throw (three-year-olds).
★ Begin to shift weight from back foot to front foot (three-year-olds).
★ Can catch balls that bounce better than those thrown by others.
★ Show increased strength, balance, and coordination and thus improve throwing distance, speed, and accuracy.
★ Can catch balls with the arms to one side (between ages four and five).

Balancing
★ Can walk heel-toe on a straight line without falling (three-year-olds).
★ Can balance on one foot (static balance) for a few seconds (three-year-olds). Can do more static balance feats (four- and five-year-olds).

Hopping and Skipping
★ Can hop on preferred foot (three-year-olds).
★ Can hop faster and for longer distances (four- and five-year-olds).
★ Can skip (between ages four and six).
★ Can do *rhythmic hopping*—hopping on one foot and then the other without breaking the rhythmic pattern (some five-year-olds).
★ Can do *precision hopping*—following a certain pathway (some five-year-olds).

16-3 (Continued.)

Weight shift is the change of weight from the back foot to the front foot. Body rotation and weight shift may begin during the third year. They become much more refined by the end of the preschool period. These two changes improve a preschooler's throwing distance, speed, and acc

Fine-Motor Development

Preschoolers' ability to **manipulate**, or work with by using the hands, is still awkward. However, as preschoolers

Attractive pictures and charts bring chapter content to life and clarify concepts

Chapter Review

Review and Reflect
helps you recall important chapter information

Making Observations
offers observation activities for use in formal and informal settings

---

Review and Reflect

Write your answers to the following questions on a separate sheet of paper.

1. Most babies add _____ (half, double, triple) their birthweights during the first year.

2. True or false. The rate of growth over the months is more important than the measurement of total growth.

3. True or false. In the first year, the baby gets longer because the legs grow.

4. What are three changes that occur in the bones during development?

5. True or false. *Motor development* is the way children learn how to play with others and share their toys.

6. True or false. There is a pattern to children's physical development.

7. True or false. Infants learn in the same sequence, but the rate varies.

8. List the following motor skills in order of occurrence: sits without support with back straight; raises the head while on abdomen; creeps; walks; rolls over from front to back; stands without help; picks up object with thumb used in opposition to finger.

9. Reflexes are _____ (learned, unlearned).

10. Voluntary movements are _____ (learned, unlearned).

Cross-Curricular Link

11. **Math.** Interview at least six parents of young children. Ask each parent what the baby's weight and height were at birth, six months, and one year. Record these figures in a master list. Showing your work, figure the average weight and height for this group of babies at each age.

12. **Science, Writing.** As a group or class project, write a one- or two-page brochure that explains at what ages parents can expect their children to learn certain motor skills. You may also find pictures or drawings to illustrate the various skills. The brochure could be checked by a physician before making copies. Find out whether copies could be given to new parents at the hospital, posted in medical offices, or printed in a local newspaper.

13. **Speech.** Find a quality infant toy that would encourage an infant to develop gross- and fine-motor skills. Make an oral presentation to the class showing how your selected toy promotes both types of skills.

14. **Technology.** Work with a partner to visit a Web site designed for parents. Search for information that would help the parents of infants understand their child's physical development in the first year. Based on what you have learned in the chapter, does the advice seem sound to you? Why or why not? Create an electronic presentation of your findings. Adhere to all copyright laws and cite any sources you may use for the presentation. Share your presentations with the class.

Making Observations

15. Observe a doctor giving a well-baby exam. Ask the doctor to explain each procedure. Note weight and length as well as head and chest measurements. Also note heart and breathing rates and reflexive and voluntary movement. How does the baby's progress compare to age norms? What progress has the baby made since the last checkup?

16. Visit a child care program that serves infants of various ages. Choose four or five babies who represent different ages. Watch the babies closely and record your observations. Compare the babies' abilities to sit, move about, and grasp objects.

17. Observe two infants who are the same age. How do they differ in their physical maturity? How do they differ in their motor skills? Does one infant have a lag in maturity or skills? If so, did the parent say anything that explains the lag, such as low birthweight or serious illness?

18. Observe how several babies move toward a toy. Describe exactly how each baby moves toward the toy. (Often babies use more than one motor skill to reach a toy.)

Thinking Critically

19. Some people believe babies should be fat. Why do some people have this perception? Can such a perception lead to problems?

20. Parents sometimes push their babies to walk early. Can this be harmful to babies? Why or why not?

21. As you read, the grasping reflex is not highly developed until almost one year of age. Does this mean parents can assume their baby is not able to grasp small objects on the floor and insert them into his or her mouth, nose, or ears? Why or why not?

Cross-Curricular Link
activities strengthen academic skills in core areas, such as history, math, science, social studies, reading, and speech

Thinking Critically
activities challenge you to use critical-thinking skills in group discussion and individual reflection

Appendices

Appendix A

Developmental Milestones Q and A

Q: Will the developmental milestones listed and the ages given vary somewhat from source to source?

A: Yes. Authors list milestones to fit the content of their writing. Ages differ even for the same milestones because researchers interpret the milestones differently. (For example, *walking* may be taking a couple of unsure steps or toddling across a room.) Depending on the researcher, the age norms may be based on the age in which 50%, 67%, or 75% of children reach the milestone; this makes for reported differences in the typical age. Thus, *developmental milestones are only a general idea of the timing of certain changes.*

Q: Do developmental milestones "fit" premature babies?

A: They do fit if you adjust the baby's age to his or her due date. For example, if a baby is born two months early, the baby will likely achieve milestones two months later during the first two years.

Q: When are developmental milestones the most precise?

A: These charts are rough guidelines for the first year and even less precise in the following years due to differences in children's environments.

Q: Do developmental milestones remain the same from generation to generation?

A: Some milestones have remained somewhat the same for many years. However, the environment can cause changes. For example, putting babies to sleep on their backs (a SIDS

preventive) has caused babies to roll over about a month later than when tummy sleeping was common. Also, due to more learning materials (games, books, media) and preschool programs, many more young children are learning colors, letters, and numbers before the kindergarten year than in the past.

Q: Is the accomplishment of the milestone or the age the most important to development?

A: The accomplishment of the milestone, regardless of age, is by far the most important factor. For example, think about this question: Among your friends can you tell who walked earlier and who walked later as a baby?

Q: Why are ages given?

A: Ages help parents discuss any possible delays with their child's doctor. Doctors usually watch a child for a few weeks or months before drawing a conclusion. If a doctor notes *significant delays*, he or she may refer the child to a specialist for further testing.

Q: If the child is ahead of the norms, does it mean he or she is gifted?

A: A gifted child continues to accelerate over the course of several years. Many children with more average intelligence learn some skills early due to an early exposure to that skill. With the exception of children who are profoundly gifted, giftedness is not usually confirmed until age nine or even later.

Q: Will the child maintain the same pace of development; that is continue to be slow, average, or above average in reaching each milestone?

A: Because development in one area reinforces and enhances develop-

in other areas, children do not maintain a steady pace in reaching milestones. Development is a journey without a cruise control.

Q: Is regression in skills a cause for concern?

A: Some brief regressions are due to an illness or to a change in the child's environment, such as a move, a change

in child care and education programs, or even a change in family make-up (a new baby, a divorce, death). Regression that continues, worsens, or spreads to several developmental areas may be a symptom of a serious developmental problem. *Parents should always discuss developmental regression with their child's doctor.*

Developmental Milestones of Children Through Age 12

Newborn Milestones	
Physical	
1 Month	Has reflexive movements.
	Startles easily (Moro reflex).
	Roots for breast.
	Stares at objects, but does not try to grasp.
	Attempts to lift head when on tummy.
2 Months	Has more voluntary actions.
	Cycles arms and legs.
	Holds head up when on stomach at 45-degree above surface.
	Uses a reflexive grasp. Holds objects placed in hands for a few seconds.
3 Months	Leans on elbows and holds chest up and head erect for 10 seconds.
	Moves arm and leg on each side of the body in unison.
	Holds hands open.
	May swipe at dangling objects.
	Explores face with hands.
4 Months	Rolls from stomach to side.
	Holds head steady for a short time.
	Turns head in all directions.
	Splashes and kicks in bath.
	Sits with support of cushions for a short time.
	Touches objects close to hand and may bat objects.
	Pulls objects placed in hand toward mouth.

Appendix A: Developmental Milestones highlights the physical, intellectual, and social-emotional developmental milestones for children through age 12

Appendix B

Recommended Childhood Immunizations

Recommended Immunization Schedule for Ages 0 Through 6
—United States • 2009
For those who fall behind or start late, see the catch-up schedule

Vaccine ▼ Age ►	Birth	1 month	2 months	4 months	6 months	12 months	15 months	18 months	19–23 months	2–3 Years	4–6 Years
Hepatitis B	HepB	HepB			HepB						
Rotavirus			RV	RV	RV						
Diphtheria, Tetanus, Pertussis¹			DTaP	DTaP	DTaP		DTaP				DTaP
Haemophilus influenzae type b			Hib	Hib	Hib	Hib					
Pneumococcal			PCV	PCV	PCV	PCV				PPSV	
Inactivated Poliovirus			IPV	IPV		IPV					IPV
Influenza						Influenza (Yearly)					
Measles, Mumps, Rubella						MMR					MMR
Varicella²						Varicella					Varicella
Hepatitis A						HepA (2 doses)				HepA Series	
Meningococcal										MCV	

▮ Range of recommended ages   ▮ Certain high-risk groups

1. Pertussis — whooping cough
2. Varicella — chicken pox
3. Human Papillomavirus — virus that can cause cervical cancer and genital warts (STD); vaccination given to females.

Note: Recommendations are reviewed and updated regularly. Check for updates at the American Academy of Pediatrics (http://www.aap.org).

Appendix B: Recommended Childhood Immunizations provides U.S. immunization schedules for children through age 18

Appendix C

Indoor Dangers

Environment

Carbon monoxide (A colorless, odorless toxic gas.)

Possible causes
★ Wood-burning, coal, gas, kerosene, and propane heating devices emit more carbon monoxide than electric heating.
★ Homes with attached garages are at higher risk because vehicles emit carbon monoxide as waste.
★ Cooking on a barbeque grill nearby the house increases risk because carbon monoxide is released in the smoke.

Childproofing measures
★ Maintain fireplaces and heating system.
★ Keep home well ventilated.
★ Keep grill farther from the home. Close doors and windows when using the grill.
★ Install a carbon monoxide detector on each floor in the home. Replace or repair as needed.
★ Learn the warning signs of carbon monoxide poisoning. Seek help at once if these are noted.

Fire

Possible causes
★ Problems with household wiring, electrical appliances, chimney fires, and space heaters are main causes of fires.
★ Accidents with matches, lighters, cigarettes, and candles often lead to fires.
★ Cooking accidents can cause fires.

Childproofing measures
★ Install smoke detectors in every bedroom and near the kitchen. Check monthly and install new batteries twice yearly.
★ Have working fire extinguishers near kitchen and fireplaces.
★ Keep matches, lighters, cigarettes, and candles out of the reach of children.
★ Do *not* leave lit candles or food cooking on the stovetop unattended.
★ Plan escape routes from various rooms of the house. Teach fire safety and escape routes to even very young children.

Lead paint (Used in buildings built before 1978.)

Possible cause
★ Lead poisoning comes from breathing lead dust or fumes or eating paint chips. (Lead causes brain damage.)

Appendix C: Indoor Dangers identifies safety concerns and suggests childproofing measures

Exploring Careers

Child Development: Early Stages Through Age 12 challenges you to plan for the future—and provides the information you need to make sound career decisions.

Chapter 26, *Making Career Decisions*, explains how to develop a career plan based on your interests, aptitudes, and abilities. You will learn about exploring careers through the career clusters—16 general groupings of occupational and career areas. The chapter also includes how to develop a résumé and prepare for successful job interviews. You will also identify skills needed for working in child-related fields and achieving career success.

Career clusters icons throughout the text identify child-related occupations. Each chapter features one occupation and highlights the typical job duties, education needed, and job outlook.

Human Services

Adoption Coordinator

Adoption coordinators facilitate the placement of children for adoption. They conduct home studies and monitor children throughout the adoption process. They must also possess a working knowledge of state laws as they relate to adoption.

Education: A bachelor's or master's degree in the human services field.

Job Outlook: Employment for social workers is expected to grow much faster than the average for all occupations.

What adults say and how they act affect babies' fears. Adults who act or look fearful in a storm, for example, will cause children to be fearful. Adults who tell babies that many situations can hurt them teach children to fear. Of course,

some fear is good. However, too much fear is not healthy. Fear affects motor and mental development because fearful babies often will not welcome new experiences.

Anxiety

Anxiety is fear of a possible future event. Sometimes the words *worry* and *concern* are used to describe anxiety.

The first anxiety of an infant is called **separation anxiety**, 10-5. This anxiety, or fear that loved ones who leave them will not return, is seen around eight months of age. The anxiety peaks between 10 and 18 months, and then fades a great deal by two years. What causes these changes? It is due to changes in mental abilities.

Very young babies have not yet become attached to certain people. They do not realize caregivers are

10-5 Older babies may find it hard to separate from their parents, even at bedtime.

26 Making Career Decisions

After studying this chapter, you will be able to

- ★ identify steps in self-assessment.
- ★ explain how to research careers and develop a career plan.
- ★ describe how to find a job.
- ★ describe careers in child-related fields.
- ★ explain how personal and professional qualifications affect your career choice.
- ★ identify skills needed for job success.

Terms to Know

lifestyle
self-assessment
values
aptitudes
abilities
career clusters
personal plan of study
career plan
goals
resources
networking
résumé
cover letter
references

portfolio
direct intervention
consultants
licensing personnel
entrepreneur
personal qualifications
career burnout
leader
professional qualifications
work ethic
codes of professional ethics
formal leadership
informal leaders

Reading Advantage

As you read the chapter, write a letter to yourself. Imagine that you will receive this letter in a few years when you are working at your future job. What would you like to remember from this chapter? In the letter, list key points from the chapter that will be useful in your future career.

Companion Web Site

Interactive Activity

Learn more about preparing for a career by completing the *Read, Discuss, and Analyze* Activity for Chapter 26 at g-wlearning.com.

629

FCCLA Activities

Family, Career, and Community Leaders of America (FCCLA) is a student organization that promotes personal growth and leadership development through family and consumer sciences education. As the only in-school student organization with the family as its focus, FCCLA is an ideal companion to *Child Development: Early Stages Through Age 12* and other courses in your school's family and consumer sciences program.

Involvement in FCCLA offers the opportunity to

★ participate in activities and events at local, state, and national levels

★ develop leadership and teamwork skills

★ help others through community service projects

★ prepare for future roles in your family, career, and community

Child Development: Early Stages Through Age 12 features *Focus On: Family and Community* activities at the beginning of each part. These hands-on FCCLA projects help students

★ apply academic and communication skills

★ strengthen interpersonal relationships

★ develop leadership and problem-solving skills

★ recognize the value of good health

★ establish positive work-related attitudes and habits

Many of the *Focus On: Family and Community* activities suggest ways to expand the projects for competitive events. For additional information about FCCLA, visit **www.fcclainc.org**.

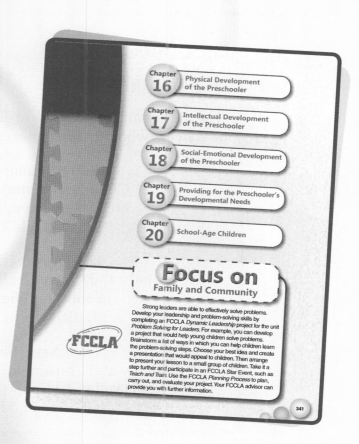

About the Author

After a 38-year career in education, Celia A. Decker retired as a professor in the Department of Family and Consumer Sciences at Northwestern State University of Louisiana. She taught courses in early childhood education, child development, and family relations. Dr. Decker was coordinator of graduate studies in early childhood education. Before her position at Northwestern State University, she taught college courses at East Texas State University (now Texas A&M at Commerce) and at the University of Arkansas at Fayetteville. Dr. Decker also taught public school kindergarten in Kansas City, Kansas.

In addition to writing this text, Dr. Decker coauthors *Parents and Their Children* with Verdene Ryder. Dr. Decker has also published other books, numerous chapters in books, and articles. She presents papers at national and state annual meetings of professional associations, such as the National Association for the Education of Young Children, Southern Early Childhood Association, Association for Childhood Education International, National Association of Early Childhood Teacher Educators, and the Society for Research in Child Development. She does extensive consultant work for Head Start, Even Start, and local school systems.

During her years of teaching, Dr. Decker was named to Who's Who in Child Development Professionals, Who's Who in Personalities of the South, Who's Who in American Women, and the World's Who's Who in Education. In 1994, she was selected as the Outstanding Professor at Northwestern State University.

Reviewers

The author and publisher are grateful to the following reviewers who provided valuable input to this edition.

Judith Solomon-Marks
Child Development Instructor
North Valley Occupational Center
Mission Hills, California

Denise Musick, CFCS
Family and Consumer Sciences Instructor
Southport High School
Indianapolis, Indiana

Amie Shea
Family and Consumer Sciences Instructor
Hazelwood Central High School
Florissant, Missouri

Contents in Brief

Contents

Features

Focus on...

Learn More About...

Featured Careers

Part 1 Children in Today's World

Chapter 1 Learning About Children

Chapter 2 Families Today

Chapter 3 Preparing for Parenting

Focus on
Family and Community

Interview an older family member. If possible, ask him or her for permission to record the interview. Share with the person what you have learned about developmental tasks. Ask the person to describe developmental tasks he or she mastered that people seldom master today. Examples might include chores, hobbies, games, and job duties of the past. Create a family history book by adding photos to written stories and memories. Take it a step further and develop an FCCLA *Power of One* project for *Family Ties*. Use the FCCLA *Planning Process* to plan, carry out, and evaluate your project. Your FCCLA advisor can provide you with further information.

FCCLA
Family, Career and Community
Leaders of America

1 Learning About Children

After studying this chapter, you will be able to

★ **list** reasons for learning about children.

★ **define** the term child development.

★ **summarize** the six stages of the individual life cycle that involve children.

★ **describe** three factors that promote growth and development.

★ **explain** how brain development occurs.

★ **identify** differences in the rate of growth and development.

★ **explain** and **give examples** of some major principles and theories of growth and development.

★ **develop** observation skills.

Terms to Know

child-centered society
socialize
culture
character
development
child development
individual life cycle
heredity
environment
genes
genetics
neurons
wiring
axons

dendrites
synapse
pruning
window of opportunity
plasticity
developmental acceleration
developmental delay
principles of growth and development
sequenced steps
teachable moment
developmental tasks
direct observation
indirect observation

Reading Advantage

Before you read the chapter, read all of the chart and photo captions. What do you know about the material covered in this chapter just from reading the captions?

Companion Web Site

Interactive Activity

Learn more about factors that influence children's growth and development by completing the *Read, Discuss, and Analyze* Activity for Chapter 1 at **g-wlearning.com**.

Child development is one of the most fascinating subjects you can study. Children are constantly changing and discovering. They are also curious and creative. Who else would use a cardboard box for a house, a car, or a hiding place? If you spend any time with children, you know they can be lovable and challenging.

How will studying children help you? You may be interested in a career in which you care for children. One of your future goals may be to become a parent. Learning about children will help you better understand them as well as yourself. As you learn, you will see that children go through many stages of growth and development. This book emphasizes the early years because these years are the most important in shaping children's lives.

Studying children will also help you learn positive ways to care for them. People like to think they live in a **child-centered society**—a society that sees children as important, cares about their well-being, and works to meet their needs. However, some children also experience a great deal of harm through abuse and neglect. Children need safe environments. They need homes, schools, and other places where they can develop to their full potential, 1-1. All children should have the chance to grow in an environment that will promote their health and well-being. By studying children, you will learn how to provide these safe places.

1-1 Activities that are fun and challenging encourage intellectual and social development.

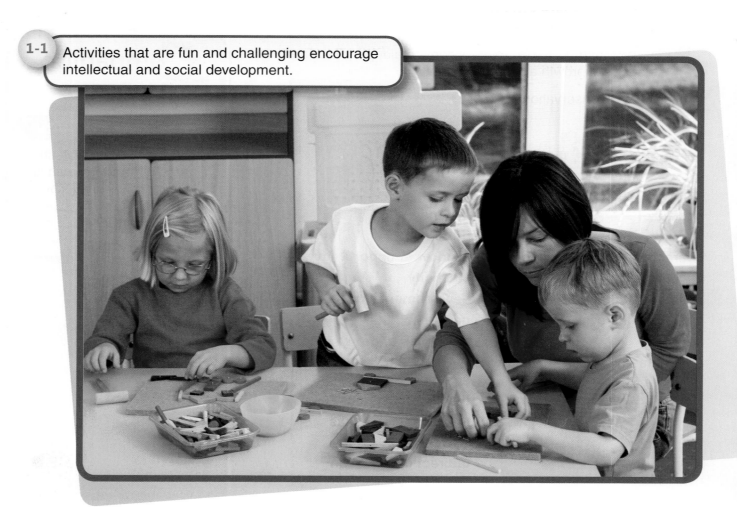

Why Study Children?

Knowing how to meet children's needs is not easy. Before studying how adults can help children develop and learn, you must understand why you should study children.

To Understand Yourself

Studying how children grow and develop can help you grow, too. It can help you appreciate all that goes into taking a first step or saying a first word. When you help a child overcome a fear or learn a skill, you feel good. Adults often enjoy just being with children. Their awe of beauty, their frankness, and their world of magic please adults.

Children can share gifts that, sadly, adults often outgrow. Many times, adults are not fully aware that who they are today is a result of the children they once were. As you study children, you can gain insight into your own growth, development, and values. You can also understand how your values affect your feelings about, and reactions to, children. This knowledge can then help you learn better ways in which to care for children.

To Be a Responsible Parent

By studying children, parents know their children's needs at each stage of development. They also know the best ways to respond to those needs. Parenting is a mind-boggling task. How much adults know about children, however, can determine the kind of parents they become. Studying children also helps parents have realistic expectations about their parenting abilities. Parents must be responsible for meeting all their children's needs, which include the following:

★ **physical needs.** Children need the right diet to nourish their growing, active bodies. They need clothes that are well-fitting. Children need shelter and physical protection, 1-2. They also need proper health and medical care. Parents must provide for these needs.

★ **intellectual needs.** Parents need to provide good learning experiences for their children. Positive learning experiences can motivate children and help them develop the necessary skills they need to become independent adults. Parents must also meet children's creative needs.

1-2 Infants and young children have many safety needs.

★ **social needs.** Learning to form relationships is a key social need. Children need to form strong relationships with their parents. These relationships can help children feel secure and teach them how to respond and relate to other people. Children also need a sense of belonging. To build this sense, parents must **socialize** their children, or train them to live as part of the group. Parents

must teach children about their **culture**, or way of life within the group. Each culture may have its own language, beliefs, attitudes, values, rituals, and skills. Parents help children learn what the culture expects of its members. (You will learn more about the role of culture in families by reading Chapter 2.)

★ **trust needs.** Children need to feel they can cope with demands of family, friends, and society. Being able to trust their parents helps children gain confidence. Trust begins early in life when parents meet their needs. Trust grows as parents allow children the freedom to develop.

★ **love/guidance needs.** Children need love and support from their parents. In loving children, parents must listen to their children, set limits, and share their reasons for limits, 1-3. As a part of guidance,

Focus on Reading
Culture

Read all or some of the chapters from Laura Ingalls Wilder's books *Little House in the Big Woods* and *Farmer Boy*. Share with your class examples of how the parents socialized their children. What skills, customs, and values did the parents hand down to the children in the stories? How are these teachings different from what your parents have passed down to you about your culture?

1-3 Setting limits is part of loving and disciplining children.

Learn More About...
Children's Rights

Children are easily hurt because they are physically weaker than adults and cannot reason as adults. Society must protect them. By learning about children, lawmakers can pass laws that will keep children safe.

The Convention on the Rights of the Child (United Nations International Children's Education Fund) wrote 54 articles that set out the rights of every child in the world. These rights can be given under 11 major categories. The following categories explain children's rights to:

★ **an identity** (government should protect children's names, family ties, and nationalities)

★ **a family** (children should be able to live with their parents unless this is not in the children's best interest; parents have the responsibility for raising children with government support)

★ **express themselves and have access to information** (children have the right to: express their views; have freedom of thought, conscience, and religion; and obtain information)

★ **a safe and healthy life** (children have the right to life; the government should do all it can to make sure children survive and develop; children should have access to medical services and a decent standard of living)

★ **special protection in times of war** (children who are refugees are entitled to special protection; children who are under 15 should not take part in armed conflict)

★ **an education** (primary education should be free and required of all children; secondary education should be accessible to all children)

★ **special care for the disabled** (children with disabilities have the right to special care, education, and training)

★ **protection from discrimination** (all rights apply to all children; children have the right to practice their own cultures, religions, and languages)

★ **protection from abuse** (children shall be protected against abuse and neglect; government shall be involved with laws and programs concerned with abuse)

★ **protection from harmful work** (children have the right to rest, leisure, play, and participation in cultural and artistic activities; children have the right to be protected from having to participate in work that threatens their health, education, and development)

★ **special treatment if arrested** (children are entitled to assistance and treatment that respect their rights)

parents help their children develop character. **Character** is the principles and beliefs that guide one's conduct and define one's personality and behavior. Through love and guidance, parents help their children grow into self-directed adults.

To Protect Children's Rights

In the United States, parents have the rights of guardianship and determine their children's upbringing. For example, they control the children's level of financial support. They also control religious and moral teachings, as well as education and health care choices. The state can come between a parent and child only if the court feels the child needs more protection. For example, the state may require foster care.

Each state can make laws and policies to protect children. For example, laws exist regarding school attendance, child labor, and illegal drug sales to help protect children and society. State laws protect children from the results of their own lack of judgment. For example, young children are not responsible legally for their contracts. Children are treated differently in court than adults. The state can make laws to develop child welfare services. For instance, a state office monitors the quality of child care programs.

Children have gained rights, too. Examples are the rights of due process and fair treatment in schools and juvenile and family courts. In some states, children may receive medical help without parental consent.

Laws can be enacted on the local level, too. An example is a curfew law. In addition, local citizen groups often become *advocates* (people who actively support a cause) of children's rights. These groups attempt to get needed laws passed and notify the appropriate people when it seems a child's rights have been violated.

To Work with Children

In the past, people thought all the knowledge and skills that adults need for child-related careers—including parenting— came naturally. Many felt just being raised in a family teaches adults all they need to know about children and child care skills.

Today, experts know that understanding children requires careful study. Changes continue to take place in society and in families. These changes require people to know more about children's growth and development than what they observe in their own families.

Adults with child-related careers should study children. Some careers focus on only one area of children's needs. For example, a school cook is concerned with children's nutritional needs, while a teacher may focus more on intellectual needs. However, the child is a whole person. Anyone preparing for a child-related career should know about all aspects of children's growth and development. Learning more about children enables workers in child-related careers to provide better care for children.

Child Care Worker

Child care workers work with young children who are not yet in school. They may also work with older children before or after school. Child care workers meet children's basic needs and provide activities to stimulate growth and development.

Education: Educational requirements for child care workers vary greatly for each state. Requirements may include a Child Development Associate (CDA) credential or a bachelor's degree.

Job Outlook: Future employment opportunities are expected to grow faster than the average for all occupations.

What Is Child Development?

Development is the gradual process through which babies become adults. The process has many stages, such as before birth, infancy, childhood, adolescence, and adulthood. Development begins at conception and continues until death.

For many years, scientists and researchers have been studying children. The goal of these professionals is to learn more about how children grow and develop. **Child development** is the scientific study of children from conception to adolescence. Child development is concerned with the whole child. It focuses on all areas of development—physical, mental, and social-emotional.

Child development focuses on changes that occur in children over time. Changes occur in both growth and behaviors. *Growth* is a change in size, such as height, or in quantity, such as vocabulary. *Changes in behavior* include any change in motor, thinking, and social-emotional skills.

By doing research, experts in medicine, education, family and consumer sciences, and sociology help gather knowledge about children. People then use these facts to learn about children. Anyone who is around children can use this knowledge. Child development teaches teens and adults how to care for children.

Individual Life Cycle

The **individual life cycle** is a description of the stages of change people experience throughout life, 1-4. To help them study development over time, experts divide life into age-related stages. These stages are based on changes in growth and behavior that occur as a result of age. The exact ages for a specific person may vary, but average ages are given. These provide a basic idea of when stages

1-4 A person will go through many changes throughout his or her individual life cycle.

may begin and end. Because this book is about child development, only the first six stages (those that involve children) are described here. The life cycle also includes stages for teens and adults.

★ The *prenatal stage* begins at conception and ends about nine months later at birth. The rate of growth at this stage is the fastest it will be in life. In this stage, a child grows from a single cell to a complete organism.

★ The *neonatal stage* extends from birth through the second week. During this period, the baby physically adapts to life outside the mother's body.

★ The *infancy stage* begins at two weeks and continues through the first birthday (12 months). The infant develops the foundation for motor, thinking, language, and social skills.

★ The *toddler stage* begins at 12 months and ends at 36 months (the child's third birthday). In the toddler stage, the child makes great strides in motor, thinking, and language skills and begins to test his or her dependence on adults.

★ The *preschool stage* begins at three years and ends at the sixth birthday. During this stage, the child becomes more self-sufficient, spends many hours in play exploring the physical and social world, and develops a rather stable self-concept.

★ The *school-age stage*, or middle childhood, begins at 6 years and ends at 12 years. This stage corresponds to the typical ages of children in the elementary school years. Achievement is the central goal of these years. School-age children master the basics of reading, writing, and arithmetic. They are exposed to many other learning opportunities, too. In school, children interact with peers more and learn by group instruction. This makes it important for them to learn self-control.

Factors That Influence Growth and Development

Why is each child different? Two main factors influence growth and development. First, each child has unique, inborn traits. **Heredity** includes all the traits that are passed to a child from blood relatives. Second, a child's surroundings also play a large role. **Environment** includes all the conditions and situations that surround and affect a child.

The way these two factors combine also makes children different from one another. Experts are studying how these two factors affect children's growth and development. They continue to learn, but unanswered questions remain.

Heredity

You have many traits in common with all the other members of your family. These traits pass to you in complex ways through your parents' genes at the moment of conception. **Genes** are sections of the DNA molecule found in a person's cells that determine the individual traits the person will have. Genes carry the inborn instructions that help make you who you are, 1-5.

Genetics is the study of the factors involved in the passing of traits from one generation of living beings to the next. In short, genetics is the study of heredity. *Geneticists* (biologists who study heredity) continue to make strides in learning which traits pass from parents to child. Almost every physical, mental, and social-emotional trait is affected by genes. Thus, genes influence your growth and development in many ways. The following points are known about heredity:

★ The genes' instructions are lifelong. They carry the same message throughout life. For instance, the genes for eye color remain the same for life.

★ Genes affect some parts of growth and development more than others. For instance, genes determine body features such as blood type, facial structure, and color of hair, eyes, and skin. Other traits, such as mental ability and social-emotional traits, are affected by both genes and the environment.

★ Some genes determine whether a person will have a trait. For example, a person either is or is not an albino. (An *albino* is a person with white skin, almost white hair, and pink eyes.) This is determined by genes.

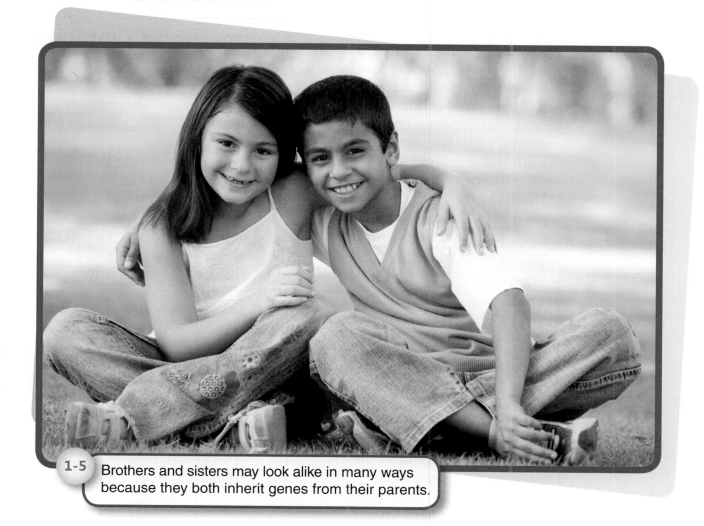

1-5 Brothers and sisters may look alike in many ways because they both inherit genes from their parents.

Child Advocate

Child advocates represent the best interests of children who have been abused or neglected. They promote and protect the rights of children.

Education: Educational requirements vary for each state. Training in laws regarding children in the state in which advocates practice is often required.

Job Outlook: Employment for child advocates is expected to grow much faster than the average for all occupations.

★ Other genes affect the range of a trait. Traits like height (very short to very tall) and athletic ability (almost no ability to greatness) come from these genes. These genes determine a trait's potential. (*Potential* is the greatest amount or level possible.) Whether a person will show or use that trait to its potential depends on the person's life. For instance, a healthful diet will help a child reach his or her height potential. However, the child cannot grow beyond this potential. On the other hand, children with poor nutrition may not achieve their full potential.

Environment

The environment affects growth and development, too. Physical conditions, such as food and rest, are part of the environment. These conditions shape children's experiences. A child's environment also includes relationships with others, as well as everything children hear or see. All these factors affect the way a child grows and develops.

Factors in the environment can affect physical traits. For example, studies show that babies' brains develop at a slower rate if no one holds or talks to them. When children receive attention and many chances to learn, their brains develop to their full potential.

Intellectual and social-emotional traits are also affected by factors in the environment. For instance, a child whose family members show affection openly may be more likely to show affection, too. A child whose family members show little affection might be less comfortable hugging or kissing others.

Heredity and Environment Combined

For years, people argued about which affected growth and development more—heredity or environment. Now, experts agree they work together.

Genes control how quickly a baby's muscles and bones grow (heredity). A proper diet is needed for the baby to grow (environment). However, a better diet does not make bones and muscles bigger than heredity allows (heredity and environment).

Going one step further, parents can exercise their baby's muscles to help strengthen them (environment). Nevertheless, the baby cannot walk until muscles and bones are ready (heredity). When the baby's body is ready, parents can help the baby walk as soon as possible through exercise and encouragement (heredity and environment).

This interaction can also be observed in the developing brain. Genes and environment work together to shape a child's brain. The effects of each are unique.

Brain Development

The command center of the body—the brain—fascinates scientists. People who study and work with children are also often curious about how the brain grows and changes in childhood. Until recently, the brain was mostly a mystery. However, in recent years, scientists have learned much more about brain development. Much of this knowledge is gained from the use of high technology and advances in biochemistry. An abundance of brain research is now in progress. Although many questions have been answered, many more remain for scientists to unravel.

Basic Wiring Occurs

The brain is responsible for controlling most body functions. These include operation of the body systems, movements, thinking, memory, and feelings. Brain cells called **neurons** control these tasks. The neurons send and receive electrical impulses throughout the brain. These impulses are like messages that tell body parts or systems what to do.

Electrical impulses can pass within a single brain cell or between two brain cells. Special chemicals send both types of impulses (within one cell or between two cells). When a message must travel between cells, however, it needs a pathway along which to travel. For this "talk" between neurons, the brain builds a web of fibers to serve as links between cells. Think of these fibers as microscopic cables that carry brain signals. This network of fibers is called the brain's **wiring**.

Each neuron can develop two types of cables, 1-6. Longer, heavier cables called **axons** send signals. Each cell can have only one axon. This axon transmits all the signals from this neuron to other neurons. Short, bushy cables called **dendrites** receive signals. One cell can have as many as 15,000 dendrites. The axon from one neuron, however, does not touch the dendrite of another neuron. Instead, there is a tiny gap between them, which is called a **synapse**. As the signal leaves the axon, it jumps the synapse to travel to the dendrite. The brain's complex wiring allows one axon to send signals to many dendrites simultaneously.

Wiring of Brain Cell

Synapse

Cell body

Axon

Dendrites

1-6 Brain cells "communicate" with one another by sending messages from the axons of one neuron across the synapse to the dendrites of another neuron.

Heredity and Environment Interact

Scientists now know that heredity and environment work together to develop the brain. Heredity affects how many neurons a baby will have throughout life. All these neurons will be present at birth. In addition, half of a person's 80,000 genes are involved in brain growth and development. These genes cause cells to divide and grow. They are also responsible for basic wiring between the axons and dendrites before birth. When the baby is born, he or she will have about 50 trillion synapses in the brain. These synapses are the ones the baby must have to survive outside the mother's body.

Unlike a computer that is built and then turned on, the brain starts working even before it is finished. The basics are present at birth, but the baby's brain continues to grow after birth. When stimulated, the axon sends electrical impulses to the dendrites of other cells. These messages help the brain form more synapses (connections) between the neurons. Repeating a positive experience causes the impulses to be sent again, which strengthens the connection.

The brain can use a stronger connection more easily than a weak one. Over time, the brain continues to strengthen used pathways, but begins to weed out the unused pathways. This process is called **pruning**. Healthy pruning allows the remaining connections to become strong. This increases the speed and efficiency for often-used brain signals. Too much pruning means the person will not be able to develop certain needed skills and abilities. Pruning begins in the very first years of a child's life and is almost completed by age 10 years.

In this system of wiring, the environment is crucial. Rich sensory experiences create new dendrites, which build new networks for learning. Examples of rich experiences are getting a hug, hearing music, learning a skill, and exploring a toy. In the first year of life, the number of synapses increases to more than 1,000 trillion. This allows for the rapid rate of learning among babies and young children.

Focus on Science
Brain Development

Rich sensory experiences strengthen and refine the brain's wiring. A lack of stimulation can prevent some connections from forming and cause pruning to other connections. In fact, early experiences have such a dramatic effect on brain wiring they can increase or decrease the final number of synapses by as much as 25 percent. The effects this has on future learning potential are lifelong. What does this say about the importance of caring for babies and young children? What effects can effective caregiving have on the future of your community, country, and the world? What results might ineffective caregiving have?

Windows of Opportunity

Timing is an important concept when it comes to brain development. The entire brain is not wired at one time. Genes control the general order and timetable in which regions of the brain develop. Each region has a specific function, such as processing a person's movement, language, memory, emotions, or sensory experiences. By observing children's skills, experts have learned which parts of the brain are being wired at various ages.

For best results, parents and people who work with children should offer specific types of stimulation at certain times. These times are called windows of opportunity. A **window of opportunity** is a prime period in a child's life for developing a particular skill. In this window, the child reaches a peak capacity to learn this skill if given the opportunity. At this time, a certain type of stimulation is more critical than others.

Each area has its own window of opportunity. Some windows are large, which means the favorable time for learning this skill is several years. Language development is a good example. Some windows are small, which means the most favorable time for learning is less than a year. For instance, wiring for vision is completed in a few months. Once the window of opportunity passes, it is more difficult (sometimes impossible) for the brain to develop this skill or acquire this learning.

Often, the windows of opportunity for various tasks overlap. This means more than one learning can happen at the same time. For instance, the window for learning to respond to stress lasts from birth to a little more than three years. Windows for basic motor skills open and close about the same time. This means a child will likely be learning those skills at the same time if given the opportunity.

Why is this information useful? Knowing when the windows of opportunity for various skills occur helps parents and teachers offer the right kinds of experiences for a child at the best possible times. They will know which skills they should encourage most and which will likely come at a later time. This can help children's brains reach their full potential.

Brain Plasticity

When working with children, it's good to know that a child's brain has the ability to change or adapt to the environment. This ability to be shaped and reshaped is called **plasticity** (technically *brain plasticity*).

Plasticity can have both positive and negative effects on brain development. This depends largely on the environment. In a favorable environment, the brain receives a great deal of stimulation. This stimulation comes from the child's experiences and surroundings. Stimulation causes the brain to send signals that strengthen the wiring for these types of activities.

The following are basic suggestions for offering a positive environment for young children:

★ The best experiences are interaction with loving adults engaged in daily tasks and family-type activities. (Even child care programs for children under three years of age should have a home-like atmosphere.) Babies and very young children need not be taught in a formal way. These children learn by playing, especially with caring adults.

★ Children need choices in what and how to learn. For example, adults should never insist that a baby or toddler play with a certain toy or listen to a certain story.

★ Children need time to practice and master skills. Repetition of experiences develops the brain. Even with a small quantity of playthings, children can learn and develop.

Because of plasticity, brain development can be easily injured by abuse, neglect, and other negative experiences. Stress has a harmful effect on brain function. When a person fears or senses a threat, the body prepares for "fight or flight." The resulting chemical change in the brain has been described as an acid bath washing over the wiring. This acid prunes away the synapses needed for caring for and understanding others. Furthermore, because stress signals occur in the brain cortex (the part of the brain in which you do most of your thinking), a child cannot learn well while distressed. If stress is constant, these unused connections will also be pruned.

Plasticity lessens with age. Even the brain of a three-year-old is far less changeable than it was at birth. Ten-year-olds have very little plasticity, and adults have even less. This short period of brain plasticity tells us the following:

★ The infant and toddler years are times of great brain activity and learning.

★ Children who have developmental delays, live in unsafe environments, or lack stimulating experiences need early professional help to overcome these obstacles.

★ A good early environment provides the best foundation for all areas of development. It also promotes *resilience* (the ability to recover from or adjust easily to change).

Cutting-edge science on brain development confirms what many parents and caregivers have known for years, 1-7. The earliest years are the most important for all areas of growth and development (physical, intellectual, and social-emotional). Prenatal care, loving relations between young children and adults, and quality experiences play a lasting role in brain development. Learning about brain development can help adults shape children's potential in positive ways.

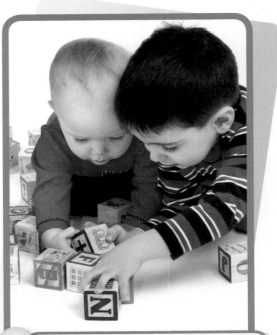

1-7 Parents can offer play experiences, such as blockbuilding, at the appropriate times to help their children master these skills.

Differences in the Rate of Growth and Development

All people change with time. They grow and develop certain skills and behaviors in expected sequences called *stages*. As you just read, many factors influence growth and development. These factors make each person develop at a unique rate.

Some people enter a stage earlier and some later than the typical age. **Developmental acceleration** is when a child performs like an older child. For example, a 30-month-old child who speaks in long, complex sentences is developmentally accelerated in language. On the other hand, **developmental delay** is when a child performs like a younger child. For example, a three-year-old who speaks in two-word sentences may have a developmental delay in language. With support and encouragement, children with delays usually catch up with other children over time.

People do not advance in all areas of development at the same rate. For example, a child may develop at a fast rate in motor skills and a slower rate in language usage. A child may be developmentally accelerated or delayed in one or more areas. It is even possible for a child to be delayed in one area and accelerated in another. Some children have a favorable heredity and environment. These children may be developmentally accelerated in most areas. Sometimes unfavorable conditions can delay most areas of development. For example, a child born too early may be developmentally delayed in most areas.

Principles of Growth and Development

Each person is unique, yet people are more alike than different. Experts study these likenesses to find patterns in the way people generally grow and develop. These patterns, or **principles of growth and development**, do not fit every person exactly. However, they are true enough to be used as a guide when learning about children. The following sections describe key principles of growth and development.

Growth and Development Are Constant

Many aspects of a person's growth and development are unchanging. This is called *constancy*. Traits that children possess today are a good hint—but not proof—of traits that will be present in the future. For example, tall two-year-olds tend to be tall adults. Children who are good students in elementary school are likely to be good students in high school. Happy, secure children tend to be cheerful, confident adults.

Why is this so? There are two reasons for constancy in growth and development. First, traits controlled by heredity do not change. Second, people often live in the same environment for years. For major changes to take place in growth and development, major changes must take place in the environment.

Growth and Development Are Gradual and Continuous

Growth and development are gradual and continuous because changes that take place happen in little, unbroken steps. A child does not grow or develop overnight. Consider a baby taking his or her first steps on a certain date. Each

day before walking, the baby grew, the body matured, and the baby practiced motor skills, such as crawling and pulling to a stand. All these small changes led to the baby's first steps, 1-8.

In a positive way, the principle also suggests development does not reverse overnight. A few mistakes or stresses usually do not cause severe problems. As an example, a one-day junk food binge does not seriously harm a healthy person.

The principle also suggests that if people do not develop when they are supposed to, they may be able

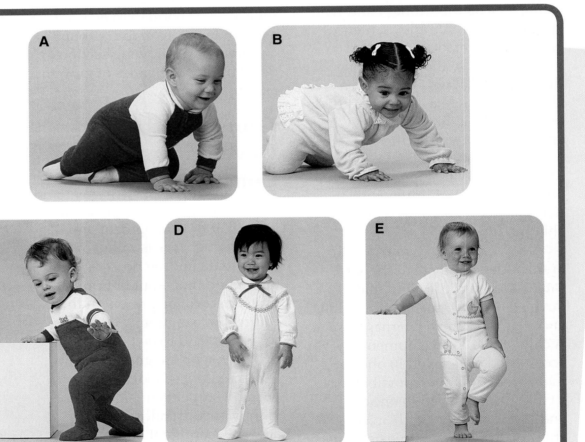

1-8 Children must practice many motor skills before they take their first steps. Before walking, children pull themselves mainly by their arms (A), creep on all fours (B), pull themselves onto their feet (C), stand without support (D), and try standing on one foot (E).

Photographs courtesy of Carter's; Photography by Bruce Plotkin to do so later in life. For instance, if children are not taught to read at age six, they can learn a few years later, although it may be more difficult. In a few cases, once an opportunity has passed, it might never be possible to gain this development.

This principle can also work to a person's disadvantage. It suggests that poor growth and development are not easily reversed. For example, consider a child with poor health due to a lifelong poor diet. It may take many months or years of eating a carefully planned diet to restore the child's health. In some cases, the body may never be able to overcome these obstacles. Consider, too, a child who lags in mental development due to the lack of quality experiences with adults and with toys and books. This child will likely need special help in early childhood in school programs in order to "catch-up."

Growth and Development Happen in Sequenced Steps

In order for growth and development to be continuous, change must build on what children have already learned. For instance, writing comes from making random marks. The steps in growth and development follow one another in a set order called **sequenced steps**. Think about the changes that happen in children in ranked stages—one stage always occurs before the next.

A **teachable moment** is a time when a person can learn a new task. It occurs when the body and mind are physically ready (during the brain's windows of opportunity), when caregivers encourage and support the child, and when the child feels a strong desire to learn. If a child has not reached the teachable moment, he or she will feel stressed when trying to master a task or skill. Waiting too long after the teachable moment occurs may cause problems, too. For example, a child who is ready to ride a bicycle is not given the chance to learn. This child may then have trouble learning the skill as an adult.

Growth and Development Happen at Different Rates

Growth and development happen at different rates throughout life. Experts know when fast and slow periods of growth and development occur. Height and weight increases are fast in infancy, for example. The increases are moderate in preschool, and fast again in junior and senior high school.

Rates of growth and development also vary from one child to another. Some children develop quickly and others slowly. Although the sequence of growth and development is similar for all children, the rates of change differ. Why do these rates differ? Children grow and develop at different rates because of heredity, environment, and motivation.

Heredity determines different growth rates. For example, girl's bones and organs are more mature than boy's at all ages because of heredity.

Children need a good environment to grow at the best rate. A good environment includes much love and care and many ways to learn. If the environment is lacking, *lags* or delays in growth and development occur. On the other hand, an adult's attempts to hurry growth and development may cause a child harmful stress.

Motivation, which is a child's desire to achieve, also makes growth and development rates vary. Some children are eager to achieve and others are more poorly motivated.

Growth and Development Are Interrelated

In this book, the physical, mental, and social-emotional aspects of growth and development are often discussed in separate sections or chapters. This is so you can better understand each aspect. In reality, however, all aspects interact in complex ways. For instance, as children's bodies grow and mature, their motor skills improve. Increased motor skills, in turn, can improve children's social skills, 1-9. As social skills improve, children talk to more people and learn about new ideas. This helps their mental skills. As mental skills improve, children can play in more complex sports, which helps their motor skills.

People who work with children must understand how areas of growth and development affect each other. For instance, a teacher's job is to improve children's intellectual growth. However, how teachers treat children also affects their social-emotional growth. Understanding these interrelationships improves the way people work with children.

Theories of Growth and Development

Many researchers have studied children. Some of the more famous include Erik Erikson (1902–1994), Jean Piaget (1896–1980), and Lev Vygotsky (1896–1934). Their theories about child development are described in later chapters of this text. Researchers Robert J. Havighurst (1900–1991) and Abraham Maslow (1908–1970) also studied children. Their research led them to form the following theories about growth and development.

Havighurst's Theory of Developmental Tasks

Each child masters skills and activities that fit his or her level of growth and development. In all cultures, children are expected to learn skills like crawling, self-feeding, and dressing at a time that is right for them. These are called **developmental tasks**, or tasks that should be mastered at a certain stage in life.

1-9 Having the needed motor skills to play hand games can lead to a fun time with a friend.

Havighurst, a well-known educator and behavioral scientist, believed achieving developmental tasks leads to happiness and success with later tasks. Failure to achieve tasks leads to unhappiness and problems with later tasks.

Havighurst identified the developmental tasks of children as coming from the following three sources:

★ **physical growth.** A baby comes into the world as a helpless being. As his or her body matures, the child is able to learn many new skills, such as walking and reading.

★ **social pressures.** Through rewards and penalties, society pressures the child to master the tasks seen as important. Developmental tasks differ from culture to culture, because each group may value different skills. For instance, playing to win has no value to Hopi Indian children. However, most other American children feel winning is important. Tasks differ from region to region, too. Over time, tasks also change to reflect changes in society.

★ **inner pressures.** The actual push to achieve comes from within children. In the end, it is the child who is responsible for mastering each task. Children work harder to learn tasks they like, 1-10.

Developmental Tasks

Area: Motor task

Task for middle childhood: Learning physical skills needed for common games

Example of task: Learning skills needed to play ball

Source: Physical growth
Child needs bone and muscle growth. The child's eyes and hands must work smoothly together.

Source: Social pressures
Other children reward skillful players (praise or accept them as friends) and punish failures (tease or reject them as friends). Parents and coaches may also expect children to master the skills.

Source: Inner pressures
Child desires to be admired by other children, parents, and coaches.

Source: Must see new possibilities for behavior
Child sees older children playing ball.

Source: Must form new concept of self
Child thinks, "I can be a player."

Source: Must cope with conflicting demands
Child thinks, "I can get hit with a ball or be teased for striking out. But if I do not play, the other kids will make fun of me, and my parents and coaches will not consider me grown-up."

Source: Wants to achieve the next step in development enough to work for it
Child now spends hours in practice.

1-10 Children master developmental tasks when their bodies are ready, when others place pressure on them, and when they want to learn a new skill.

Maslow's Theory of Human Needs

Abraham Maslow, a noted psychologist, believed that development is a result of meeting personal needs. His theory states all people work to fulfill basic needs and higher-level needs.

Maslow divides basic needs into four levels. The first level includes all physical needs. The other three levels are the *psychological* (related to feelings) needs of security; love and acceptance; and esteem.

In addition to basic needs, Maslow also created a fifth level for higher-level needs, which he called *self-actualization needs*. These are the needs to grow and feel fulfilled as a person. They include the drive to pursue talents and hobbies, gain skills, and learn more about the world. Education meets self-actualization needs. Complete self-actualization is a lifelong process. Many people never attain complete self-actualization.

Maslow ranked these basic and higher-level needs in an order he called the *hierarchy of human needs*, 1-11. This means lower-level needs (basic needs) must be somewhat fulfilled before higher-level needs can be pursued.

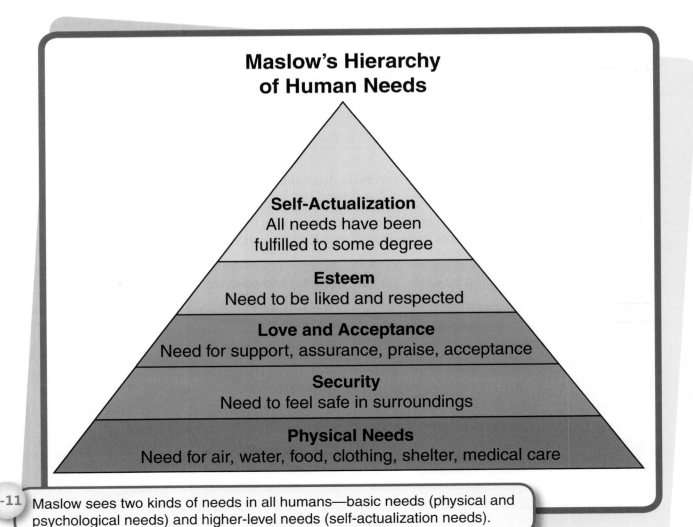

Maslow's Hierarchy of Human Needs

Self-Actualization
All needs have been fulfilled to some degree

Esteem
Need to be liked and respected

Love and Acceptance
Need for support, assurance, praise, acceptance

Security
Need to feel safe in surroundings

Physical Needs
Need for air, water, food, clothing, shelter, medical care

1-11 Maslow sees two kinds of needs in all humans—basic needs (physical and psychological needs) and higher-level needs (self-actualization needs).

All adults who study about and care for children need to understand this hierarchy of human needs. Maslow's work implies the further up the hierarchy a person can go, the more growth and fulfillment he or she will seek. Maslow sees humans as driven by the need to become more fulfilled.

Adults need to learn and practice ways to help children meet their needs. The first step is to help children meet basic needs. For instance, adults can offer children nutritious foods. Once basic needs are met, adults can help children meet higher-level needs. For example, well-fed children can turn their attention from eating to psychological needs. These might include building relationships with friends. Higher-level skills help children reach their full potential as adults, which is called self-actualization.

Observing Children

Observation is the oldest, most common, and best way to learn about human behavior, including the behavior of children. One reason observation is so commonly used is because humans enter the world with their own observation equipment—their senses. As you watch and listen to children, you can learn about their behavior. By watching carefully, you can respond quickly if dangers arise.

When you observe adults who work with children, you can learn to imitate their successful behaviors. For instance, if you observe a teacher sitting on the floor working with children, you might later try

this, too. This can help you interact with children in a more positive way. Because many skills are learned through imitation, this type of observation is important.

Because the senses are the main tools you use, you might think observation skills come naturally. To some extent, they do. You see and hear what goes on around you every day. It takes training, however, to interpret what you see and hear into information that you can use. For this reason, many observation skills must be learned. These skills come with knowledge and practice. Pretend you are looking at an X-ray with your doctor. Where you might see only shadows and lines, your doctor sees a bone fracture. Why would your doctor see more? With his or her experience, your doctor can see meaning in these images you may not notice.

You will learn more about children when you use your mind to "see" more. Observing children will help you understand what you read in this book and what you hear about children. At the same time, what you learn from your reading will help you see more when you observe, too, 1-12.

Why Observe Children?

How do researchers know so much about children? They have been observing and writing about children for many years. As you observe, you will behave like a researcher, too.

Usually, a researcher has a question and then observes children to learn the answer. What you

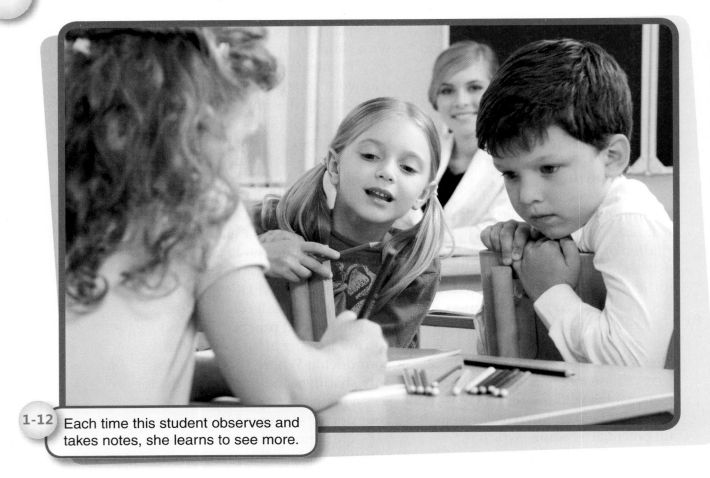

1-12 Each time this student observes and takes notes, she learns to see more.

observe will depend on the purpose of your observation. Because this book looks at the sequence of children's growth and development, you will consider these principles when you observe. Your teacher will assign you a task from the book. As you observe, you will look for answers to each task.

What Do Researchers Want to Know?

Sometimes researchers, while observing, think of another idea to study. You, too, will notice behaviors that were not part of your assigned work. You will want to ask questions about what you see. This is how researchers learn.

Other times, researchers decide to observe further because they want to know more about a behavior. For example, you may hear three-year-olds reciting numbers from 1 to 10. Does this mean they can count objects to 10? To find out, you may need to observe behavior more closely.

Researchers may also look for causes that affect behavior, such as factors that cause a child to feel secure. You may try to understand the behaviors of children or note why a certain game worked well with children.

Observing children can help you better interact with the children in your care. You can learn this by observing how others work with children and how the children react to them.

Ways to Observe

There are many ways to observe children. The best way is to observe children directly. However, many observations are done indirectly.

Direct Observations

A **direct observation** means watching children in their natural environments. These environments include home, play groups, child care programs, schools, and public places, such as shopping centers, parks, and restaurants. Most direct observations occur in these types of places.

Researchers often set up special laboratory settings where they can study what they may not see in the natural environment. They may need to observe, for example, how a baby reacts when the mother leaves the room and a stranger enters. Researchers also use laboratory observations to speed up the observation process. Suppose researchers want to observe a child's balancing skills. If they go to a park with a balance beam, they may wait hours before they observe enough children to form a sample for their study. In a laboratory, however, children would arrive at the setting, walk the beam, and leave. Researchers also use laboratory settings when special equipment is needed.

Observations set in laboratories cannot answer all questions. For instance, it would be hard for researchers to know if children really like playing on a balance beam. Although some information in this book comes from research in the laboratory setting, this is not the way you will start observing. You will begin your observations in the natural setting, as do all researchers.

Indirect Observations

Although direct observation is the main way to learn about children, researchers also use other observation methods to study them. Sometimes they want to see something in more detail or check direct observations. One important method is **indirect observation**. This may include asking questions of parents, teachers, or children. Indirect observation also includes observing products children make, such as artwork or the stories children dictate or write. This method helps you gather information you could not obtain directly from observing the child.

You can learn a lot from children's work. You can learn even more when you observe children making these products. For example, it is easy to look at a drawing and notice a child has colored outside the lines. How can you tell if this is due to lack of motor control, a damaged crayon, or a rushed coloring job? Only direct observation will tell you.

Guidelines for Observing

Anyone observing children should follow certain guidelines, 1-13. These guidelines are important for several reasons. First, they protect the rights of the subject and the observer. They also list proper behaviors you should follow when visiting a child care center. Finally, these guidelines will help you make meaningful and accurate observations.

Guidelines for Observations

Guidelines	Details About Guidelines
Know your objectives.	Objectives tell us ★ what age children to observe ★ what type of activity to observe ★ where to observe (in some cases) ★ how much time to spend observing ★ what type of records to keep
Obtain permission to observe.	In public places (a park or shopping center), you may observe children without permission. Parents or other adults are more cooperative, however, when they know what you are doing. Explain that you will keep children's names or other information confidential. To observe in private places (homes or child care programs), you will need prior approval from your teacher and permission from the adult at the home or program. Observe only on dates and times approved by your teacher. If observing in a home, call the day before to be sure the time is still convenient for the parent.
Know what to do at the site.	Remember, you are an invited guest. ★ Always introduce yourself and state your purpose. ★ Try not to distract children or adults from their activities. Move quietly, and do not talk unless you are working with the children. ★ Thank the parent or teacher when leaving. Sites also have different procedures. At some sites, you observe in an observation room looking through a one-way mirror. At other sites, you may help with the children. In still other sites, you sit away from the children. Find out in advance what you will be expected to do.
Ask staff members questions at convenient times.	Never interrupt a staff member engaged with children or an adult.
Be sure observations do not distract children from regular activities.	★ Get acquainted with the children and setting before observing. ★ Unless asked to help, do not get any closer to the children than necessary. (When making language observations, however, you must be close.) Do not smile at children or wear jewelry or clothing that will distract them. If children come to you, answer them briefly but encourage them to return to their activities. ★ Avoid talking directly to children, including giving hints about how to do an activity. ★ Your objectives should never interfere with the program objectives.
Observe carefully and objectively.	Observations require intense mental activity. You want to watch closely so you can remember the situation vividly. Many situations can affect objectivity, such as distractions, fatigue, or discomfort. Biases also affect objectivity. For these reasons, observers should not study their own children or children of close friends or relatives.

1-13 Care must be taken when doing observations.

(Continued.)

Record accurately.	Avoid the following three errors when recording information: ★ Leaving out information that may help you understand the situation. ★ Recording behaviors that did not occur. This happens when the observer does not pay close attention or relies on memory to complete notes. Sometimes biases cause the observer to use inaccurate words. Avoid using too many adjectives in your descriptions. ★ Having notes out of sequence. Control this by writing the time in your notes every three to five minutes.
Protect the rights of all observed.	People have privacy rights observers must protect in the following ways: ★ Never discuss a child in front of that child or an adult except the child's teacher. ★ Use no name or the child's first name only during class discussions. (Researchers often use letters or numbers to identify children.) ★ Respect parents' rights to refuse your request to observe. ★ Keep information confidential. Take notes discreetly so others cannot read them as you write. File notes in a secure place when you are not using them. ★ Destroy notes completely when they are no longer useful. This applies to handwritten, typed, or word-processed notes and notes on CDs. (If notes can be retrieved or are readable, they are not destroyed.)

1-13 *(Continued.)*

Summary

The scientific study of children is called child development. Children's growth and development depend on three factors—heredity, environment, and the combination of heredity and environment. Most children follow similar patterns called principles of growth and development.

Brain development research helps people better understand how to help children learn. To help a child's brain wire itself to perform at its inherited potential, adults can offer a positive environment and rich sensory experiences.

Researchers have formed a number of theories about how children grow and develop.

Havighurst and Maslow are two researchers with such theories.

Observing children is the best way to learn about their behavior. Child observations are done to answer questions, get new ideas, and look for causes that affect behavior.

Companion Web Site

Interactive Activity

Review vocabulary terms and key concepts for Chapter 1 at **g-wlearning.com**.

Review and Reflect

Write your answers to the following questions on a separate sheet of paper.

1. True or false. Only people who will be parents someday need to know how to care for and guide children.

2. List four reasons why people study children.

3. Define the term *child development*.

4. List the six stages of the individual life cycle that involve children.

5. What are the three factors that influence growth and development?

6. True or false. Genes affect the physical, mental, and social aspects of development to the same degree.

7. The environment _____ (does, does not) greatly affect growth and development.

8. True or false. Brain development is a good example of how heredity and environment interact to affect development.

9. Explain the difference between developmental acceleration and developmental delay.

10. Describe one principle of growth and development and provide an example.

11. True or false. The steps in which most children grow and develop occur in about the same order. The order of the steps in growth and development is about the same for most children.

12. What are the three sources Havighurst identified that contribute to children mastering developmental tasks?

13. Explain Maslow's hierarchy of human needs.

14. List five guidelines for observing children.

Cross-Curricular Link

15. **Social Studies, Speech.** In small groups, discuss examples of culture that are handed down from one generation to another. Examples of culture include language, beliefs, attitudes, values, rituals, and skills.

16. **Social Studies, Art.** Make a display called "Children in Our Society." In the display, use newspaper clippings, magazine articles, and other information on children and products for children.

17. **History, Technology.** Use the Internet to research the history of child labor laws in the United States. How did the needs of children lead to the development of these laws? Using presentation software, create a presentation of your findings to share with the class. Adhere to all copyright laws and cite any sources you may use for the presentation.

18. **Science (Brain Research).** Research the anatomy of the brain and create a presentation illustrating the various parts. You could also choose to research more about brain development and design a presentation showing how stimulation changes the wiring of the brain.

19. **Social Studies.** Havighurst said one source for developmental tasks comes from social pressures. Given the situations in society today, what developmental tasks do you predict will be important for future children? Why?

20. **Reading, Writing, Career Study.** Read about the life of a famous person in any career. Write a report giving examples of constancy in the person's growth and development. How did this constancy lead to fame in his or her career? Check your report for correct spelling, grammar, and punctuation.

21. **Speech, Career Study.** Interview a person working with children in a child-related career such as a child care teacher or child care provider. What characteristics does this person need to work with children? What are the job responsibilities? What are the educational and training requirements for the career? Share your findings with the class.

Making Observations

22. In small groups, observe a group of people. List characteristics you see that are due to heredity and characteristics you see that are due to environment. Compare and discuss your lists in class.

23. Observe infants or toddlers and note examples you see that illustrate the principles of development.

Thinking Critically

24. With a group of classmates, list some ways society is child-centered and some ways society is adult-centered. Discuss your lists. Can a society resolve these dual interests? How can a new family find a balance for a happier family life?

25. If you were asked to recruit other students in your school to take a child development course, what would you say or do to convince them child development is a worthwhile subject? Be specific and explain the reason behind your idea(s).

26. With a small group, discuss how areas of development are interrelated. Each group should trace the effects of a different problem, such as poor nutrition or lack of affection, on all areas of development.

2 Families Today

After studying this chapter, you will be able to

★ **describe** changes affecting families today.

★ **explain** the role of families in today's society.

★ **list** the main advantages and disadvantages of living in different types of families.

★ **explain** changes that take place during the family life cycle.

★ **describe** the major roles of parents.

★ **define** three parenting styles.

★ **list** characteristics of healthy families.

★ **describe** ways that culture influences the family.

Terms to Know

nuclear family
single-parent families
joint custody
extended family
stepfamilies
adoption
adoption agency
independent adoption
illegal market adoption
closed adoption
open adoption
foster families
guardian

family life cycle
nurturance
guidance
discipline
power assertion
love withdrawal
induction
authoritarian
permissive
democratic
cultural diversity
multicultural families

Reading Advantage

Write the main headings in the chapter, leaving space under each heading. As you read the chapter, write three main points that you learned from reading each section.

Companion Web Site

Interactive Activity

Learn more about family types by completing the *Read, Discuss, and Analyze* Activity for Chapter 2 at **g-wlearning.com**.

The family is the oldest known social group. Why did it come into being? Experts do not know exactly, but most believe people began living in families for children's well-being. Throughout history, families have held different ideas about children's needs. These ideas have changed the roles of parents and family structures. However, families continue to be the basic unit of society.

Changes Affecting Families Today

Changes in society have caused major changes in the family. Before the Industrial Revolution, many families lived on farms and met most of their own needs. They were producers who built their own homes, made their own clothing, and grew their own food. These families consisted of the *immediate family* (parents and their children) as well as grandparents and other family members. They often lived together or in nearby houses.

During the Industrial Revolution, many families left their farms and moved into the cities to work in factories, leaving behind relatives and friends. In the cities, families no longer produced most of their own needed goods and services. They began earning an income and purchasing goods from others outside the family. City families became consumers.

Away from other relatives, people began to turn to their immediate family members for companionship and emotional support. The immediate family became more important for love and security. When these needs were not met within the family, divorce rates increased.

Many changes affect families. As you look at Figure 2-1, try to picture what the data indicates about today's family life.

Changes in Family Roles

The roles of family members have changed through the years. Until the 1700s, parents were the only ones to meet children's physical needs for food, clothing, shelter, and safety. The main focus of parents was on the survival and character development of children. When children reached age four to seven years, they were expected to work long days in factories or on farms. Children were considered an asset to the family, for they helped the family earn money.

As adults learned more about children's needs, parent-child roles changed. Childhood came to be seen as a special time. Labor laws, created by advocates for children, changed the role children played in the economy. Children could now lead lives as *children*, not as a source of family income. Although families still met children's physical needs, they viewed loving care and support as highly important. Family support groups, such as schools, youth groups, and children's health providers began to support the parenting role. Today, most people believe that children's many needs are best met in a loving family encircled by a supportive environment.

A Snapshot of America's Families

Marriage Facts

Median age of marriage
- ★ 27.1 years for men
- ★ 25.3 years for women

Divorced and Widowed

45–50 percent of all marriages end in divorce

10 percent of all adults are divorced at any given time

Median age of first divorce
- ★ 30.5 years for men
- ★ 29.0 years for women

Additional marital separations and desertions occur

7 percent widowed at any given time

Remarriage

95 percent of all divorced people remarry

Divorce statistics are higher for those remarried

Family Structure of Families with Children Under Age 18

67.8 percent live with married parents

25.8 percent live with one parent
- ★ 22.6 percent live with mother
- ★ 3.2 percent live with father

2.9 percent live with unmarried parents*

3.5 percent do not live with a parent

Number of Children per Family

2.1 children per family

Slight increase in family size, especially among higher-income families

Parental Employment

All families with children
- ★ 90.7 percent had at least one employed parent
- ★ 71 percent had a mother employed
- ★ 55.1 percent had a mother of a child under age one employed

Married couples with children
- ★ 97.3 percent had at least one employed parent
- ★ 62.2 percent had both parents employed
- ★ 31 percent had father, but not mother, employed
- ★ 5 percent had mother, but not father, employed
- ★ 54.6 percent had a mother of a child under age one employed

Unmarried mothers
- ★ 76.5 percent employed
- ★ 56.5 percent with a child under age one employed
- ★ 50 percent work full-time, year round

Unmarried fathers
- ★ 92 percent employed
- ★ 74 percent work full-time, year round

Birth and Death Rates

Over 14 babies born per 1,000 people

Trend is toward a slight increase each year

38 percent of all births are to unmarried women

Births to unmarried women by age group
- ★ 15–17 years: 92 percent
- ★ 18–19 years: 81 percent
- ★ 20–24 years: 58 percent
- ★ 25–29 years: 31 percent
- ★ 30–39 years: 18 percent

Death rates of children and teens
- ★ infants: 6.9 deaths per 1,000 live births
- ★ children (ages 1–4): 20 deaths per 100,000
- ★ teens (ages 15–19): 65 deaths per 100,000

Children and Poverty

18.3 percent of all children live below the poverty level**

27.7 percent of children in mother-only families live below the poverty level

11.1 percent of children in father-only families live below the poverty level

* Before 2007, a child living with two unmarried parents was counted as a child living with a single parent.

** *Poverty level* (also called *poverty line* and *poverty threshold*) is based on a minimum amount of income a family needs for food, clothing, housing, transportation, and other necessities. The levels vary by family size and structure, such as single parents, to determine who is in poverty. If a family's total income is less than the level, then that family and every individual in it is defined as *in poverty*. Poverty levels may differ somewhat depending on whether one is referring to the levels set by the Census Bureau or the Department of Health and Human Services. Many assistance programs are tied to these poverty measures.

2-1 These data reflect the changes that affect families today.

Family Types

In the United States, children are members of many types of families. The family type describes which people live in the household and how these people are related. Families can be nuclear (two-parent), single-parent, or extended families. These families include children, their biological parent or parents, and (in extended families) other relatives.

Children usually enter families through birth and live in these families throughout childhood. Some children, however, have families who formed differently. These types of families include stepfamilies, families with adoptive children, foster families, and guardians. In these cases, children can have more than one type of family. The following sections describe each family type and its effect on children.

Nuclear Families

A father, a mother, and their biological child or children who live together form a **nuclear family**. This type of family exists in most societies, 2-2. In nuclear families, children often leave home when they become adults. When these children marry, they begin their own families separate from their parents.

When you think of the "typical family," what type of family comes to mind? Many think of the nuclear family, with a working father and a mother who cares for children at home. Is this type of family really typical in the United States? No—actually, only a small number of American families have two parents. Even fewer of those families have mothers who stay home with children.

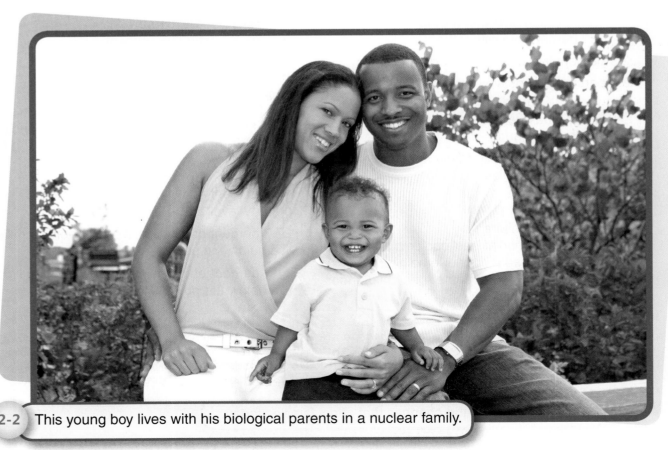

2-2 This young boy lives with his biological parents in a nuclear family.

Compared to other family types, nuclear families can have some disadvantages. In this tight family unit, relatives and others do not live in the home. Children in a nuclear family may be exposed less often to various kinds of people, including older adults. This means the children may lose out on the skills these other people can teach them. Finally, the family may live too far from relatives to rely on them for support in times of stress. This family type can also be a drawback for children if the parents do not get along. Children may be exposed to stress. This is especially true if the relationship is abusive.

On the other hand, nuclear families have advantages. Both the adults and the children may have their needs met more easily because family members can share responsibilities. Children may be apt to learn more flexible home and child care roles in the nuclear family. Adults often share these tasks, and children who see role sharing may be better prepared for the future than those who do not. Children also have the chance to see how spouses should relate to each other.

Single-Parent Families

Single-parent families are headed by one adult. These families form when a parent dies, parents divorce or separate, or a single parent gives birth or adopts children. A single parent may also head the family if the other parent deserts the family.

The number of single parents in America is growing. The greatest increase is among parents who have never been married. The high rate of marital separation and divorce is also a factor. Women head most single-parent families. However, a growing number of single fathers are gaining custody and raising their children.

Raising children alone is hard. Single parents face the responsibility of providing care, supervision, and guidance for their children alone. Both parents still have a legal responsibility to provide financial support for the children, but often one provides the bulk of the support. Single parents may lack support and feel overwhelmed. How well they handle their parenting roles depends on their family situation. For instance, a sudden change from having two parents to having only one can be a difficult adjustment for the remaining parent and the children.

Being a single parent is not easy, but it can be very rewarding. Children in well-adjusted single-parent homes are often more stable than children in unhappy two-parent homes. The relationship between the children and their parent is often very strong. In addition, recent studies show that children of single parents may show independence at an earlier age than those in other family types. In these studies, children with one parent performed some self-care tasks, such as using the toilet, earlier than children living with two parents.

Living with a single parent does not always mean the other parent cannot take an active role in the children's lives. In fact, children are often happier when both parents are involved. When possible, parents should work together to raise the children even if they do not live in the same house. Some co-parents go to court to seek **joint custody**. This is the shared legal right to provide care and make decisions about their children's lives. Joint custody avoids the issue of determining which parent will be the primary caregiver. Joint custody is becoming more common.

If only one parent participates in the child's life, he or she should be sure to find other sources of support and help. Families and friends can serve as role models for the children. These loved ones can offer help and love to the parent and the children. Often, social service agencies offer emotional, practical, and financial help, too.

Extended Families

In an **extended family**, more than two generations of a family live together. In the past, the extended family was most often an older couple with their children, in-laws, and grandchildren. Today, many other family groups may form an extended family, 2-3.

Sometimes the extended family lives in one home. Each family unit in the extended family may have some space to call its own. The extended family might cook and eat together and share some common space in the home. Extended family members may live together if they run a family business. In these families, members usually share housework and child care. Each member does a certain task, and members often may not change roles. For instance, the same person may cook each day.

Extended families are very common in many countries around the world. In the United States, these families are generally less common than they once were.

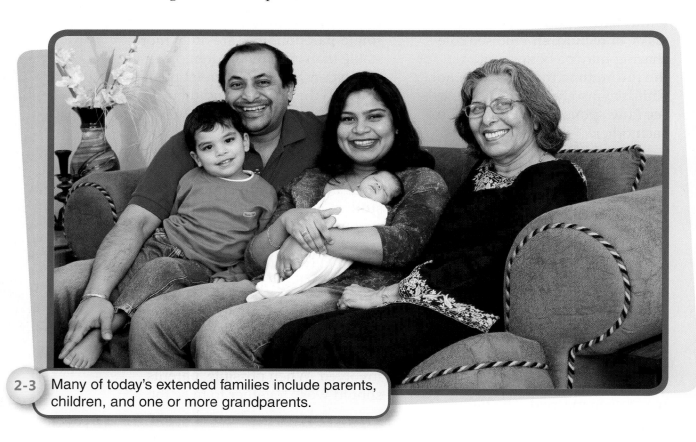

2-3 Many of today's extended families include parents, children, and one or more grandparents.

For the most part, fewer family businesses and less economic need for large families caused the decline. In some cultures and regions of the country, however, this family type is still quite common.

Sometimes an extended family forms temporarily. For example, young adults may move back home while trying to establish their careers. A divorced family member may need a temporary residence while trying to save money. Aging family members may need short-term care.

Extended families do experience certain problems more often than members of other kinds of families. Sometimes children and even adults find they must deal with too many people. Also, decisions are often made for the good of the entire family rather than the needs of each person.

These families also have many advantages. Children learn to interact with people of all ages because young and old members are in daily contact. This helps family members know and respect each other. Extended families are good at handing down family beliefs and *family history* (stories of a family's past), 2-4. Because there are so many members, extended families can perform more duties than small family groups. For example, some members can care for the children of working parents. When stressful events, such as death, happen in extended families, many people are there to help children and adults.

Stepfamilies

Stepfamilies are formed when a single parent marries another person. In many cases, two single parents marry each other. Families in which the children of both spouses will live with the couple are sometimes called *blended families*.

The stepfamily is a fairly common family form. As more single parents marry or remarry, it grows even more common. In fact, many of today's children have two stepfamilies—that of the father and his new wife and that of the mother and her new husband. Often children live with only one of these stepfamilies. Other times, children live with each stepfamily part of the year. Each situation is unique.

When a stepfamily forms, it can be a big adjustment for everyone. Family members find themselves in instant relationships—stepparents must relate with stepchildren and

2-4 Grandparents often take pride in handing down family history and sharing their talents with their grandchildren.

stepchildren must relate with each other. The parents must also adjust to their new roles of husband and wife. Children usually maintain relationships with the family of their other parent, too. All this adds up to many changes for everyone, especially the children.

Children may have problems adjusting to a new family. Many children are asked to adjust to two sets of rules. This can be a major problem for school-age children, who are weighing family and peer priorities in search of self-identity. Dealing with two families may further confuse their self-identity.

One study reported that, although they do face problems, almost two-thirds of stepfamilies have good relationships. In this study, both mothers and children tended to rate stepfathers as good parents—just as good as biological fathers. It can take special effort, however, to help the family adjust smoothly.

Families with Adopted Children

Adoption occurs when a child of one pair of parents legally becomes the child of another parent or parents. Adoption legally ends the rights and responsibilities between a child and the birthparents (biological parents). The adoptive parents are then granted these rights. Adoption gives the child a new family.

People want to adopt for a number of reasons. Among them are the following:

★ The couple cannot give birth or can give birth only with great difficulty.

★ The couple may want to add to their current family.

★ The couple knows a child who needs a home.

★ A single person wants to be a parent and provide a home for children.

Fewer birthparents plan adoptions now than in the past. This means fewer babies are available to be adopted. Many of the children available for adoption are older, have special needs, are born outside the U.S., and are living in foster families and group homes.

Adoption Agencies and Independent Adoptions

Most parents who have adopted children have spent much effort finding them. There are two ways to adopt children legally—through an adoption agency and through an independent source.

An **adoption agency** is an agency licensed by the state to handle adoptions. It is either state funded (such as the agency that also handles foster care) or private (managed by a church or organization). The agency works out the details between the birthparents and adoptive parents. Final legal aspects of the adoption are handled in state courts.

In an **independent adoption**, a person, such as a lawyer or physician, works out the details between the birthparents and adoptive parents. In some independent adoptions, there are fewer details that must be worked out. Such cases include adoption of relatives or stepchildren. All independent adoptions are handled in state courts and thus follow state laws. Foreign adoptions can be either agency or independent adoptions. You can use Figure 2-5 to

Types of Adoption

Type	Pros	Cons
Agency	★ Agency handles the legal aspects to meet the needs of all involved. ★ Children are closely matched with adoptive families to ensure good placement. Emphasis is on meeting the child's needs. ★ Birthparents can request certain types of adoptive families. (They can choose or meet adoptive parents in an open adoption.) ★ Adoptive parent can choose a child of a certain gender, age, and family background. ★ Information is exchanged between birthparents and the adoptive family (nonidentifying information only in a closed adoption). ★ Social workers counsel both sets of parents. ★ Adoptive families are supervised from the time children are placed until the adoption is final. ★ Cost may be lower for the adoptive parents. Agency may charge based on parents' ability to pay.	★ Agency sets criteria for adoptive parents. Many suitable homes may be turned down in favor of "more qualified" homes. People who are newly married, remarried, single, or older may have a harder time using an agency. ★ Income, religious, and housing guidelines may also exclude some people wanting to adopt. ★ The study of people wanting to adopt is extremely detailed and goes into all aspects of personal and married life. ★ Fewer babies are available for adoption. Also, available children may not be of the same culture as the adoptive parents. ★ When fewer children are available for adoption, long waiting periods are common. ★ People wanting to adopt may wait a long time before a good match with a child is found.
Independent	★ There are no stated qualifications for adoptive parents. Thus, many people who might not be chosen to adopt through agency (people who are newly married, remarried, single, or older) can become adoptive parents. ★ If they wish, birthparents can arrange for someone they already know as adoptive parents. ★ It may be easier to adopt a baby or to adopt a child of the same culture as the adoptive parents.	★ Less emphasis may be placed on the child's welfare. ★ Adoptive parents are screened less thoroughly. Placement occurs before a study is done, so child may be in an unsuitable home. ★ Adoptive parents may receive less information about child's background and health history. ★ Adoptive parents need to hire lawyers to help them with legal details. ★ May be less privacy for both sets of parents than in an agency adoption. ★ Counseling is not provided as part of the adoption. ★ Cost may be higher than with an agency. (Some adoptive parents unknowingly enter illegal market adoptions.)

2-5 Adoptive parents should consider the advantages and disadvantages of each type of adoption before choosing one.

help you compare the pros and cons of each type of adoption.

Adoption Options and Rights

The laws of each state govern adoption options and rights. In all states, it is illegal to buy or sell a child for adoption. This is called an **illegal market adoption**.

In an adoption of a newborn, birthparents sign forms to release the baby from the hospital for adoption purposes. They also sign papers consenting to the adoption. Then the matter must be presented in court and a judge must declare the adoption final. Each state sets laws about what papers must be signed and what waiting periods may occur between various steps of the process. When the adoption is complete, the child's original birth certificate will be placed under court seal. A new one will be issued listing the adoptive parents as the child's parents.

Both agency and independent adoptions may be either closed or open adoptions. Birthparents and adoptive parents can choose the type they prefer. The two options differ in how much information is exchanged and how much contact occurs between the birthparents and the adoptive family.

In a **closed adoption** (also called *confidential adoption*), the identity of the birthparents and adopting family are not revealed. The two sides do not meet or contact each other. The adoption agency, attorney, or doctor works out the details of the adoption. Addresses, names, and other identifying facts are kept private.

Other information can be exchanged through the agency or person handling the adoption. The adoptive family and child have a right to know the medical history and social backgrounds of the birthparents. The birthparents have a right to know about the type of family in which the child will be placed. Sometimes birthparents write a letter for the child to read when he or she is old enough to understand. (This letter would be signed with a nonidentifying signature, such as *Your Birthmom*.)

In closed adoptions, state laws govern what identifying information can be made available and to whom it can be given. Sometimes even an adult who was adopted as a child cannot obtain information about his or her birthparents.

Fewer closed adoptions occur today. These are being replaced by **open adoption**, a type of adoption that involves some degree of communication between the birthparents and adoptive family. The *openness* of the adoption refers to how much information is exchanged and how much contact occurs. In an open adoption, the birthparents might choose and meet the adoptive parents. They could also choose the adoptive parents from résumés and/or photographs.

In the last 20 years, adoptions have become more accepted. Open adoptions are more common. The birthparents feel they have more choice in the decision. Adopting families will not think of the adoption process as something secret and will also have the information and support to best parent their children. Children benefit from knowing their adoptions are loving decisions that involve open communication between both sets of parents. In open adoptions, all adoption records are usually accessible to adopted children when they become adults.

Adoption rights protect those involved in adoption. In most states, the birthfather has legal rights. State laws may permit him to deny *paternity* (fathering of a child), give all rights to the birthmother, or give permission along with the birthmother for the child to be adopted. In some states, if the father cannot be found, steps can be taken to end his rights to make decisions about the child.

Adoption Issues

Children who are adopted generally have stable, happy home lives. This is because their adopted families want them very much, 2-6. Some problems can exist, however. In most cases, adoptive parents do not have the nine months of pregnancy to make the transition to parenthood. Instead, they take on their new roles very quickly. Persons wanting to adopt may be on a waiting list for many years. Then one day the adoption agency may call and announce a child will be ready for them the next day.

Other problems may arise related to the adopted child's birthparents, especially if the adoption is closed. Birthparents may want to see the child. There is a chance they may want to become part of the child's life. Adoptive parents may not agree this is best for the child. Children who are adopted often ask questions about the adoption. They may want to know about or meet their birthparents. Older children who have lived with their birthparents

and are then adopted by a new family need time to adjust. These children may miss their birthparents or want to be with them again. Adoptive parents may need to seek counseling to help them guide the children and offer them the support needed to make the adjustment.

Adoptive parents should answer their children's questions about adoption in direct and honest ways. Adopted children should be told from the beginning they are adopted. Their adoptions should not be kept secret. This would cause more turmoil for the child when he or she found out the truth.

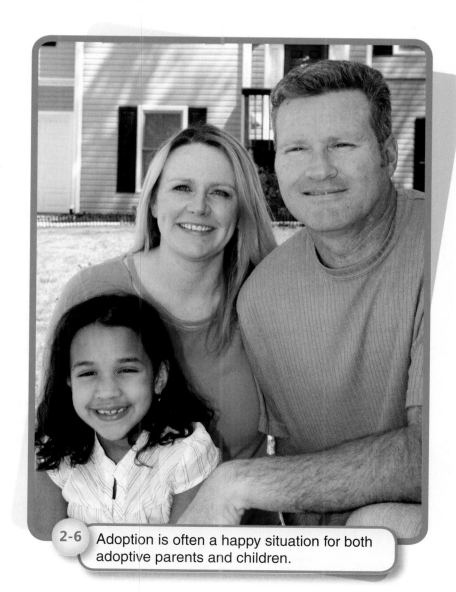

2-6 Adoption is often a happy situation for both adoptive parents and children.

It can take time for each member to adjust to living in an adoptive family. Soon, however, this family will likely adapt. Most adoptive parents create a loving family life that helps adopted children overcome any stress they may feel.

Foster Families

Some children live at least part of their lives in **foster families**. These are families in which adults provide temporary homes for children who cannot live with their birthparents.

Foster parents assume the parenting responsibilities for the children in their care. They fill these roles until the children are reunited with their birthparents or placed in adoptive homes.

Children often enter foster families because of problems in their birthfamilies. These problems often include abuse, neglect, and substance abuse by the birthparents or other family members. In these cases, the courts intervene to protect the children. The court places the children in a foster family and provides counseling, treatment, and

Learn More About...
Foster Care

In recent years, three main changes in the foster care system have greatly helped foster children. The following paragraphs describe each of these changes.

First, foster families get more support in the task of raising children. Better screening and training for foster parenting are now more common. Caseworkers are making more frequent visits to foster families to check on the welfare of the children. Therapists counsel for the foster family as a whole and each member separately.

Second, the courts have recognized that all children need permanent homes. In the past, birthparents were given many years to work out their problems. These children spent years waiting for a permanent home life, which some of them never received. Foster children were also moved from foster home to foster home due to a large number of less-than-ideal placements. Moving foster children was also meant to prevent too strong of attachments between foster parents and foster children. Such actions were not in the best interest of the children. Today,

birthparents must become fit parents more quickly or sign papers allowing their children to be adopted. Foster children who are not reunited with their birthparents are placed for adoption sooner than in the past—many as babies or very young children. Now foster parents who care for a given child may even be eligible to adopt the child.

Third, states are recognizing foster children may need help and support even after they reach 18 years of age. In most states, foster family care stops when the child reaches this age. Some young adults, however, may not have yet completed high school. Even fewer are enrolled in further education or have careers. Today, some provisions are being made to further help young adults from foster families. Programs are available to help them find housing, learn work skills, and gain life-management skills. These programs can help foster children become independent and live on their own. Having this help can make the transition from foster care to adulthood easier for them.

other help for the birthparents. The goal is to reunite children with their birthparents if possible. However, the birthparents must be able to provide a safe, secure home for their children. In serious or prolonged cases, the court may sever the rights of the birthparents. The children are then placed in a foster family until they can be adopted and given a permanent home. Sometimes children can be adopted by their foster parents.

A foster family may have one or two parents. It may include other biological, adoptive, or foster children. A foster child may be placed with brothers and sisters or apart from them, depending on the situation. Foster families can offer a stable, secure home for children. Joining a foster family is a big adjustment, however. In many cases, foster children need counseling for the problems they faced in their birthfamilies. They may also miss their birthparents and other family members. To ease separation stress, contact or visitation is sometimes granted. Other children may grieve if they know they will never return to live with their birthparents. Each situation is unique. Foster parents need to be flexible, supportive, and understanding of the children in their care.

Guardians

A **guardian** is often chosen by the biological parents to take responsibility for a child in the event of the birthparents' death or extended absence. The guardian is usually someone who has close ties to the family, such as a relative or friend. A guardian must be

legally appointed by the court. The guardian assumes parental responsibilities. Some guardians manage the child's inherited money, while others take full financial responsibility for child rearing costs. The court supervises the guardian and may even make some decisions for the child. A child remains with his or her guardian until the child becomes a legal adult or the court terminates the relationship. A child and guardian often develop a strong emotional bond because of the guardian's familiarity with the child's family.

The Family Life Cycle

Families change through the years, just as individuals do. Most families change in similar stages that are called the **family life cycle**. The family life cycle can be divided into six stages, 2-7.

In the *beginning stage*, the couple is a family of two. During this time, they get to know each other better. They also decide whether they want to become parents and how soon, if ever, they will parent. (Families without children will stay in this stage until they reach the mid-years stage.)

For families who will have children, the next stage is the *childbearing stage*. In this stage, the family grows as parents give birth to one or more children. Parents learn their roles in caring for and guiding children through their earliest years. As parents enter later stages, their roles will continue to change.

The *parenting stage* begins when the family is complete.

The Family Life Cycle

Beginning Stage
A couple marries and gets to know each other. This stage lasts until a child is born.

Launching Stage
The couple's children begin leaving home to live on their own. This stage ends when all children have left home.

Childbearing Stage
The couple starts having children. This stage lasts until the birth of the last child.

Mid-years Stage
The couple focuses on their marriage, planning for their future, and becoming grandparents. This stage lasts until the couple retires.

Parenting Stage
The couple focuses on guiding their children through the school-age and teen years. This stage lasts until children start to leave home.

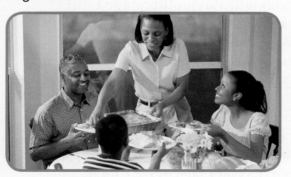

Aging Stage
The couple retires and adjusts to this change in lifestyle. This stage lasts throughout life.

2-7 Families with children pass through the six stages of the family life cycle.

Parents focus on guiding and nurturing their children. They are preparing their children to become productive members of society. During these years, parents also realize other people will be teaching and guiding their children. Children begin to learn more from teachers and peers. Parents need to stay involved with their children's growth.

Children's adolescent years can be confusing for both parents and children. Adolescents are striving to become more independent. They are not always ready to handle as much responsibility as they want to, however. Adolescents may want more privacy, but they still need to know they can talk to their parents. At this stage, parents need to begin treating their children as adults. They also need to know when to provide guidance and help.

The *launching stage* brings new feelings for parents. During this stage, children start to leave home to make their own lives. As each child leaves home, parents may feel lonelier. They may also feel their children no longer need them. In this stage, parents must acknowledge their children are adults. Now their relationships may be more equal. Parents may continue to be an important part of their children's lives.

In the *mid-years stage*, parents may find more time for themselves than they did when their children lived at home. They may devote more time to new interests or hobbies. Keeping in touch with their children is still important. They may be involved with their grandchildren. The couple also begins to focus on retirement.

The final stage of the family life cycle is the *aging stage*. This stage lasts from retirement to death of both partners. In this stage, the couple may pursue new hobbies and spend time with family and friends. They may have health problems that cause them to need help from their children. The couple may face different challenges and have new concerns. During this stage, all family members may need to make many adjustments.

A new challenge for families occurs when grown children return home after the launching stage. Economic troubles, divorce, or other situations may cause them to move back home again. Parents may have to learn new ways to relate to these children. They may have adjusted to their children becoming adults. Now, however, they may not know how to treat them as adults when they all live in the same home. Likewise, adult children may not know what parents expect of them. Family members need to communicate openly to make sure everyone continues to get along.

Roles of Parents

Parents are responsible for the well-being of their children. In American society, parents' roles mainly involve socialization, nurturance, guidance, and discipline. Children must be socialized into their culture by their parents and other members of their family. Children thrive in a nurturing environment and need guidance and discipline to learn right from wrong.

Socialization

As you learned in Chapter 1, socialization is the training children receive to help them learn to live in a group. Each group or culture has its own rules and ways of doing things. Children are not born knowing what their parents' cultural group or society expects of its members. All this must be learned, 2-8. These learnings occur early in life, with the foundation being laid by as early as five years of age. In these early years, children interact mostly with their parents. For this reason, parents are the people most responsible for socializing children.

Socialization is complex and requires the passing down of many values that work toward the same end. Socialization is a major role of parents, for it allows children to fit into their culture. As you read the next sections, keep in mind the way parents nurture, guide, and discipline their children is part of the socialization process.

Nurturance

Nurturance, in a narrow sense, includes the physical aspects of child care, such as feeding, dressing, and bathing children. In a broader sense, nurturance includes meeting mental needs, such as providing children with a stimulating environment. Nurturance also includes meeting social-emotional needs, such as helping children feel secure and loved. Physical care, love, and concern are important for children's healthy growth. Both mothers and fathers play an important role in nurturing their children.

Guidance and Discipline

Child guidance and discipline are important responsibilities of parenthood. Parents guide their children in their daily interactions with them. **Guidance** includes the words and actions parents use to influence their child's behavior. For example, when parents face frustrations but react calmly, they guide their children to do the same. By showing children they are not upset when they do not get their way, parents are modeling good behavior. Guiding children in a positive way is an important parental role.

Discipline is part of guidance. **Discipline** is the use of methods and techniques to teach children self-control. Through discipline, children learn to act in ways that society finds acceptable. Punishment

Aspects of a Person's Culture

History, folklore, heroes

Language (written, verbal, slang, body language, and gestures)

Humor

Names (surname and given name)

Holiday celebrations, traditions, and rituals

Methods of greeting (such as eye contact, handshakes, hugs, kisses, and bowing)

Preferences about personal space and touching

Foods, eating methods, eating manners

Dress and body decorations

Home furnishings and decorations

Arts and crafts

Music

2-8 Culture touches many aspects of a person's life. What others can you list?

is not the same thing as discipline. *Punishment* is a consequence for a misdeed. For punishment to be effective, the negative consequences must fit the misdeed.

The goal of guidance and discipline is to teach children behaviors that will help them guide themselves. Guidance and discipline teach children to think and act in safe and acceptable ways. There are various ways to help children learn this, and some are more effective than others.

Types of Discipline

Most parents would like to find the perfect method for handling their children's unpleasant or disruptive behaviors. Although there is no perfect method for use with every child, some forms of discipline are better than others. These methods teach children self-control. This is important because parents will not always be able to guide children, especially as they become older. Studies have found that parents and other adults use three types of discipline—power assertion, love withdrawal, and induction.

Power Assertion

Power assertion occurs when parents use or threaten to use some form of physical punishment (also called *corporal punishment*) or deny privileges. The main problem with physical punishment is that it can hurt or harm children. For this reason, corporal punishment is illegal in child care programs and some other settings. Certainly, many people can name children who were occasionally spanked and are now healthy, happy adults. Some

Family Counselor

Family counselors are professionals who work to improve the social and psychological functioning of children and their families and to maximize the family well-being. They help families to overcome stress, mental health issues, and behavioral problems.

Education: A bachelor's degree is the minimum requirement for entry into the occupation, but many positions require an advanced degree. All states have some licensure, certification, or registration requirement.

Job Outlook: Employment for family counselors is expected to grow much faster than the average for all occupations.

adults even claim spankings were good for them. If this is true, why are most parenting experts against power-assertive techniques?

There are several reasons that power-assertive techniques are not healthy forms of discipline. First, power assertion works because the child fears the adult. As the child grows physically, however, fear lessens and the technique no longer works. Even for young children, fear is based on being caught and punished. Many power-assertive adults will threaten, "Don't let me catch you doing that again!" Thus, the child weighs the chances of being caught and the likely punishment. The child is not being guided by what is right or wrong.

Another reason power-assertion techniques are poor is because, to children, being physically punished for an act of aggression, such as hitting another child, seems like a double standard. The child may think,

"You are hitting me; why can't I hit others?" This is a good example of punishment not fitting the misdeed.

In addition, power-assertive techniques are often used when parents are angry. If parents are prone to losing their tempers, their intended light physical punishment could become abusive when done in anger.

Finally, all discipline techniques are imitated or modeled by children. Children disciplined through power assertiveness are more apt to use these methods in their own relationships. If they see their parents lose control, children may become violent during the teen years or abusive to their own spouses or children as adults.

Love Withdrawal

In a discipline technique called **love withdrawal**, parents threaten children or suggest some form of parent/child separation. An extreme example is parents telling children they do not want or love them. Some parents even tell their children they are going to give them away. Milder forms of love withdrawal include ignoring the child or giving the child the "silent treatment." Experts consider love withdrawal to be emotional abuse. Even in its milder forms, the technique creates stress and prevents the expression of feelings.

Induction

The third technique, **induction**, happens when parents discipline by reasoning and explaining. If punishment is needed, these parents use logical consequences. For example, they stop an aggressive child from hitting by taking the child out of the play group. Parents may also remove a toy or object that is the center of a fight. Adults, as older and wiser people, explain to children why they should or should not use certain behaviors. Once desired behavior is achieved, play resumes. Children disciplined by this technique tend to show better self-control, display more concern for others, and take responsibility for their own failures.

By using the induction method, parents can use several discipline techniques. The technique used will vary for each age group, 2-9. These techniques are described in more detail in later chapters on meeting children's needs.

Parenting Styles

Most parents want to raise their children to become responsible, well-mannered adults. When their child leaves babyhood, parents must begin guidance and discipline. Within a year or two, parents develop a parenting style. Parenting styles can be grouped into three main categories: authoritarian, permissive, and democratic.

Authoritarian

Some parents use an **authoritarian** parenting style, in which the main objective is to make children completely obedient. These parents think obedience is the most important behavior their children should learn. They expect children to respect their authority with little or no explanation as to why children should obey. Such parents are likely to use physical punishment when children do not behave. They seldom reward good behavior.

Examples of Specific Discipline Techniques

0–3 months

None. Parents try to soothe babies with routines.

3–6 months

None. Parents try to interact with babies as much as possible.

6–12 months

None. Parents still try to interact with babies and make their houses childproof as soon as they begin to scoot or crawl.

12–18 months

Parents provide a secure base for normal exploration and childproof their houses and yards. They can also direct their babies away from undesired behavior and dangerous situations. They may introduce the word *no* for unsafe situations.

18–36 months

Parents should remove children from dangerous situations. They should say no and give one- or two-word explanation, such as "Hot!" or "Hurt baby." Parents should also keep their houses childproof.

3–4 years

Parents should explain why children cannot do or continue to do something. After the first offense, take or send children to a quiet place where they are alone but not afraid. Children should remain alone for three or four minutes.

4 years–school age

Parents should use the induction method. Adjust reasons to the child's age. Some good techniques include the following:
- ★ Listen to the child's story.
- ★ Acknowledge the child's feelings with statements such as "I know you feel angry."
- ★ Express your feelings about the consequences and your expectations with statements such as "I was furious you left your wagon outside in the rain. The wagon goes in the garage each day."
- ★ Avoid attacking a child's character. For example, do not call the child "stupid."
- ★ Allow the child to make amends.
- ★ Give the child a choice of meeting a standard or losing a privilege. For example, "If you cannot throw away your trash, I cannot let you eat a snack."

Parents may need to send some children to a quiet, safe place for about one minute per year of age, when misbehavior occurs.

2-9 At every age, parents should discipline their children with love and understanding.

Authoritarian parenting may teach children to obey their parents. However, these children may not understand why they should act as their parents wish. They may not be able to develop self-control. They may also fear their parents and even rebel against them when they become older. Authoritarian parenting does not have good outcomes for the child. As a result, most parenting experts do not recommend this style of parenting.

Permissive

Permissive parents give children almost no guidelines or rules. They feel children should make their own decisions about right and wrong. They may think setting limits for their children will make the children feel unhappy or unloved. The truth is, without guidelines, these children may feel lost. They may have trouble getting along with others later in life because they have never needed to follow rules. Permissive parenting can also give children the impression parents do not care enough to guide and teach them. Parenting experts do not recommend this style of parenting.

Democratic

Most parents find a compromise between these two styles of parenting. They use a **democratic** (authoritative) style, in which parents set some rules, but allow children some freedom. When these parents set rules, they explain to children why the rules are needed. Children may even be allowed to help set some rules and decide some punishments. These children learn self-discipline in a positive, encouraging setting. Parenting experts endorse a democratic parenting style as healthiest for children and families.

Characteristics of Healthy Families

Families may be healthy or unhealthy. What determines a

family's health? In the past, it was measured mainly by durability (family staying together for many years). Often, durability can be a sign of a family's health. Sometimes, however, families may stay together even though members may seem to be a family in name only.

There is no magic recipe to create a healthy family. Families can be very different and yet strong. Some characteristics are often seen in healthy families. The most common is that spouses enter marriage with shared values. They use these values to decide on goals throughout their marriage and guide them in parenting their children.

Closely tied to shared values is the belief that family members are individuals. Strong families accept that even people who share many values will be somewhat different. They also realize life itself can change the family's goals. Healthy families are willing to adjust as needed.

Healthy families seem to share a mutual commitment to family life. In these families, parents want their own relationship to succeed. They want to be successful parents. Part of the commitment involves growth—becoming more loving, caring, and understanding. These members also want to do many things as a family unit.

In healthy families, members want to help each other rather than being self-centered. Members share responsibilities. Although each family may divide tasks differently, healthy families seem to happily follow their own choices about duties. Each member can depend on the others to keep promises, fulfill commitments, and be honest.

Focus on Speech
Parenting Styles

Choose a classmate to help you role-play the three parenting styles. Take turns being a parent and a young child. Choose a situation in which a child might behave poorly. First, role-play how the parent would respond in an authoritarian style. Next, role-play the same scene with a permissive parent. Finally, show how a parent could respond to the situation using the democratic style. Which response seems healthiest for the child, and why?

Healthy families communicate. They are polite and consider each other's feelings. They talk about their feelings and problems. Healthy families use problem-solving skills to work on problems rather than trying to change others, 2-10. Above all, the members support each other's efforts and show appreciation for each other.

Cultural Influences on Families

Families are alike in many ways, but they may differ in the cultural groups to which they belong. Culture, a way of life for a certain group of people, greatly affects a family's life. Because not every

Steps in Problem Solving

Step 1. Identify the problem
★ What is the problem that is getting in the way of achieving a goal? Be specific.
★ How is the problem affecting me? How is it affecting others?
★ What is happening? When is it happening? What causes the problem?

Step 2. Look at alternative solutions
★ Brainstorm for as many solutions as possible.
★ Do not discard any idea at this point. Sometimes seemingly "bad ideas" can be developed into "good solutions."

Step 3. Analyze the alternative solutions
★ Write down the good and bad points for each possible solution.
★ Group alternative solutions, when possible, such as these two involve changing jobs and these three involve staying with the job.

Step 4. Select a possible solution
★ Decide which solutions might have the most impact on the problem. Decide if the solution is realistic and manageable.
★ As you consider possible solutions, think of the consequences of each. What is the extent of a risk involved in each possible solution?
★ Do not hurry this step. Talk to others, including those affected by the problem.

Step 5. Implement a solution
★ After choosing a solution, plan how and when you will implement it.
★ Be specific on the steps to implement the plan.
★ Communicate the implementation steps to all involved.

Step 6. Evaluate the results
★ Evaluate the effectiveness of the solution. Is the solution achieving the desired goal? Did the solution have any unforeseen risks?
★ If the problem has not been resolved, ask the following: Do I need to give it more time to work? Should I change the plan of action somewhat? Do I need to begin the entire process again?
★ If the problem seems to be resolved, continue to monitor. Problems do not always stay solved.

2-10 These steps can be used to solve all kinds of family problems.

family belongs to the same culture, the effects of culture differ widely from one family to the next.

People of many cultural groups live in the United States. Families who once came from many parts of the world call this country home. The U.S. is an example of a nation with great **cultural diversity**, which means it has more than one culture represented among its people.

Families often identify their culture in terms of their origin or ancestors. Some people refer to their *region of origin*. An example is saying a person has a Native American, European, or African heritage. Other people refer to culture by the *specific country* from which their ancestors came. These people might say they are Mexican rather than Latino or Chinese rather than Asian. Still other groups refer to the *language* they speak, such as Spanish-speaking or German-speaking peoples.

All families are affected by each culture to which they belong. The influence might be subtle or more profound, depending on how involved the family is in the culture. The degree of involvement can vary widely, even among members of the same culture.

Culture affects the beliefs and customs of families. Each culture's practices support its particular beliefs and customs. For example, families in some cultures view academic learnings as the top priority for children, whereas other cultures emphasize play as well as academic skills. Because they have such different views, these two families will differ in their parenting practices, modeling, praise, and criticism regarding the role of education.

Parents model, reward, and praise what their culture values. They criticize and correct that which does not fit with their cultural beliefs. In this socialization process, children learn most of their culture's values at home. These concepts are also taught indirectly by living within the culture.

Some cultural concepts, such as history and heroes, are taught more directly. The reasons behind traditions of the culture are also often taught to children from an early age. Older family members may help impart values to children through storytelling and answering children's questions about the culture or its practices.

Cultures differ in the way they view the concept of family. In some cultures, *family* includes only the immediate family. In others, this term has a broader meaning that includes extended family members, close family friends, and neighbors.

The importance of the family also varies from culture to culture, 2-11. In cultures with a group orientation, family is most important. As the name suggests, cultures with an individual orientation focus on each person as an individual more than on the family as a group.

Goals for achievement vary from culture to culture. Some cultures stress academic achievement as a way to honor the family and achieve economic success that will help the entire family. Other cultures stress achievement in social interactions. In these cultures, showing dignity and respect in interactions with others brings honor to the individual or family.

Cultures See Families Differently

Group-Oriented Culture	Individually-Oriented Culture
Family includes kin and perhaps others.	Family includes parents and their children.
Family members live in same house or near each other.	Family members may live far from kin.
Status in the family (and possibly in the group) is achieved by age and/or gender.	Status is determined by achievement.
Elders make decisions based on the welfare of the whole family (collective responsibility).	The individual considers his or her own welfare when making decisions for himself or herself (individual responsibility).
Members take pride in their family name, family history, and family honor.	Members take pride in their own talents, achievements, and status.
Conform to those in authority.	Challenge or question those in authority.
Cooperate in all tasks.	Competitive.
Family harmony is emphasized.	Individual pursuit of happiness is emphasized.
Early dependence on group is encouraged. Group members help each other, even at their own expense.	Early independence encouraged. Each person is expected to help himself or herself with little assistance from family.
Parent-child bond stressed. Children are seen as extensions of parents (children bring honor to and help family throughout life).	Husband-wife bond stressed. Children are individuals who as adults take care of themselves.
Parents ask, "What can we do to help each other?"	Parents ask, "What can I do to help you?"
Expression of emotion is more indirect (emotionally controlled; modest; formal toward elders to show respect).	Expression of emotion is more direct (emotionally expressive; more "I centered;" informal).

2-11 Group-oriented cultures see families differently from cultures that are individually-oriented. These two sets of beliefs affect family life in different ways.

Language and dialect can vary from one culture to the next, too. Families generally use their culture's native language and teach this language to their children. Using the language of their people can bring a sense of unity and belonging and contribute to their culture. Families may use language as a way to foster this involvement in the culture.

The use and meaning of body language can vary from group to group. This explains the well-known saying: *Not all people smile in the same language.* In some cultures, smiling expresses friendliness, pleasure, or understanding of humor. In other cultures, a smile is used to acknowledge a fault. Some cultures might use smiling to mask emotion (hurt or disagreement) or avoid conflict. In other cultures, people smile in response to a compliment if they feel verbal response would show a lack of modesty.

The family also teaches children how to respond to people of other cultures. Families who value diversity point out the benefit of learning from people who are not like themselves. These families teach children to appreciate people of all cultures. They believe each group is different from, but equal to, other groups. Other families do not value diversity. They believe their group is better than others and that people of different groups should not interact with one another. Whatever their viewpoints, parents should be aware they are passing these views to their children.

Multicultural Families

As the United States increases in cultural diversity, the number of multicultural families continues to grow. In **multicultural families**, two or more cultural groups

Focus on Social Studies

Cultural Diversity

Speaking different languages is not the only way communication differs across cultures. The role of language can differ, too. For instance, some cultures teach children to talk often, be open and direct, and be informal. These children might address people by their first names without asking and soon after meeting, use slang, and talk to strangers. Other cultures value silence; that is, talking only when necessary. These cultures teach children to notice other body language clues (such as "reading the eyes") to help them understand without being told. These cultures prefer formal word choice and the use of courtesy titles when addressing elders or strangers. In these cultures, children are taught to address elders in a way that shows respect. In what ways do you think your cultural background will influence the way you parent or care for children? How can children benefit from these influences?

are represented. This happens when people of different cultures marry or when single people of different cultures have children together. Children and their adoptive or foster parents might also come from different cultures.

Multicultural families are like other families in many ways. They have many of the same joys and problems as other families. In some ways, however, these families are unique. The diversity within their families can bring added joy as well as added challenges.

Everyone in a multicultural family needs to learn about the cultures of its members. Parents need to understand the roles and expectations of each of these cultures. This takes some time and effort, but it can help the family avoid misunderstandings and conflicts.

In some multicultural families, parents do not know enough about the culture into which they are marrying or from which adopted or foster children are coming. Problems in these families may occur because of the following:

★ verbal and nonverbal communication differences between cultures

★ differing cultural expectations, roles, beliefs, and values

★ differing traditions including religious beliefs, rituals, and holidays

★ differing views regarding family life

★ expressions of bias or exclusion from others, especially family members

Most children raised in multicultural homes are happy

and are high achievers in school. They grow up to respect diversity and have a strong sense of self. The strongest multicultural families seem to have much in common, 2-12.

These parents often explain to their children that people who express bias toward them may not know any better. The unkind words and actions of biased people may come from not knowing others who are different from them. Parents in strong multicultural families discourage their children from fighting in response to bias. They make it clear it is not right to hurt people who are different or assume all people in a group behave the same way.

What Makes Multicultural Families Strong?

Studies have shown the strongest multicultural families often have the following in characteristics:
* parents have strong cultural identities and feel good about their multicultural family
* the family talks about cultural issues in the home
* parents and children develop creative ways to solve problems that show equal respect for both cultures
* the family surrounds itself with supportive family and friends
* parents work with child care staff and teachers on behalf of their children
* the family celebrates all cultures
* parents tolerate no biased remarks within their circle of family, friends, and peers

2-12 Having or lacking these characteristics may influence the strength of multicultural families.

Summary

The family is the basic unit of society. Many changes affect families today. One major difference from years past is the variety in family types that occurs. Family types include nuclear, single-parent, stepfamilies, extended families, families with adopted children, foster families, and guardians. Each family type has unique problems and strengths.

Many changes take place during the six stages of the family life cycle. From the beginning stage through the childbearing, parenting, launching, mid-years, and aging stages, the family grows and develops.

Parents have many responsibilities with respect to their children. They have parental roles to fulfill. The main roles are socialization, nurturance, and guidance and discipline.

Several factors contribute to the health of a family. These include shared values, a mutual commitment to family life, shared responsibilities, and good communication.

Culture greatly influences how each family lives its life. Because the United States has such cultural diversity, the effects of culture vary widely from one family to the next. Multicultural families are also becoming more common. These families may have more challenges, but they can be as happy and healthy as other families.

Companion Web Site

Interactive Activity

Review vocabulary terms and key concepts for Chapter 2 at **g-wlearning.com**.

Review and Reflect

Write your answers to the following questions on a separate sheet of paper.

1. Describe two changes affecting families today.

2. List one advantage and one disadvantage of living in each of the following family types: (A) nuclear families; (B) single-parent families; (C) extended families; (D) stepfamilies; (E) families with adopted children; (F) foster families.

3. True or false. A guardian must be legally appointed by the court.

4. What are the six stages of the family life cycle?

5. Being responsible for their children's welfare involves the parental roles of _____, _____, and _____ and _____.

6. Describe three types of discipline and their effects on children.

7. The _____ parenting style allows children to have some freedom, but sets rules for their well-being.

8. The _____ parenting style allows children to do as they please without interference.

9. The _____ parenting style pushes children to be obedient to their parents above all else.

10. List three factors that contribute to the health of a family.

11. What is *cultural diversity*?

12. List five characteristics of successful multicultural families.

Cross-Curricular Link

13. **History.** Use Internet or print sources to research the Industrial Revolution timeline. What invention started the Industrial Revolution? What other inventions contributed to the Industrial Revolution in the United States? How did the Industrial Revolution affect families? Share your findings with the class.

14. **Writing.** Write a fiction story entitled, "The Joys and Trials of Living in a _____ Family Type." Base the story on your own family type or describe what you think it would be like to live in a family type different from your own. Check your story for correct spelling, grammar, and punctuation.

15. **Reading, Writing.** Read at least two children's books about divorce and/or stepfamilies. Give the bibliographical information, the age for which the book was written, and a few statements about the main ideas the book conveys.

16. **Speech.** In small groups, play the roles of family members in various stages of the family life cycle. Emphasize the changes that take place in each stage.

17. **Speech.** Interview parents in the midyears or aging stages of the family life cycle. Ask how their roles as parents have changed through different stages. What stages do the parents remember as the happiest? What challenges did they face in each stage? Share your findings with the class.

18. **Writing, Technology.** Use the Internet to research disciplining of children. Then use word processing software to compose a short paper on your findings. Check your paper for correct spelling, grammar, and punctuation. Adhere to all copyright laws and cite any sources you may use for the paper.

19. **Social Studies.** Research another culture that interests you. What types of music and art are significant? What are common foods? What are the traditional ways of dressing? What special events are celebrated? Share your findings with the class.

Making Observations

20. Observe how couples with young children share their responsibilities. What techniques do they use to help them meet their obligations?

21. If possible, observe a family of a culture different from your own. What similarities do you notice between this family and your own? What differences seem to exist?

Thinking Critically

22. What are some of the advantages and disadvantages of joint custody over sole custody for parents? for children?

23. What are some possible benefits and problems of open adoption for each of the following: birthparents, adoptive family, adopted child? Whose benefit do you think should take priority, and why?

24. Many adults know reasoning rather than power assertion is a better form of discipline, yet many adults still use threats to discipline children. Why do adults use threats? Can threats be justified? Why or why not?

25. Discuss with a small group what makes a family healthy or strong. Compile a checklist someone could use to "test the health" of his or her family. Have the teacher photocopy each group's list. Compare other lists to that of your group and discuss.

3 Preparing for Parenting

After studying this chapter, you will be able to

★ **explain** why parenting is more difficult than other jobs.

★ **analyze** some of the motivations for and against parenthood.

★ **identify** factors to consider before becoming a parent.

★ **describe** effects of family planning.

★ **explain** physical and psychological problems of infertility.

★ **describe** fertility methods.

Terms to Know

indirect costs
foregone income
maternity leave
paternity leave
Family and Medical Leave Act
family planning
birth control methods
infertile
sterile

fertility counseling
assisted reproductive
  technologies (ARTs)
artificial insemination
in vitro fertilization (IVF)
gamete intrafallopian transfer
  (GIFT)
surrogate mother

Reading Advantage

After reading each section (separated by main headings), write a three- to four-sentence summary of what you just read. Be sure to paraphrase and use your own words.

Companion Web Site

Interactive Activity

Learn more about the decision to parent by completing the *Read, Discuss, and Analyze* Activity for Chapter 3 at **g-wlearning.com**.

Parenting is a rewarding and difficult task. Many people invest more money, time, and emotions in their children than they do in any investment in their life. Most parents hope their children will inherit all their strengths and avoid their weaknesses. They also hope their children will have opportunities they did not have.

Before having a child, a couple must seriously consider all aspects of parenting. This chapter discusses some of the important decisions people must make to prepare for parenting.

Why Is It Hard to Be a Good Parent?

Parenting skills are not automatic. A person may be able to biologically reproduce, but that does not necessarily mean he or she will be a good parent. If a person has long, agile fingers, does that mean he or she can automatically play the piano well?

Becoming a good parent is hard for a few reasons. First, parenting involves relationships with people. In a good relationship, each person wants what is best for the other. They support each other. Sometimes, because of people's individual differences, this is hard. In addition, the parent-child relationship is difficult because it is more one-sided than other relationships. For many years, parents are the "givers" and children are the "takers," 3-1.

Parenting is hard because unlike most jobs there is no specific age requirement to become a parent. At what age can a person direct a child

care center? be a U.S. president? Most jobs provide much more training than what new parents receive. Parents probably have studied and trained more for their careers than for their roles as parents. Their job skills may be better than their child care skills, for which they have had little or no training.

Parenting is also difficult because many people today do not have the benefit of early training within the family. Years ago, extended families were much more common. Children could often see their parents handle younger brothers and sisters. They may even have helped care for them. Today, fewer children have this chance to learn. Also, in the past, most young parents turned to relatives for parenting help. Now young parents often live many miles from their relatives.

3-1 Children require much care in their first years. They are not able to give much in return.

Being a good parent is hard, but it is also most parents' greatest wish. Because of this desire, couples are becoming better informed about parenting skills and child development. A parent can best measure success if his or her adult children can say, "If I could have chosen my parent, I would have chosen you."

Deciding About Parenthood

Deciding whether to have children is a personal choice. For the sake of the couple and the future child, the adults should agree on the decision. Couples should discuss their feelings about parenthood before they marry.

The decision to parent is unlike many life decisions in two ways. First, the decision to parent is a permanent choice. Once a child is born, he or she is part of the parent's life forever. A person can choose to change careers, for example, but having a child is different. Once a person is a parent, he or she will always be a parent.

Second, a decision not to parent is not permanent. People must make many life choices within a limited amount of time. For example, if a person wants a career in ballet, he or she must begin studying as a youngster and continue for many years. Couples have a longer period of time to decide whether to become parents. Young couples have at least 15 safe childbearing years. The option of adopting a child may increase this time by a few years. Thus, some couples may want to be parents, but may choose to wait until a better time. Other couples may not be sure about parenthood and wait to decide. Even couples who decide

✓ *Learn* More About...
Parenting Skills

Many couples feel they need help learning how to become good parents. They want to find the following resources to help them learn about child care and development:

★ professionals and/or successful parents to give advice

★ literature (books, journals, magazines) that is accurate, practical, and available

★ child care and parenting classes (community colleges and local American Red Cross chapters may offer such classes.)

★ families with infants and young children (Spending time with children by babysitting and volunteering in schools and religious organizations can help you understand what it is like to care for children.)

New parents should also realize there is not one right way to parent. Although some methods may be more respected than others, many factors influence parenting. The culture in which a child is raised affects how parents raise children. The personalities of parents and children also affect parenting. The ways couples have seen their parents or friends care for children influences how they care for their own. All these factors are important to think about when learning child care skills.

they never want children can later change their minds.

Couples have different motivations for and against parenthood. Some of these are described in this chapter. In the end, each couple must make the choice by respecting their feelings and needs.

Reasons for Choosing Parenthood

Couples have various reasons for choosing parenthood. Although they may not always be able to explain why, they see children as part of their life. The following are reasons couples give for wanting to become parents. Some are better reasons than others.

"We want to share our love with a child." This is perhaps the most important reason for wanting a child. A couple's desire to share their love and time with a child is the best reason for parenthood, 3-2.

3-2 Parenting involves sharing knowledge and love with a child.

Parents should want a child with no strings attached. If parents hope a child will fulfill other needs or goals, the parent-child relationship may not be healthy.

"Wouldn't it be nice to have a cute little baby?" When some couples see others with babies, they think it would be nice to have a cute little baby, too. It is good for couples to think positively about babies. The problem is, babies are not always cute. All babies are sick, fussy, and cranky at times. In addition, children do not stay babies long.

"Our parents want grandchildren." Some couples want to fulfill their parents' wishes to be grandparents. It is fine for the parents of each spouse to want a grandchild. Grandparents can give a child much love. It is more important, however, for parents to want and love a child.

"Our older child needs a brother or sister." When a couple wants a playmate for an older child, the parents are fulfilling someone else's needs, not their own. This reason is similar to having a baby because parents want grandchildren. Although a child might enjoy a brother or sister, there are other ways to meet an only child's needs for playmates.

"A child can make us proud." Some couples see children as sources of pride. They want children to carry on the family name and customs, inherit the family business or money, or achieve certain goals. It is good for parents to be proud of their children and want them to achieve. They must be careful, however, not to let their hopes stifle their children's goals. Parenthood is not a good choice if a child is wanted only to

boost the parents' ego or meet their unfulfilled goals.

Parent-child relationships suffer when children cannot meet their parents' goals. Not meeting parents' goals can make children feel inadequate. The relationship also suffers when children meet the parents' goals, but feel they cannot be themselves. This often leads children to resent their parents.

"Others will see me as a stable, reliable person." A few couples see having children as giving them the image of stable community members and reliable employees. Fortunately, such ideas are beginning to break down. People are judged more today on their own merits and not on family status. Parents should not want children simply to help them create an image or fulfill their goals.

"A child will comfort us in our old age." Sometimes couples think of children as sources of help in their old age. It is natural for people to think about being helpless or lonely when they grow old. However, an aging parent cannot count on a child's help. In fact, parents may outlive their children.

"A child will make us love each other." Some couples hope that having a child will save a failing marriage. Children may enrich family life for stable couples. Unstable couples may find that having children makes their problems worse. Studies show couples with children often argue about parenting practices—especially discipline. Children also add a financial burden. Usually, these problems add to the instability of marriages. Couples who stay together "because of the children" may always be unhappy. Sadly,

their children often feel responsible for the problems at home.

Reasons for Not Choosing Parenthood

Some couples decide to postpone parenthood. Six percent of all couples plan to be childless permanently. These couples feel parenthood does not suit them—at least at the present time. Even couples who want children should think about how children will change their lives.

"We're not ready for a child." When couples say they are not ready for children, they usually mean they need to mature. They may want to pursue their interests before caring for a child. They may feel they need more time as a couple for their marriage to mature. They may need more time for education or job maturity. Some jobs take many years of education or training. Many people want to spend time establishing themselves in a career before becoming parents.

"A baby costs a lot." Babies do cost a lot. At one time, a large family was an economic asset because children helped with the work. Today, children cannot contribute a great deal, if anything, to family income. (Later in this chapter, you will look more closely at the cost of having a child.)

"A child will tie us down." With children comes endless responsibility. Unlike many other responsibilities, child care tasks cannot be put off until later. Children cannot be ignored while on vacation. Even with the best babysitters in charge, parents cannot completely forget their roles. They are always called if children are hurt, ill, or need help. However, the

couple can arrange to have personal time with a little planning.

"A child will interfere with our careers." Both children and careers require time and attention. When tending to both their career and children, parents face two common problems. First, it is hard for parents to have enough time and energy for both parenting and succeeding at work, 3-3. Second, it is difficult to find good child care services.

Some careers make parenting easier than others. For example, school teachers have hours and vacation times similar to those of their older children. Other careers make parenting more difficult. For example, they may require parents to work long hours, night shifts, or at irregular times. Other examples include jobs that make parents feel stressed, demand parents to travel, or frequently ask families to relocate. Jobs that require families to live in areas

that are unsafe or do not have schools are also hard for parents. Couples who combine these types of jobs with parenting must plan carefully.

"Our child could be sick or have a disability." There is no guarantee a child will be in perfect health when he or she is born. Babies can be born with disabilities or become seriously ill or injured. Good medical care before and after birth reduces—but does not eliminate—these risks. Children with disabilities or who are ill or injured, have special needs beyond those of other children. However, most parents feel that raising children with disabilities is highly rewarding.

"Our marriage could fail, and I don't want to be a single parent." Couples whose marriages are unstable may feel this way. Couples with marital problems may want to solve them before having children. Being a single parent is hard. Single parents may lack money, help with household and child care tasks, and the support of a spouse. Without these resources, the single parent cannot always take part in adult activities, which can lead to feelings of isolation. However, many single parents can solve such problems.

Factors to Consider

Parenthood happens quickly. When a child is born or placed (during adoption), the mother and father instantly become parents. Few, if any, other jobs give a beginner such responsibility. No wonder some people refer to their first child as an "experimental child." To prepare for parenthood, couples need to know how children will change their lives.

3-3 One of the challenges of parenting is having enough time and energy to devote to both parenthood and career.

How Children Affect Parents

Raising children is another name for *parenting*. This is only half the picture. Parenting is two-directional. Parents develop along with their children. Ellen Galinsky, a psychologist, describes how parents develop, 3-4. Parents must want more than to have a baby. They must want and be willing to change along with this baby over many years.

Galinsky's Parenting Stages

Stage	Timing of Stage (based on child's age/stage)	Parenting Tasks
Image-making	Before Birth	★ Prepare for changes in their lives. ★ Form images of what their child will be like and their roles as parents.
Nurturing	Birth to Age 2	★ Try to balance their baby's needs with their own needs. ★ Provide loving and consistent care to their baby. (This stems from emotional bonds.)
Authority	Age 2 to Ages 4–5	★ Change their role as the family's authority figures (called *parenting style*). ★ Teach their child the "rules of behavior" through reasoning, rewards, and punishments.
Interpretive	Ages 4–5 to Ages 12–13	★ Share their knowledge about the world with their child. ★ Interpret other authority figures, such as teachers or coaches, by explaining what they expect. ★ Teach values and morals as the need arises. ★ Help their child accept social reality, such as "life may not always be fair."
Interdependent	Teen Years	★ Cope with their teen's changing needs for closeness and distance. ★ Monitor teen's behavior and give guidance as needed. ★ Begin to give more freedom with boundaries to their teen.
Departure	Teen or Early Adult	★ Evaluate themselves as parents. ★ Redefine their relationship with their child, such as allowing their child to make his or her own decisions. Provide guidance only when asked.

3-4 According to Galinsky, parents develop in stages based on their children's age and stage.

How Children Affect Relationships

People who think about having children must look at their lives. They should look at the strengths and weaknesses of their present relationships. Couples should remember that, for children's healthy growth, their strengths should balance each other. In addition, the couple should think about other changes parenthood will bring.

Children and the Couple

Couples should begin looking at their relationships by asking questions about their feelings for others. These kinds of questions relate directly to parenting. For starters, couples might ask themselves the following:

★ Are we loving and sensitive to others' needs?

★ Are we careful not to judge people and their ideas?

★ Can we recognize and respect others' rights?

★ Are we self-disciplined?

★ Do we relate well to others?

★ Are we flexible enough to accept changes?

★ Are we brave about challenges?

★ Can we be honest about our feelings for others?

After answering these questions, couples should think about how their relationship with their partner would change if they were parents. The following questions may help:

★ Do we have the time and energy to give to children?

★ Do we want to share much of our time together with children?

★ Are we doing in our daily lives what we want our children to do? (Children model parents' behavior.)

Couples cannot set a "formula" for successful parenting. They must realize children bring extra work to a marriage. Children usually do not strengthen a weak marriage. However, if a couple can answer most of these questions positively, their relationship may be strong enough for parenthood.

Children and Relatives and Friends

Couples must also look at their present relationships with relatives and friends. Good relationships with others are positive for the couple and their possible children. Couples might want to ask themselves the following questions about their relationships with others:

★ Do our relatives and friends share our basic values?

★ Can we ignore small differences in beliefs?

★ Can we ask for advice and also use our own judgment?

★ Can we tell others about our needs and accept the help they offer?

★ Can we recognize others' needs and offer our help?

★ Can we avoid abusing others' generosity, including time and money?

★ Can we share fun times with others?

If couples can answer most of these questions positively, having a child should not cause problems in relationships outside the family. When couples enjoy their relationships with others before parenthood, then including children can further enrich the relationships, 3-5.

Couples must also think about how their relationships with others can affect their children. There are at least three advantages to children's relationships with others. First, relatives and friends provide children with their first link to the outside world. Second, grandparents and older relatives can teach children about the past. Third, when many relatives and friends care for children, they feel more rooted to their family. Because each relative and friend is unique, children learn to understand that people are different. They also learn

to accept people's unique traits. This interaction will help children get along well with others as they grow.

Sharing Responsibilities

Couples should examine how they feel about home care responsibilities. Some couples practice more traditional roles. For example, the husband brings home the paycheck and the wife cares for the home and children.

Today, many wives work outside the home. In these families, husbands often help with home and child care tasks more than they would in traditional roles. Many men enjoy taking on some of these tasks. In many families, however, wives still do far more in the home, even if both spouses work outside the home. In a few families, the wife works outside the home and

3-5 Strong relationships with other adults can provide support for a couple when they decide to have children.

the husband cares for the home and children. In this way, husbands and wives switch traditional roles.

Couples must consider how they feel about the way they share tasks. They need to ask themselves the following questions:

★ Are we happy with the way we share responsibilities?

★ Do we appreciate each other's help?

★ Do we feel equally important in efforts to reach our goals?

Next, the couple must consider how children will affect how they share responsibilities. They should ask themselves the following questions:

★ If we become parents, will there be major changes in the way we share responsibilities?

★ Can we agree on how to divide home and child care tasks?

★ If one of us works outside the home and the other cares for children, will we feel we are contributing to our goals equally? How will the full-time employee develop a close relationship with the children? How will the full-time homemaker meet personal needs for adult time and interaction?

Couples who want to share responsibilities should answer these questions. How they choose to divide tasks can depend on each person's needs. If couples plan carefully and try all ideas, they can divide tasks so both partners are happy.

Managing Finances

Couples must realize children cost a lot. The first year is expensive, and expenses grow as the child grows. The first baby is often the most expensive. Additional children may use some of the firstborn's items. However, each extra child increases the costs. A second child usually doubles costs. Couples should think about finances before becoming parents. They should ask themselves the following questions:

★ How do we currently earn and spend our money?

★ Are we happy with our budget?

★ Do we have regular savings we could use to meet child-related expenses? If not, can we adjust our budget to meet such expenses?

★ Can we expect more income or lower expenses during the next few years to help offset child-related costs?

★ What type of savings goals do we need for a child?

★ What is an estimate of child-related expenses for the first and next several years?

In addition, spouses should consider the indirect costs of having a child. **Indirect costs** are resources parents use to meet child-related costs that could have been used to meet other goals. They are not actual expenses.

If one parent stays home to raise the child, there will be the indirect cost of **foregone income**. This is the potential income lost by not being in the workforce. Foregone income is greater for the parent who could earn the higher salary.

Another indirect cost is the impact that time out of the labor force will have on career opportunities. A worker who is out of the workforce for several years may miss promotions and may even need to be retrained before working again. The cost of time out of the workforce is the most difficult indirect cost to calculate.

Couples must think about many factors when they estimate the direct and indirect costs of parenting. Each family is different, and these differences show in the way families spend their money.

Carefully planning financial resources is important for everyone, 3-6. In some ways, financial planning becomes more important when couples begin to think about children. This is because children rely on their parents for financial support for many years. Parents also model for their children either good or poor consumer practices.

Focus on Financial Literacy

Estimating Indirect Costs of Parenting

Many factors must be considered when estimating the indirect costs of having children. Indirect costs vary from couple to couple. For one couple, an indirect cost of having children might be giving up time to pursue a hobby. Instead, the couple must spend time interacting with their child. For another couple, one spouse might change work hours to take a shift opposite the other spouse. This would allow the couple to avoid child care costs, but it would have an indirect cost. The spouse with the job change might give up certain job tasks that can only be done in the previous shift. Giving up this task might have an effect on career goals. If one spouse chooses to stay home with the baby and not return to work, then foregone income becomes an indirect cost. What other factors would you consider when estimating indirect costs?

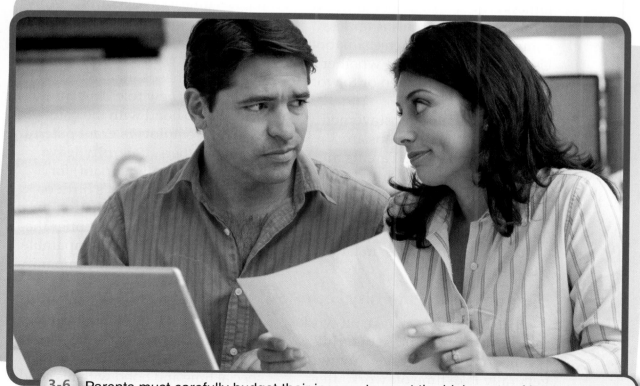

3-6 Parents must carefully budget their income to meet the high costs of having a baby.

Financial Planner

Financial planners assess the financial needs of individuals. They use their knowledge of investments, tax laws, and insurance to recommend financial options to individuals. They help them to identify and plan to meet short- and long-term goals.

Education: A bachelor's or graduate degree is required for financial planners. Most financial planners have at least a bachelor's degree in finance, business administration, accounting, statistics, or economics.

Job Outlook: Employment of financial planners is expected to grow much faster than the average for all occupations.

Managing Careers

Couples must decide whether they will both work or whether one will care for children at home. Some fathers choose to stay home while mothers work, but this is far less common than the reverse situation. Usually mothers decide whether to stay home with children or to work outside the home.

Today, because most women work, child care decisions are extremely important. Parents must decide who will care for the baby. They must also decide how much time they will take from work when the baby is born. (You will learn about child care options in later chapters of this text.)

Maternity and Paternity Leave

The time mothers take off work for the birth or adoption of a child is called **maternity leave**. Women generally take time off work after giving birth or adopting a child. Some women take time off just before the birth as well, although this is less common than in the past. Today, many pregnant women can stay on the job until just before their babies are born.

The length of maternity leave varies from company to company. Six weeks is often the minimum length offered. Maternity may be paid, partially paid, or unpaid. Some companies grant benefits and a percentage of salary during maternity leave. Others grant a longer unpaid leave. Some companies allow a maternity leave of several months or a year. Most working mothers return within three months of the birth or adoption, although many would prefer to take off more time. They may decide not to take more leave for financial or career reasons.

Maternity leave allows the new mother time to regain her strength and get to know her newborn. It takes time to recover from pregnancy, labor, and delivery. Life with a newborn is usually hectic and exhausting for the first few weeks. The mother needs time to rest and adjust to her new role. This time also helps her to bond with the baby.

Some employers grant paternity leave to fathers. **Paternity leave** is time off (usually unpaid) for a set period after a child's birth or adoption. At the end of paternity leave, the company must offer the father a job and salary comparable to the one he left. A few companies pay for this leave.

Paternity leave is growing more common. This time helps the new father care for his recovering wife and child. It allows him to share in this special time and bond with his child.

Men sometimes face some problems in taking paternity leave. One is the economic hardship caused if the leave is unpaid. Some men say their companies might not give them salary raises and promotions if they choose to take leave. These problems may change as more men take paternity leave.

A law called the **Family and Medical Leave Act** protects the rights of many women and men to take unpaid maternity or paternity leave. This law applies to U.S. companies with more than 50 employees. It grants these workers a total of 12 weeks unpaid leave per year to provide care for family members in certain situations. One of these situations is the birth or adoption of a child, 3-7. During this leave, the employee's job must be held or an equal job must be available when the worker returns.

A second federal law also applies to maternity leave. This law states employers are required to treat leave for childbirth and recovery as a medical disability. If employers have provisions for people with other medical disabilities, they must apply these same rules to a woman on maternity leave. This law may require partial pay during the maternity leave.

Before children are born or adopted, it is good for parents to review their employers' leave policies. Understanding these polices will help them calculate forgone income costs of various lengths of leave. When they know these costs, a couple can plan their budget accordingly and decide what leave each partner wants to take.

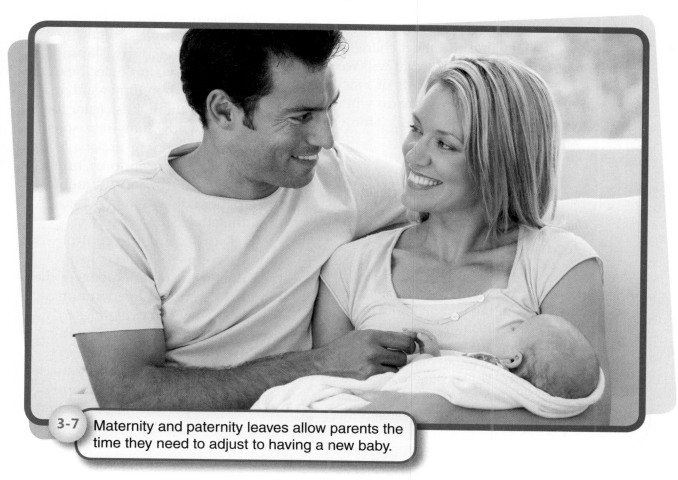

3-7 Maternity and paternity leaves allow parents the time they need to adjust to having a new baby.

Problems with Family and Work

Working parents often encounter problems as they care for their families and strive to do well at their jobs. These roles can be tough to balance. Dual-career couples will need to answer the following questions:

★ Can we find good child care during working hours?

★ Can we balance job demands and children's needs? For example, will we be able to give complete or only partial attention to our children after work?

★ Can we work out mutual responsibilities for child and home care tasks?

★ Can we make enough time for ourselves as individuals and as a couple free of other concerns?

★ Can we be organized? Can we be flexible and meet changes in our schedules? What will we do to meet the needs of a sick child? What will we do when job demands are heavy for a short time?

★ If we are uncomfortable with our answers to any of these questions, what other options do we have?

Parents may worry about how their children will be affected when they work outside the home. Studies show that, when children had good care, being separated from parents during work hours did not harm them. However, the mother's attitude about work seemed to be most important. The happiest children came from homes where the mother wanted to work and did—or wanted to stay home and could. If the mother is happy about her situation, children benefit from her attitude. Children may suffer if their mother is unhappy about her situation.

Family Planning

After considering all these factors, many couples practice family planning. **Family planning** happens when a couple decides how many children they want and when to have them. It is easier to plan a family now than in the past, because many options are available for controlling conception. Couples can use these **birth control methods** to help them delay having children until they decide to conceive.

To learn about birth control options, couples should consult their doctor or staff members of the Planned Parenthood Federation of America. They can explain each method in terms of the following:

★ how the method works to prevent pregnancy (For example, does the method block sperm's travel or provide hormones that prevent ovulation?)

Focus on Speech
Community Services for Parents

Arrange to visit a local program or agency that provides services for parents. Talk with the director or a parent educator about the services offered. What is the purpose of the program? How can parents benefit from the services provided? What costs are involved? How can a parent enroll in or join the program? Share your findings with the class.

* how successful the properly used method is at preventing pregnancy

* directions for using the method

* the method's possible side effects and risks, including future fertility

* the method's cost

Before advising a particular option, however, the doctor will review the couple's health history and give them a complete checkup. The couple should think about which method they prefer. This will depend on their religious beliefs and their likes and dislikes of certain methods.

Family planning is a couple's personal choice. There are some points couples should keep in mind as they plan families. A woman should consult a doctor about her health before becoming pregnant. A doctor may suggest an ideal pre-pregnancy weight. A doctor may also prescribe prenatal vitamins, suggest a nutritional diet, and recommend less caffeine. The doctor will also encourage no alcohol or smoking.

To protect the health of a mother and child, mothers need advice on when to have the next baby. As a general rule, doctors are now saying a woman should not try to become pregnant before 18 to 23 months after delivery.

In addition, there is often less jealousy between children when they are born about three years apart. This is because older children can help with the new baby and still feel needed. Also, some research shows this spacing may allow each child to develop better. It gives parents time to work with each child alone before they must divide their attention.

Not all couples feel they can handle another child right away. These feelings depend on their finances, emotional and physical energy, career, age, and lifestyle. Couples should not feel guilty if they want only one child. They should realize an only child would not necessarily be spoiled or lonely. The best reason for a couple to have another child is wanting to share their love and time with this child, too.

Infertility and Sterility

About 88 percent of all couples who try to conceive will do so within a year. Couples who do not conceive within a year are known as **infertile**. About 37 percent of women under the age of 35 will later conceive. This percentage drops a great deal after this age. Most will need medical assistance, but some will conceive on their own. The remaining couples will not successfully conceive, for one or both partners are **sterile**. This means the couple will be permanently unable to conceive or the wife is unable to carry their fully biological child.

People often think that women account for almost all fertility problems. In one-third of the cases, infertility is due to the woman. In another one-third of the cases, it is due to the man. The remaining cases are caused by both partners or by unknown reasons. When both adults are infertile, they have a much lower chance to conceive than couples with only one infertile partner.

Reproductive diseases and problems with the reproductive organs are the main causes of infertility and sterility, 3-8. Certain diseases, such as diabetes, and some prescription drugs, such as those for high blood pressure, may lessen fertility. Being exposed to drugs, chemicals, and radiation can hamper fertility. The same is true of sexually transmitted infections, smoking, and being overweight. Excessive physical activity, being underweight, and aging can also lead to fertility problems.

Overcoming Infertility

Infertile couples who want to pursue having biological children can seek fertility counseling. **Fertility counseling** consists of determining the reasons for the fertility problems and exploring treatment options. First, both partners are given several tests. These might reveal the fertility problem involves the woman, the man, or both partners.

If a problem is found, the doctor may suggest steps to restore fertility, 3-9. Hormones or drugs might be given to stimulate ovulation or balance hormone levels. Surgery might be able to repair problems with the reproductive organs.

If these treatments do not work, couples can look into other options. They might consider adopting a child or being foster parents. Other couples try what are called **assisted reproductive technologies (ARTs)**. These are methods to help infertile couples conceive. Three of the most common ART procedures are the following:

★ **Artificial insemination** occurs when the sperm is introduced into the vagina or uterus by a medical procedure rather than by sexual relations.

★ **In vitro fertilization (IVF)** occurs when some of the mother's eggs are surgically removed and fertilized with sperm in a laboratory dish. After a few days, the fertilized egg is implanted into the mother's uterus. Babies conceived by this method were once referred to as test-tube babies.

★ **Gamete intrafallopian transfer (GIFT)** occurs when a mixture of sperm and eggs is placed in the woman's fallopian tubes, where fertilization can occur. Because more than one egg is present, conception is more likely, but a multiple pregnancy can occur, too.

In some cases, problems exist with the sperm, eggs, or both sperm and eggs of the couple. For example, one or both partners may be sterile. When these problems

Major Causes of Infertility and Sterility

Women	Men
Lack of ovulation	Low sperm count
Hormone deficiencies	Hormone deficiencies
Irregular ovulation	Inability of sperm to move
Damage to reproductive organs	Damage to reproductive organs

3-8 Infertility can have many causes, some of which are unknown.

Fertility Methods

Method	Used to...	Problems
Artificial insemination	Provide increased number of sperm for conception in biological mother. Impregnate surrogate mother.	Slight risk of infection If sperm is not husband's, moral issues and legal issues (legitimacy and biological father's rights)
Hormone therapy (fertility drugs)	Stimulate ovaries to function properly.	Multiple pregnancies Possible increased risk for female cancers
Microsurgery	Attempt to open the fallopian tubes.	Risks of surgery, such as anesthetic and infection risks
In vitro fertilization (IVF)	Allow a woman with permanently blocked fallopian tubes to have her eggs surgically removed and fertilized with her husband's sperm in a laboratory dish. After a few days, the fertilized eggs are implanted in the mother's uterus. Impregnate surrogate mother.	Risks of surgery Multiple births Moral and legal issues
Gamete Intrafallopian Transfer (GIFT)	Increased chances of conception if men have a low sperm count or women have problems ovulating. (A mixture of sperm and several eggs are surgically placed in the fallopian tubes.)	Risks of surgery Multiple births
Surrogate mother	Replace the infertile couple's role in bearing a child. Surrogate mother (A) may bear a child who is the infertile couple's biological child conceived by in vitro fertilization, (B) may bear a child with her egg and the husband's sperm (of the infertile couple) that were introduced to the surrogate mother through artificial insemination, or (C) may bear a child not biologically related to the infertile couple by using her own eggs and donor sperm introduced through artificial insemination.	Moral issues Legal issues

3-9 Infertile couples now have many options for having children.

exist, couples may opt to use an ART with the germ cells (sperm, eggs, or sperm and eggs) that were donated by other people. These donor cells would be used to attempt conception.

If the wife cannot carry a baby, the couple might consider using a **surrogate mother**. This is a woman who bears (sometimes both conceives and bears) a child for a couple. The surrogate would carry the baby in her uterus, give birth to the baby, and sign her parenting rights over to the couple. She could conceive using an ART with the wife's eggs (or donate her own eggs if the wife's eggs cannot be used).

There are many drawbacks to ARTs. Even with advances in fertility treatments, over half of all ART attempts do not succeed. Older couples have the least chance of conceiving. Fertility, especially for the woman, declines with age and also increases the risk of birth defects. Fertility problems are emotionally painful for couples. They may feel very disappointed if they use ARTs and it is not successful. Couples may also feel their privacy is violated during fertility testing and treatment. Some couples begin to lose hope about their life plans. The partner with the fertility problem may feel damaged, defective, or guilty.

Another drawback to ARTs is the cost. These methods are very expensive—each try costs thousands of dollars. Couples may need to try the procedure more than once for it to succeed. They may have to travel some distance to major hospitals for fertility treatments. Even still, there is no guarantee the couple will ever conceive. Couples may

lessen the costs of ARTs by seeking treatment through research or teaching hospitals.

ARTs also raise some ethical and legal issues. When donor cells are used, the donor of the egg or sperm is the biological parent of the child born to the couple. Problems can result if the donor wants parenting rights or changes his or her mind. Other problems can occur if the couple decides, for whatever reason, they do not want the baby. These complex issues can lead to legal battles. Couples may want to seek legal advice before agreeing to use donor cells in an ART procedure.

Likewise, the use of a surrogate raises moral and legal issues. First is the moral issue of whether someone other than the couple wanting to parent should be involved in the pregnancy. Legal issues are raised concerning any fee and what happens if the oral or written agreement is broken. These questions include the following:

★ Who pays if the surrogate mother's and/or the newborn's medical fees are much higher than the contract fee?

★ What happens if the surrogate decides she wants to keep the baby who may be her child biologically?

★ What happens if the couple decides they do not want this child because they have conceived in the meantime or the child has a disability?

Because of these drawbacks, many couples choose not to pursue their options regarding ARTs. Others try, but find they cannot restore their fertility. Both types of couples may face or experience a crisis as they adjust to this reality. For some people who deeply desire children, there may be a lasting sense of being unfulfilled. Counseling may help them resolve these feelings. Many other couples become fulfilled parents through adoption or foster parenthood. Some childless couples find fulfillment in other endeavors involving families and children.

Summary

Parenting is more difficult than other tasks because it involves relationships. Parents usually are not trained to be parents. Most jobs require training, but parenting, one of the most important jobs of all, is often undertaken without preparation. With fewer extended families today and more mobility, having supportive relationships is more difficult.

Those considering parenting need to find out what resources are available to them. They should learn as much about children as possible. These resources include professionals, successful parents, books, magazines, or child care classes. Spending time with other infants and children will also increase a couple's knowledge of children. The way the couple was raised will affect their parenting roles.

Couples have different reasons for wanting or not wanting children. There are a number of factors couples must think about when deciding on a family. They must see how parenting will create developmental changes in themselves. They must consider how having a baby will change their relationships with each other, relatives, and friends. Couples should also think about how children will affect their shared responsibilities at home. In addition, they should also understand how children affect their finances and career.

Many couples today practice family planning. The use of birth control methods can make family planning more successful. A couple should consult their doctor when selecting a method.

Some couples who plan for children find they are infertile or sterile. These problems have many causes, some of which are unknown. In some cases, infertile couples choose to pursue an ART method, such as artificial insemination, IVF, or GIFT, to help them conceive. Some consider becoming parents of adopted or foster children or seek other ways to include time with children in their lives.

Companion Web Site

Interactive Activity

Review vocabulary terms and key concepts for Chapter 3 at **g-wlearning.com**.

Review and Reflect

Write your answers to the following questions on a separate sheet of paper.

1. True or false. For most couples, parenting is a natural, automatic response that immediately follows a baby's birth or adoption.

2. List three poor reasons people give for wanting to become parents.

3. True or false. A couple's desire to share their love and time with a child is the best reason for parenthood.

4. What does Galinsky say about parenthood?

5. What are the most common problems of meeting both career and parenthood demands?

6. Define *foregone income*.

7. Why might a woman consider taking maternity leave after the birth of a child?

8. What is the Family and Medical Leave Act?

9. How does family planning affect children?

10. True or false. Infertility is a problem that affects only women.

11. Explain how infertility might affect a couple.

12. Describe two ways an infertile couple might be able to become parents.

Cross-Curricular Link

13. **Writing.** Compose a short paper giving your views on the kinds of maturity couples should have before becoming parents. Check your paper for correct spelling, grammar, and punctuation.

14. **Speech.** Interview several couples who have young children. Ask each couple about how they learned the skills they would need for parenting before they had children. What skills did they have to learn after having children? Ask them to share some funny stories about trying to care for their children. Take notes or record the stories. Share your findings with the class.

15. **Reading, Writing.** Read a book about child care. Create a bibliography that includes the title of the publication, name and address of publisher, topics covered, age of children discussed, and other important information.

16. **Math.** Child care is an indirect cost of parenting when both parents work. Ask a local child care provider what rate is charged to provide child care for one infant full-time (all day, five days a week). Use this weekly rate to calculate the cost of child care during the first year of life (from age six weeks until the first birthday).

17. **Science.** Working with a small group, research one of the ART methods that can help infertile couples conceive. Prepare a group report on your chosen method.

Making Observations

18. In an informal setting, observe parents who are having a difficult time with a child. What parenting skills might they need to help them with their children? For example, do they need to know more about appropriate developmental tasks for the child's age, discipline methods, or how to childproof their home?

19. Observe examples of literature and professional services for parents in your local school and community.

20. Observe how dual-career families share responsibilities for home and child care.

21. Observe how an employer in your community helps parents meet their family and work obligations. For example, does the employer offer maternity leave, paternity leave, child care programs, job sharing, and/or flexible work schedules?

Thinking Critically

22. If a married couple chooses not to have children or wants to wait several years before having a child, what can they say to their parents who want grandchildren? Why do older people often want grandchildren? Besides having grandchildren, what are some ways older people can fulfill their need to be with young children?

23. What are some specific ways a dual-career couple can equally share home care tasks? What could be done to make the sharing of home tasks fair if the demands of one person's job involve travel, very long work hours in comparison to the partner's work hours, being on-call, or bringing work home?

24. Why might companies choose to offer paternity leave to their employees? Why might companies choose not to offer paternity leave to their employees?

25. Suppose you and your future spouse could not conceive. Do you think you would consider using an ART or surrogate mother to help you become parents? Explain.

Chapter 4 Pregnancy

Chapter 5 Prenatal Care

Chapter 6 Childbirth

Chapter 7 The Newborn

Focus on
Family and Community

Research organizations in your community that provide services for expectant parents and newborns. Do any of the organizations provide prenatal or childbirth classes? Are classes offered for parenting, providing daily care for infants, and first aid? Do any of the organizations use volunteers? Choose one organization to visit and learn more about its history and goals. Take it a step further and become a volunteer to help the organization. You can also participate in the FCCLA *Community Service Program*. Use the FCCLA *Planning Process* to plan, carry out, and evaluate your project. Then summarize your community service activities in a *Chapter Service Project Manual*, which you can present at an FCCLA Star Event. Your FCCLA advisor can provide you with further information.

4 Pregnancy

After studying this chapter, you will be able to

★ **describe** what happens during conception.

★ **explain** how genetic factors affect prenatal development.

★ **describe** how a person inherits traits through genes.

★ **list** the three different types of multiple pregnancies.

★ **describe** the three main stages of prenatal development.

Terms to Know

cell	identical
sperm	prenatal development
ovum	germinal stage
conception	amnion
zygote	placenta
fallopian tubes	umbilical cord
uterus	embryonic stage
genetic factors	embryo
chromosomes	cartilage
dominant traits	fetal stage
recessive traits	fetus
multiple pregnancy	quickening
fraternal	age of viability
chorion	

Reading Advantage

Find the list of terms at the beginning of the chapter. Write what you think each term means. Then look up the term in the glossary and write the textbook definition.

Companion Web Site

Interactive Activity

Learn more about a multiple pregnancy by completing the *Read, Discuss, and Analyze* Activity for Chapter 4 at **g-wlearning.com**.

Pregnancy is a special time for a couple. The feelings of parents-to-be range from great excitement to anxiety. However, when both spouses want children, they adjust rather easily to parenthood.

Pregnancy is the process through which a new human prepares to enter the world. This process begins when a baby is created inside the mother's body. During the nine months of pregnancy, the baby grows and develops at a fast rate. Before the baby is actually born, however, many complex changes must take place.

Many factors influence these changes. One factor is a baby's genes. Genes determine much about a person's looks, personality, and physical size. A baby's genes come from both the mother and father, 4-1. These genes start to control how babies grow and develop before they are even born.

Conception

A **cell** is the smallest unit of life that is able to reproduce itself. Life begins with the joining of two separate cells—one from the male and one from the female. These cells are called *germ cells* (the cells involved in reproduction). The male germ cell is called the **sperm**. The female germ cell is the **ovum** (often called the *egg*). The joining of these two cells is called **conception**. At conception, ovum and sperm combine to form a single cell called a **zygote**. Another name for the zygote is a *fertilized egg*.

How do these two types of germ cells form and unite to create new life? Ovum are produced and stored by the woman's ovaries. Inside the ovary, the ovum is stored in a small sac called a *follicle*. Hormones cause some follicles to grow and fill with fluid each month.

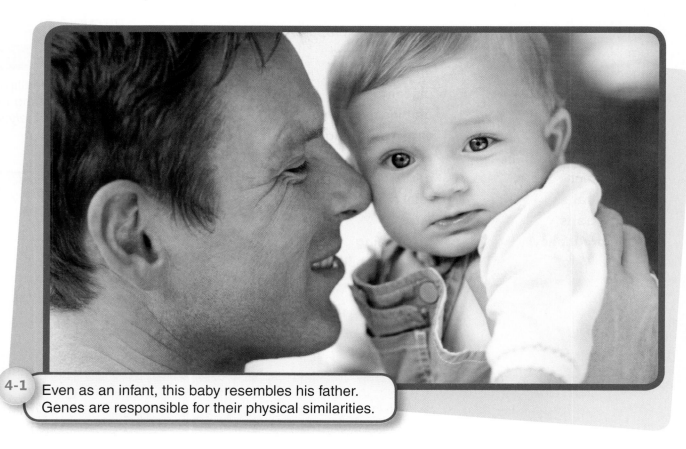

4-1 Even as an infant, this baby resembles his father. Genes are responsible for their physical similarities.

Around the middle of the menstrual cycle, one ovum is released from the follicle, and the other follicles that were growing become inactive. (Sometimes more than one ovum is released.) The release of the ovum from the ovary is called *ovulation*.

When the egg is released, it travels toward the **fallopian tubes**. These are two hollow tubes that extend from the right and left sides of the uterus. The **uterus** is the organ in which the baby develops and is protected until birth. One end of each fallopian tube is connected to the uterus. The other end of each tube has fingerlike projections. These projections lie near, but are not attached to, the ovary. The projections from the fallopian tube help gather the ovum as it emerges from the ovary. Once inside the fallopian tube, the ovum moves very slowly down the tube. Here,

the ovum is ready and available to be joined by a sperm, 4-2.

Semen, a liquid which contains over 300 million sperm, enters the woman's body during intercourse. These sperm begin a journey to the ovum that lasts only minutes. Many sperm do not survive. Only 300 to 500 reach the fallopian tube.

Sperm may meet the ovum at any point. Conception usually happens when the ovum is less than one-third of the way down the fallopian tube. After that point, conception is unlikely because the ovum has a short life span. It only lives about 24 hours after ovulation.

The sperm approach the ovum and try to break through its surface. Only one sperm successfully enters, or fertilizes the egg. Once one sperm is accepted, no other sperm can enter the ovum. Conception has occurred, and the zygote forms.

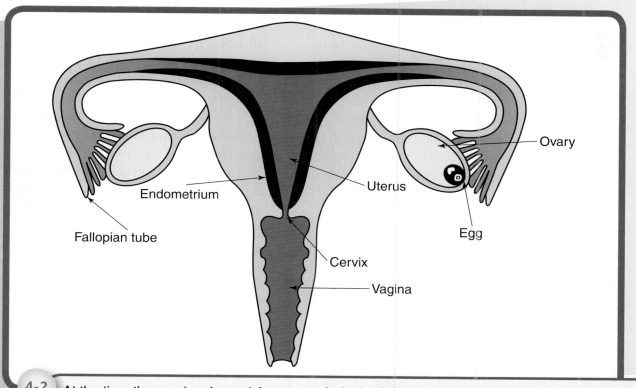

Ovary

Endometrium

Uterus

Fallopian tube

Egg

Cervix

Vagina

4-2 At the time the egg is released, hormones help the fallopian tube projections move to gather the egg. These hormones also prepare the uterus to receive and support a baby if conception occurs.

Genetic Factors and the Unborn Baby

In Chapter 1, you learned that genetics is the study of heredity. A person's inherited traits are passed to him or her at conception. The total heredity is received at this one time—no new genes will be inherited.

Genetic factors are the traits passed through the genes. These factors affect all stages of growth and development. In many ways, genetic factors influence the prenatal stage more than any other stage of life. Following certain rules, each parent's genes combine to make a blueprint for the unborn child's growth and development. During pregnancy, this blueprint, called a *genome*, guides growth and development as the baby changes from a zygote to a baby ready to be born. The unborn baby will come to look much like other members of the family. He or she will likely have abilities, interests, and personality traits that are similar to those of family members, too.

During the prenatal period, the genetic blueprint also gives the cells instructions for family-like traits that will unfold throughout life. For example, during the prenatal period a baby boy's cells receive instructions on hair loss later in life. These instructions determine whether he will be bald, what the pattern of hair loss will be, and when hair loss will occur. Some people's genes lead them to lose hair, while others have genes that promote keeping a full head of hair. What causes each person to be so different? Heredity does, and it works in complex ways. You may understand heredity better by reading about Steve.

Heredity and Steve

Steve is a five-year-old boy. Like many children his age, Steve asks many questions, enjoys pretend games, and shows interest in letters and numbers. Although Steve shares many traits with other five-year-olds, he is uniquely Steve—not Kate, Peter, Susan, or even his older brother, Chris. How did Steve become the person he is?

Like all people, Steve began life as a single-celled zygote. The *nucleus*, or center, of this cell contains a set of instructions to build a living being. These directions tell the body whether a being will be a person, an animal, or a plant. The instructions are written in what scientists call a *genetic code*.

Where does nature keep this important genetic code? The genetic code is stored in DNA (deoxyribonucleic acid). DNA is a chemical compound that is found in threadlike structures called **chromosomes**. The chromosomes carry genes in living cells. Chromosomes contain the information nature needs to make Steve a human.

Focus on Science

Genes

Because blood relatives share ancestors, they have some genes in common. These genes can cause family members to share common traits. Make a list of the traits of someone you know well. Include physical, mental, and personality traits as well as interests and talents. Beside each trait, write the relative(s) with whom the person shares a trait.

Chromosomes and Genes

All living organisms have a certain number of chromosomes. Each human baby receives a total of 46 chromosomes, which form 23 pairs. Half of these chromosomes come from the mother and half come from the father. Each sperm contains 23 chromosomes, as does each ovum, 4-3.

Each chromosome contains about 20,000 genes. These genes determine a person's individual traits. Human cells contain about a million genes. Sometimes one gene determines a trait. Other times, a group of genes decides a trait.

Steve's genes have determined he has blue eyes; light brown hair with a reddish tinge; and fair, freckled skin. His genes give him Rh positive blood, type O. They also carry a better-than-average chance of having high blood pressure. Because of his genes, Steve learns quickly. These qualities are only part of Steve's genetic information. The sum of Steve's genes, along with his environment, makes him Steve and no one else.

Steve's appearance is unique; he does not look exactly like anyone in his family. He looks like his father in some ways and his mother in other ways. Some of Steve's features do not look like either of his parents' features. Steve's hair is the same color as his mother's, but his body is built like his father's. Even though both of Steve's parents have brown eyes, his eyes are blue.

Steve's traits were passed to him through his parents' germ cells (ovum and sperm). Of the 46 total chromosomes a parent has, only half (23) will be present in his or her germ cell. Chance determines

Geneticist

Geneticists study the science of heredity and living organisms. Many geneticists perform research to develop solutions to health problems and improve the environment.

Education: A Ph.D. in biology is needed for research, but a master's or bachelor's degree is acceptable for some non-research positions.

Job Outlook: Future employment opportunities are expected to grow about as fast as the average for all occupations. Competition may be very high for grant research.

which chromosomes these will be. The baby inherits a set of 23 chromosomes from each parent. It is the final combination of these two sets of chromosomes that makes each person unique.

4-3 Every child inherits 23 chromosomes from the mother's ovum and 23 chromosomes from the father's sperm.

Dominant and Recessive Traits

In all but one chromosome pair, all the genes occur in pairs. In each gene pair, one gene originates from the father and the other is from the mother. The genes from each parent work together to determine the appearance of each trait in a child.

In the case of Steve, his genes give him blue eyes, but both his parents are brown-eyed. You may wonder how Steve's parents could pass on this trait even though neither of them has blue eyes. This is an example of how heredity can be complex.

People can pass on traits that do not show in them. This is because some traits are dominant and some are recessive. **Dominant traits** are those that always show in a person even if only one gene of the pair is inherited for that trait. **Recessive traits** typically do not show in a person unless both genes for the trait are inherited (one from each parent). In a few cases, a boy can inherit recessive traits by receiving a single recessive gene from his mother. Examples are color blindness and hemophilia. Most often, however, it takes two recessive genes for a recessive trait to show. A person who inherits only one recessive gene for a trait becomes a *carrier* of that trait. This makes it possible for the trait to show up in later generations.

People can have dominant, recessive, or both types of genes for height. Tallness is dominant and shortness is recessive, 4-4. There

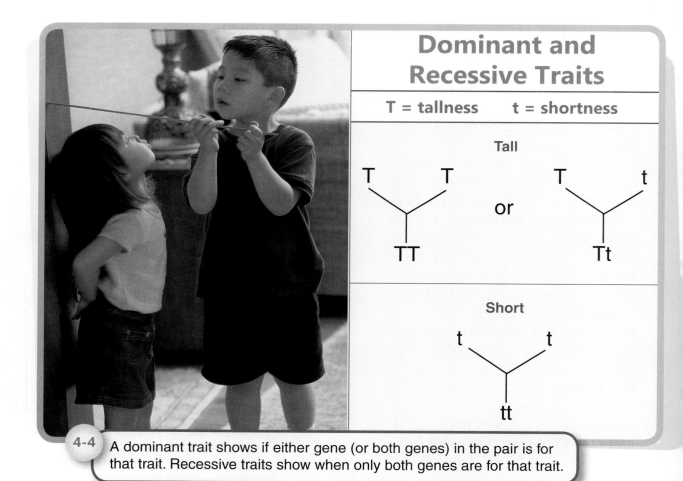

Dominant and Recessive Traits

T = tallness   t = shortness

Tall

T   T   T   t

or

TT   Tt

Short

t   t

tt

4-4 A dominant trait shows if either gene (or both genes) in the pair is for that trait. Recessive traits show when only both genes are for that trait.

were both tall and short relatives in Steve's mother's family—possibly for several generations. Because of this, Steve's mother inherited one gene for tallness and one for shortness, so she is tall. Steve's father also had tall and short relatives. He is a tall man, but also has one gene for tallness and one for shortness. Some of the ova from Steve's mother were for tallness and some for shortness. In like manner, some sperm from Steve's father were for tallness and some for shortness. Steve received both an ovum and a sperm for shortness. Because he has two recessive genes, Steve shows the recessive trait of shortness. Steve's brothers and sisters could be short like Steve or tall like Steve's parents.

Sex Chromosomes

Of the 23 pairs of chromosomes, 22 are alike in both males and females. These 22 pairs provide genetic information for both males and females, such as height and eye color. The chromosomes that make up the twenty-third pair are different for females and males. This pair is called the *sex chromosomes*. The sex of a child, however, is determined by this whole chromosome pair, unlike traits that are determined by a few genes on chromosome pairs.

Females have the chromosome pair called XX (because when viewed with a microscope, the pair looks somewhat like the letters X and X). When a female's chromosome pair splits to form germ cells (ova), all ova will be X because each chromosome pair was XX.

Males have the chromosome pair called XY (because when viewed with a microscope, the pair looks somewhat like the letters X and Y). When a male's chromosome pair splits to form germ cells (sperm), some will be X and some will be Y. This is because each chromosome pair was XY.

All the mother's egg cells will carry the X chromosome. If fertilized by a sperm carrying an X chromosome, the child will be female (XX). If the sperm cell carries the Y chromosome, the child will be male (XY). Because the father's sex chromosome is the one that can vary, it is the father's sperm that always determines the sex of the child, 4-5.

4-5 Because this child is male, his father's sperm carried a Y chromosome. When the father's sperm carries an X chromosome, the child is female.

In the XY chromosome pair, a few of boys' traits are determined only by their mothers. Think of an X as having four legs and a Y as having three legs. Genes on the fourth leg of the X alone determine these traits. There is no fourth leg of the Y to follow the laws of dominant and recessive genes. This is not the case for girls whose sex chromosome pair is XX. For boys, the genes on the unmatched fourth-leg of the X chromosome determine the *sex-linked traits*. Some sex-linked traits include color blindness and hemophilia, a serious blood disorder. Girls would only have these disorders if they received these recessive genes from both parents.

Multiple Pregnancy

Sometimes two or more babies develop in the same pregnancy. This is called a **multiple pregnancy**. Multiple pregnancies are far less common than single pregnancies, 4-6. Notice twins are more common than triplets, and triplets are more common than quadruplets. In very rare cases, as many as seven or eight babies can be conceived in the same pregnancy.

Doctors are often concerned about the health of multiple births with three or more babies. Most babies in these births are born early and have low birthweights (under 3.3 pounds for multiple births). This puts them at risk for severe vision, hearing, mental, and developmental disabilities. Twins are also almost 5 times (triplets almost 10 times) more likely to die in their first year than single-birth children.

Fraternal Births

The most common multiple pregnancy is caused when multiple babies develop from two or more ova. Each ova is fertilized with a different sperm. This means each child has a different genetic makeup. These babies are as much alike and different as any other brothers and sisters. Children born in these multiple births are called **fraternal** children. They can be twins, triplets, or higher multiple births. (*Fraternal* comes from a Latin word meaning *brother*.)

Fraternal children may or may not be the same gender. They look different at birth and show greater differences as they mature. Each child in a fraternal birth has his or her own chorion. The **chorion** is a membrane that surrounds the baby in the uterus.

Identical Births

In identical births, children develop from a single ovum that was fertilized by a single sperm. During the early days of the

Chances of Having Spontaneous Multiples*

Twins	1 in 83 pregnancies
Triplets	1 in almost 7 thousand pregnancies
Quadruplets	1 in about 572 thousand pregnancies
Quintuplets	1 in about 47.5 million pregnancies
Sextuplets	1 in almost 4 billion pregnancies

*These numbers exclude pregnancies of women using ART.

4-6 Most women have single pregnancies. Twins are by far the most common multiple pregnancy.

Learn More About...
Factors Affecting Multiple Births

Although multiple pregnancies are not as common as single pregnancies, they have become more common. This is due to several factors.

Maternal Age (*Note:* Older mothers have a greater risk than younger mothers for pregnancy problems, including the loss of the baby. Babies born to older women are at an increased risk for abnormalities compared with those of younger women.)

★ rate doubles between 35 and 40 years

★ rate decreases between ages 40 and 45 years

★ after age 45, 1 in 9 pregnancies are multiples

Better Nutrition

History of Earlier Pregnancies

★ compared to the first pregnancy, the rate increases four times for the fourth or fifth pregnancy

★ rate is four times greater for women who have had multiples over those who have had singletons

Multiple Pregnancies on the Maternal Side of the Family

Use of ART

Is there something common about these factors? Yes, they all increase the chances of multiple ovulation due to hormones. The hormones in fertility drugs stimulate ovulation. Thus, successful ART almost always produces a multiple pregnancy. In the 1990s when ART was new, it was not uncommon for some of these women to have more than three babies. Higher-number multiples are now on the decline. This is due to improvements in ART.

---

pregnancy, the ovum splits to produce two or more children. Scientists do not know why the ovum splits. The chances of identical births are much less than the odds for fraternal births, 4-7.

If the ovum does not completely split, the babies will be *conjoined twins*. The bodies of these twins are joined in one or more places. They may share external body parts, such as legs, or internal organs, such as the liver. Conjoined twins occur in about one in 250,000 *live births*.

Babies from an identical birth have the same genetic makeup. This is because they came from one fertilized ovum. These babies are called **identical**. Identical children can be twins, triplets, or higher multiple births.

Identical children are very similar in appearance. People often confuse which child is which. Even family members may confuse them, 4-8.

Chances of Having Spontaneous Identical Multiples*

Twins	1 in 250 pregnancies
Triplets	1 in almost 62.5 thousand pregnancies
Quadruplets	1 in over 15.5 million pregnancies
Quintuplets	1 in almost 4 billion pregnancies

*These numbers exclude pregnancies of women using ART.

4-7 Identical multiples are far less common than fraternal multiples.

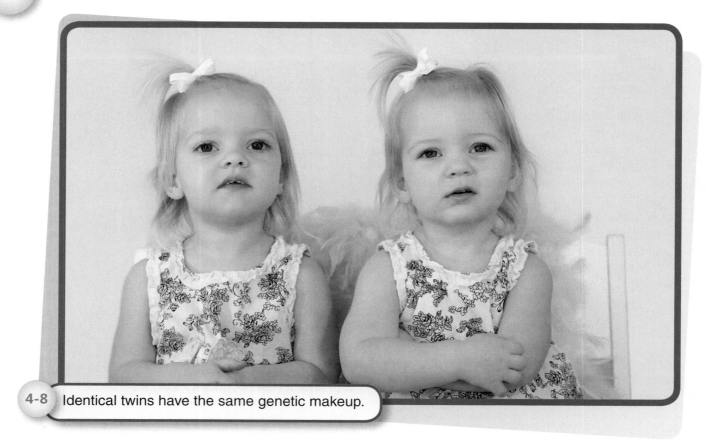

4-8   Identical twins have the same genetic makeup.

However, except for their genes, identical children are not exactly alike. Their fingerprints, palm prints, and footprints are similar, but not exactly the same. Also, environment makes identical children different. For example, one child may be larger because of better nourishment, even before birth.

Some identical twins are *mirror twins*. They look the way you and your mirror image would appear. For instance, one may have a birthmark on the right shoulder and the other may have one on the left shoulder. One may be right-handed and the other left-handed.

Sometimes it is difficult to tell whether children are identical. At birth, the delivering physician may be able to tell. If not, blood tests or skin grafting can be used for proof. Identical children are always of the same gender. Unlike fraternal children, they usually share one chorion. However, it is possible for each identical child to have a separate chorion.

Mixed Types

Multiple pregnancies may be both identical and fraternal if three or more children are born. In mixed types of pregnancies, separate sperm fertilize two or more eggs (fraternal). Then, one or more of the fertilized ova may split (identical).

If all children are identical or all are fraternal, this is not a mixed pregnancy. However, triplets are often from a mixed pregnancy, with two children identical and one fraternal.

In like manner, quadruplets may also be all identical or all fraternal. However, quadruplets are often a mixed pregnancy type. With quadruplets, there could be several combinations. Three children could be identical and one fraternal, or two could be identical with the other two fraternal. There could even be two identical pairs, but such a case has not been known.

Stages in Prenatal Development

Many changes happen between conception and birth. The development that takes place during this time is called **prenatal development**. Prenatal development is divided into the germinal, embryonic, and fetal stages. See 4-9.

Germinal Stage

The first stage of prenatal development is the **germinal stage**. Conception marks the beginning of the germinal stage. This stage covers about the first two weeks of the pregnancy.

The fertilized egg (zygote) remains a single cell for about 30 hours. Then it starts to divide. On the third day, it has formed a hollow ball of 32 cells. This ball of cells enters the uterus, where it continues dividing rapidly for about three more days. During this time, the ball of cells floats freely in the uterus.

About 10 days after conception, the ball of cells begins to embed in the wall of the uterus. The cells continue to divide. The chorion and **amnion** (a fluid-filled sac) begin to form. They surround the cells and protect the baby until birth. The **placenta**, an organ filled with blood vessels, begins to develop against the wall of the uterus. The umbilical cord grows out from the developing child, at the site of the future navel, and connects with the placenta. The **umbilical cord** contains three blood vessels that connect the child with the placenta. As the placenta develops, it will begin to nourish the baby, remove the baby's wastes, exchange gases between mother and baby, and provide the baby with needed hormones. When the baby can receive nourishment from the mother, the germinal stage has ended.

Embryonic Stage

The second stage of prenatal development is the **embryonic stage**. Experts say this is the most critical stage of pregnancy because almost all body systems develop during this stage. The embryonic stage lasts about six weeks. During this stage, the baby is called an **embryo**.

Changes happen so quickly that, when this stage ends, the embryo looks like a small human being. The embryo has tiny arms, legs, fingers, toes, and a face. All the major organs, such as the heart, brain, and lungs, are present. The heart begins beating in this stage. The embryo's body does not yet have solid bones, but is supported by cartilage. **Cartilage** is soft, elastic, flexible tissue that provides structure for the body. Cartilage is the tissue found in the tip of your nose.

The baby now receives both good and harmful substances from the mother's placenta through the umbilical cord. Because the baby's body parts are developing so quickly, passing harmful substances to the child can affect him or her for life. That is why the mother's health habits become very important during

Prenatal Development by Week

Carnegie Institute of Washington,
Dept. of Embryology, Davis Div.

4-day-old zygote

Carnegie Institute of Washington,
Dept. of Embryology, Davis Div.

4½-week-old embryo

The Germinal Stage

Conception through 2 weeks
★ Cell divisions occurring
★ Fertilized egg embedding in the wall of the uterus
★ Amnion, placenta, and umbilical cord beginning to form

The Embryonic Stage

2 weeks through 8 weeks
★ Internal organs (heart, liver, digestive system, brain, and lungs) developing
★ Tissue segments (future vertebrae) in a spinal column forming
★ Limb buds (future arms and legs) appearing
★ Ears and eyes beginning to form

4-9 Cell division results in the beginnings of a baby and a life-support system between mother and baby. The amnion, chorion, and placenta develop at the end of the germinal stage. They protect and nourish the baby until birth.

this stage. She should eat healthful foods so her baby receives the needed nutrients. She should also avoid substances like alcohol, drugs, caffeine, tobacco, and X-rays that may harm the baby. With regular medical care and by taking care of herself, a woman does her part to help her baby be born healthy.

Fetal Stage

When bone cells start to replace cartilage, the baby enters the **fetal stage** of development. This stage begins about nine weeks after conception. From this point until birth, a baby is known medically as a **fetus**.

Chapter 4 Pregnancy   **113**

Carnegie Institute of Washington,
Dept. of Embryology, Davis Div.

9-week-old fetus

Carnegie Institute of Washington,
Dept. of Embryology, Davis Div.

12-week-old fetus

The Fetal Stage

9 weeks
★ Facial features forming
★ Limbs, hands, feet, fingers, and toes developing

12 weeks
★ 3 in. long; weight 1 oz.
★ Muscles forming
★ Teeth and vocal cords developing
★ Eyelids and nails appearing

16 weeks
★ 6–8 in. long; weight 5–6 oz.
★ Lanugo (cottony growth) appearing
★ Heartbeat audible by stethoscope
★ Eyebrows and eyelashes growing

20 weeks
★ 10–12 in. long; weight 1 lb.
★ Sweat glands forming
★ Head hair appearing
★ Vernix caseosa (cheesy material) covering body
★ Skin developing

24 weeks
★ 14 in. long; weight 2 lbs.
★ Eyes maturing
★ Taste buds developing

28–40 weeks
★ Growing rapidly
★ Lanugo disappearing
★ Fatty tissue forming under skin
★ Body organs maturing

During the fetal stage, all parts of the body mature, and overall size increases quickly. Major changes happen in the fetus, 4-10. By the fourth month, the fetus has usually grown enough to give the mother's growing abdomen a pregnant look.

Two milestones happen during the fetal stage. In the third month of pregnancy, parents-to-be may be able to hear their baby's heartbeat for the first time. They can do this at their doctor's office with the use of a special listening device. In the past, parents-to-be had to wait until much later in the pregnancy when the heartbeat could be picked up by the doctor's stethoscope.

Fetus in the Uterus

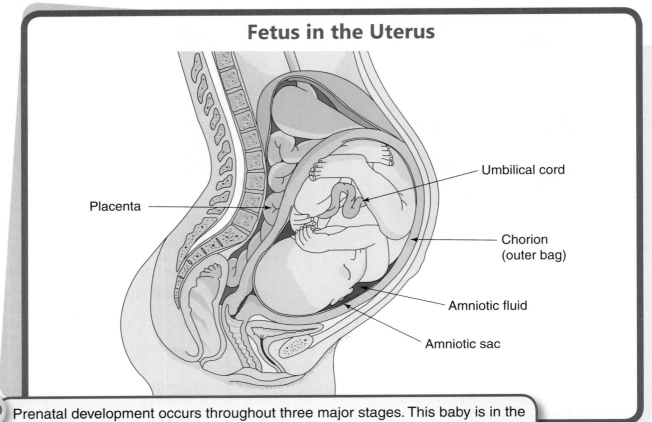

Placenta

Umbilical cord

Chorion (outer bag)

Amniotic fluid

Amniotic sac

4-10 Prenatal development occurs throughout three major stages. This baby is in the fetal stage and has already turned to a head-down position to prepare for birth.

Between the fourth and fifth months, a mother will begin to feel her baby move. Amazingly, the baby can turn, swallow, and even suck its thumb. The fetus can also move its head and push with the hands, feet, and limbs. When the mother feels these movements, it is called **quickening**. The mother should tell her doctor when she first feels movement.

A second milestone is reached when the fetus is seven months (28 weeks) old. This is the age at which most babies could survive if they were born. It is called the **age of viability**. By this time, the baby's brain has more control over body systems than before. However, most babies born at this time would need some intensive care in hospitals. With recent advances in medicine, more babies born before seven months have survived with special care.

Although a baby born at seven months can survive, the chance of surviving improves with each week closer to nine months. (This is true unless earlier delivery is needed for medical reasons.) In the last two months of pregnancy, the inner surface of the baby's lungs must produce a substance that allows the baby to breath air. A baby that is born too early experiences *respiratory distress syndrome (RDS)*. The baby also becomes larger.

In the ninth month of pregnancy, the fetus receives immunities from the mother. These help prevent the baby from catching some diseases after birth. In most cases, the baby also turns to a head-down position to prepare for birth.

Summary

The nine-month pregnancy process begins with conception. At this moment, ovum and sperm unite and combine to form a single cell.

In this one cell is all the genetic information the child will receive from each parent. These genetic factors will influence all stages of life, especially the prenatal period. Genetic factors provide a blueprint for the future unfolding of family traits.

The zygote's nucleus stores this blueprint within DNA molecules, which are part of the chromosomes. Humans have 23 pairs of chromosomes—an equal number of which are received from the mother and father. Genes within each chromosome can determine some of an individual's traits. How genes from the parents interact can also determine traits. Two types of traits are dominant and recessive. Gender of the child is controlled by whether an X or Y sex chromosome is received from the father's sperm.

Multiple pregnancies occur when one or more eggs are fertilized by one or more sperm. Two types of multiple births are fraternal and identical. Each type forms differently from the other. While fraternal twins differ genetically, identical twins share the same genetic makeup. Multiple pregnancies may include combinations of identical and fraternal children.

Prenatal development is divided into the germinal, embryonic, and fetal stages. In the germinal stage, the dividing cells of the zygote travel toward the uterus, float freely, and then embed in the wall of the uterus. Almost all body systems develop during the embryonic stage. The fetal stage lasts from about nine weeks until birth. During this stage, the fetus grows and its body systems mature. At the end of the ninth month, the baby is ready to be born.

Companion Web Site

Interactive Activity

Review vocabulary terms and key concepts for Chapter 4 at **g-wlearning.com**.

Review and Reflect

Write your answers to the following questions on a separate sheet of paper.

1. Describe briefly what happens during conception.

2. Each sperm contains _____ (23, 46) chromosomes; each ovum contains _____ (23, 46) chromosomes.

3. Explain what determines an unborn baby's gender.

4. Paul and Emily both have blue eyes, a recessive trait. They are expecting a baby. What eye color will the baby have? Why?

5. List the three different kinds of multiple pregnancies.

6. Patty and Patrick—who look almost alike in size, coloring, and facial features—are _____ (identical, fraternal) twins.

7. True or false. In the germinal stage, the zygote receives nutrients through the placenta.

8. In which stage do the baby's body systems and organs start to form?

9. True or false. The mother's nutrition does not matter during the embryonic stage because the baby has not developed enough.

10. During the fetal stage, the baby's limbs are supported by _____ (cartilage, bones).

11. True or false. By the fourth or fifth month of pregnancy, the baby begins to make movements the mother can feel.

Cross-Curricular Link

12. **Science, Career Study, Technology.** Use the Internet to research genetic counseling. What job duties do professionals in this field have, and what technologies do they use to investigate which genes a child might inherit from parents? Using word processing software, compose a short report on your findings. Check your report for correct spelling, grammar, and punctuation. Adhere to all copyright laws and cite any sources you may use for the report.

13. **Science.** Collect pictures of identical and fraternal siblings and note how alike or different they are. Try to find various pictures of the same people taken over several years.

14. **Technology.** Create an electronic presentation showing how quadruplets can be all identical, three identical and one fraternal, two identical and two fraternal, two identical pairs, and all four fraternal.

15. **Science.** Record the color of your eyes and those of each of your parents. (If you wish, record the eye colors of another person and his or her parents instead.) Based on what you have learned about dominant and recessive traits, try to determine the following: (A) What gene combinations are possible for you, given

your eye color? (B) What gene combinations are possible for your mother, given her eye color and yours? (C) What gene combinations are possible for your father, given his eye color and yours?

16. **Writing.** Write a story about prenatal development from the unborn baby's point of view. Use your creativity to explore what life might be like for the baby as new developments occur before birth. Refer to Figure 4-10 to gather ideas as you write. Check your story for correct spelling, grammar, and punctuation.

Making Observations

17. Observe your physical features. Which features seem to come from your mother's family and which from your father's family? Which features do you share with other relatives?

18. Observe brothers and sisters. Which characteristics do they share? How are they different?

19. If possible, observe identical twins. Which of their characteristics are most alike? Which are similar but somewhat different? Which are dissimilar?

Thinking Critically

20. *Conception* is sometimes referred to as the "miracle of life." Biologically, why can conception indeed be thought of as a miracle?

21. How do the stages in prenatal development follow the principles of growth and development (that is, growth and development are constant, happen in sequenced steps, happen at different rates, and have interrelated parts)? Give specific examples as part of your explanation.

22. Identical births have exactly the same heredity. What are some of the biological advantages of having an identical sibling? Are there disadvantages, too?

5 Prenatal Care

After studying this chapter, you will be able to

★ describe the early signs of pregnancy.

★ explain the role of the environment on prenatal development.

★ explain the relationship between the health of the mother and the health of the baby.

★ describe how diseases, drugs, radiation, environmental pollutants, and congenital problems can harm the fetus.

Terms to Know

obstetricians
environmental factors
premature
low birthweight
Rh factor
diabetes
pregnancy-induced
   hypertension (PIH)
sexually transmitted infections
   (STIs)

acquired immunodeficiency
   syndrome (AIDS)
fetal alcohol syndrome (FAS)
congenital problem
pre-term birth
miscarriage
stillbirth
ultrasound
chorionic villus sampling (CVS)
amniocentesis

Reading Advantage

Take two-column notes as you read the chapter. Fold a piece of notebook paper in half lengthwise. On the left side of the column, write main ideas. On the right side, write subtopics and detailed information. After reading the chapter, use the notes as a study guide. Fold the paper in half so you only see the main ideas. Quiz yourself on the details and subtopics.

Companion Web Site

Interactive Activity

Learn more about health hazards to avoid during pregnancy by completing the *Read, Discuss, and Analyze* Activity for Chapter 5 at **g-wlearning.com**.

The prenatal period, which lasts about 280 days, is the shortest stage in the life span. This formative stage is also the most critical time for a child's development. For this reason, proper prenatal care is crucial for all mothers-to-be.

At no other time are two people closer than a mother and baby during the prenatal period. Even before the mother knows she is pregnant, the baby affects her life. The mother's body changes to prepare for nine months of growth. The baby continues to affect the mother's body through delivery.

As you read in Chapter 1, the environment influences growth and development. The unborn's first environment is the mother's body. She has a great effect on her baby's development.

The mother gives the baby a safe "home" in her uterus. She eats, breathes, and gets rid of wastes for them both, and her body works to bring the baby into the world.

The March of Dimes urges mothers to "Be good to your baby before it is born." Parents-to-be should take this slogan seriously. Because experts know more about pregnancy, childbirth, and infant care than ever before, parents-to-be can take many steps to keep mother and baby healthy and safe.

Ideally, these steps should begin *before* a woman becomes pregnant. Good health habits throughout the younger years help prepare a woman for childbearing. Through a complete medical checkup, the couple's doctor will suggest how to prepare for a healthy pregnancy.

As soon as a woman believes she is pregnant, she should seek prenatal care. This medical care is important, whether it is a first, second, or later pregnancy. Starting good prenatal care early in pregnancy greatly reduces the risk of complications.

Signs of Pregnancy

A woman cannot feel the sperm and egg unite. She cannot feel cells divide as the baby begins to develop. Nevertheless, her body immediately begins to nourish and protect the new life. Hormones trigger changes in some of the woman's organs. The signs of pregnancy help a woman recognize these changes.

Pregnancy is a normal process, not an illness. If a woman is healthy and happy about having a child, she may even feel better than before she became pregnant. The signs of pregnancy are divided into presumptive and positive signs, 5-1. The *presumptive signs* could be signs of pregnancy or a medical condition. Doctors must determine their cause. However, doctors identify *positive signs* as definitely being caused by pregnancy.

Medical Care

Medical care is the best way to make childbearing safe and successful. If a woman believes she is pregnant, she should make an appointment with a doctor as soon as possible. Many pregnant women choose to visit **obstetricians**, or doctors who specialize in pregnancy and birth.

The First Appointment

The first prenatal appointment sets a foundation for medical care throughout the pregnancy. It is a

Signs of Pregnancy

Presumptive Signs

★ **Amenorrhea (menstruation stops)**—If the woman is usually regular in her menstrual cycle, a delay of 10 or more days is a sign.

★ **Nausea**—Nausea is present in about ½ to ⅔ of all pregnancies. Because it often occurs in the morning hours, it is called *morning sickness*. Nausea may happen at any time of the day. Nausea occurring at the same time daily from weeks 4 to 12 is a sign.

★ **Tiredness**—Many women feel tired during the first few months of pregnancy.

★ **Frequency of urination**—The growing uterus puts pressure on the bladder. Hormones may also cause more frequent urination.

★ **Swelling and tenderness of the breasts**—This is often the first sign women note.

★ **Skin discoloration**—Stretch marks may be seen as the breasts and abdomen enlarge. Darkening of skin may occur on the face and nipples.

★ **Internal changes**—Doctors often note softening of the cervix (Goodell's sign). There may also be a softening of the lower part of the uterus (Hegar's sign) and a bluish tinge to the vagina and cervix due to circulatory congestion (Chadwick's sign). The uterus is also enlarged with irregular areas of firmness and softness (Piskacek's sign).

★ **Other signs**—Other symptoms include backache, groin pains, dizziness, abdominal swelling, leg cramps, varicose veins, and indigestion.

Positive Signs

★ **HCG (Human Chorionic Gonadatrophin)**—HCG is a hormone found in the blood and urine of pregnant women. Lab tests may detect the hormone's presence as early as the first two weeks of pregnancy.

★ **Fetal Heartbeat**—This can be heard through a special device at 12 weeks and through a stethoscope at 16 weeks.

★ **Fetal movement**—Spontaneous movement begins at 11 weeks, but is not felt until 16–18 weeks.

★ **Fetal image**—This may be seen with ultrasound scanning.

★ **Fetal shape**—The baby's shape may be felt through the abdominal wall.

★ **Uterine contractions**—A doctor may note these painless contractions.

5-1 Presumptive signs could be signs of pregnancy, or they might be signs of other conditions. Positive signs, however, are definitely caused by pregnancy.

good idea for the couple to go to this visit together. They can share important information with the doctor and learn much about what to expect in the months ahead.

First, the doctor will gather general information, such as the age and health history of each parent. Next, the doctor will ask details about the woman's menstrual cycle and any past pregnancies. The doctor will also answer any questions the couple has about the pregnancy. First-time parents often have many questions.

The visit continues with a complete physical exam for the mother-to-be. The doctor will weigh the woman and take her pulse, blood pressure, and respiration rates. He or she will check the woman's breasts and perform a pelvic exam. The doctor may measure the woman's pelvis to be sure it is large enough to allow the baby's head through during delivery. Urine tests and blood tests will be done. The blood tests check for blood type, *anemia* (a condition caused by lack of iron), and diseases that can harm an unborn child. In some women, a test will also be done for blood sugar level.

The doctor will advise the couple on health habits to follow in pregnancy. Most of these pertain to the mother, but the father can be involved, too. For example, the couple could work together to quit smoking. This will protect their baby's health, as well as their own. The father-to-be can also encourage his partner to eat right, be active, and get enough rest. He can join her in following these healthful habits.

At the end of the checkup, the obstetrician estimates the *due date* for the baby's birth (which is now given as the expected week of birth). This date may be adjusted later.

Couples then set the date for the next appointment. Usually the doctor sees a pregnant woman once a month during the first six months of pregnancy. Visits increase to twice a month during the seventh and eighth months. During the ninth month, visits increase to once a week or more. Going to each of these appointments is important. Having a doctor monitor the pregnancy lessens the discomforts and increases the confidence of the couple. More importantly, doctor visits increase the chance of delivering a healthy baby.

The Unborn Baby's Environment

At the moment the sperm enters the egg, the baby begins to form traits from both the mother and father. These inherited traits, or genetic factors, are merged into a unique new person. They will influence the child's growth and development throughout life. However, development is not determined solely by genetic factors.

Immediately after conception, the environment begins to exert an influence on the unborn's traits. **Environmental factors** are those factors caused by a person's surroundings. The prenatal environment is the mother's body and will affect the baby, 5-2.

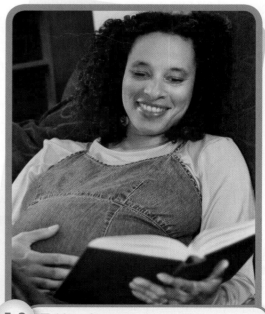

5-2 Taking time to relax and reduce stress is critical for mothers-to-be. A high stress level during pregnancy can affect the unborn in negative ways.

Factors That Affect the Baby's Health

An unborn baby depends on the mother for a healthy start. Women with good health habits before pregnancy most often have healthy babies. Some women are called *high-risk mothers-to-be*. This describes a pregnant woman with environmental factors that do not promote a healthy pregnancy. What are these factors?

Mother's Age

In regard to health, the ideal time for a woman to have a baby is between ages 21 and 28 years. Teens and women over 36 are high-risk mothers-to-be. Because pregnant teens are still growing themselves, their bodies cannot always meet the needs of babies. Very young teens tend to have babies who are **premature** (born too soon), have **low birthweights** (weigh less than 5½ pounds at birth), have disabilities, or are born dead. Women over age 36 have a higher rate of babies with health problems, disabilities, and disorders.

Mother's Physical Health

The mother's prepregnancy health greatly affects the outcome of pregnancy. Healthy women will most likely have healthy pregnancies. Unhealthy women will likely have health problems in pregnancy. Mother's health affects the baby's health before and after birth, too.

Any health problems a woman has may play a role in pregnancy. Women should ask their doctors

Focus on Health

Healthy Pregnancy Weight

Women who start pregnancy at 15 percent or more under healthy weight more often have low-birthweight infants than women of healthy weight. Being underweight can also lead to other problems that endanger the health of both mother and baby. Women who start pregnancy at 20 percent or more over their healthy weight have more complications, too. They experience more fatigue, high blood pressure, heart strain, and blood sugar problems.

Each woman should know her healthy weight, which is based on body build and age. If unsure, doctors can provide this information. Reaching a healthy weight before becoming pregnant should be the goal. However, women who are already pregnant should discuss their weight with a doctor or dietitian. Why is a large or sudden weight change not advised in pregnancy?

(before pregnancy, if possible) how these problems might affect the pregnancy. In many cases, steps can be taken to protect the unborn. The doctor will want to monitor health problems more closely during pregnancy. Special testing might be done, and medications or treatments might need to be adjusted for the safety of the unborn. With good health care during pregnancy, women can overcome many health problems.

It is also important for a woman to enter pregnancy at a healthy weight for her age, height, and body type. Being underweight or overweight before pregnancy can lead to serious health problems for mother and baby.

Closely related to healthy weight are nutrition and activity level. Women who have good eating habits and engage in regular physical activity are more likely to have healthy pregnancies. Being inactive or having poor eating habits often result in problems during pregnancy.

✷Rh Factor

The **Rh factor** is a protein substance found in the red blood cells of about 85 percent of the population. People who have the substance are called *Rh positive* (Rh+), and those who do not are called *Rh negative* (Rh–).

The only time this factor can cause the baby a problem is when the father is Rh+ and the mother is Rh–. This combination occurs in 12 percent of all marriages. If the baby inherits the Rh+ blood type from the father, the baby may develop *Rh disease*. Rh disease is a type of anemia that destroys the baby's red blood cells.

Rh disease does not affect the first Rh+ unborn. However, during any pregnancy, some of the baby's Rh+ cells may enter the mother's bloodstream during birth. This happens in about four percent of cases. These cells are foreign to the mother's Rh– system. Her body fights these Rh+ cells by making antibodies. This then makes the mother immune to the blood cells of future Rh+ babies. In the next pregnancy, these antibodies cross the placenta. If the baby has Rh+ blood, the antibodies destroy the baby's red blood cells.

A vaccine called *anti-Rh-immune globulin* now greatly reduces the danger of Rh disease. An Rh– mother receives the vaccine within 72 hours after the birth of each Rh+ baby. The vaccine blocks the growth of antibodies in her body. The vaccine is given after the loss of an Rh+ baby, too. An Rh– female should also receive the vaccine after a transfusion of Rh+ blood anytime during her life. The vaccine is almost 100 percent effective unless the woman's body has already made antibodies to Rh+ cells.

Mother's Emotional Health

Positive thoughts and feelings are important for a woman to have a healthy baby. Negative feelings can stimulate the nervous system and the flow of the hormone adrenaline. Both the nervous system and adrenaline control heart rate, breathing, and muscle tension. This makes the body ready to deal with stress.

When a mother is happy and relaxed, her adrenaline level is low, her heartbeat and breathing are slow, and her muscles are relaxed, 5-3. When the mother is

5-3 During the prenatal stage, the mother's body serves as the baby's environment. The mother should work to make this the best possible environment for her growing baby.

under stress, adrenaline crosses the placenta to the baby, carrying stress signals. The mother's stress increases her heartbeat and muscle tension as well as the baby's. Later in the pregnancy, the baby not only receives the adrenaline signal, but also hears changes in the mother's heartbeat and breathing.

Can stress harm the unborn baby? The unborn baby can handle some stress. However, if the stress is long-lasting, severe, or frequent, the mother may have a more difficult delivery. The baby may be smaller, fussy, or quite active. Thus, emotional support during pregnancy is good for both mother and baby.

Health Habits During Pregnancy

Good health habits are always important. Health habits for pregnant women are similar to good health habits for all people. However, when a woman is pregnant, health habits have an even greater effect on her health and her baby's health. In sum, there are major environmental factors affecting the unborn baby.

During pregnancy, certain health habits change. A pregnant woman may have to eat more of some foods. She may have to take vitamin supplements. A mother-to-be may also need to be more cautious about her physical activities. She may need to give up active sports, such as volleyball. Every pregnant woman should take care of herself. Because each pregnancy differs, the mother-to-be should ask her doctor for health guidelines to follow.

Nutrition

The old saying that mothers-to-be are *eating for two* (or maybe more) is correct. During the first week, the baby is fed entirely on the contents of the ovum's yolk sac. After embedding, the fertilized egg feeds on mucous tissues that line the womb. By the twelfth week, the baby completely depends on the mother for food.

Scientists now feel a woman needs essential nutrients throughout her life to prepare for pregnancy. Providing for her own needs and those of her baby may put a nutritional strain on the woman's body. Good nutrition before pregnancy builds nutrient stores in her body that will help meet these needs. Pregnant teens under 17 years of age have more nutritional problems because they are still growing. Their bodies have not had time to build these stores.

Good nutrition during pregnancy is vital. There is a direct link between what a pregnant woman eats and the following factors:

★ her weight gain

★ the unborn's weight gain

★ the infant's growth

★ the infant's mental capacity

★ the infant's physical performance

Thus, a nutritious diet is essential. Cells need proteins, fats, carbohydrates, minerals, and vitamins to help them grow. A healthful pregnancy diet includes foods rich in these nutrients. Like all Americans, pregnant women should follow the food guidance system developed by the USDA, 5-4. While this is a good basic guide,

MyPyramid For Moms

	1st Trimester Apr – Jun Based on a 2200 calorie pattern*	2nd Trimester Jul – Sep Based on a 2400 calorie pattern*	3rd Trimester Oct – Dec Based on a 2600 calorie pattern*
GRAINS Make half your grains whole	**7 ounces a day** Aim for at least 3½ ounces of whole grains a day	**8 ounces a day** Aim for at least 4 ounces of whole grains a day	**9 ounces a day** Aim for at least 4½ ounces of whole grains a day
VEGETABLES Vary your veggies	**3 cups a day** Aim for this much weekly: Dark green veggies – 3 cups Orange veggies – 2 cups Dry beans & peas – 3 cups starchy veggies – 6 cups Other veggies – 7 cups	**3 cups a day** Aim for this much weekly: Dark green veggies – 3 cups Orange veggies – 2 cups Dry beans & peas – 3 cups starchy veggies – 6 cups Other veggies – 7 cups	**3½ cups a day** Aim for this much weekly: Dark green veggies – 3 cups Orange veggies – 2½ cups Dry beans & peas – 3½ cups starchy veggies – 7 cups Other veggies – 8½ cups
FRUITS Focus on fruits	**2 cups a day** Eat a variety of fruit Go easy on fruit juices	**2 cups a day** Eat a variety of fruit Go easy on fruit juices	**2 cups a day** Eat a variety of fruit Go easy on fruit juices
MILK Get your calcium-rich foods	**3 cups a day** Go low-fat or fat-free when you choose milk, yogurt, or cheese	**3 cups a day** Go low-fat or fat-free when you choose milk, yogurt, or cheese	**3 cups a day** Go low-fat or fat-free when you choose milk, yogurt, or cheese
MEAT & BEANS Choose lean with protein	**6 ounces a day** Choose low-fat or lean meats and poultry. Vary your protein routine—choose more fish, beans, peas, nuts, and seeds.	**6½ ounces a day** Choose low-fat or lean meats and poultry. Vary your protein routine—choose more fish, beans, peas, nuts, and seeds.	**6½ ounces a day** Choose low-fat or lean meats and poultry. Vary your protein routine—choose more fish, beans, peas, nuts, and seeds.

* These are only estimates of your needs. Check with your health care provider to make sure you are gaining weight appropriately.

The calories and amounts of food you need change with each trimester of pregnancy. Your plan may show different amounts of food for different months, to meet your changing nutritional needs. Changing the amount of calories you eat each trimester also helps you gain weight at the correct rate.

Know your limits on fats, sugars, and sodium

	OILS	EXTRAS
	Aim for this much:	Limit extras (solid fats and sugars) to this much:
1st Trimester	6 teaspoons a day	290 calories a day
2nd Trimester	7 teaspoons a day	360 calories a day
3rd Trimester	8 teaspoons a day	410 calories a day

5-4 This sample diet is based on a moderately active 26-year-old woman who is 5'5" and who weighs 125 pounds before pregnancy. Nutritional needs differ slightly during pregnancy, so women should consult their doctors or dietitians about what to eat during pregnancy.

the need for some nutrients does increase during pregnancy.

A pregnant woman's doctor or dietitian can advise her what specific diet changes she should make during pregnancy. Diets for pregnant and nursing mothers provide more calcium, iron, folic acid, and protein than diets for nonpregnant women. Folic acid is a B-vitamin that can be found in most enriched breads, pastas, rice, and cereals, as well as multivitamins. Pregnant women need 600 micrograms of folic acid daily. Folic acid prevents birth defects of the baby's brain (anencephaly) and spine (spina bifida).

Pregnant women should have eight 8-ounce glasses of water daily. Caffeine intake should be limited during pregnancy. Daily intake of caffeine from all sources (including coffee, tea, soft drinks, and chocolate) should not exceed the amount of caffeine found in one cup of coffee.

Weight Gain

Experts suggest women gain between 25–35 pounds in pregnancy. More weight should be gained for multiples, such as 40–45 pounds for twins. The exact amount depends on the woman's height and prepregnancy weight. Women who enter pregnancy underweight may be advised to gain more. Overweight women may be advised to gain less than this amount.

To meet the nutrient needs for themselves and their babies, pregnant women need to eat 300 extra calories per day, starting in the fourth month. More calories are added for multiple babies.

Weight gain during pregnancy is not all stored as fat, 5-5. Much of the weight gain goes to the growing baby and the supporting tissues.

Doctors carefully watch how much weight pregnant women gain. Gaining too much puts extra strain on the heart and makes the woman uncomfortable. Doctors also watch for sudden weight gain and unusual swelling. These conditions are serious and require prompt medical attention. Gaining too little weight is not good for the developing baby, either. This can signal the baby is not growing properly or receiving enough nutrients.

A woman should steadily gain a healthy amount of weight

Weight Gained During Pregnancy

Portion of Added Weight	Weight Gain in Pounds
Baby	7.5
Uterus	2.0
Placenta	1.5
Amniotic fluid	2.0
Increased maternal blood volume	3.5
Increased maternal breast mass	1.5
Increased maternal stored fat and protein	4.0
Increased maternal fluid retention	4.0
Total weight gain	26.0

5-5 Weight gain is a necessary part of pregnancy, but this weight gain has many causes.

throughout her pregnancy. The following amounts are common:

★ during the first three months— about four pounds total

★ from four to nine months— about three to four pounds per month (with most of the weight gain occurring from seven to nine months)

Hygiene Practices

Women should continue their normal grooming and body care habits during pregnancy. Paying attention to her appearance may help the mother-to-be feel better during physical discomfort or emotional stress.

Many doctors suggest pregnant women do the following:

★ Have a dental checkup. (Recent studies show a link between gum disease in pregnancy and early birth.)

★ Avoid very cold or very hot baths and hot tubs.

★ Wear comfortable clothes with low-heeled shoes.

★ Replace tub baths with showers or sponge baths during the last four to six weeks of pregnancy. (This helps to prevent internal infection. It also helps to prevent possible falls due to the woman's larger body size.)

Rest and Sleep

A mother-to-be needs much rest and sleep. Many doctors advise eight to nine hours of sleep a night. In addition, pregnant women need at least one 15- to 30-minute rest (with or without sleep) during the day. Many women feel the most tired during the first few months and last weeks of pregnancy. Exhaustion is never good, especially in pregnancy. However, a sleepless night is not dangerous. If a woman has frequent sleep problems, she should talk with her doctor. She should never take drugs (even over-the-counter medicines) unless prescribed by her doctor.

Physical Activity and Exercise

Unless advised by her doctor to limit physical activity, a pregnant woman can and should be active. Activity helps keep weight within normal limits, strengthens muscles women use in delivery, increases energy, and relieves tension, 5-6.

Many doctors advise mothers-to-be to avoid contact sports, activities that jolt the pelvic region, and activities that could result in falls. On the other hand, doctors often advise women to walk during pregnancy. Some women take special exercise classes for pregnant women.

In childbirth classes, women may learn conditioning exercises to relieve back and leg strain of later pregnancy. They can also learn exercises that prepare the muscles for delivery.

Health Hazards to Avoid

Many health problems in the unborn can be prevented if the mother protects herself before and during pregnancy. Only about 20 percent of disabilities present at birth are caused by genetic factors. Most are caused by environmental factors.

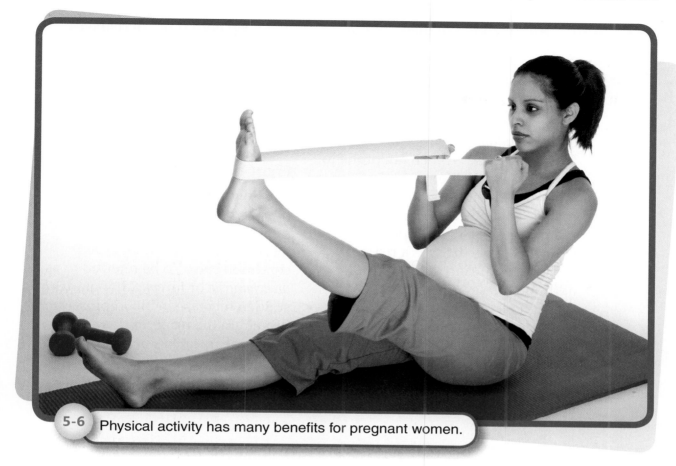

5-6 Physical activity has many benefits for pregnant women.

Harmful substances can enter the mother's body, pass through the placenta, and enter the baby's body. Some substances can pass from mother to baby during the birth process. Any substance may be harmful if passed to an unborn child at a critical time during growth. In most cases, the strength of the substance may be less important than the time when it reaches the baby. For example, in the 1950s a drug called *thalidomide* was used to treat morning sickness. Some mothers took the drug only a few times while others took it often. Taking any amount of the drug during the embryonic stage resulted in a baby born with severe birth defects. Other substances are equally dangerous throughout pregnancy.

Diseases or Illnesses in the Mother

Maternal illnesses may exist prior to pregnancy. They may also develop during pregnancy. Some illnesses have few effects on the fetus, while others severely affect the baby.

Diabetes

Diabetes is a disorder caused by the body's inability to use sugar properly. In diabetes, the body inadequately produces or uses the hormone insulin. Some women might have diabetes before they become pregnant. If so, they should talk to their doctors about how to manage the disorder during pregnancy.

Another kind of diabetes can occur during pregnancy. It is called *gestational diabetes*, and it appears in women who did not have diabetes before pregnancy. Soon after pregnancy ends, gestational diabetes usually disappears. However, these women are prone to diabetes later in life.

Women with gestational diabetes usually have larger babies, often weighing 10 to 12 pounds at birth. A large baby is a risk to the mother during delivery. In addition, these babies are at risk for high blood pressure, congenital problems, heart problems, and infant death. The chances of diabetes increase for these children.

Careful balance of diet, physical activity, and medication (if needed) will keep both types of diabetes under control. Pregnant women with this condition should work closely with their doctors and dietitians to plan for a healthy pregnancy.

Pregnancy-Induced Hypertension (PIH)

Pregnancy-induced hypertension (PIH) is the name for high blood pressure caused by pregnancy. This dangerous condition can also be referred to as *preeclampsia* or *toxemia*. It includes a sudden increase in blood pressure, protein in the urine, and swelling. PIH appears late in pregnancy, but its cause is unknown. It affects 8 percent of all pregnancies, especially those of older women and those

Learn More About...
Rubella and Other Infections

Rubella (formerly called *German measles*) is a virus that can cross the placenta and affect the baby during the first three months of pregnancy. For the mother, this disease is mild. Infected babies, however, may be born blind, deaf, with a mental disability, or with heart problems.

Chicken pox results in birth defects for 1–2 percent of babies whose mothers are infected during the first 20 weeks of pregnancy. Babies exposed to chicken pox between 5 days before and 2 days after birth can develop a very serious, even fatal, form of the disease.

The only way to protect babies is to prevent their mothers from catching these diseases. Mothers should have received vaccinations for all these during childhood. As a general rule, most vaccinations, except for flu, must be avoided during pregnancy. A pregnant woman should avoid exposure to anyone she knows that has any of these diseases.

Many other infections can be dangerous during pregnancy. These cannot be prevented by childhood vaccinations. One such disease is *fifth disease*. Women who had this disease as a child are immune. Although fetal infection is rare, the virus can be deadly for infected babies.

Another infection is *toxoplasmosis*, which is caused by a parasite that primarily infects cats. Because this infection can damage an unborn's nervous system, pregnant women should avoid contact with cats. Women should also avoid contact with the cat's litter box or soil used by cats. The parasite is also found in raw meats. Pregnant women must be very careful when they handle raw meats and must eat only properly cooked meats.

with a multiple pregnancy. If untreated, PIH can lead to damage or death of the mother, baby, or both. Early treatment can help both mother and baby avoid serious health problems. This may include bed rest, medicine, and perhaps early delivery of the baby.

Sexually Transmitted Infections (STIs)

Sexually transmitted infections (STIs) are infectious illnesses that are passed primarily through sexual intercourse. They are also known as *sexually transmitted diseases (STDs)*. Contracting an STI has very serious health consequences. A mother could be infected with an STI and not even realize it because she may not show any signs of infection. This could be extremely dangerous to her unborn baby. For example, some STIs can enter the bloodstream of the mother and cross the placenta to reach the unborn. Others infect the mother's reproductive tract and can pass to the baby during delivery. Still other STIs can be passed from mother to infant during breast-feeding.

All STIs are dangerous to unborn babies, 5-7. None is more dangerous, however, than **acquired immunodeficiency syndrome (AIDS)**. This disease is caused by the *human immunodeficiency virus (HIV)*. AIDS develops when this virus attacks the body's immune system until it is no longer able to fight illness. HIV is spread through sexual relations or by contact with contaminated blood and bodily fluids. Among drug users, HIV can spread through the sharing of contaminated intravenous needles. HIV can also pass from mother to unborn baby during pregnancy, childbirth, or breast-feeding. Among babies born to mothers with HIV, about one in four also have the virus. Scientists continue to work on a cure for AIDS. Prevention, however, is the best way to keep unborn babies safe from this disease.

Drugs

The term *drugs* includes medications, alcohol, nicotine (from cigarettes), and illegal drugs. Each of these drugs can cross the placenta and reach an unborn baby. Some drugs harm the baby in the early months of pregnancy, and many harm the baby throughout pregnancy. Other drugs, such as aspirin, are most hazardous near delivery.

Medications

The effects of most medications on unborn babies are not known. Therefore, a pregnant woman should not take *any* medication without consulting her doctor. This includes prescriptions, over-the-counter medicines, dietary supplements, and herbal products. A woman's doctor can identify the risk of taking a medication. He or she can then weigh this risk against the woman's need for the medicine. In some cases, a severely ill mother may be given medicines because the benefits outweigh the risks. This is best decided by the woman's doctor on a case-by-case basis.

Alcohol

Doctors advise women never to drink alcohol during pregnancy. Any alcoholic drink, whether beer, wine, or hard liquor, can harm an

STIs and Their Effects on the Unborn/Newborn

STI	Transmission	Effects on Baby
Syphilis	Contracted by mother through sexual activity. Crosses the placenta beginning in the eighteenth week of pregnancy.	Effects prevented if treated before the sixteenth week. Untreated infection causes deafness, brain damage, skin lesions, bone and facial deformities, and fetal death.
Cytomegalovirus (CMV)	Transmitted by respiratory contact or sexual activity. CMV crosses the placenta.	Fatal for embryo or young fetus. In older fetuses, causes brain, liver, and blood problems. No treatment or means of prevention.
Herpes Simplex (herpes)	Contracted primarily by sexual relations. Transmitted to baby at or shortly before delivery by baby's contact with infected secretions.	Newborns develop skin lesions and brain damage, and 50 percent die. May result in increased risk for mental health problems. No treatment available. C-sections may prevent contact with secretions.
Gonorrhea	Contracted by sexual relations. Transmitted to baby at or shortly before delivery by baby's contact with reproductive tract infection.	Blindness if untreated. Treatment includes placing silver nitrate in the infant's eyes and treating baby with antibiotics.
Chlamydia	Transmitted through sexual relations. (Twice as common as gonorrhea.) Women rarely experience symptoms. May lead to sterility.	Miscarriage, low birthweight, and death of infants due to lung disorders.
Acquired Immunodeficiency Syndrome (AIDS)	Acquired by mother through sexual relations or contact with infected blood or body fluids. Infected mothers transmit the virus in 25 percent of births. (Women who are pregnant usually have HIV only with full-blown AIDS following pregnancy.)	Illness and perhaps very early death of child. Treatment of symptoms. No cure.

5-7 STIs can have serious effects on the unborn baby.

unborn baby. Taking even one drink may cause the baby to be abnormal.

Almost 40,000 babies are born with damage from alcohol. **Fetal alcohol syndrome (FAS)** is a group of symptoms that occurs in infants whose mothers drank during pregnancy. Babies with FAS are shorter and weigh less than other babies. Their growth and development are slow. These babies have small heads, unusual facial features, heart defects, poor motor development, and disabilities. *Fetal alcohol effect (FAE)*, a term used to describe less severe damage, causes children to have serious learning problems.

Nicotine

When a pregnant woman smokes, her baby feels the effects. Babies of smokers are usually smaller than average or premature. Nicotine raises the mother's heart rate, blood pressure, and breathing rate, and reduces the flow of blood. While a mother is smoking, the baby's oxygen is greatly reduced. Babies need oxygen as they grow, especially during the prenatal period. Studies now show that cleft lip/palate risks are increased when mothers smoke.

Smoking, especially after 16 weeks of pregnancy, is very risky because it raises a woman's chance to lose her baby. There is also a higher risk of delivery problems when a woman smokes.

Smoking can cause a baby's brain to develop abnormally. This can lead to learning problems, hyperactivity, and poor attention spans. Ear infections and breathing problems are also more common among babies exposed to smoke during pregnancy. Newborn and infant deaths are increased in homes where parents smoke. Secondhand smoke affects an unborn baby's health in similar ways.

Illegal Drugs

About four percent of babies are born to mothers using illegal drugs, such as cocaine, crack, heroin, and marijuana. These drugs cross the placenta quickly and reach the baby. If a woman is addicted to drugs, chances are her baby is, too.

Pregnant women who use drugs often have low-birthweight and premature babies. One of the greatest problems for these babies happens after they are born. Because they are no longer receiving the drugs, their bodies go through withdrawal. This causes the baby great stress. Symptoms of the baby's withdrawal include a high-pitched cry, shaking, poor feeding, and fever.

Cocaine has devastating effects on babies. It can cause women to lose their babies or have babies born too soon. These babies also grow more slowly. Cocaine can damage a baby's brain, eyes, heart, limbs, intestines, and urinary tract. By the first month, these babies' attention spans worsen rather than improve.

Pregnant women who use illegal drugs often neglect their own health. In many cases, these women eat poorly, smoke, or abuse alcohol. Some never see a doctor during pregnancy. For these reasons, babies whose mothers use illegal drugs have a slim chance of living a healthy life.

Radiation Exposure

During pregnancy, X-rays should be avoided if possible. This is because

X-rays aimed toward the fetus increase the likelihood of childhood cancer. Some studies also link the use of X-rays in pregnancy to congenital disabilities in the fetus.

Pregnant women should always inform their doctors or dentists of possible or known pregnancy before X-rays are performed. Women should not work near X-ray machines or stay in the room when an X-ray is being taken.

If an X-ray is necessary before delivery, it must be low in intensity, taken away from the fetus, and done only when the abdomen is shielded by a lead safety drape.

Environmental Pollution

Parents should determine whether their home and workplace are safe. Lead, chemicals, pesticides, and herbicides all pose risks to the unborn baby. Pregnant women should check to be sure their environments do not harm their babies.

Complications of Pregnancy

Pregnant women can greatly reduce the chance of problems in their pregnancies by receiving prenatal care, following their doctors' advice, and practicing good health habits. However, complications (problems) can occur in any pregnancy. The major complications of pregnancy are described in 5-8. Complications can damage the mother's health. Some can result in congenital problems or the loss of the baby before birth. Prenatal care helps doctors note problems early, which allows for needed early treatment.

Congenital Problems

A **congenital problem** is a physical or biochemical problem in a baby that is present at birth. It may be inherited or caused by environmental factors. These disabilities and diseases occur with varying degrees of severity. Figure 5-9 describes the most common congenital problems.

Pre-Term Birth

Pre-term birth is a delivery that occurs before 37 weeks of pregnancy. These births account for almost 13 percent of live births in the United States. Pre-term births are increasing and are possibly due to more multiple births and to teen and older mothers-to-be.

Pre-term labor is the main cause of death in the first month of life. Pre-term labor can trigger many problems, such as cerebral palsy, chronic lung disease, and delays in development. Pre-term births take an emotional and financial toll on families. There have not been many advances in stopping pre-term births. Studies are now looking at a hormone (progesterone) as a way to prevent some pre-term births. The best preventive is good health habits in pregnancy.

Miscarriage

A **miscarriage** is the expulsion (forcing out) of the baby from the mother's body before week 20 of pregnancy. The medical term for miscarriage is *spontaneous abortion*. **Stillbirth** is the loss of the fetus after 20 weeks of pregnancy. In a stillbirth, the baby is born dead.

Complications in Pregnancy

Problem	Causes	Symptoms
Ectopic pregnancy (development of fetus outside of uterus)	Blocked fallopian tube	Spotting and cramping; uterus does not enlarge as it should; rupture of fallopian tube
Too much amniotic fluid	Uncontrolled diabetes; multiple pregnancy; incompatible blood types; congenital problems	Excessive pressure on mother's body; breathing problems, congenital problems in the newborn
Too little amniotic fluid	Congenital problems, growth problems, death of fetus	Fetal movement slows or stops
Bleeding in late pregnancy	Placenta abruptio; placenta previa; vaginal or cervical infection	Bleeding—often heavy
Placenta abruptio (placenta becomes detached from the uterine wall before it should)	Unknown. Occurs more in women who smoke, have high blood pressure, have had previous children or a history of detached placentas, suffered injury to the abdomen, and are carrying multiples	Bleeding, cramping, abdominal tenderness
Placenta previa (placenta attaches itself to the uterus near or covering the cervix rather than in the upper half of the uterus)	Scarring of the uterine wall from a prior pregnancy; tumors of the uterus; surgery of the uterus; more common among women who smoke or use drugs, are older than 35, and are carrying multiples	Bright red bleeding without pain or tenderness of the abdomen
Pregnancy-Induced Hypertension (also called *preeclampsia* or *toxemia*)	Multiple fetuses; teen pregnancy or pregnancy of woman over 40 years of age; high blood pressure; kidney disease	Sudden swelling of hands and face; high blood pressure; headache; dizziness; fever; irritability; protein in urine; abdominal pain; blurred vision; seizures

5-8 Complications in pregnancy require immediate medical treatment to protect the health of mother and baby.

Congenital Problems

Problem	Symptoms	Causes	Treatment
Cleft lip/palate	Noticeable at birth. A cleft lip occurs when the two sides of the upper lip fail to grow together properly. A cleft palate occurs when an opening remains in the roof of the mouth. This creates problems in breathing, talking, hearing, and eating.	Variable; often caused by a number of factors working together; smoking and severe dieting may be factors	Corrective surgery and speech therapy
Cystic fibrosis	A chemical failure affects lungs and pancreas. Thick sticky mucus forms in the lungs, causing breathing problems. Reduced amounts of digestive juices cause poor digestion of food. An excess amount of salt is excreted in perspiration.	Recessive gene	No cure; physical therapy, synthetic digestive enzymes, salt tablets, and antibodies can lessen the effect of the symptoms; may have shorter-than-normal life span because of higher susceptibility to respiratory diseases
Diabetes	Metabolic disorders cause high blood sugar. The person feels thirsty, hungry, and weak and usually loses weight.	A number of factors working together	No cure; can be controlled by insulin injections, careful diet, and physical activity
Down syndrome	Distinct physical features are evident. Slanting eyes; large, misshapen forehead; oversized tongue; single crease across palm of each hand; and varying degrees of mental retardation are typical.	Chromosome abnormality; more likely to occur when mother is over age 35	Special educational needs; life span may be nearly normal
Huntington's chorea	The brain and central nervous system gradually deteriorate when the person is between 30 and 40 years old. This causes involuntary jerking, loss of mental abilities, insanity, depression, and finally death.	Dominant gene	None

5-9 Congenital problems have various symptoms, causes, and treatments.

(Continued.)

Hydrocephalus	Extra fluid is trapped in the brain. The person's head is larger than normal.	A number of factors working together	Surgical removal of excess fluid; without treatment, children rarely survive
Muscular dystrophy	A group of disorders which damage muscles. They cause progressive weakness and finally death.	Often sex-linked	No cure; therapy and braces offer some relief
Phenylketonuria (PKU)	An enzyme deficiency makes the person unable to digest a certain amino acid. The baby appears normal at birth, but slowly develops mental retardation because the amino acid builds up in the body and causes brain damage.	Recessive gene	A carefully prescribed diet that balances the enzyme deficiency; the effects of the disease can usually be avoided if treatment begins within the first six weeks of birth
Sickle-cell anemia	Red blood cells are sickle-shaped rather than round. They cannot carry oxygen efficiently throughout the body. People become pale, tired, and short of breath. They have occasional pains and low resistance to infection. Their life span in often shorter than normal.	Recessive gene often seen in people of Afro-American descent	No cure; various treatments relieve some symptoms; blood transfusions are needed occasionally
Spina bifida	A condition that causes partial paralysis due to an incompletely formed spinal cord.	Heredity and environmental factors	Corrective surgery and physical therapy
Tay-Sachs Disease	A lack of a specific chemical in the blood resulting in an inability to process and use fats. Leads to severe brain damage and death, often by age two or three years.	Recessive gene often seen in people of Eastern European Jewish descent	None

5-9 *(Continued.)*

About fifteen percent of all known pregnancies end in the loss of the baby. Some miscarriages occur even before the couple is aware of the pregnancy. Miscarriage is most common in the first three months, but it can occur later. Losses frequently occur for unknown reasons. Most miscarriages result from congenital problems of the fetus. Miscarriages also occur more often with pregnancy complications and certain diseases. Habits of the mother, such as smoking, drinking, or using drugs, can also lead to fetal loss.

Having a miscarriage does not mean a couple will never have a baby. Their risk of a second miscarriage is higher than that of couples who have never miscarried. However, with good medical care, many couples can conceive again and deliver healthy babies after having a miscarriage.

Monitoring the Baby's Development

Monitoring the baby helps doctors determine the baby's health and exact age. Monitoring also indicates the size and gender of the baby. It will show if there is one or more than one baby in the mother's uterus. It will also indicate the baby's position before delivery.

Blood Test

A blood test, called a *triple-screen*, is given at 12 weeks. It measures AFP (alpha-fetoprotein), HCG (human chorionic gonadotropin), and estriol (a protein found during pregnancy). This test screens for neural tube defects, Down syndrome, and other severe abnormalities. If the results of the blood test are questionable, other tests are given.

Experts are now studying a new way to treat samples of maternal blood. The newer method may increase the amount of fetal DNA that can be studied. This technique promises to give the same information as the more invasive methods of getting DNA samples from the chorion or the amniotic fluid.

Other blood tests are used to check for conditions other than possible abnormalities in the fetus. Blood tests can screen for STIs at a mother's first medical visit. Another blood test given at six or seven months screens for gestational diabetes.

Ultrasound

One test that is done to monitor an unborn baby is **ultrasound**. This is a test in which sound waves bounce off the fetus to produce an image of the fetus inside the womb. The picture of the fetus the ultrasound produces is called a *sonogram*.

The technician holds a *transducer* over the mother's abdomen. The transducer emits sound waves. The waves are deflected or absorbed at different rates, depending on whether they hit bone, organ tissue, blood, or water. These differences are changed into electrical impulses. This produces a visual image of the fetus on a computer monitor, 5-10. From this image, the doctor can

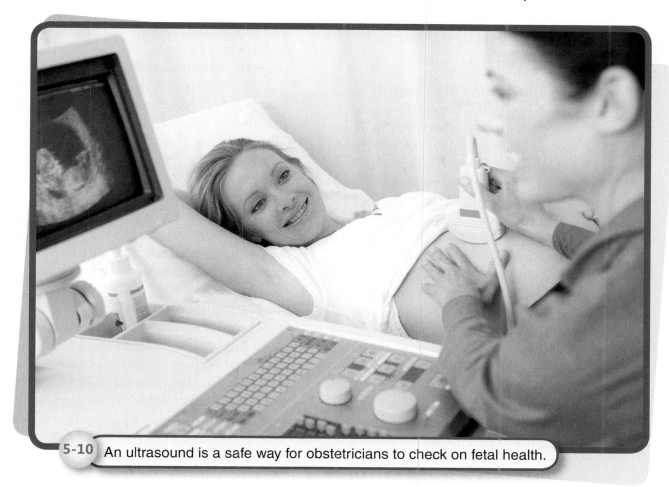

5-10 An ultrasound is a safe way for obstetricians to check on fetal health.

see whether the baby seems to be developing correctly.

A new 3-D ultrasound can help specialists look at the severity of structural defects. For example, these machines can detect the thickness of a fluid-filled area behind the unborn baby's neck (called *nuchal translucency*). This test can confirm Down syndrome early in the pregnancy.

Because ultrasounds are considered safe, they are used fairly routinely. Medical doctors discourage women from having ultrasounds made by retailers who simply make photos for parents.

Health Science

Ultrasound Technician

Ultrasound technicians use equipment to collect reflected echoes to form an image that may be videotaped, transmitted, or photographed for interpretation and diagnosis by a physician. Obstetric and gynecologic ultrasound technicians specialize in the imaging of the female reproductive system and the fetus of a pregnant woman to track the baby's growth and health.

Education: Ultrasound technicians are often trained in accredited programs and are registered. They may train in hospitals, vocational-technical institutions, colleges and universities, and the Armed Forces.

Job Outlook: Job opportunities should be favorable, as ultrasound becomes an increasingly attractive alternative to radiologic procedures.

Chorionic Villus Sampling

Chorionic villus sampling (CVS) is a procedure for finding abnormalities in the unborn. This procedure is performed by testing a small sample of the chorion, which will later develop into the fetal part of the placenta. CVS is used between weeks 10 and 12 of pregnancy. This test can detect serious problems with the fetus early in the pregnancy.

A hollow tube is inserted through the vagina into the uterus and guided to the chorion. Chorionic villi projections from the chorion transport nutrients to, and wastes from, the unborn. A small section of the villi is painlessly suctioned off and analyzed for congenital problems. CVS has a slight risk of infection, which can result in a miscarriage.

Amniocentesis

Amniocentesis is a prenatal test used to check for the presence of over 100 congenital problems. Usually it checks for problems such as Down syndrome, Tay-Sachs disease, and sickle-cell anemia.

To perform the test, a medical specialist inserts a needle through the abdominal wall into the uterus. Ultrasound is done at the same time to position the needle. The specialist draws a small amount of fluid from the amniotic sac.

Why does this fluid give so much information? Cells cast off by the fetus float in the fluid. These cells are cultivated in a lab for three to five weeks and are then checked for congenital problems.

Amniocentesis cannot be done until the fetus is 15 to 18 weeks old. At this time, there is enough amniotic fluid for the test. Due to the lab time required, the woman will be 20 to 21 weeks pregnant when she learns the results.

Amniocentesis is a safe procedure in 99 percent of cases. However, miscarriage or premature birth may result in a few cases. For this reason, amniocentesis is not a routine procedure. It is used only when problems are suspected or the mother-to-be is older.

Summary

Environmental factors begin to interact with genetic traits the moment after conception. The first environment for the baby is the mother's body. The condition of her body and her daily health habits have a great effect on her baby's development.

As soon as the signs of pregnancy are detected, a woman should seek medical care. The health of the baby depends on the health of the mother.

Good health habits need to be practiced during pregnancy. Doctors recommend most women gain between 25–35 pounds. Mothers-to-be should rest when they feel tired. They should also remain active during pregnancy.

Many diseases or illnesses in the mother can harm the baby. The health of the fetus is also endangered through drug use. Radiation exposure and environmental pollution can create possible harmful effects.

Congenital problems can occur for various reasons and occur in varying levels of severity.

Pre-term labor is the main cause of infant death in the first month of life. Developmental problems occur in varying levels of severity.

A miscarriage may occur if a pregnancy has complications. This can result because the mother smokes, drinks, uses drugs, or has certain diseases. It can also occur if the baby has congenital problems. Blood tests, ultrasound, CVS, and amniocentesis are tests that monitor the health of the fetus.

Companion Web Site

Interactive Activity

Review vocabulary terms and key concepts for Chapter 5 at **g-wlearning.com**.

Review and Reflect

Write your answers to the following questions on a separate sheet of paper.

1. Which is *not* a sign of pregnancy? (A) enlarged and sore breasts; (B) cravings for pickles and ice cream; (C) missed menstrual cycle; (D) morning sickness.

2. In terms of health, between which ages is it safest for women to become pregnant?

3. True or false. Most doctors advise women to gain as little weight as possible during pregnancy regardless of prepregnancy weight.

4. _____ is a disorder caused by the body's inability to use sugar properly.

5. What is *pregnancy-induced hypertension*?

6. True or false. During pregnancy it is safe to take over-the-counter drugs, such as cough medicine and aspirin.

7. True or false. A congenital problem is a physical or biochemical problem in a baby that is present at birth.

8. _____ is a group of symptoms that occurs in infants whose mothers drank during pregnancy.

9. Define *pre-term birth*.

10. Stillbirth is the loss of the fetus _____ (before, after) 20 weeks of pregnancy.

11. True or false. Good health practices are much the same during pregnancy as they were before pregnancy.

12. Name four tests for monitoring a baby's development before birth.

Cross-Curricular Link

13. **Health.** Create a fill-in booklet for pregnant women. Include sheets of information a pregnant woman would need to give her doctor. Also list questions she needs to ask her doctor. Use these suggested topics to start.

(A)   Information the doctor needs—family health history; history of the woman's menstrual cycle and date of last menstrual period; history of any serious or chronic diseases or conditions; history of woman's past pregnancies; current use of drugs, including prescription and over-the-counter drugs.

(B)   Information the mother-to-be needs—due date; present weight and recommended amount of weight to gain during pregnancy; recommendations regarding nutrition, physical activity, and rest; changes in the treatment of any disease or condition; information on giving birth (place, types of delivery, and arrangement for care of newborn); fees and insurance; appointment dates and how to contact doctor in an emergency.

Placing the booklet in a folder with pockets is often helpful, because many doctors give their patients charts and pamphlets.

14. **Reading and Writing.** Read at least three articles concerning prenatal care. Write a brief essay describing the main points of each article. Include the title of each article and the author. Check your essay for correct spelling, grammar, and punctuation.

15. **Health, Technology.** Create an electronic presentation entitled "Eating for Two Requires Careful Planning." Include sample menus for a pregnant woman for one week. You might also include pictures or a list of some fattening, nonessential foods she should avoid. Share your presentations with the class.

16. **Science, Writing.** Use Internet or print sources to research a congenital problem. Is the congenital problem inherited or caused by environmental factors? What is the possible severity of the disability or disease? What types of treatment are available? Write a report of your findings. Check your report for correct spelling, grammar, and punctuation.

Making Observations

17. Observe pregnant women in informal settings. What healthful activities or behaviors do you see these women use? Do you identify any activities or behaviors they use that are not healthful during pregnancy?

18. Observe a sonogram photo. Which features of the baby can you see?

Thinking Critically

19. Some of the most severe congenital problems are caused by recessive traits. Based on this statement, why is it biologically better for closely related blood relatives not to marry? Explain your answer.

20. Years ago, pregnancy could not be confirmed for several weeks. Today's tests can confirm pregnancy within days of conception. What advantages occur as a result of early confirmation?

6 Childbirth

After studying this chapter, you will be able to

★ list ways family members can be involved during pregnancy.

★ describe the birth process and some of the possible complications of delivery.

★ describe physical and emotional changes in the mother during the postpartum period.

Reading Advantage

Take time to reread sentences or paragraphs that cause confusion or raise questions. Rereading will clarify content and strengthen your understanding of key concepts.

Terms to Know

labor
certified nurse-midwives (CNMs)
natural childbirth
Lamaze method
lightening
breech birth position
dilation
episiotomy

forceps
vacuum extraction
cesarean section
bonding
postpartum care
baby blues
postpartum depression (PPD)
postpartum psychosis (PPP)

Companion Web Site

Interactive Activity

Learn more about postpartum care by completing the *Read, Discuss, and Analyze* Activity for Chapter 6 at **g-wlearning.com**.

Childbirth ends the prenatal period and begins the baby's life as a separate person. Through labor and delivery, the mother's body works to bring the baby into the world. At the end of this process, parents can finally meet their precious newborn.

Before a baby is born, all family members need to be close. Family members should help each other adjust to life with a baby. Couples who are close during the prenatal stage can actually have better marriages. Family closeness can also ensure better parenting through each stage in the child's development.

The Role of the Family

Pregnancy should be a family affair. Studies show that fathers-to-be who become involved with pregnancy and childbirth are more involved in parenting. Children enjoy preparing for the new arrival. This helps them lessen their jealousy of the new sister or brother.

Family Involvement

Long ago, when mothers delivered their babies at home, some fathers became involved. However, women relatives and friends usually helped the new mother. When hospital deliveries became common, fathers were further detached from the birthing process. It was the father's duty to call the doctor and bring his wife to the hospital. Once in the hospital, he was sent to the "pacing room" to pace the floor, nap, compare notes with other fathers, and watch the clock.

Today's Fathers-to-Be

Today, most fathers-to-be take a more active role during pregnancy and delivery. Their role changes throughout pregnancy and birth. During the first few months, many mothers are concerned about their health and that of their babies. Husbands need to reassure their wives. Husbands can also help select a doctor and decide other aspects about delivery.

The middle part of pregnancy is often the most pleasant for the entire family. Mothers-to-be often feel their best. Husbands and family members are more aware of the baby because they can see the mother's abdomen grow. They can also feel the baby move. The couple may decorate a nursery and gather items needed for the baby. At this time, young children are often told about the baby. Parents should include them in baby preparations as much as possible.

The final months are an exciting and trying period. Mothers-to-be are often concerned about their health and safety in delivery. They may also feel more tired as the due date approaches. Husbands should support their wives. Couples often become educated about childbirth by reading books and attending classes, 6-1.

Today, many fathers see their babies being born. Some research shows that it is good for mothers to have helpers during labor. (**Labor** is the process that moves the baby out of the mother's body.) Mothers with helpers have shorter and more enjoyable labors. Helpers tend to calm mothers and reduce their feelings of anxiety. Anxiety can be a problem in labor because it causes

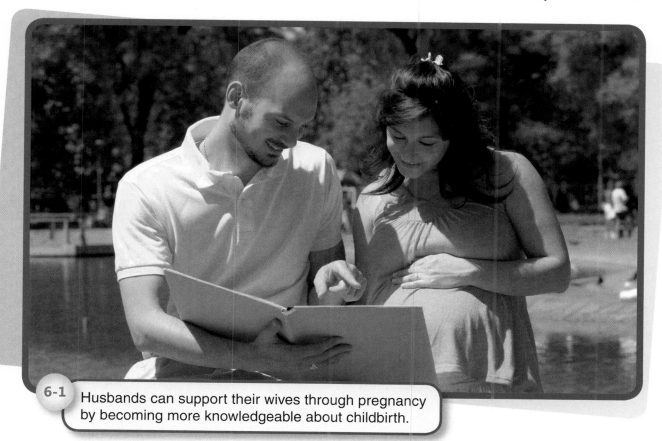

6-1 Husbands can support their wives through pregnancy by becoming more knowledgeable about childbirth.

changes in the blood chemistry. These changes

★ decrease the flow of blood to the baby, which can harm the baby

★ slow contractions, which results in a longer labor

A final benefit of fathers as labor and delivery helpers is the closeness it provides for the fathers. Fathers who participate in labor and delivery often have closer relationships with their children than those who do not.

Family Decisions Concerning Childbirth

Parents have many decisions to make before the baby is born. They must choose where the birth will take place. Parents also need to choose a method of delivering the baby with their doctor's advice. They must decide about cord-blood banking.

Choosing a Birth Place

Parents have several options about where their baby will be born. Sometimes the options are limited by where they live, who will deliver the baby, and the conditions of the mother and baby.

Hospital deliveries are the most common. In a hospital, mothers labor in a maternity room. They are taken to a delivery room shortly before the baby's birth. After the birth, they spend a short time in a recovery room before being taken back to their maternity room. Mothers who need the surgical delivery of their baby will use a surgical room. The delivery or surgical room is the best place for high-risk deliveries.

Many hospitals now offer parents the option of a homelike room in the hospital for low-risk deliveries. The birthing room is furnished like a bedroom, but has all needed hospital equipment. A nurse stays with the parents during labor. The doctor and delivery nurses are present for delivery or if problems arise. The parents stay in the room until the mother is discharged. Visitors are welcome.

Some parents want more control over their baby's birth. To them, hospital deliveries treat childbirth as an illness rather than a natural process. Mothers who have low-risk deliveries may opt for a birth center. A *birth center* provides health care before labor and delivery services. The birth center is often located near a hospital. These centers employ **certified nurse-midwives (CNMs)**. These nurses have special training in delivering babies during normal, not high-risk pregnancies. Many CNMs work out of hospitals where they can call for help if an emergency arises.

Nurse-Midwife

Nurse-midwives provide primary care to women, including gynecological exams, family planning advice, prenatal care, assistance in labor and delivery, and neonatal care.

Education: The nurse-midwife nursing specialty requires at least a master's degree. Most programs include about two years of full-time study and require a BSN degree for entry; some programs require at least one to two years of clinical experience as an RN for admission.

Job Outlook: Nurse-midwives will be in high demand, particularly in medically underserved areas such as inner cities and rural areas.

Other couples opt for a home birth, which was the norm before hospital deliveries. Home births are risky because emergency services are not always nearby. Many parents lessen the risks by having a CNM for the delivery. The infant death rate is higher for home births than for hospital births.

Choosing a Method of Delivery

Parents may be able to choose which method of delivery they would like to use. They should discuss this decision with their doctor. All methods try to make labor and delivery safer and more comfortable for the mother and baby. Labor is hard work. It requires the use of many muscles. Pain is a part of labor, but if muscles are tense, the mother has even more pain.

For any given delivery, the amount of pain cannot be known in advance. Labor may range from quick and easy to long and painful. People also feel and react to pain differently. The mother should discuss delivery options with her doctor. She should also know options may change during labor. For example, a woman may begin labor without drugs, but ask for pain relief if problems arise or labor is just too painful. The doctor, too, may opt for the use of a drug for pain relief.

Some mothers hope to be totally alert through delivery. They cope with pain by using breathing and relaxation techniques. Many drugs can cross the placenta and make the baby sluggish. In addition, most doctors like the mother to stay alert through delivery so she can help bring her baby into the world.

Newer drugs and the way they are given have made their use safer for mother and baby and labor shorter. Thus, many women opt for a more pain-free labor and delivery. Drugs used for childbirths can be grouped in three ways. *Sedatives* reduce anxiety and are used in the early stages of labor. *Analgesics* reduce pain but do not take it away. *Anesthesia* (also called *anesthetics*) blocks pain. Drugs may be used separately or in combination. All drugs can have side effects. However, general anesthesia has the most side effects.

Options for using drugs for pain relief are described in 6-2. To make sure the drug is safe for mother and baby, the doctor must know the mother's health history. The doctor must also know the mother's current health status and any food or drink intake during the last several hours. Different methods of childbirth differ in how the laboring mother is expected to handle the pain of labor.

Natural Childbirth

One method of delivery without drugs is called **natural childbirth**. Although the method was developed

Commonly Used Drugs for Labor and Delivery

Drug	Comment
Sedation	Drug given by injection or intravenously (IV) to help reduce pain and ease anxiety.
Local Anesthesia	Drug injected to numb the vaginal area when birth is near, an incision will be made, or sutures are needed.
Regional Anesthesia	Drug injected to numb one area (region) of the body.
Epidural	Drug given through a tiny tube (catheter) placed in the small of the back, just outside the spinal canal. Mothers feel touch and pressure, but not pain.
Spinal	Drug administered into spinal canal. Side effects are similar to those of epidural, but may be more dangerous. Epidural has almost replaced the spinal.
Combined Spinal Epidural (CSE Anesthesia); also called *walking epidural*	A low dose is injected below the spinal cord into the spinal fluid. A combined diluted analgesic and anesthesia are given as an epidural. The low dose allows the mother to move and walk as desired.
General Anesthesia	Drug given intravenously (by IV) or by breathing a gas that puts the mother to sleep. General anesthesia is reserved for when complications arise, such as when an emergency C-section must be done. General anesthesia has more side effects for both mother and baby than other types of anesthesia.

6-2 Many drugs are available to ease the pain of labor and delivery.

in the 1930s, the most common approach today is the Bradley® method. This method is both a prenatal care and delivery method.

In natural childbirth, the woman learns about the birth process. She is also trained to breathe and relax in a way that helps the birth process. Women need support. The father usually plays an active role in prenatal study and delivery with this method. Some parents use a *doula* (which means *female helper*) who reassures and guides the mother through labor. Doulas cannot deliver babies. Other parents use CNMs or nurses to aid the mother.

Some doctors use natural childbirth in hospitals. CNMs use this approach exclusively at birth centers. Unless attended by a doctor, natural childbirth is used for home deliveries.

Lamaze Method

Another method is called the **Lamaze method**. It is named for Dr. Fernand Lamaze, the French doctor who made the approach popular. The idea behind the Lamaze method is that women may already be conditioned to fear childbirth. In Lamaze training, the mother is taught to focus on something other than pain. This is like an injured athlete who thinks about the competition rather than a painful injury.

The Lamaze method is very similar to natural childbirth in its beliefs. Unlike natural childbirth, it does not take a hard line against pain relief drugs.

In this method, the mother and her coach, usually the father, attend Lamaze preparation classes. The classes prepare her mentally and physically, using instruction and practice. The following features describe the Lamaze method:

★ The woman's coach learns the breathing patterns and helps the mother-to-be through labor.

★ The woman receives medication when necessary. Not all women can deliver without drugs, even when they are informed about childbirth.

Learn More About... Cord-Blood Banking

Expecting parents are likely to see flyers and ads for cord-blood banking. This decision must be made well before the due date. What is cord-blood banking? *Cord blood* is blood drawn from the umbilical cord after the baby is born. This blood is taken to a blood bank. Stem cells are removed and stored for possible future use.

Research is finding ways to transplant these cells into children with some life-threatening illnesses. Stem cells help make healthy new cells. Using one's own stem cells eliminates the need for doctors to find a match. Only private banks store cord blood for a given child.

The American Academy of Pediatrics (AAP) suggests that parents use a private bank only if certain illnesses are common in their family. This is due to the high cost of banking cells, which can only be used when a child is very small. The AAP says other parents should consider donating the blood to a free, public bank. The cells can be used to help another child or aid research.

★ Training in childbirth is given in small classes—usually no more than 10 women and their coaches. Classes are held weekly for 8 to 12 weeks before the delivery date. The instructor provides information about childbirth. He or she teaches physical exercises needed for delivery. The instructor also teaches breathing patterns to use. Couples may share their feelings.

Many parents who have used this approach say childbirth was rewarding. The approach helped them avoid or postpone the use of drugs. Through this method, the mother and father shared the experience and were ready to welcome their newborn.

Time to Be Born

The months of waiting and excitement during pregnancy come to an end sooner than expected. Friends and relatives often give celebrations like baby showers. Parents may put the final touches on the nursery, 6-3. Names are often chosen. If parents are planning a hospital delivery, they pack a suitcase for the hospital. Arrangements with employers are made. Babysitters are secured for young children.

Final natural preparations are taking place, too. The mother's body makes the hormonal changes needed for labor to begin. The baby is moving into position for birth. The doctor checks these preparations and keeps the parents informed.

Labor takes most parents by surprise. It may begin any time and any place—even in the middle of sleep. The first contractions are usually so mild that many parents still wonder if the time has really come. Once begun, labor and delivery are completed within hours. Following childbirth, there is a period of readjustment for the mother to a nonpregnant condition. The baby adjusts to life outside the mother's body. The family adjusts to the changes a new baby brings.

The Last Weeks of Pregnancy

Birth occurs about 266 days after conception (or about 280 days from the mother's last menstrual cycle).

6-3 Expectant parents often keep busy during the months of waiting during pregnancy by performing tasks such as preparing the nursery.

How does this baby enter the world? A series of contractions in the uterine muscles move the baby out of the mother's body. These contractions are involuntary. In other words, the mother cannot make these contractions happen. Natural signals from the body control when they begin, how long they last, and how strong they are. Contractions happen in intervals. They are separated by periods that allow the mother's muscles to relax.

Contractions

During the last few weeks of pregnancy, the mother experiences lightening. This is especially true for a first pregnancy. **Lightening** is a change in the baby's position. The uterus settles downward and forward, and the baby descends lower into the pelvis. In most cases, the baby's body rotates so the head is toward the birth canal. In about two percent of the cases, the baby takes a buttocks-first position. This is called **breech birth position**. When lightening happens, the mother can breathe easier. However, she may have leg cramps and may need to urinate more often due to the increased pressure on her bladder.

Because her body is preparing for labor during lightening, the mother may have a few irregular contractions. These irregular contractions are known as *false labor*. The contractions are real, but true labor has not begun. Some parents-to-be have gone to the hospital only to find out the contractions were false labor. Parents should carefully time the intervals between contractions to tell whether she is really in labor.

Regular contractions occur at rather regular intervals. As labor progresses, contractions increase in both length and strength. The intervals of relaxation between contractions decrease. Parents who are in doubt about the type of contractions should call the health provider and go to the planned birth place.

Other Signs of Labor

Besides regular contractions, there are several other signs of the coming labor. One sign is the mother may feel a burst of energy due to increased adrenaline. Mothers should not become overly tired. They should save the energy for labor.

Another sign is the mucous plug in the cervix will become loose. The small amount of blood in the mucous is called *the show*. It means labor should start within 24 hours.

A third sign is that part of the amniotic sac may break before labor begins. (Often the sac breaks after labor begins.) If the mucous plug becomes dislodged or the amniotic sac breaks, the mother should not bathe. Once contractions begin, the mother should not eat food or drink liquids unless she is advised to do so by her doctor.

Stages of Labor

In medical terms, labor is divided into these three stages: (1) **dilation**, or opening, of the cervix; (2) delivery of the baby; and (3) delivery of the placenta, 6-4.

Stage One—Dilation of the Cervix

In the early part of labor, contractions come every 15–20 minutes and last about 30 seconds.

In the middle part of the first stage of labor, contractions may last 45–60 seconds and will be two to four minutes apart. The most difficult labor occurs in the later part of the stage, called the *transition*. Contractions last for 90 seconds. The spacing is so close it often feels continuous. Contractions cause the uterus to narrow. This straightens the baby's body and presses the baby's head (or buttocks) against the cervix. As the baby pushes against the cervix, the cervix flattens and opens (dilates).

If the amniotic sac has not broken, the doctor will break it when the cervix is fully dilated. Full dilation of the cervix will measure about 4 inches (10 centimeters) in width. This is the size of a small grapefruit. When the cervix is completely open, the first stage of labor ends. The length of time for this stage varies a great deal, but the average length is eight hours for a first pregnancy (less for later pregnancies).

Stage Two—Delivery of the Baby

During the delivery stage, the baby's head enters the birth canal. The mother's muscles push to move the baby down. The walls of the upper part of the birth canal are elastic. However, the arrangement of muscles in the lower part of the canal causes resistance and pain.

The doctor may have the mother use natural techniques, such as breathing, to reduce pain. Often, an incision, called an **episiotomy**, is made to widen the birth canal and prevent tearing. A new practice is to lubricate the birth canal to ease the baby out. After delivery, the doctor sutures any incision.

6-4 The three stages of labor are (A) dilation of the cervix, (B) delivery of the baby, and (C) delivery of the placenta.

The baby changes position during birth. The baby faces downward as the head emerges. Then the head rotates to the side. The shoulders, abdomen, and legs follow. The remaining fluid from the amniotic sac is expelled. The doctor helps the baby by holding and turning the baby as needed. The doctor uses instruments to suck fluid from the baby's mouth. This helps the baby take his or her first breath.

The second stage ends when the baby is free of the mother's body. The time of birth is noted. The second stage usually lasts from 30–90 minutes for a first pregnancy. The doctor clips the umbilical cord before the third stage begins.

Stage Three—Delivery of the Placenta

In about 5–10 minutes and up to 30 minutes after birth, the mother has a few irregular contractions. These cause the placenta to completely detach from the uterus and descend. The placenta and fetal membrane that are expelled following the birth of a baby are called the *afterbirth*. The drug *pitocin* is often used to help the uterus contract, which stops the main flow of blood. Nurses also massage the lower abdomen to aid contraction. As the third stage ends, mothers feel a little cold and tired. They also feel relief and joy.

Complications of Delivery

Years ago, many mothers and babies died in childbirth. Due to modern medicine, childbirth is now much safer, especially for women who have prenatal care. Most deliveries occur without complications. The rate of death is low for newborns and even lower for mothers. Still, complications may occur during or after childbirth, even in pregnancies without obvious problems. The most common complications are described in 6-5.

When complications occur, special medical care is needed to protect the health of mother and baby. This care may involve the use of delivery-aid techniques. Which technique is used depends on the nature of the problem. Each technique poses risks, but has important advantages. A woman's doctor should explain to her any technique, risks, and advantages. The woman can then decide whether to have the procedure. The most common techniques used to aid delivery include the following:

★ *version*, or manually rotating the unborn baby into the correct position for delivery

★ the drug *pitocin* can speed up labor by causing contractions to start or strengthen

★ **forceps**, a curved instrument that fits around the sides of a baby's head, aids in easing the baby down the birth canal during a contraction

★ **vacuum extraction**, in which suction is used to attach a cuplike device around the top of the baby's head, allows the doctor to gently pull the baby down the birth canal

Complications of Childbirth

Complication	Comment
Premature delivery	Baby may not be mature enough to survive. Baby is often not in the correct position for delivery.
Premature rupture of membranes (PROM)	The amniotic sac breaks, but labor does not begin. Infection is a danger. Babies who are mature will be delivered. With immature babies, drugs are given to prevent infection until delivery.
Prolonged delivery	Both mother and baby are at risk for other complications.
Abnormal position for delivery	Babies may be injured and uterus may rupture. Sometimes the position may be corrected; if not, the baby must be surgically removed.
Cephalopelvic disproportion (baby's head is too large to pass through mother's pelvic bones)	Baby is often surgically removed.
Umbilical cord problems—compression (hollow cord is wrapped around the baby's body) or **prolapse** (cord slips into the birth canal and is trapped between baby and canal)	Cord supplies oxygen. Babies deprived of oxygen may be born with cerebral palsy, visual problems, and brain damage, or may even die. If the cord cannot be returned to the proper position, the baby is surgically removed.
Asphyxia	Oxygen supply is cut off due to problems with the placenta or umbilical cord. This can cause brain damage or death. (After birth, breathing problems may result if lungs contain fluid or waste materials. Chest massage, drugs, and respirators can be used to stimulate breathing.)
Meconium aspiration	If the baby passes a stool before birth, the amniotic fluid and the baby may be covered in meconium. Swallowing sterile meconium is not a problem. Breathing it in (aspirating) will cause the baby to have mild to severe breathing problems. The problem can last for years. Doctors attempt to suction it from the baby's nose and mouth before the first breath.
Postpartum bleeding	The uterus should contract and squeeze shut the blood vessels that supplied it during pregnancy. Massage and hormones are given to help the uterus return to its original size. In rare cases, surgery may be needed to close the blood vessels and stop bleeding.

6-5 Complications may occur in childbirth and can put mother and baby at risk. Tests for the health of the baby are discussed in Chapter 7.

Cesarean Births

Many delivery problems are handled through the cesarean section (or C-section) method. In the **cesarean section**, the mother's abdomen and uterus are surgically opened, and the baby is removed. The incisions are then closed as with any other surgery. Doctors use C-section deliveries for the following reasons:

★ The mother's pelvis is small or not shaped correctly for an easy birth.

★ The baby or mother is at medical risk.

★ The baby's head is large.

★ Contractions are weak or absent.

★ The baby is in an incorrect position for birth.

★ It is a multiple birth.

★ The doctor feels that previous uterine scar(s) could rupture during labor (one cesarean birth does not mean that all later births must be C-sections, too).

C-sections are not without problems. Recovery after childbirth is longer than for vaginal deliveries. The following are risks for both the mother and the baby:

★ the risks of major surgery

★ the increasing need for surgical removal of the uterus (hysterectomy) with each C-section

★ a low, but increased risk of stillbirth with the next pregnancy

★ an increased risk of complications (loss of baby or uterine rupture) from "vaginal birth after cesarean" (VBAC)

Hospital Care

For parents who choose the hospital setting, both mother and baby can expect to remain in the hospital 24–60 hours, 6-6. The stay will be longer for a complicated or C-section delivery. Medical care is given to ensure their health and safety. The mother's body must recover from the exhausting delivery. She will be closely watched to see whether she is recovering as she should. The baby must be monitored for health problems and adjustments to life outside the mother's body.

Most hospitals have nurseries for a healthy baby's care. Nurses are on duty in the nursery at all times. Except for breastfeeding times, much of the infant's stay will be in the nursery. Visitors may see the baby through the nursery window during certain times. Young brothers and sisters may or may not be allowed to visit the hospital at all.

Focus on Health

Optional C-sections

Between 27–30 percent of births today are by C-section. Around 18 percent of these C-sections are performed due to parent option rather than for medical reasons. Optional C-sections are often done on older mothers who plan on only one pregnancy and like the idea of a scheduled delivery. The March of Dimes has reported an increase in babies born between 34–36 weeks directly linked to the use of optional C-sections. Why is it so important for parents to carefully consider this option?

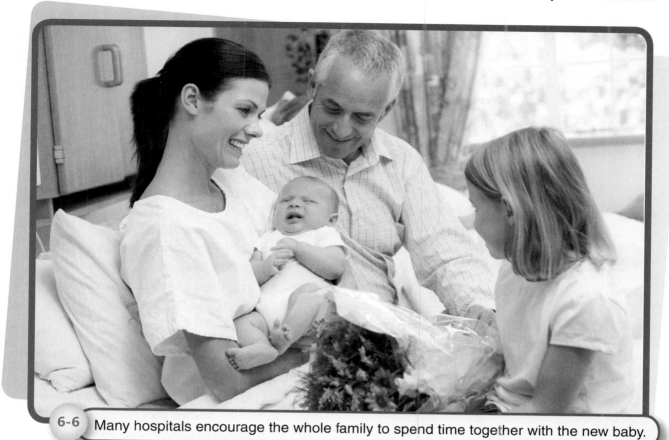

6-6 Many hospitals encourage the whole family to spend time together with the new baby.

Hospitals which have birthing rooms encourage a *rooming-in* arrangement. This means if the baby is healthy, he or she is placed in a bassinet in the room with the mother. The medical care of the baby can be given in the mother's room. Nurses will still be available to help the new mother. The father or a support person is provided with a bed. Visits are limited to certain hours, and only a few visitors may be allowed in the room at one time. Many hospitals have security measures to keep unauthorized people out of the part of the hospital used for mothers and newborns.

Babies who are born at-risk are placed in special nurseries.

(You will read about this in Chapter 7.) Most often these babies are kept beyond the normal hospital stay for mothers. Parents visit their babies in these special nurseries.

Bonding

Bonding, or developing a feeling of affection, is important for parents and their baby. The first hour after birth is perhaps the most sensitive bonding time. The newborn will watch, hear, and respond to the body movements, voice, and touch of the mother and father. Bonding continues during the next few weeks as parents become more and more attached to their babies.

Bonding helps infants and parents, 6-7. Because bonding is so helpful, many hospitals have changed their rules regarding premature or ill infants. These new policies allow parents to visit the special nursery and feed, touch, talk, and sing to their babies.

Benefits of Bonding

To Infant

★ Increased chance of survival
★ Better weight gain
★ Less crying, more smiles and laughter
★ Fewer infections
★ Possibly higher IQ
★ Better language development

To Parents

★ Less incidence of child abuse
★ Faster recovery from delivery
★ Longer breast-feeding
★ More self-confidence as a parent
★ Less depression after delivery

6-7 Bonding helps both infants and parents. It is the first step toward a healthy parent-child relationship.

Postpartum Care

Postpartum care is the care the mother receives during the six to eight weeks following the birth of her baby. In this period, the mother's body returns to its prepregnancy state. For nursing mothers, the body's complete return to normal requires more time.

The first hour after birth is a critical time for restoring body stability. Vital signs (pulse, respiration, and other body functions) are measured every few minutes just as they would be following surgery. Doctors want to make sure the uterus contracts properly.

In order to regain their strength and avoid health problems, women get out of bed soon. After a few days, the doctor might allow a new mother to begin certain exercises that will help tone the abdominal muscles. These exercises are done slowly and gradually for safety. Most mothers also want to lose some of the extra weight from pregnancy. On the average, a woman loses 11 pounds during birth and another 7 pounds within a few weeks after birth. The remaining weight must be lost through diet and physical activity.

A woman should check with her doctor about dieting. A nutritious diet is essential for all mothers. For nursing mothers, the final pounds are usually shed after weaning. A nursing mother should not diet to lose weight. Her body needs many nutrients and much energy to create the breast milk that will sustain her baby.

Rest is also important. For a few days after delivery, many mothers need a great deal of sleep.

Doctors often advise mothers to sleep when their babies sleep for the first few days. Because the baby will wake often throughout the night for feedings, new mothers will have to plan ways to get the sleep they need, 6-8. They can do this by lessening their workload. The following timesaving steps can help:

★ Ask a friend to watch the baby so the mother can take a nap.

★ Pack away nonessential items that add to housekeeping time.

★ Prepare and freeze meals before baby comes to use after the baby is born.

★ Use disposable dishes and plastic utensils for a few days or weeks.

If the mother must return to work before the end of the postpartum period, she should get special guidance from nurses and doctors. The key to complete recovery, whether the mother is at home or on the job, is to go slow with activity. Too much activity slows the reversal process.

Postpartum Mood Disorders

Closely linked to physical changes are emotional changes. Certainly, mood disorders are very common. Mood disorders are twice as common in women as in men. These disorders occur far more often in women during the childbearing years.

Many women are aware of mood changes that occur with each menstrual cycle. In addition, mood disorders peak during the postpartum period. Although

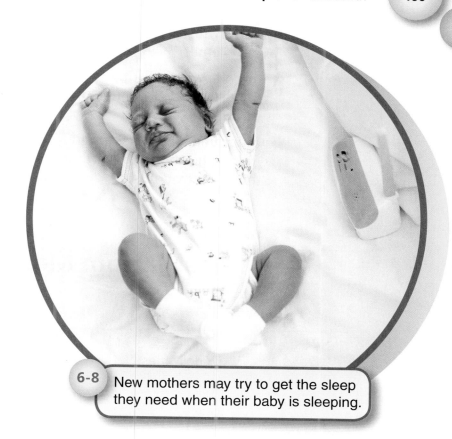

6-8 New mothers may try to get the sleep they need when their baby is sleeping.

the exact causes are not known, scientists believe the problem may be due to the following:

★ an inherited tendency for mood disorders

★ dramatic changes in the body chemistry after giving birth that affects the brain

★ stress caused by caring for a new baby while recovering from pregnancy and delivery

All women in the postpartum period are at risk. However, some women are at a heightened risk of having a postpartum mood disorder. Women with the following factors have an increased risk:

★ being a teen or over 40 years old

★ family history of mood disorders

* family history of thyroid problems
* mood swings during the menstrual cycle—often called PMS
* migraine headaches when taking hormones (including birth control pills)

* fertility problems
* severe family stress
* lack of support from family and friends
* previous postpartum mood disorder

Mood disorders range from mild to severe as described in 6-9.

Postpartum Mood Disorders

Name	Incidence	Symptoms	Appearance and Duration
Baby Blues	40–85% of all deliveries	Irritability; anxious spells; sleep and appetite problems; weeping; feeling tired	Peaks between three and five days postpartum. Often resolves itself within a few days.
Postpartum Depression (PPD)	10–15% of all deliveries (26–32% of teen deliveries)	Restlessness; exhaustion; inability to concentrate; memory loss; uncontrollable crying; trouble making decisions; lack of interest in pleasurable activities; appetite and sleep problems; overconcern or lack of interest in baby; fear of harming self or baby; guilt	Occurs within first 6 weeks postpartum. If untreated, may last a year or longer. Often happens again in future deliveries.
Postpartum Psychosis (PPP)	0.1% of all deliveries (1 in 1,000)	Severe mental illness; includes delusions that often focus on the infant dying; sees the infant as either perfect or defective; desires to kill self or infant	Occurs between 1 and 3 months postpartum with a second peak at 18 to 24 months postpartum. Continues until treated.

6-9 Postpartum mood disorders may be mild or serious. In serious or prolonged cases, medical help should be sought.

Each has its own symptoms. **Baby blues** is a mild postpartum mood disorder that goes away on its own. It is by far the most common. **Postpartum depression (PPD)** is a serious form of depression. **Postpartum psychosis (PPP)** is an extremely severe mental illness. (*Psychosis* means *mental illness*.)

PPD and PPP need immediate medical treatment.

If a new mother has intense or prolonged feelings of depression after the birth of her child, she should discuss the problem with a doctor. Her doctor can help her get the treatment she needs to overcome her mood disorder.

Summary

Family decisions to be made before birth include where the baby will be born, which method of delivery will be used, and whether to use cord-blood banking. When delivery nears, the mother-to-be will go into labor. If complications occur during or after childbirth, special medical attention will be needed. When a vaginal birth is not safe for mother, baby, or both, the doctor may perform a C-section.

During the postpartum period, the mother's body returns to normal. She will need to rest, get physical activity, and eat nutritious meals.

Having postpartum mood disorders is common. These disorders are mainly due to hormone changes in the body that, in turn, affect the brain. The more severe forms (PPD and PPP) require medical treatment.

Companion Web Site

Interactive Activity

Review vocabulary terms and key concepts for Chapter 6 at g-wlearning.com.

Review and Reflect

Write your answers to the following questions on a separate sheet of paper.

1. List two ways a father can take an active role during pregnancy and childbirth.

2. True or false. Birthing rooms and rooming-in arrangements are designed to provide the best of both home and hospital experiences.

3. In _____ training, the mother is taught to focus on something other than pain.

4. What is *lightening*?

5. Define the term *breach birth position*.

6. True or false. False labor pains do *not* really cause pain. The mother imagines them.

7. Place the following steps of labor in proper order: (A) birth of the baby; (B) the show; (C) dilation of the cervix; (D) delivery of the placenta; (E) cutting of the umbilical cord.

8. Which of the following is the most accurate statement about delivery? (A) The delivery method should mainly depend upon the condition of the mother and her baby. (B) Cesarean sections are best because childbirth should be quick and easy.

9. When complications occur, _____ may be used to ease the baby down the birth canal.

10. _____ care is essential for a healthy return to a nonpregnant state.

11. True or false. It is quite normal for women to cry and feel sad during the first few days after giving birth.

12. True or false. Baby blues is an extremely severe mood disorder that requires immediate medical treatment.

Cross-Curricular Link

13. **Speech, Career Study.** Interview a certified nurse-midwife (CNM) to discuss the advantages of a home delivery, the type of training required of a CNM, the type of deliveries the CNM handles, and what happens in an emergency if the woman is delivering her baby at home. Share your findings with the class in an oral report.

14. **Speech, Writing.** Interview two women in your family who gave birth two or three generations apart. (This might include a grandmother and cousin, for example.) Ask each to describe her childbirth experience. Where did she give birth, and who was allowed to be with her? What rules did she have to follow in pregnancy and childbirth? How much technology was involved in the birth? Summarize your interviews in a written report entitled "Pregnancy and Childbirth: Yesterday and Today." Check your report for correct spelling, grammar, and punctuation.

15. **Writing.** Write an essay on the importance of bonding for both the infant and the parents. Check your essay for correct spelling, grammar, and punctuation. Share your essay with the class.

16. **Science (Brain Research), Technology.** Use the Internet to research how changes in brain chemistry during pregnancy relate to depression. Create an electronic presentation of your findings. Adhere to all copyright laws and cite any sources you may use for the presentation.

Making Observations

17. Observe advertisements by local hospitals or health programs. What services do they offer for prenatal care, preparation for delivery, and labor and delivery? What options are there in your community (delivery versus birthing room, delivery by obstetrician or certified nurse-midwife)?

18. Observe a family that is preparing for a new baby. How does each family member help with this preparation? How do older children react to the upcoming birth?

Thinking Critically

19. At one time, pregnancy and childbirth were considered a "woman's affair." Now this event is thought of as a family affair. List ways family members can be involved.

20. Imagine a couple with a premature baby who will likely remain hospitalized for several weeks. What challenges might the couple face in terms of bonding? What can family and friends do to help the couple bond with the baby?

7 The Newborn

After studying this chapter, you will be able to

★ **give examples** of medical care and tests newborns receive at birth.

★ **describe** the characteristics of a newborn.

★ **identify** a newborn's physical, intellectual, and social-emotional needs.

★ **explain** how parents of newborns can meet their own needs.

Terms to Know

neonate
Apgar test
Brazelton scale
pediatrician
anemia
phenylketonuria (PKU)
jaundice
intensive care nursery (ICN)

neonatal intensive care units (NICUs)
neonatology
well-baby checkup
reflexes
rooting reflex
sudden infant death syndrome (SIDS)
colic

Reading Advantage

Before reading, skim the chapter and examine how it is organized. Look at the bold or italic words, headings of different colors and sizes, bulleted lists or numbered lists, tables, charts, captions, and boxed features.

Companion Web Site

Interactive Activity

Learn more about meeting the newborn's physical needs by completing the *Read, Discuss, and Analyze* Activity for Chapter 7 at **g-wlearning.com**.

When the doctor clamps and clips the umbilical cord, a baby's life on his or her own begins. From birth to age one month, the baby is medically known as a **neonate**. (Neonate is from the Latin words *neo*, meaning new, and *natus*, meaning born.)

Great changes happen in the *neonatal* (or newborn) period of growth and development. Newborns come from a world that was dark and quiet and filled with the sounds of the mother's body. They lived in a home of warm, comfortable fluid. They received food and oxygen easily and without waiting. The support of the amniotic fluid helped them move without difficulty and cushioned them from shock.

At birth, babies enter a more exciting world. They are exposed to light and noise. The newborn's life support system—the placenta and umbilical cord—stops functioning minutes after birth. The newborn's air passage is drained of water. The lungs expand as the baby takes his or her first breath. Now the baby must search for a nipple and suck when hungry. The baby's body feels different because gravity hinders movement. Suddenly the head and trunk seem heavy to the baby. This new world is different and sometimes frustrating.

The birth also turns a man and woman into parents. They must adjust to a different world, too. Parents can enjoy this time of adjustment if they do the following:

★ Plan carefully.

★ Accept the responsibility of parenthood.

★ Love and communicate with each other.

★ Live one day at a time.

★ Realize that, in time, frustrations such as sleepless nights will decrease and the joys of parenthood will increase.

Medical Care and Testing

Good prenatal care gives the baby the best chance for a healthy start. All newborns also need medical care for healthy development. Newborns must go through a few simple procedures, too.

In hospitals, the medical care doctors and nurses provide for the baby begins at birth. After delivery, the baby is often held head downward. Then the doctor suctions fluid from the nostrils and mouth. The mother may hold the baby on her abdomen until the cord

Health Science

Neonatologist

Neonatologists are physicians who specialize in the care of newborns. They often work with premature infants. They specialize in the diagnosis and treatment of a variety of ailments specific to newborns.

Education: Requires eight years of education beyond high school and three to eight additional years of internship and residency. A license is also required.

Job Outlook: The growing population will drive overall growth in the demand for neonatologists, as consumers continue to demand high levels of care using the latest technologies and diagnostic tests.

is clipped. The nurse then takes the baby to a special table with a heater. The nurse dries the newborn with warm towels.

The Apgar Test

In most hospitals, the newborn's physical condition is checked using the **Apgar test**. This test checks the baby's chance of survival. The baby scores a 0, 1, or 2 in each of five areas, 7-1. The best total score possible is a 10.

The Apgar test checks the baby's pulse, breathing, muscle tone, responsiveness, and skin color. The baby's heart rate and breathing are most important. Skin color, which is a sign of circulation, is least important. The test is given one minute and five minutes after delivery. (For the first scoring, the umbilical cord is often still working. It usually has been clipped for the second check.) The five-minute score should be higher.

Most healthy babies score 6 or 7 at 1 minute, then 8 to 10 at 5 minutes. If a baby scores 7 or less at 5 minutes, he or she is tested again at 10 minutes after birth. A low score means the baby needs special medical care.

After the Apgar test, the nurses begin health care. Antibiotic drops are put into the eyes. Because a baby's temperature is not very stable, a thermometer is attached to the chest, and the baby wears a snug cap. Most newborns receive a vitamin K injection to help their blood clot. Some receive an injection of penicillin to fight a possible strep infection. Nurses take a sample of cord blood to know the baby's blood type and antibody status. A doctor carefully checks the baby. Before the baby is taken from the

Apgar Test			
Sign	**Scores**		
	0	1	2
Heart rate	Absent	Slow; fewer than 100 beats per minute	More than 100 beats per minute
Respiratory effort	Absent	Weak cry; hyperventilation	Good; strong cry
Muscle tone	Limp	Some flexing and bending of extremities	Well flexed
Reflex irritability	No response	Some motion	Cry
Color	Blue; pale	Body pink; extremities blue	Completely pink

7-1 A newborn's condition may be quickly determined by the Apgar test.

delivery room, footprints are made. Name bands are placed around the baby's wrists and/or ankles for identification purposes, 7-2.

Neonatal Behavioral Assessment Scale

Some doctors use the Neonatal Behavioral Assessment Scale. This test is commonly called the **Brazelton scale**. The scale helps doctors spot any problems as early as possible. (This differs from the Apgar test, which predicts the chances of survival and signals the need for emergency medical care.) The Brazelton scale tests the baby in the following four areas:

★ interaction with the environment—the baby's alertness; attention to sound, light, and other factors; and tendency to cuddle

★ motor processes—the baby's general activity level and reflex behavior

★ control of physical state—self-quieting behaviors and levels of excitement and irritability

★ response to stress—the newborn's response to stress (startle reactions and trembling)

Other Screening Tests

Within the first few days after birth, a **pediatrician**—a doctor who cares for infants and children until adulthood—runs other tests to determine the newborn's health. Blood tests are run to rule out anemia. **Anemia** is a condition that occurs when the level of healthy red blood cells, which carry oxygen to all parts of the body, becomes too low. This can result in fatigue and shortness of breath. Hearing tests are often conducted. A loss of hearing without treatment will cause a delay in speech and language.

Doctors also test for certain disorders by taking a few drops of blood from the baby's heel. Screening can be done for 55 disorders, of which 29 are treatable. The number of disorders a doctor will check varies depending on each state's screening program. Currently, all states check the presence of **phenylketonuria (PKU)**, which is a disease that can cause mental retardation if untreated by diet. Many states also check for the following:

★ *Hypothyroidism*—a thyroid hormone deficiency which, if untreated, leads to slow growth and brain development.

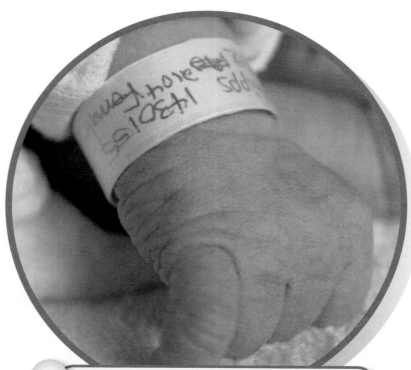

7-2 Bands on the wrists and/or ankles, labeled with the family name, help identify the baby.

★ *Galactosemia*—the inability to convert a sugar in milk into glucose. Untreated it can cause blindness, mental retardation, and death.

★ *Sickle cell anemia*—can cause anemia, pain, damage to vital organs, and death. Early and consistent treatment reduces the problems.

Most states test for more than these disorders, but do not test for all of the treatable disorders. The March of Dimes actively works with state legislators to add all 29 treatable disorders to each state's screening program. Parents can request any tests that are not required by the state, but must pay for them.

Another condition doctors check is jaundice. **Jaundice** is a buildup in the blood of a yellow pigment called *bilirubin*. Newborns, especially premature babies, have problems handling bilirubin due to their immature livers. Babies with jaundice will have a yellowish tint to their skin, tissues, and body organs. Jaundice is checked using blood from a heel prick or by a painless monitor. Doctors treat jaundice by placing the baby under bright lights, 7-3. If untreated, a severe case can lead to cerebral palsy, hearing loss, and mental retardation.

Care for Premature Babies

Over 12 percent of babies are born premature. Some are born with congenital problems involving the heart, digestive tract, spine, or brain. These babies need immediate, intensive care. They are often placed in an **intensive care nursery (ICN)**. The ICN can save these newborns' lives or prevent further damage. Newborns who need intensive care live in **neonatal intensive care units (NICUs)**. NICUs are heated,

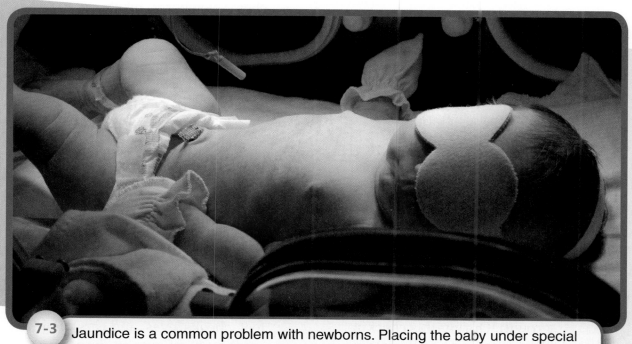

7-3 Jaundice is a common problem with newborns. Placing the baby under special lights helps to reduce the skin's yellow color. A blindfold protects this baby's eyes.

completely enclosed beds. They have two doors (which are slightly larger than an arm) that open and close to permit care. NICUs are equipped with devices for giving oxygen and monitoring breathing and heart rate. The doctors and nurses who work in ICNs have special training in neonatology. **Neonatology** is a branch of medicine concerned with the care, development, and diseases of newborns.

Circumcision

About 65 percent of newborn boys are circumcised. *Circumcision* is a surgical procedure in which the skin (called *foreskin*) is removed from the end of the penis. Except for a few genital problems, it is most often done today for religious or cultural reasons. It may be performed in the delivery room. When it is done for religious reasons, it is often done soon after discharge from the hospital. Circumcision carries the risks of surgery, such as infection. Some doctors think that circumcision is not necessary because it does not provide any health benefits. Other doctors disagree. Parents may wish to seek advice from their doctor or religious leader when deciding whether they want their son to be circumcised.

Well-Baby Checkup

Before the newborn leaves the hospital, the pediatrician will ask the parents to make an appointment for a well-baby checkup within three to five days. A **well-baby checkup** is a routine medical visit in which the doctor examines a baby for signs of good health and proper growth. During this checkup, the pediatrician will examine the baby, answer questions, and make recommendations. The pediatrician will ask for the family health history. The nurse will weigh the baby and measure the length, head, and chest. Parents then schedule their baby's next checkup.

Physical Traits of a Newborn

The songwriter who said, "You must have been a beautiful baby," was not talking about newborns. The plump, cute babies you see in advertisements are usually several months old. What does a newborn look like? Their physical traits are described in 7-4.

Newborns possess other physical traits that sometimes worry parents. They cough and sneeze to clear mucus from their air passages and lungs. They breathe unevenly, about 46 times per minute, from the diaphragm in the abdominal area. (Adults breathe about 18 times per minute, usually from the chest.) Newborns' heart rates are often between 120 and 150 beats per minute. (Adults' heart rates are about 70 beats per minute.)

Reflexes

All people have built-in behaviors they did not learn. For instance, your knee jerks when tapped with a mallet. These automatic, unlearned behaviors are called **reflexes**. Newborns enter the world with many reflexes. Some are triggered by an outside stimuli (light, touch, sound) that are directed to a body part (hands, feet, cheeks, eyes, and ears). For newborns, reflexes are important.

What Do Newborns Look Like?

Feature	Description
Size	★ Most full-term babies weigh slightly over seven pounds and are about 20 inches long. Boys are slightly larger than girls. ★ Newborns will lose weight after birth, then regain birth weight within 10 days. ★ They will grow about 1½ pounds and one inch during the first month. ★ Newborns look thin because they have little body fat.
Body Proportion	★ Newborns look out of proportion as compared to adults. The head is ¼ of total length. An adult's head is ⅛ of total length. ★ The chest is rounded. ★ The stomach protrudes, and the pelvis and hips are narrow. ★ The legs are drawn up and appear to bow because of their position before birth. ★ The legs are short compared to the arms. ★ Newborns have almost no neck.
Face	★ Newborns have a broad, flat nose. ★ They have a tiny jaw and chin. ★ These features help them suck more easily.
Cranium	★ Newborns have *fontanels* (called *soft spots*) where the skull is not closed. Fontanels allow the skull to compress while passing through the birth canal. Fontanels also allow the skull and brain to grow. ★ The fontanels fill with bone as the skull grows. The skull completely closes between one and two years of age, when brain growth has slowed. ★ The membrane that covers the fontanels moves in and out as the baby breathes. This may be seen in a baby with little hair. ★ The bones of the skull are soft and may be molded into an egg shape during birth. This makes birth easier. The molded shape of the head will disappear in a couple of weeks.
Skin	★ Newborns have thin, dry skin. ★ The skin may look blotchy and ruddy. You may see the blood vessels. ★ The skin of the feet is loose and wrinkly. ★ The wrists have deep, bracelet-like creases. ★ The scalp skin is also loose. ★ At birth, newborns have a protective, cheese-like covering called the *vernix caseosa*. ★ Down (called *languno*) on the ears, shoulders, back, forehead, and cheeks frequently is present, especially on premature babies. ★ Babies often develop a rash one or two days after birth. This should disappear in one week.

7-4   A newborn looks different from older children or adults.

(Continued.)

Skin (Continued)	★ A newborn may have pinkish marks on the forehead, eyelids, and the back of the neck. These are called *stork bites*. They fade within a year. The name comes from the mythical stork who delivered babies. However, the blotches are caused by a collection of small blood vessels. ★ Newborns of African, Mediterranean, and Asian descent may have greenish-blue spots on their backs. These are called *Mongolian spots*. ★ Many newborns look yellow because of jaundice. Stork bites
Eyes	★ Newborns' eyes appear small. ★ Their eye color is usually a dull gray-blue due to lack of pigmentation. Eye color develops around six months of age. ★ Red spots may appear in the whites of the eyes. ★ Babies do not produce tears until three months. Their eyes may drain from the side effect of silver nitrate, however. ★ A newborn's eyes may cross at times. Eyes usually begin to work together at about six months.
Mouth	★ Newborns have puffy cheeks. This is because they have sucking pads on the inside of the cheeks. ★ The tongue is short and cannot be extended beyond the gums. ★ The lining of the lips may peel. ★ Most newborns are toothless, but some are born with one or more teeth.

7-4 (Continued.)

★ Reflexes are a clue to the health and maturity of the nervous system. The absence or weakness of a reflex may result from prematurity or a congenital problem. For example, newborns jerk or withdraw their legs when the soles of their feet are pricked. This reaction is called the *withdrawal reflex*. The reflex continues throughout life, and its absence may be a sign of brain damage. However, some reflexes should disappear at a certain time. If these reflexes do not disappear, this may signal a problem.

★ Babies need some reflexes for survival. When you touch a newborn's cheeks, lips, or skin around the mouth, the baby searches for food. The head turns and the mouth moves. This is called the **rooting reflex**. After finding an object with the mouth, the baby begins to suck. Rooting should vanish in three to four months.

★ Some reflexes remain the same throughout life, such as the knee jerk. Others lead to learned, voluntary behaviors, such as the sucking reflex. The newborn learns to vary sucking strength with the softness of the object.

★ Using reflexes may give the newborn the practice needed to develop voluntary behaviors such as sitting, walking, and climbing. These behaviors are essential for development.

There are many reflexes, and researchers are observing and describing more. Several are illustrated in 7-5.

Palmar (grasping) Reflex

Newborns' fingers tighten around any object placed in the palm. Grasp is strong enough to lift them into a sitting position.

Plantar (grasping) Reflex

Newborns' toes tighten around any object when the ball of the foot is stroked. This reflex disappears between 8 and 15 months of age.

Babinski Reflex

Newborns' toes fan out if the outside of the sole is stroked from heel to toe. Reflex ends at about one year of age.

Moro (startle) Reflex

The reflex consists of two movements. Newborns fling arms and legs out (A) and pull them back again (B) when they are startled.

Walking Reflex

When babies' feet touch a solid surface, alternating steps are taken as in walking. This reflex disappears in three or four months.

7-5 Some major reflexes help infants survive and learn.

Meeting the Newborn's Physical Needs

Newborns are completely helpless. They depend on adults to meet their physical needs. New parents often feel nervous when handling their fragile newborn.

Feeding

People need nutrients to grow and stay healthy. Because newborns grow quickly, their nutritional needs are especially important. Although parents can meet these needs by either breast-feeding or formula-feeding, breast-feeding is preferred. The best first food for babies is breast milk. The American Academy of Pediatrics recommends breast-feeding for at least the first 12 months of life. This option has advantages for baby, mother, and the family, 7-6.

Breast-Feeding

Mothers who breast-feed their babies should do the following:

★ Eat a balanced diet. The quality of breast milk varies only slightly from mother to mother. Even malnourished women can provide high-quality milk, but their own bodies suffer. During the first six weeks of nursing, most mothers stay on the same diet they followed while pregnant. After six weeks, they will need about 500 extra calories to produce the amount of milk needed for the growing baby.

★ Drink at least eight 8-ounce glasses of fluid per day. The best choices are water, milk, and fruit or vegetable juices. Sugary drinks and those with caffeine should be avoided.

★ Check with a pediatrician about giving the baby a supplementary source of iron, fluoride, and vitamin D.

★ Realize that certain foods may upset the baby. For some mothers, these include coffee, tea, chocolate, cola, cocoa, herbal teas, and artificial sweeteners. The baby's intestinal tract may be irritated by foods the mother has eaten, such as broccoli, asparagus, eggplant, onions, tomatoes, garlic, and spices. If the mother notices her baby is bothered by a food she has eaten, she needs to stop eating this food while breastfeeding.

★ Tell doctors and dentists when nursing. Also, the mother should talk to her doctor before taking over-the-counter drugs. Any drug could affect her milk and the baby.

★ Rest and avoid stress. Milk supply decreases when mothers are tired or under stress.

★ Consult with a doctor, nurse, or breast-feeding expert (called a *lactation consultant*) for breast-feeding advice.

★ Use breast-feeding time to bond with the baby. During feeding, mothers should smile at, sing to, talk with, and cuddle their newborns.

Advantages of Breast-Feeding

For Babies	For Mothers and Family
Breast milk contains the right proportions of proteins, carbohydrates, fats, vitamins, minerals, and water. This makes it easier to digest than formula.	Breast-feeding helps mother rest during the day and makes night feeding easier.
Mother's immunities to certain diseases are passed to the baby. Breast-fed babies have low rates of ★ diarrhea and constipation ★ rashes ★ allergies ★ ear and respiratory infections ★ urinary tract infections ★ bacterial infections And possibly lower rates of ★ sudden infant death syndrome (SIDS) ★ childhood diabetes ★ intestinal tract diseases as adults ★ lymphoma (cancer)	Breast-feeding has health benefits for mother, such as ★ causes uterus to contract to original size ★ reduces postpartum bleeding ★ reduces menstrual blood loss ★ helps bones regain minerals ★ reduces risk of breast cancer, especially during childbearing years ★ reduces risk of ovarian cancer
	Breast-feeding can save the family money on formula, bottles, and nipples.
	Breast-feeding saves time in formula and bottle preparation.
Breast milk is always sterile (unless put in a bottle) and is ready immediately.	Due to healthier breast-fed babies, families may save money on medical bills and loss of money from wages and salary.
Breast-fed babies are usually the right weight because the milk content is perfect for baby's needs and mother does not overfeed the baby.	Because breast-fed babies are usually healthier than bottle-fed babies, parents often miss less work if the mother breast-feeds. This benefits employer and employee.
Vigorous sucking required for breast-feeding satisfies the need for sucking and promotes good development of facial structures and healthier, straighter teeth.	Breast-feeding women can offer their baby the most nutritional food, even while returning to their careers. (Mothers who work can pump the milk several times during the day and refrigerate or freeze it. The baby takes this milk in a bottle while mother is away.)
Babies rarely choke, for they can control the flow of milk.	
Mother and baby develop a warm relationship because of touch and eye contact.	

7-6 Breast-feeding has many advantages for the baby, mother, and family.

Formula-Feeding

Although most mothers can breast-feed, a few cannot, 7-7. Even when mothers can breast-feed, sometimes they choose not to do so. If parents choose formula-feeding, they should do the following:

★ Consult with a doctor about the type of formula to use. Most formulas are based on cow's milk, but some are soy-based. Soy formulas are often used for babies who have problems digesting milk-based formulas.

Formula-Feeding Is Sometimes Necessary

Adoptive and foster mothers usually formula-feed.

Some infant diseases prevent babies from breast-feeding.

Formula-feeding is recommended if mothers have the following:
★ tuberculosis (TB)
★ HIV
★ herpes
★ hepatitis
★ certain strep infections
★ silicone breast implants (in some cases)

Formula-feeding is recommended for mothers taking certain drugs for the following:
★ cancer
★ Parkinson's disease
★ migraine headaches
★ mood disorders (depression)
★ arthritis

The use of illegal drugs, smoking, or radiation treatments may make formula-feeding the better choice.

Breast disease may make nursing impossible.

7-7 In some cases, formula-feeding is necessary. Mothers should seek medical advice if they have questions about which method is safest to use.

★ Report any digestive upsets or rash to the baby's doctor. These might indicate a problem with the baby's formula.

★ Formulas are available in powdered, liquid concentrate, or ready-to-feed forms. When using powdered and liquid concentrate forms, any water added (including bottled water) should first be boiled for one to two minutes and then cooled.

★ Do not make your own formula. Commercially-prepared formulas are regulated by the Food and Drug Administration. Milk products used in purchased formulas are specially processed to make it easier for the baby to digest. Do not feed the baby cow's milk before the baby is a year old.

★ Feed newborns the right amount of formula as recommended by the baby's doctor. Two to 2½ ounces per pound of body weight in a 24-hour period is a good general rule.

★ Keep utensils, bottles, and nipples completely clean.

★ Keep mixed and ready-to-use formula refrigerated to prevent the growth of bacteria.

★ Check nipples. Large or clogged holes cause feeding problems. Torn or worn nipples could cause the baby to choke.

★ Babies do not always finish their bottles. Throw away all unfinished formula. The baby's saliva causes bacteria to grow.

★ Hold and cuddle the baby during feeding. Parents may

want to take turns feeding the baby. This helps both of them bond with the baby, 7-8.

★ Do not prop the bottle. Babies can choke while feeding. (If a baby chokes, parents should turn the baby on his or her side or abdomen, then pat on the back.)

Burping the Baby

Whether breast- or formula-fed, babies must be burped. Burping rids the body of the air swallowed while sucking or crying. To burp a newborn, do the following:

★ Place the baby in a sitting position with a hand on the collarbone and under the chin.

★ Lay the baby face down across your lap with baby's face toward adult's knees. (You may burp a newborn on your shoulder, but this position is easier when the baby is larger.)

★ Lightly pat the baby's back once he or she is in position. Pat the baby below the ribs for two or three minutes unless the baby burps sooner.

★ Burp a baby before, midway, and/or after feeding.

Clothing and Dressing

Babies' clothing should be comfortable, easy to put on and take off, suitable for weather and temperature, and safe. What clothes do babies find comfortable? Loose-fitting clothes are easy to move in, and clothes without too many ties, buttons, or snaps are also good choices. Be sure that clothes are flame-retardant and that fasteners and decorative items are secure. Because

the American Academy of Pediatrics recommends no blankets for the first year, choose warm clothes. However, do not overdress babies.

Because baby clothes are so cute, it is easy to make unwise choices. Babies outgrow their clothes quickly, so they do not need too many. Parents can stay within their clothing budget by watching for sales. They can also save money by borrowing baby clothes. Choosing clothes suitable for either boys or girls (and storing for the next child) is smart, too. Another smart idea is for parents to buy or make clothes the baby can

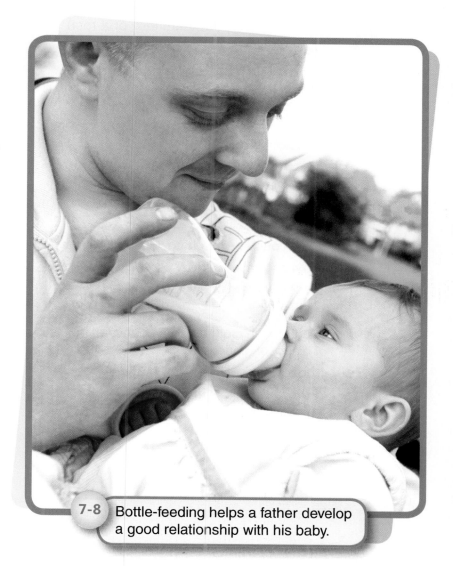

7-8 Bottle-feeding helps a father develop a good relationship with his baby.

grow into. Clothes should be easy to launder, also. Clothes that must be hand-washed or dry-cleaned are not practical. See 7-9 for a newborn's basic clothing needs.

Focus on Health

Diaper Rashes

Diaper rashes may develop from the constant use of plastic pants or from the outer layer of disposable diapers. In a diaper rash, bacteria grow rapidly on the warm, moist, and air-free skin. Most babies develop diaper rash at one time or another. The most common treatment is to wash the area with soap and water after each change, expose the area to air, and use petroleum jelly or a rash ointment before diapering. If the rash persists following several days of treatment, parents should consult a pediatrician. How can parents prevent most diaper rashes?

Basic Clothing Needs for the Newborn

★ 3 to 4 cotton knit nightgowns or kimonos

★ 3 to 4 cotton knit shirts

★ 2 to 3 sweaters or sweatshirts

★ 1 knit cap

★ 3 to 6 dozen cloth diapers or several boxes of disposal diapers

★ 1 dozen cloth diapers (for burping, protection of bedding, etc.)

★ 3 plastic pants, if using cloth diapers

★ 3 to 4 pairs of socks

★ 4 to 6 bibs

★ 1 dressy outfit for outings and pictures

7-9 Parents usually receive many baby clothes as gifts shortly before and after their baby is born.

Remember, dressing time is a chance to talk with newborns. Newborns talk with their body movements, eyes, and sounds. Tell babies what you are doing as you dress them. ("I'm snapping your shirt. Snap…snap…snap.")

Newborns are easier to dress than older babies because they do not squirm as much. The following suggestions should make dressing easy and safe.

★ Put out the baby's clothes before you begin. Undo any buttons or snaps before you get the baby.

★ Support the baby's head as you lift him or her.

★ Pull the baby's arms and legs through the openings. Newborns cannot push.

★ Cuddle fretful babies before continuing to dress them.

Diapering

Parents can use either disposable or cloth diapers for babies. There are many different brands and sizes of disposable diapers. Newborn disposable diapers have a cut-out in front so the baby's cord stump does not get wet. They all have waterproof outer layers and are easy and convenient to use. Some babies wear cloth diapers with plastic pants over them most of the time. When traveling, they use disposable diapers. See 7-10 on how to diaper a baby.

Both cloth and disposable diapers have advantages and disadvantages. Parents must consider cost and convenience. For child care, disposable diapers are often required. Parents must also consider how much time they have to wash diapers. In some places, parents have the option of using a diaper service that picks up soiled diapers and delivers sterilized cloth ones.

If a boy has a circumcision, parents must keep the penis clean with soap and water. The baby may leave the hospital with a gauze dressing covering antibiotic cream. The doctor may instruct the parents to apply new dressings for a few days. Circumcisions usually heal within two weeks.

Bathing

Newborns do not get too dirty except for their faces, necks, and diaper areas. These areas must be kept clean. Sponge baths are recommended until the navel has completely healed—up to three weeks after birth. (Keep the cord stump dry and never pull on it even when it starts coming loose. The doctor will tell parents any other procedure in cord care.) See 7-11 on how to give a sponge bath.

Sleeping

Newborns average about 17 hours of sleep per day. (Some sleep as few as 11 hours daily, while others sleep as many as 23 hours per day.) Because newborns are growing so rapidly, their tiny bodies need lots of rest.

Newborns do not sleep quietly between feedings. They usually take seven or eight naps in which they suck, wheeze, and gurgle. This pattern of light sleep continues for the first half year. Newborns adjust to regular household sounds, so it

is not necessary to whisper or tiptoe while they sleep.

Place the baby on a firm mattress in a bed with sides that will prevent the baby from falling.

How to Diaper a Baby

1. Gather diapering materials before you get the baby.

2. Place the baby on a safe, firm surface. A changing table with a safety belt is best.

3. After fastening the baby to the changing table, unfasten and remove the soiled diaper.

4. Using baby wipes, wipe the baby's genitals and buttocks from front to back.

5. With one hand, grasp the baby's ankles and slide a fresh diaper under the baby's bottom. Then pull the front of the diaper up between the baby's legs.

6. When using disposable diapers, the tape fastens from the back to the front. With cloth diapers, protect the baby from the pin by slipping two of your fingers between the baby and the diaper. (Diaper pins that have been pushed into a bar of soap will slide easily through a cloth diaper.)

7. Return the baby to a safe place.

8. Properly dispose of wet or soiled diaper.

9. Sanitize the changing area. (Scrub the changing area with detergent and water. Rinse with clean water treated with a disinfectant ($\frac{1}{8}$ cup chlorine bleach to 2 quarts of water) kept in a spray bottle. Allow the solution to stand for two minutes before wiping with paper towels. (The solution must be made fresh daily, so a reduced amount is more practical. The spray may be used on other surfaces, too.)

10. Wash your hands thoroughly.

7-10 If you unfasten a diaper and find the baby does not need to be changed, refasten the diaper with tape or diaper pins.

How to Give a Baby a Sponge Bath

1. Collect all supplies. You will need the following:
   ★ towel or sponge for baby to lie on
   ★ baby soap
   ★ cotton balls
   ★ washcloth, towel, and wrapper (a hooded cape or a hooded, front-opening "robe" to wrap around baby), or another large towel
   ★ bath oil and lotion
   ★ manicure scissors (made for babies)
   ★ hair brush and comb (made for babies)

2. Place supplies within the adult's reach, but out of the baby's reach.

3. Place the baby on a towel or a baby-sized sponge placed on a cabinet or bathing table. Never leave the baby unattended—even for a second!

4. Wash the baby's face with a washcloth dipped in clear water and squeezed out.

5. Clean eyes, ears, and nose with sterile gauze pads dipped in clear water and squeezed out.

6. Lightly soap the rest of the baby's body and rinse with a wet washcloth. Pat the baby dry as you wash each area. Keep the baby covered with a wrapper or an extra towel.

7. Moisten the baby's skin with baby oil or lotion. (Be careful when your hands and the baby's skin have lotion; it can be slippery.)

8. Shampoo the scalp once or twice a week with soap to prevent scaling, called *cradle cap*. (Newborns of African-American descent need less frequent shampoos and more moisturizing with conditioners.)

9. Brush and comb hair after you have dressed the baby.

10. Cut the baby's nails when necessary.

7-11 Gather and organize all bath supplies before placing the baby on a towel.

Water beds should never be used. Pillows, stuffed toys, flat sheets, and blankets should only be used after the baby is a year of age. Until a baby can change sleep positions easily, these items can hamper breathing. It may be best never to place pillows and stuffed toys in a baby's bed. Once he or she can stand on these items or on bumper pads, the baby can climb over the railing and fall.

Until age one year, babies should be placed on their backs for sleeping. The baby also needs a clean pacifier when put to bed. This greatly reduces the risk of **sudden infant death syndrome (SIDS)**. This is a syndrome in which a baby dies without warning while sleeping. Allowing the baby to become too hot has also been linked to SIDS. For this reason, it is best not to overdress the baby for sleep. You will read more about protecting a baby from SIDS in Chapter 11.

Bedding equipment and supplies are simple for newborns. The basic items needed are listed in 7-12.

Exercising

Movement is a large part of life—before birth and in the newborn stage. Watch the constant movement of newborns lying awake on their backs. Exercise is important for muscle development, coordination, and even relaxation. Helping newborns exercise will not cause them to crawl or walk sooner. It may help the general development of the muscles, however. To help the baby exercise, see 7-13.

Bedding Equipment and Supplies

Bed
★ Bassinets, cradles, or cribs are all fine beds.
★ A baby bed should be high and stable enough to prevent young children or pets from tipping it over.
★ If a cradle or bed with slats is used, the slats should be no further apart than 2 ⅜ inches. This prevents babies from wiggling feet first through the slats until their heads are caught. This could cause serious injury or death.

Bumper pads ~~NO~~
★ Use bumper pads in cradles or beds with slats. Bumper pads should tie securely in at least six places.
★ Do not use bumper pads until babies can lift their heads. This prevents suffocation.
★ Remove bumper pads when the baby can stand. This prevents the baby from using them as climbing devices.

Large pieces of flannelette sheeting
★ Cover the mattress or pad with two or three pieces of 25 by 30 inch waterproof flannelette sheeting.
★ Put the sheet over these pieces. (Large pieces are important once the baby begins to move around in bed.)
★ Use the sheeting until the child remains dry at night without diapers.

Small pieces of flannelette sheeting
★ Place four to six 18-inch squares of waterproof flannelette sheeting on top of the baby's sheet. Remove this sheeting when infants are asleep or when pads are soiled.
★ Use the sheeting to catch spit up or overflows from a diaper.

Sheets
★ Three or four sheets are needed for frequent middle-of-the-night changes. Sheets come in various sizes to fit bassinets, cradles, portable cribs, and standard cribs. Parents should choose the size that matches their baby's bed and has fitted edges for a tight and smooth fit. If sheets do not fit properly, they can come off the bed easily and present a safety risk. The fabric can tangle around the baby and smother or strangle him or her. Look for crib sheets approved as safe by the *Good Housekeeping Institute* and the *American Society of Testing and Materials*.

Sleepwear and blankets*
★ Sleepwear that keeps the baby warm is essential. Babies kick off their blankets while they sleep. Warm sleepwear for newborns has bottoms and cuffs that convert to mittens.
★ Sleepwear includes elastic-bottom gowns and sleepers.
★ Large blankets (36 by 50 inches) may be more economical than receiving blankets (about 30 by 40 inches), which babies quickly outgrow.

*Do not use blankets for sleeping infants under one year of age.

7-12 The bedding needs of newborns are simple.

Suggestions for Helping Babies Exercise

★ Place the baby on a foam pad or bed where he or she is comfortable and safe.

★ The baby should wear nonrestrictive clothing while exercising so he or she can move easily.

★ Select a good time. The baby should exercise for a daily total of 10 to 15 minutes. Choose a time when the baby is alert but not fussy. Watch a baby's schedule for several days before selecting a time. (Just before or after a feeding time is not a good time.)

★ Move the baby gently. If the baby shows resistance, stop.

★ Talk or sing to the baby during exercise.

★ Try the following exercises for a newborn. Be creative and use others, too.
  (A) With the baby on his or her back, lift arms above the head, straighten them from the shoulders (in the form of a cross), and down to the sides.
  (B) Draw the palms of the hands together as in clapping.
  (C) Alternately move one knee up to the chest and then the other.
  (D) Straighten the knees by holding the legs together with one hand under the calves and the other hand gently pushing the knees flat.

7-13 Exercising is good for the baby. It also gives the parents and baby time to "talk."

Helping the baby exercise has added bonuses. Exercising, if started early in life, may become a daily, lifelong habit. Daily exercise is also a way to have fun with babies and develop a warm relationship. Many families find that doing physical activities together is great family fun.

Scheduling

Babies do not come into the world knowing anything about a schedule. The following is an age-old question:

Q *Should parents try to figure out when their baby "tells them" he or she is hungry or sleepy, or should parents try to teach babies to adopt a schedule for eating or sleeping?*

A Doctors now suggest that newborns feed on demand and that mothers watch for clues of hunger (baby is alert, mouthing, and rooting). Newborns nurse about every two hours; that is, 8 to 12 times in 24 hours. They breast-feed until *satiety* (being full), which takes at least 15 minutes per breast. Sleeping should be done on the newborn's schedule, too. Doctors suggest arousing a sleeping newborn every three or four hours for feedings, however. Regular feedings are the only way to get needed nutrients.

In a few weeks, most babies begin to develop eating-sleeping patterns. These patterns change, however, as the baby's needs change. The length of time between feedings will increase, which results in fewer feedings per day. The many short daytime and nighttime naps will gradually be replaced by fewer, but longer, daytime naps and longer periods of sleep at night. Babies will spend more and more time awake.

Meeting babies' needs helps them learn to trust the world (and show less fear and anxiety). In the long run, parents who work to meet their babies' needs promptly are rewarded with happier, less fussy babies.

Meeting the Newborn's Intellectual Needs

For years, people thought newborns were sleepy, helpless, and unable to understand the world around them. The more people study children's learning, the more they realize that learning begins right after birth. In fact, the brain and some of the senses are active before birth. Because learning begins so early, parents are a child's first teachers.

What Newborns Can Do

Newborns can tell the difference between human speech and other sounds. Some studies found that babies in the delivery room responded to human speech by looking in the direction of the sound. The same babies ignored other sounds. At just 12 to 24 hours old, newborns can move their arms and legs rhythmically to human speech.

During the first few hours after birth, babies can tell the difference between a click and a tone sound. They can learn whether to turn their heads right or left for a reward of sugar water. Within a week, newborns become even better at distinguishing sounds. For example, newborns will cry in response to another baby's cry, but not to a fake cry. From birth, babies will turn toward a parent's voice over a stranger's voice.

During the first few weeks of life, babies begin to learn about space. If babies see a moving object approaching them on a collision course, they will turn their heads or pull away as much as possible. If the object is not on a collision course, babies will not defend themselves.

Imitation, or copying the actions of another person, is a common

---

Learn More About...
What Brain Research Says About Newborns

As you learned in Chapter 1, brain research shows the importance of early experiences. During the prenatal period, genetic factors and the environment of the unborn wired the brain stem. The brain stem regulates heartbeat, breathing, and reflexes. In short, neonates are wired to live in the world. They are also wired to learn, but these connections are weak. Much wiring remains to be done.

The *sense organs* (eyes, ears, nose, skin, tongue) transmit information from the environment to the brain. All the sense organs can function at birth. Thus, newborns have a great ability for learning.

Brain research indicates newborns need to be touched and cuddled, talked to, and offered sensory experiences. To prevent newborns from becoming overwhelmed, parent talk and other experiences should be slow, quiet, and repeated often. For this reason, never put an infant in front of a TV. Just as newborns sleep and eat on their schedule, they should receive this important "food for the brain" when they are alert.

way people learn. Until recently, experts thought babies did not imitate until they were at least eight months old. Now they know newborns can imitate adults' facial and hand gestures.

Newborns show they are learning by their behavior. When presented with a stimulus such as your face, an object, or a sound, they respond by becoming quiet and looking. Their heart rate increases. Newborns also show learning because they can remember for a short time. If you show newborns a stuffed dog a few times and show them the same stuffed dog and a stuffed duck, they will look at the duck. Thus, they remembered the older stimulus (the dog) and were more interested in the newer stimulus (the duck).

How Can Parents Help Their Babies Learn?

As you can see, newborns are learners. Just as parents need to meet the newborn's physical needs, they need to meet his or her intellectual needs. Parents must take time to stimulate their newborns.

Most parents ask, "When and how do I stimulate my newborn?" Babies learn in their waking, alert state. Their eyes are open and shiny, and they look around. Parents need to let their newborns take the lead. Newborns send cues about their interests. When they are overstimulated or bored, they either become more active and fretful or go to sleep. (Adults behave in much the same way.) Because newborns cannot walk or crawl, experiences must be taken to them. Newborns learn through their senses.

Most of the stimulation comes from being near parents and other caregivers. Newborns are fascinated at seeing faces, hearing sounds, and feeling warm and loved when cuddled, 7-14. Warm and expressive talk stimulates newborns. Newborns love to hear singing (and they are an uncritical audience).

Newborns enjoy looking at objects with certain features, 7-15. Because their distance vision is limited for the first three to four weeks, mobiles hung above the beds this early are almost useless. Newborns can see objects attached near to or in the corners of their bed as they turn their heads left and right. (Because newborns tilt their heads back, they see objects placed in the corners of the bed more easily than those placed on the sides.) Objects should be changed frequently. Newborns get bored, too. Because newborns have very

7-14 Babies need to be cuddled.

Visual Preferences of Newborns

Designs and Patterns		Newborns like bold, black-and-white patterns. They prefer horizontal and diagonal designs to vertical ones. Babies like spiral patterns and concentric circles more than solid-colored circles. Newborns like fabrics that have simple designs in high contrast with the background.
Objects that Move		Newborns like objects that flutter with the breeze or move with the crib's, stroller's, or car seat's movement.
Circular-Shaped Objects		Newborns enjoy balls, rings, and hoops.
Faces		Newborns' favorite visual preference is the face. Newborns enjoy seeing people, especially their parents, and even their own reflections in a baby mirror. They also like dolls or toy animals with painted or embroidered faces.

7-15 Newborns have visual preferences.

short memories, objects can be rotated. (Well into infancy, babies see rotated objects as "new.")

Grasping objects during the newborn stage is a reflex action. For added safety, objects should be securely fastened, nontoxic, and too large to swallow.

Other ways to stimulate the newborn include using colorful bed bumper pads. A wind chime, music box, or soothing music are other good sensory experiences for newborns.

Meeting the Newborn's Social-Emotional Needs

Each baby is an individual. Some babies are more active. Some like to be cuddled. Some cry a lot, and others seem happy. This individuality influences the parents' response to the baby, just like a person's personality affects the way you respond to him or her.

Alertness of Newborns

Babies seem to learn best when they are in the alert, inactive state. At this time, babies are quiet, but alert. In this state, babies also seem to develop warm relationships with others. Newborns are not much fun if they are always asleep or fussy. Parents often refer to alert and inactive babies as good babies and fussy babies as difficult ones.

Babies differ in alertness because of their individuality. For example, premature babies are often not as alert. Also, babies differ in the length of time they are alert. There seems to be a general pattern in the development of alertness. Unless affected by drugs used in delivery, newborns are usually alert for a while after their birth. Then newborns tend to sleep a lot during the next few days. With each passing week, newborns spend more time in the alert-inactive stage. They total about 11 hours in the first week and 22 hours in the fourth week.

Parents can work to establish a good relationship early in the newborn's life, even if the baby is sleepy or fussy most of the time. Time takes care of the sleepiness of healthy newborns. Parents need to cuddle and play with their babies in the alert state. Parents should try to soothe fussy newborns and enjoy them during their alert times.

Soothing a Fussy Baby

All newborns cry. Some babies cry ⅙ to ¼ of each day, even when nothing is wrong. Parents need to understand this crying is not related to their parenting abilities. Some babies just cry more and are harder to soothe than others.

Newborns cry for almost any reason because crying is the way they "talk." They may cry because they are tired, hungry, lonely, or uncomfortable. Babies also cry to relax from tension. Colic is a major reason babies cry, especially during the first three months. **Colic** is a condition (not a disease) in which the baby has intense abdominal pain. There are many causes of colic, such as allergies, tension, swallowing air when sucking or crying, and hunger. Medication may be prescribed in severe cases, but soothing often works.

Parents should try to soothe newborns. They will not spoil the baby by answering his or her cries. To soothe a newborn, try to interpret the cry, then respond. Chart 7-16 describes three distinct cries and how to respond to them. Some ways to soothe a baby are the following:

★ Rock the baby in a vertical (over your shoulder) position. Put your hand behind the baby's head and rock quickly.

★ Carry the baby around the house or yard.

★ Sing and play music. Babies like the quiet tones of lullabies or even a steady tone.

★ Take the baby for a car ride or a walk in a stroller.

Constant crying causes tension in parents. Relief from tension is good for family relationships. Using a babysitter for an hour or even an entire afternoon may help reduce tension.

The Meanings of Cries

Cause	Sounds of Cry	Ways to Respond
Pain	Cycle begins with shrill scream, followed by silence, and ends with short gasps. Cycle is repeated.	Respond immediately. Ease pain if possible. Cuddle baby to calm.
Hunger or Boredom	Slow cries that become louder and rhythmic.	Feed if near feeding time. OR Entertain by giving baby a tour of the house or yard.
Upset	Fussy, rather quiet cry. Cry sounds a bit forced.	Cuddle or entertain.

7-16 Newborns communicate with their cries.

Meeting the Parents' Needs

Parenting skills do not come automatically. They are learned. Even experienced parents find they must learn new things with each child. Each parent learns to cope in a different way. Because this learning takes time, the first few weeks are especially difficult ones. This is also the time when parents get the least amount of sleep because the baby awakes to feed often.

Parents should not forget about their own needs while learning to care for newborns. How can parents meet their own needs?

The Need for Rest

Getting enough rest is always important, especially for new parents. Newborns can tire parents. Being tired can lead to illness, irritability, and depression. Thus, it is important for parents to rest when possible. Parents of newborns need to put off unnecessary chores, such as cooking complicated meals or doing extra cleaning. They should sleep or rest while babies sleep. Parents can take turns getting up with the baby at night. Even if the mother is nursing, the father can get the baby, change the baby's diaper, and bring the baby to the mother for feeding. This allows the mother more rest.

Organize Tasks

Parents need to organize their households. Valuable time is wasted looking for misplaced items. New parents need to find a place for baby gear. If parents travel with babies, their vehicle must also be organized. Parents need to be mentally organized, too. A bulletin board used for posting doctors' recommendations, appointments, bills, shopping lists, and other reminders may help.

Taking Care of New Business

New babies bring new legal matters for parents. While in the hospital, parents should apply for their baby's birth certificate and social security number. (Social security numbers are needed for tax forms, bank accounts, savings bonds, and medical coverage.) Parents will need to add their child's name as a beneficiary to life insurance policies, investment accounts, and their will. Parents need to enroll their baby in a family health policy.

Time to Be with Adults

Parents need to spend time with other adults—especially each other. Spending some time with adults each day restores their energy. Parents should plan for extra time for each other and other adults.

Parents need to get out of the house with and without their newborns, 7-17. Spending too much time in the house often gives parents the feeling they are living in a baby's world. Going out, even for a short walk, restores physical and mental energy. It can make both babies and parents feel better. Parents also need to have competent babysitters for some outings without babies.

New parents can learn much from sharing with other parents. Many first-time parents find it helpful to call close, experienced friends for advice. In fact, studies have shown that many parents who found having children an unhappy experience were isolated from family or friends.

The successful development of newborns depends on the parent-child relationship. With their own needs met, parents are better able to meet their newborn's needs. Babies whose needs are met by loving parents are off to a good start.

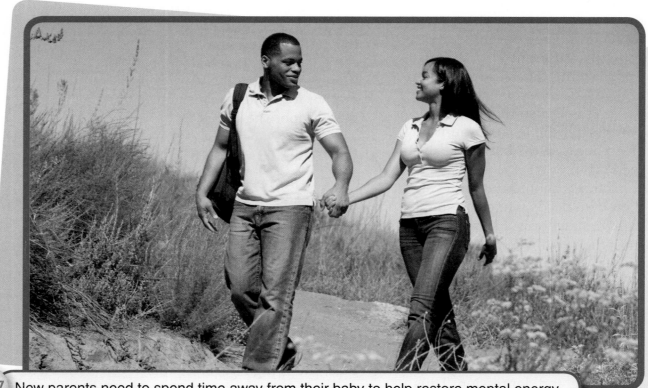

7-17 New parents need to spend time away from their baby to help restore mental energy.

Summary

Soon after birth, newborns undergo various tests to assess their health. Among these are the Apgar test, Brazelton scale, and test for PKU.

Newborns are not the plump, pretty babies shown in advertisements. Their bodies look out of proportion to their heads. Their skin may be wrinkled, blotchy, and reddish in color.

Babies have a number of automatic, unlearned behaviors called *reflexes*. How babies respond to these reflexes shows the health and maturity of their nervous system.

Although babies can thrive on both breast-milk and commercially prepared formula, breast-feeding is preferred. Breast-feeding has many advantages. Nursing mothers need to eat nutritious diets.

Newborns' clothing should be comfortable, safe, and easy to put on and take off. It should also be appropriate for the temperature and easy to launder. Using disposable or cloth diapers is a decision that parents make based on expense and convenience.

Brain research stresses the importance of the newborn period for being loved and cuddled, talked to, and having sensory experiences. Stimulation meets the intellectual needs of newborns. Most of this comes from being near parents and other caregivers. Hearing and seeing others talk and looking at and feeling objects helps their sensory awareness. Parents meet the social-emotional needs of children by enjoying babies' alert quiet times and soothing them when they are fussy.

In addition to meeting their baby's needs, parents must take time to respond to their own needs. Caring for babies is time-consuming and can be exhausting. Parents need rest. Time alone and as a couple can help new parents refresh themselves and become happier, more successful parents. Parents must also organize their household tasks and take care of new business resulting from their baby's birth.

Companion Web Site

Interactive Activity

Review vocabulary terms and key concepts for Chapter 7 at **g-wlearning.com**.

Review and Reflect

Write your answers to the following questions on a separate sheet of paper.

1. Which five areas are included in the Apgar test?

2. List the four areas that are tested in the Brazelton scale.

3. What is *jaundice*?

4. _____ is a branch of medicine concerned with the care, development, and diseases of newborns.

5. Describe four aspects of a newborn's appearance.

6. Explain the difference between reflexes and voluntary movements. Describe two reflexes seen in the newborn.

7. List three advantages of breast-feeding for the baby and three for the mother.

8. To reduce the risk of SIDS, babies should be placed on their _____ (backs, stomachs) for sleeping.

9. True or false. When parents help their babies learn, they need to let the newborn take the lead.

10. True or false. Newborns who cry a lot are just spoiled. The way to stop the crying is to let them cry it out.

11. Explain how parents may meet their own needs for the following: (A) resting; (B) spending time with each other; (C) organizing their household; (D) taking care of new business; (E) getting out of the house

Cross-Curricular Link

12. **Speech, Writing.** Interview a pediatrician about the medical care of a newborn and the importance of well-baby checkups. Write a paper summarizing your findings. Check your paper for correct spelling, grammar, and punctuation.

13. **Math.** Chris is a newborn who is formula-fed every 4 hours during a 24-hour period. He weighs 10 pounds. Based on the guideline given in the chapter, calculate how much formula Chris needs at each feeding. (This formula does not replace a doctor's advice.)

14. **Health, Safety.** Use a life-size infant doll to practice the following skills needed for newborn care: feeding, bathing, diapering, and dressing. Treat the doll as you would a newborn, such as being gentle with the baby and supporting the head. Which skills were easiest for you, and which will take much more practice? In what ways might these tasks be different with a real newborn than with a doll?

15. **Financial Literacy.** Work in a small group to make a shopping list of items needed for each of the following: (A) clothing and diapering;

(B) bedding; (C) bathing; (D) traveling; (E) toys for newborns. Then do some comparison shopping (in stores, in catalogs, or online) to find the range of prices for each item. Share your findings with the class.

16. **Science (Brain Research), Writing.** Use Internet or print sources to research brain development in newborns. What can parents do to improve newborns early learning experiences? Write a report of your findings. Check your report for correct spelling, grammar, and punctuation.

17. **Social Studies.** Poll 10 parents by asking each parent what he or she found to be the most difficult part of life with a newborn. Using your master list of responses, create a graph showing the results of your poll.

Making Observations

18. Observe a newborn. Compare the newborn's physical characteristics with those in 7-4.

19. Observe a newborn's movements. What reflexes did you observe?

20. Observe a parent caring for a newborn. How much time does each task take? Which tasks seem easy? Which tasks seem more difficult?

21. Observe a newborn being dressed. Which clothing features made dressing the baby easy? Which made dressing the baby difficult? Did the clothes look comfortable on the baby? Why or why not?

Thinking Critically

22. Some new parents have never been near newborns. How do you think advertisements posing older babies as newborns affect their perceptions of their newborns?

23. Child development experts often advise parents to follow the baby's lead. Brainstorm with classmates how you can follow a baby's lead in meeting his or her needs. Are there times when newborns should follow their parents' lead? Why or why not?

24. Sometimes one spouse becomes unhappy when the other spouse spends so much time with the baby. How can a spouse tell when this is a reasonable complaint? What are some specific ways parents can make time to meet each other's needs?

Part 3 Infants

Focus on
Family and Community

Babies are born with the ability to learn. In fact, the sooner adults provide babies with learning experiences, the more babies want to learn. Learning new skills can be very rewarding at any age. You can learn new skills that will help you now and in the future as you relate to children, family, friends, and even coworkers. Choose a new skill you are interested in learning, such as managing money, improving study habits, making friends, or speaking a different language. Take it a step further and develop an FCCLA *Power of One* project for the unit *A Better You*. You can also participate in an FCCLA Star Event. Use the FCCLA *Planning Process* to plan, carry out, and evaluate your project. Your FCCLA advisor can provide you with further information.

8 Physical Development of the Infant

After studying this chapter, you will be able to

★ describe how an infant develops physically during the first year.

★ describe the order in which an infant's motor skills develop.

Terms to Know

skeletal system
failure to thrive
body proportions
ossification
deciduous teeth
motor development
gross-motor skills

fine-motor skills
age norm
crawl
creeping
cruising
voluntary grasping

Reading Advantage

Find an article on **http://news.google.com** that relates to the topic covered in this chapter. Print the article and read it before reading the chapter. As you read the chapter, highlight sections of the news article that relate to the text.

Companion Web Site

Interactive Activity

Learn more about the motor development of an infant by completing the *Read, Discuss, and Analyze* Activity for Chapter 8 at **g-wlearning.com**.

Infancy is the period of life between two weeks and one year after birth. Children's development during this time is exciting because they grow and learn new skills each day.

Babies continue to develop physically during the first year. A human's physical growth is completed at 20 or 21 years. This growth period is longer than that of any living creature. During much of this time, others must care for the human.

Just as babies grow quickly during the prenatal and neonatal stages, they grow quickly during their first year of life. It is fun to watch a tiny newborn grow into a more chubby-looking infant. Good physical development is important during this time. A healthy baby keeps growing and developing in all areas.

Skeletal Growth

The **skeletal system** is made of bones and teeth. *Skeletal growth* refers to the changes in length, weight, and the appearance of teeth.

Length and Weight

The baby's length and weight change quickly during the first year. (The term *length* is used for the first year because the baby does not stand. After the first year, the term *height* is used.) Changes happen so quickly that even people who see the baby daily are amazed at how fast he or she grows.

All children grow at their own rates. The average length of a baby at birth is 20 to 21 inches. Most infants increase their birth lengths by 30 percent in the first five months.

They reach 1.5 times their birth lengths (adding a total of 9 to 10 inches) during their first year, 8-1. Usually boys are slightly longer and heavier than girls (by about ¾ of an inch and 1½ pounds) by one year.

Around nine months, the infant is rather chubby. This change happens because fat tissues under the skin have increased. After this time, fat tissues begin to decrease. Even at this early age, boys have more muscle length and thickness, while girls have more fat.

The rate of growth is more important than the actual length and weight. The baby's doctor will use a growth chart to record the baby's growth at each checkup. This growth chart shows several growth rates for babies as well as the measurements for this baby. The doctor will compare the baby's actual measurements to the growth rates. As long as growth seems

Average Length and Weight During First Year

Age in Months	Length in Inches	Weight in Pounds
Birth	20	7½
3	23¾	12½
6	26	16¾
9	28	20
12	29½	22¼

8-1 A baby's length and weight increase quickly during the first year.

to continue at a constant rate, the doctor will not likely be concerned.

Sometimes, however, babies experience a **failure to thrive**. This means their rates of growth slow considerably over time. This may indicate a health problem exists. In this case, the growth chart would show the baby was growing at a steady rate and then showed a decline. Possible causes of failure to thrive include the following:

★ diseases that prevent all or some nutrients from being absorbed or that cause nutrients to be quickly expelled from the body

★ the baby's food is not providing enough nutrients (diluted formula or breast milk affected by mother's malnutrition)

★ feedings are offered too infrequently or last too short a time

★ the baby is not held, touched, or talked to, or is abused or neglected

With the proper care and attention, the baby's health can often be restored. How long this will take depends on when the problem began and how severe it is.

Body Proportions

Infants do not look like small adults. Their **body proportions** (relative size of body parts) differ from those of adults. For example, an infant's head is about one-fourth his or her total length, while an adult's head is one-eighth of his or her total height. Unlike adults, the forehead of an infant is wider than the chin. The jaw is smaller and slopes backward. This is commonly called the "baby look."

More than half of the total growth of the head occurs during the first year of life. (The head circumference grows from an average of 13.5 to 18.5 inches in the first year.) From birth until six months, the infant's head is larger than the chest. In most six-month-old children, the chest becomes larger. The difference in the distance around the chest as compared to distance around the head continues to increase with age.

Besides having a large head, an infant has a long trunk, a "pot-bellied" abdomen, and short legs. The gain in length during the first year is because the trunk grows. The legs do not grow much longer at this time. The abdomen sticks out because the internal organs are large for the baby's small body. Because the center of gravity is high on the baby's body, the result is poor balance. No wonder babies toddle rather than walk!

Pediatric Audiologist

Pediatric audiologists examine children to identify those with hearing loss and other auditory, balance, and related sensory and neural problems. They then assess the nature and extent of the problems and help manage them.

Education: Individuals must have at least a master's degree in audiology to qualify for a job. However, a doctoral degree is becoming more common. Audiologists are regulated by licensure or registration.

Job Outlook: Average employment growth is projected. However, because of the small size of the occupation, few job openings are expected. Job prospects will be favorable for those possessing the Au.D. degree.

Bones and Teeth

The infant skeleton is mainly made of cartilage. That is why infants' bones do not break easily. There are large spaces between their "bones" to help the joints bend easily without breaking. Young babies can suck their toes with no trouble, but sitting and standing are impossible because their skeletons are not sturdy. Due to their softness, an infant's bones can easily become misshapen. Lying in one position all the time can flatten the baby's head in one place. This has become more common in recent years with the need for babies to sleep on their backs. (This sleep position greatly reduces the risk of SIDS.)

Changing a baby's position during waking hours can keep the head from flattening. Many doctors now recommend "tummy time" for babies. Once babies can hold their heads up (at two to four months), they should spend time on their stomachs while alert. This encourages the development of motor skills, such as rolling over, reaching, and crawling. It also aids bone growth. During tummy time, caregivers should stay close and offer the baby toys to see, reach,

and grasp. This stimulates the baby's brain.

During the first year, three changes occur in a baby's bones.

★ First, the length of the bones increases.

★ Second, **ossification** (depositing of the minerals, calcium, and phosphorus) begins. Ossification helps the skeletal frame become sturdy. This, in turn, helps the infant to sit and eventually walk.

★ Third, the number of bones changes. For example, the hand and wrist of a one-year-old infant has only three bones, but there are 28 bones in the adult's hand and wrist. Also, ossification in the skull results in several bones becoming one skull bone. This growth is completed in about two years.

Teeth, a part of the skeletal system, begin forming in the sixth week of prenatal life. By birth, all 20 **deciduous teeth** (nonpermanent teeth) and a few permanent teeth are developing deep in the jaw. Most babies begin cutting teeth during the second half of the first year, 8-2.

Focus on Science
The Senses

As you will read in Chapter 9, the senses mature very quickly during the first months after birth. Not only do the senses aid intellectual development, they aid physical development. As the senses mature, babies find their new world more interesting. They move their bodies to get closer to objects. They also learn to grasp to move objects closer to their bodies.

Both types of actions aid motor development. In what other ways can the senses aid development?

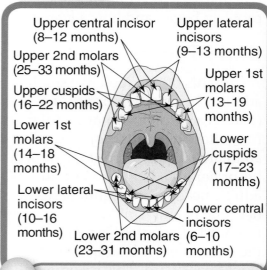

Upper central incisor (8–12 months)

Upper lateral incisors (9–13 months)

Upper 2nd molars (25–33 months)

Upper cuspids (16–22 months)

Upper 1st molars (13–19 months)

Lower 1st molars (14–18 months)

Lower cuspids (17–23 months)

Lower lateral incisors (10–16 months)

Lower central incisors (6–10 months)

Lower 2nd molars (23–31 months)

8-2 Deciduous (nonpermanent) teeth appear in a predictable pattern.

The *sequence* (order) of teething is easier to predict than *when* teeth will appear (timing). In fact, a few babies are born with one or more teeth. Other children are more than a year old when their first teeth appear.

Motor Development

Motor development is the use and control of muscles that direct body movements. Learning to use and control large muscles, such as the trunk, arms, and legs, helps babies crawl and walk. These abilities are called **gross-motor skills**. Being able to control the small muscles, such as the hands and fingers, leads the baby to develop **fine-motor skills**. Having control over the body is a sign of babies' growth and development.

The baby's motor skills develop in three main patterns. This order of motor development builds upon the order of brain development. The following list shows the pattern of motor development:

1. Babies move slowly because they must think as they move.

2. Babies' reactions develop from general to specific. At first, babies show general reactions to what they see and hear. Later in the first year, babies give more specific reactions. For example, if young infants see something they want, they wiggle all over. Older infants smile and reach for the object.

3. Motor development occurs in two directions. The first is from the head to the foot. The second is from the center of the body out to the extremities (from the trunk to the hands and feet).

Head-to-Foot Development

Head-to-foot development begins before birth. The unborn baby develops a head, then arm buds, and then leg buds. At birth, babies have well-developed facial muscles, but less well-developed leg muscles. This is why babies can suck, but cannot walk.

Figure 8-3 shows the sequence or milestones in which babies can control their head, neck, and trunk muscles. *Milestones* are sequenced steps, and the order of these steps is more constant than their timing. How do experts calculate the timing of these steps? Some babies develop when they are older, others when they are younger. Experts call the typical time when a developmental milestone occurs, an **age norm**. An age norm can be expressed as an average age or age range. The age norm predicts when development will likely occur.

Head and Neck Control

Newborns need to have their heads supported continually. Their muscles are not strong enough to hold their heads steady themselves. Some babies can raise their unsteady heads briefly when lying on their stomach. By two months, most babies spend a great deal of time with their heads and chests raised. Between three and four months, eye muscles are well developed, permitting babies to focus on objects in any direction. They can smile when they want to and make some sounds with the lips. Head control is almost complete

2 months (chin up)

3 months (chest up—arm support)

4 months (sits with support)

5 months (sits on lap, grasps object)

6 months (sits on high chair, grasps dangling object)

7 months (sits without support)

8 months (stands with help)

9 months (stands holding furniture)

10 months (creeps)

11 months (walks when led)

12 months (pulls to stand by furniture)

14 months (stands alone)

15 months (walks alone)

8-3   A baby gains control over the head and neck before the leg muscles.

when babies are about six months old. By this time, babies can raise their heads briefly while lying on their backs. They can also hold their heads steady while sitting with support.

Trunk Control

Control of the trunk develops more slowly than control of the head. Babies placed on their stomachs can lift their heads before they can lift both their heads and chests. Trunk control permits babies to achieve two major milestones in motor control—rolling over and sitting.

Rolling Over

Often between the second and fifth month, babies learn to roll over. Usually they first roll from front to back. A month later, they usually roll from back to front. It is easier for a baby to lift the head and trunk when on the abdomen than when on the back.

Sitting

Learning to sit takes several months. The baby first must gain strength in the neck and back. The baby must also be able to control the head.

Babies can sit briefly with support (being held or with pillows placed at their backs) at three or four months of age. By age seven months, most can sit for a short time without support. For longer periods of sitting, they often lean forward and support themselves with their arms and legs, 8-4. They may even topple over if distracted. Progress now becomes rapid. By nine months, most babies can sit without support.

Leg Control

Leg control is the last phase of head-to-foot development. With leg control, locomotion really begins. (*Locomotion* is the ability to move from place to place.) Babies usually go through the stages of crawling, creeping, standing, and walking.

Crawling

How can you tell when a baby is gaining leg control? When lying on the tummy, the baby's hands and feet will work together smoothly (at five or six months). This shows leg control. Babies play with their own feet and toes at about seven months. They begin to crawl well at the same time. Babies **crawl** by pulling with their arms. They do not lift their abdomens from the floor. The common term for this is "belly-crawling."

8-4 Until back muscles are strong, leaning forward helps babies to sit unaided.

Creeping

Babies may begin **creeping** between six and eight months. Creeping means to move by using the hands and knees or hands and feet. Babies begin to creep by lifting their abdomens and hips off the floor alternately. The movement may become a rhythmical, rocking motion. Within a couple of months, many babies can move forward or backward on hands and knees (or on hands and feet) with their abdomens off the floor, 8-5. The common term for creeping is "knee-crawling."

Standing and Walking

Six-month-old babies enjoy standing when supported under the arms. They push with their feet and bounce on adults' laps.

8-5 To creep, this baby must raise the trunk of his body and coordinate the movements of his arms and legs.

A few months later, babies can pull to a standing position. When babies stand alone, they often enjoy **cruising**, or walking by holding something for support.

At first, babies stand with support, holding on to a stable object. As they develop, babies stand further away from objects. They use large objects for balance by holding on with only one of their hands. They also take a few cautious steps between objects and people. Most babies first stand alone at between 12 and 14 months and begin walking a few weeks later.

Center-to-Extremities Development

In center-to-extremities development, control begins with the trunk, then arms, hands, and fingers. This control extends to the hips, then legs, feet, and toes. Children can use their arms and hands to crawl and lift objects before they can use the hand and finger control needed to stack blocks. As you can see, the ability to control the body begins with the center of the body and moves outward.

Control of the arms, hands, and fingers develops in stages. As you read earlier, the baby comes into the world with a grasping reflex called the *Palmar reflex*. With this reflex, the baby will automatically grasp whatever is placed in the hand.

Learn More About...
Differences in Physical Development

With few exceptions, the order of physical development is the same for every child. However, each child develops at his or her own rate. The rate is affected by heredity, nutrition, illnesses, and activity. Whether a child is praised and encouraged (environment) can also make a difference. Some infants develop more quickly than the age norm; others lag behind. A particular infant may also develop quickly in one area, but more slowly in another.

If a baby's development seems to be much slower than the norms, parents should talk to a doctor. Regular medical care is the best way to find and treat problems that may exist. A doctor, parent educator, or other child development professional might also advise the parents how to best encourage this area of the child's development.

At two months, babies begin to swipe at objects in an attempt to grasp them.

When the baby is about four months, the grasping reflex is replaced by **voluntary grasping** (the intentional act of grasping of an object). The first grasps are rather crude, but with practice, the baby refines his or her skills. Voluntary grasping is well developed between ages five to six months. At this time, a baby can grasp one object that is handed to him or her.

Six- and seven-month olds usually bring any grasped item directly to the mouth to explore it. At seven months, babies can accept two objects handed to them. A month or two later, babies can use the thumb in opposition to the forefingers to pick up an object. This is the most complex grasp the baby will learn. It is called the *pincer grasp*. Ten-month-olds can often accept three objects handed to them.

Summary

A baby's physical development is rapid during the first year. Length and weight increase quickly. The baby's body proportions soon change. The bones begin to develop. Teeth begin to appear in a certain order.

Motor development is the ability to control the large and small muscles. Movements using these muscles are called *motor skills*. Examples include walking; crawling; and using the arms, hands, and fingers. Motor development occurs rapidly in the first year.

Control over the body comes in a slow, predictable pattern. Babies' reactions to what they see and hear are general at first and then become more specific. Control of the body begins from head to foot and also goes from the trunk outward. There is a sequence to babies' motor development.

All children develop physically in much the same way. The rate of development may vary because it can be affected by heredity, environment, nutrition, illnesses, and activity. Parents who have concerns about the rate of their child's development should seek a doctor's advice.

Companion Web Site

Interactive Activity

Review vocabulary terms and key concepts for Chapter 8 at **g-wlearning.com**.

Review and Reflect

Write your answers to the following questions on a separate sheet of paper.

1. Most babies _____ (half, double, triple) their birthweights during the first year.

2. True or false. The rate of growth over the months is more important than the measurement of total growth.

3. True or false. In the first year, the baby gets longer because the legs grow.

4. What are three changes that occur in the bones during development?

5. True or false. *Motor development* is the way children learn how to play with others and share their toys.

6. True or false. There is a pattern to children's physical development.

7. True or false. Infants learn in the same sequence, but the rate varies.

8. List the following motor skills in order of occurrence: sits without support with back straight; raises the head while on abdomen; creeps; walks; rolls over from front to back; stands without help; picks up object with thumb used in opposition to finger.

9. Reflexes are _____ (learned, unlearned).

10. Voluntary movements are _____ (learned, unlearned).

Cross-Curricular Link

11. **Math.** Interview at least six parents of young children. Ask each parent what the baby's weight and height were at birth, six months, and one year. Record these figures in a master list. Showing your work, figure the average weight and height for this group of babies at each age.

12. **Science, Writing.** As a group or class project, write a one- or two-page brochure that explains at what ages parents can expect their children to learn certain motor skills. You may also find pictures or drawings to illustrate the various skills. The brochure could be checked by a physician before making copies. Find out whether copies could be given to new parents at the hospital, posted in medical offices, or printed in a local newspaper.

13. **Speech.** Find a quality infant toy that would encourage an infant to develop gross- and fine-motor skills. Make an oral presentation to the class showing how your selected toy promotes both types of skills.

14. **Technology.** Work with a partner to visit a Web site designed for parents. Search for information that would

help the parents of infants understand their child's physical development in the first year. Based on what you have learned in the chapter, does the advice seem sound to you? Why or why not? Create an electronic presentation of your findings. Adhere to all copyright laws and cite any sources you may use for the presentation. Share your presentations with the class.

Making Observations

15. Observe a doctor giving a well-baby exam. Ask the doctor to explain each procedure. Note weight and length as well as head and chest measurements. Also note heart and breathing rates and reflexive and voluntary movement. How does the baby's progress compare to age norms? What progress has the baby made since the last checkup?

16. Visit a child care program that serves infants of various ages. Choose four or five babies who represent different ages. Watch the babies closely and record your observations. Compare the babies' abilities to sit, move about, and grasp objects.

17. Observe two infants who are the same age. How do they differ in their physical maturity? How do they differ in their motor skills? Does one infant have a lag in maturity or skills? If so, did the parent say anything that explains the lag, such as low birthweight or serious illness?

18. Observe how several babies move toward a toy. Describe exactly how each baby moves toward the toy. (Often babies use more than one motor skill to reach a toy.)

Thinking Critically

19. Some people believe babies should be fat. Why do some people have this perception? Can such a perception lead to problems?

20. Parents sometimes push their babies to walk early. Can this be harmful to babies? Why or why not?

21. As you read, the grasping reflex is not highly developed until almost one year of age. Does this mean parents can assume their baby is not able to grasp small objects on the floor and insert them into his or her mouth, nose, or ears? Why or why not?

9

Intellectual Development of the Infant

After studying this chapter, you will be able to

★ **describe** how and what infants learn.

★ **explain** how infants express what they know through language.

★ **identify** the order in which infants learn.

Terms to Know

intellectual development	object identity
stimuli	object permanence
binocular vision	depth perception
perception	vocabulary
perceptual learning	coo
cognition	babble
sensorimotor stage	monotone
imitating	inflections
concept	reduplication babbling
object constancy	passive vocabulary
object concept	active vocabulary

Reading Advantage

Write all of the chapter terms on a sheet of paper. Highlight the words that you do *not* know. Before you begin reading, look up the highlighted words in the glossary and write the definitions.

Companion Web Site

Interactive Activity

Learn more about how babies communicate by completing the *Read, Discuss, and Analyze* Activity for Chapter 9 at **g-wlearning.com**.

Intellectual development is how people learn, what they learn, and how they express what they know through language. (It is also called *mental* and *cognitive development*.) During the baby's first year, intellectual development happens as quickly as physical development.

Babies come into the world using all their sense organs and react to stimuli with certain reflexes. **Stimuli** are changes in the environment, such as sound or light, that affect the sensory organs causing the person to react. Within 12 months, infants have highly developed sense organs and motor skills. They use these to learn about people, objects, places, and events in their world. At birth, the main sound babies make is crying. By the end of the first year, they know many words. Some can even say a few words.

How Infants Learn

For many years people have wondered how infants learn. Learning involves more than physical development. Most researchers in child development believe babies *want* to learn. Each month babies exert more and more effort to explore their world.

Brain Development Supports Learning

A baby's brain and sense organs mature a lot during the first year. This helps babies learn. As motor skills develop, infants are able to move toward many sights, sounds, and other learning experiences. Research provides support for areas of brain development that have long been recognized as major mental learnings of infancy. For example, brain research has noted much activity in the motor and vision centers of the brain.

Motor Center

As reflexes wane, much activity occurs in the motor center. Wiring here begins at two months. At this time, babies begin the multi-year process of learning voluntary gross-motor movements. Wiring for fine-motor movements begins at two or three months. This is

Learn More About...
Brain Development

As you read in Chapter 1, the complex building process of the brain does not occur all at once. Different parts of the brain get priority at different times. At given times, certain experiences are especially helpful to brain development. These times are called *windows of opportunity*. Experiences that are repeated or similar to others reinforce a baby's learning. New experiences expand a baby's knowledge.

Brain development research suggests the following three factors affect the rate of mental development:
★ the baby's physical development (mainly brain growth)
★ the baby's environment
★ the interaction of the first two factors; that is, using the windows of opportunity

when babies make their first attempts to grasp objects.

Vision Center

Vision is needed quite early in life. For this reason, the vision center is very active in early infancy. Babies' maturing eyes and brain wiring help them look at people's faces and objects. Infants need many chances to see interesting objects.

First to mature is the ability of the baby to see through each eye clearly. Although they do not have the acuity (ability to see objects sharply) of adults, by two to three months, infants can see objects at many distances very clearly.

Between one and three months of age, babies begin to look at objects with both eyes. Watching a young infant, the adult may notice the baby's eyes do not seem to work together. Often, one eye drifts off focus. At first, the baby's brain "sees" two slightly separated images of the same object. Around three months, the baby's brain can fuse the image, or see it as one object using both eyes. To fuse an image requires the eyes to stay focused together on the object. The window of opportunity for fusing images is very short. (Fusing images should happen naturally unless the baby has weak eye muscles.)

Once the baby can fuse images, he or she has what is called **binocular vision**. Binocular vision is necessary for recognizing how far away an object is. Thus, the eyes guide the hand in knowing how far the arm must extend before grasping. The eyes also guide the feet in knowing how far down, up, or away the next step will be.

Vision is highly important to learning other things, too. Activity in the vision center of the brain peaks at eight months. At this time, babies begin inspecting everything—the details of their world; thus adding to mental learnings.

Thinking and Memory Centers

Instead of just seeing, hearing, and touching, babies try to make sense of people, objects, sounds, and events. Babies not only try to figure out what is happening, they also try to cause things to happen. For example, babies may try to make their cradle gym bounce or make a ball roll. Babies like to repeat and vary these events, too. Brain development research suggests that wiring in the thinking and memory centers of the brain begins at 6 months. Because thinking and memory are so complex, wiring in these centers continues for about 10 years.

Just as an infant needs good nutrition for physical growth, he or she also needs a good mental diet. Interesting things to see, hear, and touch are "food for thought."

Child Development Specialist

Child development specialists observe and record children's behavior. They apply principles of child growth and development to plan safe and healthy learning environments for children. They focus on advancing children's physical, intellectual, social, and emotional development.

Education: Coursework in child development is required. The level of education is dependent upon the level of responsibility.

Job Outlook: Employment of child development specialists is projected to have average growth.

Because the world is new to the infant, common objects and experiences provide a rich mental diet. The adult's face, a cardboard box, some pans and spoons, or a trip in the yard can provide good learning experiences, 9-1.

Perception

Perception involves organizing information that comes through the senses. This is a major step in learning. People perceive by noting how things are alike and different in size, color, shape, and texture. Perceptions about form, space, weight, and numbers come through the senses, too.

Perception also involves how fast the brain organizes information. For example, a mature reader can tell the difference between *b* and *d* faster than a beginning reader.

9-1 Common experiences, such as interacting with a parent during daily routines, provide a rich mental diet for the infant.

Finally, perception involves the way a person reacts to different sensory experiences. As an example, a child in a room crowded with strangers may run to his or her mother. However, if the child is alone with the mother, he or she may play with a toy on the floor rather than in the mother's lap.

Perceptual Learning

The process of developing mental images is called **perceptual learning**. Perceptual learning happens because the sense organs mature and preferences for certain stimuli change.

The sense organs develop at rapid rates. At birth, infants can hear differences between high- and low-pitched sounds. They can move their bodies to the rhythm of adult speech. By three months, babies can tell the difference in the sounds of words like *daddy* and *mama*. Their vision improves as their eye muscles become strong enough to focus on objects.

Changes in Preferences

From the time of birth, babies are bombarded with all types of stimuli. In order to learn, infants must choose from among these stimuli. See 9-2 through 9-5 to learn why babies tend to choose some objects over others.

Cognition

Cognition is the act or process of knowing or understanding. Cognition gives meaning to perceptions. The baby's brain begins to piece together perceptions to form a picture in the mind.

Babies Choose One Object over Another

Babies have certain preferences. They prefer to play or interact more with one object than another. Researchers believe infants have inborn abilities to choose the stimuli that will most help them learn. Studies show the following changes in preferences, or choices, they make:

★ **Preferences change from parts of objects to complete objects.**

At first, infants react to, or study, parts of objects. Later, they pay more attention to the entire object. For instance, at two months they smile at eyes drawn on a blank background. At three months, they study a picture that has eyes and a nose. By five months they smile only at the picture of the full face. They prefer the complete objects rather than parts of objects.

★ **Preferences change from simple to complex objects.**

Until babies are almost two months old, they do not prefer one object to another. After that, babies prefer more complex objects. For example, babies prefer 3-D objects over 2-D pictures. They prefer patterned or textured cards over plain white or solid-colored cards. Babies also prefer a drawn human face over any other drawn pattern or solid-colored card. Other preferences include slow-moving objects over nonmoving objects and curved lines over straight lines. They may show little or no reaction to complex stimuli because they cannot understand them.

★ **Preferences change from familiar to new objects.**

After two months of age, babies begin to explore things that are new to them. They ignore objects that are too different because they may not understand them.

9-2 Infants change their preferences for certain objects.

9-3 When shown each of these figures, babies' preferences from least to most liked were— white circle, yellow circle, red circle, concentric circles, circle with words, circle with face. (Frantz's study.)

9-4 When shown each of these pairs of lines, infants liked the curved lines more than the straight lines. (Frantz's study.)

Infants' Preferences for Experiences

Approximate Age	Seeing	Hearing	Touching
Birth–3 months	★ Follows slow-moving objects with eyes. ★ Looks when held to shoulder. ★ Looks at hairline part of face at 1 month. ★ Looks at eyes, nose, and mouth at 2 months. Often smiles. ★ Prefers patterns to solids. ★ Follows the gaze of an adult to look where the adult is looking at 2 months.	★ Reacts physically to sounds by opening eyes widely, startling, or making other movements. ★ Is calmed by gentle voice. ★ Connects voices with faces at 1 month.	★ Lessens reflexive grasping and begins voluntary grasping between 6 weeks and 3 months. ★ Holds objects less than 1 minute. ★ Swipes at objects suspended overhead at 2 to 3 months.
3–6 months	★ Prefers red and blue to green and yellow. ★ Enjoys mirrors, but does not know his or her image until after 1 year of age. ★ Grasps what is seen. ★ Enjoys small objects. ★ Imitates facial expressions.	★ Learns the meaning of familiar sounds, such as making food and a nearby parent. ★ Reacts to differences in tones of voices. ★ Tries to locate source of sounds. ★ Repeats own sounds. ★ Tells differences in sounds, such as *ba* and *pa*.	★ Grasps with both hands and often clasps hands when object is out of reach at 3 to 4 months. ★ Takes 1 object at a time. ★ Plays with hands at 4 months. ★ Plays with toes at 5 to 6 months. ★ Mouths all objects; opens mouth well in advance of approaching objects. ★ Opens hands wider for larger objects than for smaller objects.

9-5 Babies change their seeing, hearing, and touching preferences as they try to learn about their new worlds.

(Continued.)

6–9 months	★ Examines objects with eyes and hands. ★ Recognizes drop-offs (but is not safe from falls). ★ Looks for hidden (covered) toys.	★ Learns noises different toys make. ★ Notes differences between questions and statements by changes in pitch. ★ Enjoys hearing singing and tries to sing along.	★ Handles objects by turning, shaking, and banging. ★ Enjoys toys with moving parts such as dials and wheels. ★ Holds own bottle. ★ Uses one object to work another, such as hitting a drum with a stick. ★ Transfers objects from one hand to the other.
9–12 months	★ Shows less interest in faces except to quickly identify the familiar face and the strange face. ★ Looks where crawling. ★ Watches dropped objects with interest to see whether they roll, break, or bounce. ★ Enjoys hiding games, such as hide and seek.	★ Imitates sounds. ★ Enjoys hearing own name. ★ May make sounds of some animals. ★ Knows meaning of many words and may respond to requests.	★ Predicts weight of objects with correct arm tension. ★ Enjoys self-feeding. ★ Shows held objects to others. ★ Enjoys dropping objects into pails and boxes. ★ Enjoys stacking blocks and knocking them down. ★ Takes lids off objects. Pulls and pushes roll toys. ★ Turns knobs and switches. ★ Nests (puts smaller into larger) objects.

9-5 (Continued.)

Two psychologists, who described how children learn, were Jean Piaget, a Swiss, and Lev Vygotsky, a Russian. Both were born in 1896. Vygotsky was only 38 when he died, and his work was not known outside of Russia until the 1960s. Piaget's work was well-known by the 1960s, and he continued his work until his death in 1980.

Both men agreed that children construct their knowledge from their experiences. They believed learning attempts must be respected by allowing the child to take the lead. Their ideas influence education even today.

Piaget and Vygotsky differed in other ways. Piaget felt children learn through their environment by making their own discoveries. Piaget thought the role of the adult was to provide a stimulating environment. His research led him to believe that *all* children go through four stages in their understanding of math, science, language arts, play, and even moral development.

Like Piaget, Vygotsky believed children's thinking changed. Because Vygotsky thought that changes were more individual and cultural, distinct stages were not part of his theory. Although he knew children learned some things through their own discovery, he felt children learned mainly through interactions with others within their culture. In short, adults and more advanced children guide each child's discoveries. His theory is thus known as the *Sociocultural Theory of Development*.

Piaget's Sensorimotor Stage

Because infants explore with their senses and motor actions, Piaget called the first stage of mental development the **sensorimotor stage**. This stage begins at birth, and most children complete it in two years. During this stage, infants use their senses and motor skills to learn and communicate. Learning at this time is important. This time is the basis for all future mental development.

Piaget described the learnings of the sensorimotor stage through six substages. In 9-6 you can see that children will work through four substages during their first year. In studying the chart, you will note the following key points:

★ In the first two substages, babies use their own body to learn (hence the term *primary*). That is, babies learn through their own reflexes and early voluntary actions.

★ In the second two substages, babies learn as their actions produce responses from people and objects (hence the term *secondary*).

★ At first, connections are accidental; later, babies note the repeated connection between what they do (action) and what happens (response). This is the beginning of seeing cause and effect.

★ Babies repeat their actions many, many times (hence the term *circular*) to verify the results and bring pleasure.

★ Babies begin learning by **imitating**, or doing what others do; this is an important way to learn. Between 8 and 12 months, babies have goals, such as wanting a toy, that direct their actions. They can now combine several actions they have already learned to reach goals.

Piaget's Stages of Cognitive Development

Stage 1: Sensorimotor Stage (Birth to 2 years)

Learning through the senses and physical actions in six substages.

Substages 1 and 2 involve the baby's own body.

Substage 1: Practicing Reflexes (birth to 1 month)

★ Find stimulation through inborn reflexes, such as sucking and looking.
★ Practice these reflexes making them strong and more efficient.

Substage 2: Primary circular reactions (1 to 4 months)

★ Use voluntary actions that came from the reflexes, such as sucking at will.
★ Adapt these basic actions, such as sucking with more force for nourishment and with less force for pleasure (pacifier or hand).

Substages 3 and 4 involve people and objects.

Substage 3: Secondary circular reactions (4 to 8 months)

★ Notice some responses to their actions, such as crying brings mother and kicking makes the mobile bounce. Practice their action-response sequences.
★ Can imitate some actions of others.

Substage 4: Coordination of secondary circular reactions (8 to 12 months)

★ Begin to have goals, such as wanting a toy.
★ Problem-solve by combining two or more actions, such as *crawling* toward a toy and then *grasping* it.
★ Use a few tools to attain goals, such as using an object's string to pull it within reach.

Substage 5 and 6: (12 months to 2 years)

Stage 2: Preoperational Stage (2 to 7 years)

Stage 3: Concrete Operational Stage (7 to 11 years)

Stage 4: Formal Operational Stage (11 years on)

9-6 Piaget described how infants use their senses and motor skills to learn. Infants are in the sensorimotor stage.

★ Not only do babies combine actions to *problem-solve*, they use some simple tools to achieve a goal. For example, babies may use a stick or a stool (tools) to help them reach a toy (goal).

Vygotsky's Basic Theory

Vygotsky believed that the culture in which a child is reared and his or her own social environment (family, school, community) determines how a child will think. He saw teaching of children as the basic sociocultural activity of humans. He believed that "teaching" was done through imitation of the model, instruction, and working together on tasks or projects. Helping children is called *scaffolding*.

To be effective as a "teacher," Vygotsky thought it was most important for the "teacher" to follow the child's lead. For each concept or skill, "teachers" must work in a child's *zone of proximal development* (ZPD); that is, the level in which a child can learn with help. Working in this zone shows respect for what the child is learning and his or her interests. This is *following the child's lead*. Adults must find a child's ZPD (called *finding the match*). If the match is right, children can be challenged to learn new concepts or skills, but will not be overwhelmed.

Once in the ZPD, adults should provide lots of scaffolding at first. After many experiences, some scaffolding or help is removed. Once all the scaffolding is removed for a given learning, a new ZPD appears. The gradual withdrawal of help makes the child more self-confident, too.

While their baby is an infant, parents can best scaffold through emotional communication. In the very early months, parents should try to interpret their baby's cries or sucking behaviors. Around four months, babies' signals become clearer. For example, babies use body language, such as kicking when they want out of a high chair or turning their head away when bored. If parents read the cues and respond, the foundation for learning will begin.

What Infants Learn

As babies explore their world, they learn many concepts. A **concept** is an idea formed by combining what is known about a person, object, place, quality, or event. Thinking is organized through concepts. For example, if you see an animal you believe is a cat, you immediately think of all you know about cats. Then you note how this animal is like or unlike other cats you recall. Children must learn to understand the ideas of cats, then animals, and finally living creatures.

Concepts change from simple to complex as the child's brain matures and experiences increase. A child understands the word *chair* before knowing about the many types of chairs. Concepts also change from concrete to abstract. For example, children can draw themselves and their parents (concrete) before they can draw other people (more abstract).

As children grow, their concepts change from incorrect to correct. First, a child may call all men *Daddy*. Later, they understand the concept of *men*.

Concepts are different for each person, too. No two people have exactly the same experiences. Not only do experiences differ, but also many concepts involve emotions. For example, the concept of school may be pleasant for one person, but unpleasant for another.

During the first year, infants form many concepts. These concepts help infants make sense of their world and further their mental development.

Perceptual Concepts

Information comes to infants through their senses. At this time, babies begin to make order of what they see, hear, smell, taste, and touch, 9-7. They begin to mentally organize this information. The following sections describe major perceptual concepts children learn in the first year.

Object Constancy or Sameness

Object constancy is knowing that objects remain the same even if they appear different. For example, a child may see a big airplane with bright colors take off and then look small and gray in the distant sky. Children learn that, although it may look different in size, shape, or color, it is still the same plane. Object constancy begins during the first year. It is not fully developed until the second or third year.

Object Concept

Object concept is the understanding that the world of objects, people, and events are separate from one's interactions with them. Parents are often the first "objects" with whom babies relate. Although they relate to them, they come to see they are separate from themselves. This understanding must happen before they can develop object concept about all people and objects in a general sense.

Object concept has two parts—object identity and object permanence. A child who has **object identity** knows that an object stays the same from one time to the next. For example, each time a child sees a toy bear, it is the same. Each time a child sees Daddy, he or she knows Daddy is the same although perhaps he is dressed differently or doing different tasks.

Object permanence is knowing that people, objects, and places still exist even when they are no longer seen, felt, or heard. For example, a baby may know mother is in the house, even though she is not in the room. Like most concepts, object permanence develops with many experiences over time. The concept begins to develop as early as a month or two of age. At this time, the baby will stare for a second in the place where an object or person was just seen, but has disappeared. A few months later, the baby will gleefully recover an object partially hidden. Toward the end of infancy, babies will watch an adult completely hide an object and will then "search" for it.

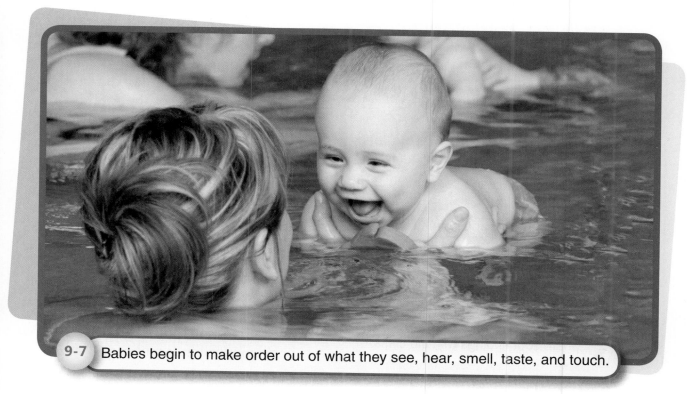

9-7 Babies begin to make order out of what they see, hear, smell, taste, and touch.

Depth Perception

Depth perception is the ability to tell how far away something is. It requires the development of binocular vision. Depth perception is needed for safety purposes. It keeps a person from stepping off an object far from the ground. People also use this skill to judge how far something is so they can reach it. Depth perception is rather well developed by seven to nine months of age. However, children are not safe from falls for many years.

Language: Brain Development Research

Language is closely related to mental development. Brain development research shows language wiring begins at birth,

if not before, 9-8. The first wiring has to do with the sounds of language, for these are needed to understand speech and to speak. The wiring follows this sequence:

★ During the first half-year, babies distinguish small differences in sounds. They are prepared to learn any language.

★ Because there are so many connections, pruning begins at six months of age. Babies come to notice only major differences in sounds in the languages they hear from caring adults. (Brain development research says they ignore language from the radio or television.) Even in adults, the brain detects small differences in sound through context clues; that is, through hearing the entire word or the word used in a phrase. For this reason, spelling words are often pronounced and then used in sentences.

★ By 12 months of age, babies complete the auditory maps needed for their own language. Learning to speak another language without "an accent" becomes much more difficult as the wiring for the sounds of other languages begins to be pruned away.

Not only does wiring for language sounds begin early, between 9 and 12 months, the brain's speech center begins the wiring process.

Language relates to mental growth in other ways, too. As people understand more concepts, their vocabularies tend to grow. A person's **vocabulary** consists of the words he or she understands and uses.

Focus on Science
Object Permanence

Try an object permanence experiment on babies who are four, six, and eight months old. To do the experiment, follow these steps:

★ *Step 1:* Place a toy in front of the baby. Let the baby play with the object.

★ *Step 2:* Take the toy and use a small baby blanket or towel to partly cover the toy.

★ *Step 3:* Take the toy and completely cover it with a blanket or towel.

★ *Step 4:* Take the toy and cover it with a box.

★ *Step 5:* Take the toy, place it in a small box, and place that box in a large box.

At any step, if the baby cannot find the toy, stop the experiment. Note the age of each baby and how many steps he or she could do. Share your findings with the class.

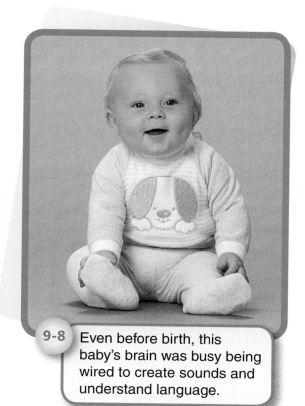

9-8 Even before birth, this baby's brain was busy being wired to create sounds and understand language.

Because language and mental growth are closely related, vocabulary words are often thought to measure mental growth. However, this is not always true. Infants can do and understand more than they can explain. Their speaking vocabularies lag behind what they understand.

There is a relationship between language and social and emotional growth. Language is used to express feelings or emotions. Before infants develop language, they show feelings by crying, laughing, clinging, and other physical signs. Even young children express many of their feelings physically. They show these feelings with temper tantrums, snatching toys from others, and hitting. As children grow older, they learn to express more of their feelings in words. Through language, children learn to make friends and get along with others.

How Babies Communicate

From the time infants are born, they are communicating. Through the sounds they make, others learn to understand their language.

Crying and Cooing

Newborns do not have control over the sounds they make. They make many noises while eating and sleeping. They swallow, smack, burp, yawn, and sigh. During the first month, babies communicate by crying. Parents can quickly learn what their baby's cries mean.

Between the sixth and eighth week, most babies begin to **coo**, making light, happy sounds. Babies coo more when others talk to, smile at, and touch them.

Babbling

Between the fourth and fifth month, babies begin to babble. Babies **babble** by making a series of vowel sounds with consonant sounds slowly added to form syllables, such as *ba*, *da*, and *gi*.

Babbling is an important pretalking skill. When babbling begins, babies practice all the sounds of all the world's languages. Babies are ready to learn any language or languages they hear, 9-9. Around one year, however, they make only the sounds needed to speak the languages they hear. This is because the brain has pruned away the connections needed to make sounds from other languages.

Babbling is not **monotone** (at a single pitch). Babies babble with **inflections** (changes of pitch) to express happiness, requests, commands, and questions. Often a baby babbles with so much feeling you can almost guess what he or she is saying.

First Words

Babies may begin talking during the last three months of the first year. Many start talking later. Most experts state that in order to count sounds as a word, the same sounds must be used each time to refer to a specific person, object, place, or event. No wonder many babies do not talk during the first year! Before talking, babies must do the following:

★ understand object permanence

★ understand that people, objects, places, and events have names

★ remember words that go with people, objects, places, and events

★ have the ability to make the sounds

★ realize that talking is important

A baby babbles all the sounds of all languages.

Reduplication Babbling

Often, first words come from babbling. Babies do **reduplication babbling**. They repeat the same syllable over and over, such as *da-da-da-da*. An adult who hears *da-da-da-da* may say, "That's right, *Dada*." The adult may point to Daddy. Daddy may pick up the baby, smile, nod, and call himself *Dada*. With practice, the baby connects the sound, which was already mastered, to the person.

The number of words babies learn varies a great deal. Studies show that most babies say about three words by the end of the first year. Spoken vocabulary does not begin to increase quickly until later in the second year.

Passive Versus Active Vocabulary

Although babies can say only a few words, they understand many, many more. The words people understand, but do not say or write, are called their **passive vocabulary**. In contrast, **active vocabulary** includes the words used in talking or writing.

Babies' passive vocabulary far exceeds their active vocabulary. Once babies get the idea that objects in their world have names, they learn these names quickly. They even understand sentences that refer to part of their daily routines such as, "Time for breakfast." Soon their favorite spoken word may be *whaddat* (What is that?) as they begin to learn language.

Baby Signing

With their limited active vocabularies, babies cannot tell others what they want or need. This often leads to screaming babies and frustrated adults. In the 1980s, Linda Acredolo and Susan Goodwin, professors in California universities, noted babies may make up signs for certain objects. Thus, they developed *Baby Signs*, a formal sign language for hearing babies. The 100-plus gestures come from American Sign Language (or ASL, the sign language for the deaf) and from baby-friendly modifications of ASL gestures.

Baby-sign language is becoming more common. Babies can use their hands before using the more intricate muscles needed for many words. Research shows that parents should begin signing when the baby is six or seven months old. Babies begin signing about two months later. Several research reports show signing babies outperformed nonsigning babies later in spoken vocabulary, sentence structure, and reading skills.

Summary

Intellectual development includes how babies learn, what they learn, and how they communicate. The rate of development is affected by the child's physical development and the environment.

Organizing information that comes through the senses is a major step in infant learning. Babies perceive whether things are alike or different in size, color, shape, and texture. They develop perceptions of form, space, weight, and number. They begin to piece this information together and give meaning to their perceptions.

In addition to the senses, children use their motor skills to know and understand their world. As their newborn reflexes give way to voluntary movement and sensory perceptions, children begin to learn. Piaget called this first stage of mental development the *sensorimotor* stage. He found that children go through a series of substages before they discover new ways to solve problems. On the other hand, Vygotsky saw children's development determined by culture and adult guidance. He thought children's learning led to changes in development.

Through children's early experiences, they form ideas, or concepts, about the world around them. As their brain matures and experiences increase, they learn various perceptual concepts. These include object constancy or sameness, object identity and permanence, and depth perception.

Language and mental development are closely related. Brain research shows that major wiring occurs in the brain's ability to distinguish the sounds of language. Toward the end of the first year, the speech center of the baby's brain becomes very active. Vocabulary tends to increase as more concepts are understood. Learning to express themselves promotes children's social and emotional development.

Crying is the baby's first communication method. Before first words are said, cooing and babbling occur. Babies have a much more extensive passive vocabulary than active vocabulary. At age one year, many babies have an active vocabulary of three words. Baby-sign language is one way to bridge the gap between what babies understand and what they can say.

Companion Web Site

Interactive Activity

Review vocabulary terms and key concepts for Chapter 9 at **g-wlearning.com**.

Review and Reflect

Write your answers to the following questions on a separate sheet of paper.

1. True or false. A baby's intellectual development is slow compared to physical development during the first year.

2. What are two factors that affect the rate of intellectual development?

3. Which of the following is an example of perception? (A) telling the difference between a mother's face and the faces of other women; (B) calling mother *mama*.

4. True or false. Babies first study parts of an object before paying attention to the object as a whole.

5. True or false. Babies would rather play with a familiar toy than try a new toy.

6. Which member of each pair do infants like better? (A) 2-D pictures or 3-D objects; (B) patterned cards or solid-colored cards; (C) straight lines or curved lines.

7. Which statement would Piaget support? Vygotsky support? (A) Children learn more by exploring on their own in a stimulating environment. (B) Children learn more when others teach them.

8. According to Piaget, children will work through _____ (two, four, six) substages during their first year.

9. Give an example of each of the following perceptual concepts: depth perception, object permanence, and object constancy.

10. True or false. Babies can make all the sounds needed to speak any language.

11. Pretalking skills begin at birth. List the following skills in the order of their occurrence: cooing, crying, reduplication babbling, babbling, and first words.

12. True or false. Baby-sign language confuses children.

Cross-Curricular Link

13. **Science (Brain Research), Technology.** Use the Internet to research brain development in the first year. (A good Web site source is: **www.zerotothree.org**.) Choose a specific research topic that interests you, such as "How is brain development affected by nutrition?" or "Which influences brain development more: genes or the environment?" Then, use word processing software to write a report of your findings. Check your paper for correct spelling, grammar, and punctuation. Adhere to all copyright laws and cite any sources you may use for the report.

14. **Science, Writing, Speech.** Choose a common word, such as *blue, school, music,* or *food.* Write a few phrases about what you think when you hear the word. Compare the perceptions of class members. Discuss your experiences and emotions associated with your perceptions of each word.

15. **Art.** Make a poster using words and/or drawings to describe the baby's learnings during the first year as stated by Piaget.

16. **Speech.** As a class, assign groups to make a recording of the sounds of babies who are 2, 4, 6, 8, 10, and 12 months old. Try to distinguish cooing from babbling. Listen for babbling sounds that are similar to words.

17. **Speech.** Interview the parents of young children about the first words their babies said and the age the babies began to talk. Share your findings with the class, and then compare them. Note the similarities and differences in the beginning of spoken language.

Making Observations

18. For one week, observe an infant exploring his or her world for 30 minutes per day. Record what the baby does during this time. What senses were used? What concepts and skills might the baby have been learning?

19. Observe infants as they see, hear, or touch objects in their environments. Compare your observations with information given in Chart 9-6.

20. Observe objects from a baby's walking and crawling heights. Describe how the objects look from each of these views. How would this help parents baby-proof their home?

21. Observe a baby trying to talk. Identify the baby's sounds as coos or babbles. What might the baby have been saying with his or her sounds?

Thinking Critically

22. Bring in several toys designed for infants. What do you think would be appealing about each toy? Make a list. What suggestions would you make to improve the appeal?

23. Hold a given object, such as a colored cube or cylinder. Turn the object in the hand and move it closer to and away from the face. How could that object look different in size? color? shape? Be specific in your explanation.

24. Suppose a friend told you it is *not* important for adults to talk to babies until babies begin to talk. Do you agree or disagree? Why? What should parents do?

10 Social-Emotional Development of the Infant

After studying this chapter, you will be able to

★ identify temperamental differences in babies.

★ describe the infant's major first-year social tasks.

★ explain the roots of four emotions—love, fear, anxiety, and anger.

Terms to Know

social-emotional development
disposition
emotions
temperament
siblings
mistrust
attachment

attachment behaviors
age-appropriate behaviors
anxiety
separation anxiety
dependence
independent

Reading Advantage

Read the review questions at the end of the chapter *before* you read the chapter. Keep the questions in mind as you read to help you determine which information is most important.

Companion Web Site

Interactive Activity

Learn more about temperamental differences in infants by completing the *Read, Discuss, and Analyze* Activity for Chapter 10 at **g-wlearning.com**.

Social-emotional development is an important type of development. It has three main parts. The first part is a person's **disposition** or mood. Some people have a more cheerful disposition, and others are more moody. The second part is learning to interact with people and social groups. These may include family members, schools, and clubs. The third part includes the ways people show feelings through emotions of love, fear, anxiety, and anger.

Emotions are thoughts that lead to feelings and cause changes in the body. For example, if you are upset at someone or something (a thought), you may become angry (a feeling). Your anger may increase your heart rate (change in your body).

Social-emotional development happens as quickly during the first year as physical and intellectual development. A baby enters the world with some unique traits. These traits are the root of the child's later personality. By the end of the first year, personality traits show even more. As a baby's social world expands the infant forms ideas about whether the world is a friendly place. The baby begins to express feelings with different emotions.

Temperamental Differences in Infants

Temperament is the tendency to react in a certain way, such as being cheerful or grumpy. Sometimes the word *disposition* also defines the ways people react. Experts think temperament is partly inherited. They also think a person's temperament may be due to prenatal conditions and ease of birth. These

Learn More About...
Characteristics of a Baby's Temperament

Some experts rate characteristics of a baby's temperament. These ratings place most babies in one of the following three groups:

★ **Easy**—Easy babies have regular habits, such as eating and sleeping. They respond quickly to a new situation. They are cheerful.

★ **Slow to warm up**—These babies take more time to adapt to new situations.

★ **Difficult**—Difficult babies are irregular in their habits. They often withdraw or protest—even scream—when facing new situations.

Researchers found that 4 in 10 babies are easy. One in 10 babies are slow to warm up, and 1 in 10 are difficult. A few babies cannot be grouped because their temperaments vary from day to day.

Easy babies usually get off to a good start with their parents. Difficult babies often have a rough start, which may cause parents to have increased feelings of anxiety. If the parents are stressed, this may cause increased stress in the child. Good, consistent care of difficult babies may make them happier. This supportive care includes extra holding, cuddling, and soothing. Easing these babies into new situations and alerting them to upcoming changes is also helpful.

factors, along with environment, shape a person's personality. A baby's temperament often shows by two or three months. In many children, but not all, temperament stays the same for years.

The Infant's Growing Social World

Infants are not truly social at birth. *Social* refers to a relationship between two or more people. Social development is shaped by how other people affect the baby and how the baby affects other people. By the end of the first year, social development is well underway. This section will focus on three aspects of social development in the first year. These three aspects are (A) interacting with others, (B) learning to trust, and (C) showing attachment.

Interacting with Others

Babies are born with tools for social development. At birth, babies can turn in the direction of the human voice. They move their bodies in the rhythm of human speech. They like to look at people's faces.

Babies understand social messages by the way others talk to, look at, or hold them. Babies send signals to others through their cries, coos, and smiles. These communications begin as early as two weeks after birth. Smiles with expressive eyes begin around the fifth or sixth week.

From the third to sixth months, babies become even better at understanding and sending social signals. They also begin to

distinguish between those who care for them and strangers.

Once babies are able to creep easily and have better arm and hand control, they *initiate* (begin) social contact. For example, they may follow others around the house. They reach with their arms to signal they want to be held.

Interacting with Adults

Babies thrive most when they are held, talked to, cuddled, and comforted. They are often happier babies, crying less than those who receive little attention. Parents and caregivers help their baby's mental development as well as social development by providing lots of loving care. As you read in Chapter 3, the parenting stage is called *Nurturing*.

Focus on Speech

The Social World of Babies

Interview two parents about the expanding social world of their babies. Prepare your list of interview questions in advance. Use the following for starters:

★ Who were the first people (not including hospital staff) to see your baby? hold your baby? feed, dress, and change your baby?

★ Besides parents, who are other important people in your baby's life?

★ How did your baby react to siblings and other children? How did siblings and other children react to your baby?

★ Did your baby become attached to an object? What object?

What do the responses of the parents tell you about the differences in the social-emotional development of their babies? Report your findings to the class in an oral report.

Grandparents, friends, babysitters, and others are helpful to babies' total development. When these people care for and show an interest in them, babies learn to understand and trust others. This helps expand babies' social environment.

Interacting with Other Children

Babies enjoy being around **siblings** (brothers and sisters) and other children. Babies tend to watch and follow children. They like to play with the toys of older children. Infants learn from older children. From infants, older children learn lessons in loving and caring for others. All children benefit in these relationships.

Learning to Trust

Trust is a key part of social development. How much a person trusts or does not trust other people affects how he or she interacts with them.

Many experts have researched the development of trust in infants. One of the most famous was psychologist Erik Erikson. He studied trust as one aspect of personality development, 10-1. Erikson viewed personality as ever-changing from birth through old age. He saw the family and other factors as major influences on personality. Erikson believed personality could develop in healthy or unhealthy ways.

Erikson described personality in eight stages that cover a person's *life span* (from birth throughout life). Each stage presents a specific developmental change for the person. The stages unfold one after another throughout a person's life. During each stage, the person faces

Erikson's Stages of Personality Development

Basic Trust versus Basic Mistrust (First Year of Life)
Consistency in having needs met and sameness in environment leads to a feeling the world is reliable. The baby develops a sense of basic trust. If the world is not seen as a reliable place, the baby develops a sense of basic mistrust.

Autonomy versus Shame and Doubt (Second Year of Life)

Initiative versus Guilt (Preschool Years)

Industry versus Inferiority (Middle Childhood)

10-1 Learning to trust while avoiding mistrust is the social-emotional task of infancy.

an important task that must be met. This task can have either a positive or negative outcome. No one is completely successful in any stage, but the more one is successful, the healthier the personality will be. If unsuccessful, the personality is more vulnerable during other stages. Erikson believed a person can overcome unsuccessful past tasks, but positive changes later in life are more difficult.

Each of Erikson's stages has a descriptive title that shows both outcomes of the task. For infants, the first stage is called *trust versus mistrust*. In this stage, infants learn whether to trust others or mistrust them. **Mistrust** is most serious for it includes a lack of trust and feelings of suspicion.

Erikson stated that two key factors are essential in whether infants learn to trust. First, infants learn to trust by having a consistent environment. This is an environment that includes sameness in routines, caregivers, and surroundings. Second, infants learn to trust by having their basic needs met promptly each time. Babies' basic needs include food, clothing, warmth, sleep, cleanliness, cuddling, playing, and communicating with others.

According to Erikson, if a baby's basic needs are consistently met, then babies feel the world is a good and happy place. This helps them learn to trust others and adapt to their world. If basic needs go unmet or partly met and the surroundings are less than stable, then babies feel helpless and confused. They develop mistrust.

Showing Attachment

Attachment is closeness between people that remains over time. In Chapter 6, you learned about a special type of attachment called *bonding* (the feeling of love parents have for their baby that often begins soon after birth). During the first year, babies come to care for their parents, too. This is called *attachment*, 10-2.

Brain development research indicates that healthy brain development depends on attachment. Overcoming stress throughout life is easier for those babies who formed strong attachments early in infancy.

Babies develop an attachment to those who care for them. They

Bonding and Attachment	
Relationship	**Term Used**
Parents come to love their babies soon after birth. Parents ⟶ Baby	Bonding
Babies whose needs are met come to love their parents. Children realize this tie after six months of age. Baby ⟶ Parents	Attachment

10-2 *Bonding* and *attachment* are terms used for two loving relationships between parents and babies.

show this in a number of ways. **Attachment behaviors** are actions one person demonstrates to another to show closeness to that person. Attachment behaviors include trying to stay close to, following, or clinging to the adult. Smiling, crying, or calling are other attachment behaviors. However, babies who cry the loudest are not always the ones with the strongest attachment. For example, a strongly attached baby who is sure of the parent's return may not cry much when left alone. Attachment is developmental; thus attachment behaviors often occur in a set order, 10-3.

Attachment is closely related to fear of strangers and fear of being left alone. These somewhat negative emotions are described in the next section.

Attachment can be positive, too. For healthy social-emotional development, attachment is important. Everyone needs to love and be loved. Attachment also helps mental development. Attached

Development of Attachment Behaviors

Approximate Age	Attachment Behaviors
1 month	Baby can recognize familiar and unfamiliar voices.
2 weeks to 2 months	Baby smiles.
3 months	Baby gives joyful sounds and movements, such as kicks, coos, and gurgles. Baby may even laugh.
4 to 5 months	Baby becomes still and breathing becomes shallow when unknown people are close.
7 to 8 months	Baby cries when a stranger is nearby or when the baby is left alone.

10-3 Attachment behaviors are closely related to the baby's mental development.

During the first three or four months, babies have two basic responses to their worlds. The first is distress, shown by crying and muscle tension. The second is excitement, shown by smiling, cooing, and wiggling the body. By the end of the first year, babies can express love, fear, anxiety, anger, jealousy, joy, and sadness. Babies who express a range of emotions, from happy to unhappy, show healthy development.

Because thinking changes, the situations that cause emotions change over the years. Four-year-olds may fear monsters in their rooms at night, but older children do not. As people mature, the way they respond to their emotions changes, too. For example, a two-year-old may throw a temper tantrum when angry. Adults show their anger in more mature ways. When people act their age, they use **age-appropriate behaviors**. These are proper or expected ways to express emotions at certain ages.

babies tend to explore their worlds through play more than babies who are not attached to others.

Infants Express Emotions

Long before feelings are expressed, the emotion center of the brain becomes active. Brain development research shows that by two months, babies begin to construct emotions. Babies first get visual cues of emotions in others at this age. Feelings are complex, and they are tied to thinking, memory, and even language. For this reason, emotions are wired over a rather long period.

Love

Before love can develop, babies must realize they are separate from caregivers and others. (This is an example of object concept, which was described in Chapter 9.) Over time, babies come to know that other people make them feel full, clean, and comforted. As babies associate these feelings with their caregivers, they become attached to these adults. They begin to feel and show love and affection, 10-4. Babies show love not only to important adults but also to children who keep them company.

Besides loving people, babies become attached to objects, including pacifiers, stuffed toys, and even blankets. Babies seem to

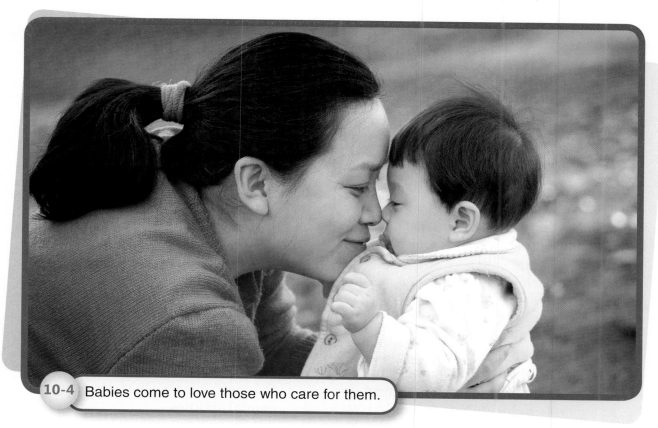

10-4 Babies come to love those who care for them.

need these objects even more when they are upset or afraid. They also seem to need them when routines change. Sometimes adults worry about children's love for these objects. However, such attachments tend to give babies security and are important to them. Children will give up these objects in time.

Fear

At birth, babies react with the startle reflex when they hear loud sounds or do not have support for their bodies. Babies are not showing true fear with this reflex. This is because the change in their bodies is caused by reflex rather than by a feeling, which would be driven by a thought (emotion). However, certain fears are thought to have their roots in the startle reflex. By four or five months, some babies fear adult strangers. They may even fear adults

they know who have new hairstyles, hats, sunglasses, or other such changes. Babies do not seem to fear young children they do not know.

Fear as an emotion occurs at around six months. To be fearful, babies must know they can be hurt. The following are the two kinds of fear:

★   Fear of the unknown. Infants fear adult strangers, a new bed, or a sudden movement. They also fear different sounds, such as the crack of thunder or a screaming siren.

★   Fear learned from direct experiences or teachings. Infants may fear getting soap in their eyes, a doctor's office, or a snapping dog because of a negative past experience. They also fear hot stoves and bad dogs because of an adult's constant warning.

Adoption Coordinator

Adoption coordinators facilitate the placement of children for adoption. They conduct home studies and monitor children throughout the adoption process. They must also possess a working knowledge of state laws as they relate to adoption.

Education: A bachelor's or master's degree in the human services field.

Job Outlook: Employment for social workers is expected to grow much faster than the average for all occupations.

What adults say and how they act affect babies' fears. Adults who act or look fearful in a storm, for example, will cause children to be fearful. Adults who tell babies that many situations can hurt them teach children to fear. Of course, some fear is good. However, too much fear is not healthy. Fear affects motor and mental development because fearful babies often will not welcome new experiences.

Anxiety

Anxiety is fear of a possible future event. Sometimes the words *worry* and *concern* are used to describe anxiety.

The first anxiety of an infant is called **separation anxiety**, 10-5. This anxiety, or fear that loved ones who leave them will not return, is seen around eight months of age. The anxiety peaks between 10 and 18 months, and then fades a great deal by two years. What causes these changes? It is due to changes in mental abilities.

Very young babies have not yet become attached to certain people. They do not realize caregivers are

10-5 Older babies may find it hard to separate from their parents, even at bedtime.

somewhere else when out of their sight. They do not know how long they will be gone. Thus, these very young babies are accepting of all who care for them. By eight months of age, babies develop these ideas about their loved ones. They also begin to anticipate future events. During this time, babies become anxious when the adults they love must leave them for a time. This is common when a parent goes to work or leaves the house on an errand. The anxiety begins when the baby sees clues of the upcoming separation, such as a parent picking up car keys or telling the baby good-bye. Separation anxiety is more intense when strangers, such as new babysitters, are near. However, they cannot anticipate a reunion with their loved ones. Thus, during separations, these babies cry as though their heart will break and are most difficult to console.

Once separation anxiety begins to fade at 18 months, young children react less intensely to regular separations. What mental changes occur? It may be due to the following:

★ Babies younger than two years of age cannot understand why parents must leave.

★ Unlike two-year-olds, who remember their parents have returned after each separation, babies do not have the memory of past events.

★ During the first year, babies need someone to fulfill their needs. (Relying on someone else to meet your needs is called **dependence**.) Two-year-olds are more **independent** (want to do things for themselves).

★ Two-year-olds can express their needs better. Young babies cannot express their needs to others well; especially to those adults they do not know. Being unable to express themselves can lead to anxiety.

Anger

Almost from birth, babies show what is called *infant rage*. Infant rage occurs when the baby is distressed. When they feel distressed, babies may swing their arms and legs excitedly, turn red, and cry loudly, 10-6. Infant rage is not anger, for there is no thought.

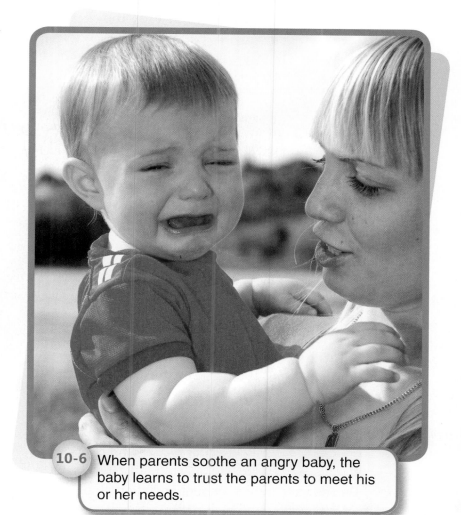

10-6 When parents soothe an angry baby, the baby learns to trust the parents to meet his or her needs.

By 8 to 10 months, babies begin to develop true anger. At this age, infants direct their anger toward a certain person or object. Babies may express anger in physical ways, such as trying to get away from the person holding them. They may also grab, shake, or hit an object. Babies often show anger when

★ they are held against their will. They may be angered if held when they want to be down. They may also be angered if being diapered or dressed when they do not want to be. In addition, being left in a crib when they want to be out makes them angry, too.

★ toys are taken from them. Babies show anger when they cannot reach a toy they want.

★ they are being distracted when they want their needs met. For example, showing a crying, hungry baby a toy may cause the baby to cry louder and push the toy away.

All babies express their anger in physical ways because they lack language skills. Some babies with calm dispositions seem to show little anger during the first year, 10-7. Babies whose moods are more negative may show much more anger. Meeting the baby's needs quickly often prevents anger. Staying calm, by talking in a quiet voice and not looking upset, helps children see how to control their anger. Parents can sometimes reduce a baby's anger by holding him or her close for a short time.

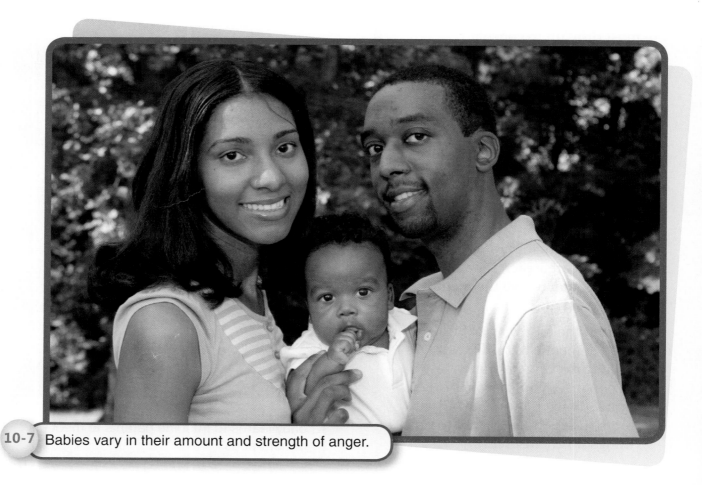

10-7 Babies vary in their amount and strength of anger.

Summary

Social-emotional development involves a person's basic disposition, the way they interact with others, and how they show their feelings. Babies vary in their temperaments. Some are easy, others are slow to warm up, and still others are difficult. Temperaments, along with the environment, help shape personality.

An infant's social development is affected by interacting with others, learning to trust, and showing attachment. Babies interact with others at an early age through crying, cooing, and smiling. They need the loving care provided by parents and other caregivers. These people give babies attention they need.

Babies learn trust by having their basic needs met and living in a consistent environment. These basic needs include physical needs of food, clothing, warmth, sleep, and cleanliness. Psychological needs, such as cuddling, loving, playing, and being talked to, are also important in their development. Having the baby's needs met makes the baby happier, which makes parents happier, too.

Many babies develop an attachment for their parents and others who are close to them. These attachments are important for healthy development, including brain development. Babies who form attachments tend to reach out and want to explore their world.

The emotional center of the brain begins to be wired at two months of age when babies see emotions in others. Emotional development is complex and depends on brain development in other areas, such as thinking, memory, and language. Thus, emotions are slow to develop.

Emotions of love, fear, anxiety, and anger arise in all children. These emotions consist of thoughts that lead to feelings and, in turn, cause changes in the body. It is healthy for babies to express a wide range of emotions, from unhappy to happy. Emotions are handled differently throughout life.

Companion Web Site

Interactive Activity

Review vocabulary terms and key concepts for Chapter 10 at **g-wlearning.com**.

Review and Reflect

Write your answers to the following questions on a separate sheet of paper.

1. True or false. Babies enter the world with unique traits.

2. Name two factors that affect a baby's temperament.

3. What are three pretalking social signals babies can send to the parents?

4. True or false. Giving babies love and care helps their intellectual and social development.

5. True or false. Meeting an unhappy baby's needs by soothing his or her cries will spoil the child.

6. Adults can help a baby develop trust by (A) meeting the baby's needs as soon as possible; (B) changing all the baby's toys once a week so the baby does not get bored.

7. Give two examples of attachment behaviors.

8. True or false. Babies who cry loudly when parents leave them are more strongly attached to their parents than babies who do not.

9. Which statements about emotions are true? (A) Feelings occur before thoughts. (B) Over the years, the causes of emotions remain the same. (C) Over the years, the ways a person expresses emotions remain the same. (D) Over the years, causes and expressions of emotions both change.

10. True or false. Babies are as afraid of unknown young children as they are of adult strangers.

11. What is *separation anxiety*?

Cross-Curricular Link

12. **Writing.** Write a one- or two-page brochure about the importance of trust in the infant's life. Explain how adults can promote trust in the infant. Check your brochure for correct spelling, grammar, and punctuation.

13. **Speech.** Interview a child care provider. Ask the provider about his or her experience with separation anxiety among the children in his or her care. At what ages has the provider seen this anxiety the most? What techniques proved successful and unsuccessful at comforting children in these situations? Share your findings with the class.

14. **Science (Brain Research), Technology.** Use Internet sources to search for information about how brain development affects social-emotional development in the first year. Then create an electronic presentation of your findings to share with the class. Adhere to all copyright laws and cite any sources you may use for the presentation.

15. **Speech.** Have a class discussion on how emotions are useful. Compare the usefulness of emotions to those emotions that can hinder abilities to work and play to the fullest.

16. **Social Studies.** People's expression of emotions should change as they mature. Each stage of life has age-appropriate behaviors. List behaviors considered mature for an infant, but immature for a high school student.

Making Observations

17. Observe a group of infants. Note differences in temperament. Do some infants seem easygoing? Do other infants seem more difficult?

18. Observe an infant with a parent or regular caregiver. How does the baby show attachment? How does the adult encourage attachment (for example, by soothing the baby or showing affection)?

19. Observe a baby showing fear, anxiety, or anger. What seemed to trigger the infant's reactions?

Thinking Critically

20. Babies' temperaments seem to shape their personalities. How would you describe your temperament? Have you had these characteristics for a long time? Do others in your family (such as a grandparent, parent, or cousin) have the same temperament?

21. Some parents believe babies can be spoiled if people hold them when they do not have physical needs. Do you agree with this idea? Why or why not?

22. Your friend has a cute baby you would like to hold. As you approach the baby, you see obvious signs of stranger anxiety. What are some things you can do to lessen the baby's anxiety?

11 Providing for the Infant's Developmental Needs

After studying this chapter, you will be able to

- ★ **plan** ways to meet the developmental needs of babies in their first year.
- ★ **demonstrate** skills that meet babies' physical needs.
- ★ **stimulate** babies' mental development.
- ★ **enhance** babies' growing awareness of themselves.

Terms to Know

nutrients
solids
intolerance
stimulants
depressants
weaning

finger foods
enriched environment
sensory stimulation
coordination
self-awareness

Reading Advantage

Arrange a study session to read the chapter with a classmate. After you read each section independently, stop and tell each other what you think the main points are in the section. Continue with each section until you finish the chapter.

Companion Web Site

Interactive Activity

Learn more about how to handle special problems that babies may have by completing the *Read, Discuss, and Analyze* Activity for Chapter 11 at **g-wlearning.com**.

Because babies develop so quickly in the first year, they have many needs. To meet their physical needs, adults must understand babies and respond to their signals. Adults must also meet baby's mental needs with activities that help infants learn and develop. To meet their social-emotional needs, parents must touch, hold, and look at babies lovingly. Galinsky calls this the *nurturing stage* of parenting.

Babies develop best when they feel the love and joy of their caregivers. By meeting a baby's needs promptly, adults help the baby develop trust. From learning to trust others, the baby becomes more aware of his or her own abilities.

Physical Needs

Babies need others to meet all their physical needs. *Physical needs* are the most basic needs of humans. These include the needs for food and sleep. Babies who are hungry, tired, or sick suffer in physical, mental, social, and emotional ways. For example, a baby who is fed late may not want to play and explore. The baby may also act fussy.

Feeding

The need for food is the baby's most basic physical need. This is because a baby's body grows so quickly in the first year. In fact, the body grows three times faster in the first year than in the second or third year. The baby is also busy exploring and developing, 11-1. A healthful diet provides the nutrients the baby needs to grow, explore, and develop. **Nutrients** are the substances in food that give babies energy and help them grow.

Meeting a baby's food needs quickly alleviates hunger. Some studies indicate that, for very young babies, the sensation of hunger may be physically painful. A hungry baby may cry until fed. This cry of hunger differs from other cries, which makes it easy for parents to recognize. Responding promptly to the baby's need for food teaches the infant his or her needs will be met. Erikson calls this learning a sense of *basic trust*.

Feeding times can also be comforting for babies. As adults feed a baby, they should show warmth and concern. This helps deepen their relationship with the baby. Being cared for by gentle, loving adults promotes a baby's social and emotional development.

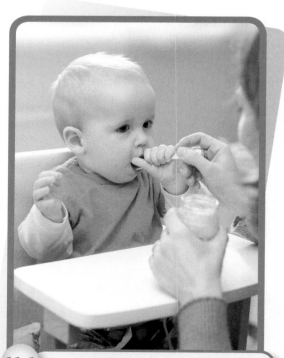

11-1 A healthful diet is essential for meeting the physical needs of the baby's body as he or she grows, develops, and explores.

Feeding During the First Year

How much food does a baby need? It all depends because each baby has unique needs. These needs depend on the baby's size and how fast he or she is growing. The baby's health, heredity, and level of activity also affect his or her food needs. A pediatrician or dietitian can help parents learn what and how much to feed a baby.

First Foods

Most babies begin "eating" an all-liquid diet of milk (either breast milk or formula). Between six months and one year, the baby begins to eat cereals, fruits, vegetables, meats, and breads. These foods are called **solids**. Solid foods for infant feeding are semiliquid, mushy foods, including commercially prepared baby foods and table foods that have been mashed, pureed, or strained. Many doctors advise parents to wait until their baby is at least six months old before starting solids. (See 11-2 for a basic first-year feeding plan.) Doctors do not suggest solids for the first six months for the following reasons:

★ Babies are not born with the ability to swallow solids. Their jaw and throat muscles must develop before swallowing is easy and safe.

★ In the first six months, babies do not need solids for nutritional reasons. Their immature digestive systems cannot process the complex nutrients found in solids.

Basic Feeding Plan for Baby's First Year

Step 1

★ Mother's milk or formula only (often for the first half year)

Step 2

★ Mother's milk or formula, plus infant dry cereals mixed with strained juice, mother's milk, or formula

Step 3

★ Mother's milk or formula, cereals, and strained single-ingredient fruits, vegetables, and meats (These are added gradually, with the baby's doctor often suggesting which to try first.)

★ When the baby can eat a variety of cereals, fruits, vegetables, and meats, breast milk or formula is cut to between a 16-ounce minimum and a 25-ounce to 30-ounce maximum per day. Babies should take ½ of their calories from milk and ½ from solid foods

Step 4

★ Mother's milk or formula, cereals, and foods with two or more ingredients combined, such as apple-banana juice or chicken and noodles

Step 5

★ Mother's milk or formula, cereals, and foods with some texture

★ Foods have small pieces rather than a strained texture (Some companies call these "junior foods.")

11-2 Babies begin with a liquid diet and advance gradually in a step-by-step pattern to eating many solids.

★ Starting solids too early may cause physical problems.

★ Some solids have too much sodium. This may increase the baby's chance of high blood pressure as an adult.

★ Solids may be too high in calories. This may make the baby gain weight too quickly.

★ Holding a baby close while formula- or breast-feeding gives the baby a warm feeling of physical closeness. Spoon-feeding does not do the same.

Introducing New Foods

When babies are ready for solids, parents should introduce one food at a time. They should feed the new food in small amounts, such as a bite or two.

Parents should not add another new food for at least five days.

This helps the parent see whether the baby has an intolerance for the food. **Intolerance** is a negative physical reaction that eating a certain food can cause. A food may cause fussiness, a rash, or an upset stomach. If the baby's stools become looser, more watery, or contain mucous, parents should inform the baby's doctor.

Food intolerance among infants often shows in one to four days. Many doctors suggest waiting until after the first birthday to try an offending food again. If babies react to many foods, doctors can test the baby and give him or her a special diet.

Foods to Avoid

Babies should not eat some foods, 11-3. For example, small or hard foods may cause the baby to choke. Some foods and beverages may have too much sugar, sodium,

---

Foods Babies Should Not Eat

Choking
★ Raw, hard fruits and vegetables (apples, berries, carrots, celery)
★ Thick-skinned fruits unless peeled
★ Marshmallows
★ Hard candy
★ Grapes and raisins
★ Hot dogs sliced in rounds (rounds should be quartered)
★ Pretzels
★ Nuts and peanut butter
★ Whole kernel cooked corn and popcorn

Too much sugar
★ Cake, in excess
★ Candy, in excess
★ Cookies, in excess

Too much sodium
★ Saltine crackers, in excess

Little or no nutritional value
★ Artificially flavored fruit drinks
★ Soft drinks

Hard to digest
★ Yeast or unpasteurized yogurt

Stimulants
★ Coffee
★ Tea
★ Soft drinks with caffeine
★ Cocoa

Depressant
★ Alcohol

11-3 Some foods are not good for a baby's health.

or artificial flavors. Unpasteurized yogurt and foods that contain yeast are hard for babies to digest. Substances called *stimulants* and *depressants* are harmful for babies whether found in breast milk or given directly to babies. **Stimulants** (such as caffeine) speed up the functions of organs, such as the heart, and the nervous system. **Depressants** (found in alcohol) slow the functions of organs and the nervous system.

The Feeding Schedule

The daily feeding schedule should fit the baby's needs. Some babies like smaller, more frequent meals. Others eat more food less often. When the baby's growth rate slows toward the end of the first year, his or her appetite will decrease, 11-4. Most babies will establish an eating pattern, but some days they will be hungrier than others.

Homemade Versus Store-Bought Baby Foods

Parents today can choose from a variety of commercially prepared baby foods in the grocery store. Still, many prefer to make the baby's food at home for health or economic reasons. See 11-5 for advantages to both methods.

When buying commercially prepared baby food, check for freshness. Check the *sell-by date* on the cap or the side of the container. This date is the last date the store should sell the product. (You can still safely use the food for a few days after this date.) Make sure food containers are sealed properly and have not been opened. Check to see whether the safety button on

First-Year Daily Feeding Schedule

Months	Hours Between Feedings
1 to 3*	3 to 4
3 to 5	5**
6	6**

*Often sleeps through the night in about 3 months. Babies are given a late evening feeding (about 11 p.m.). They sleep until early morning (5:30 or 6:00 a.m.).

**Nutritious snacks of regular baby food (fruit juice, fruit, etc.) or milk and water should be offered about halfway between feedings (2½ to 3 hours after each feeding) if the baby is awake.

11-4 A baby's feeding schedule changes during the first year.

unopened jars has risen. If so, the food is unsafe to eat. It may have been tampered with or spoiled.

When you are giving the baby store-bought food, spoon out the amount of food you need. Do not feed the baby from the jar. Bacteria in the saliva from the baby's spoon can spoil the food. Most babies like food at room temperature. If the food needs to be heated, test the temperature by putting a small drop on your wrist before serving. After baby food jars have been opened, store them in the refrigerator. Use the leftover baby food within two days.

Weaning

Weaning is the process of taking a baby off the bottle or breast. The process should be gradual because the baby must learn a new way to drink. A slow pace allows the baby time to get used to this change.

When do you start to wean a baby? Age at weaning will

Advantages of Baby Food Methods

Commercially Prepared

★ Food is easy to buy and use. In fact, commercially prepared foods were first introduced as "convenience foods."

★ The food may be more economical than homemade food if the cost of ingredients, gas or electricity, and time used to prepare the food are considered.

★ Many foods are available in all four seasons. (Some fruits and vegetables may not be available year-round for preparing homemade foods.)

★ Foods can be bought with the right texture for the baby's age.

★ Foods are sterile until opened.

★ Unopened foods can be stored without refrigeration for a long time before they lose quality.

★ Foods, except dry cereals, are packaged in small amounts for one or two servings.

★ Possibly harmful additives have been removed or reduced.

Homemade

★ Possibly harmful additives are not used.

★ Food is usually less expensive to prepare.

★ ' Food can be prepared while making foods for other family members.

★ No special appliances are needed to prepare baby food.

★ Making your own food saves storage space required for baby food products.

★ If the baby has allergies, it may be necessary to prepare special food.

★ Recipe books are available with many tasty recipes.

★ A creative cook is not limited to commercially prepared foods.

★ Making food brings a sense of satisfaction to those who like to cook.

11-5 Commercially prepared and homemade baby foods both have many advantages. Parents choose the method that best meets their family's needs.

depend on whether the baby is fed breast milk or formula. Parents should also consult their baby's doctor about what age he or she recommends for weaning.

Weaning from the Breast

The American Academy of Pediatrics recommends mothers breast-feed their babies for at least 12 months. Mothers may nurse longer, however. Often the baby is completely weaned from the breast by 18 to 24 months.

Age at weaning will determine which fluid is offered. If weaned before one year of age, babies should receive iron-fortified infant formula for the remainder of the first year. Babies weaned after one year should be offered whole cow's milk. Children between one and two years of age should drink only whole milk rather than milk with reduced quantities of fat. Formulas designed for toddlers are not better for children than cow's milk after age one year.

Whether the baby is weaned to a bottle or directly to a cup will also depend on age. Babies who are weaned before they are skilled enough to use a cup will be weaned from the breast to the bottle. Older babies can be weaned directly to a cup.

Weaning from the breast cannot be abrupt either for the baby or the mother. Abrupt weaning for the baby is stressful. For the mother, abrupt weaning can cause blockage of the milk ducts and possible depression. A woman may need to consult her doctor during the weaning process.

When weaning begins, parents should offer the new liquid (formula or whole milk, depending on age) as part of one feeding. (The early evening feeding is usually best, because there is less breast milk.) Increase the amount of liquid offered at this feeding until the baby has taken an entire feeding by bottle or cup for several days.

Parents should wait at least three days before replacing another feeding with the bottle or cup. Then apply the same steps to another feeding until the baby is weaned. (The early morning feeding is often the last one to stop.) Often, breast-fed babies accept a cup sooner than bottle-fed babies.

Weaning to a Cup

For formula-fed babies, weaning from a bottle to a cup may begin as early as the child can use the cup and shows interest in doing so. Although this may be as early as 9 months of age, a recommended age to start weaning from the bottle to a cup is 12 months. At this time, cow's milk can be given instead of formula. This process is often completed by 18 months.

Parents often teach babies to drink from a cup in the following ways:

★ Give the baby a special baby cup. The cup may have two handles and be weighted to keep it from tipping. Some cups also offer special features that make liquid less likely to spill.

★ Praise the baby when he or she tries to handle the cup. Parents should not expect this to be an easy task for several months. Even after that age, many accidents will occur.

★ Give the baby a few sips of liquid (about one tablespoon in the bottom of a cup) at about six months. The small amount is less scary if it splashes against the baby's nose. It is also less messy if spilled.

★ Let the baby drink small amounts of milk at one feeding. If the baby already drinks small amounts of juice or water during a feeding, choose that feeding for putting milk in the cup. A baby should work up to at least four ounces of milk from the cup at one feeding.

★ Gradually replace other bottle feedings in the same way. The last bottle of the day is often the last to be replaced.

Spoon Feeding

Parents are often eager to see their babies eat solids. Why? Parents probably see this as a transition to a more grown-up stage of eating. Like many other skills, eating from a spoon is developmental. Most pediatricians recommend the baby be six months old before being introduced to solids, 11-6. This is the time when most babies are developmentally ready to begin learning to eat with a spoon and just before solids are nutritionally needed. The closer the baby is to six months old, the better he or she will

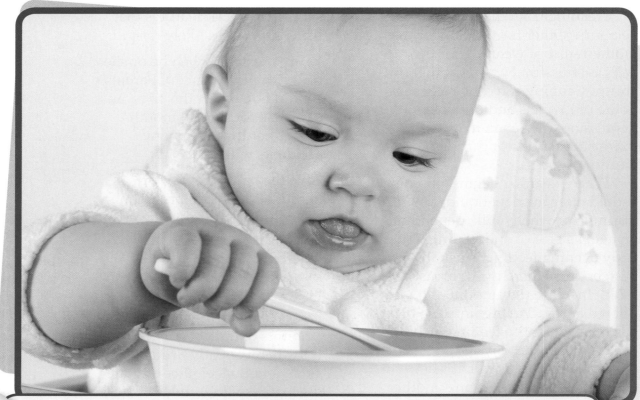

11-6 In the second half of the first year, babies begin to experiment with feeding themselves.

do with this developmental task. This is true for the following reasons:

★ Until babies are 16 to 18 weeks old, they have an *extrusion reflex* (the tongue thrusts forward when it is touched by an object). Also, babies will not open their mouths when they see food until they are about five months old. If solids are not introduced before eight or nine months, however, the baby may reject them.

★ Babies do not need more nutrition than breast milk or formula until they reach 13 to 15 pounds.

★ Before six months of age, babies do not have the needed *enzymes* (special proteins that aid digestion) or saliva for digesting solid foods.

The American Academy of Pediatrics recommends as the first solid food a commercial iron-enriched rice cereal. For the first feedings, the cereal should contain so much liquid that it "pours" from the spoon. To get this consistency, use about one teaspoon of rice cereal mixed with two tablespoons of breast milk or formula. Although water could be used, breast milk or formula will be more nutritious and offers a familiar taste. Very gradually make the cereal thicker at each feeding as the baby learns to use his or her tongue and tolerate the texture. The baby's pediatrician will recommend when to introduce other solids. As cereal and other solids are introduced, the baby will need water for proper kidney action. The baby's doctor can advise how much water to offer each day.

Solids are always fed from a spoon. Solids should not be diluted with liquid and fed using a bottle with a large hole in the nipple or an "infant feeder." These practices defeat the purpose of having a baby learn to use his or her tongue and throat muscles to chew, swallow, and breathe. Nonspoon methods present a risk of choking, too.

For the first spoon feeding, the baby should be held in the adult's lap in an almost upright position. Later, parents can feed babies from infant seats or high chairs. Use a small spoon with a long handle to make feeding easier. A plastic-coated baby spoon is better for the baby's sensitive gums than a metal spoon. Place a small amount of food on the tip of the spoon. A few bites are enough for the first feedings.

Parents should start these early feedings at times when the baby shows signs of hunger, but is not too hungry. Waiting too long can make a baby too upset to learn something new. Parents often try feeding the baby a few bites of cereal about halfway through the milk or formula feeding. They should give the baby a sip or two of water after the cereal, but before resuming the feeding of breast milk or formula. Thus, the baby's meal begins and ends with the familiar taste of breast milk or formula.

Most doctors recommend offering the baby new solids early in the day and no later than early afternoon. They advise this because babies are more apt to have colic in the evening hours. Also, an allergic reaction following a night feeding would occur in the wee hours of the morning rather than during the early evening.

During the first spoon feedings, babies often thrust their tongues forward, pushing the spoon and food out of their mouths. This is a reflexive response to having strange objects in the mouth. This does not mean the baby does not want the food or is being stubborn. Thus, parents can continue to offer a bite or two as long as their babies continue to cooperate. Once babies turn their heads or close their mouths, parents should stop feeding the solids and resume feeding from the breast or bottle. Waiting a day or two before trying solids again is often best. Frustrated babies are not good learners. During the developmental process, parents must remain calm and pleasant. Babies should see eating solids as loving as drinking from the bottle or breast. Soon the baby will be eating easily from the spoon.

Self-Feeding

Babies begin self-feeding by eating finger foods. **Finger foods** are foods a baby can self-feed using the fingers. Near the end of the first year, babies often develop the skill of self-feeding finger foods at the

Nanny

Nannies generally take care of children from birth to age 12, tending to the children's early education, nutrition, health, and other needs. A few may also perform the duties of a housekeeper, including cleaning and laundry.

Education: Training requirements range from a high school diploma to a college degree.

Job Outlook: Nannies are expected to experience job growth that is faster than the average for all occupations.

same time they develop the pincer grasp. Some babies, however, will simply rake the food into their mouths. Finger foods aid the baby's growing independence as well as grasping and chewing skills.

Eating finger foods is fun, but it can also be hazardous. As babies are learning to eat these foods, they may choke or gag at the new textures. For this reason, adults should keep their babies in full view when they are eating. Adults should also offer only "safer" foods. These foods include small pieces of melba toast; crispy, unsalted crackers; bagels; zwieback; and fruits and vegetables that have been cooked and diced. (Adults should choose from the foods they know their babies already tolerate.)

Self-feeding with a spoon begins in the second year. Younger babies may want to help adults by grabbing the spoon during a feeding. Adults can often solve this problem by giving the baby a spoon to hold as they feed. Babies may even hold a spoon in each hand. Some parents

then let the baby use the spoon on the last few bites. The spoon rarely reaches the mouth, but this is good practice for later self-feeding.

Mealtimes should be pleasant for the baby. Caregivers should try to stay calm regardless of what or how much the baby accepts or rejects. If the adult is unpleasant when the baby rejects a food, the baby is more likely to refuse the same food next time. Kindness makes new foods easier to accept.

Clothing

Infants grow quickly and outgrow their clothing several times in the first year. Because babies grow at different rates, infant clothing should be bought by length and weight rather than by age. (Sewing patterns should be bought by length and weight, also.) Companies use different sizes; thus, it is important to read the hangtags carefully before buying to select the right size for the baby. Chart 11-7 shows examples of clothing sizes.

Typical First-Year Clothing Sizes

Sizes of Clothes Other Than Sleepwear

Size	Newborn	0 to 3 mo.	6 to 9 mo.	12 mo.
Length (inches)	20 to 22	22½ to 24	24½ to 28½	29 to 30½
Weight (pounds)	5½ to 8½	9 to 12	12½ to 19	19½ to 20½

Sizes for Sleepwear

Size	XS/S	M	L
Age	0 to 3 mo.	3 to 6 mo.	6 to 9 mo.
Weight (pounds)	0 to 11	12 to 15	16 to 19

11-7   Length and weight are better indicators of clothing size than age.

From three months to the end of the first year, babies move more with each passing week. Therefore, they should wear comfortable and roomy clothing. The basic points given in 11-8 can be used to select baby clothing.

Style and Color

The style and color of baby clothes is a personal choice. Almost any style has advantages and disadvantages. For example, two-piece outfits (tops and bottoms) often can be worn longer because they do not get as tight in the crotch as one-piece outfits. Two-piece outfits make changing the diaper easy, too.

One-piece outfits, such as jumpsuits and overalls, look neater on crawlers because they do not separate. These outfits are also warmer.

Shoes

Shoes are not needed until a baby begins to walk outdoors. Shoes protect and cushion the feet from outside dangers. Indoors, babies should walk without shoes to prevent flat-footed walking. Most shoes worn in the first year are for decoration. These shoes have soft, cloth soles. Babies need to wear socks or footed clothing in cool weather to keep their feet warm.

Points to Consider When Choosing Baby Clothes

Feature	Examples
Safety	★ Fire retardant ★ Not tight or binding ★ No loose buttons or other fasteners ★ No loose trim ★ No drawstrings
Comfort	★ Soft (made of knitted fabric) ★ Nonirritating clothes (flat seams and fasteners) ★ Garments without too much extra fabric, so that baby does not rest on the bulk ★ No fuzzy trims that tickle ★ Neck openings large enough for easy dressing ★ Right weight for needed warmth (Several layers of lightweight clothes, such as an undershirt, a t-shirt, and a sweater are warmer and more comfortable in warm weather than one heavy garment.) ★ Roomy for active body movements ★ Antistatic ★ Absorbent (Manufactured fibers, such as polyester or nylon, should be blended with cotton to increase absorbency.)
Easy Care	★ Machine washable ★ Can be washed with other clothes ★ Soil-release finish (to make stain removal easier) ★ Shrinkage control ★ Little or no ironing needed ★ Easy to mend

11-8 Babies need clothing that meets their special needs.

Caring for Baby Clothes

Parents can care for baby clothes properly by following these practices:

★ Before cleaning clothes, read labels and tags. Follow directions. Pretreat stains before washing clothes to prevent the stains from setting. Also, mend tears before washing to prevent them from getting larger.

★ Infants' and children's clothes often need to go through more rinses than other clothing. Extra rinses help remove detergent from clothes. Babies' skin is more sensitive than adults', and detergent residue may cause skin rashes. Parents might also want to choose a gentle detergent designed for infant clothes.

★ When washing baby sleepwear, do not add fabric softener to the load. The chemicals in fabric softeners can reduce the flame-retardant qualities of the clothing.

★ Many parents store baby clothes for future children or as keepsakes. Before storing, clean the clothes. Soiled spots change over time, and then stains cannot be removed. When clothes are clean and dry, they are ready to be stored. Do not use plastic bags. Fabrics need air to maintain their strength and oils. Store light and dark clothes separately to prevent the transfer of dyes. All clothing should be stored away from damp areas. Dampness promotes mildew and insect damage.

Diapering a Baby

Babies require frequent diaper changes throughout the first year. This is a skill parents will soon perfect. (You may want to refer to Chapter 7 to review the steps used in diapering.) When using disposable diapers, the baby will change sizes as he or she grows. Cloth diapers can be folded differently to accommodate older babies.

Older babies wiggle more and may protest when diapered. This makes the task harder for adults. To keep a baby's interest, it is a good idea to talk, sing, and play with the baby during diaper changes. Offering the baby a toy may also help the baby keep still during the change.

Adults must keep diaper-changing areas very clean. This is crucial to prevent the spread of germs. To do this, dispose of any paper used on the changing table. Clean visible soil with detergent and water and then rinse with water. Spray the entire changing surface

Focus on Financial Literacy

Good Consumer Sense

Because babies quickly outgrow clothing, good consumer sense is important. The following tips can be helpful when shopping for quality and comparing prices. What other tips would you add to this list?

★ Look for built-in growth features. These include a double row of snaps or buttons at the waistline to lengthen the garment from shoulder to crotch. Two buttons on straps used for lengthening is a good feature. Also look for stretch waists and stretch leg and arm openings.

★ Choose more stretch knit garments than woven garments. Babies can wear these longer.

★ Look for flame-retardant finishes on clothing.

★ Look for ease-of-care labels.

with a sanitizing solution, such as one teaspoon of household bleach per one cup of water made fresh daily. Leave it in contact with the surface for two minutes. The surface may be air dried or wiped dry. Caregivers should also wash their hands (and the baby's hands) after each diaper change.

Tub Bathing

Tub bathing can begin as soon as the baby's navel and circumcision have healed. When preparing for a tub bath, the steps are the same as those used for sponge bathing listed in Chapter 7. The only difference is that a small tub is filled with about three inches of water. The water should be comfortably warm. You can test the water's temperature by dipping your wrist or elbow into the water. Have everything (shampoo, washcloth, towels, skin care products, and diaper) ready before getting the baby. See the steps for tub bathing listed in 11-9. Put the baby in a safe place before cleaning the tub area.

Like diapering, bathing is a good time to play with babies. As babies are bathed, they enjoy parents who talk, sing, cuddle, and smile. Babies often respond well because warm water is relaxing. As babies get older, they enjoy kicking and splashing in the water as their parents hold them. Water play is good for baby's developing motor skills as well as being lots of fun.

Establishing Routines

A routine helps children feel secure because it teaches them what to expect. Routines, such as having one's physical needs met promptly, help infants develop basic trust. Although babies do not know clock time, they do develop a sense of rhythm in their lives formed around routine care. Schedules also help adults get their baby-care tasks done with greater ease. A schedule is important, but remember to adjust it as needed.

Routines should fit babies' and adults' needs. Schedules should also change as babies mature. For older babies, feedings are more widely spaced, daytime naps grow shorter, and more playtime is needed.

Rest and Sleep

Rest and sleep are important to a baby's health. Like others, babies vary in the amount of rest and sleep they need. From one to three months, babies need a total of 14 to 16.5 hours of sleep. For the remainder of the first year, babies need 14 to 15 hours of sleep. Many babies begin sleeping through the night at twelve weeks, but some sleep fewer hours for many months. If the baby does not sleep well at night, parents may try to rearrange their baby's schedule. Awakening babies after four hours of daytime sleep should help the baby sleep longer at night. (If a baby sleeps well at night, parents should not interfere with daytime naps.)

Some babies who have slept through the night may begin to awaken and cry during the night. This often happens between five and eight months. Hunger is seldom the reason for this awakening. As babies awaken, they may feel lonely and long to have a parent near. Parents should check on their crying babies, comfort them for a few minutes, and then put them down. Playing with a baby during the night is not a good habit to form.

Many babies take long naps in both the morning and afternoon until

How to Give a Tub Bath

Doctors usually recommend tub baths as soon as the baby's navel and circumcision are healed. Fill the tub (often a large dishpan) with about three inches of comfortable warm water. Test the water temperature with your elbow or wrist. Also, place a towel on the bottom of the tub to keep the baby from slipping.

Step 1: On the Table

Undress the baby, except for the diaper. Cleanse the eyes, nose, ears, and face as you would in a sponge bath. Apply liquid baby bath to head with hand, or use washcloth after about first two months. Note: When the baby is older and has more hair, use a liquid baby shampoo that will not irritate the eyes.

Step 2: Into the Tub

After removing the baby's diaper, you can place the child in the tub. Use a safety hold—slip your right hand under the baby's shoulders. Place your thumb over the right shoulder and your fingers under the right armpit. Support the buttocks with your left hand, grasping the right thigh with your thumb and fingers. Lower the baby into the tub feet first, keeping the head out of the water. With your left hand, rinse the head, letting water run back into the tub.

Step 3: Bathing the Body

Soap the front of the baby's body, being careful to wash inside all the skin folds and creases, then rinse. Reverse your hold to soap and rinse the baby's back. It is not necessary to turn the baby over. Clean the genital area during the bath, just like the rest of the baby. In the external folds of a baby girl, a white substance may gather. If it remains after bathing, gently wipe it away with a washcloth or with a cotton ball dipped in baby oil. Be sure to wipe from front to back. When cleansing a baby boy who has not been circumcised, do not push back the foreskin unless your doctor tells you to.

Step 4: Out of the Tub

Use the same safety hold to lift your baby onto a warm, dry surface. Cover the baby with a towel and pat dry, paying special attention to folds and creases.

Step 5: Diaper Area Care

To keep the diaper area dry, use baby cornstarch to help prevent irritation and redness.

Step 6: General Skin Care

Moisten fingers on a cotton ball dipped in baby oil or baby lotion. Apply it to all tiny creases, such as around the neck, armpits, arms, hands, legs, and feet. Use a little baby oil on a cotton ball to help remove cradle cap. Apply baby cream to any irritated part. Sprinkle baby powder on your hand and pat lightly over large areas of the body.

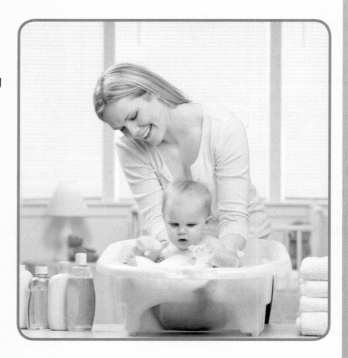

11-9 Tub baths should be given carefully and quickly for the baby's comfort and safety.

five or six months. At this age, babies often take a short morning nap and a long afternoon nap. Most babies drop the morning nap between 9 and 15 months. They may continue to take an afternoon nap until three to five years of age. This nap may gradually shorten as a child grows.

Sudden Infant Death Syndrome

Sudden infant death syndrome (SIDS) is a major cause of deaths in infants during their first year of life. In many cases, seemingly healthy babies simply stop breathing in their sleep. Unfortunately, the cause of SIDS is unknown. Some experts think the cause may be a virus or bacterial infection that attacks the brain stem (where breathing is controlled) before or shortly after birth. The most common age for SIDS to strike is between two and four months. Some children even die for unexplained reasons after one year of age. Such deaths are called *Sudden Unexplained Death in Childhood (SUDC)*.

Although the exact cause of SIDS is still unknown, some risk factors are known, 11-10. For example, studies have noted a danger in babies who sleep on their stomachs. Stomach-sleeping may put pressure on the baby's jaw and thus narrow the airway. It also increases the risk of the infant rebreathing exhaled air. This exhaled air (which contains carbon dioxide rather than oxygen) might become trapped in a pocket around the baby's mouth by a soft mattress, fluffy blanket, stuffed toy, or pillow near the face. The pocket holds the exhaled carbon dioxide, which the baby then breathes back into the lungs. Many babies and older children

Risk Factors for Sudden Infant Death Syndrome (SIDS)

Caregivers should discuss with their doctors ways to protect infants who are at high risk for SIDS. These are infants who meet any of the following conditions:
* being born to a teen mother
* lacking prenatal care
* being exposed to tobacco, alcohol, or illegal drugs (especially cocaine) before birth
* being born more than two weeks before due date
* being born at a low birthweight (less than 5½ pounds)
* being part of a multiple birth (especially if weighing less than 3.3 pounds)
* being exposed to cigarette smoke after birth
* having an older sibling who died of SIDS
* being male and having other risk factors listed above
* being between 2 and 4 months of age

11-10 Certain conditions put infants at a higher risk for SIDS.

would awaken if they lacked oxygen. However, SIDS babies may have a brain abnormality or immaturity that prevents them from awakening and moving. Furthermore, some very young babies may not be able to raise their heads, leaving them trapped to rebreathe the exhaled air.

Research continues for the cause and prevention of SIDS. Until a prevention is found, parents can take the following positive steps to protect their infants:
* Avoid as many of the risk factors as possible both before and after the baby is born.
* Place baby on a firm mattress.
* Do not use fluffy blankets, comforters, throws, stuffed toys, or pillows in the bed. (Display

these baby gifts or purchases somewhere else in the room.)

★ Make sure the baby does not get too warm while sleeping. The temperature of a baby's room should be between 68 and 72 degrees. (Babies who become very warm may go into a deeper sleep and thus find it more difficult to awaken.)

★ Offer a pacifier for sleep from birth and continue its use for sleep even after the baby no longer uses a pacifier while awake.

★ Avoid sharing a parent bed with a baby (called *co-sleeping* or *co-bedding*). Young babies are safest in their own crib in their parent's room.

★ Encourage adequate sleep. (Sleep deficits of even two hours on a given day are associated with SIDS.)

★ Have regular well-baby checkups.

★ Breast-feed the baby for at least seven months and preferably for one year.

★ Use a breathing monitor and alarm if recommended by your doctor.

★ Place baby on his or her back to sleep. If you see a baby roll onto the stomach, turn the baby to his or her back. (Since the American Academy of Pediatrics recommended back sleeping, SIDS has decreased almost 40 percent. The rate would likely decrease more if all parents and caregivers followed the recommendation. It is easy to remember—"back to sleep.")

Places for Sleep and Play

Where do babies sleep and play? Space for sleep and play is based on a family's lifestyle

Learn More About...
Play Spaces for Babies

When choosing play spaces for babies, adults should keep the following points in mind:

★ Ensure that all spaces are safe. For example, use eco-friendly paints and natural fabrics. Put the crib in a safe place. A house must be childproofed by the time a baby can crawl. (Childproofing and safety measures are described in Chapter 22.)

★ Make all spaces for children washable. Babies are messy by adult standards.

★ Decorate the nursery with the idea that a child grows quickly. Today, most parents are choosing a décor that flows into the rest of the house and one that they, as adults, enjoy. For example, parents are using brighter colors and

tone-on-tone shades that stimulate the baby's perceptions. Polka dots, stripes, and swirls are replacing small prints. Colors are achieved by objects used on or near neutral-colored walls or through the use of brighter wall paints and paper. As the baby grows, the décor should include his or her interests. Rooms should be bright and cheerful. Place pictures and wall hangings at the child's eye level. Floor coverings should allow play with blocks and wheeled toys.

★ Consider convertible furniture which is often more economical than replacing all baby furniture. Convertible furniture is usually very sturdy, too, and thus safe even for babies.

and housing. However, a few guidelines are important.

Babies should sleep away from major activities. Parents might use a screen to section off part of their bedroom to make a private sleeping area for the baby. Others have babies share space with an older sibling. Another option for some parents is providing the baby his or her own bedroom or bedroom/playroom.

The sleeping area should be large enough for a full-size crib and other furnishings. Children often sleep in a crib until they are three years old or 35 inches tall. Many parents like to have a dressing/changing table. Some parents are purchasing convertible furniture that will grow with the child. For example, some cribs can be converted to youth or even adult beds. Dressing/changing tables can be made by attaching a vinyl-covered pad and safety belt to a dresser. Later it can be changed back into a dresser or an entertainment center. An adult-size rocker is convenient for the baby's sleeping area. Parents also need storage space for clothing and baby products. Purchasing a closet system allows for adapting storage as the child's needs change.

If adults plan a playroom, they should not expect a baby to stay there all the time. Children like to be near others. During the first year, babies need places to play and toys in several rooms where household activities take place. A playyard may be used for short periods of time, especially when babies need a safe place to play. Parents should limit total time spent in a playyard to no more than two hours per day, however. Babies need to be able to move and explore freely in order to develop crawling, creeping, and walking skills.

Intellectual Needs

Babies need more than physical care to help them grow. Experts know that babies are born with the ability to learn. They also know babies need an environment that offers them chances to learn. This is called an **enriched environment**, 11-11. One study found that babies whose caregivers expected them to learn at an early age developed more quickly than other babies. This may be because adults who expect more provide more activities to help babies learn.

Adults can provide learning experiences for babies soon after birth. In fact, the sooner adults

11-11 In an enriched environment, babies are eager to explore the age-appropriate toys offered to them.

provide activities, the more babies want to learn. Adults should not forget, however, that babies learn at different rates. The rate of learning cannot be increased with lots of activities and toys. Babies can take in only so much. Too many activities and toys can confuse or bore the baby.

Weave words, singing, and activities into daily routines, such as feeding, bathing, and diapering. Adults do not need to have a set schedule of daily games. The number and types of games are not as important as the warmth and caring that adults show for babies.

A skillful caregiver knows how to use activities to meet babies' intellectual needs. Adults can use the following methods:

★ Watch for signs of the baby's interest in certain experiences. To check for interest, show the baby how to use a toy, and then give him or her a turn. Repeat several times. If there is little or no interest, the toy or game is probably too advanced for the baby. Try it again in a few days or weeks. Parents who match a toy or game with their child's abilities and interests are working in Vygotsky's ZPD.

★ Let the baby begin most activities, then expand them. For example, the baby may be patting a high chair tray. Expand the activity by patting a different object (that makes a different sound). You may also pat the tray harder, softer, faster, or slower than the baby.

★ Repeat games many times. Using games over many months helps the baby retain the skills each game helps build.

★ Let babies try things on their own. This helps them learn to solve problems. Piaget thought this was crucial for learning.

Activities to Stimulate the Senses

Sensory stimulation involves using the senses to learn about the environment. According to Piaget, babies use their senses as a major way of learning. Infants use their senses to explore objects offered to them and discover how objects operate.

For the baby to develop fully, all five senses (sight, hearing, touch, taste, and smell) must be stimulated. One example of a sensory stimulation activity is to let the baby touch a number of safe objects. This can be done while walking around the room or outdoors. For example, letting the baby touch the bark of a tree helps improve sensory development. See 11-12 for other ways to help children stimulate their sensory learning.

Focus on Science
Brain Development

Interview a *child development professional* (person with a college degree in child development, child and family studies, or early childhood education) regarding ways parents and caregivers can stimulate brain development in infants. What types of stimulation appear to be best for babies? What is the professional's opinion regarding the use of "brain development aids," such as flash cards, videotapes, and kits marketed to "boost a baby's brain power." If the professional does not recommend these techniques, what techniques does he or she recommend that parents can use instead?

Sensory Stimulation Activities

Activity		Sense
Mobiles Place mobiles on crib and playpen. Keep them out of the baby's reach. Change the objects on the mobile often. Try to visualize them from the baby's point of view.		Sight
Tracking Objects Hold an object like a yarn ball, small flashlight, or rattle about 12 inches from the baby's eyes. Move it in a short arc and gradually extend the arc to a half circle. The baby's eyes should track or follow the object.		Sight
Wind Chimes Hold the baby near wind chimes blowing outdoors. Hearing wind chimes and seeing them move is interesting for babies.		Hearing and Sight
Face Hoop Draw a face by decorating fabric with fabric scraps or paint. Insert the fabric between round embroidery hoops. Hang the face down or hold it for the baby to see. (The face hoop is not safe for the baby to mouth.)		Sight
Sound Can Place some large wooden beads or large spools of thread in a juice can. Tape on the lid. The baby can hear the objects move inside the can. Other baby-safe objects can be used, too.		Hearing

Mobiles

Tracking Objects

Wind Chimes

11-12 Sensory stimulation activities help babies learn about their environment.

Problem-Solving Activities

As babies use their senses to observe their world, they try to make sense of what they see, hear, smell, touch, and taste. In an enriched environment, babies learn how their world works as they begin to explore.

A number of games and activities can help babies begin to organize and understand their world. Peek-a-boo is one of the first games babies love to play. To play this game, cover your eyes, or go out of sight, saying, "Where did (baby's name) go?" The baby will wait expectantly for you to uncover your eyes or come out of hiding and say, "Peek-a-boo, I see you!" Through this game, babies learn to understand a person is still there even though he or she cannot be seen. This is an example of an object permanence activity.

Babies need to repeat games with many objects and with some changes in order to test how something works. There are many kinds of problem-solving activities. More activities are found in 11-13.

Problem-Solving Activities

Spatial Relationship Activities

Stacking and Nesting

Stacking and Nesting
Find or purchase three cans or boxes that are different sizes. They must fit inside each other. These can be stacked by placing one on top of the other. They can also be nested by placing one inside the other. Show the baby how to stack and how to nest. (For young babies, the boxes should differ greatly in size. If there are many pieces, start with only the smallest, the middle-size, and the large pieces. After the baby can work with three pieces well, add others one at a time.)

Far and Near
Hold a toy close to the baby's eyes. Move it back slowly and say, "There it goes." Move it forward slowly and say, "Here it comes." The game helps babies see size differences in near and far objects.

Other Performance Activities

Where's the Object?

Where's the Object?
Hide a favorite toy, starting with simple ways of hiding and moving. Advance to more complex ways as the baby masters each. During each game, let the baby watch you hide the toy. If the baby finds the toy, move on to the next step. (1) Partially hide the toy under a blanket. (2) Next, totally hide the toy under the blanket. (3) Wrap the toy in paper so that the shape of the object shows. (4) Place the toy in or under a box. (5) Place the toy in a box that is in another box.

Hide and Seek
Hide from the baby, leaving some part of yourself visible. Let the baby find you. Once found, make the reunion happy, with lots of hugs and kisses. (This helps the baby overcome anxiety when left with others.) After partially hiding yourself during many games, hide yourself completely. Choose a hiding spot where the baby can find you easily.

Activities Using Objects as Tools

Making Sounds with Objects

Pulling Strings
Babies can learn to get an object by pulling a string in many ways. You may buy toys that are pulled on a string. You may also attach any toy or safe household object to a string for the baby to pull.

Making Sounds with Objects
By hitting objects together, babies can learn to make different sounds. They will learn to vary the sounds by hitting softer or harder, or by changing the objects. Different objects to use include a pan with a spoon, a box with a spoon, a drum with a stick, and a block with a block.

11-13 Problem-solving activities help babies understand their world.

Motor Activities

Movement is important for infants. Babies begin moving even before birth. Although motor nerves are not fully developed for four or five years, coordination improves quickly after birth. **Coordination** is the working together of muscles in movements, such as walking. As infants explore, motor activity helps their coordination and mental development. As motor skills improve, babies feel better about their abilities, which boosts social-emotional development.

If they are free to move, babies will engage in many motor activities on their own. However, they need some encouragement from caregivers. Babies use their large muscles as they perform gross-motor skills, such as rolling over, sitting, crawling, standing, and walking. An example of an activity that encourages gross-motor skills is crawling in and out of boxes or cartons. Coordination in the small muscles, especially those in the fingers and hands, is evident in the use of fine-motor skills. Playing with blocks is a fine-motor skill that requires coordination of the small muscles. See 11-14 for other activities for gross- and fine-motor games.

Language Activities

Hearing spoken words is important for the child's language development. Babies learn language by hearing people talk. This is best done during baby's routine care. Adults can talk about the foods, toys, people, and routines that are part of the baby's world. Exact words are not as important to the infant as hearing language. While dressing a baby, the adult

Gross- and Fine-Motor Games

Gross-Motor Games

★ **Knock the Toy.** When a baby can stand by holding a playpen or crib railing, place a stuffed toy on the railing. Tell the baby to hold the railing with one hand and to knock the toy off with the other.

★ **Cartons or Boxes.** Place a large carton or box on its side. Let the baby crawl in and out of the carton.

★ **Dance to the Music.** Tell the baby to dance to the music. You may want to dance with the baby.

Fine-Motor Games

★ **Cups.** A baby can improve fine-motor skills by playing with a plastic infant cup. When the baby can handle the hand-to-mouth movement, add a teaspoon of water to the cup. As the baby becomes more skilled, add more water.

★ **Blocks.** Show the baby how to use blocks in different ways. Then let the baby try. Blocks can be stacked, hit together, or placed in a line and moved by pushing the last block.

11-14 Gross- and fine-motor games help babies' coordination and mental development.

could make any of the following statements and questions:

★ "I'm putting on your green shirt."

★ "Isn't this a pretty shirt?"

★ "Are you ready for the shirt to go over your head?"

★ "Here's a button, here's a button, and here's one."

★ "Do you like green?"

Although it does not matter exactly which words parents use, words should be pronounced correctly. Changing pitch or singing also varies the sound and adds interest.

Adults can encourage babies to talk, too. Often, the baby will babble in response. When the baby babbles, encouragement should be given such as, "That's right!"

Reading to infants daily exposes them to new words and ideas. Even babies who cannot comprehend the words benefit from being read books, magazines, and newspapers. Time spent reading and hearing words is important at all ages.

Language games can be worked into daily routines. These routines can include a special time of sharing for babies and adults. Perhaps one of the earliest language action games babies enjoy is *pat-a-cake*. See 11-15 for this and other language games.

Social-Emotional Needs

Babies have needs that must be met for healthy social-emotional development. During the first year, social and emotional development seems to center on the baby-adult interaction, the baby's developing self-awareness, and adults' ways of handling special problems.

Language Games

★ **Verbal Imitation.** Imitation of verbal (and even nonverbal) signals helps language development. Two stages are used during the baby's first year.

Stage 1 (0–6 months)—Imitate the baby's gestures and babbling. If you see a gesture or hear a sound, repeat it with a smile or laugh. See whether the baby repeats it. If the baby has not repeated the gesture or sound in return, repeat the sound. Once the baby catches on, the baby will imitate sounds after you.

Stage 2 (6–12 months)—In this stage, you can begin by making a gesture or sound. See whether the baby imitates it. If the baby has not repeated the gesture or sound in return, make the same gesture or sound again. The baby should catch on quickly.

★ **Books.** Begin looking at books while the baby is still young. At first, talk about the pictures. As you talk, point to the pictures. Later, begin to read if the story is short. Go on to the next page as the baby loses interest in one page. Between 9 and 12 months, you can ask the baby to find certain pictures, such as cars, pets, or people.

★ **Puppets.** You can make or buy a puppet to talk to the baby. At first, the baby will just look and listen. Later, he or she will talk to the puppet.

★ **Action Rhymes.** Children can enjoy action rhymes toward the end of the first year. Action rhymes combine the rhythm of language with a few motor actions. An example follows:

Pat-a-Cake

Pat-a-cake, pat-a-cake, baker's man.

(Help baby clap hands on the words "pat-a-cake")

Bake me a cake as fast as you can.

Roll it, and pat it, and mark it with a "B."

(Help baby roll hands on the word "roll.")

Put it in the oven for baby and me.

11-15 Language games expose babies to words.

Baby-Adult Interaction

Each baby comes into the world with a unique temperament. Adults may respond positively or negatively toward the baby's temperament. Adults' feelings are conveyed mainly through the way they hold, touch, and look at the baby. The baby reacts to adults' feelings and actions. For example, if adults are tense or the baby's needs are unmet, the baby becomes fussy and difficult. On the other hand, when adults are relaxed and the baby's needs are promptly met, the baby is more often quiet and cooperative.

Adults who have good relationships with babies seem to respect their temperaments. Two nationally-known infant educators, Alice Sterling Honig and Magda Gerber, have taught the need to respect each baby's individual temperament and interests. For example, active babies often get into places they do not belong. They require more watching than less active children. These parents should adjust their own behaviors to provide this extra level of care.

Babies feel love through physical contact with the adult, 11-16. Physical messages shape feelings between adults and babies. A single or seldom-sent message does not determine the relationship. The quality of the relationship is influenced more by the total number of messages and the strength of these messages. Even the most loving adults can be hurried and tense at times. In a healthy relationship, the balance must be on the positive side.

Adults should realize that relationships with children are rather one-sided for many years. Babies may

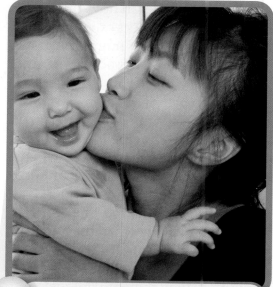

11-16 The feeling of love and joy between a baby and an adult can be shared through physical contact.

give some smiles and hugs, but adults must do most of the giving. This giving is important, though, because the feelings adults show for babies help to shape babies' self-concepts. Fostering good feelings in babies seems to increase the joy and love between babies and their caregivers.

Helping Babies Develop Self-Awareness

In the first year, a baby begins to develop **self-awareness** or an understanding of himself or herself as a unique person. As babies develop self-awareness, they form a mental picture of themselves. They form an idea of who they are and what they can do.

Babies gaze at their hands for hours, making slight movements. As their brains process the sight and sensation of these moving hands, babies learn their hands are a part of them. This discovery helps babies become more aware of their bodies.

Infants also learn how their movements can affect other objects. For example, a baby might move a hand, bat a toy on a cradle gym, and make the toy turn. This discovery teaches the baby which objects are part of himself or herself (the hand) and which are not (the toy and the cradle gym). When a baby crawls to get a toy, the baby learns his or her actions can make things happen.

At eight or nine months of age, babies start to learn they are individuals separate from others (known as *object concept*). They begin to realize they are not just extensions of their parents. Feeling separate leads babies to express anxiety when caregivers leave them.

Adults can promote self-awareness by using the baby's name as much as possible. Calling the baby by name during happy times gives the baby positive feelings about his or her name. Happy times include reunions between adult and baby, such as after a nap or when the adult returns from work. Parents can also call the baby by name when talking to him or her during child care tasks or games.

Looking in mirrors also increases self-awareness. Babies enjoy seeing themselves in mirrors even before they know the images they see are their own. Calling the baby's image by name is helpful. Adults may also place babies in front of mirrors so they can watch themselves eat, dress, and move. Babies also enjoy having nonbreakable play mirrors as toys. They like to point to their eyes, ears, nose, mouth, and toes. They also like finding these body parts in the mirror.

Toward the end of the first year, babies become possessive about some objects. This should be encouraged, because babies' understanding that some objects belong to them is part of self-awareness. Also, babies must possess things before they can learn to share in a few years. Adults can help teach possession by making statements like "Here's Barbara's dress," or "Where are Keith's blocks?"

Handling Special Problems

All babies have some problems. These may include feeding and sleeping problems, fear of strangers, or lots of crying. When problems arise, these tips may help.

★ Decide if the problem is temporary. Wait a few days, unless the baby seems ill. Babies do have mood changes. Also, the problem may be because of a hurried or tense caregiver. In these cases, the problem will likely end as soon as the adult slows down or relaxes.

★ If the problem continues, talk to an expert. Start with your pediatrician or a family doctor.

★ Get help when needed. For example, parents who have a fussy baby may need to use loving babysitters to give them time to rest or leave home for a few hours.

★ Give in to a baby's demands sometimes, if the results are not serious. Even babies have wills of their own, and letting them have their way sometimes is not going to spoil or harm them. For example, if a baby refuses to eat peas, try other vegetables with similar nutrients.

★ Remain calm. This helps the baby and the adult.

Experienced caregivers tend to almost ignore many common, not-too-serious problems. Experience teaches that all babies are different and many problems solve themselves in time.

Recognizing Developmental Delays

As you read in Chapter 1, a *developmental delay* simply means a child's development falls far behind typical children of his or her age in one or more areas. A larger gap indicates a more serious delay. Infancy is the best time to begin watching for delays and treating problems. Seeking help early can keep some problems from worsening. If an infant's development seems to be much slower than the norms, parents should consult a doctor. See the *Infant Milestones* in Appendix A to learn about some typical infant behaviors that may help parents to recognize delays.

Summary

With the rapid development during the first year, the baby has many needs. Adults must meet their physical, intellectual, and social-emotional needs.

Only breast milk or formula is recommended for the first six months. After that, adults can introduce solid baby foods one at a time. Learning to drink from a cup, eat finger foods, and use a spoon takes time. These tasks require the child to use a different set of throat and tongue muscles and develop coordination.

Babies outgrow their clothing quickly. Good consumer sense is important when buying baby clothes. Parents should read labels for care instructions and check for flame retardant and anti-static finishes. Clothing must be clean and free of detergent residue before wearing.

Other needs include bathing, sleeping, and playing. When giving a tub bath, make sure the water is comfortably warm and the child is safe from slipping. Children should have their own sleep area away from distracting noises. Keep the child's bed free of soft, fluffy products, and put all infants on their backs to sleep. All play spaces for babies and young children should be safe, yet provide stimulating play.

To develop intellectually, children need an enriched environment. They need activities that will stimulate all the senses. Problem-solving activities help them learn about the world around them. Activities that develop motor skills are encouraged. For language development to take place, it is important to talk to children and encourage them to make sounds and words.

Babies' social-emotional needs center on their interaction with others and their growing self-awareness. Adults and those around them help babies develop their self-identity.

Different problems in feeding, sleeping, and crying may develop. Parents and caregivers need to try a number of methods to handle these problems calmly, yet effectively. If a problem persists, or a delay is suspected, parents should contact the child's doctor for advice.

Companion Web Site

Interactive Activity

Review vocabulary terms and key concepts for Chapter 11 at **g-wlearning.com**.

Review and Reflect

Write your answers to the following questions on a separate sheet of paper.

1. Babies' most basic needs are in the _____ (physical, intellectual, social) area.

2. Give three reasons for not starting solids before babies are six months of age unless advised by a baby's doctor.

3. True or false. Weaning is a physical and social-emotional process.

4. True or false. Generally, SIDS occurs in babies between 10 and 12 months of age.

5. List three suggestions in planning sleep and play spaces for a baby.

6. True or false. Activities and games should be woven into child care routines.

7. List two methods caregivers use to meet babies' intellectual needs through activities.

8. Learning to sit is an example of a _____ (fine-motor, gross-motor) skill.

9. True or false. Babies learn language by hearing people talk.

10. List two ways to help a baby learn to talk and understand words.

11. List three ways in which parents can help their child develop self-awareness.

Cross-Curricular Link

12. **Financial Literacy.** Examine five articles of baby clothing and list the good features noted in each piece. Create a hangtag for each item that lists its best features. Show each piece to the class as you read its hangtag aloud. Which articles of clothing would you purchase?

13. **Health, Safety.** After viewing a demonstration of tub bathing for infants, practice the steps using a doll. Remember to talk and play with the baby as you give the bath.

14. **Reading, Writing.** Read at least three articles that provide information about sudden infant death syndrome (SIDS). Write a two-page report based on your findings. Check your report for correct spelling, grammar, and punctuation.

15. **Financial Literacy.** Imagine you are a parent of an infant and you have $150 allotted in your budget for first-year toys. Use a catalog, shop online, or visit local stores that carry infant toys. List the items you would purchase, giving a description of each item and listing its price. Consider the various areas of development and ability levels of infants in the first year. Which items would promote the development of

fine-motor skills? gross-motor skills? Present your list to the class and explain the reasons behind your choices.

16. **Speech.** Ask a pediatrician or child development expert to identify various signs that would indicate a child might have a developmental delay that requires professional help. Why is seeking help early so important? Ask the expert to share any experiences he or she has about working with infants who have developmental delays. Do delays in infancy always guarantee lifelong delays? Share your findings with the class.

Making Observations

17. Observe a baby trying to drink from a cup or handle a spoon. What problems does the baby experience? How are these problems related to messiness?

18. Observe several babies wearing different types of outfits. Describe the outfits and list the advantages or disadvantages of each.

19. Visit the home of a 6- to 12-month-old. Observe the places designed for the baby's sleep and play. Ask the parent whether he or she likes these arrangements, and why. Describe your findings to the class.

20. Observe a baby playing. What senses are being stimulated? Which motor and language skills are being developed?

21. Observe an infant and parent playing. How does the adult encourage a positive relationship?

Thinking Critically

22. Some parents believe that feeding babies solids early is the best way to ensure they sleep throughout the night. How can this belief be harmful to babies?

23. In the text, *peek-a-boo* is described as a good game for developing object permanence in babies. What other games promote object permanence?

24. Adults need to respect babies' temperaments. What are some ways parents can respect the temperament of a happy baby? a shy baby? a fussy baby? an active baby? a quiet baby?

Part 4 Toddlers

Focus on
Family and Community

Eating nutritious foods and getting plenty of physical activity can help you now and in the future. Learn to make healthful choices by preparing your own daily menu with plenty of nutritious foods. Become more physically fit by developing your own daily fitness plan. Create a "food diary" and write an entry each day, recording the number of calories you consume according to the menu you prepared. You can also record your level of physical fitness. How do your health habits compare with your nutritional needs according to MyPyramid? What can you do to develop a more healthful lifestyle? By maintaining your own personal health, you will be better able to teach young children to do the same. Take it a step further and get involved with the FCCLA national peer education program, *Student Body*. You can complete projects in the units *Eat Right* and *Be Fit*. Your FCCLA advisor can provide you with further information.

12 Physical Development of the Toddler

After studying this chapter, you will be able to

★ describe the physical changes that occur between the first and third years of life.

★ identify the toddler's major gross- and fine-motor skills.

Terms to Know

muscle development
large-muscle development
small-muscle development
eye-hand coordination

Reading Advantage

As you read the chapter, write a "top ten" list of important concepts.

Companion Web Site

Interactive Activity

Learn more about the toddler's small-muscle development by completing the *Read, Discuss, and Analyze* Activity for Chapter 12 at **g-wlearning.com**.

Children between ages one and three years are called *toddlers*. This name fits them, because toddlers toddle during almost all their waking minutes as they explore the world around them. As toddlers develop physically, their bodies mature. This helps them handle more complex tasks. Although toddlers do not grow as quickly as infants, they go through many important physical changes.

Babies do not have much control over their muscles when they are born. By the end of their first year, infants are just learning to control voluntary muscle movements. Both the gross- and fine-motor skills of toddlers improve. These skills improve so much that, by the end of their second year, toddlers can run, jump, throw, and feed themselves, 12-1.

Body Growth and Development

After the first year, babies continue to grow quickly. Their organ systems continue to mature, too. However, they do not grow as quickly as they did during their first year.

Height and Weight

Toddlers grow at different rates. This is due to environment and heredity. What does heredity affect? Heredity affects a baby's height. It also affects how fast the baby grows taller. Because genes determine height, they also influence weight. (A person who is taller usually weighs more than a person who is shorter.) However, the environment (diet,

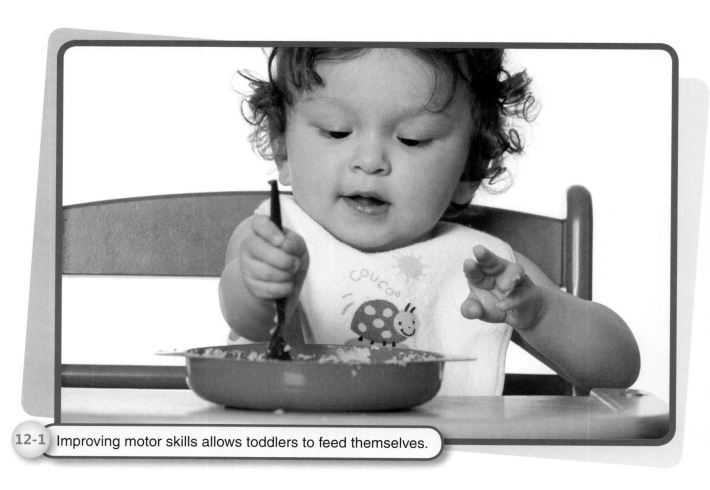

12-1 Improving motor skills allows toddlers to feed themselves.

physical activity, health, and even emotions) affects a person's weight more than genes. Because of these factors, toddlers sometimes grow at different rates than norms predict for their age.

Years One and Two

Body growth begins to slow after the first year. Babies grow about half as much in height during the second year as compared with the first year. Most babies triple their birthweight during the first year, then gain only one-fourth of that amount during the second. Some babies grow a little faster than these norms in their second year. (They may be "catching up" to norms after a premature birth or first-year illness.) Most girls reach half of their adult height by age 20 months. Boys reach half of their adult height by age 27 months. However, many factors affect growth rates.

After Year Two

After 24 months, children grow at a slower, but steadier rate. They tend to gain two to three inches and about six pounds per year throughout childhood. (This rate of growth continues until about 11 years for girls and 13 years for boys.) Chart 12-2 shows the height and weight norms from 12 to 36 months.

Other Body Changes

The body proportions of a two-year-old still differ from those of an adult. At 24 months, the head is a little more than one-fifth of the total height. An adult's head is one-eighth of his

Average Height and Weight from One to Three Years

Age in Months	Height	Weight
12	30 in.	21 lbs.
18	32 in.	24.5 lbs.
24	34 in.	27 lbs.
30	36 in.	30 lbs.
36	38 in.	32 lbs.

12-2 Children's height and weight increase steadily from ages one year to three years.

or her height. A 24-month-old's chest and abdomen are about the same size. By 30 months, the chest is larger than the abdomen. As the child matures, the difference between chest and abdomen size will become even greater. The child's body-build type will become apparent during the toddler years.

Bones and Teeth

As toddlers grow, their bones continue to become harder, though

Focus on Science
Brain Development

By the end of the second year, the brain is four-fifths of its adult weight. The brain is closer to maturity than any other organ. The other body organs continue to mature, but they do so at a slower rate than the brain. (This is an example of the *head-to-foot* or *cephalocaudal principle*—development is completed from the brain down the spine.) How can early experiences affect a toddler's brain development?

the degree of ossification is not the same throughout the body. Due to the cartilage, the toddler's bones are more flexible and less likely to break than an adult's bones. However, the softer bones are more prone to disease or deformation. The toddlers' *fontanels* (gaps between the skull bones, also called *soft spots*) are closed or almost closed. The toddler's spine changes from the infants' C-shaped spine to S-shaped like an adult's spine. The S-shape allows the posture to become straighter and more upright. This makes standing and walking easier. Shortly after two years, a child has the full set of deciduous teeth (often called *baby teeth*).

Fat and Muscle Tissue

Fat deposits under the skin decrease rapidly between 9 and 30 months. The chubby baby becomes a slender child if the child's diet and level of physical activity are appropriate, 12-3. After 30 months, a chubby child is either overweight or obese. **Muscle development** (the lengthening and thickening of muscles) is slow during the toddler stage.

Motor Development

Toddlers improve the motor skills they developed as infants. However, they also learn many new skills. Motor skills develop as the child grows and develops. As the child practices new skills, motor development improves even more.

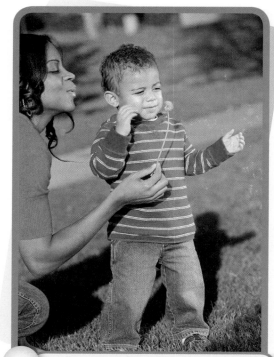

12-3 The toddler will slowly become slender because fat deposits under the skin are decreasing.

Large-Muscle Development

Large-muscle development refers to the development of the trunk and arm and leg muscles. Movements, such as crawling, walking, jumping, and running, mainly depend on these large muscles. (These movements are examples of gross-motor skills.) During the first year, most babies develop these muscles at least to the point of standing and walking with support. After one year, babies master walking and begin learning other motor skills. Toddlers love to run, jump, and use other large muscles. When they are held in one place too long, they begin squirming, as if to say, "I want down!" (Squirming is an example of a large-muscle movement.)

Walking

Most toddlers begin to walk without support within two or three months before or after the first birthday. Why do babies begin to walk at different ages? Some children are frustrated or even fearful when they fall while trying to walk. Others who creep quickly may not walk early because creeping gets them where they want to go. Often, girls begin to walk a couple of months earlier than boys. Also, lighter babies may walk earlier than heavier babies.

Although some conditions are helpful, babies learn to walk in their own time and way. To do so, they need warm adult support, a positive reaction to the baby's attempts, and a safe area. Pushing a baby to walk early will not help. Preventing a baby from practicing pre-walking skills due to adult concern about little falls does not help either. Both may delay walking and will surely frustrate both the baby and adult.

Beginning Walkers

Regardless of age, all beginning walkers share some common traits.

They stand with their feet wide apart, which gives them a wider base of support. They turn their feet outward and slightly flex their knees. Some children walk on their tiptoes. This is not because they want to stand taller (which they learn to do). Babies stand on their tiptoes because they have not learned to lower their heels. A baby's first steps often seem like staggers. The baby may step to the side or backward. He or she may also take irregular steps, lurch forward, and weave. Arms are often held up or out and do not swing alternately with foot movement. Because it is hard for babies to balance their large heads, they often fall.

A flat spine causes the toddler to tilt forward slightly when walking. As the toddler grows, this walking posture changes as the lower back curve takes on the S-shape, called the *lumbar curve*. As it does, the walk becomes more upright. This, plus improved ability to balance, helps the toddler to walk steadily. The toddler's stance also becomes narrower, the feet are positioned straighter, and the knees are less flexed.

Learn More About...
Walking at Two Years

At two years, a child's walk may look like a run, but it is not a run. Toddlers take about 170 steps per minute. Their stride is half the length of an adult's stride. Can you imagine doubling your steps, taking 170 steps per minute, and having someone hold onto your hand above your head? Yet, this is how many toddlers walk with adults. No wonder walking tires young children before it tires adults.

Toddlers rarely go around small obstacles on the floor, such as a toy or book. They simply walk over these objects, which increases their chances of falling. Toddlers must watch their foot placement while walking until almost three years of age. They must watch each step the same way you would if you were walking on stones across a creek. Being distracted is another reason toddlers fall.

Running

True running (not just a hurried walk) begins around two years of age. Two-year-olds are not skillful runners. This is due to their arm placement. They tend to hold their arms up or out as they run. Running is also awkward because toddlers cannot start or stop quickly.

Jumping

Stepping off low objects at about 18 months is the way children learn to jump. Before two years of age, children may step off a low object and remain suspended in air for a brief moment. At two years, children can jump off low objects with two feet. However, they move their arms backward instead of helping the jump by swinging their arms forward.

Climbing

Babies may begin to climb as soon as they can crawl or creep. Between 15 and 18 months, babies will climb onto furniture. They will walk up and down stairs with help. They often hold onto the stair railing and the adult's hand, or turn to the side and hold the railing with both hands, 12-4. For toddlers, going up stairs is easier than coming down stairs. Toddlers do not change feet while climbing until after the second birthday.

When does climbing begin? There really is not a set time. Climbing ability relates to the kinds of stairs and other objects near the baby. Babies can climb more easily if stairs are enclosed and not too steep. Climbing also relates to courage. A courageous baby is likely to try climbing sooner than a timid baby.

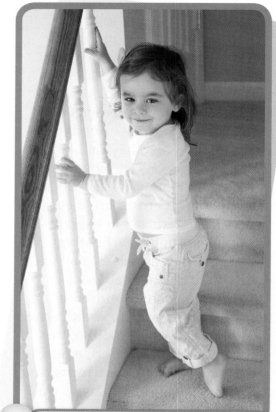

12-4 Toddlers can climb more easily if the stairs are not too steep and if there is a railing or an adult's hand to hold.

Throwing and Catching

Infants begin throwing by accident. They forget to hold onto an object while swinging their arms. They enjoy seeing the object move and hearing the sound it makes when it lands. Then, babies start to throw on purpose. Planned throwing begins around one year of age.

Year-old babies usually throw from a sitting position, such as from the high chair. After babies feel secure standing or walking, they throw from standing positions. Children under three years are not very skillful throwers. These children usually use a rigid throw and do not shift their weight. In fact, when throwing with one hand, they often step with the same-side foot. They also cannot release the ball at the right time, which sends the ball in almost any direction.

For almost a year after children begin to walk, they "catch" an object by squatting and picking it up, 12-5. Around two years of age, the child will bend at the waist to pick up the thrown object. Two- and three-year-olds may try to catch by standing in one position with arms extended and elbows stiff. For the child to catch a ball, it must be exactly on target. The child does not move toward the ball. In fact, many children close their eyes as the ball comes toward them.

Small-Muscle Development

Small-muscle development refers to the development of small muscles, especially those in the hands and fingers. The movements that depend on these muscles are fine-motor skills. Fine-motor skills also depend on a child's level of eye-hand coordination. To have **eye-hand coordination**, children must coordinate what they see with the way they move their hands. As eye-hand coordination and small muscles improve, toddlers can better handle complex fine-motor skills. With time and experience, clumsy and difficult movements become smoother and require less effort.

By the end of the first year, babies can hold objects between the thumb and index finger. This helps them learn many new fine-motor skills. Between 12 and 18 months, toddlers can hold spoons in

12-5 Toddlers squat to pick up thrown objects until they are about two years old.

their fists. They can feed themselves and drink from cups, although they may often miss their mouths and spill food. With practice and better eye-hand coordination, however, toddlers become better at feeding themselves. By 15 months, they can fill and empty containers. They can also make marks on paper by holding a pencil or crayon in their fists. At this age, the toddler can do the following:

★ remove a hat and socks

★ insert rather large objects into holes

★ turn pages of a book several at a time

★ begin to fit objects together

★ build a tower of two to three soft blocks

Between 18 months and 2 years, fine-motor skills improve even more. By this stage, toddlers can string large beads on cords. They can turn the pages of books one at a time. They can open doors by turning knobs. Most two-year-olds can hit pegs with a hammer. After two years, many children hold crayons or pencils with the thumb on one side and fingers on the other side. They still cannot hold or write with a crayon or pencil the way an adult can, 12-6.

By two years, most children begin to show a definite hand preference (also called *handiness* or *hand dominance*). Hand preference is developmental and requires the use of both hands in various activities. During activities, the dominant hand is called the *worker*, and the other hand is called the *helper*. Think about how you use both hands while handwriting. Because hand preference is developmental, toddlers use both hands to some extent and often switch hands. For example, their right hand tends to be used for drawing or throwing a ball and the left hand for holding a cup and eating. With each passing year until the school years, more and more children use the right hand for most activities.

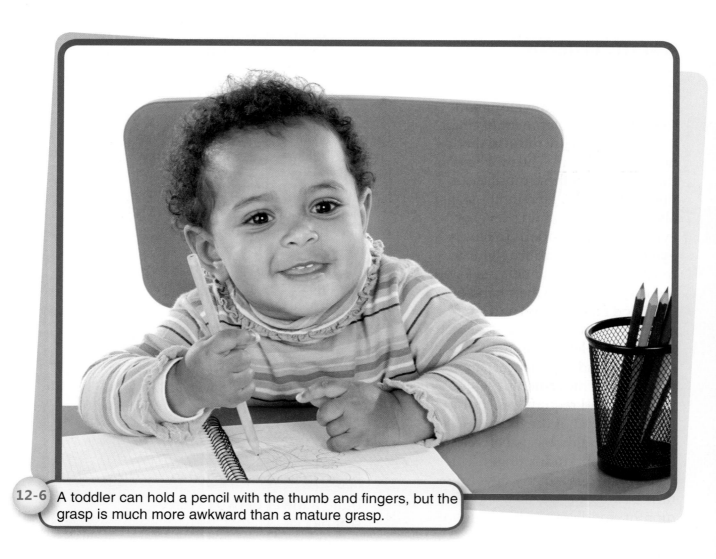

12-6 A toddler can hold a pencil with the thumb and fingers, but the grasp is much more awkward than a mature grasp.

At that time, 85 to 90 percent of all children are right-handed. (This is the same percentage as found among adults.)

Because hand preference is determined by brain wiring, each child should determine his or her own preference. Adults can help by placing or holding objects at a child's midline (center of body) rather than to the right or left of the child. This gives the child an easier choice in hand use. Adults can also encourage activities that require the use of both hands doing different actions, such as bead stringing. Certainly, adults should never force a change in preference.

Speech Pathologist

Speech pathologists assess, diagnose, treat, and help to prevent disorders related to speech, language, cognitive-communication, voice, swallowing, and fluency. Many work with children who cannot produce speech sounds or cannot produce them clearly; those with speech rhythm and fluency problems, such as stuttering; and those with voice disorders.

Education: A master's degree is the most common level of education among speech pathologists. Licensure or certification requirements also exist, but vary by state.

Job Outlook: Average employment growth is projected. Job opportunities are expected to be excellent.

Summary

Children tend to grow more slowly after their first year. Individual differences are due to heredity and environment. A toddler's bones continue to harden. Fat deposits under the skin decrease, making the toddler more slender. Body build becomes more apparent. The brain matures at a faster rate than other body organs. A full set of baby teeth may be present shortly after age two years.

Toddlers refine gross-motor skills, such as walking, climbing, and throwing. Many new skills are emerging, such as running, jumping off objects, and catching objects.

Fine-motor skills depend on the child's level of eye-hand coordination. Most children begin to show a definite hand preference by their second year. Hand preference is developmental and may not be stable until the school years.

Companion Web Site

Interactive Activity

Review vocabulary terms and key concepts for Chapter 12 at **g-wlearning.com**.

Review and Reflect

Write your answers to the following questions on a separate sheet of paper.

1. A person's height and the rate of increase in height are mainly due to _____ (heredity, environment).

2. A person's weight and the rate of increase in weight are mainly due to _____ (heredity, environment).

3. True or false. A baby's rate of growth slows after 12 months.

4. True or false. Between 12 and 24 months, a toddler will gain only about one-fourth of his or her total weight.

5. The fastest organ to develop is the (A) heart; (B) brain; (C) liver; (D) lungs.

6. True or false. Children are usually chubbier after their first year than before.

7. Give two possible reasons babies might begin to walk at different ages.

8. Explain why toddlers may fall if they do not think about what they are doing as they walk.

9. List four movements that depend mainly on the large muscles.

10. True or false. One-year-olds have well-developed eye-hand coordination.

11. True or false. Year-old babies can grasp objects between the thumb and index finger, so they hold flatware and crayons the same way adults hold them.

Cross-Curricular Link

12. **Social Studies, Writing.** As a group or class project, write a one- or two-page brochure explaining toddlers' motor skills. Include information on the order (and approximate age) when toddlers learn motor skills. Also, explain the motor actions used when walking, running, jumping, climbing, throwing, and catching. (Illustrations may help.) Have the teacher check your brochure, then make copies. Give copies to parents and adults at a program that serves toddlers, such as a child care program or preschool.

13. **Social Studies.** The text indicates toddlers walk at a rate of about 170 steps per minute. Walk quickly while counting your steps for one minute as your partner times you. Next, time your partner for one minute as he or she walks quickly counting steps. How do your results compare with your partner's and with the average rate for toddlers? What conclusions can you draw from this experiment?

14. **Health, Safety.** Visit Web sites of manufacturers of toddler play equipment. What kinds of equipment can you find that

provides safe opportunity for toddlers to climb both indoors and outdoors? Share your findings with the class.

15. **Science, Speech.** Ask a pediatrician or child development expert to explain whether it is desirable for parents to push toddlers to use a particular hand or if they should let the child's natural preference determine hand use. Share your findings with the class.

Making Observations

16. Observe infants and toddlers. Describe how children from the two age groups differ in appearance.

17. Observe several 24-month-olds with their parents. Do the taller toddlers have taller parents? Do the shorter toddlers have shorter parents?

18. Observe two toddlers—a new walker and an experienced walker. How do their posture and walking skills and style differ?

19. Observe the gross- and fine-motor skills of toddlers between 12 and 36 months of age. Note the kinds of movements they make compared to those of adults. Share your findings with the class.

20. Observe toddlers with materials that require fine-motor skills. How do they grip pencils, crayons, or markers? How messy is their self-feeding? Are large beads and puzzle pieces hard to manage?

Thinking Critically

21. Two-year-old Sarah has a shorter-than-average mother and a taller-than-average father. Her parents wonder whether Sarah will be a tall, average, or short adult. Can they predict her height? If so, how? Do you think such a prediction will be very accurate? Why or why not?

22. When toddlers walk or run, they usually hold their arms out. Why? In what situations might adults do this?

23. Why is coloring within the lines an impossible skill for toddlers?

13

Intellectual Development of the Toddler

After studying this chapter, you will be able to:

★ describe how and what toddlers learn.

★ describe the sequence of language development.

Terms to Know

deferred imitation
attributes
language
parentese

articulation
communication
grammar

Reading Advantage

Read the summary at the end of the chapter *before* you begin reading. Reading the summary helps identify main points and important information.

Companion Web Site

Interactive Activity

Learn more about the different rates at which toddlers learn to talk by completing the *Read, Discuss, and Analyze* Activity for Chapter 13 at **g-wlearning.com**.

In previous chapters, you have read about how babies learn. Much of what babies learn begins in the neonatal period. By the end of infancy, learning becomes much more advanced. All areas of development are closely linked. During the first two years, motor skills are highly linked to mental skills because very young children act upon objects within their environment. Also, walking and other motor skills expand the child's physical and social worlds.

Toddlers are eager to learn. They are curious about everyone and everything. They may not always be interested in learning what adults want them to learn. However, when working at a task they choose, toddlers will stay with the task until they are satisfied with the results.

In this chapter, you will see that toddlers truly begin to understand their environment. They learn about the properties of objects and what happens when they manipulate them. Because they learn to think before acting, toddlers plan new ways to achieve goals. Toddlers also become able communicators as they learn new words and speak in short sentences.

How and What Toddlers Learn

Through stages of development, Piaget has described how children's thinking changes as they mature. He called the first stage the sensorimotor stage. It includes children from birth to two years of age. As you read in Chapter 9, children in this stage learn through their senses and motor actions.

During the toddler years, Piaget believed children completed the last two substages of the sensorimotor stage, 13-1. From about 12 to 18 months, toddlers are in substage 5. They learn by discovering new ways to solve problems. Substage 6 begins when toddlers start to think mentally. This occurs from 18 to 24 months. A few older toddlers may enter the preoperational stage, which you will read about in Chapter 17.

Discovering New Ways to Solve Problems

From 12 to 18 months, children are busy exploring. They show lots of interest in new actions. Toddlers are active explorers and experimenters. Piaget called them "the little scientists." Toddlers use physical trial and error methods of solving problems. They seem to get into everything. After discovering one way they can use an object, toddlers seem to want to know what else they can do with the same object. Piaget called the substage *tertiary* simply because it is the third major change in mental development. They also enjoy repeating their actions—hence *circular*. Repeating actions helps them verify their observations in much the same way that scientific findings are verified through additional research.

Working Toward a Goal

In this stage, children's actions involve reaching a goal. The goal may be obvious to an adult. For example, a child may pull an object by its string in order to grasp it. Sometimes the goal may

Piaget's Stages of Cognitive Development

Stage 1: Sensorimotor Stage (Birth to 2 years)

Learning through the senses and physical actions in six substages.

Substages 1 and 2 involve the baby's own body.

Substages 3 and 4 involve people and objects.

Substages 5 and 6 involve creative actions and thinking before acting.

Substage 5: Tertiary Circular Reactions (12 to 18 months)

★ Sometimes called the substage of the "little scientist." Experiment with objects to receive various results.

★ Notice some attributes of objects (sometimes color, sometimes size).

★ Use physical trial and error to solve problems.

★ Imitate behaviors they have never done before; imitate only in the presence of the model.

★ Look for hidden objects in the last place seen.

Substage 6: Mental Imagery or Representation (18 to 24 months)

★ Can think about different ways to solve problems without using physical actions in a trial and error way.

★ Can think through the sequence of a few steps to solve a problem.

★ Begin to do some deferred imitation.

★ Know all objects and people are someplace. Hunt for objects in every possible place (completion of object permanence).

Stage 2: Preoperational Stage (2 to 7 years)

Stage 3: Concrete Operational Stage (7 to 11 years)

Stage 4: Formal Operational Stage (11 years on)

13-1 According to Piaget, many children complete the sensorimotor stage in the toddler years.

not be obvious. It may seem as if the child is only playing with or throwing objects. However, children play with objects to see how they work, 13-2. They want to know what happens to objects when they are rolled, shaken, thrown, or moved in other ways. Repeating actions with little changes helps toddlers learn the best way to reach their goals.

As toddlers learn more about objects, their thinking skills improve.

They can now help themselves more. For example, toddlers learn how to feed and dress themselves. They discover how to open doors and put objects in containers. They can find ways to grab out-of-reach objects. They solve their problems the best way they know how, but do not think about the consequences of their actions. To get a cookie on the kitchen table, a toddler may pull on the tablecloth until the cookie falls (along with other items on the table).

13-2 Children learn by playing with different objects.

Developing Other Skills

As young toddlers make discoveries and work toward goals, they develop other important skills. These skills include the following:

★ Imitation develops quickly. With the model present, they can imitate a short sequence of actions, such as giving a doll a bottle and then burping the doll.

★ Noticing the properties of objects is just beginning. Usually the first properties to be noticed are a few colors, such as *red* and *blue*. Toddlers also notice major size differences in objects, such as *big* and *tiny*.

★ Understanding object permanence is *almost* complete. Young toddlers will look for a completely hidden object where they last saw it or found it. They cannot, however, imagine it might be hidden in some other place.

Beginning of Thought

Around 18 to 24 months, toddlers enter substage 6. They now think about what they do before they do it. When you see toddlers pause in mid-action, they are probably thinking. Unlike younger children who have not developed thought processes, these children will "figure things out" mentally instead of actually testing them physically. For example, the two-year-old will think that a large object will not fit through a small opening in a container. On the other hand, a one-year-old would try to push the object through the opening to realize that it would not fit.

Older toddlers' thinking skills are far from mature because they think mainly in terms of actions. In the example you just read, the two-year-old would mentally see himself or herself trying to put the object through the opening before concluding it was too big to fit. These older toddlers even identify objects in terms of actions. For example, a 30-month-old may answer the question, "What is a ball?" with the reply, "To play with," or "To roll."

Thinking and Imitation

Children also show they can think by imitating what someone else has done at an earlier time. The ability to recall an observed behavior and later imitate it is called **deferred imitation**, 13-3. (*Deferred* means postponed.) Deferred imitation is used in both pretend play and language.

Thinking and Goals

Thinking also shows in the child's way of reaching goals.

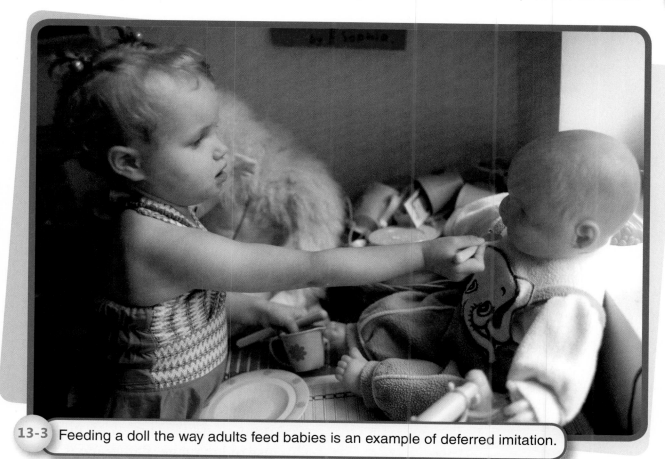

13-3 Feeding a doll the way adults feed babies is an example of deferred imitation.

A child may want to reach a toy on a high playroom shelf (goal). He or she may have used a stepstool in the bathroom, but not in the playroom. The child thinks about the stool and how it works in the bathroom. Then the child gets the stool to reach the object. If the child cannot bring the stool into the playroom, he or she may use another object as a stool. The child has thought through how to reach the goal.

Thinking and Hiding Games

Thinking is evident in hiding games, too. Children at this stage will search for objects they have not seen someone hide. This might happen when the adult pretends to hide a toy in one place, but really hides it in another. The child knows the object still exists (object permanence) and thinks about where the adult could have hidden it. To find hidden objects, the child must also think in terms of spatial concepts. For example, the child must consider which objects would be large enough to conceal the hidden toy.

Thinking and Shape, Size, Color, and Texture

Toddlers continue to use their senses to learn about their world. They are learning about the **attributes** (properties) of objects, such as their shape, size, color, and texture. A toddler might often refer to these attributes when talking about a red ball or a big dog, for example.

Toddlers begin to perceive differences in attributes. Noting these differences is a thinking skill, for it requires comparison. This skill is needed for the identification of objects. Mentally comparing differences comes before the use of terms such as *ducks* and *geese* or *red* and *pink*. Although toddlers sometimes use the wrong word for an attribute, they do note the differences among objects.

Thinking and Object Exploration

Toddlers also learn more about what will happen as they handle objects. They learn by throwing, rolling, shaking, or moving objects, 13-4. Toddlers learn that round objects roll and flat objects slide. They also learn that hard objects will make a loud noise when hit together, but soft objects will not.

A toddler often knows the attributes of new objects based on prior experience. He or she uses this knowledge in play. Suppose a child has already been exposed to the noise made by metal objects and the lack of noise made by soft objects. He or she will use this knowledge when given new objects for play. The child would immediately bang metal pans together, but would not bang together two balls of yarn. This is a very valuable thinking skill.

Thinking and Language

Finally, the way children think is observed through their use of language. **Language** is a symbol system in which words are used as labels for people, objects, and ideas. Unlike other symbol systems, such as pictures, words do not sound or look like the people and objects they represent.

In order to learn language, children use two thinking skills. First, they must associate the word with the person or object to which it refers. For example, toddlers must understand the word *milk* refers to a certain liquid, not water or juice. Second, children must recall the word and its meaning when they hear the word or want to say it. Language requires high-level thinking skills.

13-4 Toddlers use their motor skills to explore playthings. They learn important concepts as they stack, nest, hit, bang, and manipulate these objects.

Language Abilities

As you read in Chapter 9, babies begin to learn language

Learn More About...
Helping Toddlers Learn

As you read in Chapter 9, Vygotsky saw the need for adults to recognize a child's ZPD and then to scaffold the child's learning within it. Although Vygotsky did not talk about each stage of learning, there are ways to recognize a toddler's ZPD, which include the following:

★ Note the toddler's explorations and interests and favor interests that are extended.

★ Observe the toddler's goals.

★ Watch the toddler's body language and vocal cues for signs of pleasure or frustration during play.

★ Recognize the toddler's learning style, such as a liking for visual things, a liking for sounds and fun words, or a liking to move, touch, and do.

Once the ZPD is determined, the adult is ready to support the learning. Some possible ways include the following:

★ Watch and show interest through eye contact, smiles, and a few words if the toddler is involved in play.

★ Change the level of toy difficulty as needed. Find a similar, but simpler activity if the toddler is frustrated with the current activity. Find a similar, but more challenging activity if the toddler shows repeated success with the activity and now appears less interested.

★ Introduce novelty into an activity if the toddler appears uninvolved. For example, a toddler who seems bored with blocks might like balls. If the toddler seems bored with certain props for play, add a new prop.

★ Demonstrate the use of a toy, but do not interrupt a toddler's use of a toy in a safe but perhaps different way than usual.

★ Consult with a toddler when help is needed in solving a problem, such as fitting, building, or sorting toys.

★ Show delight and pride in a toddler's discovery or new skill.

★ React with patience to a toddler's frustration.

In Chapter 16, you will read about some specific activities that meet many toddlers' needs.

---

as infants. Newborns will turn toward the sound of human speech just minutes after delivery. Babies react to differences in sounds during the first couple of months. Then they begin to babble these sounds at about six months. Toward the end of the first year, they understand many words and sentences. They may also say a few words.

Language is often used to distinguish infants from toddlers. Learning language is important for children's mental and social development.

Research emphasizes the importance of parents as the first language teachers. Parents speak in a high-pitched style known as **parentese**. While speaking, parents put their faces closer to children, use shorter sentences, and speak in a singsong fashion, 13-5. As a way to help toddlers learn the meanings of words, parents should look at objects they are describing.

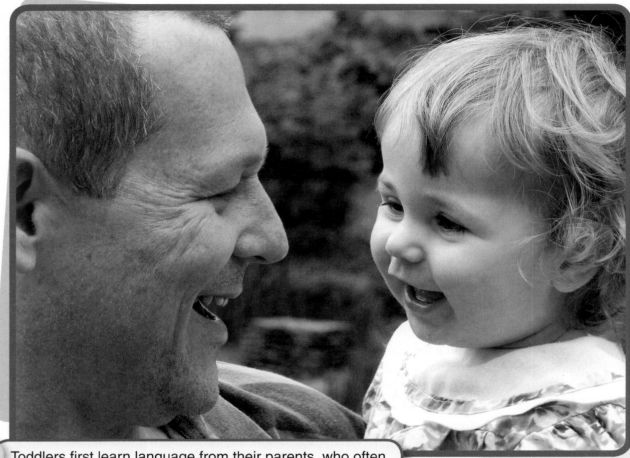

13-5 Toddlers first learn language from their parents, who often speak to their children in a style known as *parentese*.

Learning Spoken Language

Spoken language develops at a faster rate between one and three years than at any other time in a person's life. However, learning to talk takes time and effort. This is because speaking involves **articulation** (making the sounds of language) and learning the meanings of words.

Learning to Articulate

Babies can make all the sounds of any language. They learn the words and language of those around them through imitation. Learning to control the tongue, lip muscles, and vocal chords to form words takes practice. Babies do not pronounce sounds accurately each time.

Children who cannot make one sound will substitute another. For example, they may use *d* for *th*, such as *dat* for *that*. Sometimes children can articulate the right sound in one place in a word, but not in another. A toddler may have no problem with *m* at the beginning of a word such as *milk*. However, the toddler may have trouble making the *m* sound in the middle of *hammer* or at the end of *broom*.

Toddlers may also change the sound order of a word. They may say *perslip* to mean *slipper*. They may even change an entire word, such as say *book* and mean *bird*. Sometimes toddlers will drop a sound if they cannot pronounce it. For example, they may say *seepy* instead of *sleepy*.

A few children articulate most sounds correctly from the beginning. Most children make substitutions. They tend to correct themselves in time. Adults should pronounce words correctly, even if the toddler's way of saying words sounds cute. Children need good examples to follow. In time, the child will learn from listening. Forcing children to repeat a word again and again is not a recommended way to correct pronunciation, because it may cause the child stress.

Learning Meanings

Learning the meanings of words is hard. To do so, the child must link certain features with a name. This is difficult because many objects with different names share common features. For example, both lambs and ponies run outside and have four legs. Sometimes children confuse the meanings of words they hear. They may use a wrong name for an object, such as call a cow a *moo* or a stove *hot*. Without meanings attached to spoken sounds, there would be no language. These meanings give the child two new tools—communication and a new way to think.

Communication is the skill needed to understand others and be understood by them. Already, toddlers can understand many words and sentences. When they begin to talk, they want to be understood. Toddlers often use their

communication to achieve three goals, 13-6.

As you read, language is part of the thinking process. In other words, people learn to think in words. As the child learns to talk, words go with actions. For example, the toddler will say *goodbye* while waving. Later, children talk to themselves as they play or lie in bed. They then often whisper words. Finally, they think about words without saying them.

Young children develop both vocabulary and grammar. As children learn language, they attach meanings to words and to the order of words. This process is gradual, however.

Vocabulary

Most children's vocabularies grow slowly until 18 months to two years of age. The fastest growth occurs around 30 months of age.

Focus on Science
Brain Development

Many studies support recent research in brain development. Wiring for language is very active in the toddler years. Studies support the window of opportunity for language learning. How many words a child understands or speaks is related to how much parents and other caregivers talk to him or her. The most important thing for word growth is the number of times a child hears given words. At age 20 months, toddlers of chatty mothers or caregivers knew more words than children of less talkative ones. By 24 months, the gap had doubled in favor of talkative adults. The same results held for grammar. Mothers and caregivers who use complex sentences have children who use them, too. Why do you think it is important for adults who talk to toddlers to pronounce words correctly, as opposed to "baby talking" to them?

The Tool of Communication

Reasons to Communicate	Examples of Communication
To achieve a goal	"Want cookie." (I want a cookie.) "Go bye-bye." (I want to ride in the car.) "No!" (I don't want _____.)
To identify an object	"See doggie." (I see a dog.) "Big!" (That is big.) "What dat?" (What is that?)
To create a bond with another person	"Mommy?" (Where are you mommy? I want you.) "Kiss." (I love you.) "Hurt." (Please help me.)

13-6 Reading to toddlers helps them learn about the usage and meaning of words. It also provides a special time for parents and toddlers to share a quiet closeness.

Toddlers will vary in the number of words their vocabularies include at different ages. This can also depend on whether all spoken words or only those used correctly are counted as part of the vocabulary. Children may use words for a while, drop them, and pick them up again months later. The size of the vocabulary can be measured most easily in children three years of age and older.

Grammar

Grammar is the study of the preferred word usage and order in a given language. Each language has grammar rules. Children begin to learn these rules in the toddler period. This learning begins with single-word "sentences" and will often progress to simple sentences of a few words during the toddler years. Within six months of saying their first words, toddlers usually begin to put words together. Combining words is an advanced skill because word order affects the meanings of sentences. By listening to adults and having good books read to them, toddlers learn the basic rules for the language they hear. They then apply these rules to their own phrases and sentences.

Arts, A/V Technology & Communications

Author of Children's Books

Authors of children's books are often self-employed and sell their work to publishers, publication enterprises, or manufacturing firms. Authors of children's books must be able to express ideas clearly and logically and should enjoy writing. Creativity and curiosity are valuable traits. They must demonstrate good judgment and a strong sense of ethics in deciding what material to create for children.

Education: Education can vary greatly.

Job Outlook: Employment of authors of children's books is expected to grow about as fast as the average for all occupations.

Single Words

From 12 to 18 months of age, toddlers use sentences of only one word. This single word is often used by the toddler to mean different ideas at different times. A child may say *bye-bye* both to identify a moving object (a car) and to make a request ("Let's go!"). To understand these meanings, the caregiver must note how the child says the word, what gestures he or she uses, and what is happening at the time.

Children use words that represent the actions they see and the people and objects they know, 13-7. First words are usually nouns and simple action verbs. Nouns may include words like *mama*, *daddy*, and *kitty*. For toddlers, action verbs may include *run* and *fly*. Next, the child learns descriptive words (adjectives and adverbs), such as *big*, *hot*, *pretty*, *loud*, and *fast*. Young children quickly learn words for human interactions, such as *hi* and *bye* and words for love and affection, too, such as *hug*.

Two or More Words

After 19 months, many children begin combining two or more words to form sentences. At the early stage of combining words, toddlers use only the most necessary words. By 24 to 30 months, many toddlers begin using three or more words in their sentences. When the child begins to use these multi-word sentences, the words that are added fill in the gaps. "All gone milk" becomes "Milk is gone." By the time the child uses three-word sentences, word order is often used correctly. The child may say, "Bird is flying," instead of saying, "Fly bird."

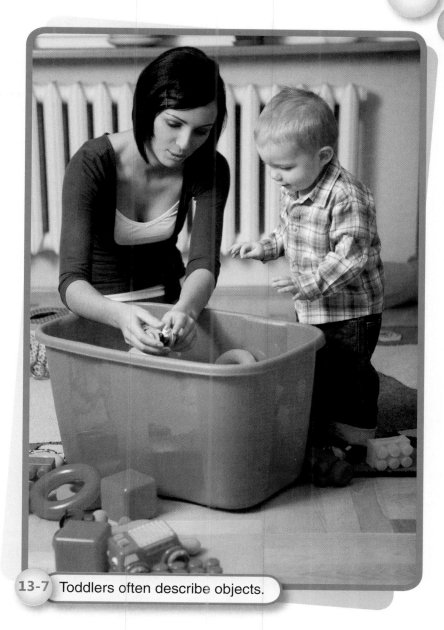

13-7 Toddlers often describe objects.

Different Rates of Learning to Talk

The rate at which toddlers learn to talk can vary by several months. Many adults worry about a slow talker, only to see the toddler become a nonstop talker a few months later. These toddlers are hearing sounds and learning meanings all along. When they begin to talk, they progress quickly.

A number of factors can affect language development. Learning to talk depends on the following:

★ **hearing.** A child must hear human speech clearly in order to learn to talk without special training, 13-8. Even ear infections can delay speech in toddlers.

★ **interest.** Some active toddlers are more interested in motor skills than in talking. Within a few months, they often catch up to earlier talkers.

★ **mental abilities.** Because language is so closely related to thinking, a child with a mental disability is often slower to talk. On the other hand, early talking does not mean a child is bright. Children of average and even below average mental abilities may talk at a young age simply by repeating what they hear.

★ **gender.** From the first year of life, girls tend to excel in verbal skills more than boys. Researchers do not know whether this is due to heredity or the environment. (For example, adults may talk to girls more than to boys.)

★ **need for speech.** Some children get what they need without saying anything. For example, if a toddler receives milk by pointing, holding a cup, or crying, there is no need to learn to say, "I want milk."

★ **interesting environment.** Just as adults have more to say when they have new experiences, so do toddlers.

In some cases, the rate of language development may lag far behind the norms. In these situations, the child should receive professional help. Each child needs the best opportunity to develop language because language is essential to healthy mental and social-emotional development.

13-8 Children must hear speech clearly to be able to learn how to talk.

Summary

As toddlers explore and learn more about the world, they discover many new ways to solve problems. Through their actions, they find out what and how things work. You can see children begin to think by the way they work through problems to reach goals. Their language development is a good indication of the way toddlers think. Vygotsky's theory would encourage adults to find a toddler's ZPD and then support the child's learning with objects, such as toys and books.

Language is one of the most difficult skills children must learn. Articulating sounds and learning meanings of words takes time and practice. The peak age of language development occurs between one and three years of age. Recent brain research supports this concept. Toddlers need many experiences in hearing words and sentences, especially from parents who use parentese. Children first use single words of familiar people, objects, and actions before joining words to form sentences.

A number of conditions can affect language development. These include hearing problems, interest in talking, and mental abilities. Girls tend to talk sooner than boys. Having a need for speech and an interesting environment also affect when and how toddlers learn to talk.

Companion Web Site

Interactive Activity

Review vocabulary terms and key concepts for Chapter 13 at **g-wlearning.com**.

Review and Reflect

Write your answers to the following questions on a separate sheet of paper.

1. True or false. Toddlers use past learnings and increased motor skills to help them learn.

2. True or false. Trying to see how something works helps toddlers develop intellectually.

3. According to Piaget's developmental stages, how is problem solving achieved?

4. Give one example of how adults can find a toddler's ZPD and one example of how to support his or her learning.

5. Give two reasons language development is one of the most difficult skills toddlers learn.

6. Describe what the term *articulation* means.

7. Replacing one sound with another sound, such as saying *wed wabbit* instead of *red rabbit*, is (common, uncommon) among toddlers.

8. True or false. Good language development is reinforced when adults repeat and encourage children's cute sayings, even when they are wrong.

9. In each of the following groups of words, which word would the toddler probably learn to say first? (A) happy or daddy; (B) bye-bye or empty; (C) kitty or pretty.

10. Describe three reasons children may be late talkers.

Cross-Curricular Link

11. **Writing.** Write a brief essay describing the toddler's learnings between 12 and 24 months. Check your essay for correct spelling, grammar, and punctuation.

12. **Writing.** Write a story from a toddler's point of view in which the language used shows typical toddler language development as described in the text. Share your story with the class.

13. **Speech.** Interview the parent of a toddler. Ask the parent to describe the toddler's language skills, providing examples. What words and sentences does the toddler use? Which words are commonly misused or mispronounced? Does the child demonstrate a larger passive vocabulary (words understood) or active vocabulary (words used)? In what ways does the parent encourage the child's language development? Has he or she ever tried any techniques that were unsuccessful? Share your findings with the class.

14. **Speech.** Work with a partner to role-play both positive and negative ways parents can respond to their toddler's language usage errors. Show how toddlers might react to each of these responses.

15. **Speech.** Interview a speech professional. Ask this person to explain both average language skills of a toddler and signs that professional assistance should be sought. Share your findings with the class in an oral report.

Making Observations

16. Observe a toddler playing with an object. Which senses did the toddler use? How did the toddler handle the object (shake, hit, or squeeze it)? What might the toddler have learned about the object (color, texture, rolls when dropped, soft when squeezed)?

17. Observe a toddler talking. List words the toddler says. Did the toddler seem to understand each word's meaning or incorrectly name some items? What type of words did the toddler mainly use (nouns, verbs, adjectives)?

18. Observe two or more toddlers of the same age. After listening to them talk, compare their vocabularies, articulation skills, and abilities to speak in sentences (versus words or phrases).

19. Observe a toddler exploring his or her world for 30 minutes. Record your observations. Especially note answers to the following questions: What senses were used? What activities interested the toddler most? How did the child try to solve problems? What were some possible learnings?

Thinking Critically

20. Parents often think their toddlers throw objects to see how often they will pick them up. Do you agree with this idea? Why or why not? What might a toddler learn from throwing objects?

21. Why is imitation an important mental skill? What things do toddlers learn by imitation? What are some things you have learned by imitation? Why is deferred imitation a more advanced mental ability than imitating while seeing an action performed?

14

Social-Emotional Development of the Toddler

After studying this chapter, you will be able to

★ **describe** how toddlers develop self-will.

★ **explain** the way toddlers extend their social relationships with others.

★ **describe** how toddlers develop a sense of self-worth.

★ **identify** how toddlers reveal their emotions.

Terms to Know

autonomy
self-esteem
temper tantrum

Reading Advantage

Make a list of everything you already know about the topic of this chapter. As you read the chapter, check off the items that are covered in the chapter.

Companion Web Site

Interactive Activity

Learn more about how toddlers express their emotions by completing the *Read, Discuss, and Analyze* Activity for Chapter 14 at **g-wlearning.com**.

Most babies begin life surrounded by people who meet all their needs. Babies' needs are rather simple, so caregivers can meet most of them promptly. When their needs are met and their environments are consistent, babies become attached to their caregivers. They then learn to trust their world.

As babies become toddlers, two changes happen. First, toddlers find out more about their world and themselves as individuals. Second, toddlers find the world is not solely devoted to meeting their needs. Toddlers learn that caregivers cannot always give them what they want right away, 14-1. However, if love and trust are established by the end of the first year, toddlers will reach out in this new world. They will learn about themselves and others.

Toddlers will begin to meet their needs without always depending on others. They will show emotions to others and learn how people respond to those emotions.

Self-Awareness

By the first birthday, toddlers have rather highly developed physical and mental skills. They can move around by themselves and reach objects they want. They are beginning to talk, which also helps them express their needs. These fast-growing skills influence the toddlers' relationships with others. In turn, others' reactions to them affect how toddlers see and understand themselves.

The self-awareness that begins to develop at birth continues to build throughout life. In the toddler

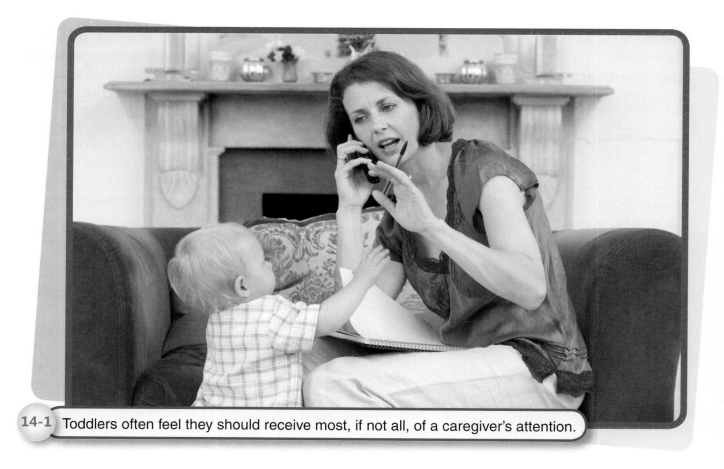

14-1 Toddlers often feel they should receive most, if not all, of a caregiver's attention.

years, self-awareness emerges as a separate, possessing self (concerned about *me* and *mine*) and as a drive for independence. Toddlers become aware of how they look, what belongs (and does not belong) to them, and what they can and cannot do (especially physically).

Toddlers are also becoming more aware of others' feelings toward them. They realize they can be praised, thwarted, and hurt emotionally by others whom they love. This lays the foundation for feelings about oneself, such as pride, shame, guilt, and jealousy. Toddlers are more often aware they can affect others, too. Thus, at times they show positive emotions, such as true affection for others. At other times, they show negative emotions, such as defiance when they are angry.

Achieving Autonomy

Erikson states that social-emotional development begins in infancy when the baby learns to trust or mistrust. As you read in Chapter 10, babies whose needs are met and who have consistent environments develop a sense of trust. This sense of trust helps them as they enter the second stage, called *autonomy versus shame and doubt*, 14-2. For most children, this stage begins sometime between 12 and 18 months and is completed at about 3 years of age.

Autonomy is a form of self-control in which a toddler seeks to do his or her own will. Autonomy builds on the toddler's expanding motor and mental skills. Toddlers are proud of their new skills and want to use them. They have the energy to carry out their goals. Because toddlers have much more

Erikson's Stages of Personality Development

Basic Trust versus Basic Mistrust (First Year of Life)

Autonomy versus Shame and Doubt (Second Year of Life)

★ Toddlers seek some autonomy so they can use their new skills and knowledge.
★ Toddlers seek control over whether to rely on others as they see fit.
★ Autonomy learned at this stage leads to self-pride.
★ Failure to achieve autonomy leads to feelings of shame in front of others and self-doubt.

Initiative versus Guilt (Preschool Years)

Industry versus Inferiority (Middle Childhood)

14-2 Learning to become more independent while avoiding shame and doubt is the social-emotional task of toddlerhood.

"know how" than infants, they feel very independent. The independent feeling comes from the toddlers' increasing self-awareness of their abilities. Thus, Erikson explains autonomy as the toddler's feeling of being able to do some tasks without help from others. He feels that caregivers should recognize toddlers' desire to be more independent and allow them to do what they can at their own pace.

Although toddlers want to be independent, they can misjudge their skills. They also do not understand possible results of some of their actions. For example, they can spill or break objects and harm themselves or others. Thus, adults must set limits on some of their actions. Toddlers often become defiant in response. Sometimes, toddlers find limits to their actions through their own failed attempts. This is most frustrating for them, too. Parents and their toddlers may also have conflicts when adults offer to help or take over tasks for toddlers. Because many of the toddler's activities center on routines, many of these conflicts concern eating, sleeping, toileting, and dressing.

During this stage, parents may wonder why a child turns negative and yells or kicks when told what to do. When limits need to be set or when things do not go the toddler's way, negative attitudes surface. At these times, toddlers need help to control their negative impulses. Calm controls are helpful and not damaging to the toddler. As you read in Chapter 3, Galinsky calls this parenting stage the *authority stage*.

On the other hand, Erikson says that when impatient caregivers do for toddlers what toddlers can do for themselves, damage occurs. Consistently criticizing or overprotecting toddlers leads them to feel they cannot control themselves and their world. Erikson calls this feeling a sense of shame and doubt.

Promoting a Toddler's Autonomy

Adults can promote autonomy by giving toddlers safe choices. Caregivers must find creative ways to build toddlers' feelings of independence and allow them to use their new skills. First choices offered should be simple, such as indoor play versus outdoor play. The toddler should be offered two alternatives and allowed to choose.

Before offering the toddler a choice, however, caregivers must be sure they can stand by either option chosen. If they fail to honor the child's choice or try to talk him or her out of it, this can be damaging. It undermines the toddler's sense of autonomy.

Caregivers should also step in and redirect a toddler before he or she engages in a forbidden or unsafe action. This is more helpful than waiting to intervene after the child is already performing the action. It is also more helpful than simply reacting to the consequences.

Extending Social Relations

As children get older, their growing motor and mental abilities help them interact with others more. These interactions teach them

Early Head Start Teacher

Early Head Start teachers work to promote healthy prenatal outcomes for pregnant women, enhance the development of very young children, and promote healthy family functioning. They work to prevent and detect developmental concerns at the earliest possible time.

Education: High school and a current preschool, center-based Child Development Associate Credential (CDA); or an associate, bachelors, or advanced degree related to early childhood education are most often required.

Job Outlook: Job prospects are expected to be favorable.

Learn More About...
Ways to Promote Autonomy in Toddlers

Adults may find it hard to help toddlers achieve autonomy while keeping them safe and preventing conflicts. Erikson feels adults should firmly reassure the toddler. They do not need to give in to the child's will all the time. However, when they confront a child, they should stay calm. Parents must also assure the child they still love him or her. This protects children from harm without making them feel ashamed or guilty. The following ways show how to help the toddler in this stage:

★ Make sure the indoor and outdoor environment are safe. This will help you avoid having to warn or threaten the toddler constantly.

★ Set some important limits for the toddler, but do not make everything off limits. Let the toddler know what is off-limits beforehand.

★ Follow through on limits set for the toddler by making sure the toddler does as told each time in these areas. Avoid inconsistent enforcement of limits.

★ Allow the toddler to make some minor decisions and abide by the toddler's choices on these matters. Avoid making all the toddler's decisions for the toddler.

★ Let the toddler make mistakes without scolding or being criticized. Avoid making demands that are too rigid for a toddler to follow or correcting the child for every mistake.

★ Give the toddler the freedom to play in safe places with safe playthings in his or her own way. Avoid directing or interfering with the toddler's safe play.

★ Praise the toddler for becoming more autonomous. Avoid mixing praise with criticism, however.

---

new skills and attitudes, which help toddlers get along with other people. This process of interacting with others socializes children.

Toddlers with a healthy attachment to caregivers have a safe base from which to meet people. Although toddlers continue to look to their main caregivers for social interaction, they now spend more time with other adults. These adults include babysitters, relatives, and neighbors. Having more than one caregiver often helps toddlers adjust to others. This also helps children to expect differences among people. When children have positive experiences with many adults, they develop trusting relationships with them.

Getting Along with Other Children

During the second year, toddlers tend to interact more with other children. Their first interactions are brief. They often imitate each other's actions with a toy. Later, they talk as they play.

Toddlers are possessive of their toys and belongings when they play. Between ages 30 and 36 months, toddlers become good at keeping their possessions by holding them firmly or retrieving them from others. Often toddlers are not quite ready to share all the time.

Some studies show that toddlers are not as self-centered as experts once thought. Toddlers can share sometimes. They may return a snatched toy if the owner cries. They praise other children and show concern for someone who is hurt. When toddlers have loving relationships with their caregivers, they seem better able to show concern for other children.

Self-Esteem

Children become more aware of themselves, especially as physical beings, as they approach the first birthday. They enjoy hearing their names and seeing themselves in mirrors. With the help of caring adults, children develop good feelings about themselves. Feeling good about yourself and what you can do is called **self-esteem**. People with a high level of self-esteem believe they are worthwhile people, 14-3.

14-3 When provided with a nurturing environment, toddlers learn to like themselves and feel good about what they can do.

As you read in Chapter 10, babies sense how others feel about them from the way they are spoken to and held. Toddlers must feel loved, even when they are difficult or make mistakes. If adults scold toddlers each time they do something wrong, toddlers will feel they are beyond being loved.

When toddlers feel good about themselves, they seem to admire themselves and their growing control over their bodies. They are confident and like to show off their physical feats for others. They will often clap for themselves and laugh with delight at their new skills.

Toddlers become more aware of their bodies and what their bodies can do. They can name some body parts. Toddlers also know they can see, hear, touch, taste, and smell, but may not know which body part controls each sense. (For example, they may not know that eyes are used for seeing). Toddlers seem to have little awareness of their own weight. Toddlers will run and thrust themselves on the laps of adults. They may also run and cling to standing adults, causing adults to lose their balance. They can feel pain, but do not always know where it is. Unless they can see a cut, scrape, or burn, they cannot tell someone where it hurts. A toddler with a throat infection may even deny having a sore throat. More advanced body concepts develop later.

Emotions

Toddlers' mental abilities seem to result in the following changes in emotions, which are different than those of adults or infants:

★ Toddlers react to more stimuli than infants. Toddlers know more people to love. They experience more things and people to fear, have more things to make them anxious, and find more to anger them.

★ Toddlers can better sense emotions in others. Toddlers can detect fear in adults. They may even sense something is wrong when adults are anxious. Toddlers respond to emotions in other children. They can imitate others' emotions, too.

★ Toddlers' motor skills allow them more physical responses. For example, they can run or hide when fearful, or they can hit or kick when angry. The toddler's ability to talk allows a verbal response. Even the single word *no* shows feelings.

★ Toddlers' abilities to imagine increase the number of negative emotions, such as fear of the dark and fear of monsters. Toddlers cannot totally separate what is real from what is pretend. Emotions caused by imagination are just as real as the feelings they may have when a prized toy is broken.

Affection

Toddlers are still attached to their caregivers. They express affection for their caregivers by wanting to be near them. They seek caregivers when faced with a strange situation. This attachment seems to help other aspects of social-emotional development.

This is because the love a toddler feels for caregivers extends to non-caregiving adults, children, and pets, 14-4.

Fear

Many fears that began during infancy are evident after the first birthday. Fears increase quickly after age two because toddlers know about more things to fear. They know of more objects and situations that can hurt them. They can also imagine things that do not exist, such as monsters. Toddlers may also fear animals, darkness, nightmares, "bad people," injury, gestures, and startling noises.

Instead of talking about their fears, toddlers tend to act them out in play. It is common to see a two-and-a-half-year-old who fears

14-4 Toddlers begin to show affection for beloved toys as well as people and pets.

dogs barking and growling in play. Toddlers may imitate bad people seen on television or in books. Adults should handle these fears in a matter-of-fact way. Never tease toddlers about their fears or push them into scary situations.

Anxiety

Most two-year-olds show less separation anxiety than younger children. Some separation anxiety continues into the toddler stage and sometimes beyond, 14-5. Many toddlers overcome some of their separation anxiety if they feel a caregiver's love and know the caregiver will return. Increased language skills help toddlers understand why parents sometimes leave. Parents must make sure their toddler receives good and loving care during separations.

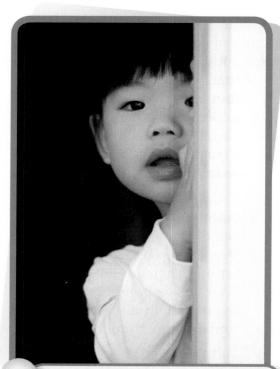

14-5 Being separated from caring adults still causes anxiety in the toddler.

Focus on Science
Brain Development

To decrease toddlers' fears, adults may want to keep them from watching too much TV. The American Academy of Pediatrics advises parents to avoid TV viewing for children younger than two years. For children two years and older, parents are advised to limit TV viewing to two hours or less daily. This is especially important because brain development is rapidly occurring during the early years of a child's life. Watching too much TV can cause children to fear that the world is scary and people are bad. As a result, children may be less willing to explore their surroundings. In addition, when children are watching TV, they are inactive and not interacting with others. This detracts from a child's physical, intellectual, and social-emotional development. In what ways do you think too much TV is harmful to children?

Nightmares may begin around two years of age. Nightmares may stem from fear of being left alone, getting hurt, or angering adults. The details of the nightmare are unreal, often including unknown lands and monsters. If toddlers are content during the day, nightmares do not reveal a problem. These bad dreams are a way of dealing with anxiety. For most children, nightmares decrease in time. A trip to the library or bookstore may result in some humorous books to help the child deal with nightmares.

Anger

Toddlers desire more independence and have a strong will. When thwarted in their goal-seeking behaviors, toddlers react with anger. Sudden emotional outbursts of anger, called **temper tantrums**, often appear during the second year of life. The child may lie on the floor, kick, and scream. Tantrums tend to happen when something does not go a toddler's way. Because this is often the case, temper tantrums are common for toddlers.

Temper tantrums are meant to attract attention. Often they are not directed at anyone. Because tantrums are done to seek attention, ignoring the toddler may cause him or her to stop. After the tantrum is over, give the toddler love and reassurance. More ideas for handling tantrums are given in Chapter 15. Remember that a child's anger is not purposefully directed toward others until the child is three years old.

Summary

The second period of social-emotional development begins when children develop wills of their own. Erikson called this period *autonomy versus shame and doubt.* During this time, toddlers become independent. They do not always understand the dangers their actions may cause. Because of this, many conflicts with caregivers occur.

Toddlers begin to interact with others besides their parents and caregivers. Through socialization, they learn to get along with others. Having positive experiences with others helps them develop trusting relationships. Toddlers' interactions with other children are brief. They often imitate each other before they interact by talking. Toddlers are possessive of their toys and belongings, but can show concern for others, too.

The good feeling children develop about themselves is called *self-esteem.* Toddlers are becoming aware of their bodies, but cannot always tell adults where they feel pain.

Toddlers experience a wider range of emotions than infants. They are still attached to their caregivers, but are also beginning to show affection for others. Fears tend to intensify during this period, including the fear of the unreal, such as monsters. Being separated from parents continues to make toddlers anxious. Nightmares are a way toddlers often deal with their anxieties. Anger occurs when events do not go how the toddler wants. These frustrations often result in temper tantrums. Ignoring tantrums may make them end sooner.

Companion Web Site

Interactive Activity

Review vocabulary terms and key concepts for Chapter 14 at **g-wlearning.com**.

Review and Reflect

Write your answers to the following questions on a separate sheet of paper.

1. True or false. Toddlers find their world is solely devoted to meeting their needs.

2. True or false. Adults' reactions to toddlers affect how toddlers feel about themselves.

3. True or false. *Autonomy* means being able to do some things without the help of others.

4. Identify the correct statement. (A) Autonomy often happens during new activities. (B) Autonomy often involves trying to work beyond the ability level.

5. List three ways adults can help the toddler develop autonomy rather than shame and doubt.

6. True or false. Adjusting to others is easier if the child has only one main caregiver, such as the mother.

7. Which of the following does *not* promote social development? (A) insisting that toddlers play alone more; (B) often spending time with others.

8. Shaming toddlers for their mistakes _____ (does, does not) affect their self-esteem.

9. Toddlers' sense of self-esteem is centered on their awareness of their _____ (physical, mental) abilities.

10. What four general changes in emotion occur during the toddler stage?

11. List three fears common to toddlers.

12. How should adults react to toddlers' temper tantrums?

Cross-Curricular Link

13. **Speech.** Toddlers often admire themselves in mirrors and enjoy their new abilities. In small groups, discuss how adults admire themselves and whether self-admiration is good when expressed by older children and adults.

14. **Writing.** Some people refer to the toddler years as the "terrible twos." Write an essay explaining why people use this term to describe toddlers. Also discuss why this term is incorrect. Check your essay for correct spelling, grammar, and punctuation.

15. **Reading and Social Studies.** Use the dictionary to find the definitions of the terms *autonomy*, *shame*, and *doubt*. List common situations that toddlers might experience. Identify whether each experience promotes autonomy or shame and doubt. Compare your list to that of a classmate.

16. **Reading and Writing.** Read three children's books that relate to the social and

emotional development of toddlers. List the title, author, publisher, and copyright date of each book. Then, write a paragraph describing the message of each book. Conclude the paragraph with your opinion of the book. Check your paper for correct spelling, grammar, and punctuation.

17. **Speech.** Work with a partner to role-play a situation in which a toddler fears the dark and monsters in the closet. Take turns playing the toddler and the parent coping with the toddler's fears. Discuss the role-play in class.

Making Observations

18. Observe two or three toddlers of the same age. How do they show their attachments to several people? How do the strengths of these attachments differ for a parent versus a babysitter?

19. Observe several toddlers playing together. Are they possessive about toys? How do they reclaim a special toy from another child? How do they react when a toy is reclaimed from them? How do adults settle toddlers' disputes?

20. Observe several toddlers playing. Describe actions that would show self-esteem. Describe actions that would show the toddler does not feel good about him- or herself. What did the adults do to promote positive self-esteem in toddlers?

21. Observe toddlers in a group care situation. How do the toddlers try to achieve their goals? How is the adult showing authority? How do the toddlers react to this authority?

22. Observe a toddler showing affection, fear, anxiety, or anger. What seemed to trigger the emotion? Compare what you noted with your text.

Thinking Critically

23. A conflict of wills between children and adults often occurs during routine care times such as meals and dressing. How much freedom should parents give toddlers? How much permissiveness might result in spoiled babies?

24. Why is it impossible to explain to toddlers that monsters and other unreal creatures exist only in their dreams or minds?

25. What are various means people use to seek attention? Why do toddlers use temper tantrums to get attention rather than other means?

15 Providing for the Toddler's Developmental Needs

After studying this chapter, you will be able to

★ **plan** ways to meet toddlers' physical needs.

★ **stimulate** toddlers' growing mental abilities.

★ **help** toddlers adjust to their first social controls.

Terms to Know

food allergy
registered dietitians
MyPyramid
ritual
toilet learning
regression
training pants

spatial
transitional stage
self-restraint
self-assertion
obedience
contrariness

Reading Advantage

As you read the chapter, record any questions that come to mind. Indicate where the answer to the question can be found: within the text, by asking your teacher, in another book, on the Internet, or by reflecting on your own experiences. Pursue the answers to your questions.

Companion Web Site

Interactive Activity

Learn more about how to help toddlers control their emotions by completing the *Read, Discuss, and Analyze* Activity for Chapter 15 at **g-wlearning.com**.

Children continue to develop quickly between their first and third birthdays. Toddlers still depend on adults to provide for their needs. During these years, however, toddlers begin learning some self-care skills, such as self-feeding, self-dressing, and toileting. They will even help with washing their hands and bathing.

At this age, intellectual abilities seem to blossom. Toddlers learn to use language to talk with others and help them think. They learn many concepts through daily routines at home and then practice these concepts in play.

Toddlers have many social-emotional needs. They try to do tasks on their own, but they find some too hard for their immature bodies and minds. Toddlers need loving adults who understand their wills. Adults need to allow some freedom. They need to praise toddlers when they master a new skill. They need to help toddlers when they cannot manage a task.

This chapter will give examples of ways to assist toddlers' development. Adults need to help toddlers begin to think independently and practice self-care. They need to help children find a balance between their own will and the limits to self-will society expects.

Physical Needs

Caregivers must meet toddlers' physical needs to keep them healthy and safe. Meeting physical needs also keeps toddlers mentally and socially fit. To meet toddlers' physical needs, adults must make sure toddlers are fed, clothed, cleaned, and rested. Adults must also guide toddlers' self-care skills, such as self-feeding, self-cleaning, and toileting. As toddlers learn self-care skills, they can meet their physical needs. Self-care skills also help toddlers advance in intellectual and social-emotional development.

Feeding

During the toddler years, the eating experience changes. Toddlers graduate from a bottle and baby foods to a cup and *table foods* (foods prepared for the entire family). They begin to feed themselves. In addition, toddlers often join the family for meals instead of eating at other times.

Focus on Health

Preparing Table Foods for Toddlers

In preparing table foods for toddlers, parents can use the following helpful hints. What other hints can you add to this list?

★ Avoid adding salt, sugar, or spices to the food served to toddlers. (Parents can separate the toddler's serving from the dish before adding these for other family members.)

★ Cook and refrigerate all foods properly.

★ Continue to introduce new foods at five-day intervals to check for allergies and intolerances.

★ Mash foods or cut them into bite-sized pieces for the toddler.

★ Offer the toddler six offerings of food (meals and snacks) per day using a toddler-sized plate to avoid overwhelming the toddler with too much food.

The Eating Style of Toddlers

The toddler's appetite decreases as the physical rate of growth slows. Infants usually gain about 15 pounds in the first year. In contrast, toddlers gain only about 11 pounds in two years. The energy needs of toddlers are incredibly high, however.

Typically, toddlers are picky eaters. They develop definite food likes and dislikes, just as they do about most things in their world. For example, they may settle on a diet of only a few foods for days or even weeks. Being assertive about foods and eating is part of what it means to be a toddler.

Toddlers' eating patterns are not at all like those of adults. In fact, toddlers seem to have odd eating habits. Erratic eating habits are as normal as toddler mood swings. They may skip a meal or two and then eat as though they are starved a few hours later. These busy explorers often do not like to sit down to a feast. They prefer to eat on the go. Although these habits may concern the adult, the habits should not harm the child. Most toddlers who are offered nutritious meals and snacks will eat enough over time to meet their food needs.

Most toddlers want to feed themselves (*self-feed*), 15-1. They want to control their own eating. Toddlers can pick up food with fingers and learn to use a spoon. However, a toddler's fine-motor skills are not mature. Therefore, playing with food—including smearing it on the wall or dropping it on the floor—is part of self-feeding.

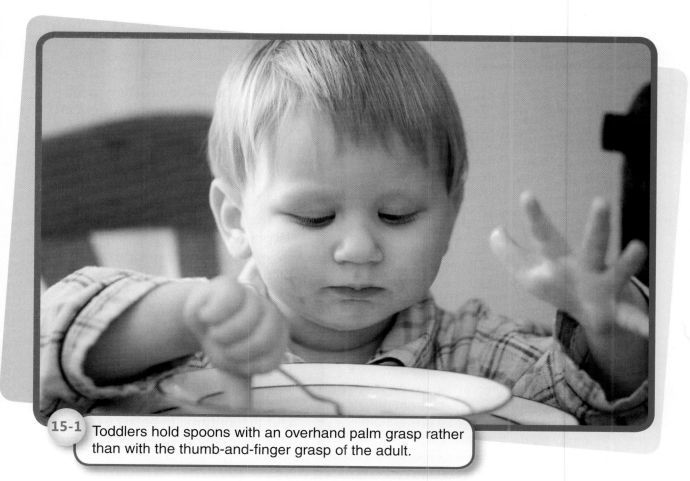

15-1 Toddlers hold spoons with an overhand palm grasp rather than with the thumb-and-finger grasp of the adult.

When mishaps occur, parents must remember the toddler is not being naughty. He or she is learning about the texture, color, and qualities of food. Self-feeding also helps the toddler show independence. It boosts the toddler's self-esteem, too.

Providing for Toddlers' Food Needs

Food intake should always meet a child's nutritional needs. Toddlers eat smaller amounts of food than infants or adults. Adults must give toddlers nutritious foods. These foods are needed for the body's growth and repair. Foods that are high in calories and low in nutrients should be avoided. (These foods are said to contain *empty calories* because they are not nutritious.) Eating too much of these foods may cause the child to gain too much weight now or in the future.

The toddler's pediatrician often makes food recommendations based on height and weight of the toddler, as well as other factors. These factors include history of weight gain, physical activity level, anemia, illnesses, and food intolerances and allergies. A **food allergy** is an abnormal response to a food that is triggered by the body's immune system. Allergic reactions can be very severe, sometimes causing serious illness or even death. The most common foods that are responsible for a large percentage of food allergies include milk, eggs, peanuts, fish, crustacean shellfish, wheat, soybeans, and tree nuts. All food labels are required to list the presence of these eight ingredients. For children who have special food needs, a physician or registered dietitian should plan the child's diet. **Registered dietitians** have special training in nutrition and diet. They meet the qualifications of the American Dietetic Association (ADA).

Providing for the Needs of One- to Two-Year-Olds

As you read in Chapter 11, by the time infants weigh about 15 pounds, they begin to need more nutrition than is provided by breast milk or formula. Solids are called *complementary foods* because they provide the nutrients needed in addition to formula or breast milk. During infancy, the number of calories received from complementary foods is rather low.

From 12 to 24 months, toddlers should continue to breast feed or start drinking whole cow's milk.

Registered Dietitian

Registered dietitians plan food and nutrition programs, supervise meal preparation, and oversee the serving of meals. They prevent and treat illnesses by promoting healthy eating habits and recommending dietary modifications.

Education: A bachelor's degree in dietetics, foods and nutrition, or a related area is usually required. Graduate degrees are also available. The Commission on Dietetic Registration of the American Dietetic Association awards the Registered Dietitian credential to those who pass an exam after completing coursework and an internship.

Job Outlook: Average employment growth is projected. Job growth will result from an increasing emphasis on disease prevention through improved dietary habits.

(Toddler formulas or reduced fat cow's milk are usually not recommended until after two years of age.) Toddler's daily caloric intake varies depending on age, size, and activity level. Complementary foods should provide about half of the calories consumed.

Toddlers should have about two cups of whole milk each day. Toddlers should not be given fruit juices or drinks in place of milk. This is because these drinks do not provide the calcium and other minerals toddlers need for proper bone growth and ossification. In addition to milk, calcium-rich foods (such as yogurt or cheese) can be offered as part of meals and snacks.

Between one and two years of age, a toddler's diet is transitioning. Parents may have difficulty determining their toddler's varying food needs. It is important that parents always follow their toddler's cues for fullness and hunger. Parents should let toddlers eat a variety of nutritious foods until they are full. The exception to this recommendation would be if a toddler has a health concern that merits a special planned diet.

To better help parents meet their young toddler's nutritional needs, the ADA recently worked with Gerber® Products Company to develop a "Start Healthy" program. This program provides nutritional guides and menu plans to meet the toddler's needs, as well as feeding advice from experts.

You can learn more about how to meet the nutritional needs of one- to two-year-olds by visiting the "Start Healthy" Web site at **www.gerber.com/starthealthy**.

Meeting Nutritional Needs of Older Toddlers

Older toddlers (those who are two to three years old) can follow the **MyPyramid** food guidance system in order to determine their nutritional needs. The United States Department of Agriculture (USDA) designed this system to help people make more healthful food and physical activity choices.

By going to the Web site at **MyPyramid.gov**, you can create a personalized eating plan based on a person's age, sex, and activity level. After you enter this data, a daily food intake plan is created, 15-2. It indicates what and how much the person needs to eat.

MyPyramid has five major food groups. Fats are also included, but foods in this category should be eaten in limited amounts. The following groups are included in the MyPyramid plan:

★ **Grain Group.** This group includes breads, cereals, rice, and pasta. These foods provide carbohydrates (starches), which are a good source of energy and fiber. They also provide many needed vitamins and minerals.

★ **Vegetable Group.** Foods in this group provide vitamins, folate, minerals, and fiber.

★ **Fruit Group.** Fruits and fruit juices provide needed amounts of potassium and vitamins A and C. The American Academy of Pediatrics advises no more than one of these servings should come from fruit juice. This is because the actual fruits are more nutritious and less likely to cause dental caries than fruit juice.

MyPyramid
STEPS TO A HEALTHIER YOU

Based on the information you provided, this is your daily recommended amount from each food group.

GRAINS 3 ounces	VEGETABLES 1 cup	FRUITS 1 cup	MILK 2 cups	MEAT & BEANS 2 ounces
Make half your grains whole Aim for at least **1½ ounces** of whole grains a day	**Vary your veggies** Aim for these amounts **each week**: **Dark green veggies** = 1 cup **Orange veggies** = ½ cup **Dry beans & peas** = ½ cup **Starchy veggies** = 1½ cups **Other veggies** = 4 cups	**Focus on fruits** Eat a variety of fruit Go easy on fruit juices	**Get your calcium-rich foods** Go low-fat or fat-free when you choose milk, yogurt, or cheese	**Go lean with protein** Choose low-fat or lean meats and poultry Vary your protein routine—choose more fish, beans, peas, nuts, and seeds

Find your balance between food and physical activity Be physically active for at least **60 minutes** every day, or most days.	**Know your limits on fats, sugars, and sodium** Your allowance for oils is **3 teaspoons a day**. Limit extras–solid fats and sugars–to **165 calories a day**.

Your results are based on a 1000 calorie pattern   Name: _____

This calorie level is only an estimate of your needs. Monitor your body weight to see if you need to adjust your calorie intake.

15-2 For good health, a two-year-old needs physical activity as well as these recommended amounts from each food group of the MyPyramid every day.

★ **Milk Group.** Foods in the milk group provide protein, vitamins, and minerals.

★ **Meat and Beans Group.** This group includes meat, poultry, fish, dry beans, eggs, and nuts. (Nuts, however, are a choking hazard, and are not recommended for this age group.) Meat, poultry, and fish provide protein, B vitamins, iron, and zinc. Dry beans and eggs provide protein, vitamins, and minerals.

★ **Oils.** Oils are fats that are liquid at room temperature, like the vegetable oils used in cooking. Foods that are mainly oil include mayonnaise, certain salad dressings, and soft (tub or squeeze) margarine. Because oils contain essential fatty acids, there is an allowance for oils in the food guide.

The USDA recommends offering smaller serving sizes to two- and three-year olds. This might be one-half to two-thirds the full serving size. Regardless of the amount offered, an older toddler will likely eat as much as he or she wants and play with the rest.

Preventing Feeding Problems

Toddlers need to be carefully watched while they are eating; they can easily choke on foods. Toddlers should sit or stand still while eating. They should not crawl, creep, walk, or run while eating. The ADA recommends that parents avoid certain foods that are choking hazards for this age group. These foods include the following: popcorn; grapes; raisins; nuts; spoonfuls of peanut butter; hot dogs; small, hard candies; and chunks of raw carrot. Softer raw foods may be safer in larger pieces than in finely chopped pieces because they are easier for the older toddler to hold.

Sometimes toddlers develop feeding problems. Most problems stem from the toddler's stage of development—the slowing growth,

improving motor and learning skills, and changing social needs. See 15-3 for some common feeding problems and suggestions to solve them. Toddlers work out most feeding problems in time with the help of patient adults.

Clothing

Choosing the right clothes and shoes for toddlers is important. Proper clothing helps toddlers stay active, comfortable, and safe. It also stands the strain of constant movement and messy play.

Choosing Garments

Although toddlers grow more slowly than infants, they still outgrow their clothes quickly. Fit is important for the toddler. Clothes that are too tight will bind and restrict movement. Clothes that are too loose will be uncomfortable and perhaps unsafe. To check for fit, let toddlers try on garments.

When it is not possible for the toddler to try on the garment, parents have to choose the garment based on size alone. Sizing can be confusing. Some companies use descriptive terms, such as *small*, *medium*, and *large* as their sizes. Other companies set sizes by age, such as *18 mo. (1T)*, *24 mo. (2T)*, *3T*, and *4T*. The most accurate sizing method is the weight range or weight and height ranges. A few companies provide more than one type of sizing on their labels for easy comparison. Sizes vary from one company to the next, but an example is provided in 15-4.

Quality features include safety, comfortable fabric and construction, growth features, durability, attractive style, and easy care.

Feeding Problems of Toddlers

Problem—A toddler refuses to eat a meal or takes only a few bites.

Possible solutions—

★ Keep records of all the foods the toddler eats during the week. (The toddler may be getting enough of the needed foods.)

★ Break meals up by offering part of the meal early and the rest of the meal in two or three hours.

★ Make snacks high in nutritional quality.

★ Eat foods of high nutritional quality. Toddlers imitate adult food habits.

★ Serve small portions and let the toddler ask for seconds. Too much food can be discouraging.

★ Make mealtime pleasant even when the toddler refuses to eat.

Problem—A toddler refuses to eat new foods.

Possible solutions—

★ Offer a taste or two of new foods on a regular basis to help the toddler to accept them over time.

★ Offer only one new food at a time.

★ Serve a taste or two of a new food on a plate that also has favorite foods.

★ Model proper food attitudes for toddlers. Saying, "Eat your spinach, it's good for you," may give the toddler the idea that spinach is a must, but not good tasting.

★ Try a new way of preparing foods. For example, toddlers usually like simple foods more than mixtures (casseroles). Toddlers prefer finger foods to foods eaten with flatware. They like less salty and spicy foods more than highly seasoned foods.

★ Remain pleasant with the toddler. Force-feeding and anger do not work.

Problem—A toddler shows lack of self-feeding skills and plays with food.

Possible Solutions—

★ Give the toddler time to learn how to self-feed. (Most children cannot hold flatware in the mature way until five years of age or older.)

★ Provide a comfortable setting for eating. The correct chair provides support (so the child is not sliding down), is the correct height, and has a place for feet to touch rather than dangle.

★ Provide suitable eating equipment, such as small plates (especially those with sides), small cups (perhaps with handles or spill proof features), and baby or junior flatware (or small spoons and salad forks).

★ Use a high chair or table and chair that can be cleaned easily. (Nearby floor and walls should also be easily cleaned.)

★ Keep cleaning supplies handy during meals.

★ When possible, prepare foods in easy to manage form, such as finger foods. (Runny foods, foods that must be cut, and foods that are hard to pick up will be messy for the toddler.)

★ Praise the toddler for successes. Never laugh at mishaps.

★ Prevent playing with food by staying near the toddler during eating time and removing food once the toddler is playing more than eating.

★ Be firm in saying *no* when the toddler goes too far with playing. You may even say, "Balls are for throwing; food is for eating," or "I want the kitchen to stay clean; food on the floor is messy." If the toddler does not control the play, remove the food or the toddler. (Toddlers learn quickly when eating rules are fair and consistently enforced.)

15-3 Feeding problems are common for toddlers.

Toddler Clothing Sizes

Size	Height	Weight
18 mo./1T	30¾ to 32 inches	22 to 24 pounds
24 mo./2T	32½ to 35½ inches	24½ to 28 pounds
3T	36 to 38½ inches	28½ to 32 pounds
4T	39 to 41 inches	32½ to 36 pounds
5T	41½ to 43 inches	36½ to 41 pounds

15-4　When they are given, height and weight ranges provide more accurate sizing than a size based on age alone.

See 15-5 for some examples of each of these features.

Some adults consider self-dressing features when choosing a toddler's clothes. Such features make dressing and undressing without help easier. However, toddlers are better at taking clothes off than putting them on. By 18 months, toddlers will help by extending arms and legs while being dressed. They will also unzip zippers and remove mittens, hats, socks, and untie shoes. A few items are designed to teach self-dressing to children under three. Adults should accept self-dressing efforts of the toddler even if the results are incorrect.

Some self-dressing features are critical when toddlers begin toilet learning. Toddlers must be able to remove clothing very quickly to avoid toileting accidents. Teachers of toddlers in group settings often request no jumpsuits, overalls, or belts. Difficult clothing fasteners are also a problem. The best clothes are elastic-waist pants or shorts. Parents, too, will find this type of clothing the most workable.

Fitting Shoes

Because the bones and muscles of the foot are developing, shoe fit is important for proper growth and comfort. Shoes that fit improperly can cause permanent damage to the child's feet. Toddlers often outgrow their shoes before they wear them out. The average rate of foot growth for toddlers is one shoe size every three to four months.

The toddler has flat feet because the arch is relaxed. This flat-footed look disappears around age three years. Going barefooted or wearing socks without shoes is good for the development of the arch. Shoes, even high-top shoes, do not provide support. Parents often choose high-top shoes because they are more difficult for the toddler to remove.

Toddlers need shoes to protect their feet from cold, dampness, and harmful objects. Shoes that fit properly have ½ inch of space between the large toe and shoe when the toddler stands. They also have a flexible sole and snug-fitting heel. Except for rain or snow boots worn over shoes, new shoes are recommended over hand-me-downs. Each foot is

Important Features in Toddler Clothes

Safety

★ Fire retardant (will burn, but smolders slowly rather than flaming when on fire)
★ No drawstrings or loose buttons, fasteners, or trim
★ Belts, ties, and sashes fastened to the garment securely to prevent tripping, choking, or strangling
★ Bright-colored clothing (increases ability to see toddlers)

Comfort

★ Made of lightweight and absorbent fabrics
★ Made of stretch fabrics
★ Elastic encased or nonbinding
★ Fullness in pant legs to permit knee bending and stooping with ease
★ Collars and sleeves that do not rub or bind
★ Coats, sweaters, and jackets that can fit over clothes without binding
★ Underwear that is not binding
★ Neck openings large enough for ease of dressing

Growth Features

★ Made of stretch fabrics
★ Dresses without definite waistlines
★ Pants and skirts with elastic or adjustable waistbands
★ Adjustable shoulder straps
★ Clothes with deep hems, large seams, and pleats or tucks that can be easily let out
★ Two-piece outfits

Quality Construction

★ Reinforcement at points of strain such as seams, knees, pockets, and pocket edges
★ Stitches that are even and not too long
★ Seams that are flat, smooth, and finished
★ Securely attached fasteners and trims
★ Built-in growth features, such as deep hems
★ Patterns are matched at seams

Easy Care

★ Washable (especially machine washable with other colors)
★ Little or no ironing needed
★ Easy to mend

15-5 Toddlers' clothes need to have certain features.

shaped differently. With even a little wear, shoes conform to a person's foot.

Rest and Sleep

Toddlers often sleep fewer hours and take fewer naps than babies. Chart 15-6 shows the general trend in sleep patterns. The sleep needs of toddlers vary. Toddlers may sleep less when under stress and more than average when recovering from an illness.

How much sleep does a toddler need? Parents should not use age

Average Sleep of Toddlers

Age	Night	Naps
9 to 12 months	12 to 14 hours	1 to 4 hours, morning and afternoon
13 to 30 months	10 to 12 hours	1 to 3 hours, afternoon
31 to 36 months	10 to 15 hours	Naps beginning to disappear*

*Two-thirds of two-year-olds take a nap; 10 percent of three-year-olds take a nap.

15-6 A toddler's sleep needs change over time.

to figure this. Instead, they should awaken toddlers at the same time each morning for about a week and then note when they become sleepy. The amount of time between the average "sleepy time" and the same waking time is close to the amount of sleep needed.

Toddlers are more likely than babies to resist rest and sleep, even when they are tired. Bedtime problems stem partly from the toddlers' struggle for autonomy. Often adults become physically tired from coping with toddlers who resist sleep. Adults may even feel stress if bedtime becomes a battle of wills. These ideas may help solve problems.

★ Accept that adults cannot force toddlers to sleep. Resistance often disappears after the toddler years.

★ Have a definite hour for bedtime. Use a neutral sign, such as a clock (not a person), to signal the hour.

★ Set a bedtime **ritual** or routine. The ritual should last about an hour a night. Include only restful activities, such as a warm bath, drink of water, story, song, and hug. Naptime rituals can be developed, too.

★ Provide a comfortable place for sleep.

★ Tell toddlers who do not want to sleep they do not have to sleep, only stay in bed. Toddlers usually accept this.

★ Comfort fearful toddlers. Tell them where you will be while they sleep. Provide a night-light in their room. Place a stuffed animal in their bed. Tell fearful toddlers you are there to keep them safe and will check on them every 10 to 15 minutes. (Toddlers are often asleep after two or three check times.)

★ Comfort toddlers who awaken with nightmares. Do not ask them to tell you about their nightmares. It is best to forget them. (If they want to tell you about their nightmares, listen. Assure them these are just bad dreams.)

★ When children get up, return them to bed. Meet any real needs, such as a drink for a child who is thirsty, but turn down nonessential requests. Be firm, but calm.

★ Keep the child away from active areas, such as where others are watching TV or talking.

Adults' actions will determine whether toddlers learn the tricks to get what they want or learn that adults will insist on their staying in bed. Learning to stay in bed helps toddlers get their needed rest. Adults also need time to meet their own needs, too.

Hygiene

One of the most important parts of hygiene for toddlers is bathing. Bathing is fun for most toddlers. Although toddlers can sit and stand easily, they are not safe when left alone while bathing, 15-7. Young

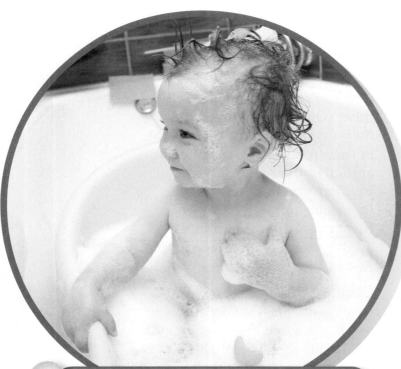

15-7 Keeping children safe in the tub is extremely important. A secure toddler usually enjoys bathing and splashing in the water.

toddlers may feel more secure being bathed in a child's tub. This tub can be placed inside the regular bathtub for easy bathing and less messy splashing. Other parents find their toddlers enjoy special bathtub seats designed for toddlers.

Toddlers may want to help bathe themselves. A bath mitt is the easiest for them to use. Most toddlers have fun trying to hold slippery soap. Some toddlers enjoy rinsing themselves with a handheld shower.

Water Play

Toddlers also need some time for water play during baths. They have fun playing in water and learn a great deal, too. From playing in the bathtub, toddlers can learn that

★ some toys float and some sink

★ water power can push toys

★ water can be held for a brief time in the cupped hand

★ water makes all things wet

★ they can make water splash, squirt, and drip

★ the bottom of the tub can be seen through water

★ soap makes bubbles

Many bath toys are sold for toddlers. Toys can be made easily from household objects, too.

Dental Care

Dental care is also important for toddlers. Many dentists recommend a first dental checkup by two years of age. Eating nutritious foods helps teeth stay healthy. However, cleaning teeth regularly is also needed. When the toddler is about 18 months of age, a caregiver can brush the toddler's teeth with a child-sized brush, 15-8. At this age, brushing can replace wiping the teeth. The toddler may begin to "help" brush his or her teeth around 30 months of age. (Adults should supervise and assist with brushing throughout the preschool years.)

Toilet Learning

Toilet learning is one of the most discussed aspects of the toddler years. **Toilet learning** is the process by which adults help children control their excretory systems, namely bowel movements and urination. Over the years, adults have tried to help children at different ages. They have tried helping children early—before age one. Adults have let the child choose when to learn. They have also tried every age between these extremes.

Experts have found that two things are certain in toilet learning.

First, the timing of learning varies from toddler to toddler. Second, many toddlers do not complete the learning process quickly. Learning may take most of the toddler years and perhaps even longer to complete.

Procedure for Toilet Learning

Caregivers have tried many methods for toilet learning. Although many work, certain proven ideas help the toilet learning process. Adults should realize that toilet learning is not a one-way street. Toilet learning is something adults do *with* a child. Adults cannot do the learning for the toddler. The toddler must be ready.

Toddlers are ready to learn at different ages. Many toddlers are ready to start toilet learning around two years of age. Age three years is often a difficult time to begin for there is a brief, but intense stage of **regression** (going back to an

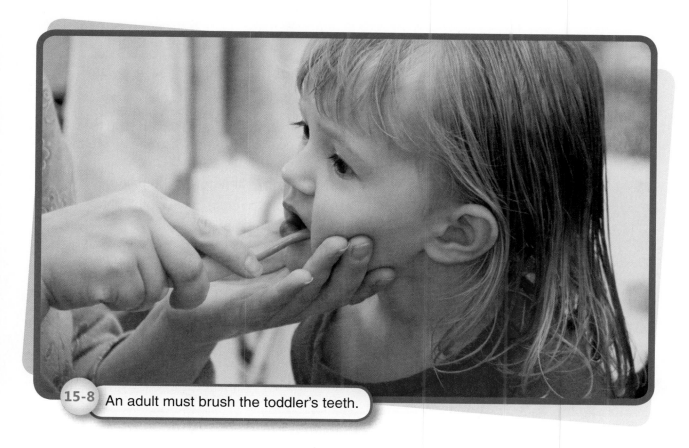

15-8 An adult must brush the toddler's teeth.

earlier stage) in the child's desire to be independent. A toddler should not begin toilet learning during periods of family or child stress. Furthermore, adults should also accept that toddlers vary in age of complete control. The average age for complete day control is 28 months, but the normal range varies greatly. No relationship exists between being a smart child and learning to use the toilet early. A rule of thumb is that a child must be able to stay dry two or more hours before he or she can begin to learn.

If the toddler is in a group program, toilet learning must be a team effort—child, family, and caregivers. A constant exchange of information between the home and the program is needed. Child care programs are often good places for toilet learning. This is due to the experience of the staff, child-sized bathrooms, and the program focus on helping children develop competence in self-care.

Even before toddlers are ready for toilet learning, adults can help them see what is expected. If an adult notes the child is eliminating, he or she should say something to make the child aware of it. When a diaper gets wet or soiled, the adult should say to the child as he or she changes the diaper, "Try to tell me next time, that way we can use the toilet."

When the Toddler Is Ready

When the toddler is ready for toilet learning, caregivers should borrow or buy a child-sized potty

Learn More About...
Physical and Emotional Factors of Toilet Learning

Toilet learning involves factors like physical development, motor skills, and emotional readiness. The physical and motor skills include the ability to

★ feel a full bowel and bladder. Until about 15 months, children move their bowels and pass urine without knowing in advance or realizing they have done so. Today's disposable diapers and disposable pull-up pants do not help with the feeling of wetness because they are designed to keep the skin drier.

★ know what the sensation of needing to eliminate means in time to get to the potty.

★ control muscles used for holding in or letting go. These muscles, which are low in the body, are among the last to develop. (This is a good example of the head-to-tail or cephalocaudal development principle.) Nerves can control these muscles around 18 months of age. Children tend to learn to control bowel movements before they learn to control their bladders.

★ walk (or often run) to the potty.

★ remove or push down clothes as discussed earlier.

For toilet learning to work, emotional readiness must occur at the same time the child is physically developed. Toddlers must see the need to use the potty. Busy toddlers often do not want to sit the needed time. Saying *no* to using the toilet is part of the self-will toddlers want to express. Toddlers may also need to master fears of falling in, the flushing water, and even the stools passed.

for him or her. Toddlers find regular toilets difficult to use and sometimes scary. A potty designed for toddlers is the easiest to use.

"Chairs" or potty rings that fit on standard toilet seats are also made for toddlers, 15-9. Potty rings have some advantages over potty chairs that are placed on the floor. The rings can be carried to places that do not have child-sized toilets. They are also more sanitary and do not require cleaning after each use. Because the ring is placed on the toilet seat, it eliminates the extra step of learning to use the regular toilet after using the potty chair.

When standard toilets are used (with or without toddler seats), toddlers will need help. Getting on the standard toilet is difficult for a toddler. Also, his or her legs can hurt after dangling for even a few minutes. Parents or caregivers can build a simple wooden platform for use in front of the toilet. This is easy for the toddler to climb onto and turn around before sitting. It can be pulled away after use or for cleaning. If a platform is not used, adults should choose a step stool with a wide base that is sturdy and will not tip.

Show the child the potty he or she will use. Some toddlers want to sit on the potty first with their clothes on to check it out. Bathroom light switches should be easy to reach. You may also want to use a night-light in the bathroom.

Easy-to-manage clothing is crucial. Many adults wait until warm weather to start the toilet learning process because toddlers can wear fewer clothes. They can also wear elastic-waist shorts or pants, which are easy to manage.

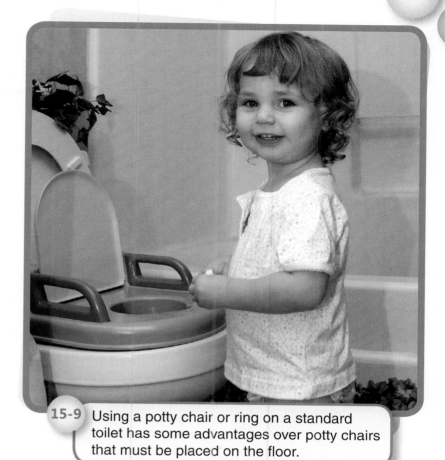

15-9 Using a potty chair or ring on a standard toilet has some advantages over potty chairs that must be placed on the floor.

Once Toilet Learning Begins

Once toilet learning begins, adults should encourage the toddler to use the toilet. However, they should not put requests in moral terms such as, "Be good and use the potty." Take toddlers to the toilet at set times until they go on their own. Before and after meals and sleep times, and every two hours are good times. Adults must remind children to use the toilet for many years after they learn.

Adults need to accept success and failure in a matter-of-fact way. Toddlers need some praise, but too much praise adds to the pressure to achieve the next time. Adults should not let failures make children feel bad or little. They should stop the learning routine during an illness or if a child shows signs of stress. Using diapers during sleep times, when traveling, or when away from home for long periods makes learning less stressful.

Accidents

No matter how much care is taken, accidents will happen. Being prepared, however, helps prevent accidents from causing too much stress for toddlers or adults. **Training pants** (pants made of disposable diaper material, pants with a multi-layered cotton fabric crotch, or specially designed ones for wading or swimming pool use) help lessen the mess of accidents. Keep household cleaning products on hand, but safely stored out of the toddler's reach, to clean accidents.

Toilet learning helps children handle their elimination needs cleanly, without help, and without fuss. Complete learning is a long process.

Indoor and Outdoor Spaces

Toddlers still enjoy being near adults and other children for most of their waking hours. However, between the second and third birthdays, many toddlers begin playing more on their own. They need a place where they can rest and sleep without being disturbed. Thus, many families plan indoor and outdoor play spaces and bedrooms for their toddlers.

Bedrooms and play spaces must be safe. (See Chapter 22 for safety tips.) If possible, these areas should fit toddlers' needs for play, rest, and learning self-help skills. Open floor and yard spaces make it easy for the toddler to be active. A cozy chair, fuzzy throw rug, corner area, and toddler bed are examples of quiet places.

Self-help features include low shelves for toys and low hooks for coats. They also include a sturdy footstool for climbing one step and light switches within reach.

Toddlers like furniture and room decorations chosen especially for them, 15-10. As you read in Chapter 11, some families are buying convertible furniture. This can be less expensive, when used

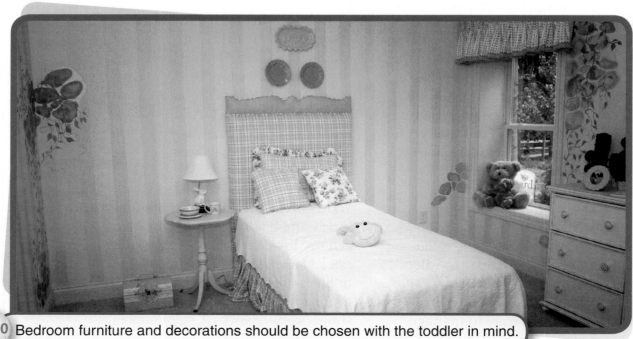

15-10 Bedroom furniture and decorations should be chosen with the toddler in mind.

for many years, compared with replacing furniture as the child grows. Furniture designed for toddlers is often made smaller than other furniture. It may also be brightly painted. Choose bedspreads, window coverings, wallpaper, floor coverings, lamps, and night-lights the toddler will like. Wall hangings and pictures can be chosen with the toddler in mind. Even a few of the toddler's toys or books on display can make the room or area special.

Intellectual Needs

For the most part, toddlers learn during daily activities. They learn as they are eating, bathing, dressing, "helping" with household tasks, and running errands with adults. Adults should use everyday activities to help toddlers learn. Toddlers can learn during meals. They can talk with others at the table (language learnings). They can see, taste, smell, and feel foods of many colors, shapes, sizes, and textures (perceptual learnings). They can make choices about the foods and amounts of each they want (decision making). Toddlers can handle finger foods and flatware (motor skills). They hear comments such as, "Food helps you grow and become strong," (a nutrition lesson). They even join in celebrations involving food, such as eating birthday cake (a social time).

Learning Through Activities

Many other activities help toddlers learn, 15-11. Bathing and dressing provide the means for language, perceptual, health, and

15-11 Playing in the rain teaches toddlers about science and their world.

motor learnings. Helping with household tasks develops **spatial** (pertaining to space) concepts as toddlers put items in drawers or laundry in a basket. Vocabulary increases as toddlers learn the names of common objects found in the home and yard. Science becomes a part of everyday life as toddlers see how the vacuum cleaner picks up dirt, how air dries clothes, and how heat makes dough change into cookies.

Learning Through Play

Toddlers also learn as they play in a safe environment with many objects to explore. Play lets the toddler check and recheck learnings. A toddler may fill a plastic pail with the same toys many times to check how much space the toys need. Adults may play with toddlers sometimes. For the most part, however, they should let toddlers play on their own, stepping in only when toddlers need help or show they desire adult participation. They may show a toddler how to put a piece in a puzzle or introduce new ideas to play.

Adults may need a few ideas for games to enrich a toddler's learnings. They can use adult-planned games when they seem to fit the toddlers' interest and skills (Vygotsky's principle). These planned games should never be forced on the child, however. Adults should keep ideas in mind and use them only to enrich toddlers' learnings. This method is the best way to meet their intellectual needs.

Sensory Stimulation Activities

The senses help toddlers learn about the qualities of objects. Through sight, they learn about an object's color and darkness or lightness. Touch teaches them if objects are rough or smooth. They use hearing and touch to find out if objects are hard or soft. Toddlers use taste to learn about sweet, sour, salty, and bitter. Using the senses helps toddlers form concepts about objects. For example, they learn that when peeled, oranges are round, orange colored, sweet smelling, sweet tasting, and juicy (wet).

Games can enrich what toddlers are learning on their own. As toddlers play games, adults should teach them by talking through the activity.

When a caregiver notices a toddler hears a sound, the caregiver should stop briefly and listen. Then say, "Do you hear that? I hear a _____. Do you

hear it, too?" Point in the direction of the sound. This helps stimulate the toddler's sense of hearing. As another activity, when cooking a food with a distinct odor, sniff loudly and tell the toddler what you smell. Say, "I smell chicken frying," or "I smell a cake baking." Later, ask the toddler, "What's cooking? What smells so good?" Variations of this include smelling and talking about other odors. Flowers, an outdoor barbecue, and the rain all have distinct smells. See 15-12 for other examples of sensory stimulation activities.

Problem-Solving Activities

Toddlers can solve many problems by testing their ideas. They are not ready to solve problems just by thinking alone. Many of the best problem-solving games involve motor actions, such as opening and closing containers, finding hidden objects, and watching how objects move.

Simple puzzles are another good problem-solving activity for children. Begin with a few pieces and work up to puzzles with five or six pieces. For toddlers, each puzzle piece should be an entire picture of an object rather than a jigsaw piece. A knob on the puzzle piece helps fine-motor control. See 15-13 for other problem-solving activities.

Motor Activities

Toddlers develop motor skills quickly. Because most toddlers are always on the go, they need few planned motor activities. Some games can improve gross-motor skills whereas others improve fine-motor skills.

Sensory Stimulation Activities

Activity	Sense
Looking at Objects	**Sight**

Ask a child to look in a certain area (such as out a window) and name something he or she sees. When the child points to or names an object, say, "That's right, it's a _____." Then talk about the qualities of the object. You may include color, size, the sound it makes, and what it does. Talk about other times when the toddler has seen the object. Three or four objects at one time are enough for most toddlers.

Animal Sounds	**Hearing**

Sing "Old MacDonald Had a Farm" and point to pictures of each animal as you sing. Start with a few of the toddler's favorite animals and gradually add others.

Recognizing Objects by Touch	**Touch**

Put three or four familiar objects in a paper bag or pillowcase. Pull an object out of the bag. Ask the toddler to name it. Then show the toddler how to feel the object using the fingers. As the toddler feels the object, the adult should describe the texture. For instance, a ball may feel "round and soft." Continue in the same way with the other objects. After feeling all the objects, put them back into the bag. Have the child identify each one by feeling without peeking.

Variations: (1) Place pictures or identical objects outside the bag. Have the toddler feel an object in the bag and point to the object or picture outside the bag. (2) Describe and name an object and have the toddler find it. You may say, "Put your hand in the bag and see if you can find the comb."

Recognizing Objects by Smell	**Smell**

Select three or four familiar objects that have distinct odors. Show the toddler how to smell by sniffing loudly. First, smell and talk about each object's odor. Then have the toddler close his or her eyes and identify each object by smelling it. If the toddler needs help, name two objects from which the toddler can choose. You may say, "Is this soap or a banana?"

Sweet and Sour	**Taste**

Give the toddler a sugar cube and refer to it as *sweet*. Then have the toddler taste lemon juice mixed with water. Refer to it as *sour*. (Use equal parts of lemon juice and water. Pure lemon juice is too sour and can be hard on teeth.) Sweeten the lemon juice and water with sugar and serve as lemonade. Although the toddler may not understand, explain, "I am making this sour lemon juice sweeter with this sweet sugar. Now we have lemonade. It is sweet." *Variation*: Give the toddler a small amount of salt to taste. Give the toddler a bite of a salty food, such as a salty cracker. Use the term *salty* to describe both flavors.

15-12 Sensory stimulation activities help toddlers learn about the qualities of objects.

Problem-Solving Activities

Opening Lids

Place a small object in a container with a snap-on lid. Show the toddler how it works. Then let the toddler try to open it. When the toddler has mastered one type of lid, try another. You may use screw-on lids and plugs. (Do *not* show toddlers or even older preschool children how safety caps work.)

Opening Lids

Stacking and Nesting

If the toddler can nest and stack two or three objects as described in Chapter 11, add a few more pieces for nesting and stacking. Rings can also be sequenced. The toddler should start with two or three rings. Slowly add the other rings as the toddler masters the game. (If there is very little difference in the size of the objects, the task becomes much more difficult. These objects can be saved for children who are a little older.)

Stacking

Where am I?

Hide from a toddler who is involved in another activity. Call out. The toddler will look for you. Praise the toddler for finding you. (Of course, do not hide behind locked doors or other places where the toddler cannot search.)

Rolling Cars

Place small cars or trucks on a board that is flat on the floor. Chair cushions, sturdy cardboard lids, or trays can be used as the board. Say, "The cars do not go." As you slowly raise the board on one end say, "Here they go." After the toddler has played with the cars in this way many times, ask, "Can you make the car go down the hill fast (slow)?" See if the toddler increases (decreases) the slope of the board.

Through the Tunnel

Using a mailing tube with both ends removed, show the toddler how to roll objects through it. The toddler will learn how objects can go in one open end and come out the other open end. After much play, some toddlers may learn to vary the slope of the tube to control the speed of the object's roll.

15-13 Problem-solving activities encourage toddlers to try out their ideas.

Riding toys help children develop their gross-motor skills. Toys that can be pushed with the feet or pedaled also help develop gross-motor skills. Interlocking blocks help develop fine-motor skills while sparking creativity. See 15-14 for other suggestions for gross- and fine-motor games.

Language Activities

Parents and caregivers can enhance the toddler's use of language. Early childhood programs that let children explore and play help language learning. Parents can organize their homes to promote language learning, too.

Gross- and Fine-Motor Games

Gross-Motor Games

Push and Pull
Push and pull toys aid the motor skills of walking and crawling. Push toys seem to be easier because the toddler can see the toy's action without walking backward or looking back over the shoulder.

Fine-Motor Games

Pounding Pegs
A hammer and peg set can help the child coordinate what is seen with the action. Toddlers should use both hands on the hammer to prevent getting the fingers hit.

Pounding Pegs

Blocks
Building a tower with three to five blocks and knocking it down is fun for toddlers. As toddlers grow, they will build taller towers. Balancing the blocks in towers requires good fine-motor control.
Variation: Push three or four blocks in a "train" while saying, "choo choo." Pushing blocks in a train requires much fine-motor control.

Blocks

Making a Face
Putting the eyes, nose, and mouth on a felt face can be much fun. The parts of the face are made out of felt with a hook-and-loop tape backing, such as Velcro®. Because the pieces are rather small, the toddler should be supervised during play.
Variation: Many other "pictures" can be made using felt pieces. For instance, the toddler can put wheels on cars or trains. They can also put flowers on stems.

15-14 Gross- and fine-motor games help toddlers improve their skills.

Good feelings between the child and caregivers may also increase the child's verbal skills.

Toddlers Need to Hear Language

The toddler's active world needs a background of language. Adults should talk during many games played with toddlers to improve toddlers' skills. Adults and children should talk during daily routines, too. As adults do things, they should say what they are doing and what the toddler is doing.

Adults can begin talking in a conversational manner even before the child can respond verbally. They can pause as though the child will answer, as in the following example:
Adult—"Aren't you hungry?"
Pause about half a second.
Imagined response from toddler—"Yes."
Pause about half a second.
Adult—"Surely you are. Lunch smells good, doesn't it?"
As adults talk to toddlers, they should use all types of sentences. Using statements, questions, and

exclamations helps the toddler hear the rise and fall of the voice. Adults can also help toddlers learn to make different sounds. For example, they can make sounds that go with toys, such as *rrr* for a siren.

Clear and Simple Speech

Speech should be clear and simple. Most adults match their sentences to the child's level. For example, new words are explained using words the child already knows. ("A bus is like a big car.") However, mispronouncing words is harmful, as is talking beneath the child's level. Challenging children slightly helps their development. (This is the principle of using the child's ZPD.)

Adults should model language for toddlers. However, they should be relaxed about toddlers' language errors. These examples show ways to model language.

★ Toddler—"My wed (red) sooes (shoes)."
Adult—"Yes, these are your pretty red shoes."
Purpose is to correct pronunciation.

★ Toddler—"I singed a song."
Adult—"You sang a song about a rainy day."
Purpose is to correct grammar.

★ Toddler—"See the plane go."
Adult—"The plane flies fast."
Purpose is to introduce a new word.

★ Toddler—"See the smoke."
Adult—"It does look like smoke." Sniff loudly. "It doesn't smell like smoke, though. We see fog. Fog is a cloud near the ground. Can you say fog?"
Purpose is to correct meaning.

In each case, the adult guides by expanding the toddler's sentence. Toddlers (and even older children) often feel defeated when adults only correct errors.

Children learn what they hear and will repeat it, too. Parents and other caregivers must not use any word or phrase that they do not want the child to use. If children repeat "forbidden words" from other sources, adults should say, "These are not words we use here (at home, at school)."

Choosing Books for Toddlers

Reading books and saying poems and rhymes helps toddlers develop language. These activities should begin early in the toddler years. When choosing books, look for the following features:

★ Pictures must be colorful and simple. Young children's books are called *picture books* because pictures, rather than words, carry the story. Some picture books do not even have words.

★ Story lines should focus on toddlers' favorite subjects. Subjects may include animals, toys, fun places to visit, cars and trucks, or home and family.

★ Books should be durable. They should be sturdy and washable. Books made of cloth, vinyl, and heavy cardboard with a plastic coating are best. You can make books by purchasing an inexpensive album with 5 X 7 inch, or 8 X 10 inch sleeves. Another option is to use top-loading sheet protectors (available at office-supply stores). Some photos may need to be mounted on cardstock. Then slip photos into the sheet protectors. (These books have the added bonus of being able to change the pictures.)

★ Pages should be easy for the toddler to turn and keep open.

How Toddlers "Read"

Toddlers will not sit still and look at books for a long time. Young toddlers may enjoy glancing at a page and turning it. (Using the motor skill of turning the page is more fun than looking at the pictures.) Later, toddlers look at the pictures for a little longer, but they still may not want to hear the story. Adults can name one object and point to it. Then they can ask toddlers to point to the objects named. As language develops, toddlers can name objects in the pictures and even make some sounds of animals or other objects. A two-year-old often enjoys hearing the whole story, as long as it contains only a short sentence or two for each picture page, 15-15.

Reading to Toddlers

Many older toddlers (and even preschool children) insist on hearing the same story over and over. They often request the same story at bedtime. Routines, including favorite, repeated stories, help the toddler feel secure. The child knows what will happen in the story's beginning, middle, and end. Sometimes children will insist that not even a word be changed. The loving adult who reads daily to a child is likely to bring more security than the story itself.

Singing with Toddlers

Songs that act out the meanings of words are helpful to toddlers. An example is "Here We Go 'Round the Mulberry Bush." This common song lets toddlers sing and act out lines

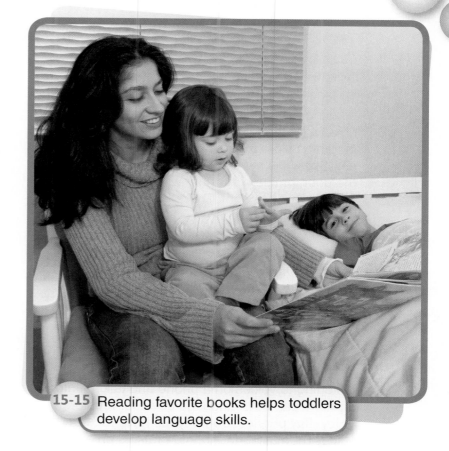

15-15 Reading favorite books helps toddlers develop language skills.

such as, "This is the way we eat our soup," and "This is the way we wash our hands." Toddlers can sing many other verses, too. Adults and sometimes children can make up new words to fit almost any activity by using "mileage tunes." (Some other common tunes are: "Oh, Do You Know the Muffin Man?"; "Twinkle, Twinkle Little Star"; and "London Bridge is Falling Down." See 15-16 for other language games that are fun and encourage children to use language.

Social-Emotional Needs

Toddlerhood is like the teen years because the toddler is in a **transitional stage** (passing from

Language Games

Show Me

Young toddlers enjoy running around and pointing to objects. When an adult names objects for the toddler to touch, the toddler's language skills improve. Make statements such as, "Show me the door." As the toddler touches the door, praise him or her with a statement such as, "You're right. That's the door."

Follow Directions

Give the toddler simple directions using familiar objects. For example, say, "Bring me the ball." Praise the toddler for following directions promptly. You may also play the game "Follow the Leader." Give simple directions such as, "Clap your hands," or "Pat your Head."

Telephones

Listening to voices on a phone and talking into a phone can help language develop. Toddlers enjoy play phones. Some types have recorded voices that talk to the toddler. Talking on a real phone with adult supervision is also a good language practice.

15-16 Adults and toddlers can enjoy language games.

one stage to another). Adults cannot treat toddlers as if they are babies or five-year-olds. Toddlers are somewhere in-between. They want to do things for themselves, but this desire exceeds what they are able to do. Toddlers are trying to become separate persons. They go back and forth between wanting to be totally independent and wanting to be totally dependent.

These changes in toddlers' wills confuse adults. Most adults find they have to give toddlers freedom at times and be firm at other times. Their actions depend on the toddlers' needs.

Discipline

Toddlers do not have **self-restraint**. In other words, they cannot always control themselves. They also do not know all the rules of acceptable behavior. Parents are in Galinsky's *authority stage* of parenting. They must set limits for toddlers. Limits keep toddlers safe and show them how to become more socially acceptable.

Balancing Self-Assertion and Obedience

Adults must help toddlers balance **self-assertion** (doing as one chooses) and **obedience** (acting within the limits set by others). The best way to do so is to meet toddlers' needs, not punish what they do wrong. Although each toddler has his or her own unique needs, some needs are common.

Toddlers Need to Feel Loved

Toddlers need to feel loved by caring adults. They seem to sense love that is shown to them physically and directly. For example, most toddlers respond to cuddling, loving words, and special times each day when attention is focused on them. Toddlers do not seem to sense love shown in indirect ways, such as having cooked meals or clean clothes (although these are important).

Toddlers Want to Feel Lovable

When toddlers are always made to feel they are "bad," they may grow to dislike themselves. Adults should label incorrect behavior as a mistake. They should not call the child *bad*, *selfish*, *naughty*, or *mean*. Harsh punishment may cause toddlers to feel they are bad, too.

Toddlers Need Respect

Toddlers are worthy of the same respect other people receive. Adults should not respond to toddlers' mistakes with hurtful teasing or anger. Respecting toddlers helps them like themselves. It also serves as the model for the growing child's relationships with others.

Toddlers Need Understanding and Patient Guidance

Toddlers need some freedom. Giving toddlers choices allows them to express their tastes. For example, adults can let toddlers choose between two green vegetables for lunch. A toddler may also choose between self-control and adult-control. The adult may say, "You may color on the paper, or I'll have to put the crayons away." Toddlers seem more willing to accept a firm no when given choices at other times. Limits given in one situation will seldom carry over to similar cases. For example, a toddler pulling books from a shelf may be told *no* as the adult gently moves the child's hand away from the books. The toddler may pause a moment, then reach for the books with the other hand. Adults must give limits for each case. They must also repeat limits again and again before they become part of the toddler's life.

Toddlers Need Consistency in Discipline

Consistency helps people feel secure. However, people also need flexible rules at times. Toddlers may need flexible rules when they are ill or when other problems occur. Once the situation is back to normal, rules should become consistent again. Of course, discipline changes as children grow. As they grow, children are often allowed more freedom.

Toddlers have good days and problem days, just like adults. When limits are set and discipline is firm, yet kind, the toddler will begin to have good days more often. Good days are a sign that toddlers are getting better at balancing self-assertion and the need to obey, 15-17. Balancing the two is a skill they will need throughout life.

Guidance: Helping Toddlers Control Their Emotions

Understanding toddlers' emotions is the first step in helping toddlers control them. To do so, caregivers must also control their emotions. Problems with toddlers often include contrariness, temper tantrums, and fears and anxieties.

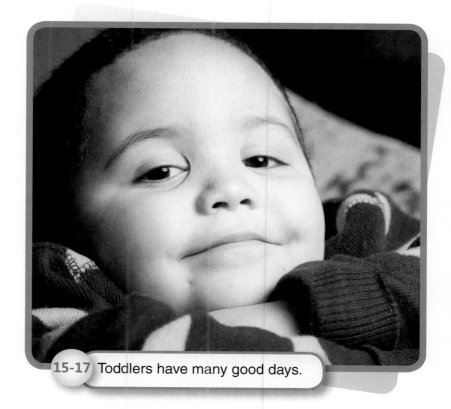

15-17 Toddlers have many good days.

Contrariness

By 18 months, many toddlers show definite signs of **contrariness**. They tend to oppose adults and even other toddlers. They replace *yes* with *no*, even when *yes* is what they really mean. *Me want* is replaced with *No want*.

Let the Toddler Choose

Certain methods often reduce contrariness. The simplest way is to let the toddler make some choices. As long as results are not harmful, allowing toddlers some freedom makes obeying easier.

Tell the Toddler in Advance

Telling the toddler about upcoming events, such as lunchtime, a few minutes in advance helps reduce contrariness. This time allows the toddler to prepare emotionally for the change of activities. Saying *no* is often a toddler's response to sudden changes. Once they say *no*, it is more difficult for them to back down. If toddlers say *no* when you tell them about a change, ignore the reply until the change happens. If children say *no* again, express toddlers' feelings. Adults can say, "You are really having fun in the sandbox, but we must eat now." If the toddler still resists, use calm actions, such as picking up the toddler.

Use Pretend Games

Another way to reduce contrariness is to play a pretend game of obedience. The adult might say, "I'm going to wash my hands before you do." (Of course, after much scrubbing, the toddler wins.) Sometimes pretend games of obedience become rituals, such as a "chase" to the bedroom at naptime.

Temper Tantrums

As toddlers discover the powers of self-assertion, they may have temper tantrums. Many two-year-olds have temper tantrums, but some do not. Toddlers who are lively, under stress (even the stress of being hungry), and cannot yet talk are prone to tantrums. Trying the following ideas may help reduce the number and frequency of tantrums:

★ Reduce or avoid demands when the toddler is tired, hungry, or ill.

★ Make requests in a pleasant tone of voice.

★ Remove toys or play equipment that seems to frustrate the child.

★ Have enough toys or ideas to prevent boredom.

★ Offer help when the toddler seems to need it. (Waiting until the child shows frustration is often too late.)

★ Give in on small demands. (Toddlers need to get their way sometimes.)

★ Praise the toddler for signs of control.

Once a temper tantrum is underway, allow the tantrum to continue. It is a form of release for the child. Ignoring the child's tantrum may help, because tantrums are often done for attention. Toddlers have been known to follow adults from room to room, throwing the tantrum each time. If a tantrum occurs in public, the adult and child should go to a quiet place for the toddler to become calm.

Comforting the Child

Adults should acknowledge the feelings of toddlers and show comfort. The adult may say, "I know you really wanted to stay outside. I'm sorry you are so upset about coming in the house." After the tantrum, hugs are often helpful. When adults hold back this comfort, toddlers may feel unlovable.

Do not use spankings to punish tantrums. If the adult expresses displeasure (or even anger) in a physical way, he or she is modeling that behavior for the toddler.

Tantrums, when handled calmly, often decrease during the preschool years. Also, adult calmness serves as a model for children of ways to deal with anger.

Fears and Anxieties

Adults should not dismiss children's fears and anxieties as silly. They should not tease children about them, either. They should handle the toddler's feelings in a matter-of-fact way.

Reducing Fear and Anxiety

Adults should show differences between real and pretend things in the toddlers' world. For example, adults should explain that dreams are not real. This will help reduce toddlers' fears of pretend things. Toddlers will often ask whether something is real or pretend. They will even ask about the same thing many times just to be certain.

Giving toddlers security also reduces fear, 15-18. Night-lights, toys in bed, and familiar caregivers add security. Avoid situations that cause much fear or anxiety. However, some situations, such as going to the doctor, cannot be avoided. These should be

15-18 A toddler's attachment to a well-loved toy can provide relief from fear and anxiety.

explained in a simple, honest way. As they are explained, address only fears the toddler has already shown.

Overcoming Fear and Anxiety

For toddlers to overcome fears and anxieties, they need to see and talk about their fear in safe ways. Telling toddlers that other children have the same fear may comfort them. Gradual exposure to a feared subject may also help. If the toddler is afraid of dogs, the adult may talk about dogs. Later, the adult may read the child a book about dogs or give the child a toy dog. After some time, the toddler may stand near a friendly puppy or small dog that is behind a fence. This method is better for the toddler than suddenly exposing the child to fearful situations.

Toddlers should be praised for small steps toward overcoming fears. For example, toddlers can be praised for only crying a little or for not running from the puppy behind the fence.

Most of the toddler's fears and anxieties will disappear with age. If parents handle fear and anxieties in understanding ways, toddlers will be better able to cope with present and future fears and anxieties.

Planning Self-Awareness Activities

A person's self-awareness begins at birth and continues throughout life. The roots of self-awareness seem to form in the toddler years. Self-awareness grows mainly out of the toddler's daily contact with his or her world. A few planned activities may enhance self-awareness.

Examples of self-awareness activities include placing photographs of the toddler on the refrigerator or another viewing area at the child's height. Keeping a photo album of the child's early years is fun for all family members. The parents and child can sit together and talk about how the child has grown and how important the child is to the family. Measuring the child's height on a chart and keeping a running tally of his or her height also helps the child gain self-awareness. See 15-19 for other examples of self-awareness activities.

With help from loving adults and their increasing mental abilities, toddlers can smoothly leave babyhood behind. Toddlers emerge as happy, confident young children.

Self-Awareness Activities

Name the Parts of the Face

Place the toddler's hands on your face. Name aloud each part of your face as the child feels it. Ask the child to name the parts.

Mirrors

With the toddler on your lap, hold a mirror to reflect the toddler's face. Ask, "Who is that?" If the toddler does not answer, say, "That is you." Say the toddler's name.

Dressing Up

Children under age three enjoy dressing up with old purses, hats, necklaces, and large flat shoes. To help the toddler play while dressing up, show the child one object. For example, show the toddler a hat and say, "Look at this pretty hat. I'm going to wear it." Place the hat on your head and talk about how pretty it is. Then say, "Do you want to wear a hat?" Place a hat on the toddler's head, saying how nice it looks. If the toddler enjoys this, try other items.

Pretend

Have a pretend tea party with a toddler. Talk about the pretend foods in much the same way you would talk about real food. If the toddler looks confused, say, "How funny! We can pretend to have a party!"

A Book About Me

Take pictures of the toddler's daily activities. Place the pictures in a photo album. (Toddlers often take these albums to child care programs to reduce separation anxiety. Be sure to include photos of parents, siblings, and other loved ones.)

15-19 These activities enhance a toddler's sense of self.

Developmental Delays

Toddlers with developmental delays may show some of the behaviors of infants as listed in Chapter 11. As you may have noted, infant development is judged mainly by gross-motor skills. During the toddler years, gross-motor skills are still important behaviors to observe, but fine-motor skills and language become more important in indicating healthy signs of development. See the *Toddler Milestones* in Appendix A to learn about some typical toddler behaviors that may help parents recognize delays and bring their concerns to the attention of a doctor.

Summary

Toddlers practice self-care skills, such as self-feeding, self-dressing, and toileting. These skills also help them advance in their intellectual and social-emotional development.

Toddlers eat table food and can feed themselves. Parents should offer toddlers nutritious foods. The MyPyramid food guidance system provides parents with guidance on a healthful diet and physical activity for their toddlers. A number of feeding problems can arise because of the toddlers' growing independence.

Clothing and shoes that fit and allow for growth are important. Other features to consider when purchasing clothing for toddlers include safety, comfort, fabric, attractive style, and ease of care.

The sleep and rest habits of toddlers have changed since infancy. Bedtime problems can develop, but if adults establish quiet nighttime rituals, bedtime is less stressful.

For bathing, place a small tub inside the regular tub. Toddlers help a little in their bathing and use this time for play. Eating nutritious foods and cleaning teeth regularly are part of good dental health. Dental checkups can begin at age two years.

Before children can begin toilet learning, their bodies must be physically ready. They must also see the need to go to the bathroom. This generally occurs sometime after age two years. Children should not be shamed or punished when they have accidents. They need praise and encouragement.

Toddlers' mental abilities are stimulated by using daily routines. Parents should also give toddlers time to check and recheck learnings through play. Adults can enrich their toddler's learning environment by providing appropriate materials and planning a few activities for the toddler. Language development is a key part of mental development in the toddler years.

Parents need to give toddlers some freedom while still setting limits for them. Contrariness and temper tantrums are typical problems at this age. Feelings of fears and anxieties should be handled in understanding ways. As toddlers become more aware of themselves and their abilities, they become more confident.

Companion Web Site

Interactive Activity

Review vocabulary terms and key concepts for Chapter 15 at **g-wlearning.com**.

Review and Reflect

Write your answers to the following questions on a separate sheet of paper.

1. True or false. Teaching self-care skills is part of meeting the physical needs of toddlers.

2. Which statements about feeding toddlers are true? (A) Because toddlers are larger than infants, their appetites increase. (B) Toddlers want to feed themselves. (C) Toddlers who play with their food are being naughty. (D) Empty calorie foods provide energy, which make them a nutritious choice for toddlers. (E) Many of the toddler's feeding problems work themselves out in time.

3. Are toddlers better at putting on clothes or taking off clothes?

4. True or false. Shoes help toddlers walk by providing good support.

5. List four suggestions that may help toddlers go to bed.

6. What is the average age for toddlers to begin feeling the sensation of needing to use the toilet?

7. True or false. Potty chairs do *not* make toilet learning easier for toddlers.

8. True or false. Intellectual needs are best met when toddlers are involved with household activities on a day-to-day basis.

9. List two ways to reduce contrariness in toddlers.

10. Describe three ways to reduce the number of temper tantrums in toddlers.

11. True or false. Toddlers become less fearful when quickly exposed to the feared situation again.

Cross-Curricular Link

12. **Health, Technology.** Plan a one-week menu (meals and snacks) for a two-year-old by using the menu planner feature on the **MyPyramid.gov** Web site. Print your menu. Post your menu as part of a classroom display.

13. **Health, Safety, Art.** Create a poster or mobile of healthful and safe finger foods for toddlers.

14. **Financial Literacy.** Borrow three items of toddler clothing and bring these to class. Examine each garment for the features listed in 15-5. List the good features included. Compare your list with others in the class. Create a hangtag for each clothing item that lists its best features. Which clothing items do you think are the best buy?

15. **Reading, Writing.** Read two toddler books on toilet learning. Record the title, author, publishing company, and copyright date of each book. Along with this information, provide a brief summary of each book that includes your opinion of the book. Why do you think toddlers would enjoy (or not enjoy) this book? How

could parents use the book to help children learn to use the toilet? Does the book provide more information or motivation? Prepare a written report of your findings. Check your paper for correct spelling, grammar, and punctuation.

16. **Speech.** Select a partner and role-play various scenarios where a parent tries to teach a child a self-care skill. Take turns being the parent and the toddler. After a few of these role-plays, discuss with your partner whether teaching toddlers self-care skills is harder or easier than you imagined.

17. **Social Studies, Speech.** Plan one activity that would help promote a toddler's sense of self-awareness. Present your activity to the class, explaining how the activity is done and how it promotes the development of self-awareness.

Making Observations

18. Observe a toddler at home or in a child care setting. How does the toddler show independence? In what ways does the toddler depend on adults?

19. Observe a toddler in his or her bedroom or playroom. What decorations seem to have been chosen with a toddler in mind? What things seem to especially fit this toddler?

20. Observe a toddler playing and identify what types of learnings he or she demonstrates in play (examples are perceptual, problem solving, motor, language, and self-awareness learnings).

21. Observe an adult reading a story to a toddler. Which features of the book did the toddler like? Was there anything about the book that did not seem fit for toddlers? Explain.

22. Observe adults caring for toddlers who are having a hard day. What adult actions seem to work best? Why? What adult actions do not seem to work? Why?

Thinking Critically

23. Examine some items used to teach self-dressing. Although these items teach some skills, how are they different from actual dressing? (Be specific about each item.)

24. Examine several pieces of equipment that can be used for problem solving, such as a puzzle. What specific skills does a child need to have or develop in order to use the materials? (As you answer this question, visualize each step.)

25. What are some of the ways adults fail to respect toddlers? What might be the outcome if adults treated their friends in this way? How can they be respectful to toddlers? (Be specific.)

Focus on
Family and Community

Strong leaders are able to effectively solve problems. Develop your leadership and problem-solving skills by completing an FCCLA *Dynamic Leadership* project for the unit *Problem Solving for Leaders*. For example, you can develop a project that would help young children solve problems. Brainstorm a list of ways in which you can help children learn the problem-solving steps. Choose your best idea and create a presentation that would appeal to children. Then arrange to present your lesson to a small group of children. Take it a step further and participate in an FCCLA Star Event, such as *Teach and Train*. Use the FCCLA *Planning Process* to plan, carry out, and evaluate your project. Your FCCLA advisor can provide you with further information.

16 Physical Development of the Preschooler

After studying this chapter, you will be able to

★ describe the physical development that occurs in preschool children.

★ describe preschool children's gross- and fine-motor skills.

Terms to Know

preschool children
internal organs
reaction time
dynamic balance

static balance
body rotation
weight shift
manipulate

Reading Advantage

Describe how this chapter relates to a chapter you read earlier in the semester.

Companion Web Site

Interactive Activity

Learn more about a preschooler's fine-motor development by completing the *Read, Discuss, and Analyze* Activity for Chapter 16 at **g-wlearning.com**.

Preschool children are those between the ages of three and five years. As you can imagine, they are becoming grown-up. The bodies of preschoolers continue to mature, which make them able to handle harder tasks. They are changing in ways that make them more like adults and less like small children.

Toddlers have gained many gross- and fine-motor skills. However, they do not have as much control over their movements as they would like. In the preschool years, children improve their skills of walking, running, balancing, and self-dressing.

Body Growth and Development

Preschool children grow even more slowly than toddlers. (If the growth rate did not slow, people would grow to be as big as giants!) Instead of growing much larger,

the preschooler's body proportions change and the organ systems mature.

The growth rate slows in almost the same way for all preschool children. This means children who are larger than their peers at age three years are likely to be larger at age five years, too.

Height and Weight

Most preschool children grow steadily at about 2½ to 3 inches each year. On average, girls are shorter than boys, but the difference is ½ inch or less.

The rate of weight gain also slows during the preschool years. Preschoolers gain about 3 to 5 pounds per year. Seventy-five percent of the weight gained during the preschool years is due to muscle development. Because boys have greater muscle development, even during the preschool years, they are, on average, a pound heavier than girls their age, 16-1.

Average Height and Weight from Three to Five Years

Age in Years	Height		Weight	
	Boys	Girls	Boys	Girls
3	38 in.	37¼ in.	32¼ lbs.	31¾ lbs.
3½	39¼ in.	39¼ in.	34¼ lbs.	34 lbs.
4	40¾ in.	40½ in.	36½ lbs.	36¼ lbs.
4½	42 in.	42 in.	38½ lbs.	38½ lbs.
5	43¼ in.	43 in.	41½ lbs.	41 lbs.
5½	45 in.	44½ in.	45½ lbs.	44 lbs.

16-1 The height and weight of children from three to five years increase rather steadily. Boys tend to be slightly taller and heavier than girls.

Other Body Changes

As toddler features begin to disappear, the preschooler's body proportions begin to look more like those of an adult. The lower face grows more rapidly than the head. This helps the preschooler's face look more like an adult's. Until age 30 months, the waist, hips, and chest measure almost the same. By age five years, the waist is smaller than the shoulders and hips. The trunk grows to allow more space for the **internal organs** (heart, lungs, liver, and others). As the trunk grows, the abdomen protrudes less. The legs grow rapidly, too. By 5½ years, most children's legs are about half the length of the body. This is the same as the adult's leg-to-body proportions.

Bones and Teeth

The bones continue to ossify and grow larger and longer. Deciduous (baby) teeth begin to fall out between ages four and five years. Although permanent teeth may not erupt until the early school-age years, they are growing under the gums. Bone and teeth development can be harmed by malnutrition and other health problems during the preschool years. Bones, muscles, and joints are more prone to injury in preschool children than in older children.

Organs

Other organs are maturing, too. The heart rate slows and becomes steady. Blood pressure increases. Breathing slows and is deeper. Although the digestive tract is maturing, it lags behind the maturity of other organs. Therefore, the preschooler's

Health Science

Pediatric Dentist

Pediatric dentists are the pediatricians of dentistry. They are primary and specialty oral care providers for infants and children through adolescence.

Education: Dental schools require a minimum of two years of college-level predental education prior to admittance. Dental school usually lasts four academic years. Pediatric dentists have two to three years of specialty training following dental school. Licensing is required to practice as a dentist.

Job Outlook: Average employment growth will generate some job openings, but most openings will result from the need to replace dentists expected to retire.

digestive tract is more irritated by high-fiber foods and seasonings than the adult's. The preschooler's brain continues to grow, too, but at a slower rate than before.

Fat and Muscle Tissues

The ratio of fat to muscle tissue continues to decrease slowly. Boys lose baby fat more quickly than girls. With good nutrition and physical activity, most of the baby fat will have disappeared by the first day of kindergarten. At age 5½ years, the preschooler's fat deposits are less than half as thick as they were at age one year.

The tall, lean body of the preschooler is strengthened. This is due to the *skeletal muscles* (muscles attached to the bones) and bones that are made stronger by ossification. Muscle fiber, which consists mainly of water, is now being replaced with more protein. Preschoolers' activity level also affects muscle development.

Besides content changes in muscle tissue, the fiber size of muscles responds to physical activity. Thus, a three-year-old's skeletal muscles develop rapidly because children are more active at this age than at any other age in the life span.

Motor Development

The motor development of preschoolers improves. This is due to physical activity and increasing body growth and development. Preschoolers have an increase in muscle development and develop better balancing skills. Their eye-hand coordination becomes more refined. Their **reaction time** (time required to respond to a sight, sound, or other stimuli) becomes shorter. Preschool children are able to perform many physical activities. Through play, preschool children's motor skills develop quickly, 16-2.

Gross-Motor Development

At the same time preschool children's large muscles develop, balance develops, too. This complex skill requires both signals from the eyes and the movement of fluids in

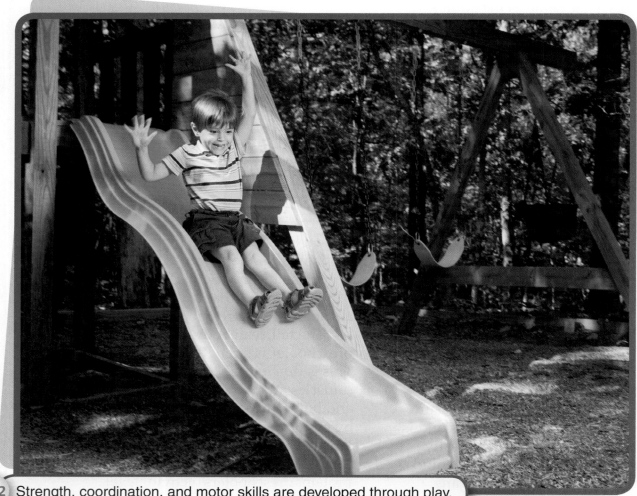

16-2 Strength, coordination, and motor skills are developed through play.

the semicircular canals of the inner ears. These signals are sent to the brain and then transmitted to the muscles of the body. Based on these signals, the muscles make constant adjustments to maintain balance. Balance keeps a person upright and affects many gross-motor activities. It is also a measure of the eye, ear, and brain health. Several studies have reported a relationship between balancing skills and the ability to start reading, too.

During the preschool years, children differ widely in their balancing skills. Through regular physical activities, preschool children will develop two kinds of balance. **Dynamic balance**, which is balance while moving, is developed when preschoolers walk a line or balance beam. **Static balance**, or balance maintained while being still, is learned when preschoolers stand on one foot with arms outstretched or folded across their chests. Dynamic balance is easier to develop than static balance. You may realize this if you have ridden a bicycle or watched or participated in dance or gymnastics.

Through muscle development and balancing skills, preschool children become stronger and more coordinated. Their gross-motor skills, such as walking, running, jumping, climbing, throwing, catching, balancing, hopping, and skipping improve. Chart 16-3 shows how these motor skills develop and improve.

You will notice that preschoolers walk more smoothly than toddlers. They like to try more challenging ways to walk. They run faster, and their arms and legs alternate in rhythm. Four-year-olds use a forward arm action to jump higher.

Focus on Social Studies

Comparing Gross- and Fine-Motor Skills

Observe gross- and fine-motor skills of children ages three, four, and five years. Make a chart to record the advancing skills. The chart might look like the following sample:

Age and gender of child_____

Motor Skill—

Hopping
Can hop _____
Distance hopped _____
Can hop rhythmically _____
Can hop with precision _____

Jumping
Length of broad jump _____
Height of hurdle jump _____
Forward movement of arms seen _____

Compare the skills of each age by using the average for each skill. Share your findings with the class.

With increased courage and better balance, climbing becomes easier. They can catch balls that are bounced better than those thrown by others. Three-year-olds begin hopping. Older preschoolers can hop and skip faster and for longer distances than younger preschoolers. Their actions become more advanced in all areas.

Two new actions help the preschooler's throwing ability. One is body rotation, and the other is weight shift. **Body rotation** is the action of turning the trunk of the body to one side when the hand on the other side is used to throw.

Preschoolers' Gross-Motor Skill Development

Walking

★ Gain skills in balancing.
★ Hold hands close to the body.
★ Begin to swing arms in alternate rhythm of foot placement.
★ Like to walk sideways, backward, and on tiptoes.
★ Like to spin around and try to become dizzy, which helps balance (three-year-olds).

Running

★ Have short stops and starts.
★ Can turn corners quickly.
★ Begin to swing arms in alternate rhythm of foot placement.
★ Increase speed a lot (five-year-olds).

Jumping

★ Have stronger muscles.
★ Increase distance of broad jump (with girls often lagging behind boys).
★ Increase height of hurdle jump (with boys and girls almost equal).

Climbing

★ Can climb with more skill due to longer legs.
★ Can alternate steps going up stairs (three-year-olds).
★ Can alternate climbing down steps (four-year-olds).

16-3 Compared to the toddler, the gross-motor skills of the preschool child are smoother and less awkward.

(Continued.)

Throwing and Catching

★ Begin to turn body to one side (body rotation) when the hand on the other side is used to throw (three-year-olds).

★ Begin to shift weight from back foot to front foot (three-year-olds).

★ Can catch balls that bounce better than those thrown by others.

★ Show increased strength, balance, and coordination and thus improve throwing distance, speed, and accuracy.

★ Can catch balls with the arms to one side (between ages four and five).

Balancing

★ Can walk heel-toe on a straight line without falling (three-year-olds).

★ Can balance on one foot (static balance) for a few seconds (three-year-olds). Can do more static balance feats (four- and five-year-olds).

Hopping and Skipping

★ Can hop on preferred foot (three-year-olds).

★ Can hop faster and for longer distances (four- and five-year-olds).

★ Can skip (between ages four and six).

★ Can do *rhythmic hopping*—hopping on one foot and then the other without breaking the rhythmic pattern (some five-year-olds).

★ Can do *precision hopping*—following a certain pathway (some five-year-olds).

16-3 *(Continued.)*

Weight shift is the change of weight from the back foot to the front foot. Body rotation and weight shift may begin during the third year. They become much more refined by the end of the preschool period. These two changes improve a preschooler's throwing distance, speed, and accuracy.

Fine-Motor Development

Preschoolers' ability to **manipulate**, or work with by using the hands, is still awkward. However, as preschoolers play with small objects, their small muscles develop and fine-motor skills improve. Improved

Learn More About...
Sequence of the Development of Fine-Motor Skills

The following list shows what to expect in the fine-motor skills of preschool children. (Remember the ages at which children develop may vary. The order of development is almost the same for all children.)

Three-year-olds
★ Builds uneven tower of blocks.
★ Pours water from a pitcher.
★ Copies a circle (with some skill).
★ Draws a straight line.

Four-year-olds
★ Cuts on line with scissors.
★ Washes hands.
★ Copies a letter t.
★ Makes a few letters.

Five-year-olds
★ Folds paper along the diagonal.
★ Copies a square and a triangle.
★ Traces a diamond shape.
★ Laces shoes and may tie them.
★ Copies most letters.

eye-hand coordination also helps fine-motor skills.

Age Three Years

At age three years, most children can feed themselves using a spoon and fork, but they are still rather messy. They can build towers from small blocks, but the towers are crooked. Three-year-olds can draw straight lines and roughly copy circles. They can unbutton buttons and pull large zippers.

Age Four Years

By four years, movements are steadier. Four-year-olds may try to use knives when they feed themselves. They are able to build straight towers and place blocks with steady hands. Four-year-olds

begin to cut along lines with scissors. (Scissors used at this age should have rounded tips.) These children can comb their hair and wash their hands. They can also begin to lace, but probably not tie, their shoes.

Age Five Years

At age five years, eye-hand coordination is greatly improved, 16-4. Right- or left-hand preference is definite by this age for many children. Five-year-olds use a spoon, fork, and knife to feed themselves. They can build towers and place other small toys with skill. They can make simple drawings freehand. Five-year-olds can fasten large buttons and work large zippers. They may even be able to tie shoelaces.

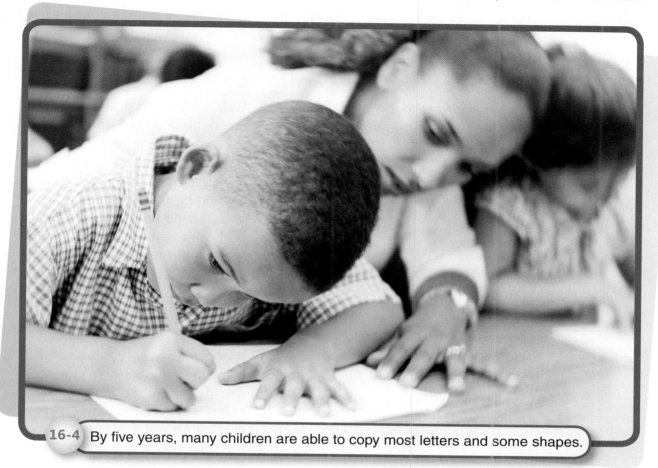

16-4   By five years, many children are able to copy most letters and some shapes.

Summary

Preschoolers gain in height and weight much more slowly than toddlers. They begin to look less like babies, and their faces begin to look more like those of adults. The waist becomes smaller than the shoulders and hips. Bones grow harder, larger, and longer. Deciduous teeth begin to fall out. Other organs and systems continue to mature. Fat deposits decrease, and muscle tissue increases in size.

Dynamic and static balance develop. Large muscles become stronger and more coordinated. Preschoolers are better able to walk, run, jump, climb, throw and catch, balance, hop, and skip.

As preschoolers manipulate small objects, their fine-motor skills improve. Better eye-hand coordination helps skills develop. Their fine-motor skills develop in a certain order that is similar for all children. Three-year-olds can build uneven towers of blocks. Five-year-olds may be able to lace and tie shoes. Hand preference is often definite by age five years.

Companion Web Site

Interactive Activity

Review vocabulary terms and key concepts for Chapter 16 at **g-wlearning.com**.

Review and Reflect

Write your answers to the following questions on a separate sheet of paper.

1. True or false. Compared to the toddler years, the rate of growth speeds up during the preschool years.

2. True or false. Preschool children's weight increases because of head (brain) growth.

3. True or false. At the end of the preschool years, the child's legs equal about half the total body length.

4. Which of the following matures most slowly: brain, digestive tract, or heart?

5. _____ (Fine-, Gross-) motor skills refer to how well a child can balance and jump.

6. List the two kinds of balance that preschool children develop through regular physical activity.

7. What two new actions help the preschooler's throwing ability?

8. List four fine-motor skills developed in the preschool period.

9. True or false. A four-year-old can cut following a line with round-tipped scissors.

10. True or false. Most four-year-olds can tie their shoelaces without help.

Cross-Curricular Link

11. **Writing.** Write a one- or two-page brochure about the motor skills of preschool children. Illustrations may help. Give copies to local programs serving preschool children for parents and other adults to use. (Ask your teacher to check the brochure before making copies.)

12. **Math.** Choose one of the age groups listed in Figure 16-1. Survey 10 parents of children in this age group. Record each parent's answers to each of the following questions: (A) What are the age and gender of the child? (B) What are the child's current weight and height? Use the data gathered to calculate the average height and weight for children of each gender. How do your figures compare to those of the text?

13. **Speech.** Interview a teacher of preschool children. Ask this person to describe eye-hand coordination of preschoolers at various ages. What changes has the teacher noticed in the children he or she serves from the beginning of the school year until now? Share your findings with the class.

14. **Social Studies.** Create a set of shape cards by drawing each of the following on a separate index card: circle, square, rectangle, equilateral triangle (three sides of equal length),

and diamond. Ask three children, ages three years, four years, and five years, to help you. Ask each child to look at each shape shown in the cards and draw it on a sheet of paper using a pencil. Write a paragraph summarizing your observations. Make a poster that includes this paragraph and the children's drawings (labeled by age). Display your poster in class.

15. **Writing.** Write a short story from the point of view of a preschooler. The story should describe the child's recent experiences with physical growth and development. Check your story for correct spelling, grammar, and punctuation.

Making Observations

16. Observe a group of preschoolers playing. What motor skills have they developed? What motor skills need improvement?

17. Observe the skills of three-year-olds and five-year-olds in handling scissors, pencils or crayons, and a paintbrush. What changes happen in this two-year period? Describe your findings in class.

Thinking Critically

18. Why are the preschool years important ones for providing children with many opportunities for gross-motor development? (Think of this question in terms of all areas of growth and development—physical, mental, and social-emotional.)

19. If you were writing a magazine article about gift suggestions to aid in preschoolers' fine-motor development, what gifts would you suggest?

20. Why do preschoolers feel so grown-up? More specifically, what physical changes (appearance and skills) give them this idea?

17 Intellectual Development of the Preschooler

After studying this chapter, you will be able to

★ **relate** how new thinking skills emerge in preschool children.

★ **identify** the major concepts learned at this stage of intellectual development.

★ **chart** the increasing language skills of preschoolers.

Terms to Know

mental images
internalized
abstract
preoperational stage
preconceptual substage
intuitive substage

egocentrism
logical thinking concepts
classifying
monologue
collective monologue

Reading Advantage

Look at the table of contents for this chapter. Use the detailed contents as an outline for taking notes as you read the chapter.

Companion Web Site

Interactive Activity

Learn more about the grammar of preschool children by completing the *Read, Discuss, and Analyze* Activity for Chapter 17 at **g-wlearning.com**.

Cognitive

Preschool children build mentally on what they have learned as infants and toddlers. Because preschoolers have better motor skills, their world broadens. Preschoolers can interact with more objects and people. They can participate in more events. This enables them to observe more and develop more advanced ideas about the physical attributes of things in their world. Preschoolers' mental development also broadens their world. They no longer rely only on their senses and motor actions to learn about their environment. Preschoolers can now solve problems mentally. Their more mature brains give them longer attention spans and help them recall more. Growing language abilities are also a major bonus, not only in communicating, but also in thinking with words.

Focus on Social Studies

Pretend Play

Work with three group members to draw or collect pictures of items that can be used in pretend play. Sort the items into two groups. In one group, place purchased items that often stand for one thing in play, such as a doll. In another group, place household items that can be many things in play, such as a box. Mount each group of pictures on a separate poster. Discuss with your group the following questions—(A) Are purchased items or household items more apt to be used in one way? Which are more likely to be used in many ways? (B) From which type of items do you think children mentally profit more—items that are often used in one way or items that are used in many ways?

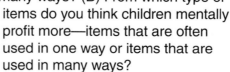

New Abilities Emerge

As you read in Chapter 13, older toddlers begin to think in their heads around 18 months of age. By three years of age, preschoolers can think in their heads better than before. They do not always have to go through physical actions in order to solve problems. Their problem-solving skills depend on their memories of past sensory and motor experiences, however. The preschoolers' thinking is marked by a number of new abilities— pretend play, mental images, drawing, and language.

Pretend Play

Pretend play begins with deferred imitation. Deferred imitation is when the child uses the actions and words of a model who is not present. These actions and words are stored in the child's mind to be acted out later.

Preschool children play many pretend games. While playing, they change things in some way from the real world or dreams. Pretend play is developmental. The following changes occur:

★ Older toddlers and young preschoolers prefer rather realistic objects, such as a plastic horse over a stick. Later, objects may stand for anything the child wants. For example, the same block can be a car, a boat, or a box.

★ Early pretend play takes place within the context of the real experience, such as pretending to eat in the kitchen. Later, children will pretend to eat in other rooms of their home or even outdoors.

★ Early pretend play involves the self. For example, younger children pretend to feed themselves, but will later feed a doll. Older preschoolers take on many adult and even animal roles.

★ Early pretend play starts with one action, such as combing hair. Later, this action evolves into a sequence of actions, such as several grooming tasks.

Pretend play is also called *symbolic play*. These mentally changed objects and roles are symbols used to represent the pretend world and the child's role in it. Because children make up their own symbols, such as a leaf for a plate or the child as Baby Bear, pretend play is a mental step beyond imitation.

Mental Images

Mental images are symbols of objects and past experiences that are stored in the mind. They are the pictures in the mind when words or experiences trigger the image. Unlike imitation and other play, mental images are private and **internalized** (thought about only). Mental images are not exact copies of real objects and experiences, but they do relate to the real world. For example, what mental images do you have when you hear the following words: *cat, thunderstorm,* and *flower*?

Drawing

Preschool children no longer scribble. They now attempt to draw objects and depict their world through these drawings, 17-1. Preschoolers intend their drawings to be realistic. They draw what they

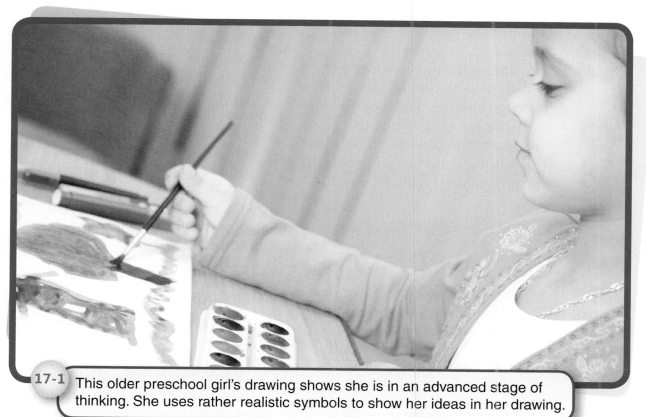

17-1 This older preschool girl's drawing shows she is in an advanced stage of thinking. She uses rather realistic symbols to show her ideas in her drawing.

think or know about a person, not what is visually accurate (like a camera view). For example, a side view of a goldfish in a drawing may show both eyes and even a smiling mouth. Drawing is a step between pretend play and mental images. This is because preschool children draw first and then decide what their pictures represent. This is in contrast to older children who decide what to draw, form a mental image of the object, and then draw it.

Language

Spoken words are symbols used to represent something. The symbols used in language are the most difficult of all symbols to understand. Unlike symbols used in pretend play, children do not decide on language symbols, but must use symbols that already exist. Words are also more **abstract** (do not relate to what they represent) compared with many other symbols. For example, the word *car* does not look, sound, or move like a car.

Although words are abstract, they do help in talking. Once language abilities develop, the child can exchange ideas with others and thus learn. The child can also think with words. Thinking is faster using words compared with actions, too.

How Preschool Children Learn

Both Piaget and Vygotsky noted how children learn by developing abstract meanings separate from their real world. They both noted the new mental abilities preschoolers have gained. Piaget focused on the limitations of these abilities, whereas Vygotsky looked at the abilities as the beginning of abstract thinking. Thus, both theories help us understand the preschooler's mental world.

Piaget's Preoperational Stage

Piaget has described the second major stage of mental development as the **preoperational stage**. This is the stage children reach before they acquire logical mental actions, which Piaget calls *operations*. These logical mental actions (operations) require the mind to think through problems and act accordingly. Operations are what most people consider logical thinking. *Logical thinking* includes combining ideas or objects, placing them in order, and doing "if-then" thinking. Preschool children have not entered the logical thinking stage yet. Just as toddlers who are walking are prone to missteps, preschool children who are thinking are prone to thinking errors in logic. (Many examples are given in this chapter.)

The preoperational stage occurs during the preschool years. For some children, it begins in the last toddler year; and for others, it includes the first year or two of school. Chart 17-2 shows the two parts of the preoperational stage—the *preconceptual* and the *intuitive substages*.

Piaget's Preoperational Substages

The **preconceptual substage** is a substage in which children ages two to four years are beginning to develop some concepts. These children are able to form a mental

Piaget's Stages of Cognitive Development

Stage 1: Sensorimotor Stage (Birth to 2 years)

Stage 2: Preoperational Stage (2 to 7 years)
Learning through symbols, such as pretend play, mental symbols, drawing, and language, but with logical limitations. The word *preoperational* means before *(pre)* logical mental actions *(operations)*.

Substage 1: Preconceptual (2 to 4 years)
* ★ Begins to develop concepts.
* ★ Has rapid development of language.
* ★ Does not think logically. (See "Obstacles to Logical Thinking" in text.)

Substage 2: Intuitive (4 to 7 years)
* ★ Figures things out through perception more than through logic; that is, cannot explain "Why."
* ★ Shows improvement, especially in classifying, ordering, and numerical skills.

Stage 3: Concrete Operational Stage (7 to 11 years)

Stage 4: Formal Operational Stage (11 years on)

17-2 The preschool child functions in the preoperational stage.

image of what they see around them. However, many of these concepts are incomplete or illogical. Children may call any animal that plays with a ball, *a dog*. They may see different members of the same group as identical, such as all collies as *Lassie*.

In the **intuitive substage**, children sometimes are able to grasp a problem's solution by how they feel about it. Through their intuition, they base their solutions on "feeling their way through" problems rather than on logic. For example, a child standing on the ladder of a slide may say to his or her parent, "I am taller than you," because he or she can see over the parent's head. The intuitive preschooler does not use logic, such as, "I may look taller,

but my feet are higher than my parent's feet; thus I am still shorter than my parent." They may even solve problems correctly, but do it through their intuition, not through logic. For example, a child can be shown three balls—blue, yellow, and red—placed in a tube with the red ball on top and held vertically. The child is told the tube will be rotated and that he or she needs to know whether the red ball is on the top or the bottom. The child watches as the tube is turned and keeps track of the red ball in his or her "mind's eye." However, the child does not use logic concerning complete and half turns to know where the red ball is, such as each complete turn means that the red ball is on top and any half turns means that it is on the bottom.

Obstacles to Logical Thinking

Piaget's work focused on the obstacles to logical thinking seen in preoperational children. What obstacles did he note that must be overcome before children can think logically? First, preschool children, especially those under four, are *egocentric*. Piaget describes **egocentrism** as the preschooler's belief that everyone thinks in the same way and has the same ideas as he or she does. *Egocentrism*, in this sense, does not mean children are selfish or too concerned with themselves. It means they simply view the world in relation to themselves. They may offer others candy from their mouths because they are enjoying it and think others would, too. If children think the slide is tall, they think adults think it is tall, too. They do not recognize that an adult who is taller may see the slide as small.

Second, preschoolers center their attention on only one part of an object or event (called *centration*). They do not see all parts at the same time. Look at the example in 17-3. The preoperational child can see that two same-size glasses hold the same amount of liquid (A). However, when one glass is poured into a beaker of smaller diameter, the child sees the liquid higher in the beaker (B) and thinks the tall container holds more. The child does not understand that the thinness of the beaker affects the level of the liquid. (The child can, however, tell you how the two containers differ in appearance.) The same thinking occurs when the child sees the liquid in the wider diameter bowl. The child thinks the quantity of liquid has changed (C). Children usually think that *wide* means *more* liquid; some children think the lower height means *less* liquid in the bowl than in the glass. Suppose the adult pours the liquid back and forth from the original glass to the beaker or bowl. The child may continue to say the quantity changes with each pour. The child cannot reason that the quantity remains the same because no liquid was added or taken away. The needed logic for this thought does not usually develop until the school-age years.

Third, preschool children tend to focus on single steps, stages, or events, rather than see the order of changes (called the *inability to follow transformations*). Piaget says the focus is as though they are seeing each frame of a film as a separate, unrelated picture rather than as a running story. As shown in 17-4, if an object is held upright and falls, it passes from an original state (vertical) to a final state (horizontal). This happens through a series of angled states. Preoperational children, after watching the object fall, will draw only the first or the

17-3 Preschool children know the amount of liquid in the two equal-sized glasses is the same (A). When the liquid of one container is poured into a tall tube (B) or a wide bowl (C), preschool children incorrectly think the amount of liquid has changed.

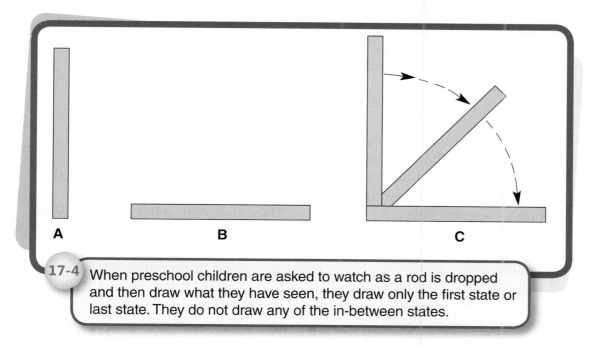

A   B   C

17-4 When preschool children are asked to watch as a rod is dropped and then draw what they have seen, they draw only the first state or last state. They do not draw any of the in-between states.

last state. How something happened or what something was like before a final change took place does not enter their minds.

Fourth, preschoolers cannot follow a line of reasoning back to where it starts (called *lack of reversibility*). They cannot retrace the steps to undo the task. For example, adding two to three equals five. To reverse the problem, a logical thinker would subtract two from five to equal three. Because the preschooler cannot see why subtracting can "undo" addition, Piaget says the preschooler cannot *reverse* (undo an action).

Finally, preschoolers link events without using logic (called *transductive reasoning*). Reasoning this way causes flaws in logic. An example is when a mother makes coffee just before a father comes home from work each day. The child may conclude that it is the coffee that brings Dad home. The events are linked to each other because they occur close together in time. A preschooler cannot come

to logical conclusions when given facts. For example, tell a child that a bug with six legs is called an *insect*. Then show a child a ladybug and say, "The ladybug has six legs. What is a ladybug?" The child will probably say, "It's black." "It's small." "It has spots." The child has the information, but cannot conclude the ladybug is an insect.

Vygotsky's Ideas on Preschoolers' Learning

During this time in childhood, Vygotsky noted the origins of thought. He saw the objects used in pretend play as pivots to *imaginative thinking* (play in the mind without action) and abstract concepts. As you read earlier, during pretend play children move from very realistic props to more abstract ones.

Vygotsky also noted that the language of preschoolers is more than an *expression of knowledge* (names of objects) or a *means of communication* (vocalizing needs and wants). Vygotsky saw that language helped thought and vice versa. Children want to know the names of things so they can express their actions. Preschoolers talk to themselves as they perform tasks. For example, a child may say, "I am drinking from my cup" as he or she takes sips. In time, this speech becomes silent (just thought) although sometimes even adults whisper or talk quietly to themselves while working on challenging tasks.

Finally, Vygotsky saw the imitative acts in pretend play as a way of learning skills. These learnings are very unique to a culture. For example, people in different cultures prepare different foods and may use different tools in the process.

What Preschool Children Learn

Preschoolers have learned a lot by now. Many new concepts begin to emerge. However, many errors and gaps still exist in the preschooler's concepts. During

Children's Television Producer

Children's television producers are responsible for facilitating children's television shows. They are involved in every stage of the television program, film or video, overseeing the project from start to finish, both in the studio and on location.

Education: Education varies. Formal training can be a great asset to workers in filmmaking and television production, but experience, talent, creativity, and professionalism usually are the most important factors in getting a job.

Job Outlook: There is keen competition in this area.

these years, learning is exciting and stimulating.

Noting Physical Attributes

Preschool children develop concepts about size, shape, color, texture, and other physical attributes (qualities) of objects. They also learn what happens when objects are acted upon by people, such as tossed in the air (they fall) or pushed (they roll or scoot). Piaget called this *physical knowledge*. These attributes are in the objects themselves and can be observed.

Preschool children are limited in their thinking about physical attributes due to having a single focus or center (called *centration*). This is seen in two ways. First, the child may not note the object's most important features. For example, the child must note a zebra's stripes to distinguish it from a horse. If the child notes the zebra's ears, this will not help, as horses have similar ears. Second, because preschoolers tend to look at parts of an object, they cannot always mentally "see" the whole object. Preschool children were shown drawings such as those in 17-5. They recognized the parts, but not the whole. (Nine-year-olds could see both.) The ability to see parts as well as the total figure is important for accurate perception.

Using Logical Thinking Concepts

Logical thinking concepts are those not experienced through the senses, but understood mentally. They require the thinker to see a relationship. Logical thinking

17-5 Most preschool children will see only parts of these drawings. They do not see the faces in the whole drawings.

concepts include classifying; arranging by size; understanding number, spatial, and time concepts; seeing cause and effect relationships; and understanding natural events. When compared to physical knowledge concepts, logical thinking concepts are much more difficult for preschool children to understand. In fact, most logical thinking concepts are not mastered until the school-age years.

Classifying Objects

Classifying is the ability to choose an attribute and group all the objects from a set (either physically or mentally) possessing that attribute. Because most preschool children become good at matching like objects, they can learn to sort. Sorting is a skill that must be mastered before classifying. Classifying is a much more difficult skill to master than sorting.

Arranging by Size

Often preschool children cannot arrange objects by increasing or

Learn More About...
Classifying Objects

To classify, the child must see how objects are alike in one attribute while disregarding other attributes. For example, while using geometric shapes in many colors and sizes, the child decides on one attribute, such as *blue*. The child would classify by grouping all blue things regardless of shape or size. Preschoolers are more apt to consider more than one attribute and end up *sorting* (putting objects into many like groups, such as red squares or blue circles). They may also begin by classifying, such as by one color, and then change attributes in midstream. For example, the child may start putting *blue* shapes together. Then he or she notices that one of the blue shapes is a *square*. Now he or she begins including *squares* of other colors in the group. Piaget would say preschoolers cannot really classify although they can point to each blue item or each square regardless of its color.

decreasing size, weight, or volume. Again, arranging by size requires mentally seeing two relationships. For example, suppose the task was to line up three people by height. The person in the middle must be shorter than one person (first relationship), but taller than the other (second relationship). You can imagine how difficult this must be for young preschoolers.

Toward the end of the preschool years, many children can arrange dowel rods or sticks in order of their lengths. To do this, however, the preschooler must physically lay the rods beside one another and hold all the bottom ends even, which is perceptual, not logical.

Understanding Number Concepts

Many preschool children can count. However, counting does not show they understand numbers. For example, a preschool child may be able to count to five by saying the numbers (called *rote counting*). The same child may have trouble when asked to find five apples in a basket or drawn on a page. Young preschoolers do not understand the one-to-one relationship that takes place when counting objects (called *rational counting*). Preschoolers may have seen older children or adults count while touching objects. They may not understand that one (and only one) number is said for each object touched and that all objects must be touched once (and only once).

Once preschoolers can count objects successfully, they still do not completely understand number concepts that also require seeing relationships. Unlike each object that

has its own name, numbers refer to groups. The number does not really refer to just the last object named, but also to the entire group. Thus, the child must mentally see that one is in two and two is in three. In fact, true counting is really adding.

Furthermore, number concepts may be made more difficult for young children by the use of many indefinite terms, such as *less*, *few*, *many*, and *some*. Adults need to realize how difficult it really is for preschoolers to understand number concepts.

Understanding Spatial Concepts

Preschool children understand the words *up*, *down*, *left*, *right*, *under*, *over*, *here*, and *there*. However, they have problems with spatial concepts. For example, until about five years of age, preschoolers may not know what is on the other side of a wall in their own homes. Preschool children also draw what they think about space rather than what they see. For example, chimneys on houses are often drawn at right angles to the roof, 17-6.

17-6 A preschool child often draws trees and other objects at right angles to the slope of the hill.

Preschool children think of the location of an object or person in relation to themselves. Learning left and right from another's perspective is hard—especially if the person is facing them. Simple tasks, such as setting a table, help children grasp these concepts.

A relationship between understanding spatial concepts and music has been noted in brain development research. Children who studied a musical instrument (not singing) have better understandings of spatial concepts throughout life. Music learnings, begun at ages three or four years, seem to produce long-term changes in the brain.

Understanding Time Concepts

Preschoolers can recall the recent past. Yesterday is recalled, but a week or a year ago may be forgotten. Children link time to events, such as time to eat lunch. They cannot see time passing. There is no physical change in the days of the week. Morning, afternoon, and seasonal changes are gradual. For these reasons, time concepts are hard to understand. They are among the last concepts to develop.

Seeing Cause and Effect

Preschool children try to understand cause and effect. Asking questions helps them to do this. Preschool children often reverse cause and effect. They may say, "Because I am staying in bed, I am ill." Reversing cause and effect may occur because many causes and their effects happen at almost the same time. In some cases, the preschooler's reversal of cause and effect may come from the difficulty in using the sentence structure to express the concept.

Understanding Natural Events

Natural events are too complex for young children to understand. Children ask questions, such as "What causes the rain?" and "What will happen to my dead fish?" Although adults may give them scientific answers, these children seem to settle on their own ideas. Some of these ideas are not even part of the real world. The following are some illogical ideas many preschoolers have about natural events:

★ **Animism.** Preschool children may assign human qualities to nonhumans, such as plants, animals, and objects. For example, the child may say, "The bike was mad at me and made me fall." Sometimes animism is used to avoid being punished or having to do something they do not want to do. For example, a preschooler may say, "My teddy bear left my toys outside."

★ **Artificialism.** Preschool children believe everything is made by real or imaginary people. For example, the child may say, "The sun was rolled into a ball by giants."

★ **Finalism.** Preschool children believe that everything has a purpose. For example, the child may say, "The ball *wanted* to roll into the street."

Language Abilities Increase

Some preschool children speak rather well. They use language to express their needs and feelings to others, 17-7. Age three years is an important time for language use.

Preschoolers' speech is as egocentric as their thinking because language often reflects thinking. In other words, they talk as though the listener would understand as they do. Thus, they often do not communicate all the needed information. *Egocentric speech* includes telling a story from the middle instead of the beginning because preschoolers assume the listener knows the beginning of the story. These young children may also use pronouns without naming the person, such as "She is eating." Again, they assume the adult knows who *she* is. The preschooler may even become impatient with the adult's lack of knowledge.

Other types of egocentric speech include repeating words without speaking to anyone. Sometimes children use **monologue** (talk to themselves as though thinking aloud). Other times they engage in a **collective monologue** (talking to another person, but not listening to what the other person has said). All children go through this stage of language development.

Toward the end of the preschool stage, egocentric speech gradually disappears. This makes communication easier. Better articulation, a larger vocabulary, and advanced grammar also make communication easier.

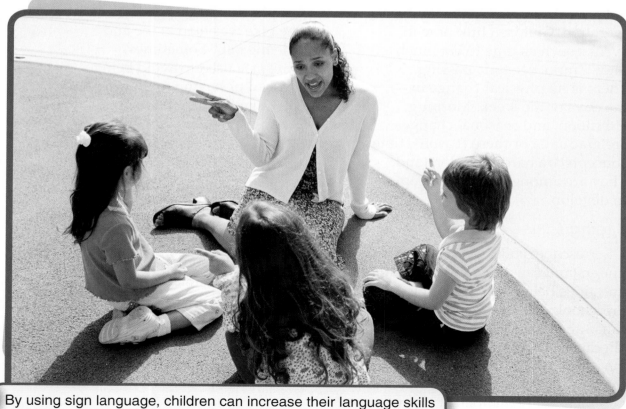

17-7 By using sign language, children can increase their language skills while learning how to express their needs and feelings to others.

Articulation of Preschool Children

Articulation refers to a person's ability to pronounce words that are understandable by others. Most toddlers have some problems making all the sounds in their spoken language. Most children substitute one sound for another for a time. In the English language, children master sounds between ages three and eight years. How fast preschool children master the sounds varies. However, the order in which they master them is about the same for most children. *Total mastery* means the child can articulate the sound in different positions within words. (Most sounds, but not all, are found in the beginning, middle, and end of words.) Chart 17-8 shows the sounds that most preschool children have mastered.

Vocabulary of Preschool Children

Experts study vocabulary growth. They have found that children know about 900 words at age three years, 1,500 words at four years, and 2,000 words at five years. Words for concrete items (such as names for objects and people) are learned before those that symbolize abstract ideas (such as names for emotions). Also, preschool children often assign their own meanings to words. A three-year-old may use the terms *less* and *more* to mean *more*, or *yesterday* to mean *anytime in the past*. Brain development research shows the window of opportunity for vocabulary growth never closes.

Articulation Mastery of Preschool Children

Age	Sound	Word Examples
3 Years	m	monkey, hammer, broom
	n	nails, penny, lion
	p	pig, happy, cup
	h	hand, doghouse
	w	window, bowl
4 Years	b	boat, baby, tub
	k	cat, chicken, book
	g	girl, wagon, pig
	f	fork, telephone, knife
5 Years	y	yellow, onion
	ng	fingers, ring
	d	dog, ladder, bed

17-8 Ninety percent of all preschool children master these sounds by the given age.

Grammar of Preschool Children

Sentence structure becomes much more complex during the preschool period. At the beginning of this stage, preschool children do not seem to notice word order. Young children will respond to "Give doll the Mommy," as quickly as they do to "Give Mommy the doll." By five years, children will not respond to "Give doll the Mommy." Preschool children's use of grammar matures a great deal between ages three and five years.

Brain development research shows the window of opportunity to learn grammar through listening to others closes at five or six years of age. Perhaps this is why grammar problems are difficult to overcome in the school-age years.

Grammar at Three Years

As shown in 17-9, three-year-olds begin to have some ideas about grammar rules. Once they learn the rules, they tend to apply them even to the exceptions. Three-year-olds may know *-ed* means past tense. Once they know the rule, they apply it to all verb forms. They may even say, "I eated." Adding *-ed* to all verbs simply shows the child has learned this grammar rule. In time, the child will learn the exceptions to the rules.

Children may have a hard time with questions because the word order is switched. Three-year-olds use question words like *when* and *why*, but they do not switch the word order. A three-year-old may ask, "When Mary will come?"

Negatives are very difficult for children, too. Once children know about negatives other than *no*, they add extra negatives. Sentences such as *I don't never want no more spinach* are common at this age. Three-year-olds do not understand the concept of multiple negatives.

Grammar at Four and Five Years

Four- and five-year-olds speak in longer, more complex sentences. They lengthen their sentences by using clauses, conjunctions, and prepositions. Instead of saying, "We play games. I had fun," the older preschool child says, "I had fun because we played games."

Four-year-old children may still find the word order of questions confusing. They often form questions by simply moving the question word to the beginning of the statement, such as "What the dog is eating?" By age five years, many children begin using tag questions. *Tag questions* are asked by making a statement and then adding *yes* or *no* to ask the question. An example of a tag question is, "The baby is small, yes?" Late in the preschool years or early in the school-age years, children begin to form questions using the proper word order. They move the question word to the beginning of the sentence with the verb following next. For example, they would say, "What is the dog eating?"

Grammar Problems

Older preschool children continue to have two problems with grammar. They have trouble

---

Grammar of Three-Year-Olds

The *-ing* verb ending used.
★ Rolling, falling

Past tense for regular verbs (*-ed*) used.
★ Rolled, walked

Past tense for some irregular verbs used.
★ Sank, ate

Verb *to be* used to link noun to adjective.
★ Truck is red; I am good

The *-s* for making plural used.
★ Cars, dolls

The -*'s* for possessive used.
★ Bob's, Daddy's

Articles used.
★ A, the

Prepositions referring to space used.
★ On, in

17-9 Three-year-olds are learning many of the rules of grammar.

with pronouns. They use objective case pronouns where subjective case is correct. For example, the child may say, "Him and me went to town," instead of "He and I went to town." Pronouns may cause problems for children into the school years.

Children also continue to apply grammar rules to every case. They may say *eated* instead of *ate*. Once the child learns the irregular form, he or she may even say *ated*. A five-year-old may learn to use the plural form *feet* and ask, "May I go barefeeted?" The many irregular forms in the English language will trouble some children for years, even if they hear the correct grammar.

Summary

Preschoolers are beginning to think in their heads rather than depending on actions. Through their new abilities, such as pretend play, mental images, drawings, and language, they are better able to solve problems and communicate. According to Piaget, preschool children are in the preoperational stage and do not yet think logically. They learn by developing some mental concepts, but many concepts are incomplete or illogical. They solve problems by "feeling their way through" instead of using logic. Vygotsky saw pretend play as a pivot toward thinking and abstract concepts. Vygotsky also noted the child's monologues, when connected to actions, aided thinking.

Preschoolers develop many concepts about the physical attributes of objects, such as size, shape, color, texture, and other qualities. Older preschoolers are also beginning to learn logical thinking concepts, such as classifying; arranging in order; and understanding numbers, space, time, cause and effect, and natural events. Because these tasks involve complex mental relationships, preschoolers will make many errors even into the school-age years.

Preschool is an important time in language development, which is now linked to thinking. Most children at this age are ready to express their needs and feelings to others. Communication is easier because preschoolers can now articulate better and their vocabulary has increased. Sentence structure and grammar rules tend to be difficult for many preschool children as well as older children.

Companion Web Site

Interactive Activity

Review vocabulary terms and key concepts for Chapter 17 at **g-wlearning.com**.

Review and Reflect

Write your answers to the following questions on a separate sheet of paper.

1. List four new abilities that mark a preschoolers' thinking.

2. True or false. Piaget believed preoperational children often base their solutions on "feeling their way through" problems rather than on logic.

3. Vygotsky believed _____ play was the pivot to abstract thinking.

4. True or false. Preschool children tend to see the entire picture rather than concentrate on its parts.

5. List four logical thinking concepts that children begin to understand in the preschool years.

6. True or false. It is difficult for preschoolers to subtract numbers because their concept of reversing is *not* fully developed.

7. True or false. Preschool children tend to settle on their own ideas for answers to scientific questions.

8. True or false. Preschool children often talk to themselves.

9. True or false. Preschoolers learn words for emotions, such as *love* and *hate*, before they learn words for objects and people.

10. Which of the following sentences is a three-year-old most likely to say? (A) "I'm never going no more to your house!" (B) "I'm not ever going to your house again!"

Cross-Curricular Link

11. **Social Studies.** Ask a preschool center director for permission to visit with children about their drawings. (If possible, ask permission to videotape or photograph a few pieces of their art.) Ask the children to tell you about the drawings. (Say, "Tell me about your picture," rather than, "What is it?") Take notes on their responses. Using your notes and the photos or videotape of the art, share with the class what symbols were used in the drawings. Point out ways in which the artists attempted to show reality, but were not visually accurate. For example, children may draw all four wheels on a car as complete circles.

12. **Science.** Try the liquid task (as described in 17-3) with a three-year-old and a five-year-old. Report your findings to the class.

13. **Social Studies.** Borrow or make a set of rods or dowels in different sizes. (Their lengths should vary at least ¼ inch.) Demonstrate (only once) for children ages three, four,

and five years how to put the sticks in order from longest to shortest. Then ask the children to place the sticks in order. What differences do you note in the children's ability to do this task? Are these differences age-related? Report your findings to the class.

14. **Speech.** Make an audio recording of the speech of preschool children in play. Listen to the tape and then answer the following questions. What sound substitutions did you hear? Did you hear complex sentences—both statements and questions? What incorrect grammar did you hear? What concepts seemed to be correctly understood by the children? What, if any, incorrect ideas were expressed? Share your findings with the class.

Making Observations

15. Observe a group of preschool children playing a pretend game. What symbols did they use? (Examples are material symbols, such as a block for a boat; sound symbols, such as sirens; and action symbols, such as pretending to eat.) In what ways were the symbols realistic? Discuss your findings with the class.

16. Observe a group of three- and four-year-old children. As they play and talk, note what they do or say that shows they still do not think logically. Which concepts seem difficult for these children (time, classifying, and cause and effect)?

17. Observe a three- or four-year-old. Note errors in articulation and grammar. Compare your findings with Charts 17-8 and 17-9.

Thinking Critically

18. Why do adults sometimes confuse preschoolers' egocentrism with selfishness? What, if anything, might an adult say or do to help these children develop a less egocentric point of view?

19. How can a preschool teacher who has many dramatic play, art, and literature/ language activities justify these as intellectual and not "just play" activities?

20. How is collective monologue an egocentric behavior? Would selfish adults tend to engage in collective monologues? If so, how might an adult monologue differ from the definition of children's monologue?

Social-Emotional Development of the Preschooler

After studying this chapter, you will be able to

★ **analyze** the problems preschoolers face as they develop initiative.

★ **explain** how adults can help children become more responsible.

★ **describe** how preschool children learn gender roles.

★ **discuss** the growing importance of friends.

★ **describe** how feelings and emotions change during the preschool years.

Terms to Know

initiative
guilt
gender-role learning
sex typing
sexual stereotyping

peers
stressors
emotional dependency
repressed jealousy

Reading Advantage

Think of a movie you have seen that relates to this chapter. Sketch a scene from the movie or write a brief description. As you read the chapter, visualize the characters in the movie. How would the scene be different if the characters had read this chapter?

Companion Web Site

Interactive Activity

Learn more about how preschool children express their emotions by completing the *Read, Discuss, and Analyze* Activity for Chapter 18 at **g-wlearning.com**.

Preschool children continue to relate socially with people outside the family circle. As they reach out, they learn more about themselves as individuals within adult and child social groups. Preschoolers start to think and act on their own. They also start to show some responsibility and begin to learn to control their emotions. Preschoolers start to understand that temper tantrums are among the ways of showing feelings that are not acceptable to adults. Preschoolers' emotions also become more complex as they understand more about their world.

Developing Social Awareness

Children's social awareness grows during the preschool years. Their feelings about themselves and how they fit into social groups are beginning to emerge. They are becoming more dependable and can complete simple tasks in the home. Through better use of language and social skills, they start to make friends with other children.

Taking the Initiative

Between ages three and six years, children become even more independent. Because of their improved abilities and limitless energy, they have a strong desire to learn, explore, and do. These children want to experience many things. They may show never ending curiosity, talk a lot and loudly, move all the time, and even "attack" others to get what they want.

When children are in this stage, which Erikson calls *initiative versus guilt*, they are eager to try

new activities. Initiative motivates them to do so. **Initiative** is the ability to think or act without being urged. Developing initiative is important because it sets the stage for ambitions later in life. Yet, initiative can lead to failures. Too many failures may lead to **guilt** (blaming oneself for something done wrong) and fear of trying new things, 18-1.

When the preschool child makes mistakes, he or she may feel badly about himself or herself. If the child feels too guilty, obedience becomes

Erikson's Stages of Personality Development

Basic Trust versus Basic Mistrust (First Year of Life)

Autonomy versus Shame and Doubt (Second Year of Life)

Initiative versus Guilt (Preschool Years)

★ Preschool children have growing abilities, much energy, and desire to engage in activities.
★ They begin trying things on their own initiative.
★ The sense of initiative learned at this stage leads to ambition and purpose.
★ Too many failures and too many negative responses from adults lead to guilt and fear of trying new activities.

Industry versus Inferiority (Middle Childhood)

18-1 Showing initiative while avoiding guilt is a major social-emotional task of the preschool years.

so important the child is afraid to try new things. This fear and guilt stifles initiative. To prevent guilty feelings, children must know it is okay to make mistakes.

Children develop initiative when they are allowed to ask questions, experiment, and explore. However, their initiative can sometimes lead to actions that are dangerous or beyond their abilities. In these cases, adults need to set limits. Galinsky's *authority stage* of parenting continues in the preschool years. At this time, children can better understand parents' explanations for limits.

Showing Responsibility

During the preschool years, children often take the first steps toward becoming dependable people. They begin to show responsibility, which is a sign of being dependable. Learning to show responsibility takes time and calls for experience. Children will have many successes and failures before they learn responsibility.

Adults help children become responsible by setting examples and giving children chances to learn. For this to occur, adults must select tasks the child can do. The child should have both the ability and the time to do each task. He or she must also be shown how to do tasks. Any requirements must be made clear. Adults must follow through with praise or other rewards for successes. They must also offer support after failures.

Preschool children are often given responsibility for household tasks, such as helping in the kitchen, putting toys away, and folding laundry. In preschool programs, children are often required to put away toys, books, and other materials. They help hand out snacks and care for plants and animals. Erikson believes children should take part in the routines of their world in real and important ways, 18-2.

18-2 Children learn to be dependable when they can help with real tasks in their world.

Learning Gender Roles

Learning about yourself is an important part of social awareness. This is because you learn how to fit into certain social groups (family, school, clubs, and others). In order to fit into any social group, people learn what is expected. For example, some behaviors are expected from people based on their gender. **Gender-role learning** means knowing what behavior is expected of a male or a female.

Gender role is a major concept children learn in the preschool years. Until age two years, most children cannot identify whether they are male or female. By age three years, gender-role learning begins. At this age, children know there are physical differences between boys and girls. They are also beginning to sense that boys and girls act differently in many situations.

How Does Gender Role Develop?

Children learn their gender roles by how others treat them and how they see others in their male or female roles. Some families treat boys and girls differently (**sex typing**). In these families, big differences exist in the clothing worn, toys received, and ways parents react to boys and girls. Other families do not distinguish between what a boy and girl can do, play with, or wear, 18-3.

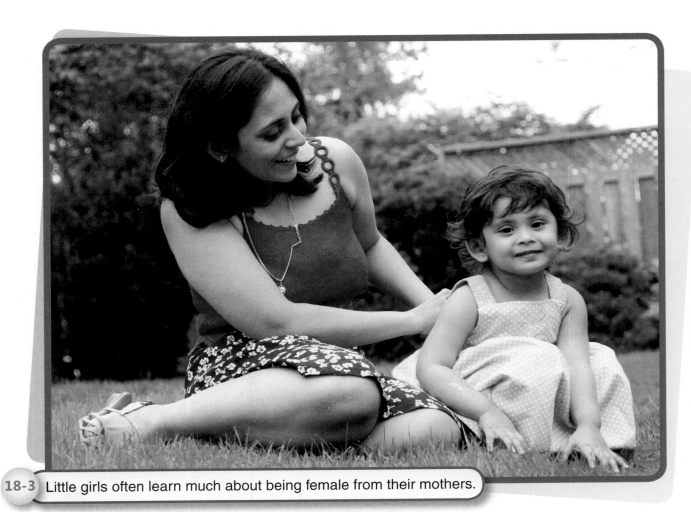

18-3 Little girls often learn much about being female from their mothers.

Children most often identify with and imitate models of the same gender. They begin to think and behave as though the traits of another belong to them. They identify with and model themselves after family members and friends. They may also model teachers and characters from television, movies, and storybooks.

Cultural Factors

The U.S. society's view of male and female roles is not as clearly defined as it once was. Traditional gender roles see the male as more aggressive and the economic head of the family. The traditional gender role sees the female as the wife and mother who stays home. **Sexual stereotyping** is a statement or even a hint that men and women always do or should do certain tasks. You can find examples of sexual stereotyping in books, television shows, and in some people's conversations.

These traditional roles are changing with the increase in the number of women employed outside the home. Also, more men have been sharing household and child care duties. Many people believe that, in order to thrive within today's lifestyle, roles must adapt to the situation. Both men and women may want to show assertive traits (such as sharing opinions) on the job. They both may want to show loving, gentle traits with their children.

Within the U.S. society, different cultures or groups hold different beliefs about gender roles. Some groups stress differences between male roles and female roles. Others stress similarities between male and female roles.

Extending Social Relations

Preschool children not only improve motor skills and knowledge through social activities, but they also increase their social learnings. These social learnings include sharing, controlling anger, thinking of other's feelings, and making friends.

Adults Are Still Important

Preschoolers continue to depend on adults to meet many of their needs. Adults serve as social models, too. They teach children by example. Besides responsibility and gender role, adults can model relationships, morals, self-control, manners, and much more.

Other Children Become More Important

Siblings and peers are more important to preschool children than to toddlers, 18-4. (**Peers** are

18-4 Warm relationships with siblings are important to the preschool child.

others near the same age.) Preschool children's reactions to other children at this age are different. Some preschoolers have fun playing with other children, others do not.

Making Friends

The ease of making friends depends on a child's friendliness, ability to follow group rules, and lack of dependence on adults. Preschool children also prefer friends of the same gender.

Preschool children have a rather self-centered view about friendships. They see friends as people who play with you, help you, and share their toys. Because of this self-centered view, usually two or three preschool children form a close circle of friends. After all, if there are too many friends, a child may not get enough from a friend. (For example, a toy may be shared more easily with one

child than with several children.) To protect their interests, preschool children will often call out, "You can't play with us." When a friend does not do as the child desires, feelings quickly change. The child takes a new best friend—at least for the moment.

Feeling and Controlling Emotions

Preschool children feel many emotions and express them in intense ways. Preschoolers still react to common childlike **stressors** (situations that cause stress). These include short separations from caring adults and fear of monsters. Short-term stressors also include "bad days" for preschoolers. These occur when their initiative requires more "nos" or when their emotions seem out of control. Besides these stressors, preschool children will react to many more long-lasting and serious stressors. These may include illness, moving, death, adult quarrels, and divorce.

Preschool children feel many emotions and are expected to control many of their intense feelings. Controlling outward signs of emotions, such as crying, screaming, or hitting, helps children become socially acceptable. However, if children control emotions without admitting their underlying feelings to themselves and others, they may become emotionally troubled. Children need to express feelings. Statements such as, "I am angry,"

Focus on Social Studies

Learnings from Play Groups

The peer group offers many learnings. As preschoolers play together, play experiences become richer. Children get new ideas and can play with more than one child. Group play teaches preschoolers how to behave with peers. Because peers are equals, children can simply refuse to play with a child who does not play fairly. Children become less self-centered in peer groups. They hear other children's points of view. Finally, children learn that

 friends are fun. A child can play with friends, sit and talk with friends, and celebrate with friends. What are some other ways in which children can learn from play groups?

or, "I'm afraid you'll leave me the way you left daddy," are healthy. How should the parent respond? Parents should affirm the emotions and address the concern. For example, parents could say, "I understand why you are angry (or afraid). I am so sorry your daddy and I could not work out our problems. I can tell you that we will always love you and make sure you are cared for and loved."

Dependency

Preschool children often feel a conflict between their needs for dependence and independence. Like toddlers, three-year-olds most often show their dependence in emotional ways. **Emotional dependency** is the act of seeking attention, approval, comfort, and contact. In emotional dependency, the child is often dependent only on one or two people. Unlike toddlers, preschoolers are more apt to accept comfort from strangers. However, they still prefer a loved adult or peer.

By age five years, children more often seek help in achieving a goal than they seek contact or approval. Older preschool children may ask an adult to button their coat or reach a toy on a high shelf. In most cases, the child really does need help. The child may also ask for help that is not needed. He or she may do this to check the adult's love or concern. In other words, emotional dependency is sometimes disguised.

Fear and Anxiety

Many of the toddler's fears disappear by the preschool years.

Child Psychologist

Child psychologists study behavior of children to analyze processes of learning, development of language in children, and parents' influence on children's behavior. They often administer intelligence and performance tests to establish and measure patterns of intellectual and psychological growth and development.

Education: A master's or doctoral degree and a state license are required for most child psychologists.

Job Outlook: Faster-than-average employment growth is expected for psychologists.

New fears and anxieties replace the previous ones. Boys often report a greater variety of fears as they grow older. Girls report more intense reactions to the fewer fears they have. Although fears are individual, fears in the preschooler years do share some common features.

★ Fear of the known, such as vacuum cleaners, disappears. However, fear of the imagined, such as monsters and robbers, increases. Children often associate these fears with the dark.

★ Fears of physical injuries become more common. Examples include the fear of death by fire, an auto accident, or drowning, and the fear of bites and stings of animals and insects. These fears emerge as children know they can be hurt, 18-5.

★ Fear of pain caused by medical and dental work occurs.

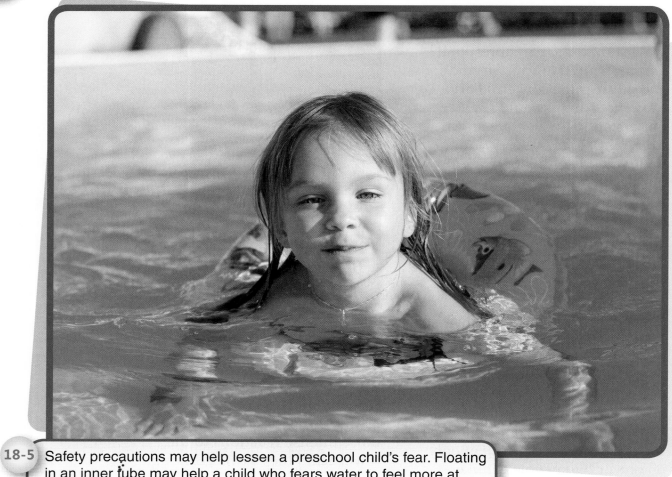

18-5 Safety precautions may help lessen a preschool child's fear. Floating in an inner tube may help a child who fears water to feel more at ease in a pool. Constant adult supervision is still needed.

★ Anxiety of a general nature is experienced. Children's specific fears may become general anxieties. For example, fear of a tornado may spread to general anxiety during a thunderstorm or even a strong wind.

As you can see, these fears and anxieties are due to the growing mind. Preschoolers understand many new concepts, but their understanding may still be limited. On the negative side, lack of understanding often creates fears and anxieties. For example, a preschool child would not understand that only certain weather conditions cause tornadoes. On the positive side, some fears may help protect children from trying unsafe activities.

Anger and Aggression

Anger and aggression begin around 10 months of age. They peak with displays of temper in the toddler years and continue in the preschool years. Expression of anger and aggression change in the preschool years to some extent.

Preschool children tend to hit or bite less than toddlers, but they threaten and yell more. Increased language skills cause this change.

Learn More About...
Causes of a Preschooler's Anger and Aggression

Children often use aggression to get their way or intentionally hurt another. Intentionally hurting someone else is the most serious form of aggression. Adults should seek to determine the underlying causes of such aggression and take action to help the child.

Children may be aggressive to gain attention or affection. Determining what a given aggressive act means can be difficult without knowing the context of the act or the traits of a given child. For example, some preschoolers may use a playful shove or hit as an affectionate greeting rather than as an aggressive act. In some cases, the child receiving such a greeting may not recognize it as a friendly sign. Fights can start from these innocent behaviors.

Sometimes objects cause a preschooler's anger. Preschoolers are in the *initiative* stage and often go beyond

their abilities only to find that objects, as well as people, may frustrate them. For example, a child may blame a bike for a fall rather than his or her lack of skill. This can result in anger and even aggression toward the object or person. Sometimes this aggression is taken out on other nearby people or objects.

Several conditions cause, or at least strengthen, anger and aggression. Having goals blocked can cause anger. One study shows that preschool children have 90 of their goals blocked each day. Preschool children who like to take charge are affected most by not getting what they want when they want it. The more carefree child is seldom unhappy when goals are blocked. This type of child simply changes the goal. For example, if a peer takes a toy, the child simply finds another toy.

However, boys tend to be more physical than girls, whereas girls tend to be more verbal than boys. It appears that girls are using more physical aggression now than in the past. This may be due to a more aggressive society or to a lack of clear distinction between gender roles.

Anger and aggression seem to be directed toward siblings and peers more often than toward adults. Preschool children appear to have learned that aggression toward adults, especially the physical type, is not acceptable. Also, anger and aggression are directed more at siblings and close friends than at casual peers.

Jealousy

Jealousy begins when people realize they must share with others the love, attention, possessions, and time once given only to them. What makes preschoolers so jealous? Preschoolers are trying to figure out who they are as individuals. To do this, they compare themselves with others. They often compete with other family members for love, which they may see as limited in amount. They compete with siblings and friends for attention and this can lead to jealousy, such as over another child's birthday party.

They are jealous about material things, such as someone else's new toy.

Jealousy often develops when there are changes in the family. The most common time for jealousy is when a new brother or sister is born. Now children must share their parents' love with this new sibling. Babies take a lot of time and energy. Children translate this as love. Preschoolers may feel there is more love for a baby and less for them.

Preschool children show fewer attachment behaviors than do toddlers, but attachment has not disappeared. In times of stress, preschool children may try to recapture the early attachment feelings. They may cry, cling, show signs of emotional dependence, and have toileting accidents, 18-6.

Some preschool children may feel jealousy, but ignore the feeling. **Repressed jealousy** is jealousy that is not directly expressed and may even be denied. Children may show this type of jealousy through nightmares or physical problems, such as upset stomachs, headaches, fevers, and changes in appetite.

Parents should note any of the symptoms of suppressed jealousy. Parents need to find ways to make each child feel special. Unlike toddlers, preschool children are better able to understand

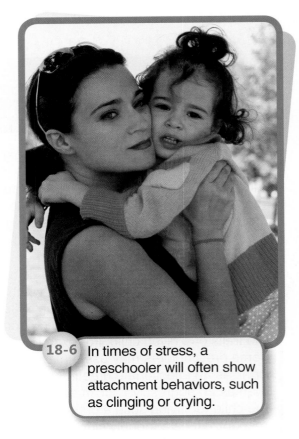

18-6 In times of stress, a preschooler will often show attachment behaviors, such as clinging or crying.

their parents' explanations. For example, a preschooler is more likely to understand when parents explain why the baby gets so much attention. Preschoolers are able to talk about some of their feelings. They can feel important by helping with a new baby. Preschoolers who are in group programs have more contacts outside the family than do other preschoolers. This often makes it easier for them to adjust to a new family member or situation.

Summary

Preschoolers who are allowed to try new activities develop a sense of initiative. If they have too many failures or limits from adults, they may feel guilty and fear trying new things on their own.

Adults need to help preschoolers become dependable. Gender roles are not as clearly defined as they once were. However, they are an important part of learning. Children learn gender roles by how others treat them and through their associations with others. They begin to identify with and model the thinking and behavior pattern of others. In this way, they learn family and workplace gender roles.

Preschool children increase their social learnings. They are still dependent on adults, but other children have become more important. Play experiences help preschoolers learn how to get along with others and develop friendships.

The preschoolers' emotions are becoming more complex. They want to be independent, but are still dependent on adults, especially for emotional support. Some of their old fears and anxieties have disappeared, but others have appeared. Anger and aggression surface during the preschool years. Jealousy stems from competition within the family and with friends over love, attention, and material things. Also, family changes bring about feelings of jealousy. However, preschoolers are better able to talk out their feelings, which helps them adjust to the changes.

Companion Web Site

Interactive Activity

Review vocabulary terms and key concepts for Chapter 18 at **g-wlearning.com**.

Review and Reflect

Write your answers to the following questions on a separate sheet of paper.

1. True or false. When limits are given to preschool children, they will quit showing initiative and feel guilty.

2. True or false. Responsibility is learned quickly if parents assign preschool children household tasks to complete.

3. True or false. When adults show preschoolers how to do something, they are teaching them about dependability and responsibility.

4. True or false. Preschoolers need some praise when they meet goals.

5. True or false. In gender-role learning, children learn what is expected in the boy or girl role.

6. True or false. A preschool child identifies with and imitates only the father role model.

7. Preschool children tend to have a closed circle of friends because (A) too many friends overwhelm the child; (B) children's games are usually played with only two or three children; (C) children have a self-centered view of friendships.

8. What can children learn from group play? List four learnings.

9. Which of the following fears are most common in preschool children? (A) loud sounds; (B) monsters; (C) physical injury and pain; (D) flushing toilets and vacuum cleaners; (E) teasing by other children; (F) darkness.

10. True or false. Anger in the preschool years is always a sign of frustration.

11. Preschool children direct their anger more at (known, unknown) children and adults.

12. True or false. Jealousy over a new baby is common.

Cross-Curricular Link

13. **Social Studies, Speech.** Work with a small group to find examples of sexual stereotyping in magazine advertisements. Discuss with your group how sexual stereotyping affects gender-role learning. Present your findings to the class.

14. **Social Studies, Writing.** Interview a teacher of preschool children. Ask this person to give examples that illustrate ways in which the program's indoor and outdoor space, equipment, and materials do the following: (A) encourage children to take the initiative for their own learnings; (B) lessen children's feelings of guilt about mistakes made; (C) give children a way to show responsibility. Write a brief report of your findings. Check your report for correct spelling, grammar, and punctuation.

15. **Social Studies, Speech.** Interview a preschool child about something scary that happened to him or her. Have the child draw a picture. Write a brief summary of the interview, including quotes from the child about the scary incident. Display the child's drawing and your report on a bulletin board.

16. **Research, Writing.** Use Internet or print sources to research the development of phobias. Write a one-page report of your findings. Check your report for correct spelling, grammar, and punctuation.

Making Observations

17. Watch children at play in a group program. List some of the gender-related differences you noted in the children's play activities, discussions, and interactions.

18. Observe a preschooler interacting with an adult at home or in a group program. What tasks was the child asked to do? How did the adult explain the task? Was the child able to do it, and why or why not? Did the child seem to feel successful?

19. Observe preschoolers in a group program. What emotions were expressed? How did adults handle the intense emotions? Did they help the children find more acceptable ways of expressing feelings?

Thinking Critically

20. How have gender roles changed over the last two or three generations? Do you think learning gender roles is easier or more difficult for today's children than for children 50 or more years ago? Why? (To help students respond, they may need to watch a sitcom episode of the 1950s, such as *I Love Lucy* or *Leave It to Beaver*.)

21. How do you think preschoolers benefit from their interactions with older adults? How do you think older adults benefit from the interactions?

22. How might adults lessen the possibilities of jealousy in preschoolers? How can adults help preschoolers deal with their jealousies if they occur? How is uncontrolled jealousy harmful in the teen and adult years?

Providing for the Preschooler's Developmental Needs

After studying this chapter, you will be able to

★ **plan** ways to meet the developmental needs of preschool children.

★ **help** preschool children care for their own physical needs.

★ **stimulate** preschool children's mental thinking.

★ **assist** preschoolers in meeting their social-emotional needs.

Terms to Know

enuresis
compare
contrast
passive observing
problem solving
transformation
class
class complement

reversals
divergent thinking
convergent thinking
cooperation
altruistic behavior
anger
aggression
assertive

Reading Advantage

As you read the chapter, put sticky notes next to the sections where you have questions. Write your questions on the sticky notes. Discuss the questions with your classmates or teacher.

Companion Web Site

Interactive Activity

Learn more about how a preschooler's intellectual needs are met by completing the *Read, Discuss, and Analyze* Activity for Chapter 19 at **g-wlearning.com**.

As you have seen, preschool children's motor, mental, and social skills develop at rapid rates. These skills help preschoolers meet their own needs. Preschoolers want to do things for themselves and others. They like to use their motor skills to feed and dress themselves and help with everyday tasks.

Mental thinking (as opposed to using physical actions to solve problems) is well underway in the preschool years. Preschoolers can mentally see objects and actions. They can even begin to solve problems in mental ways. Concepts become more correct. Language helps preschoolers expand concepts. Language is also a sign of a preschooler's progress in learning concepts.

Social skills also grow in the preschool years. Preschool children's social world includes many new adults, close friends, peers, and perhaps younger siblings. Adults expect preschool children to become more independent, responsible, and in control of their feelings. Peers and siblings treat children more as equals. Peers do not give each other the special favors adults often do. For example, a child will not always be given the first turn when playing with peers as he or she would when playing games with adults.

Preschool children are learning a whole way of life in which needs in one area of development affect needs in other areas. Thus, preschool children's changing physical, mental, and social needs demand a great deal of support and much time from caring adults.

Physical Needs

Preschool children no longer completely depend on adults to meet all their physical needs. As the body matures, motor skills are refined and the mind grows. Preschoolers are better able to help care for themselves. At this age, children want to help meet their own needs. They want to help prepare meals and dress themselves.

Children will take the initiative in learning how to meet their physical needs. However, adults must help. This is the first chance the child and adult have to work as a team and meet the child's physical needs.

Meeting Nutritional Needs

To meet the preschool child's nutritional needs, adults must be prepared to provide a variety of healthy foods at regularly scheduled meal and snack times. However, parents must be flexible and listen to their preschooler. Children grow at different rates and their energy output can vary from month to month. In addition, preschool children become more interested in foods prepared in different ways. However, eating *junk foods* (foods low in nutritional value) may become more of a problem in the preschool years.

You Are What You Eat

The slogan *you are what you eat* is correct. What you eat affects how you grow. Growth slows during the preschool years as compared to the first three years of life. However, a preschooler is not finished growing. In the preschool years, height increases about seven inches, and weight increases about 13 pounds. Other body systems must keep pace with skeletal growth. If the diet does not meet the body's needs, the body may conserve fuel needed for its own upkeep. This may slow the rate of growth. Children are also more prone to diseases when nutritional needs are not met. In addition, their recovery time is slower when ill.

The preschool child is an active child, 19-1. Watch preschool children at play. Their bodies twist, turn, and bounce as they walk. Thus, their energy needs are high. This energy must come from the foods they eat.

Nutritious foods are needed for brain growth, too. A person's daily diet affects general alertness. Diet seems to affect emotions, too. When daily food needs are met, the child seems less irritable and restless.

Basic Food Choices

MyPyramid.gov offers individualized eating plans for preschoolers as well as sample menus and tips for healthy eating. These plans show how much a child needs from each group. At this age, children often get hungry between meals and snacks, 19-2. Both the meals and snacks should be nutritious in order to meet the needs of growing children.

19-1 Preschool children have high energy levels.

Meal and Snack Pattern A

These patterns show one way a **1200 calorie MyPyramid Plan** can be divided into meals and snacks for a preschooler. Sample food choices are shown for each meal or snack.

Breakfast	Breakfast Ideas		
1 ounce Grains ½ cup Fruit ½ cup Milk*	**Cereal and Banana** *1 cup crispy rice cereal* *½ cup sliced banana* *½ cup milk**	**Yogurt and Strawberries** *½ cup plain yogurt** *4 sliced strawberries* *1 slice whole wheat toast*	**Applesauce Topped Pancake** *1 small pancake* *¼ cup applesauce* *¼ cup blueberries* *½ cup milk**

Morning Snack	Morning Snack Ideas		
1 ounce Grains ½ cup Fruit	*1 slice cinnamon bread* *½ large orange*	*1 cup toasted oat cereal* *½ cup diced pineapple*	**Frozen Graham Cracker Sandwich** *2 graham crackers (4 squares)* *½ cup mashed banana*

Lunch	Lunch Ideas		
1 ounce Grains ½ cup Vegetables ½ cup Milk* 1 ounce Meat & Beans	**Open-faced Chicken Sandwich and Salad** *1 slice whole wheat bread* *1 slice American cheese** *1 ounce sliced chicken* *½ cup baby spinach (raw)* *¼ cup grated carrots*	**Soft Taco (meat or veggie)** *1 small tortilla* *½ cup salad greens* *¼ cup chopped tomatoes* *¼ cup shredded cheese** *1 ounce cooked ground beef* *or ¼ cup refried beans*	**Bagel Snake** *1 mini whole grain bagel* *¼ cup sliced cherry tomatoes* *¼ cup diced celery* *1 ounce tuna* *½ cup milk**

Afternoon Snack	Afternoon Snack Ideas		
½ cup Vegetables ½ cup Milk*	*½ cup sugar snap peas* *½ cup yogurt**	*½ cup veggie "matchsticks"* *(carrot, celery, zucchini)* *½ cup milk**	*½ cup tomato juice* *1 string cheese**

Dinner	Dinner Ideas		
1 ounce Grains ½ cup Vegetables ½ cup Milk* 2 ounces Meat & Beans	**Chicken & Potatoes** *2 ounces chicken breast* *¼ cup mashed potato* *¼ cup green peas* *1 small whole wheat roll* *½ cup milk**	**Spaghetti & Meatballs** *½ cup cooked pasta* *¼ cup tomato sauce* *2 meatballs (2 ounces)* *½ small ear corn on the cob* *½ cup milk**	**Rice & Beans with Sausage** *½ cup cooked brown rice* *¼ cup black beans* *¼ cup bell pepper* *1 ounce turkey sausage* *¼ cup broccoli* *½ cup milk**

*Offer your child fat-free or low-fat milk, yogurt, and cheese.

19-2 Parents should offer foods to their preschoolers as determined by **MyPyramid.gov**. This sample meal and snack pattern from MyPyramid is designed for a four-year-old boy or girl who is active less than 30 minutes daily.

MyPyramid for Preschoolers
Eat Right. Exercise. Have Fun.
MyPyramid.gov

To help children learn healthy eating habits, let them eat only as much as they want. When old enough, allow children to serve themselves. Parents should suggest children take small portions at first and come back for more if they are still hungry. Allow them to stop eating once they feel full and do not force them to finish all their food. A child who learns to pay attention to what his or her body is signaling is more likely to maintain a healthy weight. When a child needs a special diet for health reasons, adults should consult a doctor or registered dietitian.

Foods that are offered to preschoolers for meals and snacks should be nutritious. Experts say preschool children as well as adults should lessen their intake of sugar, salt, and fats. Why limit these items? Eating excessive amounts of sugar can lead to tooth decay, obesity, and other health problems. These health problems often last for years. For example, a majority of overweight preschoolers are still overweight at age 12. Consuming too much fat and salt early in life may increase chances of high blood pressure in later years. This chance increases if high blood pressure exists in the family's health history. Snack foods that are high in sugar, salt, and fats should be avoided.

Food Attitudes Are Learned

The food attitudes preschoolers learn may last a lifetime. Offering a variety of foods in a pleasant atmosphere helps preschoolers form good food attitudes.

For the most part, people like variety in their lives. This includes what they eat. Some children may go through phases where they want the same food(s) day after day for a time. Others eat or drink a few of the same foods daily, but vary other foods.

Many options are available within each food group. Children should be able to eat foods they like and still meet their nutritional needs. Forcing children to eat foods they do not like can cause them to have negative feelings toward healthy foods. Using food to reward or punish can also have a bad effect. Children who are rewarded and punished with food may learn to eat as a way of bribery. For example, some parents reward with food by saying, "If you pick up your toys, we will get an ice cream cone." It would be better to say, "We'll go to the park and play catch as soon as you pick up your toys." Many parents punish their picky eaters by threatening to withhold food. For example, imagine the following conversation:

Adult: "You can't have dessert until you eat your peas!"

Child: "How many cookies do I get if I eat my peas?"

Preventing Eating Problems

Adults can prevent some eating problems in preschool children. Adults need to know that children and adults have different senses of taste and smell. For example, many adults wonder why some children do not like spinach. There is an acid in spinach (oxalic acid) that leaves a bitter aftertaste in the mouths of children, but not adults. Children often prefer mild flavors and aromas over stronger ones. They tend not to like foods that are too spicy. Children are influenced by other food tastes and qualities as well.

Food That Looks Good

How food looks may influence whether children think they will like it. Children like attractive-looking foods. Foods of different sizes, shapes, colors, textures, and temperatures look better than foods that look the same. Plates should have some empty space. Full plates can give children the feeling of too much before they take one bite. (Children can have second helpings.) Children also enjoy foods prepared especially for them, 19-3. Special dishes, napkins, or centerpieces may make eating a meal or snack even more special.

Separate Rather Than Combination Foods

Children often prefer foods that are eaten separately rather than foods that are combined. If children see or taste one food they do not like in a casserole, soup, or salad, they may reject the whole dish. They accept mixtures of fruits more easily than mixtures of vegetables. Children may eat what they choose to mix more readily than adult-prepared mixtures.

For example, children may prefer to mix their own salads from several bowls of precut vegetables.

Foods Served at Acceptable Temperatures

Preschool children do not like foods that are served at extreme temperatures. In fact, they can easily burn their mouths on foods that are too hot. Some of these foods (such as hot drinks) can simply be avoided for most children do not like them anyway. Soups are good for children, but young children cannot manage a steamy bowl or cup of soup. One easy solution is to drop a few ice cubes into hot soup just as the child begins to eat. As the ice melts, the temperature of the soup will drop to an acceptable level. Very cold foods present a problem, too. Children eat these foods very slowly, because eating large bites can cause a sharp headache. Thus, there may be more ice cream on the outside of a preschool child than on the inside. Parents can start offering suggestions for managing hot and cold foods during the late preschool years.

19-3 Foods that look fun to eat also seem to taste better.

Foods Prepared in Different Ways

Children show likes and dislikes for ways to prepare food. A child who turns down cooked carrots may eat a crisp, raw carrot. A salad dressing or dip that is not too tangy may make almost any vegetable or fruit easy to eat. Dressings made from yogurt and cheese help meet the calcium needs of young children, too.

New Foods in Small Amounts

Children will often take one bite or a small amount of a food just to see whether they like it. Give children new foods in small amounts (one slice or a tablespoon). Serve new foods with ample portions of foods children like to eat. The new food may be rejected, but do not give up. Foods may need to be offered many times before children accept them.

Easy-to-Eat Foods

Foods should be easy for preschoolers to eat. Bite-sized and finger foods are preferred over foods that are harder to eat. Most children at this age cannot cut food. They may not hold spoons and forks the right way. These problems make eating messier for preschoolers than for older children and adults.

Selecting the Right Clothes

Selecting the right clothes for preschool children is important. Clothes protect the child's body from harsh weather conditions and scrapes and cuts. Clothes are also important to a child's growing self-concept.

Learn More About... Making Meals Fun

Children enjoy helping to prepare food. By helping, children learn about colors, shapes, tastes, aromas, textures, and appliance names (*blender, oven*). They learn food preparation terms (*cut, boil, poach, bake*) and food names. Cooking teaches math concepts (*measurement, numbers, temperature, time, shapes*). It also introduces children to science as they see changes in foods (*rising, baking, freezing, boiling*). As an added bonus, children often eat what they help prepare.

Children should enjoy eating with others. Meals should be a time to relax, share, and have fun. There should be a quiet time before and after meals. Enough time should be given for the meal itself, because eating with children takes time.

Setting an example of taking turns talking and other table manners allows children to learn at mealtimes. However, punishment and scoldings should not take place at the table. All talk should be pleasant.

An attractive room for eating helps, too. Dishes and flatware suited to the child's hands make mealtime easier and also lessens the chance of accidents. Preschool children may want to help make the table attractive by choosing the napkins, picking a flower from the garden for the table, or helping set the table.

Food becomes a part of many celebrations. Preschool children may look forward to helping prepare a special holiday dish or choosing their birthday menu. Trying different eating styles is fun, too. A restaurant, cafeteria, picnic, clambake, or cookout provides children with more food experiences.

Fit

Fit is an important feature of preschool children's clothes. Clothing must give the active child freedom to move. Fit children by size, not age. Sizes for preschool children's clothes are often given as 4 through 6X or 7. Preschool boys and girls often have similar measurements. Therefore, measurements for a given size are often the same for both.

Hangtags and charts on children's sizes often give several measurements (chest, waist, hips, inseam, and others) rather than just height and weight. You may note some overlap of sizes, such as toddler size 4 (4T) and children size 4 (4). Often the chest and waist measurements are the same in toddler and children sizes. However, children sizes are often longer, and both the shoulders and back are wider than in toddler sizes. In addition to regular sizes, some clothes for children are sold in more specialized sizes to fit the slender child and the heavier child.

Chart 19-4 shows one example of typical preschool clothing sizes. Clothing varies slightly by retailer, so parents should carefully read the measurements for the best fit.

Fabric and Construction Features

Preschool children's clothes must have most of the same quality fabric and construction features as toddler clothes. (Review the clothing section in Chapter 15.) Preschool children grow mainly in the length of the arms and legs and the width of the shoulders. For these reasons, their clothes should have the following growth features:

★ wide hems that can be let out as arms and legs grow

★ kimono or raglan sleeves that allow for increase in the width of the shoulders

★ adjustable shoulder straps and waistbands that allow for both length and width increases

Typical Preschooler's Clothing Sizes

Size	Height in Inches	Weight in Pounds	Chest in Inches	Waist in Inches	Hips in Inches
4	39 to 41½	32½ to 37	22½ to 23	21 to 21½	22½ to 23
5	42 to 44½	37½ to 42	23½ to 24	21½ to 22	23½ to 24
6	45 to 46½	42½ to 47	24½ to 25	22 to 22½	24½ to 25
6X or 7	47 to 48½	47½ to 54	25½ to 26	22½ to 23	25½ to 26

19-4 These sample measurements are used by one retailer to determine sizing. Parents should check for fit by using the measurements on the label or hangtag rather than buying by the child's age.

Also, because preschool children explore indoors and outdoors, their clothes need more safety features. Outdoor clothing worn after dark should be light-colored or have a trim of reflective tape that will reflect the light from cars or other vehicles. Hoods attached to coats and rainwear should easily detach if caught on large objects. (Children have suffered neck and back injuries from nondetachable hoods.) Floppy headwear can prevent children from seeing traffic or other hazards. Floppy or wide legs and long shoelaces can cause tripping. Long, wide sleeves that are not gathered into a cuff; drawstring ties; long sashes and scarves; and extra large clothes are also dangerous.

Self-Dressing Features

By the end of the preschool years, many children can dress themselves with only a little help from adults. Of course, adults should always be near to help the child and check the child's attempts. The following features aid self-dressing:

★ Large openings, especially for slipover garments.

★ Easy-to-recognize fronts and backs of garments, such as labels, threads, or tape sewn inside.

★ Front rather than back openings, such as front buttons and attached belts that hook in front.

★ Elastic in waistbands and in sleeves (at wrist).

★ Easy-to-work fasteners. (Fasteners children can work easily include zippers with large pull tabs; smooth, flat buttons at least the size of a nickel; and shank or sew-through buttons sewn with elastic thread for a little give. Easy-to-work fasteners also include gripper snaps, the size of a dime, that do not fit too tightly together and hook-and-loop tape fasteners.)

★ Shoes with self-adhesive straps. (Children will need to practice tying shoes, however.)

In addition to self-dressing features in garments, special toys can help children learn to button, snap, zipper, and do other closings. These give children extra dressing practice.

Shoes and Socks

Most preschool children grow one shoe size every four months. By the preschool years, children may have more than one style of shoe. Along with size, check for certain features in each style, 19-5. When you buy bigger shoes, you may also need to buy bigger socks. Sock size corresponds to shoe size. Parents should have children try socks on for fit. Socks fit properly if they allow ½ inch of space beyond the child's longest toe.

Clothes and Self-Concept

Preschool children are well on their way to developing a unique personality. Clothes are one way to express their personality. Preschool children show off their clothes and talk about the clothes worn by others. Children may make comments about pockets or trim.

Style and Fit for Children's Shoes

Style	Fitting Features
Activity shoes	Flexible soles that are ¼- to ⅜-inch thick to absorb the pounding of walking, running, and jumping.
Sneakers and athletic shoes	Arch support in correct position. Check fit with the socks to be worn with the shoes. Socks are often bulky, requiring larger shoes.
Sandals	Adjustable straps and buckles that do not press into the foot.
Dress shoes	As flexible a sole as possible. (Thin soles of dress shoes do not absorb pounding. For this reason, dress shoes should only be worn for short periods.)

19-5 Shoe fit includes more than the right length and width.

Preschool children should make some choices about their clothes. Perhaps they can choose the color they want from similar outfits. If the outfit is to be sewn, a child could choose between two pattern views or among a few trims. Not only will children enjoy clothes they have chosen, but they also learn to make decisions.

Handling Sleep and Toileting Problems

The routines of meeting sleep and toileting needs are often in place by the end of the toddler years. Most preschool children still have a few problems in these areas from time to time.

Preschoolers need plenty of sleep. Research shows: three-year-olds need 12 to 12½ hours, four-year-olds need 11½ to 12 hours, and five-year-olds need 11 hours. Most children give up daytime naps during the preschool years. If bedtime rules have been enforced in the toddler years, most

preschool children accept them. The bedtime ritual is still wanted (and needed). Fears of the dark and monsters still exist, but many preschool children develop their own routines to help ease such stress. (Locking windows or having a doll watch over their sleep may comfort the child.)

Toileting accidents occur once in a while with most preschool children. Daytime accidents are most often caused by waiting too long to visit the bathroom. Adults may need to remind children to go to the bathroom after awakening in the morning or from naps. In addition, they should remind children before going outside, and before and after meals.

Time seems to be the major cure for bedtime accidents. Most children are not night-trained until at least age three years. Any instance of involuntary (by accident) urination of a child over three years of age is called **enuresis**. Sometimes, people use the term to apply to bed-wetting when the child no longer has daytime accidents. There may be many causes of bedtime accidents in the late preschool years (and even in the school-age years). Some problems include deep sleeping, fear of getting up in the dark, and too much liquid before bedtime. In a few cases, physical causes may exist. Most children outgrow these problems within a few years. For those who do not, medical help may be needed.

Providing Needed Space and Furnishings

Unlike babies and toddlers who want to be in the almost steady company of adults, preschool children want to be on their own more. Often preschool children have more toys and belongings than younger children. They need to be able to safely reach and return many of their own things. Adults must plan carefully for storage and furnishings.

Preschool children want a little space to call their own. This may be anything from a drawer or chest of drawers to one or more rooms. Even when a bedroom is shared with another child, a screen, storage cabinet, or curtain can divide the room. This allows some private space for times when the child wants or needs to be alone.

Learning Responsibility

Preschool children can learn self-help skills and become responsible for the care of their belongings. However, they need

Focus on Social Studies

Designing Spaces for Children

Visit some homes with bedrooms or playrooms designed for preschool children. If you cannot arrange any of these visits, look at such rooms in furniture stores, magazines, or catalogs. Based on what you have seen, answer the following questions:

★ How was storage space planned?

★ How did the design meet the child's desire to be more independent?

★ Did the room offer privacy for the child?

★ What, if any, changes might you recommend to make the room more appropriate for a preschool child?

some storage space that is easy for them to use. A pegboard wall with holders for equipment helps children store toys neatly and keeps them in sight. A window can be flanked with storage shelves. A window seat or desk can be used in front of the window. Strips of hook and loop tape tacked to a wall of the closet or other places can hold lightweight toys. Storage ideas are limited only by the imagination.

Plan storage so preschool children can help themselves. Lower clothes hooks and rods for a child's use. Place often-used toys and items near where they will be used and within the child's reach. There can be some order to their clothes and toys—one the child can understand and follow. Remember that dual-duty items help conserve space.

Playground Designer

Playground designers design play spaces for children, often at schools or parks. They work with architects, surveyors, and engineers. They analyze who will be using the space and the nature around the space. They make sketches, models, and photographs to explain their ideas.

Education: Most playground designers have a college degree in landscape architecture or a related subject. Most states require landscape architects to be licensed or registered.

Job Outlook: Jobs for playground designers are expected to grow faster than the average for all occupations.

Intellectual Needs

Adults must help preschool children meet their intellectual needs. As they did during the toddler years, adults direct children's attention to things to do and problems to solve. Preschool children may be enrolled in special programs. However, the home and neighborhood play groups are still the most important places for learning. Preschool children's mental abilities can and do develop any time and any place. Think about how much a child can learn from a simple shopping trip. While shopping, the child can do the following:

★ observe attributes of items, such as color, size, shape, and texture

★ sort and classify items

★ learn number skills

★ learn language skills in naming and describing items

Learning Through Observing

Children must learn to observe by seeing, hearing, touching, smelling, and tasting. During the preschool years, children should be able to see details. They then can **compare** (see how objects or people are alike) and **contrast** (see how objects or people are different). Games and activities can improve these skills. As an example, give a child a magnifying glass. Help the child look at a leaf, penny, fingernail, piece of food, or other small object. Use a pencil to point to details you want the child to see. Later, ask the child to describe the objects he or she saw. See 19-6 for other suggestions for observation activities.

Television Viewing

Children also observe by watching television. Attractive characters, animation, movement, repetition, and many sounds used on children's television programs and many commercials cause children to observe. However, **passive observing** (attending without responding) is not the same as learning. Most television shows do not require responses from children. Even if a show encourages a child to respond, the child may not.

Children need more time to digest an idea than the few seconds a television image may provide. Caring and teaching adults are more important to children's learning than any television program. Thus, television should not be used as a babysitter. However, when a quality program is viewed with a sharing adult who builds on the concepts, a learning boost will likely occur.

Observation Activities

Alike and different

Gather pairs of objects or pictures that are exactly alike. Mix up the objects and have the child sort into like pairs. Books can be made where detachable pieces can be matched to those that are attached to the page.

Variation: Have the child explain how some items are the same in some ways and different in others. Examples of objects to compare include a fork and spoon, a poodle and collie, an apple and orange, two different hats, two different coins, or two different types of leaves.

Alike and Different

Shape sorting

Shape sorters have holes that fit various shapes, such as square, circle, and pentagon. Have the child match an object with the hole through which it will drop. As children master simple shape sorters, more advanced ones can be used.

Variation: (A) Use precut shapes of paper, plastic, or wood to make other shapes, designs, or pictures. Ask older children to name shapes and explain how they recognized each shape. (B) Cut shapes out of ½ inch sponges. Using a clothespin, dip in tempera paint, and stamp on paper. (C) Using a pegboard and rubber bands, make shapes.

Varieties of liquids

Show the child varieties of liquids, such as water, milk, fruit juice, molasses, cooking oil, tempera paint (in one or more thicknesses), and dish detergent. Using two or more liquids, set up the following experiments: (A) rub a drop of liquid between the thumb and forefinger; (B) drop each liquid using an eyedropper on wax paper; (C) move a drop or two of liquid placed on wax paper by blowing through a straw; and (D) use a cookie sheet for a ramp and allow a drop or two of each liquid to flow down the ramp. Have the child describe similarities and differences in the liquids in each experiment.

19-6 Observation activities help children learn to compare and contrast.

Even the viewing of quality programs should be limited to no more than 30 to 60 minutes a day.

Learning Through Problem Solving

Problem solving is a broad term. It most often includes noting a problem, observing and questioning what you see, and solving the problem. Almost from birth, babies are action-oriented problem solvers as they physically try to make items work. By the preschool years, children use both mental and action-oriented problem-solving skills.

Mental problem solving depends on basic skills described in Chapter 17. These basic skills are classifying; reversing; and arranging objects according to increasing or decreasing size, weight, or volume. As you learned, these concepts will not mature during the preschool years. Knowing about transformations is another basic skill. **Transformation** is the sequence of changes by which one state is changed to another. For example, a caterpillar is transformed into a butterfly. Heat transforms ice to water. Understanding transformation is logically difficult for preschool children because the child focuses on single steps, stages, or events rather than the process as a whole. In like manner, natural events are observed and questioned. These, too, are difficult for preschoolers to understand.

How Adults Can Help Preschoolers Solve Problems

Preschool children, especially three- and four-year-olds, can often sort items. However, most preschool children find classifying objects difficult. Adults can help them solve these problems. For example, adults can help children sort any number of household items. These items could be laundry, toys, flatware, and groceries. To turn a shopping trip into a lesson, adults might say, "Let's put together all the food that came in boxes and then put all the canned food together. Now let's put the fresh fruits and vegetables together." Because preschoolers often feel overwhelmed when asked to pick up all their toys or clothes, parents can modify clean-up time with a sorting lesson. For example, parents can ask the child to pick up all the blue or square shapes while they get the others.

Helping Children Classify Items

Adults can help children classify items. After showing the child small blocks that may be classified by color or shape, the adult can ask, "Are any of these alike in some way?" The child may respond by saying that some of the objects are *red*, *smooth*, or *round*. When the child singles out a common attribute, the adult might say, "Would you like to find all the round pieces and put them in this box? Then we will put all the other blocks that are not round in the other box." When classifying items, there are only two groups. The **class** is a group of items that are alike in some way (the attribute). The **class complement** are groups of objects that do not belong within the class being considered. See 19-7 for other sorting and classifying activities.

Helping Children Put Items in Order

Preschool children have trouble putting items in order. Many activities can help children with this concept. Children may line objects from shortest to tallest or from tallest to shortest. The keys on the piano are ordered by pitch from high to low or low to high. Children can see and hear this. In retelling a story, events must be put in order. The number system is a series, too.

Adults can help preschoolers learn to put items in order through games and activities. However, they should keep two points in mind. First, restrict the number of items to be put in order to five or fewer. Second, make the differences in the items easy to notice. As an activity, adults could read to children about

Sorting and Classifying Activities*

Button sort

Use an egg carton or other sectioned container for sorting buttons into three or more groups. You may have the child sort according to color, size, way sewn on, or shape. (Buttons can be sorted using pieces of paper or boxes if sectioned containers are not handy.)

Variation: Sort many other objects for fun and even as a household task. Flatware, laundry, toys, and groceries can all be sorted.

Sorting

Make a book

Children can cut or tear pictures from newspapers, catalogs, and magazines. The pictures can be mounted by groups, such as fruits, cars, dogs, and toys. (The child should decide on the groups.)

Does it belong?

After the child can easily classify, bring out another object and put it with the class. Ask the child, "Does this belong?" The child should explain why it does or does not belong.

*Having children describe objects from their left to right aids developing the directionality involved in reading and writing.

19-7 Sorting and classifying activities enhance children's problem-solving skills.

The Three Bears. After reading the story, talk about the sizes of each bear, chair, and bed. See 19-8 for other activities.

Helping Children with Reversals

Before the child can mentally handle **reversals** (mentally doing and undoing an action), they need to perform some physical reversals. Reversals must be experienced— not taught. An example might be letting the child pour water or sand from one container into a different container and back again. See 19-9 for other reversal activities.

Helping Children with Transformation

Transformations happen in the natural world on a daily basis. Adults can point these out to children. For example, while watching birds perch on a feeder or in a tree, an adult could ask the child, "What happened to the bird's wings when it perched?" (They were outstretched and now are folded.) As a transformation activity, the adult and child could look at pictures of the child. The adult could point out changes in size, hair length, and motor skills. He or she could ask the child to point out other changes from one picture to the next. Non-hardening clay and sand are wonderful materials for noting transformations, too. See 19-10 for other transformation activities.

Activities for Putting Objects in Order

Make yourself little

Help a child act out different sizes with his or her body. Show how to make yourself little (by crouching down), bigger (by standing), and biggest (by stretching).

Little, bigger, biggest

Gather three boxes—one small, one large, and one even larger. Place the boxes in front of the child so the smallest box is to the child's left, the medium box is in front of the child, and the largest box is to the child's right. Ask the child to find the little box, then the bigger box, then the biggest. If the child makes a mistake and does not correct it, try nesting the boxes to compare sizes for him or her. To vary the game, you may reverse the box order or use four or five boxes that vary in size. (Box shapes should be similar unless the box sizes are extremely different.)

The Three Billy Goats Gruff

Read this story to a child. A copy with illustrations will help the child better see the sizes of the goats. After reading the story, talk about the sizes of the goats that crossed the bridge.

Ordering blocks

Cover three blocks of wood with different grades of sandpaper. Have the child put the blocks in order from least rough to roughest by rubbing them. Then ask the child to put the blocks in order using only sight. For a variation, the child may stack items in order of weight and size.

19-8 These activities enhance children's concepts of order.

Reversal Activities

Tower of blocks

Help a child build a tower with blocks. Have the child take the stack of blocks down, one by one, to reverse the order of building.

Lacing cards

Make or buy lacing cards. To make one, draw a picture on cardboard, then punch holes in the cardboard over the outline. Use a shoestring to lace through the holes and create the picture's outline. Children can lace, undo, and relace the card.

Non-hardening clay

Have the child roll clay back and forth from a long rope to a ball to reverse the order.

19-9 These activities help teach children about reversals.

Helping Children Understand Natural Events

Scientific understandings usually begin after nine years of age.

Preschoolers are fascinated by natural events and ask many *why* questions. Often they come up with illogical thoughts of their own. What should a parent do? Smile at the illogical

Transformation Activities

Growing plants

Help a child plant a fast-growing seed, such as a bean. You may also put a sweet potato in water. Look at it each day. Talk about the changes you see. Taking pictures can also help the child see the progress.

Seeing nature's changes

Ask the child to observe one of nature's many changes, such as: leaves growing on a plant or tree; leaves falling from a tree; birds from eggs to fledglings; butterfly stages (butterfly housed in an indoor container); and snow covering an object. Taking photos or having the child draw and describe is a good way to document these changes.

Cooking

Ask the child to help you cook. Point out changes that happen. Baked goods increase in size in the oven. Liquids freeze to make ice. Gelatin becomes firm as it sets. Sugar dissolves. Eggs boil and become firm, or heat and stir eggs to make them scrambled.

Making new colors

Gather paints, crayons, or colored water. Show a child how to make a new color by combining two different ones. Let the child combine different colors. Combining two primary colors is often done to create secondary colors for egg dyes and frosting.

19-10   These activities help children grasp the concept of transformation.

thinking and record it for a child's scrapbook. If the child asks about natural events give simple, but correct information and realize the child may or may not understand. For example, you can tell a preschooler, "Lightning comes from dark storm clouds," but do not say, "Lightning is an atmospheric discharge of electricity." You can say, "Thunder is the sound made by lightning." However, do not try to explain how the sound is made. In short, keep it simple. Children have many more years to learn all of these facts.

Learning Through Symbolizing

Intellectual needs are also met as the child begins to think in terms of symbols or signs. There are a number of ways children think in these terms.

The way in which children pretend is a form of symbolism. Through play, children take on the representation of another person or object, 19-11. They need many chances to pretend to be other people and objects. Many children begin pretending around their first birthday, but pretending does not reach a peak until the preschool years.

For the most part, children need only a little help in pretending. For example, adults can have the child pretend to be any person or thing. If they suggest an underwater diver, they may see the preschooler putting on a pretend deep-sea fishing outfit. Soon the child will be diving after lost treasures, being careful not to be attacked by sharks.

Helping Children Through Symbolizing

I'm a monster!

Begin by asking the child, "How do you think monsters look? How do you think they move? What sounds do you think they make? Show me." (Pretending to be a monster may help children overcome the fear of monsters.)

Variation: Have the child pretend to be any person or thing.

Pantomime

Have the child act out an action. The adult may suggest one, or the child may choose one. Have others try to guess what the action is.

Ballet

Ballet is acting out a story or idea through dance. Play some music and let the children act out something in the form of dance. The child can choose what to be and how to dance it. You may need to give a few ideas to get the child started.

19-11 These activities help meet children's intellectual needs.

Using Symbols in Art

Children use symbols when they paint, color, or do other art work. Younger children make their art products first and then sometimes decide what they represent. As children mature, the idea comes before the product is made. As is true of all representations, the child decides on the symbol, not the adult.

When children use objects, such as building blocks, clay, or dolls, to represent who or what they want to, a form of symbolism is used. Children's play materials may or may not be like the real world, but they symbolize the real world for them.

Using Symbols in Language

Words are highly abstract symbols. One of the issues of early childhood education is whether children should be taught to read and do simple math problems at an early age. Many experts feel most preschool children need more time to deal with their world using less abstract forms of symbols. They question early reading and math for the following reasons:

★ Young children must arrive at their own meanings and develop their own skills. Repeating without meaning is not real learning. Adults need to provide materials and ask *open-ended questions*. (Questions that require more than a one-word response, such as *yes* or *no*.) Adults also need to present problems for children to solve.

★ Problem solving in the real world gives a practical reason for learning. By setting the table, the child may see the need for counting forks. However, the child may not see the need to count objects in a picture shown by an adult.

★ **Divergent thinking** (coming up with different possible ideas) is more often developed through rich, everyday experiences. On the other hand, **convergent thinking** (coming up with only one right answer or way to do a task) is more often seen in formal lessons. Answers to many of life's problems require divergent minds.

★ Children need time to deal with their real world.

★ Some children feel stress as a result of formal lessons. If young children see learning as fun, this attitude may carry over to the years ahead.

Unless the child sees the mental link between a real object and its symbol (such as a real cat and the word *cat*), the symbol means nothing. When learning is meaningless or too difficult, it is stressful rather than fun. For these reasons, children need many experiences with real objects first. Next, the child should deal with the abstract symbols of his or her own choosing or making (such as pretending to be a cat or drawing pictures of cats). Children should use spoken words when handling real objects and when pretending and drawing. This prepares the child for reading words and math symbols with comprehension.

Learning Through Motor Skills

As children move and do things, they become more skillful in both mental and physical ways. Children learn as they move their bodies in space. They learn as they manipulate objects.

Because preschool children are in almost constant motion, they learn many gross-motor skills through play and play activities. Play is a fun way to learn. However, a few planned activities may be fun and help mental development as well. For example, adults can help children plan an obstacle course of tables, chairs, and sturdy boxes. Have the child go under, around, through, and on top of the obstacles.

Other suggestions for games and activities that promote gross-motor skills are found in 19-12.

Fine-motor skills should be enjoyed, too. Some of the best items are art materials, puzzles, small wooden beads to string, pegboards, and lacing cards. Small construction toys, such as plastic snap-together blocks and other building materials, also promote fine-motor skills.

Learning Through Language

Preschool children learn language from what they hear—the articulation of sounds, vocabulary, and grammar. For this reason, adults must be the best language models they can be.

Gross-Motor Games

Skipping
Teach the child to skip by doing a step-hop on one foot and then a step-hop on the other. After the step-hop is mastered, add music or a rhythmic beat. The pattern of the sound should help the child skip with the beat.

Hopping
Teach hopping in the following progression:
1. Hop on the balls of both feet and land lightly. (This is a little jump, not hopping.)
2. Hop on one foot without letting the heel touch the ground.
3. Hop high like a bouncing ball.
4. Hop as far as possible in two hops.

Throw and catch
For throwing, have the child throw beanbags or balls at targets. Have the child catch thrown beanbags or balls and bounced balls.

19-12 Gross-motor games promote children's physical skills.

Preschool children need many daily chances to talk with adults and older children. When preschool children only play with peers or younger children, they do not learn as quickly as they do by talking with adults. For this reason, only and firstborn children are often more advanced in language.

Language needs to be a part of all activities. For example, important words include names of attributes and opposites. When language is only used to give orders, learnings are not expanded. When activities and speech are combined, children's concepts and skills grow.

Television and Reading

Adults should monitor the types and amount of television children watch. Although children can hear speech on television programs, it is one-way speech. This is because the child hears, but does not respond. Children's shows that urge children to respond ask for one- or two-word responses. Studies show that children who watch less than five hours of television per week do much better in school. (Some children watch five or more hours per day.)

Reading to children every day increases language learnings. Books take us beyond the day-to-day world. Reading helps to expand concepts. It also helps children see books and reading as important. Libraries and bookstores are filled with wonderful picture books for young children on almost every topic imaginable.

Computers and Learning

Many preschool children have access to computers in their homes and in their early childhood programs. During the preschool years, children are just learning about technology. Most children, even preschoolers, develop a special liking for computers for the following reasons:

★ Computers are part of their everyday world. Even before the preschool years, many children look at the computer monitor as adults use the computer.

★ Children are in control as they work on the computer. When they push a button or click the mouse, something happens. They receive instant feedback.

★ The computer is patient and permits repetition. The child can look at the pictures, hear and see a story, draw and color, play a game, or work on learning shapes, numbers, or colors countless times. The computer is perfectly matched to the child's attention span, too, for the child can leave the computer at any point.

Hardware designed with the young child in mind makes the computer easier to use. Because of children's small hands and not fully developed fine-motor skills, a standard mouse and keyboard can be difficult to use and somewhat frustrating. Specially designed products are available for young children and children with physical disabilities. This equipment is much more expensive than standard equipment and is quickly outgrown by preschoolers. Yet it is worth considering for the child's comfort and ease of use if the child will be using the computer often.

In order to operate the computer, the hardware must also be at the right height for children. Unless children have their own computers and computer furniture, stable and comfortable stools that have seats at the right height may be the best option. A footstool or footrest is also needed if children's feet do not rest flat on the floor without one.

Many software programs are now available for children that have excellent formats and good content for the ability and interest level of the child. Because software is relatively expensive, it should be selected with care. Some general suggestions are given in 19-13.

Before purchasing, parents should decide what type of program they want. Some examples are drawing and coloring, interactive stories, learning basic skills (shapes, colors, numbers), and learning concepts (such as pictures and names of animals). They should read the evaluations from independent sources rather than from the publishers or distributors of the software.

Parents and caregivers introducing preschoolers to computers need to teach the basics, such as names for the hardware—*computer*, *CD-ROM drive*, and *monitor*—and how to handle CDs. They need to install programs, run them, and show children how they work. Until children are skilled at using a program alone, adults need to stay nearby to answer questions. However, adults should give the minimal assistance needed and avoid taking over. Adults also need to keep children safe while using computers. (This topic is described in Chapter 22.) Parents need to remember to limit the child's total media exposure (TV, computers, video/DVDs) to one hour or less per day.

Selecting Software

★ Does it fit your computer's hardware requirements (Macintosh or PC; needed operating system; processor type and speed; memory capacity; hard drive space needed; display type; and sound card type)? The sound and color used in children's software require much memory.

★ Can the child use it without much adult help (controls work quickly; icons are large and easy to select; graphics make sense; instructions are easy to follow)?

★ Is it designed for children (under child control; files not intended for child are childproof; children know whether their answers are right or wrong)?

★ Is it of value to the child (content is good and challenges; child can explore and experiment; content is free of bias; feedback is given; required skills are at child's ability level)?

★ Does it contain a variety of activities and levels so the child can move forward when ready?

★ Is the program appropriate for young children? For example, does it avoid "drill and practice," competition, violence, and flashing images?

★ Is the program enjoyable for the child?

★ Does it have good design features (high quality music and speech; keeps a record of child's work)?

19-13 Parents should carefully investigate any software purchases.

Social-Emotional Needs

During the preschool years, children's personalities seem to blossom and become more stable. Preschoolers begin to learn more about themselves. Questions, such as "Who am I?" and "What can I do on my own?" are more fully answered in the preschool years. Through successes and mistakes, preschoolers test their skills. They begin to see themselves as boys or girls with role differences.

Adults need to meet the social-emotional needs of preschool children. They must often explain reasons for limits or requirements and repeat these. Firmness and fairness must be the adult's rule if the child's self-concept is to remain healthy.

Discipline

Preschool children define themselves in terms of what they can do. In order to find out what they can do, almost all children try many activities. (In other words, they show initiative.) Active preschool children are curious. They do many things on impulse without thinking about the results of their actions. In trying new things, preschool children go beyond their abilities and make mistakes. These mistakes are self-defeating because preschool children see almost everything as within their control. Too many mistakes may bring on guilt.

When children are successful, they need to hear positive statements from adults. Children need adults to tell them what they are like. For example, parents can say, "It was *nice* of you to be so *loving* toward your baby sister." Parents might also say, "You were showing *kindness* when you shared your toys. *Kindness* helps make people like you—want to be your friend." In every case the parents should use the adjective to refer to a specific case. It is best not to over generalize, such as saying, "You are *always* nice, loving, and kind." Case descriptions refine their self-image and promote feelings of self-esteem.

Children learn more by their own attempts than by having adults do for them or tell them what to do. Preschoolers learn from both successes and mistakes. Thus, children must be given some freedom to try. Adults must accept that children will try some things even when told *no*. Some preschool children decide the pleasure of doing something is worth the punishment. Children can even dream up new activities not presently covered by the rules.

Limits

Preschool children should be given reasonable limits. This is a major responsibility of parents at this time who are in the *authority* stage of parenting. Preschoolers need limits for safety purposes and to prepare them for the real world. These rules should be spelled out. When children fail to obey, they need to be disciplined in a loving, yet firm, way.

Honest Communication

Parents and other adults need to communicate honestly when guiding and disciplining children. Being honest helps children build trusting relationships. It also helps children realize they should be truthful.

Children need to be aware that adults, too, make mistakes. Children learn this when they hear adults say, "I goofed!" or "I'm sorry." They begin to understand that all people make mistakes. They also start to see that making mistakes does not make them bad.

Sharing Responsibility

Preschool children see tasks as new skills to learn, as being fun, and as a way to please others. Adults can help children become more dependable and able to handle more responsibilities.

Some adults offer few, if any, opportunities for children to help. These adults may see preschool children as not having the desire to help. The child may stop in the middle of a task to play. Perhaps the adult thinks children lack the ability. The child may break a dish. A few adults think of children as servants who should perform tasks upon demand and to adult standards. Most, however, agree that family life and school life are made better when both adults and children help each other.

The following suggestions will help children share responsibility:

★ Children may suggest tasks, but adults must decide which tasks are safe and within children's grasp, 19-14.

★ Physical conditions should help children perform tasks. Low hooks or clothes rods, a place for each item, and a sturdy stool for reaching a cabinet are examples.

★ Adults can talk about tasks planned for the day, and they can tell children what they

19-14 A preschool child should have some pet-care responsibility only if the pet is right for the child and family and if the parents think the child can handle the task.
Photo © John Shaw

should do. Young preschoolers often help the adult do a task, but five-year-olds can work alone on some tasks.

★ Adults should not expect perfection. The finished task should remain as it is, or the task can be explained again for the child to do over. (When adults redo tasks, children feel a sense of failure.)

★ Adults can make some tasks seem more fun by creating a game. For example, blocks can be hauled to the "lumberyard" (the shelf).

★ At times, adults should respect children's priorities. There may be no harm in letting a child do a job 10 minutes later.

Children need to be rewarded for tasks completed. Adults must decide whether work is done for love only (and thus should not involve pay) or work should have pay (with money or other wants fulfilled). Some adults compromise on this issue. They expect certain jobs to be done without pay. Then they may consider other jobs—those elected by the child—to be beyond the call of duty. The extra jobs may involve pay. Whether adults pay or do not pay, children need to be thanked and skills need to be praised.

Aiding Gender Role Learning

Due to changes in society today, many parents and other adults are questioning the more rigid gender roles of the past. As is true with all personal values, parents need to be informed about the issues and make decisions. Adults make their feelings about gender roles known to children in many ways. The roles they allow or encourage their children to try and the day-to-day attitudes they convey affect children. For example, parents who value traditional gender roles might not want their son playing with a doll or their daughter engaged in rough and tumble games. These parents will model traditional roles in the home with the father not doing housework or child care tasks and the mother not doing heavy outdoor work. On the other hand, parents who believe in and practice less-defined gender roles allow their children to choose toys and games according to their own interests. In these homes, children do not see home tasks "for fathers only" or "for mothers only."

Preschool children learn their gender roles mainly through observing adults of the same gender. They learn as they help their same-gender parent with household tasks and errands. Seeing parents and other adults at work also shows children adult gender roles. Toys and books related to jobs allow children to learn about many gender roles.

Providing Time for Friendships

Living in a social world involves balancing between self-assertion (insisting on one's rights) and **cooperation** (joint effort). Because preschool children must learn to see from another person's point of view, the balance between a child's will and the wills of others takes a long time, often years.

Seeing differences in people helps children learn to see from another's point of view. The process begins in the infant and toddler years. At this time, children expand their social world beyond parents to include other family members. Friendships with peers help children see even more differences in people. Friction, which almost always occurs in play groups, shows children in a direct way that others see issues differently. In peer groups, children also witness **altruistic behavior** (actions that show concern for others). This helps children learn that others are important, too.

Friendship is a way to learn from others. Preschool children's ideas are expanded through play. In play groups children also have fun times, which are an important part of their lives, 19-15.

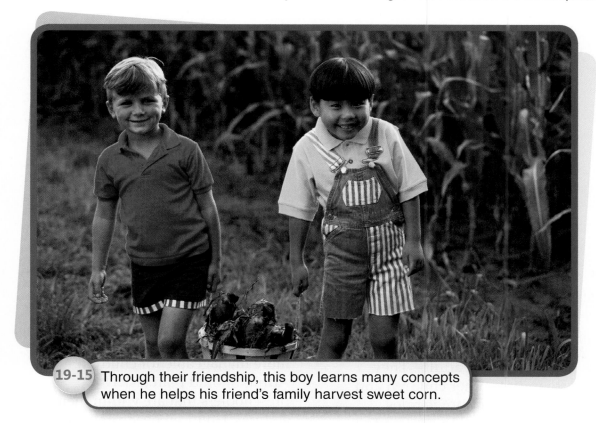

19-15 Through their friendship, this boy learns many concepts when he helps his friend's family harvest sweet corn.

Helping Children's Social Relations

Adults can help children's social relations by giving them time to play with friends. These friends may be neighborhood playmates. They may also be friends from the preschool, special interest group (such as swimming or dance class), or house of worship. Adults should allow children to interact with each other and not interfere with little conflicts (except for safety reasons).

Reducing Conflicts

Adults can reduce the conflicts of preschoolers in these ways:
* Teach children they do not always have to share, any more than adults do. Sometimes adults expect children to share all their toys even with casual friends. Adults are not expected to share all their belongings even with close friends.

* Model concern for the hurt child rather than shaming the one who has done wrong. Children learn more when adults show real concern for the hurt or wronged child while ignoring the child who was in the wrong. They see that care is given to children who are harmed.

* Explain feelings of both children wanting the same toy or wanting to do the same thing. Often toys are given up rather quickly when the adult says, "Maria needs to play with the car for a little while, but when she's ready to give it up she will let you know."

Helping Children with Emotional Control

Emotions are intense in the preschool years. The growing minds of preschool children broaden their emotions. They also help children control how they express their emotions. People cannot control feelings. They must, however, learn to control how they express these feelings. Better control of expression is a major task of the preschool years.

Adults can help children control how they express feelings by setting an example. Children imitate control, or the lack of control, seen in adults. They also imitate other children and television and movie roles.

Adults need to explain to children it is all right to feel sad, angry, hurt, and happy. They should also tell children it is all right to express some emotions. ("It is all right to cry when we feel sad." "We laugh when we're happy." "You should tell Tabitha, 'It makes me mad when you take my toys.' Then ask her to give them back.") However, children need to hear that people must not hurt others even when they are wronged. ("Hitting hurts," or "It makes others feel sad when you call them names.") Adults should talk about how all people have to work to control their feelings. There are many books on this topic.

Dependency

Knowing when and how to help preschoolers can be difficult. Some children are unable to handle some tasks on their own, but do not want the help adults offer.

Other children, however, will not let go of help from adults even when they do not need it. These preschool children need to become more independent. It is a challenge for adults to find a balance between helping and not helping.

Adults can help by loving and respecting children, 19-16. This gives children a secure base from which to try things on their own. When children ask for help, adults should be willing to help. Adults need to judge how much help children need. (Adults must avoid being too helpful or protective.) Physically arrange the house in ways that make tasks more manageable for children. Adults should plan tasks for preschoolers that are within their abilities. Children need praise and encouragement when they try tasks on their own.

Fear and Anxiety

Some fear and anxiety helps protect people. However, too much may be harmful. The following ideas may help keep children's fears and anxieties in check:

★ Accept the expressed fears and anxieties of children. (Never make fun of them.)

★ Assure children you will help keep them safe. (Never threaten to leave a child, even in a playful way.)

★ Model courage. Children learn fears from adults.

★ Handle one fear at a time. Repeat reasons children need not be afraid. Small steps taken slowly in dealing with fears and anxieties may help.

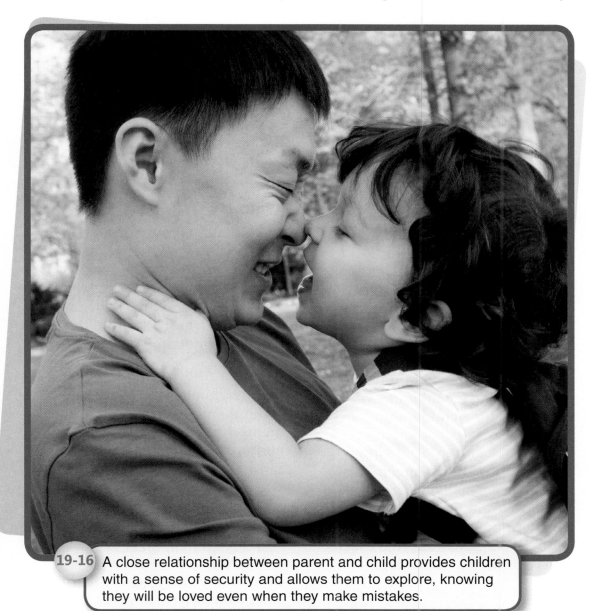

19-16 A close relationship between parent and child provides children with a sense of security and allows them to explore, knowing they will be loved even when they make mistakes.

★ Consult a doctor if fears seem too prolonged or too intense.

Anger and Aggression

Handling children's anger and aggression is not only draining, but often stirs up angry feelings in adults. Adults should note the difference in **anger** (a feeling caused by frustration) and **aggression** (an attempt to hurt or an act of hurting someone). They should not try to stop anger in children. Instead, they need to help children try to manage anger in ways other than aggression. Look for reasons the child feels angry. Does the child want attention? Is he or she frustrated in reaching a goal? Is he or she looking for revenge? Understanding motives makes finding ways to manage anger easier.

Competitive situations between peers should be reduced.

Enough toys should be supplied so children do not have to wait too long for a turn. Play should be de-escalated. Some games that begin on a rather low key become aggressive. Other games can calm children or encourage cooperation. Watch peer play groups closely. Adults can stop aggression before it occurs (and the child gets some satisfaction from the act). If children need to be corrected, adults should use nonphysical ways. However, a child should know that adults disapprove of aggressive acts. Likewise, adults need to praise cooperation.

Spanking

Studies show that punishment by aggression (spanking), especially for a child's aggressive act, increases aggression in preschool children. Spanking increases the child's anger. This produces a negative, aggressive response from the child. Furthermore, adults are serving as models of aggression—the exact behavior they wish to stop.

Modeling Aggression

Children see aggression modeled in many ways including adults' acts, peers' acts, and acts on television programs, including those by cartoon characters. All studies show that children learn to be more aggressive by example. Even letting a child hit a pillow or kick a tree trunk says that aggression is all right. Instead, teach children it is all right to feel angry, but acts of anger must be controlled.

Society tries to teach an attitude of being **assertive** (speaking out, standing up for your rights, and defending yourself), but not being hurtful to others. Trying to find the line between assertiveness and aggression can be most difficult for preschool children. (It can even be difficult for adults at times.) Because of this, preschoolers may act in an aggressive way when they are trying to be assertive.

Jealousy

Jealousy is common among preschoolers and often leads to anger. Learning to tame jealousy is a life-long process. The preschool years are the best time to begin helping the child to control this powerful emotion.

Jealousy among Friends

Preschoolers are learning about themselves by comparing themselves with friends. Even a minor inequality among friends can seem like a big deal. Love, attention, and material goods are coveted things.

Preschoolers cannot always keep their emotions under control. After parents talk with their children they may behave in acceptable ways. However, jealousy may bubble up later causing the child to be sullen or aggressive.

What can parents do? Validate the child's jealous feelings. Parents should not placate the child by giving in to jealous wishes, however. Giving a preschooler plenty of love and attention can lessen the insecurity that often breeds jealousy.

Jealousy over a New Baby

A preschool child needs help in accepting a new baby into his or her family. Parents should tell the child about the new baby before the event. They should sound pleased, but not overly excited, because children may think new babies are more important than they are.

The new baby should be described in realistic ways in terms of the work involved and other facts. Some preschool children are led to believe the new baby will be an instant, able playmate. If possible, seeing a friend's new baby can help. The child should be involved in plans for the new baby.

Preschool children seem to be happier when they can stay in their own home or near their own home and visit their mother in the hospital (even by telephone). They prefer not to be sent to stay with friends or relatives for several days. (A preschool child can imagine only so much, and separations from loved ones are always difficult.)

When the new baby arrives, parents can help prevent jealousy in these ways:

★ Provide time alone with the preschooler. This is the best way to say, "I love you."

★ Allow the preschooler to help with the new baby. Adults should sincerely thank those extra feet and hands that help so much, 19-17.

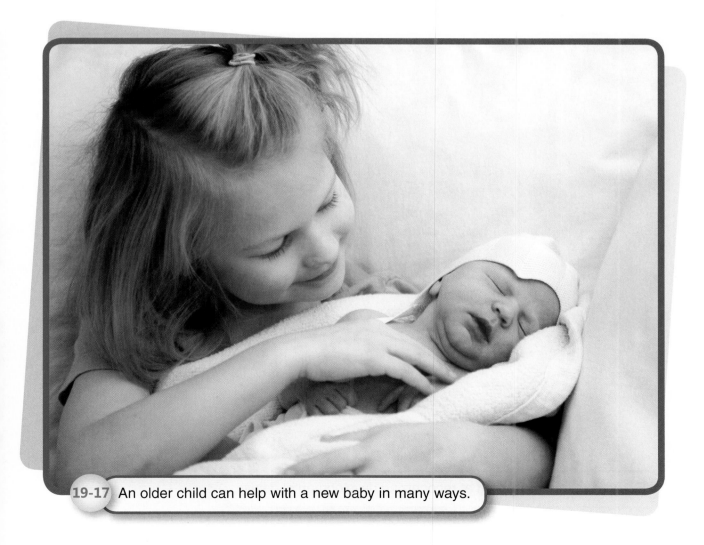

19-17 An older child can help with a new baby in many ways.

★ Expect a preschooler to show some regressive behaviors. It is natural for preschoolers to wish for the attention given to the new baby. Preschoolers enjoy being told or shown with photos how they were once cared for in the same ways.

Recognizing Developmental Delays

Preschool children with delays may show some of the behaviors of average toddlers as listed in Chapter 15. Because preschoolers are becoming more social, these behaviors as well as gross- and fine-motor skills and language are observed. If preschool children are attending child care or preschool programs, their caregivers are often good judges of developmental delays, 19-18. Parents should consult with caregivers on a regular basis and observe their own children working and playing with other children of the same age. See the *Preschool Milestones* in Appendix A to learn about some typical preschooler behaviors that may help parents to recognize delays.

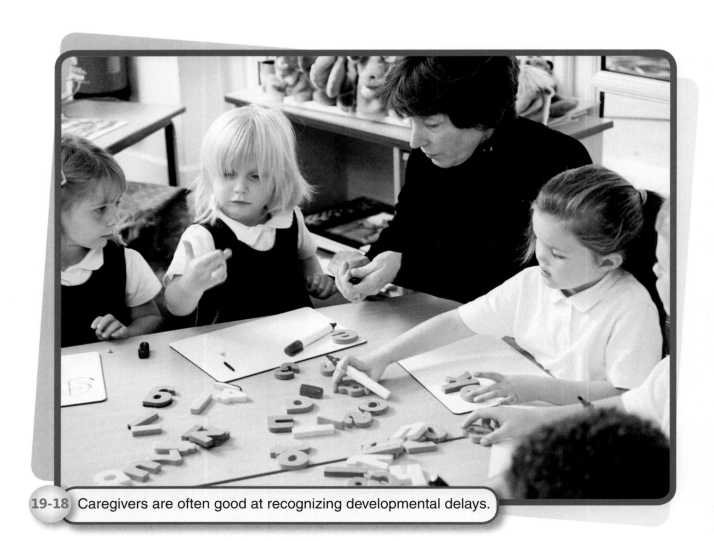

19-18 Caregivers are often good at recognizing developmental delays.

Summary

Preschool children are active and need to eat nutritious meals and snacks. They learn attitudes about food likes and dislikes from others. Preschool children like food that is easy to eat and looks attractive.

Clothing must fit properly and allow room for the child to move and grow. When selecting clothing for children, adults should look for safety features and those that promote self-dressing. Adults should allow preschool children to make some choices about their clothes.

Bedtime rules and rituals continue to be important. Toileting accidents sometimes occur. Children need to be reminded at times to use the bathroom.

Preschoolers need some space to call their own. Their area should feature storage space that is easy for them to use.

Adults need to offer opportunities for children to learn. They need to provide materials, encourage observation, and present problems for children to solve. Learning by developing symbols is critical for preschoolers because it prepares them for handling more abstract symbols, such as words. Language skills improve through modeling and using language as a part of daily activities.

When guiding and disciplining preschoolers, adults must set limits. When children fail to obey the rules, reasonable actions by a loving, but firm, adult should be taken.

Adults should give children responsibilities that suit their age and ability. They need to be praised and rewarded for completing their responsibilities.

Children learn gender roles at this age. Books and toys help children have a wider view of gender roles in various work situations. Books and toys help children have a wider view of gender roles in various family and work situations.

Adults should see that children have friends to play with and not interfere with their small conflicts. By playing with others, children learn different points of view and ways that others think and behave.

When children have fears and anxieties, adults should never make fun of them. Modeling courage and handling one fear at a time is helpful.

Adults can teach children about anger and control. Adults also need to help children learn how to express their feelings without hurting others. When acts of aggression occur, adults should always use nonaggressive means to end these acts.

Jealousy over love, attention, and material goods is common among preschool friends. Plenty of love and attention lessens the insecurity that leads to jealousy. Giving in to children's demands will only make the jealousy problems worsen. Jealousy over a new baby can be lessened if the preschool child is prepared in advance. Spending time alone with the preschool child and having the child help with the baby will ease feelings of jealousy.

Companion Web Site

Interactive Activity

Review vocabulary terms and key concepts for Chapter 19 at **g-wlearning.com**.

Review and Reflect

Write your answers to the following questions on a separate sheet of paper.

1. True or false. Because of the preschooler's steady growth pattern, he or she needs exactly the same food from month to month.

2. True or false. Forcing children to eat a food they do *not* like does little or nothing to help them learn to like that food.

3. Which of the following features should garments for preschoolers have? (A) short zippers; (B) narrow hems; (C) raglan sleeves; (D) wide shoulders; (E) adjustable shoulder straps.

4. List three clothing features that could cause accidents.

5. List two ways adults can help children have fewer toileting accidents.

6. True or false. Most television programs do *not* involve children's minds in an active way.

7. True or false. Mental problem solving is mastered in the preschool years.

8. List two examples of activities that always involve symbolizing.

9. Hardware and software that have been designed especially for preschoolers _____ (are, are not) available.

10. The best resources to help preschoolers learn language skills are _____ (other children, adults).

11. Adults _____ (should, should not) redo tasks that preschool children have done below the adults' standards.

12. List two things adults can do to make children's mistakes less self-defeating.

13. True or false. Gender roles are learned mainly by example.

14. Describe two ways to reduce conflict among preschoolers.

15. True or false. The way adults control their emotions does *not* affect children's emotional control.

Cross-Curricular Link

16. **Social Studies.** Make or gather the materials for one or more of the examples of planned activities for preschool children given in the chapter. Use the planned activity with preschool children in a group program. Discuss with the class what did or did not work and why.

17. **Technology.** Use the Internet to research books and videos or DVDs designed for preschool children who are expecting a new baby in the family. What materials are available for parents to use with their preschoolers as they talk about the changes to come?

Use word processing software to compile a bibliography of the materials you find.

18. **Speech.** Role-play a situation in which a child is angry and hits a friend. Have one person be an adult who is supervising the children. Have the adult demonstrate both good and poor discipline methods.

Making Observations

19. Observe preschoolers in a child care program eating lunch or a snack. What foods are they provided? Did they seem to like the foods or reject some? Why do you think a certain food was rejected? How did the adult encourage eating?

20. Observe preschoolers in a group program. How do their space and furnishings meet preschoolers' needs? Which features could or should be used in the home?

21. Observe preschoolers playing in a group program. Which materials help them solve problems (classify, put things in order, and symbolize)? Which materials help their motor skills?

22. Observe two or more preschoolers playing. What examples of self-assertion did you see? What conflicts occurred? Why did these conflicts occur? How were they resolved? What examples of cooperation did you see? Why do you think the children were cooperative (ages of children or enough play materials)?

Thinking Critically

23. Your text states that food attitudes learned in the preschool years may last a lifetime. What is meant by a food attitude? What food attitudes do you have that perhaps began as early as the preschool years?

24. What types of clothing did you like or did not like as a preschooler? How did your clothing tastes reflect your personality? In your opinion, to what extent should parents permit or encourage their preschoolers to make clothing choices?

25. How can adults support preschoolers' learnings through friendship? When should adults "back off" and allow children to learn how to make friends and resolve conflicts with friends?

20 School-Age Children

After studying this chapter, you will be able to

- ★ **describe** the physical development of school-age children.
- ★ **describe** the intellectual development of school-age children.
- ★ **describe** the social-emotional development of school-age children.
- ★ **explain** how adults and parents can help school-age children meet their developmental needs.

Terms to Know

school-age children	inductive reasoning
middle childhood	scientific reasoning
growth spurt	visual
permanent teeth	auditory
six-year molars	conservation
orthopedic problems	hierarchical classification
growth pains	shortcomings
precision	industry
flexibility	inferiority
concrete operational stage	scapegoating
formal operational stage	psychological security
deductive reasoning	

Between 6 and 12 years of age, children are called **school-age children** as they progress from dependent first-graders to independent preteens. Their motor, mental, and social skills develop quickly during this time, which is called the school-age years or **middle childhood**.

The school-age years are filled with fun, adventure, school, friends, family, and other events. Disappointments, challenges, and hard work are also part of this scene.

Many physical changes happen in children during the school-age years. All body systems are maturing. In addition to excelling in gross-motor activities, older children become skillful at fine-motor tasks, such as model building and handicrafts.

School-age children begin to think more logically and rely less on perception. This helps them learn new skills. Language skills are refined during middle childhood. Soon, children can articulate all English sounds. Their vocabulary continues to grow.

Children mature a great deal socially, too. Self-evaluation becomes more common during the school-age years. Children judge themselves in relation to others. They deepen their social relations with adults, including parents, and with peers. Guiding and directing them during these crucial years are important tasks.

Physical Development

Middle childhood is a period of many changes in the body.

Although these changes sometimes seem awkward as they happen, they help school-age children become more coordinated.

Body Growth and Development

The slow, steady growth rate continues in school-age children. Toward the end of middle childhood, some children—mainly girls—begin a growth spurt and other body changes of the preteen and teen years. (A **growth spurt** is a period of rapid growth, usually linked with adolescence.) During these years, body proportions change and organ systems mature.

Height and Weight

School-age children's height increases more steadily than their weight, 20-1. This is because, for the most part, genes determine height. (Height is not easily affected by the environment, except by long-term conditions, such as malnutrition or certain illnesses.)

Weight seems to parallel height somewhat. Taller children tend to be heavier and shorter children tend to be lighter. The environment also influences weight because of factors such as nutrition, illness, activity, and stress.

Boys are taller and heavier than girls until 10 or 11 years of age. At this time, most females enter a growth spurt. Many girls are taller than boys at this age. Children are often sensitive to the size difference, especially if they are becoming interested in those of the opposite gender. In reality, the average difference is only about one inch at 12 years of age. The difference

Average Height and Weight from Six to Twelve Years

Age in Years	Height		Weight	
	Boys	Girls	Boys	Girls
6	45¾ in.	45 in.	45½ lbs.	43 lbs.
7	48 in.	47½ in.	50¼ lbs.	48½ lbs.
8	50 in.	49¾ in.	55¾ lbs.	54¾ lbs.
9	52 in.	53 in.	62 lbs.	62¾ lbs.
10	54¼ in.	54½ in.	69¼ lbs.	71¾ lbs.
11	55¾ in.	57 in.	77¾ lbs.	81¼ lbs.
12	59 in.	60 in.	90 lbs.	92¼ lbs.

20-1 The height and weight of children from six- to nine-years increase rather steadily. Around age ten, girls enter the growth spurt and tend to be slightly taller and heavier than boys by the end of the school-age years.

shows mainly in a boy who matures slowly and a girl who matures quickly. Most boys catch up in growth during the early teen years.

Body Proportions

During middle childhood, body proportions become even more similar to those of an adult. A child's waist and head begin to look more in proportion to his or her body. The arms and legs grow longer, which gives the child a lower center of gravity and better balance. During these years, the trunk grows until it is two times as long and two times as wide as it was at birth. The abdomen protrudes even less than it did in the preschool years because of the longer trunk.

Bones and Teeth

The skeletal system continues to mature. The bones continue to ossify and grow larger and longer. The most significant growth is in the teeth and jaw, which results in a more mature-looking face. School-age children constantly lose deciduous teeth and grow permanent ones. Girls often lose and replace teeth before boys do. The first two teeth, often the bottom front teeth, fall out during the late preschool years. The last of the 20 deciduous teeth, the *cuspids* (shown in Chapter 8), fall out around age 12.

Unlike deciduous teeth, **permanent teeth** are intended to last a lifetime. They are harder and less sharp than deciduous teeth.

The first permanent teeth to come in are called **six-year molars**. They do not replace any lost teeth. Their name tells the age at which they usually appear. They grow behind the second set of deciduous molars, 20-2. The next permanent teeth replace lost deciduous teeth. The permanent teeth change the look of the lower part of the face.

Muscle Growth

Muscles grow and become more firmly attached to bones during middle childhood. However, the muscles are not mature and are easily injured. **Orthopedic problems** (those relating to the bones and muscles) are the most common physical problems of this age.

The skeleton grows more quickly than the muscles. The lag in muscle growth gives a loose-jointed, somewhat awkward look. Children of this age cannot completely keep their muscles from moving. This makes sitting still almost impossible.

School-age children may complain of aches and pains. These muscle aches are called **growth pains**, which are caused by muscles trying to catch up with skeletal size.

Organ Growth

Brain growth slows during middle childhood. The brain reaches 95 percent of its adult weight by age 10. The wiring is almost complete, and the brain has become more specialized. One area of the brain serves as the visual center, another as the speech center, and so forth. From this time, rewiring the brain is difficult, if not impossible.

Other organs continue to mature, too. The heart grows slowly and is small in relationship to the rest of the body. Too much strain on the heart is dangerous.

The eyes mature, enabling the child to have good visual acuity and binocular vision. The ears mature by age seven. The maturity of the eyes and ears aids perception.

Other changes include a decrease in fat deposits. Skin becomes less delicate or fine in texture. Often light hair becomes darker, too.

Motor Development

The maturing of the body leads to refined motor development. Children have a surplus of energy, too. They use this energy in motor activities.

Gross- and Fine-Motor Skills Improve

Motor skills improve during middle childhood. Children who are six to eight years old enjoy active games that use their large muscles.

Six-Year Molars

20-2   Six-year molars are the first permanent teeth.

They are more developed in large-muscle coordination than in small-muscle coordination. For this reason, they enjoy running, jumping, climbing, and playing simple games, such as tag and catch.

Children ages 9 through 12 begin to develop interests in more specific motor skills. This is due to increased mental ability as well as improved large-muscle coordination. They tend to prefer organized sports, skating, or bicycling rather than running or jumping.

Motor skills become better in middle childhood for the following reasons:

★ faster reaction time. *Reaction time* is the time required to respond to a stimulus, such as a thrown ball.

★ improved precision. **Precision** is the ability to perform motor skills accurately. It is shown in skills such as balancing, steadiness, and aiming at a target.

★ greater speed and improved strength.

★ improved flexibility. **Flexibility** is the ability to move, bend, and stretch easily.

Older school-age children have highly developed fine-motor skills. Improved skill helps them do arts and crafts, write, play musical instruments, dress themselves, and handle other tasks that need fine-motor precision. These skills seem to increase steadily during the school years. Improvement in writing ability is shown in 20-3.

Skill Performance

In the early part of middle childhood, boys perform better than girls in tasks requiring power, force, and speed. After girls begin their growth spurt, they often equal or excel boys of the same age in these tasks. Girls of all school ages tend to perform better than boys in tasks requiring flexibility or rhythm. Experts do not know whether these motor differences in the genders are due to genes or environment. Studies do show a girl or boy who is highly skilled in one motor activity will likely excel in others.

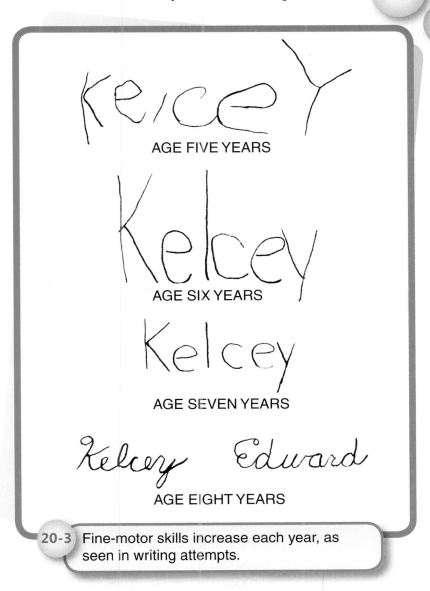

AGE FIVE YEARS

AGE SIX YEARS

AGE SEVEN YEARS

AGE EIGHT YEARS

20-3 Fine-motor skills increase each year, as seen in writing attempts.

Providing for Physical Needs

Although most school-age children have outgrown the need for direct physical care, they still have many needs that adults must meet. As children begin to think for themselves and as peers become more important, meeting needs becomes more complex. For example, school-age children see having a coat that fits in with what everyone else is wearing as more important than whether the coat will keep them warm.

Encouraging Health and Safety Practices

Good health habits, such as diet and physical activity, strongly influence how school-age children develop physically. Health habits affect their weight, posture, complexion, hair, and energy levels. Adults must promote safe living habits. They can do this by explaining good habits, setting examples, and offering chances for practice.

A Healthful Diet

Eating nutritious foods helps the school-age child's body meet its growth needs and increased energy demands. School-age children also need to store some nutrients for the rapid growth that will occur in their teen years. Healthful diets help school-age children resist infections. Healthful diets also reduce the risk for obesity and diseases associated with obesity, such as heart disease and Type 2 diabetes. Being underweight can also contribute to health problems. Children may not be getting all the nutrients they need for their bodies to function properly. In addition, children who are over- or underweight are more likely to suffer social and emotional effects than their normal-weight peers.

Parents can base the diets of their school-age children on the **MyPyramid.gov** recommendations, 20-4. As each child's needs may differ slightly, adults may need to adjust the child's diet somewhat. They should consult with the child's doctor or a registered dietitian for advice.

When children start school, adults are no longer in control of what their children eat at lunchtime. Some schools publish their weekly menus to help parents plan other meals and snacks of the day. However, children may not always eat what is on their lunch plate. Even children who carry their lunches to school may give or throw away some of their food. Parents and school staff should urge children to make nutritious food choices while away from home.

Snacking is often unsupervised. Many children buy snacks with their spending money. These often include junk foods that are high in calories and low in nutrition. Children who eat too much junk food can lose their appetite for nourishing food. These children may be receiving adequate calories, but not enough of the nutrients their bodies need for growth. Junk food can also contribute to tooth decay.

Adults can promote healthy snacking by keeping nutritious, ready-to-eat snacks on hand. Examples are cheese cubes, fresh fruit, and raw carrots or celery sticks. Adults can urge children to prepare their own nutritious snacks, too.

MyPyramid
STEPS TO A HEALTHIER YOU

Based on the information you provided, this is your daily recommended amount from each food group.

GRAINS	VEGETABLES	FRUITS	MILK	MEAT & BEANS
5 ounces	2 cups	1½ cups	2 cups	5 ounces
Make half your grains whole Aim for at least **3 ounces** of whole grains a day	**Vary your veggies** Aim for these amounts **each week:** **Dark green veggies** = 2 cups **Orange veggies** = 1½ cups **Dry beans & peas** = 2½ cups **Starchy veggies** = 2½ cups **Other veggies** = 5½ cups	**Focus on fruits** Eat a variety of fruit Go easy on fruit juices	**Get your calcium-rich foods** Go low-fat or fat-free when you choose milk, yogurt, or cheese	**Go lean with protein** Choose low-fat or lean meats and poultry Vary your protein routine—choose more fish, beans, peas, nuts, and seeds

Find your balance between food and physical activity

Be physically active for at least **60 minutes** every day, or most days.

Know your limits on fats, sugars, and sodium

Your allowance for oils is **5 teaspoons a day**.

Limit extras–solid fats and sugars– to **130 calories a day**.

Your results are based on a 1600 calorie pattern   Name: _____

This calorie level is only an estimate of your needs. Monitor your body weight to see if you need to adjust your calorie intake.

20-4 School-age children need a nutritious diet to meet their growth and energy needs. The recommended amounts shown in this sample are for an eight-year-old boy who is active 30–60 minutes daily.

Because school-age children like to eat, they often enjoy cooking. Many good cookbooks are written for this age group. Simple recipes allow children to prepare foods on their own or with a little help.

Physical Activity and Other Good Health Practices

In addition to providing nutritious foods and promoting a good diet, adults can promote other health practices. School-age children need moderate physical activity daily. Physical activity is a major contributor to physical fitness. Adults must see that children spend time being active rather than sitting in front of the television or computer for too long each day.

Research shows that the amount of sleep needed daily by school-age children varies by age. Six- and seven-year-olds need 10½ to 11 hours; eight- and nine-year-olds need 10 to 10½ hours. Ten- through twelve-year-olds need 9½ to 10 hours. When school-age children do not get the sleep they need, the following problems often occur:

★ They are unable to concentrate, which affects both learning ability and the quality of work.

★ They are more likely to be overweight.

★ They are more irritable and even more prone to bully others.

Safety Practices

Safety rules need to be modeled and practiced. For example, adults must insist on seat belts and bicycle helmets, 20-5. Adults need to keep the home safe from potential hazards. Most home accidents are due to falls and fire. Other dangers include those from poisoning, drowning, firearms, and electricity.

Selecting the Right Clothing

Like children of all ages, school-age children need clothing that fits and is well constructed. School-age children are active, so clothing should have growth features and be able to withstand stress and strain. Most school-age children have developed self-dressing skills except for a hard-to-reach button or a specially tied bow. Younger school-age

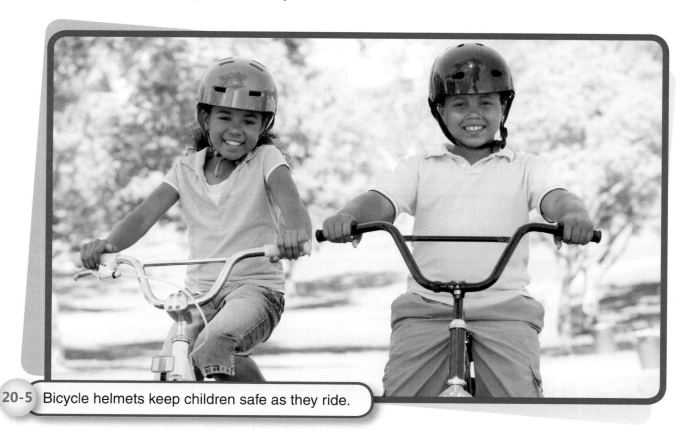

20-5   Bicycle helmets keep children safe as they ride.

children may still need to have clothes with some self-dressing features. Shoe and sock sizes change on the average of every six months for children ages 6 to 12.

Children of this age develop their own preferences for color and style. They want to fit in with their peers. The right clothing and shoes help make children feel part of the group. If clothing and shoes are too different from what others wear, children may feel rejected. Compliments from others on their clothing help boost children's self-confidence.

Due to children's emphasis on clothing, many school systems are instituting school uniforms. This is an effort to improve school performance and reduce negative behaviors. Uniforms seem to improve children's focus on learning, not on clothing choices. Uniforms are also often cheaper for parents than an individual school wardrobe.

Providing Needed Space and Furnishings

School-age children want and need space of their own. Adults should think about the following features when planning a space for school-age children:

★ Space that may be used for many purposes—playing, working on hobbies, studying, daydreaming, sleeping, and dressing. Children often want space for their friends to visit even overnight.

★ Storage space for clothes and shoes, play and hobby equipment, and books. Display areas for photos, pennants, collections, hobbies, and keepsakes are often prized.

★ Space that is attractive to school-age children. They like to choose their own color schemes and accessories.

★ Easy-to-clean rooms help children who are just learning home-care skills.

★ Furniture and accessories that can also be used in the teen and young adult years may be a wise investment.

Intellectual Development

Children make dramatic gains in mental development during the school-age years. To a large extent, this is due to the rapidly maturing brain. Children's mental development is also dependent on the environment. The environment includes the learning opportunities provided and supported by peers and adults. Mental development is also dependent on children's interest in the materials to be learned. Finally, mental development is dependent upon how well the new learnings mesh with children's prior experiences.

Children's Thinking: Piaget's Ideas

Piaget noted that between ages 7 to 11, children's thinking depends more on logic and less on perception. Piaget called this third stage of mental abilities the **concrete operational stage**, 20-6. The term *concrete* means that logic is based on

Piaget's Stages of Cognitive Development

Stage 1: Sensorimotor Stage (Birth to 2 years)

Stage 2: Preoperational Stage (2 to 7 years)

Stage 3: Concrete Operational Stage (7 to 11 years)
Stage in which children begin to think logically, but base their logic on past experiences.
★ Can see things from various perspectives.
★ Focus on more than one aspect of something at the same time.
★ Invert a sequence of steps (reversibility logic).
★ Gradually note transformations (conserve).
   Number—5 to 7 years
   Continuous quantities (liquid)—6 to 8 years
   Mass (like clay)—6 to 8 years
   Length—6 to 8 years
   Area—7 to 9 years
   Weight—8 to 10 years
   Volume—10 to 14 years
★ Use better reasoning skills.

Stage 4: Formal Operational Stage (11 years on)
Stage in which older children, teens, and adults reason abstractly.
★ Can hypothesize.
★ Do scientific and mathematical abstract reasoning.

20-6 The school-age child functions in the concrete operational stage.

what the child has experienced at some previous time. The transition between the preoperational and concrete operational stages is very gradual. Young school-age children do not apply logical thinking to all tasks. With each age, children are becoming more logical rather than depending upon their perceptions.

Piaget called the last stage of mental development the **formal operational stage** (ages 11 and older). Some child development experts place the beginning of formal operations at 12 to 14 years. In fact, many adults almost always function in the concrete operational stage. In the last stage, a person can reason more abstractly. The difference between concrete and formal operations can be seen in how a child plays a game of checkers or chess. At the concrete operational stage, the child can play checkers or chess by the rules. He or she makes each move based on what is on the board at that time. He or she does not think in terms of the next three to five moves. Older players in the formal operational stage can think ahead and plan strategies. A person using formal operations plans game strategy by thinking, "If my opponent does such and such, then what will my options be?"

Seeing from the Viewpoint of Others

School-age children begin to see others have ideas that differ from their own. Realizing that others have different ideas leads children to question their previous thoughts and search to find the right answers. School-age children work to prove or deny answers by using logic.

Piaget believed contact with peers is the greatest help in freeing children from egocentric thinking. For real communication with others, a person must recognize the point of view of others and notice how it compares or contrasts with his or her own ideas.

Focusing on More Than One Part

During the school years, the child comes to focus on more than one aspect of something at a time. This means the child can see more than one change in an object at one time. Refer again to Piaget's liquid task with a short, wide glass and a tall, thin glass, shown in Chapter 17. In the school-age years, the child knows the greater width in the first glass makes up for the greater height in the other glass. Because the child can note both diameter and height changes at the same time, it is easier to understand how the same amount of liquid looks taller in a thinner glass.

Using Reversibility Logic

School-age children are better able to understand reversibility logic. As you read earlier, *reversibility* is the ability to follow a line of reasoning back to where it started. They can carry out a task in reverse order. There is the understanding that if something is put back the way it was to begin with, it will be the same. The child who flattens a clay ball knows the clay can be made into a ball again. (In math, this concept is carried out in subtraction.)

Reversibility also means knowing that one change, such as in height, can lead to another change, such as in width. The child knows the clay can be bigger in diameter because it is flatter. (In math, this concept is carried out in division.)

Noting Transformations

School-age children can mentally put together a series of events to see changes in an object, 20-7. For example, children begin by seeing two identical glasses with equal

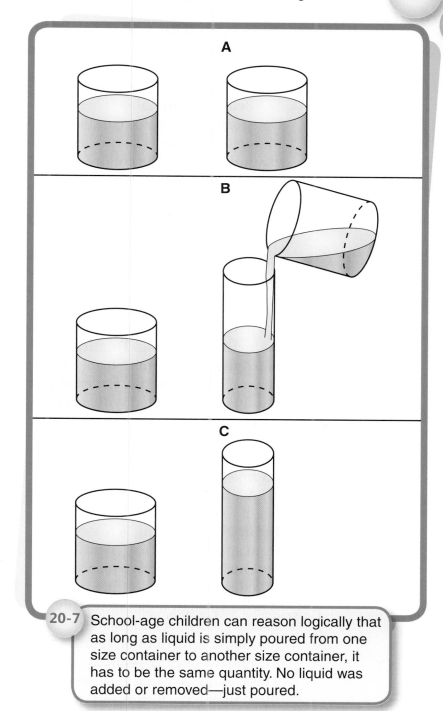

20-7 School-age children can reason logically that as long as liquid is simply poured from one size container to another size container, it has to be the same quantity. No liquid was added or removed—just poured.

amounts of water (A). Then as they watch, the water is poured from one of these glasses into a taller, but thinner glass (B). As they look at the completed transformation (C), they logically understand no liquid was added or removed—just poured. Although the amount in each of the two glasses may look different (perception), it has to be the same amount (logical reasoning). As shown in 20-6, children understand certain transformations earlier than others.

Being able to note transformations helps children understand other concepts. For example, school-age children can accept their parents were once babies. They can believe a tree grew from a seed. They understand many natural transformations, such as water turning to ice.

Using Deductive and Inductive Reasoning

The school-age child uses deductive reasoning. **Deductive reasoning** is reasoning from the general to the specific. For example, the child is presented with a general statement that all fish live in water. If the child knows that guppies are fish, then he or she can deduce that guppies live in water.

Older school-age children may begin to use inductive reasoning. **Inductive reasoning** is reasoning from specific facts to general conclusions. Inductive reasoning is called **scientific reasoning** because it is the form of logic commonly used by scientists. Inductive reasoning is most often found in children over 11 years of age. These children can weigh several ideas they have tested and draw a conclusion. For example, a child may know that people make ice cubes by putting water in a freezer. The child may put fruit juice in the freezer and find that it becomes solid, too. After trying other liquids, such as soft drinks or milk, the child may use inductive reasoning to conclude that cold temperatures change liquids into solids.

Children's Learning: Vygotsky's Ideas

As you read, Piaget thought children's mental learning was mainly due to brain development at certain ages. Unlike Piaget, Vygotsky believed that children always learned best when their minds are "stretched," but always within their ZPD.

Vygotsky believed collaboration among peers and between adults and children had a major impact on learning in addition to the role of brain development. Like Piaget, Vygotsky believed that children learn by doing, but he also thought that children learn by talking and working with others. He also felt it was important for children to persist at a task until they "got it."

Piaget felt *language reflected learning*. On the other hand, Vygotsky saw *language as a way of learning*. Through verbal interactions children learn the process of learning, such as explaining what they know and questioning others to clarify. Children also learn the needed tools—what works best. Finally, children learn the most effective way to do tasks. Vygotsky felt that after learning how to do a task, using silent words is important in doing it independently.

What School-Age Children Learn

Because school-age children are beginning to use logic in their thought processes, they are able to learn many new things. Logic helps them learn school subjects, such as language arts, reading, math, geography, science, and the arts. School-age children's concepts are clearly more advanced than preschool children's concepts. However, they still have trouble grasping some concepts, such as events in history, scientific logic, and value systems.

Physical Knowledge Concepts

As you recall, physical knowledge concepts include concepts about size, shape, color, texture, and other attributes of objects and people. It also includes knowing what happens to objects when they are acted upon, such as hit, squeezed, or dropped. Physical knowledge concepts become more advanced in school-age children because their perception has matured, 20-8. Their senses mature, making sight, sound, smell, and touch more accurate. The brain, too, processes what is seen and heard in more defined ways.

Perception

Perception in school-age children changes in many ways, especially in accuracy. Accurate perception aids physical knowledge concepts.

★ Children do more in-depth exploring of their world. For example, by age nine years, they use the eyes or fingertips to trace the outline of an object rather than glancing at it quickly. This more thorough examination helps them note details in objects.

★ Children learn what information to act upon and what to ignore as they examine an object. For example, if children are identifying geometric shapes, the color of the shapes is ignored.

★ Children learn to correctly pair **visual** (seen) and **auditory** (heard) stimuli, such as written letters and their sounds or written music notes and their pitches.

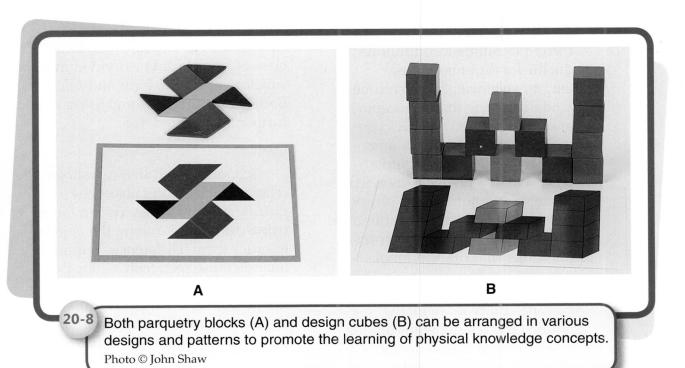

A   **B**

20-8 Both parquetry blocks (A) and design cubes (B) can be arranged in various designs and patterns to promote the learning of physical knowledge concepts.

Photo © John Shaw

Memory

School-age children have an improved memory that helps them develop physical knowledge concepts. These children are beginning to see the need for a good memory. Remembering the attributes of objects, people, and places is important. Without remembering these attributes, children cannot identify, describe, classify, or order them. Children also develop methods to help them remember. Such methods include singing the alphabet or learning a rhyme about the number of days in the months of the year.

Logic

Logic allows school-age children to form better, more accurate concepts. For example, the ability to use logic helps children master the concept of conservation. **Conservation** means that changing the shape, direction, or position of an object or objects does not alter the quantity. Children must be able to understand conservations before they can form accurate concepts related to number, continuous quantities (liquids), mass, length, area, weight, or volume. Understanding these concepts is gradual, as noted in 20-6.

Perception, memory, and logic work together to help a child develop physical knowledge concepts. With increased physical knowledge, the child is better able to give more meaning to words, drawings, and other symbols.

Logical Thinking Concepts

The ability to mentally understand relationships among objects becomes well developed in the middle childhood years. School-age children better understand classification, order, numbers, space, distance, time, and speed. These logical thinking concepts become more accurate as children replace perceptual thinking with logic.

Classification

As you read in Chapter 17, classification is the grouping of objects into a class and its complement. As school-age children classify, the attribute (shape, color, way used) that defines the class remains stable. For example, school-age children do not group by shape and switch to color in the process. School-age children also include all objects that meet the attribute for that class. By middle childhood, children fully understand the class and the complement, 20-9.

School-age children learn hierarchical classification. **Hierarchical classification** is having classes within other classes; that is a class may have many subclasses. For example, the large class of *animals* can be divided into subclasses, such as *birds* and *fish*. Both the groups *birds* and *fish* can be further subdivided, too.

Order

School-age children can show relationships among objects by putting them in order. This involves using differences among the objects to order them. Differences might include those seen (color, shape, size), heard (pitch, loudness), and felt (texture and temperature). Other differences involve time or order of events. Children can now arrange

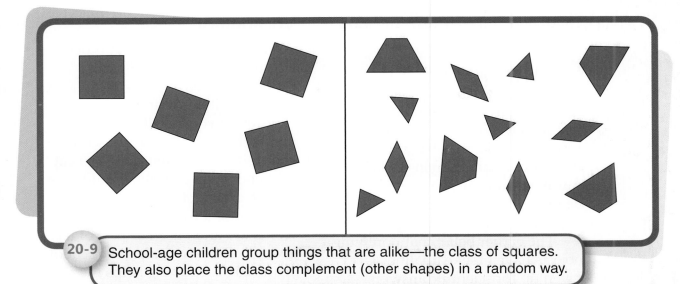

20-9 School-age children group things that are alike—the class of squares. They also place the class complement (other shapes) in a random way.

objects with small differences. School-age children use ordering in their daily lives, such as in calendars, lists, and alphabetizing.

Number

During the last part of the preschool stage and the early part of middle childhood, children learn many basic concepts about numbers. They need to learn number concepts, such as *greater than, less than, equal to,* and others. Some of these basic ideas must be grasped before children can understand math.

Children also learn that groups are changed in number if more objects are brought into the group (adding). They also learn the number changes if objects are taken away from the group (subtracting).

Space

School-age children have many correct ideas about space. They can tell whether objects are *open* or *closed* and whether they are *far* or *near*. They can also see the relationship of two or more objects. They understand such

concepts as *close to, connected, behind, in front of, above, below, left,* or *right.* They know, too, that objects, such as flying jets, do not get smaller as they move farther away.

Distance, Time, and Speed

Children who are younger than eight years of age have problems grasping distance, time, and speed concepts. They mainly have trouble understanding the ways these concepts relate. Time and distance are often confused. For example, the young school-age child may say that walking some place is *far,* but that running makes it *near.*

Children often learn clock time and calendar time in the first or second grade. However, they do not understand calendar time well until age 10 or 11. The time of historical events seems difficult to grasp until the teen years. Stories written for children often reflect their understandings of time. Stories for the young child often begin with "Once upon a time." Stories for school-age children give hints about seasons or years. Books for the later childhood and teen years mention exact time periods.

Cause and Effect Relationships

School-age children begin to resolve many cause and effect relationships. As children become less egocentric, they begin to understand that humans do not cause natural happenings. They begin to have more of a scientific approach to their thinking.

The earlier belief that nonliving objects have lifelike qualities is given up for scientific answers. However, some aspects of nature (sun and stars, oceans, mountains) that are thought of as powerful may be seen as lifelike by older children.

Language Is Mastered

Around six or seven years of age, children's speech becomes more social. They want to talk with their friends and adults. The speech of school-age children is not as involved or intellectual, however, as many adult conversations.

Focus on Reading
Using Words Effectively

Ask a librarian from a public or elementary school library to show you some books for school-age children in which the authors use puns and word play effectively. (You might start by reading some of the writings of Dr. Seuss and Shel Silverstein.) After selecting a book, select one of the following activities:
★ Share some examples of the author's plays on words with your class.
  ★ Read the book to school-age children (or one child) and share their reactions to the story with your class.

Vocabulary

Active vocabulary continues to grow in middle childhood. Children of this age give more exact definitions than do younger children. If you asked children to define the word *orange*, preschool children would often say, "You eat it." School-age children would give a more exact definition, such as, "It is a color or a fruit." Definitions of words are often used as part of tests given to children during the school years, 20-10. Reading helps the vocabulary grow, as does learning to spell words and write sentences.

Articulation

Articulation of all English sounds is often mastered by age eight. Children with the most articulation problems at the end of the preschool years often continue to have speech problems in the school years. Speech problems are also related to reading problems. This is because children need to *articulate*, say sounds, in order to decode the sounds of letters, a skill that is needed for reading and spelling.

Grammar

Around nine years of age, children have mastered the grammar they hear. They use their own set of grammar rules to make plurals, use pronouns, and show tense. These rules may or may not be those of standard grammar. Changing grammar habits after this age requires relearning.

Middle childhood is also the age of having fun with words. Children learn different word rhymes, raps, and chants. Name-calling can even become a word contest that may turn a fight into laughter. Humor is

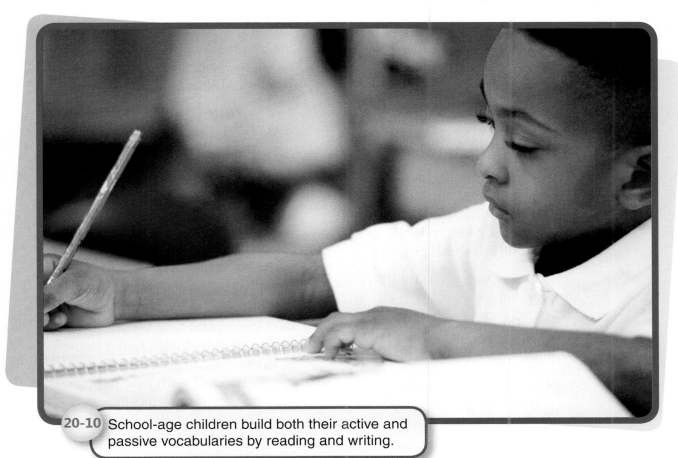

20-10 School-age children build both their active and passive vocabularies by reading and writing.

expressed more in words during the middle childhood years. Children come to enjoy many kinds of jokes, riddles, and simple puns.

Meeting Intellectual Needs

Children have intellectual needs to meet. School meets many of the mental needs of children. Home is an important learning environment, too. Children need a rich out-of-school world of things to do and see, which includes motor activities, hobbies, socializing, and daydreaming. Even day-to-day activities can be rich in learning experiences.

Guiding Intellectual Development

Adults can help school-age children meet their intellectual needs in many ways. For example, adults can do the following:

★ Provide opportunities for children to participate in activities that require effort over longer periods. Such activities might include learning to play a musical instrument or being involved in sports. It might include beginning a hobby, such as stamp collecting, model building, or other projects.

★ Allow children to choose the activities they find most rewarding.

★ Encourage children to learn. However, adults should not overuse rewards and praise. The feeling of doing a good job is often the best reward.

★ Show an interest in and support the school's program.

★ Show interest in their (the adults') own activities. Adults whose skills and satisfactions grow over long periods of time are children's best models.

Adults can enrich children's language in many ways. Sharing ideas and experiences with children can be mutually rewarding. Reading to children and listening to them read is helpful. Adults can encourage children to express themselves correctly. Children learn the language they hear, speak, and read.

There are many language games that are fun as well as helpful.

Individual word puzzles of all types are available, too. These include crossword puzzles, word finds, and scrambled words.

Preparing the Child to Enter School

Between late August and September each year, several million five- and six-year-olds enter school. Many older children also enter new schools because their families have moved. Starting school is exciting and perhaps scary for many children.

Entering school is a new developmental task for children. They must deal with new people—both children and adults. They must also deal with new concepts and skills and with a different daily structure, 20-11. School-age children spend 44 percent of their waking hours at school.

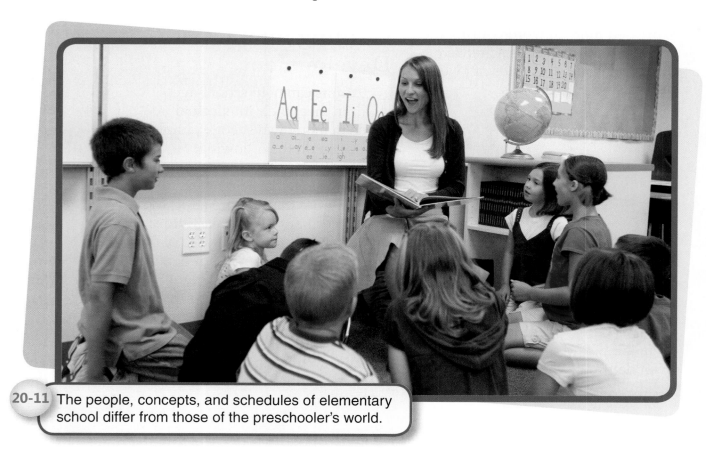

20-11 The people, concepts, and schedules of elementary school differ from those of the preschooler's world.

Adults need to help children make the transition from home to school as enjoyable as possible. Stress may accompany the new hours and routines. Adults need to realize children may manage anxiety at school, but they may show anxiety and stress at home. Extra patience is needed during the adjustment time. This is a poor time to add new learnings or tasks, such as music lessons or a new pet, to a child's life.

Adults can help children have a good basis for their school experiences in many ways. For example, they can do the following:

★ Develop a secure and trusting relationship with children.

★ Allow children to have more independence.

★ Teach children to accept the authority of adults other than parents.

★ Help children overcome separation anxiety.

School also means getting along with peers for many hours. Children sit, line up, work, eat, and share with other children. Unlike the preschool play groups, where children choose their own friends and play when they want, school relationships are more teacher directed. Children who are adaptable and have had contacts with others find it easier to adjust than those who have not had this opportunity.

Getting the Child to School

Adults need to make transportation plans clear to children. Younger children who walk or catch a bus need instructions and practice. Some adults or older children who are known to the child should be nearby. Children should be reminded not to talk to or go with strangers. They should know their full name, parent's names, address, and phone number.

School should be viewed as a natural course of events—everyone goes to school. Adults should create a normal routine for the first few days of school. Overdoing photos, sounding anxious, getting the child ready too early (or too late), or serving a special breakfast are not ways to make school a matter-of-fact event.

Adults should say goodbyes at the bus stop, on the schoolyard, or at the classroom door. These goodbyes should be warm, but not clingy. The teary-eyed child often regains control soon after the adult is out of sight, 20-12. Picking up a young child on time is very important, especially on the first

20-12 Saying goodbye in the schoolyard helps children enter the classroom in a composed, positive state.

days of school. Parents should also show a strong interest in their child's reports about his or her school days.

If the first days go well, children look forward to school. Experiences that are not good may lead to situations where children want to avoid school and stay home.

Reinforcing School Tasks

School children need daily encouragement and help. Adults must continue working with and helping their children. Help is not effective if given only a few days after the teacher shares negative reports with parents. The teachers and parents and other adults close to children have the same goal. They all want to give children the best possible education. Children are best helped when all those concerned work as a team.

Adults can ensure that children follow through on any activities the school sends home with the child. They need to supervise children's homework, but not do it for them. In the elementary school, homework most often is assigned to reinforce skills learned in class. Doing children's homework makes them rely on adults to solve their tasks. It also prevents the child from getting needed practice. (If homework is often too difficult, adults should talk to the teacher.)

Guiding Television Viewing

Parents should limit television viewing on school nights. Several studies show that as hours of television viewing increase, grades drop at the same rate. Children who do not watch as much television tend to concentrate better and use their imaginations more. Also, school-age

Learn More About...
Responsibilities Concerning Children's Schooling

Adults have a number of responsibilities concerning their children's schooling. Among these are the following:

★ See that children attend school regularly and follow the rules.

★ Take an interest in what children are learning.

★ Talk with children about schoolwork, look at their papers, and stay in close contact with the school.

Adults and children need to plan a quiet place for study. Space with a desk or table for doing work, such as writing, is important. Many children also enjoy a place to stretch out while reading.

A certain amount of time needs to be set aside for doing homework. This amount varies with the age of the child. Elementary school children need time to play and perhaps have a snack or evening meal as a short break between school and homework. However, homework should be done before most leisure activities. School-age children who do not have homework can use the set time for reading or being read to, drawing, or doing other activities that complement school tasks. Household tasks can fit with school tasks, too. For example, adults may plan a cooking project to reinforce fractions.

children who learn to budget their work and leisure times develop healthy lifelong work and play habits.

Television can be a useful tool for learning and entertainment, however, in limited amounts. It is not healthful to let television watching replace many other worthwhile activities, especially involvement with others and hands-on activities.

Assisting Computer Use

Most school-age children are becoming comfortable with computers and use them for learning and fun. Quality software and Web sites can be used to support school learnings and enhance problem solving, decision making, creativity, concepts, language learnings, and even social skills. With good software and access to the Internet, children can do the following:

★ access information

★ communicate (send and receive e-mails, "talk" with experts, and compose stories and poems)

★ publish their work

★ visit interactive sites

Teachers need to help parents learn to assist their children in the use of computers. Parents need to see software and Web site evaluations (as discussed in Chapter 19) and have lists of software and Web sites used in their children's classrooms. Teachers need to explain to parents how children can use computers in doing homework and projects and in having fun. Many librarians have helpful computer information for parents, too. Much literature on children's computer use is available through parenting magazines,

Game Programmer

Game programmers plan and write video game software. They turn ideas, art, and music into games that work. When designers describe an event in a game, programmers translate the idea into mathematical equations the computer understands.

Education: Most game programmers have a bachelor's degree in computer science, electrical engineering, or mathematics.

Job Outlook: Due to the demand for video games and industry growth, the job outlook is good.

children's magazines, newspapers, and on the Internet. This information provides reviews of software and Web sites and makes suggestions for online activities.

Although computer use is a useful tool, parents and other adults must keep children safe while using the computer. Safety is discussed in Chapter 22.

Social-Emotional Development

A whole new social experience begins in middle childhood. Children need to make many new adjustments. School-age children have to be much more independent. They are concerned about what others think of them. Friendships are fun, but sometimes difficult. They find that mastering skills needed in order to fit into society can be stressful.

In many ways, social development becomes the most important aspect of development in middle childhood. The peer group becomes more and more important as children progress through the school years. Relationships with peers affect all aspects of development. School-age children's physical skills are often judged by how well they can play sports and games with peers. Through their school activities, they make daily judgments of their own learnings compared with those of peers. Some school and youth organizations use peer-group projects. Peer groups also act as a source of socialization. Each group teaches its own rules of conduct needed for acceptance.

Developing Self-Esteem

School-age children take a close look at themselves, 20-13.

20-13 School-age children often spend much time alone thinking about themselves.

They become keenly aware of their **shortcomings** (areas in which a person wants or needs to improve) and failures. Self-evaluation becomes more complex for the following reasons:

★ School-age children become almost totally concerned with what others think of them. Peers can judge harshly. Adults cannot often change how peers judge each other.

★ Abilities in reading, math, music, computer literacy, and other skills are more difficult for children to measure. Earlier, they could tell how they compared with other children in their motor skills, such as playing baseball. Now it is much harder to compare because their school studies are more abstract.

★ School-age children are generally evaluated in comparison to other children's skills. School grades are earned more in comparison to other children's work than in comparison to the child's own previous work.

Showing Social Awareness

During middle childhood, children begin to show a greater awareness of what is going on around them. School-age children develop a sense of work and industry as they learn some of the skills needed to become ready for adult life. Social relationships grow and become more complicated.

Sense of Work and Being Industrious

As you read in Chapter 18, Erikson described the preschooler's sense of initiative as thinking and acting without being urged. The preschool child's ability to initiate experiences prepares the child for later development. In the school-age years, children enter Erikson's fourth stage of development, *industry versus inferiority*, 20-14. **Industry** means joining others in striving to become a competent member of society. **Inferiority** is feeling incompetent and less valued as a member of society.

Like initiative, industry involves doing and making things. However, industry builds on the strides made in the *initiative stage*. Thus, it differs from initiative in three major ways. These include the following:

★ Industry involves the drive to accomplish school tasks and other projects, whereas initiative involves learning tasks that will reduce the need for adult help.

★ Industry involves joining others and working as a team member, whereas initiative is more personal.

★ Industry focuses on recognition from peers and important adults, whereas initiative focuses on pleasing self and parents.

If school-age children are successful in this stage, they feel confident and productive. Being industrious increases children's feelings of self-esteem and responsibility. They see that what they do makes a difference. If children's efforts and work are

Erikson's Stages of Personality Development

Basic Trust versus Basic Mistrust (First Year of Life)

Autonomy versus Shame and Doubt (Second Year of Life)

Initiative versus Guilt (Preschool Years)

Industry versus Inferiority (Middle Childhood)

Middle childhood is the time for developing the tools of society in preparation for adult work. If children are encouraged to use these tools, they develop a sense of industry. If too little is expected or if children are criticized for their efforts, a sense of inferiority develops. Inferiority results in poor work habits, avoidance of competition, and the inability to cope with later tasks.

20-14 Being industrious, while learning to avoid feelings of inferiority, is the major social-emotional task of the school-age years.

demeaned or ignored, the outcome may be a lasting sense of inferiority.

School-age children want to satisfy themselves while being acceptable to society. The play of earlier years is replaced with more meaningful work (at least by adult standards). However, play is still important in middle childhood.

Children learn their lifelong attitude toward work at this time. Those with a sense of industry see work as the way to learn new ideas and skills and to perform in worthwhile ways. These children also see work as a way to win approval from others. Parents, teachers, and peers encourage the learning of skills. Even social organizations, such as 4-H,

Boy Scouts, or Girl Scouts, make learning skills the route to success and higher status.

School-age children like to learn to do things with and for others. They are learning and practicing cooperation as they enjoy the interaction with others.

Peers Become Important

As children spend more time with peers, they depend less on adults for company. Children in the elementary school years like to form groups. The nature of friendships changes as children mature.

Close friendships are beginning to develop in the early school years, 20-15. By age eight years, there is more separation of genders. Peer groups are informal and often include children who live near

each other. Groups are often within walking or cycling distance. The groups change as families move in and out of the neighborhood.

In this stage, children often see a friend as someone who helps them. They seldom think in terms of how they can help the friend. Give and take does occur, but it serves the individual rather than the mutual interest of friends.

Between 9 and 11 years of age, more close friendships form. Boys choose boys for friends, and girls choose girls. Children also show dislike for the opposite gender. However, girls may become interested in boys around age 11 years. Similar interests and tastes determine friendships more often than physical nearness. Some formal groups, such as team sport groups, form at this time, also. The nature of these friendships becomes one of cooperation and helping each other in order to achieve group goals.

Peer Groups Serve a Purpose

Peer groups are important to children and may serve the following purposes:

★ Belonging to a peer group gives children a feeling of sharing and loyalty. Special friends may huddle, talk, giggle, argue, and fight as they share times together. Children feel a sense of security and self-esteem when working or playing with others in their group.

★ Peer groups reinforce self-esteem. School-age children are highly concerned about how they appear to others. In peer groups, children tag others with labels, such as captain of the team or the last one chosen.

20-15 In the school-age years, children begin developing close relationships with a few special peers.

These labels make children aware of how others feel about them. Once they absorb these peer attitudes, children react to themselves as others have reacted to them.

★ Peer groups provide emotional support. Adults cannot provide the comfort that children feel when they realize others their age share similar feelings. Their group members understand how they feel.

★ Peer groups share information with each other. Children learn from their peers as they work on group projects. They not only want to be part of the group, but they want to be the best in the group. This makes children want to learn all they can from their peers.

★ Through their peer groups, children learn how to deal with rules and get along with others. Even the earlier play groups become more organized as children participate in games with rules. These groups teach children that social relationships involve rules and rules help groups work as teams. Peer group codes contain more rules about what not to do than what to do. Children learn consequences of what can happen, such as being removed from the group, if rules are broken.

★ Peer groups help school-age children gain self-control and depend less on adults. The peer group serves as a sifter for thinking through adult-taught values. Peers help children decide which values to keep and which to adjust. As children consider values, they learn to conform to others at times and stand firm in their own beliefs at other times.

Controlling Emotions

By the time they enter school, children show patterns of emotional behavior. These patterns are fairly well established. Their emotional development and personality continue to merge. Thus, the emotions felt by school-age children affect all their behavior, which influences their personality.

Love

All school-age children need love. They show love to adults and peers who care for them and accept them as they are, 20-16. School-age children do not seek relationships in which they must give too much in return. They do care for others who share common interests.

The need for love is shown in school-age children's great desire to be accepted by others—adults and peers. Most of these children, however, do not express their love as openly (with hugs and kisses) as younger children. They may be embarrassed about being openly affectionate with family members. School-age children show love for adults by kindness and doing activities with them. They show affection for peers by wanting to be with them and sharing secrets. They also show affection by staying in touch through the telephone and other available technologies, notes, and giving small presents.

20-16 School-age children show their love to family members and other close people by spending time with them.

School-age children who do not feel loved have a narrowed emotional range. They experience little or no joy, grief, or guilt. Thinking abilities are hurt because these unloved children cannot concentrate. These children often turn to antisocial behavior, such as hostile acts. These children may seek acceptance from peers who are poor role models. In order to be part of this "circle of friends," these children continue the negative behaviors of the group.

Fear and Anxiety

Some of a child's earlier fears and worries become less threatening. There is a greater separation of fantasy and reality. Thus, fear of the dark disappears after age seven years. Fear of the supernatural declines by 9 or 10 years of age. Fears of physical harm (disease, injury, or death) continue from the preschool years into the school-age years. School-age children's fears and anxieties also center on the future, embarrassment, and people and their actions, 20-17.

The fears and anxieties of middle childhood often do not disappear with age. Some studies report over half of the school-age children's fears and anxieties persist into adult years.

Anger and Aggression

Expressions of anger and aggression change with age. School-age children do not display their anger as physically as younger children do. They are better able

Fears and Anxieties in Middle Childhood

The future
★ Any new situation, such as a new school or new neighborhood
★ The world, in general, such as war, pollution, and economic changes

Embarrassment
★ School failure
★ Remaining unchosen for a team sport, part in a play, or other event
★ Mistake made in a game, recital, or other performance
★ Poor personal appearance
★ Physical examinations and fear of changing clothes in a locker room or public place
★ Personal shortcomings

People and their actions
★ Family quarrels
★ Divorce/disagreement of parents
★ Fear that custodial parent may leave
★ Kidnappers and child enticers
★ Abuse
★ Gangs and bullies

20-17 The major fears and anxieties of middle childhood are the future, embarrassment, and people and their actions.

to control their bodies and express themselves verbally. By this time, they know what is and is not acceptable. Therefore, children in middle childhood show their anger in less direct ways. For example, anger may be expressed in the forms of disrespect, sulkiness, and **scapegoating** (blaming others for their own mistakes). School-age children also show anger by gossiping, plotting, and even imagining the downfall of their enemies. Withdrawal from a situation, such as quitting or using less ability, may be another sign of anger. Some older children are physically aggressive, and their acts can have devastating outcomes.

As children grow older, they become angry about different things. Like preschool children, school-age children are angered when their wants are denied or their possessions are threatened. However, unlike preschool children, school-age children are also angered by what they see as wrongs to others. In later years, anger at social wrongs may be turned into positive social action.

Helping with Social-Emotional Needs

Although the peer group becomes an important part of school-age children's social lives, adults are still important. Adults need to help children in their activities and schoolwork. Parents often pay for children's training or participation in activities. They arrange for safe transportation to and from these activities. Adults give children support and encouragement in their social-emotional development.

School-age children enjoy just being with familiar adults. Elementary school children are still interested in doing things with and for their families, 20-18. These children also enjoy being with other adults, such as teachers and youth leaders.

Guiding and Modeling Behavior

Galinsky stated that parents of school-age children are in the *interpretive stage* of parenting. (See Chart 3-4, *Galinsky's Parenting Stages*.) Adults model their values and attitudes about almost all aspects of life. School-age children watch and listen to important adults in their lives. They pattern many of their thoughts and actions after these adults. School-age children still need a certain amount of guidance.

Balance Dependence with Independence

School-age children often question adults' guidance. Yet, school-age children need adults to listen to them and, at times, to advise and set limits. Adults must learn the balance between letting go and being there for children. This is not easy. Adults do not know whether they should protect children from problems with friends or let them cope on their own. Adults may be torn between trying to enforce their teachings and allowing children to make some of their own decisions.

Extend Gender Role

Adults help extend the gender role development in the school years. Mothers and other female adults close to school-age girls affect the girls' feminine gender role learnings. These learnings include goals in the world of work. Fathers and other male adults close to school-age boys affect boys' masculine gender role learnings. Fathers and other adult males who model warmth and sureness in their masculine roles directly affect femininity in girls. Warm, masculine-type models also help girls in their teens relate well to males in their age group. The same is true for female adults and their effect on school-age boys' learning.

20-18 Taking part in family activities is still important to school-age children.

Encourage Work and Industry

In middle childhood, children develop attitudes that prepare them for adult work. To help children develop positive feelings about work, adults must help the child focus on abilities rather than on their faults. They should set reasonable standards. When standards are too high, children feel they cannot reach them and will not try. If standards are set too low, children may not work at their potential. Even small successes help children feel good about their work, which increases their self-esteem.

Adults can help by encouraging children to succeed in school. Children do better in school when they have loving, caring parents who want them to do well than when parents show little or no concern.

Expand Children's Horizons

Adults should plan activities that can develop children's physical, mental, and social skills. By the school years, children begin to develop more unevenly. A child who has developed advanced reading skills may lag in motor skills. Children still have a wide range of talents, so they could achieve in many fields. On the other hand, children should not be expected to excel in all areas. Adults need to encourage children to test and expand their abilities.

Adults can suggest hobbies where children can succeed, 20-19. Children enjoy the steps involved in hobbies, such as making and finding objects. They like to display their new learnings.

Focus on Social Studies

Changes in Work and Home-care Tasks

Discuss with two professionals who work with school-age children how the world of work and home-care tasks have changed during the last two or three decades. (Guidance counselors, principals, and family and consumer sciences teachers are good resource people.) Ask each adult how these changes have altered the value of skills needed by adults in society. How have these changing skills affected the knowledge and skills needed by school-age children? What courses have been added to the school curriculum in the last thirty years to address these concerns? Share your findings with the class.

Keep Family Communication Open

It is important for parents and children to talk and express their feelings openly. If good communication patterns are established during middle childhood years, later teen-parent relationships will be much better.

During the early school years, children view their parents as the greatest in every way. By 9 or 10 years of age, they begin to see their parents' mistakes. Relationships between parents and children become somewhat strained. However, good communication can help ease the strain.

To communicate clearly, adults must talk to children honestly and openly. This is what Galinsky meant by being *interpretive*. They need to explain why they feel a certain way

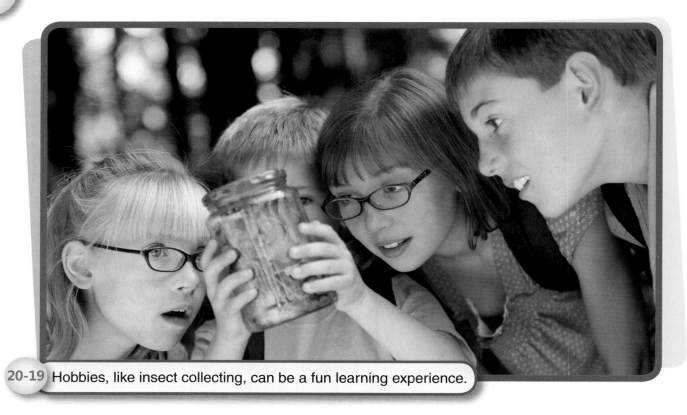

20-19 Hobbies, like insect collecting, can be a fun learning experience.

and show willingness to listen to their children's feelings. Parents may be upset because their child went to a friend's home after school without telling them. They should explain they become worried when they do not know where their child is. Parents should also let the child have input on how to avoid the problem in the future.

Listening

Listening is an important part of communication. Parents may pick up on children's emotions by listening to their comments. A child may say, "You always pick on me!" Parents can use such comments as a chance to ask children what is on their mind. They may learn that certain actions bother their children. Parents may also clear up misunderstandings at these times.

When children realize their parents will listen, they are more likely to come to their parents with problems. Children will have some problems with friendships or school. They often look to parents in these situations. Giving advice and assuring children can help them bounce back from problems. Children see their parents as people who have weathered some of the same problems.

Throughout the school years parents are still admired. This is true even though children feel that parents create many of their problems. Open communication allows children to build strong bonds with their parents that will last a lifetime.

Enjoying Family Ties

School-age children think of their families as home base. They think of home as a place for food, clothing, shelter, and psychological security. **Psychological security** is a feeling that someone cares and will help when needed.

The family provides a balance between letting go and holding on in the school years. In this role, the family provides security for trying new skills. They also need to be available when children need support.

Family activities can extend the skills children learn in school-age peer groups. In addition to direct help, parents can help by organizing the child's schedule, seeing that needed equipment is ready (washing uniforms, buying ballet slippers), and driving children to and from activities.

School-age children enjoy just being with family. They want to learn home-care skills. Children are pleased when they are old enough and skilled enough to do many things they were not allowed to do in the preschool years. Children

also enjoy family times, 20-20. They enjoy family meals, weekend outings, yearly vacations, and family celebrations. The special plans and surprises are all part of taking a major role in family rituals. School-age children may even think about how they will continue these customs when they are adults.

Providing Time for Friendships

Children need time to be with friends. If adults have many other plans for children, then they do not have a chance to form friendships. Making friends welcome in the home and encouraging peer activities is important. Parents must understand children will like their best friends almost as much as the family and will want to include them in family outings.

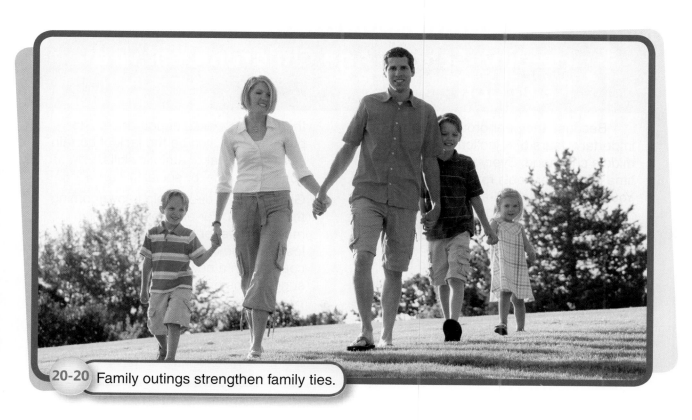

20-20 Family outings strengthen family ties.

Loss of Friendship

Children also need help when they lose their best friends through conflict, new interest, moving away, or death. School-age children can suffer great pain, even depression, from such a breakup. Depression can cause a decrease in eating, sleeping, working, or playing.

Adults can help in many cases. Children may talk to adults about the loss of a friend. Adults should choose words carefully when they discuss the breakup. For example, they should not say, "It's not as bad as you think. You'll feel better soon." Many children will tune out well-meaning adults at this point. Instead, adults should try to talk about the emotions felt without mention of getting over them.

Adults need to stay neutral if the breakup was caused by conflict. Joining a child's anger or hurt places all the blame for the breakup on the former friend. It may also say to the child, "You made a poor friendship choice."

Adults can prepare children in advance for breaks in friendships. Preparation should begin in the preschool or early school years. Parents can begin by talking about why people become friends and sometimes end friendships. Adults can also tell children about some of their friendships and breakups (or read stories about loss of friends and the hurt it causes). Preparation can also include encouraging children to play with more than one child so the loss of one friend will not be too crushing.

Learn More About...

Helping School-Age Children Deal with Rejection

Because the peer group is so important, fears of rejection are real in middle childhood. Every child, at one time or another, feels rejected by peers. You often hear school-age children say, "Nobody likes me," or "I can never do anything right!" Such statements from a child who is usually accepted are best ignored. However, adults do need to help when children experience general rejection, especially if the rejection lasts over a week. How to help depends on the child, but the following ideas often work:

★ Try to discover the problem behind the rejection. The problem may be the child's physical appearance. The problem may also be the lack of certain skills—physical or athletic skills, academic skills, or social skills.

★ Give the child direct help in overcoming the problem. For example, the child may need better grooming tools and lessons. The child may also need coaching in a new skill or step-by-step suggestions on how to make friends.

★ Plan games and activities where there is not so much pressure on a child's skills. For example, play dodge ball rather than softball.

Helping Children Control Their Emotions

Adults should continue to guide and help children control their emotions in middle childhood. They should explain to children that all people have strong feelings. Adults can talk about some of their own emotions, too. School-age children may also be helped when they read about the struggles of other children and adults to control feelings. Adults can also point out that a person needs to control his or her emotions out of respect for others.

Children need to observe parents modeling control of their own behavior. They learn by watching adults handle frustration and anger. Parents should talk about the child's problem. If they use nonphysical means to let the child know he or she has done wrong, they model acceptable ways of behavior. These are better methods than physical punishment, which often shows loss of control.

Control of emotions can be helped in indirect ways, too. Physical activity and creative tasks help children release their anger. Children show less fear of the physical world as they gain skills and knowledge. For example, fear of water is overcome when a person learns to swim well. As children improve skills, they develop healthy self-concepts. Having healthy self-concepts helps children overcome many social fears because children are not as worried about being embarrassed or rejected.

Helping Children Improve Their Self-Esteem

Children's feelings about themselves are influenced by how others, who are important in their lives, treat them, 20-21.

20-21 When children are treated well by friends and loved ones, it helps them feel good about themselves.

Parents and other adults who provide love, appreciation, and encouragement form the base for a positive self-esteem.

Every child has special talents and abilities. Parents and adults need to praise and encourage those traits. They can offer positive feedback for what the child is doing well. Saying, "You did a good job," is an important message for children to hear.

Parents need to communicate their love and acceptance to their children. School-age children still seek parental affection and approval. Children need to know they are important to their family.

Adults should discipline children privately, not in front of their peers or others. If criticism must be given, the act should be criticized and not the child. In this way, they learn that what they have done was wrong, but they can still be trusted and loved as a person.

Parents and adults need to help school-age children continue to build their confidence. They need to help children learn to believe in their own abilities. With their love, praise, and support, adults can help school-age children in their struggle for self-esteem.

Recognizing Developmental Delays

Although it is hoped that children's developmental delays have been recognized and successfully treated prior to the school years, many school-age children have delays. Some of these children's delays were identified at younger ages, but these children have not yet caught up with their peers. Regrettably, some children's developmental delays may not be recognized until the school-age years.

Many teachers are seasoned judges of developmental delays in all areas. Most teachers have had some training in child development. Also, because they teach so many children, teachers are often more experienced than parents in recognizing whether children are average or delayed.

Parents are usually informed of delays during the formal parent-teacher conferences. They may also be informed through more informal contacts with teachers, coaches, or youth leaders. Although developmental delays are not the only reason children fail to achieve in school, parents should note the achievement of their children. Parents who note their children do not seem to be achieving should contact their children's teachers as soon as possible. Through the sharing of information about children's home and school life, problems can be more accurately identified and actions planned. See the *School-Age Children Milestones* in Appendix A to learn about some typical middle childhood behaviors that may help parents to recognize delays.

Summary

School-age children's physical development continues slowly and steadily. They go through many body changes that seem to make the body appear awkward. The skeletal system is maturing. Bones are growing and hardening. Permanent teeth are coming in and changing the look of the face. Motor skills become better because of faster reaction time, precision, and improved flexibility. Their fine-motor skills begin to be highly developed.

Adults should encourage good health habits, such as a healthful diet, physical activity, and adequate rest. Parents and adults need to emphasize good safety habits and basic rules of safety in the home.

Piaget's theory brought many insights about *how children think*. School-age children are beginning to realize others have ideas different from their own. They are beginning to think more logically. Deductive and inductive reasoning become more accurate.

Vygotsky's ideas focused on *how children learn*. He saw interactions between children and adults, as well as among peers, have a major impact on learning. He also noted the power of language as a way to learn.

What children learn during the school years is astounding. Children's understanding of physical knowledge and logical thinking concepts improves. School-age children can use reversibility skills to see more than one change in an object. They can mentally join a series of events to see a transformation. By middle childhood, children have mastered most of the rules of language, including grammar and articulation.

Parents and adults need to provide activities that will help the school-age child grow mentally. Common experiences can help children learn. Helping children prepare for school and creating an environment that encourages learning are important.

Children face the challenge of *industry versus inferiority*. They show greater social awareness during middle childhood. Adult and peer relationships deepen. Peer groups are important. Children's feelings about themselves are reinforced by how peers treat them. Their sense of work and industry increases as they develop attitudes that prepare them for adult work. The major emotions of love, fear and anxiety, anger, and aggression are fairly well set and affect their behavior.

Parents and adults can encourage their school-age children to take part in peer activities and help them get along with friends. Activities that challenge their physical, mental, and social skills can be planned. Adults can model emotional control when dealing with discipline problems. Creating an atmosphere of open communication builds strong bonds between adults and children. With their love, respect, and guidance, adults can help children maintain a strong self-concept.

Companion Web Site

Interactive Activity

Review vocabulary terms and key concepts for Chapter 20 at **g-wlearning.com**.

Review and Reflect

Write your answers to the following questions on a separate sheet of paper.

1. True or false. Boys are taller and heavier than girls throughout middle childhood.

2. True or false. The first permanent teeth to erupt replace lost deciduous teeth.

3. List four reasons school-age children need an adequate diet.

4. Upon hearing another person's point of view, a child in the *concrete operational stage* thinks his or her own ideas are _____ (always right, possibly wrong).

5. True or false. When noting change in an object, school-age children begin to take in more than one aspect of the change at the same time.

6. According to Vygotsky, school-age children learn through their social interactions with _____ and _____ and through the use of _____.

7. List three reasons entering school for the first time is stressful.

8. _____ (Physical, Mental, Social) development is the most critical aspect of development in middle childhood.

9. Children can learn healthful work attitudes when adults encourage them _____ (to just get by, to do their best) in everything.

10. List six purposes of the peer group.

11. True or false. Adults affect the gender role learnings of children, even in the school years.

Cross-Curricular Link

12. **Health, Art.** Make a collage of pictures of children from ages 6 through 12. What physical changes do you notice?

13. **Health, Art.** Create a poster called "Qualities Needed in Motor Skills." Divide the poster into five areas labeled *reaction time*, *precision*, *speed*, *strength*, and *flexibility*. Find pictures or draw sketches of activities that fit each quality.

14. **Math.** Create a list of common gross- and fine-motor activities. Ask a class of fourth- or fifth-grade students to choose their three favorite activities from the list. Tabulate the results. Which activities were chosen most often? Were these gross- or fine-motor skills?

15. **Technology.** Visit the Web sites of various manufacturers of computer products for children. Using an educational software evaluation sheet, compare the features of three software products designed for school-age children. Based on your findings, which item would you recommend most, and why?

16. **Speech, Career Study.** Compile a list of 12 interview questions to ask a professional who works with school-age children who have developmental delays. If possible, record the interview on audio- or videotape. Share the tape or describe your findings to the class.

Making Observations

17. Observe school-age children eating their school lunches and choosing snack foods. How nutritious are the foods they eat (not just buy)? What problems do you see with their diets in terms of sugars, fats, or lack of nutrients? What physical problems, if any, can you observe?

18. Observe school-age children playing a table game, such as checkers, chess, or cards. What evidence of the use of logic (strategy) do you see? How would this be different for a five-year-old attempting to play the game?

19. Observe the play of six- and seven-year-olds and that of eleven- and twelve-year-olds. How does play differ between these age groups in terms of motor skills?

20. Observe a group of school-age children. What rules are being set for acceptance in the group?

Which aspects of development are being the most critically judged by peers (body appearance, physical skills, intellectual abilities, or social skills)? Explain your answer. What is happening to children on the fringe of the group?

21. Observe school-age children in the classroom. Which emotion or emotions seem the hardest to control? Give examples of displays of anger, aggression, fear, or anxiety you observe that may be the child's way of asking for love and attention.

Thinking Critically

22. How do you think girls who mature early feel when they are taller and more mature looking than their classmates? How might they feel when they excel in skill performance over these same peers?

23. Some parents give their kindergartners a crash course (often a few weeks or even a few days before school starts) in learning the alphabet, naming colors, counting, and writing their names. Do you think this is helpful or harmful to children? Why?

24. Why do you think school-age peers judge each other so harshly? What societal factors do you think contribute to this behavior?

Part 6   Guiding and Caring for Children

Focus on
Family and Community

Research child-related careers and choose the ones you would like to learn more about. Compile a list of questions that could be used to interview a person about his or her child-related career. For example, you might ask when and why the person first became interested in the field. You might also want to ask about the personal and professional qualifications required for entering the career. After you have compiled your list of questions, arrange to interview two or more people working in the child-related careers you are interested in the most. Take it a step further and develop an FCCLA *Power of One* project for *Working on Working*. Use the FCCLA *Planning Process* to plan, carry out, and evaluate your project. You might even want to try presenting your project at an FCCLA Star Event. Your FCCLA advisor can provide you with further information.

After studying this chapter, you will be able to

★ **describe** the importance of play and play activities in children's lives.

★ **explain** how adults can help children learn through play, art, music, science, and literature.

★ **give examples** of creative activities that stimulate children's physical, intellectual, and social-emotional development.

Terms to Know

active-physical play
manipulative-constructive play
imitative-imaginative play
play therapy
language-logic play
prop box
visual arts
manipulative stage

scribbling
representation stage
transparencies
percussion instruments
rhythm instruments
melody percussion instruments

Children are curious. They want to explore new objects, places, and people. Children are also eager learners. They ask countless questions as they strive for self-direction. Children express their learnings in many ways, such as through play, art, music, science, and literature.

Learning and expressing are closely related. Learnings are reflected in the way children express themselves. Their expressions expand and refine their learnings, 21-1.

Children need adults to encourage self-expression and help them learn. Adults can see what each child is ready to do. They can provide the time, space, and materials for activities. Adults can give children ideas, if needed. For the most part, children learn more from their senses and actions than from being told. Adults need to provide play experiences that teach children as well as those that simply amuse them.

Children and Their World of Play

Through play, children interact with the world of people and objects. Play can even take the form of ideas, such as word play and problem-solving games. Play is a self-chosen activity that children do for its own sake. Most of all, play is fun.

Importance of Play

Years ago, experts had not studied the value of play. They had not given it an important place in a person's life. Play—even for children—was not accepted in early history because children were expected to work. In the more recent past, play was seen as something children and adults did in their spare time. Today, experts know that play is important.

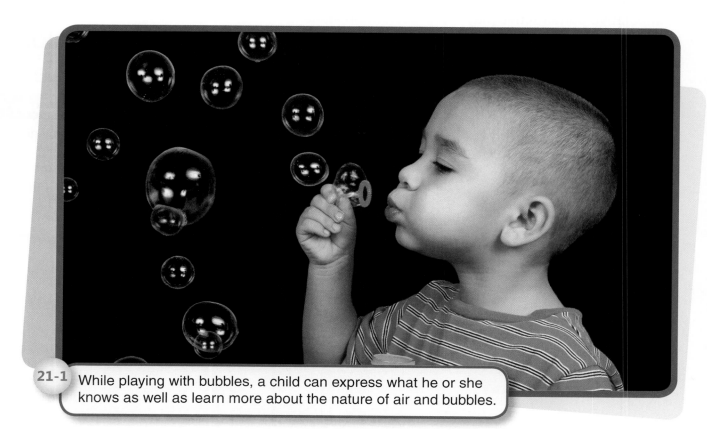

21-1 While playing with bubbles, a child can express what he or she knows as well as learn more about the nature of air and bubbles.

Play and Physical Development

One reason play is important is because it helps a child's physical development. Play improves muscles and nerves. Activities help the heart and lung systems. Active children who play often are more likely to maintain a healthy weight. Play also improves balance and coordination, 21-2. Active children and adults tend to feel better physically than those who are not active.

Play and Intellectual Development

Children learn through play. In turn, children's play reflects what they have learned. Play helps children learn concepts about their physical world. Play also brings children in contact with objects. Children can cause objects to do many things. They observe the results of actions. Children soon see how objects differ. They also learn how objects are made and about their physical limits.

Logical Concepts

Through play, children learn logical concepts. For example, children classify objects as they set up a grocery store or repair shop for pretend play. Children order objects by size as they nest measuring cups in their play kitchens. Number concepts form as children see that adding more blocks makes a higher tower or longer train. In filling a sand pail, children see that small objects fit inside, but large ones will not. They may conserve as they pour objects from one container to another. Other logical concepts also develop.

21-2 Pretend play can promote motor skills and help children learn about the roles of others.

Symbol Systems

Symbol systems are used in play, too. In symbol-type play, children select the most important aspects of an experience. For example, when playing with dolls, a child mostly feeds, bathes, clothes, and rocks the doll. When pretending to be a wild animal, a child may make loud sounds and engage in pretend attacks. Children make props to go along with their pretend play that are symbols for objects in the real world. Symbol-type play helps children prepare for the more abstract written and spoken language symbols.

Language

Play helps children learn language. For the infant, the sound of peek-a-boo comes to signal the return of a person. Infants begin with babbling sounds, which are often heard during their play with adults. Toddlers may repeat one or two words as they march around the room or pretend to read a book. Preschool children try out new rhythm and sound patterns in language. They often repeat favorite lines of stories and nursery rhymes. School-age children try rhymes, jingles, and other forms of language sound patterns.

Humor and Creative Thinking

Humor is mental play. This type of play cannot begin until the child's thinking skills are well underway. Usually it begins between the second and third year. When a child makes a change from reality or the usual, such as drawing a dog with wings, the child is showing humor. This type of humor is often called *absurdities*. Young children very much enjoy the type of absurdities found in Dr. Seuss' books (such as green eggs or an elephant hatching an egg in a bird's nest). As children develop, they see humor in language itself. School-age children, for example, like simple puns and idioms taken literally.

Play also improves creative thinking. Through play, children try new ideas. For this reason, children who play are apt to become artists and scientists as adults. During play, children can make mistakes without being corrected. Making mistakes is part of the creative process. Because they do not feel pressure, children enjoy learning new concepts through play. They also learn more through play than through any drilling process.

Play and Social-Emotional Development

Children become aware of others through play. Through this greater awareness, they develop trusting relationships. Babies play games only with people they trust, such as parents and other caregivers. Parents who play with their children during the childhood years seem to be close to them in later years.

In the preschool and school-age years, children play more frequently with peers than with adults. Playing with peers teaches children the concepts of rules, rights and property, sharing, and settling disputes. Children also learn acceptable and unacceptable behavior, as well as skills in teamwork and being a leader. In play, children learn to detect others' feelings, too. Children who play well with others seem to have the most friends, 21-3.

Cruise Ship Children's Activities Counselor

Cruise ship children's activities counselors create children's programs and implement new and existing youth activities. They supervise the activities of children onboard the ship and occasionally escort children during on-shore excursions.

Education: Educational and training requirements vary widely. Full-time career positions usually require a college degree in an area related to child development.

Job Outlook: Job opportunities for part-time, seasonal, and temporary workers will be good, but competition will remain keen for career positions. Average growth is expected.

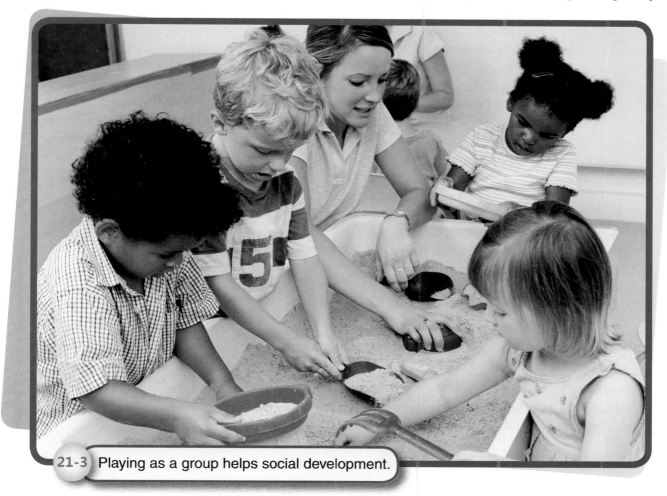

21-3 Playing as a group helps social development.

Children work out many of their feelings and problems in play. They also use playtime to make things happen their own way. For example, preschool children often feel limited in what they can do or make happen. By pretending to be dinosaurs, children can identify with the dinosaur's size and strength and make up for their own shortcomings.

Stages of Play

Did you ever think about all the different ways children play? One way is to look at the stages of play. Children's play reflects changes that take place in their physical, intellectual, and social-emotional development. In a real way, play pulls together all aspects of development. For this reason, one expert referred to play as the highest level of child development.

Children go through stages of play as they grow. These stages build on each other. Babies do not begin to play in advanced stages. Older children learn to play in higher stages, but they can still play in earlier stages, too. When older children play with younger children, the stage of play most often fits the ZPD of younger children. Older children may provide ideas that slightly "stretch" younger children's thinking. When children play with new objects, the stage of play may also become less advanced.

Stages of play are described in terms of the child's play with objects and people. Chart 21-4 shows stages of play with objects and people and how these two areas compare with each other. The chart shows only one way to view the stages of play. Other child development experts may describe stages of play in different ways.

Types of Play

Besides stages, another way to think about play is by types of play and the skills involved with each type. Types of play include *active-physical play*, *manipulative-constructive play*, *imitative-imaginative play*, and *language-logic play*.

Stages of Play

From a few months to 35 months

Play with objects

Practice play. Babies explore objects by picking them up or tracking them with their eyes. Play activities are repeated.

Play with people

Solitary play. Babies ignore other children who are nearby. Sometimes babies treat others as objects to be pushed or walked on, to be poked in the eyes or nose, or to have hair pulled.

Onlooker play. Toddlers watch others play, but do not join in their play.

Parallel play. Children play near other children and often play with the same or similar toys. They note that others have interests and skills much like their own. However, there is no real interaction among children.

From age 3 through elementary grades

Play with objects

Symbolic play. Children engage in fantasy play. They pretend they are someone else. Also, they project mental images on objects. For example, a stick can become a horse.

Play with people

Associative play. Two or more children play at a common activity. The children share ideas. However, the play is not well organized. For example, one child may decide to run a food store and another may be a mother, but the mother never shops at the food store.

Peaks at age 9 or 10

Play with objects

Rule play. Children make rules to govern their games or carefully follow the rules already established.

Play with people

Cooperative play. Two or more children share common goals and play complementary roles, such as the chaser and the chased.

21-4 The stages of play can be described in terms of how children play with objects and how they interact with peers in play situations at each age.

Active-Physical Play

In **active-physical play**, children use gross-motor skills. These skills use the large muscles for movements, such as walking, running, hopping, jumping, twisting, bending, skipping, galloping, catching, throwing, balancing, pushing, pulling, and rocking.

Through active-physical play, children learn about the space around them. They also learn about objects in this space and the movement of the body. Names for movements and positions in space take on meaning. These names include *forward, backward, big, little, fast, slow, under, over, up, down, behind, in front of, through, beside,* and *between.*

Through play, children improve and test many physical skills. They learn how strong they are by pushing, pulling, lifting, and carrying. Children learn how to spring-up in order to lift their body, which is a skill they often need. They also learn how to catch themselves on impact. Catching themselves the right way when they land protects the body from injury. Active-physical play also improves reaction time and balance. Reaction time improves as the body matures and the child practices. Children need balance for almost every gross-motor movement, 21-5.

Active-physical play helps children become more graceful. Grace improves when the gross-motor skills are developed. Grace is pleasing to see. It also helps a person engage in many more fun activities.

Manipulative-Constructive Play

Manipulative-constructive play involves fine-motor skills. These skills develop after the

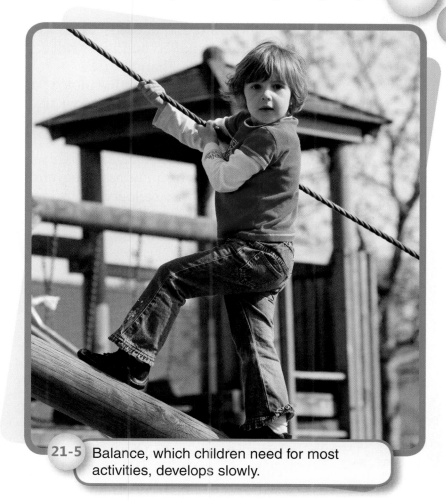

21-5 Balance, which children need for most activities, develops slowly.

basic gross-motor movements. For example, the fine-motor skill of writing develops after the gross-motor skill of walking. However, some fine-motor skills start to develop early in life. Crawling babies can pick up small objects (such as gravel and paper) on a carpet. Then they carefully put these objects in their mouth, ear, and nose. Eye-hand coordination is also involved in manipulative-constructive play.

Many toys and materials promote fine-motor skills. These include jigsaw puzzles, small blocks and other construction materials, beads for stringing, pegs and pegboards, art tools, woodworking tools, and cooking tools. Toys that promote fine-motor skills are made for little, unskilled hands as well as for more skilled hands.

Besides promoting fine-motor skills, manipulative-constructive play helps children to mentally picture objects. Many visual and mental concepts, such as shapes, distance, numbers, sorting and classifying, and reversibility, are developed. This play also helps children make abstract models of what they see.

Imitative-Imaginative Play

In **imitative-imaginative play**, children pretend to be objects or persons other than themselves. They carry out this play verbally and in actions. Imitative-imaginative play has great value. Creativity is involved as children invent their own worlds. Planning, problem solving, and decision making take place as children put themselves in different settings. For example, children choose roles, props, and actions in their play. Leadership roles in group play often emerge. Children can use play to try out many roles. They imagine or picture themselves as if they are other people and objects (symbolizing). In this way, children get some feel for others' real-life roles. Children join in holiday and other rituals as they act out roles. Many adult work and family roles began in childhood as play roles.

This kind of play helps memory because children must recall events in play. It also helps language because children must listen and speak during play. There is much freedom in expression, too, as children try to bridge the gap between what they know and do not know. Children can use their bodies to extend their language. For example, a child may say, "I'm a barber," while using the fingers as if to cut hair.

Through imitative-imaginative play, children can also express fears, resentments, and even hostile feelings in ways that are socially approved. In fact, role-play can even have some healing qualities. For example, **play therapy** is the use of play between a child and a trained counselor to help the child resolve certain problems.

There are three stages of imitative-imaginative play. These stages are called *imitative play*, *dramatic play*, and *socio-dramatic play*.

Imitative Play

Imitative play begins at about two years of age, or just as children begin to use symbolic thought, 21-6.

21-6 For toddlers and young preschoolers, symbolic play is simple. Often, they use only one object and one action to symbolize the real object or event.

Symbolic thought allows the child to let one thing stand for another. For example, a stack of books may become a spaceship. In a similar way, symbolic thought also allows the child to do one imitative action to an object, such as feed a baby doll. Toddlers and young preschool children engage in imitative play for very short periods. However, they tend to repeat the same imitative play symbols and actions over days, weeks, and even months.

Dramatic Play

The second stage, dramatic play, begins when the child is three or four years of age. *Dramatic play* involves role-playing with more than one child. Each child's role, however, is independent of the others' roles. For example, three children may be space creatures, but each child plays the game in his or her own way. These children may engage in collective monologue. Dramatic play often involves several behaviors associated with a role, such as a father who makes repairs, goes to work, and mows the grass.

Socio-Dramatic Play

In the last stage, socio-dramatic play, a group of five- to seven-year-olds plays with a theme. They assign roles to each child. Instead of just being space creatures, the children may pretend to look for new planets together. In this form of play, each child has a special role.

Language-Logic Play

Language-logic play is the form of mental play most often seen in school-age children. There are many different types of language and word games. In some language games, children compete by using vocabulary skills. Other language games include humor that is based on language, such as puns. Logic games, such as chess and checkers, require much thought about one's actions. Children must think ahead and plan strategies for sports and table games. Logic games also include object puzzles and word problems.

The Adult's Role in Children's Play

Adults have a major role in children's play. They need to allow children a great deal of free expression in play. Adults need to allow children time to explore materials and ideas. Adults' attitudes toward play influence how children view an activity. What adults do and say can promote or hamper children's creativity. Adults should provide play experiences through toys and activities that fit the children's stages of development

Toy Designer

Toy designers bring toy ideas to life. They design everything from infant toys to action figures to games. Toy designers use information about children's stages of development to create toys that are safe and encourage physical, intellectual, and social-emotional growth.

Education: Many toy designers have a bachelor's degree in either toy design or industrial design. No formal education is required, but many employers prefer to hire workers who have one of these degrees.

Job Outlook: Job outlook is good for graduates with an industrial design degree.

and unique interests. Sometimes parents can join in their children's play when invited by the children. At these times, parents should let children choose the activity and lead the play. Usually when an adult takes too much of a lead or becomes too involved, children stop playing and simply watch the adult.

Allow Freedom to Play

During play, children should be allowed as much freedom as possible, 21-7. Toys that have only one use, such as coloring books, can restrict children's play. Adults restrict play by setting many rules for safety or other reasons. Peers, too, restrict play by telling each other what and how to play. Although play can never be totally free, adults should help keep restrictions to a limit.

Allow Time to Explore

For the most part, adults should give children time to explore

materials on their own. Adults can observe play and, at times, add ideas or materials. Children should decide whether to use them. One example of how to add ideas and materials is modeling an action, such as pretending to eat make-believe food. Adults can increase a child's language skills by adding to a child's growl. They may say, "Growl! I am a tiger looking at you with my big, green eyes." Adults can also explain new concepts. They can describe airplanes as objects that go quickly down a special road called a *runway* so they can fly in the air. They can use blocks and a toy plane to explain. Adults need to rotate toys or add new toys from time to time.

Display the Right Attitude Toward Play

Adults need to see the importance of play and express that feeling to children. Think of the attitude an adult expresses to a child when the

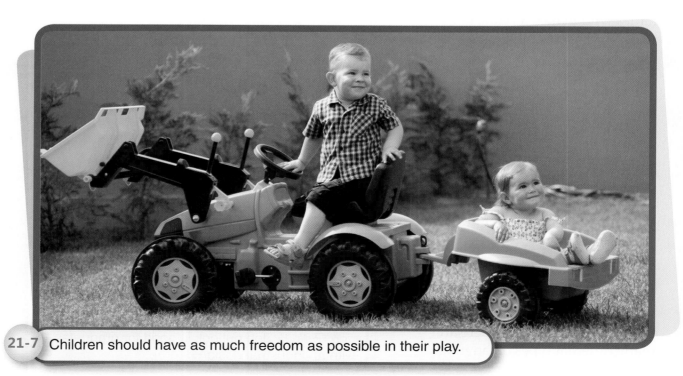

21-7 Children should have as much freedom as possible in their play.

adult says, "Can't you see I'm busy? Go away and play." Toys and play need to be seen as important, too.

Select Toys with Care

In daily play, children will use their toys extensively. For this reason, adults should select toys with care. Toys should be safe and fun. (See Chapter 22 for more details about toy safety.)

Toys should be developmentally appropriate. Some examples are as follows:

★ Infants and toddlers like texture toys, squeeze toys, stuffed toys, large balls, dolls, and toys that make sounds. Toddlers like push and pull toys, too.

★ Preschool children like toys for gross-motor play (balls, pedal toys, and climbing toys) and fine-motor play (puzzles, beads, and pegs). They also like floor blocks, dress-up clothes, puppets, toy cars, trucks, planes, animals, and people. Children can use prop boxes for role-playing, too. A **prop box** contains a set of realistic objects related to a certain role for children to use in play. For example, a prop box might contain the props needed to role-play a store clerk or nurse.

★ School-age children like sports equipment, bicycles, board games, computer games, crafts, advanced construction sets, puzzles, and collectibles.

Because each child is unique, children like different types of toys. Children's toy collections should be balanced, however. Children need to have various toys that aid all aspects of development.

Adults need to avoid giving too many toys that "perform." Examples of performing toys are battery-operated toys that perform one or more actions when switched on and toys that talk for the child. These toys do not allow much child involvement or stimulate creativity. Children need toys that let them be the "performers." Children can use open-ended toys, such as building blocks, art supplies, and balls in many ways, 21-8.

Toys should be planned for different play settings, such as indoors, outdoors, and travel. Travel toys must be chosen with much thought. These toys must be held in children's hands or laps. They must be safe in a moving car. They cannot make too much noise for a small space or distract the driver. Toys must be able to withstand the temperature of a closed car. Some toys and games are designed for travel. These toys include music and stories on CDs, magnetic game boards, and toys that attach to car seats or the back of the vehicle's front seat.

21-8 In their play, these children are using balls in one of many creative ways.
Courtesy of GameTime, Fort Payne, Ala., USA

Providing Enrichment Activities for Children

Adults can provide many learning experiences that enrich children's lives. They can encourage creativity with the types of play they provide and the ways they value these activities. Experiences in art, music, science, and literature help children learn aesthetic, creative, and scientific concepts. These experiences can also help children appreciate both natural and created beauty. Having rich and fulfilling experiences in these areas also reinforces other basic learnings and helps children develop.

Art

Art is important in children's lives. **Visual arts**, such as painting, molding, and photography, create products that appeal to the sense of sight. Visual arts help children in many areas of development. For example, fine-motor skills improve as children handle paintbrushes, scissors, and crayons.

The arts increase intellectual learnings, too. Sensory experiences help children expand their concepts of color, line, shape, form, texture, and size. Because children create what they know, visual arts cause children to think about their world. Children then record their ideas in their finished products.

✓ Learn More About...
Selecting Toys

All toys should reflect positive social attitudes. Toys and equipment should be antibiased. The toys should represent people of both genders, all ages, and all cultural groups in a positive way. Toys should avoid stereotyping of any kind. For example, both male and female clothes (and even some gender-neutral clothes) should be provided for children's dramatic play. Props for role-playing should extend beyond the kitchen and reflect many other home tasks and work roles. Dolls and manipulatives with illustrations should reflect the diversity of society. Art materials should be available to represent various skin tones. Holiday materials should be included for various cultures.

Toys should also be nonviolent in nature. Guns and knives, for example, encourage playful aggressive acts in children. Sometimes, too, young children cannot tell the difference between a real weapon and a realistic toy or can mistake a real weapon for such a toy with devastating consequences. Toys should encourage cooperation with and respect for others.

Adults must be wise when purchasing toys. Toys are expensive and quickly outgrown, and thus overbuying goes against good consumer sense. Because children often spend many hours in child care and school programs, children may not need as many home toys. Finally, adults should consider play space and storage needs for each toy.

Older children can learn many useful skills and have fun while making toys. Sometimes children spend as much time making toys as they do playing with them. Making toys also teaches children to save and recycle useful items that are often just thrown away.

Finally, art helps children develop in social-emotional areas. Children make choices about what they want to do and how they want to do an art activity. Art helps them to express feelings, too. Taking pride in their art and knowing that others accept their products builds children's self-esteem, 21-9.

Stages of Development in Visual Arts

Experts study the stages of children's development in the visual arts by watching children use art materials and looking at their finished products. A child's total development determines how he or she uses crayons, paints, clay, and other art materials. At first, children play with the art materials. They then use the materials to represent objects, experiences, and feelings. For these reasons, development is divided into the manipulative stage and the representation stage.

Manipulative Stage

In the **manipulative stage**, children play with art materials rather than use them to create artwork. Early in this stage, children under two years of age enjoy art for motor reasons. They cover paper with marks and pinch, pat, and even eat clay.

Soon the child begins to see what happens as a result of certain actions. At about 24 to 30 months, children begin the second step in this stage, called *scribbling*. **Scribbling** consists of dots, straight and curved lines, loops, spirals, and imperfect circles. Scribbling is important because the child must make the eyes and hands work together.

About 30 to 42 months, the third step in the manipulative stage occurs. Children begin to use basic shapes,

21-9 Children express their feelings through art.

such as crosses, rectangles (including squares), and ovals (including circles). They combine shapes in drawings, too. Many of these shapes are lost in the layers and layers of crayon marks and paint.

In the transition step between the manipulative and representation stages, children ages 42 to 60 months create their first symbols. Because the children often decide what the symbol is after it is made, the symbol may or may not be named. The face is often the first and favorite symbol seen in children's drawings. Even when children draw a body, it appears to be an afterthought. Children add lines to the face to draw arms, hands, body, and legs. They use circles for feet or shoes. The head remains the largest part of children's drawings for years. Although drawings contain symbols, there are no spatial relations among objects. Symbols seem to float.

Representation Stage

Most five- or six-year-old children have reached the **representation stage**. In this stage, children create symbols that represent objects, experiences, and feelings. Adults can see a child has entered this stage when the child decides what the symbol is before creating it. ("I'm going to draw a tree.")

Another signal of this stage is the showing of spatial relations among objects. In a simple spatial relationship, children show what is on the ground by using a *baseline* (a line or strip of ground or water). Typically children use baselines in these three ways:

★ Children draw a baseline near the bottom of the paper. The baseline can also be the lower edge of the paper itself. The sky often appears as a strip of color across the top of the paper. Children envision air between the objects on the baseline and the sky, 21-10.

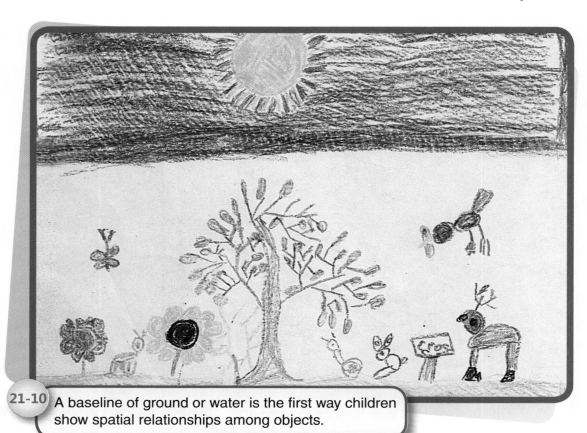

21-10 A baseline of ground or water is the first way children show spatial relationships among objects.

★ Children may draw two or more baselines, which show objects at varying distances. The closer objects are always drawn on the baseline closest to the lower edge of the paper.

★ Sometimes children draw objects perpendicular to the baseline, even when it means drawing objects upside down. This is called *folding over* because objects would appear standing if one folded the paper along the baseline.

In the early part of the representational stage, children also draw what they *know* or *feel* about people and objects rather than what is *visually true*. To do this, children's drawings have the following special features:

★ Children draw from *mixed perspectives* (from more than one view). For example, in drawing a table and chairs, the chairs are often shown from the side view. The table, however, is often drawn from the top view, but with table legs sticking out in all directions. Place settings and foods may be seen on the table, too. These objects may be drawn in mixed perspective. Children also mix front and profile views of a person, animal, or object. For example, the child may draw a fish mainly in the profile, but with both eyes on one side.

★ Many times children *exaggerate* (or increase) size to show importance. For example, children may exaggerate the size of their parents in a drawing. Certain body parts may be exaggerated, too, such as arms that reach to the clouds to catch a ball or fly a kite.

★ Children often draw symbols pictured as transparencies. **Transparencies** are pictures that show the inside and outside of an object at the same time, much like an X-ray. A drawing of a house may have windows, but it may show people and furniture below the window level. Children may also show a head inside of a cap and a hand inside a ball glove, 21-11.

21-11 Transparencies are common drawing styles of preschool and young school-age children.

★ After seven or eight years of age, representation becomes more advanced. Children draw a more detailed human face that shows expression. Visual depth also becomes a part of these more advanced drawings. Children begin to draw with more accurate perspectives. By nine or ten years of age, children can draw objects from their perspective and from the perspective of others.

The Adult's Role in Stimulating Art Experiences

Adults can stimulate art experiences by introducing children to artistic skills and art activities suited to their stages of development. They should provide art materials that allow children to explore and enrich their art skills. Adults can encourage children in their artwork in many ways.

In introducing children to art activities, adults should provide children with the right environment and supplies, 21-12. They must show children how to use artistic tools, such as scissors and paintbrushes. Once children understand how to use tools, adults should let children do their own work. They should not add to children's work or make models for them to copy. Children's work reflects their skill in handling tools and their way of seeing the world. See 21-13 for suggested art activities.

Adults should encourage children by showing interest in their artwork. They can help children try new techniques by saying they have confidence in the children.

Adults can show interest by joining children in art activities. (However, adults should never compete.) They can also display children's artwork, which increases self-esteem.

Reacting to Children's Art

When children show adults their artwork, what should adults say? A good response is to ask children to tell you about their work. Adults can say, "Can you tell me about your drawing (painting, clay project, or other)?" This is a better response than asking, "What is it?"

When children do not know what they should draw or color and ask for ideas, adults can suggest three ideas. Children then can choose the one or ones that appeal the most. This may even inspire more creative thinking, and children may come up with their own ideas.

Music

Sounds in many pitches, rhythmic patterns, and degrees of loudness are the parts of music. These parts surround people from birth. Children hear sounds and respond to them by paying attention, moving to music, and making sounds. Thus, musical development is like all other development. Those children who have had a rich world of sound and movement will have a good background for later learnings and pleasure.

For young children, there is a oneness between movement and music. Even toddlers move to music without being prompted by adults. Because young children need chances to move, music can be a fun way to support this need.

Environment and Supplies for the Visual Arts

Environment

★ *Space.* Find a place to draw, paint, model clay, cut, and paste. The space must be easy to clean, such as a kitchen, playroom, or outside area.

★ *Art smock and table cover.* Use an old, long-sleeved shirt. Cut sleeves to child's wrist length and put on backwards. Button only the top button. Use a piece of vinyl to cover the worktable.

★ *Display.* Hang pictures on the refrigerator with magnets, mount pictures on a bulletin board, or display them in a picture frame. Change artwork frequently.

★ *Storage.* Use a large cardboard box to store supplies. You may decorate the box with the child's favorite artwork. Select artwork you want to keep and store it in scrapbooks or photo albums.

Supplies

★ *Paper.* Buy newsprint and construction paper, shelf paper, and paper bags.

★ *Crayons.* Buy large crayons (suited for small hands) in the eight basic colors. (For young children, nontoxic, washable crayons are best.)

★ *Paint.* Buy dry tempera that is mixed with water for brush painting and with liquid starch for finger painting. You can make edible finger paint by using the following recipe:

Pudding Finger Paint

Ingredients

1 box instant vanilla pudding
Food coloring

Directions

1. Prepare instant vanilla pudding according to directions on the package.
2. Add a few drops of food coloring.
3. Stir until well blended.

★ *Scissors.* Buy quality child-sized scissors. Scissors are available for left- and right-handed children. Depending on a child's age, select either blunt or pointed styles.

★ *Paintbrushes.* Buy three or four brushes with short handles and bristles that are about one inch wide.

★ *Glue.* Buy glue that works on paper and cloth.

★ *Clay.* Buy Plasticine® (clay that remains soft due to oil) or play dough. You may also make edible play dough using the following recipe:

Peanut Butter Play Dough

Ingredients

2 cups peanut butter
1 cup flour
1 cup confectioner's sugar

Directions

1. Combine all ingredients in a bowl.
2. Mix until well blended.

★ *Collage materials.* Collect alphabet cereal, pasta, dried beans or peas, seeds, boxes, cloth, yarn, ribbon, paper, flowers, leaves, twigs, straws, and other objects that children can glue to a flat surface.

21-12 The right environment and supplies enhance art learnings.

Art Activities

Squeeze-bag art

1. Use a self-locking, clear food storage bag. Put a few tablespoons of finger paint inside.
2. Smooth the bag until paint covers the inside of the bag with a solid film.
3. Press air out, lock the bag, and seal the bag with tape.
4. Place the bag on a flat surface. The child can draw on it with fingers.
5. Renew drawing surface by rubbing the bag lightly with your hand.

Deodorant-bottle pens

1. Gather deodorant bottles that have rings and balls.
2. Remove the rings and balls.
3. Fill bottles with tempera paint mixed with water and then replace the rings and balls. (Do not use starch in tempera.)
4. Roll paint on paper to make designs.

21-13 Children enjoy art activities such as these.

Benefits of Music Experiences

Music provides chances for sensory and expressive experiences. Listening to music is the basis of all musical learning. As children become more attuned to the sounds around them, they learn to translate the sounds in musical ways. They may say that sounds have a high or low pitch or an even or uneven rhythm. Also, listening to the sounds of music can improve children's listening skills in general.

Making music is fun. Even babies invent ways to make sounds. They shake or hit objects and make sounds with their voices and hands.

Many instruments require more finger strength and skill than young children have. For these reasons, the first instruments children use are often percussion instruments. The tones of **percussion instruments** are produced when struck. Percussion instruments without a definite pitch, such as most drums, are called **rhythm instruments**. In contrast, **melody percussion instruments**, such as xylophones, produce various pitches when certain bars are struck, 21-14. By using these instruments, young children see how sounds are made, play rhythmic patterns, and perhaps play simple melodies.

With special training, some young children become quite skilled in playing an instrument. In fact, many professional musicians began playing instruments between three and five years of age. There are special music programs developed with young children in mind, such as the Suzuki Method® and Kindermusik®, as well as traditional music instruction.

Singing seems to make children feel good. They often sing or chant to tell what they are doing. ("Feed…ing ba…by.") They use the same words for singing as they do for speaking. Thus, singing helps language learnings.

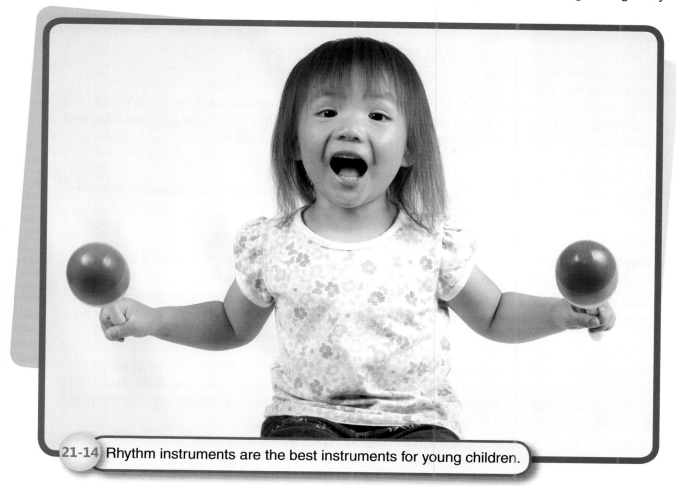

21-14 Rhythm instruments are the best instruments for young children.

Although young children do enjoy singing, they often cannot carry a tune. They are not able to match their voice pitch to the notes of the music. Until young children find a singing voice, they simply talk in a sustained hum they call *singing*. When the singing voice is found, the range is often limited to about six tones (from middle C to A). By practicing and listening, children will develop singing skills over time.

Preschool children may also have problems singing with other voices or with musical instruments. In order to sing with others, children must hear their own voice, the voices of other singers or instruments, and the unison sound.

The Adult's Role in Guiding Music Experiences

To guide music experiences, the adult must introduce children to music activities suited to their interests. These areas include listening, singing, playing instruments, and moving to music, 21-15. In addition to providing activities, adults can provide an environment that is rich in sound. They can model enthusiasm and an enjoyment of a variety of music.

Perhaps the adult's most difficult role is listening to and praising children's musical attempts. Children need adult encouragement if they are to

Music Activities

Hearing sounds

Play tapes that feature sounds in nature and sounds that manufactured products make. Talk about the tones heard in terms of sound qualities, such as *high-low, loud-soft, near-far*, and *continuous-discontinuous*. Also talk about the direction of the sound.

Story sounds

Read stories that mention sounds. Ask children to make the sounds mentioned in the story using their voices, their bodies, or objects.

Matching sounds

Play different tones using an instrument. Ask the child to match his or her voice to the pitch. (Notes should be between middle C and one octave above middle C.)

Variation: Match rhythms by tapping a simple rhythmic pattern and having the child echo the pattern. After the children echo several patterns, ask a child to play a pattern and let you echo.

Finding the sound

Have children pretend to be kittens or other animals that make sounds. Have the kittens hide while mother cat (one of the children) pretends to be asleep. After the kittens have hidden, the mother cat awakens and meows to her kittens. Kittens meow in response, and the mother cat must find the kittens by following the sounds.

Variation: Have the children point in the direction of a sound they hear. You may also have children locate a loudly ticking clock or metronome you have hidden.

21-15 Music activities provide rich sensory and expressive experiences.

practice enough to gain musical skills. Especially during the school years, parents and other adults may listen to many less-than-perfect performances. However, with loving acceptance children can become skilled musicians or, at least, learn to appreciate music.

Science

Children are born scientists. They wonder and seek answers. They test their answers repeatedly. The raw materials of science surround children in their homes, yards, group programs, and schools.

What Is Science?

To children, science is wondering about the world and everything in it. Before they can wonder, children must progress through a few steps. They must be aware, then focus on an object or happening by ignoring other things, and then observe.

Science is part of everyday life. Children experience science when they catch a cricket, put it in a jar, and watch it. They experience science when they watch water freeze and see snow melt. Children can learn about science when they ask, "Why do I need to eat my green beans?" or, "How do clouds move?"

Science is appreciating beauty. Most children are awed by the world of living and nonliving matter. They are eager to share what they find with others.

Science is caring for the world. For the most part, children translate beauty into caring. However, because of their young minds, children may not know living things can be hurt or even killed. They may not understand that resources such as water, land, and air can be damaged. They may not realize people can spoil beauty when they are not careful.

The Adult's Role in Encouraging Science Activities

Adults should encourage children to wonder, appreciate the beauty of their world, and focus on science in everyday life. Adults can call attention to the beauty of many science concepts. These include light coming through a prism, colors on butterflies' wings, the fragrance of roses, and the songs of birds. Adults can also read books on nature to children. They can visit zoos, gardens, and forests together. (Some places have special children's tours.) Adults can help children form collections of beautiful things, such as seeds, rocks, and shells.

Lessons on caring for nature should begin early. Adults can begin by giving children tasks in caring for living things starting in the toddler years, 21-16. (The task must match the child's development.) Adults should also model care for the environment. This includes saving energy in the

Focus on Science
Helping Children Explore Their World

Children usually explore and ask questions without being led by adults. However, adults can use some methods to help children explore. What methods can you think of to add to this list?

★ Adults can ask children to name the sense(s) used in learning about many objects—a *bell*, a *rainbow*, the *rain*, *foods*, a *frog*, or any other object.

★ Adults can encourage children to classify objects. Adults may ask, "How are these two objects alike? How are they different?"

★ Adults should ask many questions to encourage children to test ideas. Adults may ask, "What goes through a sifter?" "What do magnets pick up?" "Which objects float?" "What would happen if…?"

home by reminding children to turn off lights and running water. Families should also help with cleanup work around the home and in their community.

Focus of Science Activities

Science activities should focus on what children see and question around them. Science should never be a magic show. Instead, adults should explain science so children can learn about the world. For this reason, the topics and their order may differ from child to child. Generally speaking, topics should focus on children's questions and play activities.

Children like living creatures of all sizes. They need to watch, listen to, and touch animals, when appropriate. Most of all, children

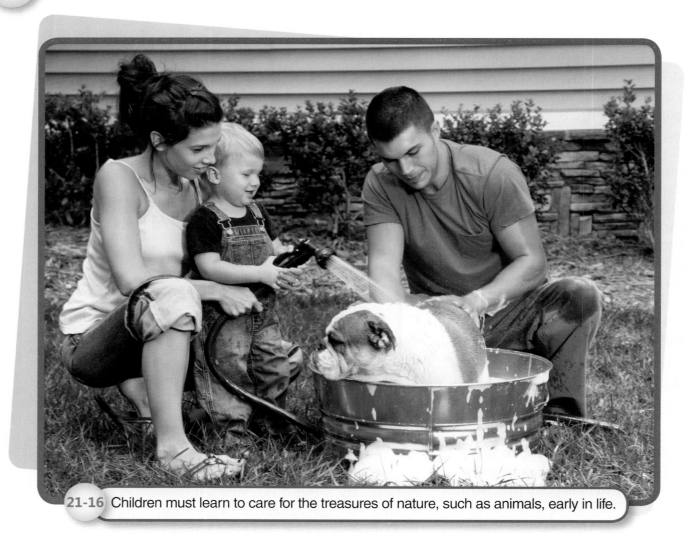

21-16 Children must learn to care for the treasures of nature, such as animals, early in life.

need to develop a respect for living things.

Children should focus on substances (physical matter of things). As children play, they handle liquid, granular, and solid substances. Activities can focus on the attributes of substances. An adult may ask, "What is water like?" Other activities can focus on what objects can be made from (or with) a substance or how the substance is used. When children are doing these activities, they are learning physical knowledge concepts.

Children can overcome some fears with science facts. For example, many children fear thunderstorms. By the early school years, children can understand the causes of thunder and lightning with adults' help. Many "why and how" books are available for children and adults.

Children should focus on fun activities that can involve many learnings. For example, cooking is one of the best ways to learn many science and math concepts, and both preparing and eating food is fun.

Children's books and magazines are filled with science learnings and activities. Television programs and the Internet are great learning resources, too. Children's interests can be easily matched with these resources.

Literature

Literature opens up a world of magic and new ideas for children. What child is not enchanted with stories and poems? Literature entertains and is an important learning tool for children. Through books, children learn pleasant lessons in concepts and language.

Benefits to Children

Books enrich life and help children appreciate beauty. Books answer children's endless questions and cause them to want to learn. Through quality stories and poems, children hear the rhythm of language, the rise and fall of the voice, and tongue-tickling phrases.

Reading to children builds their active and passive vocabularies. Children then may make up their own stories and poems at an early age, 21-17. A young child made up this poem while watching water flow from a water hose. "Water drip, water fall, running down my outside wall." (Keith, age three years.)

Children who have learned to love books can express themselves through dramatic play, art, music, and other experiences. They are able to express themselves and their feelings in many forms.

Young children like to hear stories about others their age and about people and things with which they are familiar. They better understand themselves by hearing stories that draw on their backgrounds. Older children may want to expand their learning by reading about topics that are less familiar to them.

Selecting Books for Children

In order for books and other literature to stretch the mind and stir creativity, adults must choose them with care. A children's librarian can help adults make good choices.

The Sad Pumpkin

Once there was a pumpkin. He hated any pie. One day someone gave him some pie and he began to cry. The cook asked, "Why are you crying?" He said, "Because I hate this pie." And when the cook heard this, she too began to cry. The maid came in, and when she saw the mess she said, "What's the meaning of this? I really cannot guess." And when the maid heard, she too began to cry. When the wise man came in, he gave a big, long sigh. He said, "This pumpkin hates it 'cause it's pumpkin pie."

—Keith, age seven

21-17 Children who are read to often use their rich source of background material for original works.

Books need to be on the child's level. Babies and toddlers enjoy hearing nursery rhymes. Toddlers and preschool children enjoy picture books with quality pictures. First picture books need only simple captions (or perhaps no captions at all). Later picture books have simple plots. In picture books the pictures tell the story. Books for older children have more involved plots and more written description. Now the mind creates the pictures, 21-18.

Children should experience books with delight. Story time should help children relax. Adults should hold young children as they read or seat children close to them. They should also read in interesting ways, using inflections and different voices. Children should be able to see pictures clearly. Adults can encourage remarks or laughter as they read.

Adults can plan some follow-up activities after reading a story or poem. These activities do not immediately have to follow the story. However, they should occur while the book is still fresh in the child's mind. Follow-up activities include talking about the story, finding details in the pictures, and relating the book to the child's own experiences. Other activities are drawing, making a model, or enjoying a cooking activity related to the story. Children can also do activities discussed in the book, such as going to the zoo. This makes the story or poem more meaningful to them.

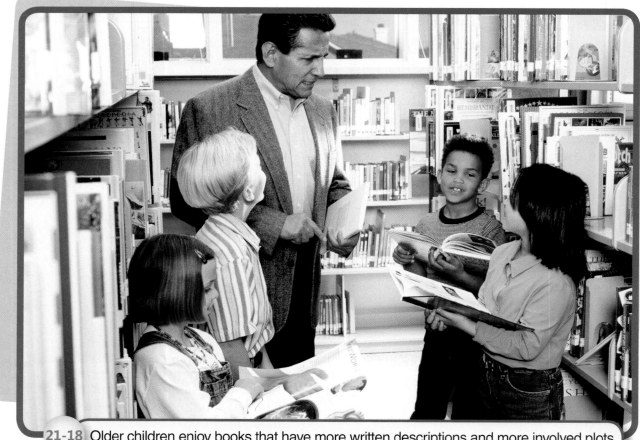

21-18 Older children enjoy books that have more written descriptions and more involved plots.

Summary

Play helps children develop in many ways. Children's play tends to reflect the changes in their developmental levels. Thus, play itself has stages. Basic skill types of play include active-physical, manipulative-constructive, imitative-imaginative, and language-logic play.

Adults need to allow children freedom to play and time to explore. Their attitude should reflect the importance of play. Adults should choose safe and fun toys. Selections should also be based on the ages of the children and type of play settings. Children can also make many toys from objects found at home.

Adults should promote learning experiences in art, music, and science and through literature. Children can learn many skills that enrich their lives through these activities.

As their art skills develop, children will progress through stages. Adults need to provide the right environment and supplies to help children with their art activities. They should be supportive and show interest in their children's artwork.

At an early age children move to the sound of music. Most children enjoy singing and making music. Adults can introduce music activities and provide an environment that is rich in sound and movement.

Children's exploring and observing lead to many questions about science concepts. Adults can encourage children's curiosity about the world and help them seek answers to their questions.

Children who have stories and poems read to them increase their language development and self-expression. Adults should choose quality literature with the children's ages and interests in mind. Follow-up activities help to reinforce learnings.

Companion Web Site

Interactive Activity

Review vocabulary terms and key concepts for Chapter 21 at **g-wlearning.com**.

Review and Reflect

Write your answers to the following questions on a separate sheet of paper.

1. True or false. Play helps children with physical, intellectual, and social-emotional development.

2. List the four types of play described in the chapter.

3. True or false. Different types of skills develop through different types of play.

4. What are the two stages of development in visual arts?

5. True or false. Scribbling does *not* have any value in children's art development.

6. When children use a _____ in their artwork, they are showing spatial relationships.

7. True or false. Children begin to use transparency symbols in their artwork when they are between two and three years of age.

8. Listening to the sounds of music _____ (can, cannot) improve children's general listening skills.

9. _____ instruments are often the first musical instruments children use.

10. True or false. Children's science learnings are mainly made up of special activities planned for children.

11. Children's spoken language reflects what _____ (has, has not) been read to them.

12. List two types of follow-up activities for children after reading literature.

Cross-Curricular Link

13. **Speech.** Work with a small group to role-play the various stages and types of play as described in the chapter.

14. **Math, Financial Literacy.** Use Internet or print sources to find art recipes for finger paint and play dough. For each recipe, calculate the cost of the ingredients if you were to buy them in a grocery store. Next, shop online to price commercially-prepared finger paint and play dough. Compare the prices of the homemade and store-bought supplies. How would the costs compare if you already had on hand the items needed to prepare the recipes yourself?

15. **Social Studies.** Help an older preschool or school-age child make a simple musical instrument. The books *Music and Instruments for Children to Make* (Book 1 and Book 2) by John and Martha Faulhaber Hawkinson are good resources. Your music teacher may also have more resources you could use.

16. **Science, Writing.** Shop online or visit a local library to search for books adults can use to guide children in science activities. Write a bibliography

listing at least three such books. For each book, include the title, author, copyright date, publisher, and a brief paragraph describing the book.

17. **Reading.** Select and read a book to a child. Use a follow-up activity with the story. Report to the class how the child responded to the story and follow-up activity.

Making Observations

18. Observe children of different ages at play. Using Chart 21-4 as a reference, identify each stage of play you observe. Also identify the type or types of play involved. Support your findings with information from the text.

19. Observe a teacher encouraging children's creative development in visual arts or music. How does the teacher guide the children's development? How are the children reacting? What skills are children developing? Do the children seem to enjoy the experiences? Why or why not?

20. Observe children as they select books in a preschool center. Listen to the children talk with each other about the books. Describe the types of books that interest young children. (Note subject matter; illustrations; novelty items, such as pop-up pictures; or fun language, such as rhymes.)

Thinking Critically

21. If you watch a group of children during free-play time, you will note they show preferences for active-physical, manipulative-constructive, imitative-imaginative, and language-logic play. What connections do you see between the children's personalities and their play choices? Which type of play did you prefer as a child? Do you see any connection between preferred play as a young child and your preferences for study, leisure, or work activities now? Explain.

22. The text states, "A child's total development determines how he or she uses crayons, paints, clay, and other materials." Make a collection of children's creative artwork. How is the child's physical, intellectual, and social-emotional development reflected in each piece of art?

23. Why is play one of the best ways to learn? Can you still learn through play? Give some examples.

22 Protecting Children's Health and Safety

After studying this chapter, you will be able to

★ **explain** ways to protect children from diseases and illnesses.

★ **create** a safe environment for young children.

★ **teach** young children simple safety practices.

★ **discuss** the steps in preparing a child for medical care in the doctor's office, in the hospital, and at home.

Terms to Know

dental caries
orthodontist
immunity
antibodies
naturally acquired immunities
artificially acquired immunities
antigens
immunization
active immunity
passive immunity
symptoms
contagious disease
allergy

allergen
childproofing
restraint systems
certified child safety seats
safety recall
LATCH system
child passenger seat (CPS) technician
filtering program
first aid
diagnosis
terminally ill

Today's advances in health and safety are greater than ever before. However, growing up is still risky business. Each day, infants and children face the risks of illness, injury, and even death. Sometimes adults can control these risks, while at other times they cannot. In particular, careful supervision and childproofing can help children avoid many risks altogether. Adults who care for children have a huge responsibility when it comes to keeping them healthy and safe.

Protecting Children from Disease and Illness

How can a disease, an injury, or an abnormal condition affect a child? Any one of these may cause pain, lifelong physical health problems, and damage to self-esteem. When health problems are prevented, detected early, or treated properly, children have a better chance of leading a healthy and happy life.

Basic Needs for Good Health

What are a person's basic needs? For good health, a person must meet his or her needs for good nutrition, rest, cleanliness, and physical activity. People must meet these basic needs throughout life. However, paying careful attention to them may be more important in childhood than at any other time, 22-1.

Basic health care is important because it helps children grow and develop properly. In turn, good health provides children energy

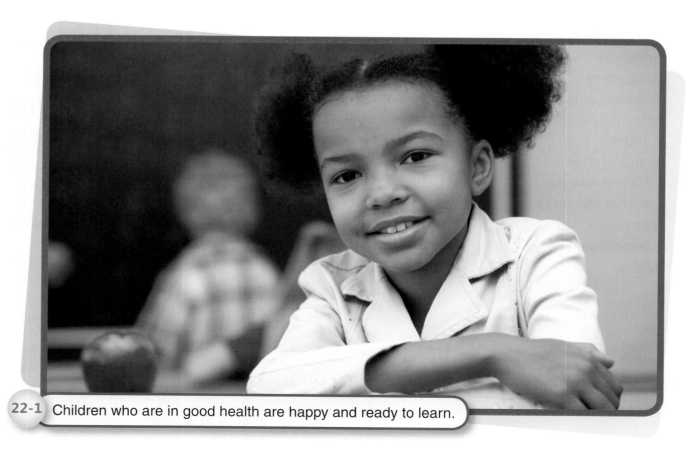

22-1 Children who are in good health are happy and ready to learn.

for their daily activities. When a disease or injury occurs, children who are otherwise healthy tend to recover quickly and completely. Also, neglecting health needs for long periods could cause health problems with lasting effects. For example, obesity is considered America's most important children's health issue. Children who are obese are at risk for high cholesterol, high blood pressure, early heart disease, type 2 diabetes, bone problems, skin conditions, and self-esteem issues.

Adults need to help children meet their basic physical needs starting early in life. In addition, adults must model good health practices. These actions positively affect children's health. Parents' actions may also help children develop good, lifelong health care habits.

Medical and Dental Care

The goal of health care is to keep children well. To do so, doctors examine children regularly, not just when they are sick. Well-child checkups may find possible health problems before they become serious or cannot be repaired. They may even prevent problems altogether.

Doctors check children's growth and development. They protect children from certain diseases. They also note eating, sleeping, and playing habits. Doctors answer parents' questions about their child's development.

Because well-child checkups are so important, doctors suggest a schedule for regular visits. The schedule varies slightly among doctors, but the American Academy of Pediatrics suggests some general guidelines. The AAP recommends at least nine well-child checkups during the first three years. (This does not include checkups made between birth and discharge from the hospital.) The schedule usually includes 1-, 2-, 3-, 6-, 9-, 12-, 18-, 24-, and 36-month checkups. A yearly examination is recommended after three years of age. Babies of nursing mothers may have extra checkups during their early weeks. These checkups are to make sure babies are gaining weight properly (a sign they are getting enough milk). Also, premature babies are often seen by their doctors more frequently because their health and development are more vulnerable than full-term babies.

Parents should locate a pediatric or family dentist for their six-month-old child. The dentist can educate parents on proper tooth care. Dental care usually begins by the first birthday and should be repeated every six months afterward. Early checkups make children less likely to fear dental care. Dentists clean teeth. They inspect and X-ray teeth, if necessary, for **dental caries** (decayed places in teeth). Dentists repair damaged teeth and teach children how to care for their teeth. After the permanent molars come in, many dentists recommend sealants. These are plastic coatings that protect the chewing surfaces of the teeth and thus, prevent dental caries.

If a child's teeth are irregular, the child's dentist may refer him or her to an orthodontist. An **orthodontist** is a dentist who specializes in correcting irregular teeth by making crooked teeth straight. When teeth

Learn More About... Dental Hygiene

Dental hygiene should begin at birth. The American Academy of Pediatric Dentistry recommends wiping a baby's gums and teeth with water-dampened gauze or a soft, clean baby washcloth after each feeding for the first year. For children ages one to seven or eight, they recommend the following:

★ Brush teeth twice daily with a baby toothbrush. If only one brushing can be done daily, it should be before the baby goes to sleep each night.

★ Brush without toothpaste until the child is two years old or learns to spit. (Low fluoride toothpaste should be used until three years of age to keep children from swallowing too much fluoride, which can discolor the teeth.) Begin with a tiny smear of toothpaste and gradually increase the amount to the size of a pea by six years of age.

★ Brush in a circular motion on both the inside and outside surfaces of teeth and gums. Brush teeth from gum line to biting and chewing surface and from back to front. Brush the top of the tongue. Brushing should last a couple of minutes. Swish with water.

★ Rinse mouth after eating if not brushing.

★ Floss adjacent teeth as soon as they erupt.

★ Avoid offering bottles in bed. If a bottle is needed, use boiled unsweetened water at night.

★ Give milk and juice only at mealtimes. Sweet drinks, such as fruit juices, should be served only in a cup. Offer milk from a cup beginning soon after age 12 months.

★ Because brushing is a complex fine-motor skill, children cannot begin brushing their own teeth until they are about five years old. (Of course, before this age they can practice after each adult brushing.) Parents should continue to supervise and help with brushing until children are seven or eight years old.

★ Adults should practice good dental hygiene. This sets an example for the child. It also reduces the spread of bacteria from the parents' mouth to the child's mouth in kissing.

★ Wash toothbrushes once a week by dipping in hydrogen peroxide and letting air dry bristle-end up. Replace brushes every three to four months.

are straight, a pretty smile is not the only benefit. Straight teeth allow people to chew food properly and clean teeth more easily, thus reducing the chance of tooth and gum disease, 22-2.

Immunization

Immunity is the body's defense against disease. Scientists speak about several types of immunity.

The body has some *general immunities*, which defend against many diseases. These defenses include skin, some types of cells, fever, and inflammation. For the most part, however, the body needs *specific immunity* to defend against a particular disease. To form these immunities, the body must develop or receive specific **antibodies**, which are proteins in the blood that fight disease.

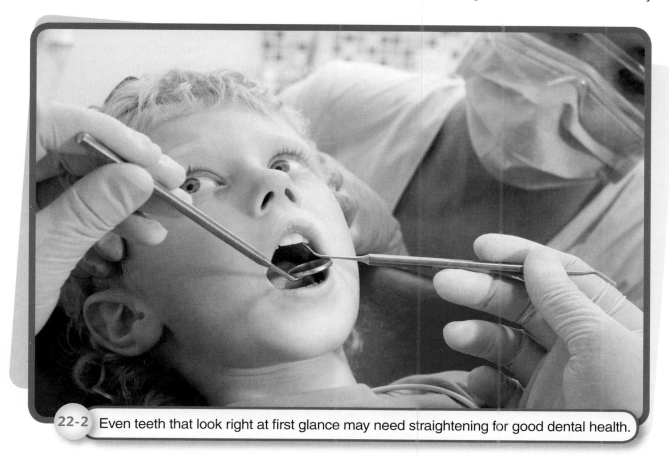

22-2 Even teeth that look right at first glance may need straightening for good dental health.

Specific immunity can be one of two types. **Naturally acquired immunities** (sometimes called *natural immunities*) are developed after direct contact with infection or by receiving antibodies from the mother during pregnancy or breast-feeding. Naturally acquired immunities can be quite long-lasting, sometimes lasting a lifetime.

Natural exposure to some diseases is dangerous or deadly, however. A person would not risk exposure to these diseases as a way to build immunity. Instead, the person might receive **artificially acquired immunities** (sometimes called *acquired immunities*). These immunities form as a person's reaction to antibodies or an antigen received through medical care. **Antigens** are substances made in a laboratory and transferred to people in the form of an injection (shot). An antigen is made from the bacteria, viruses, or toxins that cause diseases, but it is not as strong as the disease itself. When the antigen is injected into the body, the body builds antibodies to fight it. These antibodies will remain in the body to protect the person against the illness in the future. Doctors call this type of protection **immunization**. Other terms with the same meaning are *vaccination* and *inoculation*. For some illnesses, the body needs a series of immunizations to build a strong defense.

Specific immunities can also be described as *active* or *passive*. **Active immunity** is when the person's own body must produce antibodies. This occurs during direct exposure to the illness or the antigen in a vaccine. Active immunity takes several days or even weeks to become effective. This is the time when the body needs to react by making antibodies. Once developed, this immunity lasts several years or a lifetime. **Passive immunity** results when antibodies are produced by one person's exposure to a disease and then passed to another person. This is what happens when mothers pass antibodies to their unborn babies across the placenta. It can also happen for a few days after birth when mothers breast-feed their newborns. A person can also receive a transfusion of antibodies, called an *antiserum*, made by someone else's body. The antiserum is given when people need immediate immunity and cannot wait for their bodies to build antibodies, such as in the treatment for rabies. Passive immunity lasts only a few weeks.

Immunizations prevent some serious diseases. They include tetanus, diphtheria, pertussis (whooping cough), polio, measles, rubella (German measles), mumps, and chicken pox. Some parents are choosing not to have their children vaccinated. They believe vaccinations can lead to other diseases. Parents should understand, however, that if a child becomes infected, these diseases can cause serious illness and even death.

Most doctors agree that immunizations beginning at birth give children the most protection from disease. Immunizations should protect the baby without competing with antibodies received from the mother. Children's doctors keep records of immunizations. Doctors check these records before giving more doses. Schools and camps also require official records of immunizations before admission. Parents should keep a record, too, for their own information.

See the *Immunization Schedule* in Appendix B for a list of recommended childhood immunizations for birth through age 18. Recommendations are reviewed and updated regularly. You can check for updates at the American Academy of Pediatrics Web site at **www.aap.org**.

Medical Attention During Illness

Sometimes children need special medical attention. Many childhood illnesses end quickly without cause for worry. However, many **symptoms** (evidence of an illness or injury) may reveal a need for prompt medical help. Chart 22-3 lists some major symptoms for which adults should consult a doctor. Even if they notice vague symptoms, adults should call a doctor if the child's behavior seems abnormal.

In order to understand a child's condition, doctors need specific information. The adult should think of questions the doctor may ask, such as the following:

★ What are all the child's symptoms? (Give exact information, such as, "Hannah has vomited five times in the last two hours. Each time she has lost about one cup of fluid.")

★ When did you first notice these symptoms?

★ Has the child recently been exposed to a **contagious disease** (disease that can be caught from another person)?

Symptoms Indicating Possible Illness

Area of Concern	Symptom
Blood	★ Large amount lost in bleeding ★ Bleeding will not stop
Body movement	★ Convulsions (seizures) ★ Immobility in any part of the body ★ Shaking ★ Stiffness of the body
Bones and muscles	★ Swelling ★ Pain ★ Difficulty in movement
Brain	★ Dizziness ★ Visual problems ★ Strange actions or appearance ★ Unconsciousness ★ Headache
Breathing	★ Difficulty in breathing ★ Slow or rapid breathing ★ Continued coughing, sneezing, or wheezing
Digestive system	★ Sudden decrease in appetite ★ Nausea or vomiting (forceful vomiting as opposed to spitting up foods) ★ Vomits for several hours with inability to retain fluids ★ Abdominal pain or tenderness ★ Sudden increase or decrease in number of bowel movements ★ Stools or urine unusual in amount, color, odor, or consistency
Eyes	★ Irritated or red ★ Sensitivity to light ★ Blurred vision
Fever	★ Rectal temperature of 101°F or above ★ Mild fever that lasts several days
General behavior	★ Unusually quiet, irritable, or drowsy ★ Strange behavior after a fall or other accident ★ If already ill, has a rise in fever or new symptoms appear ★ Sharp screaming ★ Ear rubbing, head rolling, or drawing of legs toward abdomen
Nose	★ Nasal discharge (note color, amount, and consistency), congestion, or bleeding
Skin	★ Dry or hot ★ Excessive perspiration ★ Rash or hives ★ Severe cuts or abrasions ★ Deep bruising ★ Flushed or pale in color
Throat	★ Sore ★ Red ★ Choking or coughing

22-3 When certain symptoms appear, children may need medical help.

★ Have you treated the child's illness in any way? How? Have you given the child food, liquid, or medication? When? Does the child take any medication regularly?

★ Do you know whether the child is allergic to any medication? (A new doctor will not know about a child's allergies.)

★ What is the name and phone number of your pharmacy? (The doctor may phone in a prescription.)

Adults need to write down all this information before calling a doctor, except in extreme emergencies. They should also take pen and paper to the phone to write the doctor's instructions. After receiving instructions from the doctor, adults should ask the following:

★ Is there anything I should know about giving this medication or treatment? What other measures should I take (such as keep the child lightly covered; use a humidifier; keep the child in bed)?

★ When should I expect an improvement?

★ What changes would merit another call or office visit?

Adults should repeat the instructions for the doctor to be sure they have understood the directions correctly. They should follow the doctor's advice exactly. If questions arise after the call, adults should not hesitate to call the doctor again and ask him or her to clarify.

Childhood Diseases

Adults who care for children should be aware of diseases that are often contracted during childhood. These are called *childhood diseases*, 22-4. Most childhood diseases are contagious. If left untreated, children can suffer negative effects and even die from these diseases. This mainly occurs when adults are unaware of the diseases and their symptoms and do not seek early treatment. Besides the diseases listed in Chart 22-4, other common childhood illnesses and disorders include the following:

★ **Coxsackievirus.** A digestive tract virus that is spread on unwashed hands and surfaces contaminated by feces. The symptoms often include high fever, headaches, and muscle aches. Painful red blisters may appear in the throat and mouth. Although the disease often runs its course in a few days, parents must watch their child carefully and get medical help if other symptoms appear.

★ **Diabetes.** *Type 1 diabetes* is a condition in which the pancreas produces little or no insulin. It typically appears before the adult years. The cause is mainly genetic, but other unknown factors may contribute as well. *Type 2 diabetes* occurs when the body becomes resistant to the effects of insulin or when the pancreas does not produce enough to maintain a normal blood sugar. The onset is often in the adult years, but recently school-age children are becoming more and more vulnerable.

Childhood Diseases

Condition	Cause	Symptoms	Comments
Bronchitis	Reaction of air tubes in the chest	Cough after a cold that lasts for more than 2 weeks	Seek medical treatment.
Chicken pox	Virus	Fever; runny nose; cough; rash (pimples, blisters, and scabs)	Seek medical treatment. Keep child away from others for 6 days after rash begins. Vaccine can prevent.
Colds	Virus	Runny nose; scratchy throat; coughing; sneezing; watery eyes	Seek medical treatment if child looks and acts very ill.
Conjunctivitis	Virus and bacteria	Watery eyes; mucus in eyes; red or pink color in whites of eyes; eyelid redness	Seek medical treatment. Keep child away from others for 24 hours after starting treatment.
Diaper rash	Secondary infection may be caused by bacteria or yeast	Redness, scaling, and pimples or sores in diaper area	Seek medical advice if rash persists or worsens. If rash is caused by infection, keep child away from others for 24 hours after starting treatment.
Diphtheria	Bacteria	Headache; fever; severe sore throat with white fluid over tonsils and throat; cough; bloody nasal discharge	Seek medical treatment. Keep child away from others for 2 weeks after fever starts or when throat cultures are clear. Vaccine can prevent.
Earaches	Bacteria and virus	Fever; pain; difficulty in hearing; drainage from ear	Seek medical treatment.
Haemophilus influenza type b (Hib)	Bacteria	Fever; lethargy (tired); vomiting; poor appetite; earache; breathing and swallowing difficulties; cough; purple area on skin near eyes	Seek medical treatment. Keep child away from others until fever is gone or physician approves contact. Vaccine can prevent.
Hepatitis B	Virus	Fever; jaundice (yellowing of skin and whites of eyes); loss of appetite; nausea; joint pain; rash	Seek medical treatment. Keep child away from others until fever is gone and skin rash is dry.
Impetigo	Bacteria	Red, cracking, oozing blister-like pimples often seen on the face	Seek medical treatment. Keep child away from others until 24 hours after starting treatment.

22-4 Childhood diseases can be serious illnesses in the early years.

(Continued.)

Measles	Virus	Fever; cough; runny nose; watery eyes; brownish red and blotchy rash that begins on face and neck and spreads downward; white spots in mouth	Seek medical treatment. Keep child away from others for 6 days after rash begins. Vaccine can prevent.
Meningitis	Virus and bacteria	Fever; lethargy (tired); poor appetite; vomiting; irritable (fussy); headache; stiff neck	Seek emergency medical help. Physician will determine if child can have contact with others. Vaccines may prevent.
Mumps	Virus	Fever; swelling of one or more salivary glands; earache; headache	Seek medical treatment. Keep child away from others for 9 days after onset of swelling. Vaccine can prevent.
Pertussis (whooping cough)	Bacteria	Runny nose; coughing spells; vomiting	Seek medical treatment. Keep child away from others for 3 weeks after onset of cough. Vaccine can prevent.
Poliomyelitis (polio)	Virus	Fever; vomiting; irritable (fussy); headache; stiffness of neck and back; paralysis in some cases	Seek medical treatment. Physician will determine when child may have contact with others. Vaccine can prevent.
Reye's Syndrome	Virus (often within 3 to 5 days after other viral infections)	Vomiting; sudden fever; mental confusion; lethargy (tired); drowsiness; irritable (fussy); body rigidity; coma	Seek emergency medical help. Aspirin has been linked to onset in over 90 percent of cases. For this reason, never give medicines containing aspirin to children.
Roseola infantum	Virus (seen in children under 2 years as suggested in the name "infantum")	Fever followed by rash	Seek medical treatment. Keep child away from others until fever is gone.
Rubella	Virus	Red rash; enlarged lymph nodes; joint pain	Seek medical treatment. Keep child away from others for 6 days after rash begins. Vaccine can prevent.
Scarlet fever (scarlatina)	Bacteria	Fever; rash that causes skin to peel	Seek medical treatment. Keep child away from others until 24 hours after starting treatment.
Strep throat	Bacteria	Sore throat; skin infections	Seek medical treatment. Keep child away from others until 24 hours after starting treatment.

22-4 *(Continued.)*

The causes are often genetic and lifestyle factors, such as a poor diet and lack of physical activity. A person's ethnicity and age can also be risk factors. The symptoms of both types of diabetes are similar—increased thirst and urination, intense hunger, weight loss, fatigue, blurred vision, and slow-healing sores. If blood sugar drops too much a person can go into a diabetic coma and die. Type 1 diabetes requires consistent care, blood sugar monitoring, and insulin delivery. Type 2 diabetes is treated by diet and physical activity to manage weight. If it worsens, oral medications or insulin treatments are needed.

★ **Epilepsy.** Epilepsy is a disorder caused by abnormal activity in brain cells. It often begins in childhood. Symptoms, known as *seizures*, vary in intensity from a blank stare for a few seconds (*petit mal*) to convulsions with loss of consciousness (*grand mal*). Seizures vary in frequency, too. Most people have repeated cases of the same type of seizure, but some people have differing intensities of seizures. Epilepsy may be due to defective genes or may be traced to an accident, diseases with high fever, or medical trauma (stroke). Medications help control the problem. Patients with severe seizures may wear helmets to prevent head damage during a seizure. Some children have service dogs who sense and warn them of an upcoming seizure; this allows children to get to a safe place quickly.

★ **Head lice.** Head lice are very common among children enrolled in group programs and schools. Head lice are parasites that live and feed on a person's scalp. The disease is *not* due to personal hygiene. It is spread through touching contact with an infected person or their infected belongings, such as wearing another child's cap or hat and through touching coats or napping cots and pads. One can see the lice and lice eggs (nits) on the scalp and hair. Infected people often have small red, itchy bumps on their head and shoulders, too. Medications are used to treat head lice on the person. However, head lice have become resistant to some standard medications. Therefore, a newer prescription medication that suffocates the lice is now available. Special laundering is required to kill them on possessions.

★ **Oral thrush.** Oral thrush is a fungus infection seen mainly in babies and toddlers. It forms painful lesions in the mouth and throat. Breast-feeding mothers can develop symptoms on their nipples. If a woman has a vaginal yeast infection during delivery, she may pass it to her baby. Thrush is treated with antifungal medications.

★ **Ringworm.** Ringworm is a fungal infection that affects the skin, nails, and scalp. It forms scaly patches on the scalp. It is spread through contact and shared things with those who have ringworm. Unlike head lice, ringworm can spread through pets, too. Treatment requires about six weeks of oral medications.

Allergies and Asthma

Allergies affect over one-fourth of all children and are the greatest cause of chronic long-term health problems in young children. An **allergy** is a condition that results when a child's immune system is very sensitive to an environmental allergen and reacts negatively when it comes into contact with it. An **allergen** is a substance that causes an allergic reaction. Agents include food, insect bites and stings, medications, latex and other touch substances, and airborne allergens (pollen, animal dander, dust mites, and mold), 22-5.

Symptoms vary and include upset digestive tract, cold-like symptoms, nose bleeds, dark circles under the eyes, wheezing, and even life-threatening shock (called *anaphylaxis*). Immediate treatment for severe reactions requires epinephrine injections. In addition, allergies are treated by

★ removing or limiting contact with the substance (not having a pet or staying inside as much as possible when the pollen count is high)

★ using drugs for allergies (antihistamines, decongestants, and bronchodilators)

★ receiving injections for some allergens (called *desensitization therapy*)

Asthma, the inflammation of the airways, is the most common chronic illness of childhood. Symptoms vary from coughing and wheezing to shortness of breath. Common asthma triggers are viruses, airborne allergens, tobacco smoke, physical activity, and cold air. Asthma may lead to other respiratory problems.

Types of Allergens

Agent	Symptoms
Foods (often milk, citrus fruits, chocolate, wheat, and eggs) and medicines taken by mouth	★ Tingling mouth ★ Swelling of tongue, face, or throat ★ Hives ★ Anaphylaxis
Insect bites and stings, thorns, and medicines that are injected	★ *Edema* (swelling) at the site of the injection ★ Cough, wheezing, or shortness of breath ★ Hives ★ Anaphylaxis
Latex and other touched substances	★ Itchy skin ★ Flaking or peeling skin ★ Redness of skin
Airborne allergens	★ Congestion ★ Itchy, runny nose ★ Itchy, watery eyes ★ Dark circles under eyes (called *allergic shiners*)

22-5 Children may suffer from one or more of these types of allergies.

Oral, inhaled, and injected medications are used to help prevent attacks and to treat ongoing ones. If airborne allergens are the cause, children are often given allergy treatments, too.

Accident Prevention

Accidents claim the lives of more children than any of the major killer diseases of childhood. Several factors lead to the high accident rate among children. Some equipment and toys are not safe. Most homes have some hazards even after adults attempt to correct them. Children are energetic and curious. By the toddler years, they have the gross- and fine-motor skills to reach almost anything and get into it. Thus, children depend on adults to protect them by creating a safe environment and by supervising, modeling, and teaching safety practices.

How Do Accidents Happen?

Parents worry about how to protect their children from violence and strangers who kidnap. Many parents do not think about the two major threats to their children's safety—home hazards and lack of constant and adequate supervision. Children are much more likely to be injured in an accident at home than by a stranger's crime.

Children are the most prone to accidents before they are old enough to learn about safety practices. For this reason, adults need to take extra care to prevent these accidents. They can do this by removing hazards, supervising children, and taking safety measures. Later they can make children aware of the need for safety.

Creating a Safe Environment

Infants are totally dependent on safe equipment and clothing and on their parents' constant attention to safety matters. Creating a safe environment is also crucial for toddlers and preschool children. These children cannot make sound safety judgments. Children may not understand why they must be careful. They may be too busy reaching their goals to remember warnings. Adults must do all they can to keep the environment safe for children. In such an environment, accidents are reduced and children can play without being too concerned about safety. Older children can help protect themselves.

Supervising Children

Although safety devices are helpful, they do not take the place of adults' eyes and ears. Accidents happen more often when adults do not supervise children carefully. When adults are talking on the phone, watching television, working on the computer, visiting a friend, feeling ill, or in any way preoccupied, accidents are more likely. They happen more often in the late afternoon and early evening hours when parents make dinner or do other household tasks.

Accidents happen more often when supervision is unsuitable or lacking. For example, accidents happen more often when older children supervise younger ones. Accidents also happen when children (especially school-age children) are home alone while their parents work or run errands.

Anticipating Possible Hazards

Creating a risk-free environment is impossible. Even if it were possible to remove all hazards, this would not teach children to face and cope with risks. However, risks must not be too great, or serious accidents may happen. To prevent serious accidents, adults must look for possible hazards.

Children's developmental changes lead to certain types of accidents. Babies face hazards at birth. These hazards multiply as babies' motor skills, curiosity, and independence increase. Chart 22-6 shows accidents that are likely to occur during each stage of development. Adults must watch each child's development carefully. As they see growth stages occur, the adult must take certain safety measures. A child who can crawl up one step or onto any low object can soon climb an entire flight of steep stairs. However, an adult can keep the child safe from falling by blocking off stairs when the child begins to crawl.

Helping Children Meet Goals Safely

Adults should help children meet their goals safely. Young children learn about the world by climbing and putting objects in their mouth. Adults need to provide children with safe environments rather than change the children's goals. When babies want to climb, adults should let them climb up and down a single carpeted step. This environment is safe for them to explore, even if they take small tumbles. In addition, it helps children meet their goals. Also, small risks teach children to cope with possible dangers. A steep staircase, however, poses too great of a risk.

Childproofing the Environment

Adults must note dangerous objects in children's worlds. Moving unsafe objects out of a child's reach or preventing dangerous situations is called **childproofing** the environment.

Childproofing should start before the baby is born. Professional childproofing is a service available

Focus on Health

Childproofing

Instead of hiring a professional, many parents choose to childproof their own environment. To childproof, adults must do the following:

★ Childproof every part of the environment—inside and outside the home and vehicle.

★ Stay at least one step ahead of a child's development. A child who is just learning to stand may grasp a tablecloth for balance and pull off dangerous objects, such as hot soup.

★ Look for dangers from the child's physical perspective. Thus, if children are going to crawl in the kitchen, parents need to get down on their hands and knees and look for dangers from the child's perspective.

★ Check the child's belongings, including baby furniture, clothing, baby care equipment, supplies, and toys.

★ Choose pets carefully.

★ Stay up-to-date on the latest safety and product information.

 Accidents or injuries can occur in any part of the home. Look for potential health and safety hazards in your environment and develop a safety checklist that your family can follow.

Accidents Children Are Likely to Experience

Age of Child	Child's Traits Leading to Possible Accidents	Major Accidents
Birth to 3 months	★ Skin is much more sensitive to heat than adults' skin ★ Wiggles and rolls off flat surfaces, but cannot move away from danger ★ Puts objects in mouth and swallows them	★ Bath scalding ★ Falls from changing tables or carriers ★ Injuries from swallowing small objects ★ Drowning ★ Strangling on cords or smothering from items, such as dry cleaning bags or balloons ★ Suffocation under blankets, pillows, or soft objects
4 to 6 months	★ Skin is more sensitive to heat than adults' skin ★ Moves by rolling over and may crawl or creep ★ Grasps any object and places it in the eyes, ears, nose, or mouth ★ Hits objects, including breakable ones	★ Bath scalding and burns from hot water faucet ★ Falls ★ Injuries caused by swallowing small objects or putting them into eyes, ears, or nose ★ Injuries from broken objects, such as glass or plastics
6 to 12 months	★ Sits alone ★ Grabs anything in sight ★ Looks for objects hidden or fallen out of sight (around 10 months) ★ Puts objects in eyes, ears, nose, or mouth ★ Hits, pokes, and pushes objects ★ May walk with or without help	★ Falls from stairs or high places ★ Injuries caused by pulling on cords of kitchen appliances, pulling or grasping containers filled with hot foods or beverages ★ Burns from open heaters and floor furnaces ★ Injuries caused by swallowing small objects or putting them into ears, eyes, or nose ★ Injuries from dangerous objects, such as knives, sharp-edged furniture, breakable objects, and electrical outlets ★ Mishaps while using walkers, strollers, and riding toys
1 to 2 years	★ Walks ★ Climbs ★ Throws objects ★ Pulls open drawers and doors ★ Takes items apart ★ Puts objects in mouth	★ Drowning in bathtubs, water features, or pools ★ Falls on stairs, in tubs or pools, and off high objects, such as crib railings or tables ★ Burns from grabbing handles of pots on stove ★ Poisoning from medication and cleaning agents ★ Injuries from dangerous objects, such as knives, electrical outlets, breakable objects, toys with small parts, and sharp-edged objects inside and outside ★ Injuries caused by being on driveways and roads and in outside storage areas

22-6 Children of various ages differ in the type of accidents they are most likely to experience.

(Continued.)

2 to 3 years	★ Can rotate forearm to turn doorknob ★ Likes to climb on objects ★ Likes to play with, and in, water ★ Fascinated by fire ★ Moves at fast speed ★ Does not like to be restrained ★ Likes ride-on toys	★ Injuries caused by getting into almost anything that is not locked or equipped with special devices ★ Injuries caused by falls from high places, jumps onto dangerous surfaces (such as concrete), falls off ride-on toys and swings ★ Burns from cigarette lighters, matches, and open flames ★ Injuries caused by playing in driveways and roads and darting across streets ★ Injuries caused by swallowing small objects or putting them into eyes, ears, and nose ★ Eye injuries due to dust and sand ★ Injuries due to falls from swings and slides
3 to 6 years	★ Explores neighborhood ★ Plays rougher games ★ Plays with other children ★ Tries to use tools and equipment of the home	★ Poisoning from medicines and household products ★ Injuries from being around or using home, shop, and garden tools ★ Injuries related to action games, bicycles, and rough play ★ Various injuries from interesting hazards, such as old refrigerators, deep holes, trash heaps, and construction sites ★ Drowning ★ Burns from electrical outlets, appliances, and open flames ★ Traffic injuries
6 to 12 years	★ Participates in sports ★ Likely to try stunts on a dare in traffic as a pedestrian or on bicycle ★ Interested in firearms and fireworks ★ Uses tools in home and yard care	★ Sports-related injuries ★ Drowning ★ Firearm and fireworks accidents ★ Traffic injuries

22-6 *(Continued.)*

in many large cities. A professional childproofer inspects the home so he or she can assess the need for safety devices and do the childproofing. The service is expensive, but includes the costs of the advice, safety devices, and installation.

Indoor Safety

The indoor environment is often the greatest hazard to a child.

Each home is alike in some ways (doors, windows, electrical outlets) and different in others (stairs or no stairs, furnishings). Thus, parents must look for dangers in their own homes. Babies not only differ in their development at certain ages, but in their traits. Sometimes a baby's personality calls for additional childproofing measures. For example, some babies are extra curious and explore everything. Others are climbers who will try to scale everything in your home. Still other babies put more things into their mouth than others.

No home is safe. Problems can be found in the home structure, general furnishings, each room, and items kept in or near the home. Refer to Appendix C at the end of this text for a list of indoor dangers and how to prevent them.

Preventing Poisonings

Poisonings of children under five years of age account for more than half of all accidental poisonings in the home each year. Poisonings can occur due to lead paint used before 1978 on walls of homes and on toys. Young children eat paint chips or mouth toys and develop lead poisoning, which causes brain damage. At this age, children like to examine other objects, too. When attractively packaged household items catch their attention, children will often eat or swallow these products. Products that look (or even taste) like candy are especially enticing.

If adults take safety measures, children are less likely to be poisoned. Adults need to learn which products are dangerous, 22-7.

Poisons Cause Accidents

Cleaning Products	Garage and Garden Products	Medications	Personal Products
Air fresheners	Antifreeze	Acetaminophen	Aftershave
Ammonia	Caustic lime	Amphetamines	Baby and bath oils
Bleach	Fertilizer	Analgesic creams	Cosmetics
Cleaners	Gasoline, kerosene,	Antibiotics	Deodorant
Dishwasher and	lighter fluid,	Anticonvulsants	Hair coloring
dishwashing	oil, and other	Antidepressants	products
products	petroleum	Antidiarrheals	Hair removal
Disinfectant	products	Aspirin	products
Drain opener	Oils	Blood pressure drugs	Lotion
Floor wax	Paint	Camphor	Mouthwash
Furniture polish	Pesticides	Cold preparations	Nail polish and
Laundry products	Putty	Cough medications	polish remover
Lye	Strychnine	Diabetes drugs	Perfume
Metal polish	Turpentine	Ear medications	Permanent wave
Oven cleaner	Varnish	Heart drugs	solution
Rust remover	Weed killer	Iron, vitamins with iron	Powder, talcum
Spot remover	Windshield solution	Nasal sprays	(baby and body
Toilet bowl cleaner		Oil of wintergreen	powder)
Water softener		Pain relievers	Rubbing alcohol
		Sleeping pills	Shampoo
		Tropical anesthetics	Soap
		Tranquilizers	
		Vitamins	

22-7 Many common substances are poisonous. If you are not sure about a substance, ask your pharmacist or doctor.

Read all product labels and heed warnings. Store household products high above floor level (rather than under sinks) to keep them away from crawling babies. Lock up household products when children can walk and climb. (Once children can climb, their reach is almost without limits.) Leave an unattended, unsafe product stored in a safe, out-of-reach place. Do not leave the unattended product within reach, even for a minute.

Poisonous products must be kept in their original containers with the labels intact. Never transfer poisons to food or drink containers (such as a box, jar, or bottle). Do not put a safe substance in a container that originally held a poisonous product. For example, do not put water in a bleach bottle because a child might then assume the contents of all bleach bottles are safe. Keep medication in childproof containers. Store household products in safety containers. Carefully check containers after use to ensure each container is in good condition and closes properly.

Do not keep products that are lethal in the house. The risks are too great. For example, one teaspoon of oil of wintergreen contains six grams of salicylates. This equals the amount in 20 adult aspirin. This amount of oil of wintergreen would kill a child.

Medication is safer when adults take the following safety measures:

★ Dispose of medications properly. Disposal sites vary greatly by your locale, but may include pharmacies, hospitals, trash services, or the Environmental Protection Agencies mail-back program.

★ Replace childproof caps carefully after use.

★ Lock medication in a cabinet, a small chest, or suitcase.

★ Never give a child medication in the dark.

★ Never refer to medication as *candy*.

★ Do not give medication in baby bottles or juice glasses.

★ Do not take medication (even vitamins) in front of young children.

★ When carrying medication, store a limited amount in a childproof container and keep it in a purse or pocket. Keep your purse and the purses of visitors out of children's reach.

Standing Water Safety

Young children are not clumsy, but their body proportions make them top-heavy. If young children lose their balance near water, they may fall in and be unable to get out. Children can drown in even two inches of water. Never leave unattended buckets of water (for mopping or other chores) or filled bathtubs, sinks, or washing machines. Use a latch on toilet lids or install locks high on the outside of all bathroom doors. Eliminate or plan barriers to other standing water containers, such as indoor fountains, aquariums, or swimming pools.

Firearm Safety

Guns kill more than 10 children every day. Most firearm accidents happen when children discover a loaded gun at home. Firearm safety, in part, involves adults teaching children that guns are not toys and must not be handled by children. (Realistic toy guns can confuse children about the difference between these and real guns.) Children, however, are curious and often want to experiment even with "forbidden" objects. Thus, childproofing ensures the safest environment for the child and his or her visitors. The safest childproofing measures include the following:

★ Take ammunition out of firearms.

★ Lock the firearms out of the reach of children and use quality trigger locks.

★ Store the ammunition in a locked container apart from firearms.

★ Keep keys to firearms and ammunition cabinets in an area separate from other household keys.

★ Lock gun-cleaning supplies because they are poisonous.

Outdoor Safety

Adults must do safety checks of the outdoor areas, too. Common unsafe objects in the outdoor area include rocks, broken glass, ruts, holes, and bumps. Nails and other sharp objects can puncture children. Areas may become slippery and unsafe when wet.

If the outdoor area has pools, ponds, wells, or deep holes, adults should be sure they are enclosed by a fence the child cannot climb. The areas should also be closed and safely locked or covered to provide complete safety. To prevent falls from decks, use safety netting from the top of the railings to the deck floor. A safety gate or deck gate should be installed at the top of the steps. Open steps (common for decks) are also more risky for young children than closed stairs. Remove doors and trunk lids from old refrigerators, freezers, stoves, and cars even if stored temporarily. This prevents children from getting trapped inside and suffocating. All cars used by the family should be kept locked, too.

Plant Safety

Outside plants present a special safety problem. Many flowers, vegetables, shrubs, and trees are poisonous or have poisonous parts, 22-8. It is not always obvious to adults when children have eaten a plant leaf. However, many plants are dangerous when eaten. Some plants, because of their chemical

22-8 Before allowing their children to play outdoors, parents should check to make sure the plant life in the area is not poisonous for children.

makeup, harm the digestive tract in ways similar to eating ground glass. Other beautiful plants are deadly. Eating even one leaf of these plants may kill a child. Children need close supervision when playing outside, especially in wooded areas, gardens, and greenhouses. Remember, too, that many plants and lawns are treated with poisonous pesticides and fertilizers.

Adults should remove poisonous houseplants where children live or visit. Parents can check with their pediatrician or the Poison Control Center to learn which types of plants are poisonous. Adults should choose only nonpoisonous houseplants and keep these out of children's reach.

Safe Play Areas

Making sure children will not wander out of a safe area provided for their play is a great task. Yards with enclosed fences are best. Gates should be locked or equipped with childproof safety devices to keep children from opening them. For example, attach a screen door latch on the outside of the gate. Adults may also fit a gate with a bolt from the inside to the outside where the nut is attached. Because these devices require an adult to reach over a gate to unlock it, they are out of a child's reach.

When young children play in driveways or carports with pull and push toys or riding toys, adults should watch them closely. An extension ladder laid across the driveway a few feet from the street can help remind a child to turn around. Adults can replace the extension ladder with a play stop sign for older preschoolers.

Remember, ladders and signs are only reminders, not safety devices. Children still need close, constant supervision when outdoors.

Traffic Safety

For young children, traffic safety is another outdoor concern. Young children are not able to see ahead or react with caution to moving traffic. This is especially true when they are riding tricycles and bicycles. Children first must know that traffic can be unsafe. Traffic safety skills depend on perceptual judgments of space, speed, direction, and distance. In addition, these perceptions must interact. A child's brain and body must react quickly and correctly. Needed perceptual skills for traffic safety are not completely mastered until about 11 years of age.

Scoldings and warnings will not solve these safety problems. Rather, adults must set limits for play areas, supervise children closely, model safe behavior, and teach safety. (Teaching safety is discussed later in this chapter.) With experience and guidance, children will gradually learn traffic safety rules and practices.

Vehicle Safety

Car accidents are the leading cause of death for infants and children. Experts say protecting children with proper restraint systems could reduce that rate by 90 percent. **Restraint systems** include car seats, seat belts, and other devices that hold children safely in place while traveling in a motor vehicle. Approved restraints have passed crash tests and are designed especially for children of a certain size.

Infants and young children should be secured in certified car safety seats *every* time they travel in a motor vehicle, 22-9. This is the law in all 50 states and the District of Columbia. This law extends to taxis as well as personal cars. Additionally, the Federal Aviation Agency (FAA) recommends child safety seats be used in planes for children under four years of age.

Certified child safety seats are restraint systems for infants and young children that have been tested and approved by federal agencies. Certified child safety seats are commonly known as *car seats*. (Car seats are described in the next section.) Infant feeding seats and carriers offer no crash protection and should not be used in vehicles. Car beds should only be used with premature infants whose condition does not enable them to ride upright. In these cases, only federally approved car beds should be used.

While in a motor vehicle, adults should *never* hold a child in their arms or on their laps. This provides no protection for the child in the event of a crash. Adults cannot hold children on their laps and protect them during a crash. In a crash or hard stop, any loose objects will fly about inside the car. These moving objects exert tremendous force. For example, in a 30-mile-per-hour crash, a 10-pound baby moves forward with a force of 300 pounds. Such force is impossible for an adult to contain, meaning the baby will fly out of the adult's arms. At the same speed, an adult who weighs 125 pounds is thrown forward with a force of between one and two tons. This means a baby who rides on an adult's lap is apt to be

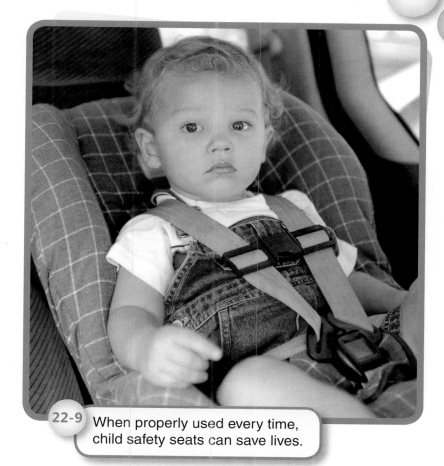

22-9 When properly used every time, child safety seats can save lives.

crushed in a crash. A baby sharing a seat belt with an adult is in equal danger, even when the car is moving slowly.

Types of Child Safety Seats

All child safety seats have a chairlike frame (seat back is higher than the child's head) made of a high-impact material. They are covered with a polyester-filled cushion. The frames have multiple slots for adjusting the harness and vehicle seat belts. The harness and vehicle seat belts keep the car seat securely in place inside the vehicle.

Many types of child safety seats are available. To provide protection, a seat must be selected to fit the child's age, height, and weight, 22-10. *Infant-only seats* are rear-facing and recline at a 45-degree angle.

Selecting Child Restraint Systems

	Birth to 1 Year	1 to 4 Years	4 to 8 Years[1]
Weight[2]	5 to 20 or 22 pounds	20 to 40 pounds	40 to 80 pounds
Height[3]	Up to 27 inches	28 to 34 inches	35 to 57 inches
Type of Seat	Infant-only or rear-facing convertible seat	Convertible rear-facing seat until at least one year[4] or forward-facing after one year[5, 6]	Belt-positioning booster seats
Seat Position	Rear-facing in middle of the back seat	Rear- or forward-facing in the back seat	Forward-facing in the back seat
Notes on Correct Use	★ Baby's head must be 2 inches below top of the seat. ★ Harness straps should come through the slot at or below shoulder level. ★ Chest harness clip should be at infant's armpit level.	★ Harness straps should come through the slots at or above child's shoulders. ★ Use top harness slots of safety seat for front-facing children. ★ Chest harness clip should be at the child's armpit level.	★ Use with vehicle's lap and shoulder belt. ★ Shoulder belt should cross the chest and rest snugly on the shoulder. ★ Lap belt should cross the upper thigh area. ★ The American Academy of Pediatrics recommends shield booster seats be used without the shield.

1. Although children may outgrow booster seats before 9 years of age, all children age 12 years and under must ride in the back seat of vehicles and be buckled.
2. Weight is more important than age in selecting the correct safety seat.
3. Height is most important for seat to fit properly with the head in a safe position and straps crossing the child's body in safe places.
4. Many new convertible seats are designed to hold infants and toddlers up to 30 or 35 pounds in a rear-facing position. A rear-facing position is a must for infants, but is also recommended for toddlers under 30 to 35 pounds. In a head-on collision, a rear-facing seat allows the force of the crash to spread evenly over the spine. Because the spine is so prone to injury in young children, a rear-facing seat can mean the difference between minor and severe spinal cord injury. Parents need to know that 20 pounds and 1 year is the bare minimum for using any forward-facing seat.
5. Some newer models of forward-facing only seats can be used by children from 20 to 60 pounds.
6. Some high-back booster seats with built-in harnesses can also be used for children 30 to 40 pounds.

22-10 Parents should choose the proper type of restraint based on their child's age, weight, and height.

Some of these seats come with detachable bases, making it easy to remove the seat while leaving the base still secured in the vehicle. *Convertible seats* face the rear in a semi-reclining position for children under 30 or 35 pounds and then face forward in an upright position for heavier children. These seats, which are bigger and heavier than infant-only seats, can be used from infancy through the preschool years. As the name suggests, *forward-facing* seats can only be used in a forward-facing position. These seats are not suitable for infants, but can be used for older children.

Although the law may permit older children to ride in the back seat with a standard seat belt, adults need to understand that seat belts were designed for adult bodies. Buckling an older child into the center back seat in no way matches the safety of proper equipment. Regular seat belts do not protect children who weigh less than 80 pounds for the following reasons:

★ Young children can slip through a regular seat belt because they do not have long, heavy legs to anchor them.

★ Regular seat belts can ride up to a young child's abdomen, where there are no bones to protect the child from the strain of the seat belt if a crash occurs. In a crash, the child's internal organs could be damaged.

★ The standard shoulder harness of a regular seat belt can move across a child's face or neck, which is unsafe. Young children need a harness designed for their size and body proportions to protect the neck and head.

To protect older children, *booster seats* are used to position children who are between 35 and 57 inches tall and who weigh between 40 and 80 pounds. Booster seats are used to elevate the child so the vehicle seat belt will be fastened in the right position. Thus, they are often called *belt-positioning booster seats*. Some parents prefer the newer *combination seats*. These seats can be used by preschool children with the harness. When children are large enough, they can safely use the same seat without the harness as a booster seat.

Choosing a Child Safety Seat

Adults may buy new child safety seats in many stores. Because babies can arrive unexpectedly, parents should choose, obtain, and install the child safety seat several weeks before the baby's due date. Hospitals will not release a newborn unless the parents have the proper child safety seat.

Parents will not want to buy a car seat more than a few months in advance, however. This is because car seats are often subject to safety recalls. In a **safety recall**, the manufacturer of a product issues a notice stating the product has been found to be unsafe. For safety reasons, consumers are asked to stop using a recalled product unless the manufacturer can provide additional parts that will make the product safe.

Before purchasing a car seat, parents can check the National Highway Traffic Safety Administration Web site at **www.nhtsa.gov/**, 22-11. For new purchases, they should always send the registration card that comes with the seat to the manufacturer.

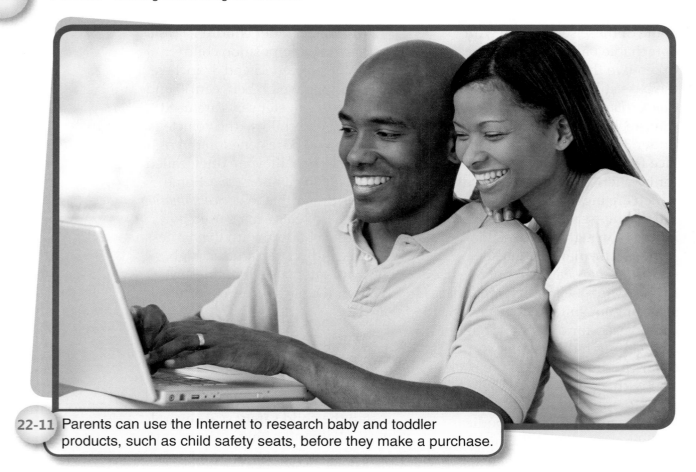

22-11 Parents can use the Internet to research baby and toddler products, such as child safety seats, before they make a purchase.

In turn, the manufacturer will notify the buyer of any problems or recalls.

In some towns and cities, adults may rent or borrow restraint systems from various programs or agencies. Parents may also borrow or buy used child safety seats. This practice is not advised, however, because the safety of the seat is unknown. Any child safety seat that is more than six years old or has ever been in even a minor accident is unsafe. If parents know a seat's owner and history, they might decide to borrow a newer, accident-free seat. They will need the owner's manual for the seat, however. If the manual is not available, parents can order another manual from the manufacturer.

Installing and Using a Child Safety Seat

Unless child safety seats are installed and used properly, they offer little or no protection for a child in a crash. For this reason, the American Academy of Pediatrics advises adults to read the directions carefully to install child safety seats correctly. Photos on the packaging should not be followed because these may be misleading. Adults should also read their vehicle owner's manual to ensure they are using the seat belts correctly. This is true whether the seat belts are used to restrain an older child or secure the child safety seat of a younger one.

A child safety seat attachment, called the **LATCH system** (LATCH stands for Lower Anchors and Tethers for Children), makes child safety seats easier and safer to use. In the LATCH system, hardware is mounted into the vehicle to hold straps that are attached to a LATCH-designed child safety seat. These straps hold the car seat in place without the use of the vehicle seat belt. The LATCH system must be installed in all new cars. For cars older than model year 2002, parents can check with the dealer about prices for installing the system.

For LATCH systems and other child safety seats, parents may want to seek help from a certified **child passenger seat (CPS) technician**. This professional can provide information on child safety seats and inspect them after installation. Parents can consult the National Highway Traffic Administration to find CPS technicians in their area. The American Academy of Pediatrics Web site (**www.aap.org/**) also provides useful information on child safety seats for all children, including those who are premature or have special needs. This Web site also provides an online shopping guide for child safety seats.

All restraint systems are designed for the back seat of the vehicle. Placing children in the back seat is important due to air bags installed for front seat passenger safety. If these air bags inflate, children under age 12 who ride in the front seat are in danger of serious injury or death. This is true even if they are in certified child safety seats.

Air bags are designed to work with lap and shoulder belts to protect teens and adults. Air bags inflate with such force they can injure or kill babies and young children who are riding in the front

seat, even in rear-facing child seats. Newer model cars may have "smart air bags" that measure the weight and closeness of the passenger and deploy more gently. Although these "smart air bags" are helpful, children should be in the back seat.

If adults have a vehicle with no back seat, such as a sports car or truck, they should realize these are not safe vehicles for children. If using another vehicle is not an option, these adults should have the "smart air bags" and properly use the rear-facing seat in the vehicle. In older model cars, turn off the passenger-side air bag when using a rear-facing seat. For older children in forward-facing seats, adults should use any air bag, but move the vehicle seat back as far as possible. They should advise children not to lean toward the dashboard.

Each time before starting any vehicle, an adult must make sure the child is buckled into the restraint system properly.

Public Information Specialist

Public information specialists arrange and conduct programs to maintain contact between organization or business representatives and the public. They handle organizational functions, such as media, community, consumer, industry, and governmental relations. Public information specialists often conduct research, prepare materials, maintain contacts, and respond to inquiries.

Education: Most public information specialist positions require a bachelor's degree, preferably in communications with broad liberal arts exposure.

Job Outlook: Employment is projected to grow faster than average.

Each buckle and strap exists for a purpose. Proper use of these is important to the child's safety. For this reason, adults should take time when needed to adjust restraint systems to fit the child properly.

Additionally, adults should set an example by always wearing a seat belt and driving safely. Children are less likely to resist using restraint systems if they and others in their lives have always used them. These children do not see using restraint systems as a choice. Children who have not always used restraint systems must be taught to do so.

Other Safety Measures

In addition to restraint systems, adults should set some other guidelines for safe travel in motor vehicles. First, they should make sure doors are locked at all times. They should never allow passengers—especially children—to ride in the following ways:

★ with any part of the body hanging out an open window

★ in cargo areas of cars, vans, or trucks

★ kneeling on the floorboard of the vehicle

If adults need to attend to a child's needs, they should pull the vehicle to the side of the road. They should not try to reach into the back seat while driving to offer assistance. When purchasing a car, adults should consider safety options, such as the following:

★ anti-pinch power windows, doors, and lift gates

★ anti-lock brakes

★ electronic stability control and anti-roll control

★ extra LATCH fixtures

★ back-up warning system

Baby Items and Toy Safety

Children's products cause many injuries each year. Many injuries can be avoided if adults choose baby items and toys carefully. Also, adults must realize that even safe products become dangerous when misused. This means supervision and safety lessons are crucial.

Selection

Selecting safe baby and toddler items and toys is important, 22-12. Some safety features are now required by law. For example, the slats in cribs and playyards must be spaced no more than 2⅜ inches apart. The law requires paint on baby items and toys to be nontoxic (without lead). Items and toys made prior to the enactment of a law may not meet the law's standards. Also, certain homemade toys may be unsafe if they do not follow the guidelines of the law. Similarly, adults must be extra careful about purchasing older toys at garage sales.

Most new toys that are unsafe for infants and toddlers must carry warnings, such as "Not Intended for Children Under Three Years of Age." Other items, such as lawn darts, cannot be sold in toy departments or toy stores because they are dangerous for children to use.

When selecting baby and toddler items and toys, adults should do the following:

★ Carefully examine items for safety features. Safety features are especially important on items for babies and toddlers.

Safety Standards for Baby and Toddler Items

Item	Safety Standards
Baby vehicle (carriage or stroller)	★ Should be pretested for balance and weight distribution. ★ Safety brake can be quickly set. ★ Protective bumpers should pad.
Bassinet	★ Sturdy bottom and wide, stable base. ★ Smooth surfaces. ★ Secure leg locks. ★ Firm mattress with snug fit.
Bed (toddler)	★ Use detachable rail with openings no more than 3½ inches apart. ★ Put padding on floor next to bed in case child rolls out.
Changing table	★ Sturdy. ★ Guardrails that are at least 2 inches high. ★ Safety strap. ★ Toiletries are out of reach of babies.
Crib	★ Slats must not be more than 2⅜ inches apart. ★ Height of crib side from bottom of mattress to top of railing no less than 26 inches. ★ Child has outgrown crib when side rail is less than three-fourths of child's height. ★ Children 35 inches and taller must be removed from portable cribs. ★ Latch on drop sides should be releasable only on outside and require a double kick. (This prevents young children and large dogs from tripping the latch.) ★ Crib sides should lock at maximum height. ★ Paint should be lead free. ★ Teething rails are preferred. ★ Crib should not have horizontal bars inside, because a baby can climb on them. ★ Bumper pads with 6 or more ties are the safest. They are not recommended until the baby can raise the head and should be removed once the baby can stand. ★ Corner posts are 1/16 inch or shorter or 16 inches or higher for canopy beds. ★ Place cribs away from windows, heaters, lamps, wall decorations, curtains, blinds, cords, and climbable furniture; a thick carpet extending beyond the crib could cushion a fall. ★ Remove crib mobiles, hanging toys, and bumper pads at 5 months; do not use stuffed animals or pillows until the toddler years. ★ No cutout designs on head- or footboards. ★ Buy cribs designed after 1987.
Crib mattress	★ When rail is in lowest position, the top of the mattress support and the top of the rail should be no less than 9 inches for standard crib and 5 inches for portable crib. ★ Mattress should be covered with durable plastic with air vents, which is then covered with a fitted sheet. ★ Torn mattress covers should be discarded. ★ Mattress should fit snugly in crib. Space between crib and mattress should be smaller than two adult fingers held together. ★ Should be firm rather than soft. ★ Move mattress to the lowest point once child can pull himself to standing.

22-12 Baby items must meet these standards to keep children safe.

(Continued.)

Diaper pails and wastebaskets	★ Keep out of reach of children. ★ Choose models with child-resistant lids.
High chair	★ Wide-spread legs improve stability. ★ Tray should lock in place. ★ Crotch snap and wrap-around seat straps are needed. ★ Nonskid rubber mats (available for bathtubs) placed on seat help prevent baby from sliding.
Playyard	★ Slats should be no more than 2⅜ inches apart. ★ If playyard has mesh netting, the weave should be smaller than tiny baby buttons and pierced earrings. ★ Floor should not collapse. ★ Hinges on folding models should lock tightly. ★ Check playyards for rivets (screwlike fasteners). If a rivet sticks out ¼ inch or more, stop using the playyard. (Pacifier strings and clothing can catch on rivet and cause strangulation.) ★ Stop using playyard when child can crawl out of it.
Vaporizer	★ Has Underwriters' Laboratories (UL) seal. ★ Cold water models are safer than steam models.
Miscellaneous	★ Replace metal hangers with strong plastic hangers. ★ Remove dry-cleaning bags or any dangerous product wrapping. ★ Use finger-pinch guards for door hinges. ★ Use UL listed night-lights.

22-12 (Continued.)

★ Carefully read labels and heed recommendations.

★ Check toys for durability. Make sure small parts are secure on all toys—even for older children.

★ Find age-stage appropriate toys. Age is only a clue to stage. Toys should be appropriate for the child's physical skills (ability to use the toy), mental abilities (understand how to use the toy), and interests. They should also have the needed age-stage safety features, 22-13.

★ Throw toy packaging away. Styrofoam®; plastic; small, plastic ties; and other packaging materials are safety hazards for young children. These materials are not meant to be played with and should be discarded. Parents should keep the identifying or safety information on baby or toddler items in a file folder. This allows them to check recall information or make a complaint.

Supervision

Adults should consider each toy in terms of how much supervision the child will need to use it. If a great deal of long-term supervision is needed, the toy may not be appropriate for the child's stage.

Safety Features for Toys

For Infants and Toddlers

Size should be larger than the child's two fists. Even large toys can break, exposing small parts. The law bans small parts in new toys intended for children under age three. Older and handmade toys may still have small parts.

Nonbreakable. Toys that break may expose small parts or break into small pieces. Toys made of glass or brittle plastic are the most unsafe.

No sharp edges or points. The law bans new toys with sharp edges or points intended for children under age eight. Broken toys often have sharp edges. Wires with sharp points are often inside stuffed toys.

Nontoxic. Painted toys should be labeled *nontoxic*. Avoid all painted toys for children who put playthings in their mouth.

No long cords or strings. Toys with long cords or strings should not be used with infants and young children who can wrap them around the neck.

Nonflammable, flame retardant, or flame resistant. Dolls and stuffed toys should be made of materials not likely to ignite.

Washable and hygienic materials. Dolls and stuffed toys must be clean when bought and must be easy to keep clean.

No broken or uninflated balloons. These balloons are the most dangerous objects for suffocation. (Inflated balloons are not safe for children under age five.)

No toys or games with marbles or balls smaller than 1¾ inches in diameter. These items are a choking hazard.

No parts small enough to fit inside a cardboard bathroom tissue tube. (Special measuring tubes are also available.) The law bans small parts intended for children under age three. Older and handmade toys may still have small parts.

No detachable clothing on dolls or stuffed animals. Fasteners used on clothing items for dolls or stuffed animals are very small and thus present a choking hazard.

No toys with springs or hinges. Springs and hinges can pinch fingers.

Sounds at acceptable levels. The law requires a label on toys that produce sounds above a certain level. The label warns, "Do not use within one foot of the ear. Do not use indoors." Toys making sounds that can result in hearing damage are banned.

For Older Children

Safe electric toys. Electric toys must meet requirements for maximum surface temperatures, electrical wiring, and display of warning labels. Electrical toys that heat are intended for children over age eight.

Items used for age intended. Chemistry sets, hobby sets, balloons, and games and toys with small parts are extremely dangerous if misused or left within the reach of younger children.

Sturdy, safe, large outdoor equipment. Space between moving parts is wide enough not to pinch or crush fingers. Bolt ends would be covered with plastic end caps. Swing seats should be lightweight and have smooth, rolled edges. All swing sets, gyms, and other large equipment should be anchored firmly to the ground.

Paints and crayons marked with designation ASTM D4236. The designation means the material has been examined and is either nontoxic or carries a warning.

No toys that are projectiles. Projectiles cause many eye injuries.

Safe tricycles and bicycles. Tricycles and bicycles should have proper assembly. Seats should be adjusted to the rider's height. (Adults should never purchase a tricycle or bicycle for the child to "grow into.") Pedals should have skid-resistant surfaces. Reflectors (at least two inches in diameter) should be used on bicycles. A proper fitting helmet should be worn at all times.

22-13 When selecting toys for infants, toddlers, and older children, adults should note special safety features.

Parents should consider waiting to purchase the toy or putting the toy away for a later date.

Supervision involves answering these questions:

★ Can an adult teach the child to use the toy properly?

★ Can an adult watch the child as he or she uses an electrical toy?

★ Can toys meant for older children be kept out of the reach of younger siblings?

Use and Storage

Adults need to think about the space needed to use and store equipment. In some cases, the size of a piece of equipment during use and nonuse is about the same, such as stringing beads, a xylophone, and a stuffed animal or doll. In other cases, toys in use require much more space than they do when stored, such as a puzzle with many pieces, large floor block sets, and toy tea sets and dishes. Adults must ask themselves other questions, too, such as the following:

★ Is there a safe place to ride a wheeled toy?

★ Is there a place to store outdoor toys when not in use?

★ Are there places to store toys to prevent accident-causing clutter?

★ Are special storage cabinets or shelves needed? (Storage items can be expensive, too.)

Maintenance

Baby and toddler items and toys should be checked to ensure they do not have the following:

★ recalls issued by the manufacturer or the U.S. Product Safety Commission (**www.cpsc.gov/**)

★ sharp points, jagged edges, and loose parts

★ any removable parts that are small enough to fit inside a child's mouth

★ rust on outdoor equipment, which weakens the structure

★ stuffed toys and dolls that must be repaired and cleaned

★ batteries not secured by a cover with a screw to prevent removal by the child

Adults should remove any broken toys from use. Children can seriously injure themselves with broken toys. Adults must properly dispose of those that cannot be fixed. They should repair any other broken items before they are put back into use.

Adults can add a few safety devices to baby items and toys, too. If a toy chest is not properly ventilated, drill a few airholes. Place a piece of adhesive tape around the wheel edge of skates to slow them. To remind children not to hold the chains of a swing too low (and thus be thrown off balance), mark chains with tape on the proper holding place.

Pet Safety

Because pets can bite, transmit diseases, and cause allergic reactions, adults must choose them carefully. Adults should choose breeds of animals that are less apt to bite. Dogs that are one year and older and cats that are nine months and older have developed immunity to many diseases. These animals make better children's pets than puppies and kittens. If children show an allergy to a pet, adults must keep the animal away from them.

Couples must realize that even happy-go-lucky pets may have difficulty adjusting to a new baby. They may resent being displaced by a new family member, especially one who gets so much attention, and may take aggressive actions. Pets may act out of instinct, too. For example, several babies in baby swings have been attacked by their family dog who grabbed the baby swing as though it were a thrown toy. Pets may try to protect themselves from children's rough play by biting. Parents need to talk with a reputable animal trainer about how to desensitize their pet in the months before a child is born. Parents must constantly supervise any situation in which their pet is near the child.

Veterinarians (animal doctors) should see pets on a regular basis.

The veterinarian will advise on regular care of pets. A sick pet should be examined at once.

Children should learn how to treat a pet, 22-14. Adults should not expect young children to care for a pet. This responsibility exceeds their development. In the lower elementary grades, children can begin to learn some pet-care duties from adults. Adults must also remind children to wash their hands after each time they handle a pet, pet housing (such as a fishbowl or cage), or pet items (toys and feeding containers).

Computer Safety

Millions of children use computers on a daily basis at home and at school. With the increase in children's computer use, both physical safety and

22-14 Pet safety includes teaching children how to handle and care for pets.

protection from adult content have become a concern. Parents can take steps to make computer use safer for their children.

Protecting Physical Safety

Children's posture and eyes can suffer when using computers. Computer work areas in homes are often designed with the adult in mind. Instead, the work area should be arranged with all users in mind.

To prevent posture strain, the work area should be at the right height for the child to reach the keyboard and mouse with ease and still keep his or her feet flat on the floor (or on a step stool or footrest if the chair or stool is too high). The monitor (screen) should be adjusted so the child does not have to tilt his or her head backward or forward. (Adults can readjust the monitor position for each user.) If the child uses books or other written materials at the computer, a document holder should be located close to the monitor so the child does not twist his or her neck.

Special care should be taken to prevent eye problems, too. To protect the eyes, adults should do the following:

★ Adjust the room lighting to match the lighting of the monitor. Bright overhead lights are often too bright. Use a dimmer switch on the overhead light, use a lamp with less wattage, or use a lamp with a three-way bulb that is on the lowest setting during computer use.

★ The screen should be glare-free. Reposition work area or use a glare-reduction filter on the computer. The filter should have the American Optometric Associations (AOA) Seal of Acceptance.

★ Children need to take breaks. Experts suggest a 10-minute break each hour. This is because lengthy viewing times can result in eye problems. Problems seeing clearly at various distances can occur if focusing at a particular viewing distance for too long. Computer users often do not blink enough while staring at a monitor. Eye irritation is more likely to occur with reduced blinking because blinking allows eye fluid to wash over the eyes.

Protecting Children from Unacceptable Content

The content of software and the Internet is constantly growing and varied. Most people have mainly positive experiences in using the computer, but there are risks.

One thing to keep in mind is that anyone in the world can publish on the Internet. Thus, some content can be erotic, violent, or even illegal. Children can access this content whether they are seeking it on purpose or happen onto it by accident.

Another danger happens when children connect online to strangers who have bad intentions. Adults have posed online as children to befriend children and lure them to meet face-to-face. At these meetings, these adults have committed sex crimes, kidnapped, or even killed their victims. Thus, parents have two roles in children's computer use—protecting children from the dangers and guiding children toward the benefits.

To help protect their child, parents may need to create technological barriers by using a **filtering program**. This is a program that prevents a child from accessing inappropriate material on the Internet. These programs can do the following:

★ block access to Web sites with adult content

★ block access to the Internet totally during set hours

★ create a log of visited sites

★ track Internet discussions in chat rooms

★ monitor software downloaded to a personal computer

Adults have several options when it comes to filtering systems. They can use any of the following:

★ a closed-system filtering program in which parents first approve the sites their children can visit, such as *Shared Access* or *Net Nanny*

★ a server-level filtering system

★ a closed-system and server-level filtering system together

★ an Internet filtering system restricting children's access to search engines that are not designed for children

Adults need to know that no filtering program or system is foolproof. However, parents can also guide their children by doing the following:

★ Locate computers in an open area of the house where use can be observed.

★ Monitor any software children are using.

★ Make sure there is a balance between computer use and other activities; some parents use time controls, such as *Bob* (Hopscotch Technology).

★ Set rules and guidelines for the child's computer use, 22-15.

★ Set a good example as an adult because children watch parents' behaviors on the computer as well as in other activities of life.

★ Plan special projects for children on the Internet. Special projects reduce time spent exploring the Internet aimlessly. Some experts estimate that as much as 90 percent of exposure to inappropriate content occurs accidentally while children are exploring without a specific goal.

Computer Safety Rules for Children

To promote the safety of children when using computers, parents should set rules, such as the following:

★ Use the computer only at times approved by adults. (Late-night or unsupervised use should be off limits.)
★ Do not give out any personal information or send any photos. (Children should use a pen name when on the Internet.)
★ Do not use chat rooms or bulletin boards unless approved by adults.
★ Tell parents about any uncomfortable images, information, or message and never respond to such messages.
★ Do not meet in person with anyone you have communicated with online without a parent with you.

22-15 By setting rules to govern their children's computer use, parents can help protect their children from the dangers of the Internet and guide them toward the benefits.

Safety Devices and Safety Measures

Installing and using safety devices are helpful. To help prevent possible accidents, adults must always anticipate upcoming hazards. Safety devices can aid in childproofing before the child is endangered. Parents can use developmental milestones to recognize the *sequence of skills*. For example, once a child can pull up, many more things are within the child's easy reach, such as doorknobs that give access to other dangers. Adults should never rely on *age norms* or past experiences to tell them when to childproof. Children develop at different rates, even within the same family. Also, some children explore more than others.

Appropriate safety devices for a given child's stage can help prevent accidents. For example, babies and very young children need electrical outlet covers and safety latches on cabinets and drawers. They also need safety knobs that require an older person's grip to open. Preschoolers and older children need computer safety devices. All children need gun and vehicle safety devices. Although safety devices, as well as room monitors, Webcams, and intercoms, are helpful, they do not take the place of careful supervision. Smoke and carbon monoxide detectors must be installed and kept serviced, too.

Adults also need to know safety measures for handling emergencies. Medical emergencies arise from both illnesses and accidents. Adults need to recognize symptoms requiring emergency treatment, 22-16. Adults

Symptoms Requiring Emergency Treatment

Seek emergency treatment when a child exhibits the following symptoms:

* ★ Looks or acts very ill or seems to be getting worse quickly
* ★ Acts very confused
* ★ Breathes so fast or hard that it interferes with making sounds or drinking
* ★ Has uneven pupils
* ★ Has a high fever (for infants under 4 months a rectal fever of 101°F or higher; for children over 4 months a fever of 105°F or higher)
* ★ Has forceful vomiting (for infants under 4 months—once; for children over 4 months—continuous vomiting)
* ★ Has severe headache or neck pain or stiffness
* ★ Has a seizure for the first time or has a seizure that lasts more than 15 minutes
* ★ Has a blood-red or purple rash *not* associated with an injury
* ★ Has hives or welts that appear rapidly
* ★ Has a stomachache that causes screaming or doubling up or has a stomachache after a blow to the stomach region
* ★ Has bleeding that does not respond to first aid
* ★ Has black or blood-mixed stools
* ★ Has not urinated for 8 hours
* ★ Has continuous clear drainage from the nose after a head injury
* ★ Has a fracture (broken bone)

22-16 Adults who note these symptoms should seek emergency medical treatment for the child.

must also take proper action. These steps include the following:

★ Apply first aid. **First aid** is emergency treatment for an illness or accident that is given before professional medical help arrives. Training in first aid can be very helpful to parents and is required as part of teacher training. First-aid supplies, including a first aid chart or book, should be kept current and nearby as well, 22-17.

★ Call the Emergency Medical System. Adults need to keep emergency phone numbers updated and quickly available, 22-18. When an emergency occurs at school or in child care, staff must read and follow the child's Emergency Medical Form; seek emergency medical help if needed; stay with the child until a parent arrives; and complete an incident report.

★ Continue first aid until professional help arrives and then do not interfere with the assistance.

Sometimes emergency situations occur due to fire, explosion, or weather situations. In these cases, parents or teachers should conduct evacuation or safety plans that have been practiced with children. They should comfort and reassure children who are frightened. A parent or teacher should have a flashlight and first-aid kit next to the evacuation door(s) or in the safety area for easy access. (A tote bag filled with these supplies makes it easy to carry while helping children.)

First Aid Items

★ Adhesive bandages (various sizes)
★ Adhesive tape
★ Antiseptic for cuts and scratches
★ Calamine lotion (for insect bites)
★ Gauze bandages and squares
★ Scissors
★ Activated charcoal (prevents poisons from entering the blood stream)
★ First-aid chart or book (for quick reference)

22-17 A few first-aid supplies are needed to treat minor mishaps.

Emergency Phone Numbers

Local emergency number: 911
Poison control center: (800)222-1222
Dentist: 555-6473
Doctor: 555-7654
Drugstore: 555-8901
Hospital: 555-7302
Neighbors: Mrs. Rodriguez 555-4060, Mr. Petersen 555-3867
Relatives: Grace Taylor (Grandma) 555-2323
Mr. and Mrs. Mason (Uncle Dan and Aunt Dianne) 555-3374
Taxi: 555-4222

22-18 Posting the correct emergency phone numbers near the telephone saves time in a crisis.

Safety Lessons

Teaching safety is an ongoing process that begins almost at birth and continues for life. The first lessons occur in the home and yard. They expand to include the total environment, such as school, water, traffic, and job safety.

Adults are models for children. A child will absorb the adult's approach to everyday actions and safety measures, such as buckling seat belts and looking before crossing streets. Adults may even exaggerate behavior to make safety measures clearer for the child. They may stop, look, and say, "I don't see a car coming, so we can cross now," before walking across a street.

Adults should carefully explain the boundaries of play. They must show as well as tell children what they can and cannot do. Warnings are more helpful if they are stated in positive ways. An adult may say, "Grass is for playing, and streets are for cars and trucks." Warnings stated in negative ways may tempt children to act in unsafe ways. Also, warnings that are repeated too often lose their meanings.

All warnings should be coupled with reasons, or the child may think a given action is okay if the adult is not watching. For example, adults should explain the importance of safety devices like seat belts, crash helmets, and life jackets. They should also explain how to use these devices properly.

Adults need to insist on obedience. Children want and need to be protected. Parents require obedience when they take action against wrong doings instead of simply threatening children. Taking action does not call for physical punishment. It can mean making the child come inside for a short time. Insisting on obedience is a way of saying, "I care about you."

Practice Safety Measures

Adults should practice safety measures with children. These measures might include a fire drill or a safe walk to school. Adults can also read books on safety to children. Adults and children can watch special segments on safety in children's television programs. To support the safety lessons, adults can have children talk about, act out, or draw the safety actions.

Preparing a Child for Routine or Hospital Care

Medical care should be part of children's lives on a routine basis as well as when problems arise. Going to the doctor or dentist can be stressful for both child and adult. However, there are ways to ease the stress.

Routine Care

Depending on their ages, children react in different ways to routine care. Children under two years of age often cry while being examined. (They may begin crying when undressed and placed on cold scales.) Two- and three-year-olds often cry, too. They may also hide from, kick, or push the doctor. (Hiding, kicking, and pushing are attempts to get rid of those who are checking or treating them.) Older children are better able to understand what going to the doctor means. These children are apt to become anxious ahead of time. They may become more anxious in the car or walking in the office. They often cry or kick during routines that are not comfortable. Many children are relaxed about procedures that are painless. Following the visit, older children may act bossy. This may help relieve the feelings of powerlessness they felt during the visit.

Adults can lessen some of the stress of routine care in several ways. First, they can select capable and caring health care professionals. Adults should feel free to ask questions. They should also feel the doctor answers their questions completely and clearly. The doctor and dentist should appeal to the child, too. Children often like doctors and dentists who greet them by name and in a friendly way. They also like caregivers who notice something personal, such as a child's new haircut or pretty dress. Talking to the child during the checkup and remaining calm, even if the child does not, are other positive qualities. Colorful waiting rooms and examination rooms also appeal to children, 22-19.

Adults should bring books and toys to appointments to make waiting more pleasant for the child. They should also bring a change of clothes, if needed. They should not give their child any candy or gum that changes the color of the mouth and throat. This may make **diagnosis** (identifying the cause) of an illness more difficult. Adults should arrive at the appointment with information and prepared questions.

Adults can reassure the child it is okay to feel sick. Pain or other sick feelings may frighten a child. Adults can explain a little about procedures and relate them as much as possible to everyday life. They may say, "X-rays are pictures," and, "The dentist will look at your teeth." Too many explanations, such as, "The doctor will use a large machine to make the X-ray," can add to a child's fear.

22-19 Waiting rooms that appeal to children make medical care less stressful.
Photo © John Shaw

Helping the Child During the Examination

During the actual examination, the following will help the child feel more comfortable:

★ Stay with the child and stand where the child can see you. (Dentists, however, usually prefer adults stay in the waiting room.)

★ Use a soft, soothing voice. A child may stop crying to hear whispered words.

★ Hold the child if the doctor asks.

★ Do not tell the child a procedure will not hurt if, in fact, it will. Instead, tell the child, "It will be all right," or "Soon it will be over." If the child cries, reassure him or her that crying is all right. Say, "I know this hurts, but it will stop hurting soon."

★ Do not distract a baby or child by making noises, such as jingling keys. Such sounds interfere with a doctor's ability to hear internal sounds.

Some babies and children cry louder when an adult tries to distract them. (Perhaps they feel the distraction means the procedure will be painful.)

Hospital Care

Hospital care is often a special problem for both parents and children. Parents see hospitals as places where people experience separation from loved ones, pain, and even death. Hospitals may also seem large and *impersonal* (not concerned about the child as a person). Parents tend to feel they are no longer in charge of their child's care once the child enters the hospital. Also, doctors or nurses often ask parents to assist during painful treatments, which can be almost unbearable for parents.

Parents or other adults may also feel guilty about the cause for needed hospital care. For example, they may feel they could have prevented a fall if they had watched more carefully. Adults might think they should have sought care earlier to keep symptoms from becoming more serious.

Children may also fear being cared for in a hospital. A child under four years of age might be most fearful of separation from parents. Older children worry about what doctors will do to their bodies. Children react to medical tests and treatments in the hospital in even more intense ways than they react to office visits. This can be because of the new people caring for the child. Also, the child may endure more frequent and painful tests and procedures. Hospital stays are longer than office visits, and the surroundings are unfamiliar, too. Children may think of hospital care as punishment.

Easing the Stress of Hospital Care

Parents can ease the stress of hospital care in many ways. First, they should find out as much as possible about the stay. This will prepare them to better help the child. If possible, they should tell the child about the stay ahead of time. The talk should focus on good points (time in the hospital will help the child feel better). However, adults should never be dishonest about what they tell the child. This can damage the child's ability to trust.

Allowing children to explore the idea of hospital care through play can be helpful, too. Using a toy doctor's kit and reading books about hospital care may relieve some of children's fears. Some hospitals have playrooms where children can act out hospital care. (The rooms also provide art activities, games, and books.)

An arranged hospital tour of the children's area may make the child feel more comfortable. The nurse who will care for the child should give the tour, if possible. Children need to develop friendships with those they will be seeing most often. This helps hospitals seem less threatening.

Parents should plan to room-in with their children when possible. Many hospitals provide a bed or reclining chair, food service, phone, television, and magazines for the parents of hospitalized children. Members of service groups may help parents by serving snacks or shopping for small purchases. They may also volunteer to sit with the child for a while so the parent can take a break.

During the Hospital Stay

While the child is in the hospital, parents can often meet the child's nonmedical needs, which may include feeding, bathing, and toileting. They should go with the child for tests and treatments when allowed. In some hospitals, parents can go with the child to the surgery room and stay with the child until he or she is unconscious. Parents may also be present in the recovery room as the child awakens.

During a hospital stay, children need items that comfort them and remind them of home, 22-20. Adults should bring some of the child's toys, pajamas, or other items to the hospital. If the child can have visitors or phone calls, adults can arrange for friends, adults, and siblings to stay in contact.

Older children may want to keep a scrapbook or box to help them remember their stay. The book or box might include pictures, hospital bracelets, covers to disposable thermometers, and syringes without needles. Children can show hospital items when telling others about their stay. Talking about a hospital stay, like talking about any other experience, is healthy for children.

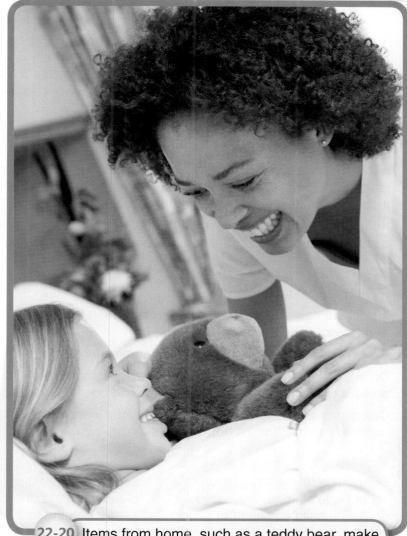

22-20 Items from home, such as a teddy bear, make a child's hospital stay more comfortable.

Caring for an Ill or Injured Child

Parents and adults who work with children will need to care for ill or injured children at some time. Children will experience many scrapes, bumps, and bruises as they learn what their bodies can and cannot do. Young children, especially those under age seven or eight, have many common illnesses, such as colds and digestive upsets. Adults often handle such small problems. Doctors also expect adults to follow through with care for more complex problems.

There are several common conditions adults must frequently treat in children. See 22-21 for practices doctors recommend. Adults should use a current first-aid chart or book to give first aid for major injuries. Taking a first-aid class is also very helpful.

Caring for Children's Health Problems

Fever

Fever is a temperature above normal body temperature. This is 97.6°F when taken under the arm (auxiliary), 98.6°F when taken orally, and 99.6°F when taken rectally.

Fevers under 101°F usually do not need treatment. Very young infants may be an exception. Ask the child's doctor for guidelines.

For higher fevers, use ibuprofen (unless child is dehydrated* or vomiting) or acetaminophen, **but not aspirin**. (Dosages are best based on weight, but child's age may be used for dosage unless the child is very light or heavy for age.) Sponge bathing can be done with medication or in place of medication if child is vomiting. To sponge bathe, use only tepid water (85°F to 90°F) in a room that is about 75°F.

Keep child's room cool; dress child lightly; encourage the non-vomiting child to drink fluids, avoid fatty diets that are difficult to digest, and keep child from exerting himself or herself.

Diarrhea

Mild cases: Continue normal diet.

Moderate cases: Use commercial rehydration fluids in generous amounts unless the child is vomiting and cannot keep these down.

Severe cases: May require IV fluids administered at the hospital.

Do *not* make special fluids to treat diarrhea, offer boiled milk or salty broth, treat with antidiarrheals, or prevent child from eating if hungry. As child begins to recover, put on BRAT diet.**

Call doctor if child is dehydrated,* has blood in stool, has a high fever (over 102°F), or diarrhea continues more than 24 hours.

Vomiting

Offer fluids frequently. (Toddlers and preschoolers can drink commercial rehydrating fluids and school-age children may have a 50/50 blend of sports drink and water. Avoid caffeine and high-sugar drinks.) If child vomits after taking fluids, offer nothing for one or two hours and then try ice chips or spoonfuls of liquid. After several hours without vomiting, begin solids, such as BRAT diet.** Do *not* offer raw fruits or vegetables, bran cereals, or dairy products until the child is able to keep down other solids. Call the doctor if baby vomits after every feeding in a 12-hour period or if vomiting is associated with swelling or a sharp abdominal pain, blood or bile in vomit, confusion or listlessness, signs of dehydration,* or combined with diarrhea for more than 12 hours.

Runny Nose

Use a nasal aspirator (rubber bulb syringe) to suck mucus from nose. Make saltwater drops by combining ¼ teaspoon salt with 4 ounces water. Place a few drops in each nostril five times per day. The drops will cause sneezing, which will clear the nasal passages. Use a cool-air humidifier in the child's bedroom. Call the doctor if other symptoms appear. (Do *not* use OTC decongestants or cold or cough remedies.)

Scrapes and Scratches

Wash with soap and water; rinse well. If desired, apply an antiseptic spray, cream, or ointment to the affected area. Cover with an adhesive strip or small piece of sterile gauze held with adhesive tape. Call the doctor if the wound is deep, puncture-like, or does not heal as it should.

Dehydration is the loss of fluid due to diarrhea, fever, and vomiting. Signs of dehydration include high fever, little urine output, dry mouth, crying with no tears, and "sunken eyes."
BRAT diet includes **bananas, **r**ice, **a**pplesauce, and **t**oast (plain).

22-21 Doctors often expect adults to care for these health problems.

Giving Medication and Proper Care

For many illnesses, adults are expected to give medication. They should use accurate measuring devices. A medically defined teaspoon contains exactly 1 teaspoon of liquid, but a household teaspoon varies from ½ teaspoon to 1½ teaspoons of liquid. For this reason, adults should use medically defined measuring devices (available at pharmacies) to give liquid medicines. This ensures they will give the correct dosage each time. Incorrect dosages may prevent infections from clearing up (from too little medication). They may also cause a child to be poisoned (from too much medication).

Adults should give medication to children in ways that make it easy for them to take. Babies may suck medication through a nursing nipple with ring attached. Some may take medication from a dropper or syringe (without a needle) inserted far back at the side of the mouth. Older children often receive medication from a medical measuring spoon. Before children can swallow tablets, adults can crush the tablets and mix them with sugar or a bite of food. An older child can learn to swallow a tablet by tipping the head back. This action causes the tablet to sink in the back of the throat. Children can also learn to swallow a capsule by bending forward. This causes the lightweight capsule to float toward the back of the throat.

Keeping an active child in bed is a challenge for most parents. As children begin to feel well, they do not want to stay in bed. Quiet games, books, DVDs, music, and paper and crayons can help children pass time. Visits from adults and other children (if the illness is not contagious) also help.

When children are ill or injured, they need a little extra attention. Babies and young children often need lots of holding and rocking, 22-22. Older children may need their illness or injury and the treatment explained to them. Most children enjoy little surprises, too. These might include a small gift, a special dish (if they can eat), or a get-well card. Above all, adults should appear cheerful and confident so they will not cause children to worry. If the child's attitude is positive, this can also speed recovery.

Caring for a Terminally Ill Child

Despite great advances, medical science cannot cure every illness. Among those who are **terminally ill** (have diseases that will result in their deaths) are children. Terminal illnesses in children may include congenital problems, such as heart and liver problems and cystic fibrosis. It may also include AIDS and some forms of cancer.

Facing the death of a child is one of the most profound emotional experiences a family can ever encounter. Often the family feels this period more keenly than the ill child. They feel a sense of loss before the death occurs. They show this by going through the stages of coping with death. Families show denial. ("The doctors are wrong.") They may try bargaining with their faith. ("Just let my child live and I will…")

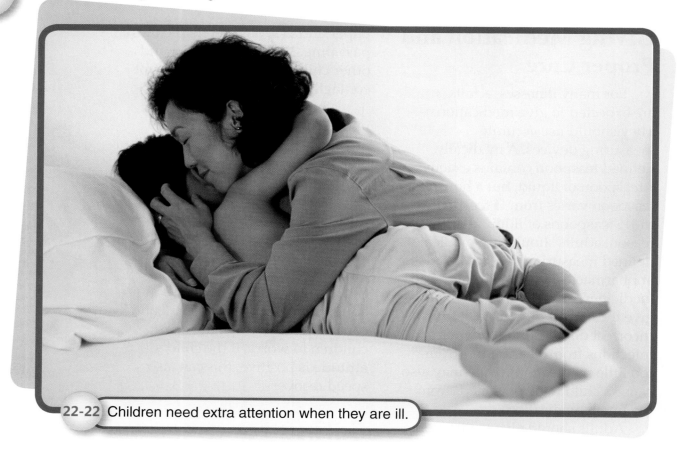

22-22 Children need extra attention when they are ill.

Families feel depressed thinking about the loss and its impact. Finally, they accept the idea of their child's death. Although family members feel sad, they usually want to appear cheerful for the child's sake or the sake of others. They also want to remain hopeful.

Helping the Ill Child Cope

Besides trying to cope with their own feelings, family members must help and seek help for the ill child. How a child perceives his or her condition greatly depends on his or her age. Children begin to understand death in the preschool years, but their understanding is rather limited until the school-age years. What and how much should a family tell a child? That is a personal decision best made after the family discusses the child's case with professionals and each other.

Parents need to find out how much the sick child wants or needs to understand about his or her illness. Older children often realize what may happen. They may fear possible tests and treatments, the separation that death brings, and being left alone. Ill children may be concerned about their parents' feelings of loss. Families must allow sick children to do all they can physically tolerate and as much as possible for themselves. They should try to help their terminally ill child experience his or her remaining life to the fullest.

Helping the Family Cope

Family members need the help of professionals during this time of crisis. Many hospitals that treat terminally ill children hire professionals, such as medical staff, religious leaders, and social workers to help the family. Parent support groups are also available. Members of these groups often provide much comfort. These people have gone through or are going through the same problems.

The family needs the help of friends at this time, too. Friends should learn as much as they can about the disease and its treatments. This will help them better understand what family members share with them. The role of friends can be described best as listening rather than advising. Certainly friends should not stop visiting. They should express their concern and sorrow with carefully chosen words. For example, saying, "I understand how you feel," may prompt a hurt response, such as, "How could you? Your child is healthy!"

If possible, friends should offer help. They should consider the family's needs and suggest a concrete way to assist. This might be an offer to cook the family dinner, mow the lawn, run an errand, or drive a healthy child to an after-school activity. Such offers are easier for the family than the vague offer of, "Let me know if there is anything I can do." Most of all, friends must remember that family members will need emotional support through calls, cards, and stopping by during the weeks and months before and after the child's death.

Summary

Protecting and maintaining children's health and safety is one of the major responsibilities of adults. In addition to teaching and modeling good health practices, adults need to provide a safe and healthy environment.

In order to monitor growth and development, adults should have children checked by health care professionals on a regular basis. Getting children vaccinated will protect them from many diseases. Children need prompt medical attention when they show certain or prolonged symptoms of illness.

Adults need to anticipate and remove possible hazards in their home. Childproofing the environment will help prevent many accidents.

Preparing children for routine or hospital care will help lessen their fear and anxiety. Ill or injured children should be treated as doctors recommend. Families experience severe emotional stress when a child is terminally ill. Caring friends and others can help family members at this time.

Companion Web Site

Interactive Activity

Review vocabulary terms and key concepts for Chapter 22 at **g-wlearning.com**.

Review and Reflect

Write your answers to the following questions on a separate sheet of paper.

1. True or false. Good nutrition serves as a physical support when an accident or injury occurs.

2. List the two best ways for adults to prevent accidents. (A) Warn or threaten a child. (B) Create a safe environment. (C) Prevent the child from doing dangerous acts. (D) Let the child learn lessons from dangerous experiences. (E) Teach safety. (F) Remove all unsafe items from the home and yard.

3. Why does the time of day affect the number of accidents children have?

4. True or false. The type of accidents a child commonly has changes with the child's age.

5. Poisonings of children under the age of five account for _____ (more than, less than) half of all accidental poisonings in homes each year.

6. True or false. Poisonings from plants are harder to detect than poisonings from household products.

7. What is the number one cause of death for infants and children?

8. Explain why holding a child on your lap or sharing a seat belt in a car is unsafe for the child.

9. List five ways parents can protect and guide children in computer use.

10. List four ways an adult can lessen the stress of routine medical care for a child.

11. Give three reasons that hospitals are stressful for the parents of sick children.

12. True or false. Teaspoons from household flatware are suitable for measuring liquid medication.

13. List two guidelines for helping the family of a terminally ill child.

Cross-Curricular Link

14. **Health, Speech.** On your own, list 10 guidelines you think parents should follow in promoting their children's health. Share your list with a small group of classmates, and listen to the lists of other members. Then, work with your group to create a "Top 10 List" that includes the best ideas of each member. Plan a creative way to present your group's list to the class.

15. **Financial Literacy, Safety.** Go shopping online, in person, or in catalogs to research the latest childproofing devices. Describe your top three picks to the class and explain how each of these devices works.

16. **Financial Literacy, Technology.** Compare the specifications and prices on two closed-filtering programs. Which one would you recommend, and why?

17. **Safety, Art.** Design a poster that illustrates a safety practice young children can learn. If approved by your teacher, display your poster in a local elementary school.

18. **Health, Safety.** Create a list of emergency telephone numbers for your home. Place a copy of this list near each telephone. (Use Chart 22-18 as a guide for the numbers needed.)

19. **Reading, Safety, Speech.** Select a children's book on a safety topic to read to children ages three to five years. Read the book to a child or a group of children. As a follow-up lesson, have the children dramatize or draw pictures about safety practices. You could also plan a different follow-up activity if approved by your teacher. Share your experience with the class in an oral report. Tell about the children's responses to the book and activity and your opinions about how well these worked.

Making Observations

20. Observe a group of toddlers or preschoolers at play. What traits of this age group make them prone to accidents? Give specific examples. How did adult actions or the environment prevent or lessen potential accidents?

21. Visit the home of a 6- to 12-month-old infant. What signs of childproofing are evident? What additional measures of childproofing would you recommend?

22. Observe toddlers or preschoolers in a doctor's waiting room. What environmental factors lessened children's stress? Did any environmental factors increase the stress? How did parents increase or decrease stress in children?

Thinking Critically

23. Explain the difference between a risk and a hazard. For a given child, can a hazard ever become a risk? Are some risks necessary for growth and development?

24. If a young married couple plans to have children soon, what advice could you give them regarding choosing a vehicle? Be specific.

25. Why are people often fearful of medical procedures or hospital care? How are the causes of these fears perhaps similar to those of young children? How might the causes be different?

23 Child Care and Education in Group Settings

After studying this chapter, you will be able to

- ★ **trace** the history of the major types of group programs for young children.
- ★ **describe** what to look for when choosing a quality program.
- ★ **explain** the effects of group care and education on children's development.
- ★ **describe** ways to help children adjust to group settings.

Terms to Know

child care programs
in-home child care
au pairs
nannies
family child care
center-based child care
for-profit programs
not-for-profit programs
work-related child care programs
school-age child care (SACC) programs
child care resource and referral (CCR&R) agencies
child development laboratories
Head Start

Montessori schools
kindergartens
private programs
fingerplays
regulations
public programs
adult-child ratio
developmentally appropriate practices (DAPs)
developmentally inappropriate practices (DIPs)
field trips
culture shock
bias
hidden added costs
hidden cost credits

Reading Advantage

Imagine you are a business owner and have several employees working for you. As you read the chapter, think about what you would like your employees to know. When you finish reading, write a memo to your employees and include key information from the chapter.

Companion Web Site

Interactive Activity

Learn more about comparing types of child care services by completing the *Read, Discuss, and Analyze* Activity for Chapter 23 at **g-wlearning.com**.

Why do some parents enroll their children in group programs? Some may work outside the home and need child care while they are gone. Others may need relief from caring for children full-time because of health (or other) reasons. Still others may use group care to challenge their children in all areas of development.

Programs for young children have not always been common. Today, the picture has changed. In the last three decades, the number of group programs has increased. Why? One reason is the public's growing concern about the need for quality education for children. Another reason is the growing number of parents in the workforce. Yet another reason is that quality group programs can affect children in many positive ways.

Along with the increased number of children enrolled in group settings, the types of programs have changed. Programs are now available to meet the needs of infants and toddlers as well as school-age children. These programs also serve more children from diverse cultures and children with special needs.

Types of Group Programs

There are all kinds of group programs for children, including child care programs, child development laboratories, Head Start, preschool (pre-kindergarten) programs, Montessori schools, kindergartens, and primary schools, 23-1. Descriptions of how these programs differ follow.

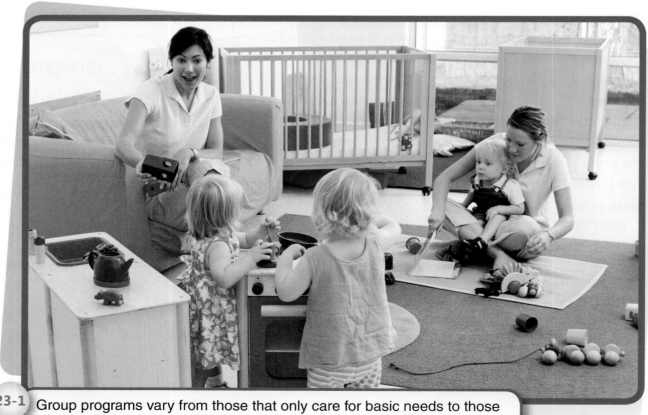

23-1 Group programs vary from those that only care for basic needs to those that provide many special activities to enhance all areas of development.

Child Care Programs

The term **child care programs** refers to programs that operate to care for children for extended hours, usually between 9 and 12 hours a day. The main purpose of child care programs is to provide basic care for children when parents are not available. More and more child care programs are providing education as well as care services, however. Child care programs offer services for children from infancy through preschool age. They may even serve school-age children at times when school is not in session.

Historical Overview

In Europe in the late 1700s and early 1800s, child care programs were called *Infant Schools*. These programs served poor children from toddlerhood to five or six years, at which age children entered the workforce. By the middle of the nineteenth century, child care for children of poor parents existed in urban areas of the United States. Many of these programs included programs to teach adults how to care for their home and children. Federal funds aided child care programs during the Great Depression of 1929 and World War II (1941–45 for the U.S.).

After World War II, child care programs declined until the 1960s. At that time, women entered the workforce in great numbers. The number of programs increased, but many were not high-quality child care programs. Currently, the increase in the number of children needing care is still larger than the increase in quality child care placements.

Types of Child Care Programs

Parents use four main types of child care—*in-home child care, family child care, center-based child care*, and *school-age child care*. Some parents use combinations of arrangements, such as center-based for work hours and relative care for other times. The type of care parents choose depends on many factors. These include the number and ages of children, cost of care, family goals for children, location of employment, work hours, and types of child care available in the local area. No one type of child care is best for every family; each type has its advantages and disadvantages, 23-2. In each type of child care, the quality of care may range from high to inadequate. Thus, parents must carefully check any child care arrangements before and during enrollment.

In-Home Child Care

In-home child care takes place in the child's own home. This type of child care can be provided by parents, relatives, or nonrelatives.

In some families, one parent stays at home to care for the children. Even among families in which both parents work, however, about 27 percent of all children younger than age five are cared for in their homes by a parent. Dual-career parents can provide this type of care by working alternate schedules so one parent is always home, taking children to work with them, or working from home. In-home care by a parent is more common for infants and toddlers than for preschoolers.

A little more than one-fourth of the children in child care are cared

Comparing Types of Child Care Services

Type of Care	Advantages	Disadvantages
In-home child care—A person is hired to care for children in the children's home.	★ The children receive all the caregiver's attention. ★ Chances of health and safety problems are small. ★ Children can be cared for when they are ill. ★ Children are not taken outdoors in inclement weather or during early or late hours. ★ Children stay in the home atmosphere.	★ Quality care can possibly be a problem due to the caregiver's limited education or training. ★ Parents must make alternative plans if the caregiver cannot work. ★ Parents must pay Social Security employer taxes. ★ Education activities are rarely offered unless the caregiver is well trained and does not have major housekeeping duties.
Family child care—A small number of children are cared for in another person's home.	★ A good selection of family child care services may exist. ★ Usually all children receive the attention they need. ★ This type of program suits after-school care. ★ Hours of operation are often flexible and meet parents' needs. ★ Children from the same family who are different ages may be cared for together. ★ Children stay in a homelike atmosphere.	★ Quality care may not be given in all family child care programs. ★ Many family child care programs are not licensed. ★ Parents must make alternative plans if the caregiver cannot work. ★ Children must leave the house each day. ★ Children may not be allowed to attend the program if they are sick. ★ Education activities may not be offered.
Center-based child care—A fairly large number of children are enrolled in a center.	★ Caregivers emphasize cooperative play and social living. ★ Centers are often licensed so basic quality may be ensured. ★ The center director makes any needed alternative plans when staff members are absent. ★ The center may provide special services, such as an educational program. ★ Facilities and equipment are designed for children. ★ Education activities are often offered.	★ Parents are often concerned about their children's health and safety. ★ The day may involve too many structured activities, especially for younger children. ★ A homelike atmosphere is usually missing. ★ A child may not receive the attention he or she needs. ★ Hours and days of operation are not flexible. ★ Payment is often expected in advance and even for days when the child is absent. ★ Ill or injured children may not be able to attend the center. ★ Children must leave their home each day. ★ Some centers are costly.

23-2 Each type of child care service has its advantages and disadvantages.

(Continued.)

| School-age child care (SACC)— Part-time care for school-age children while parents are employed or not at home. | ★ Children do not experience the risks of self-care.
★ In quality programs, children receive care, recreation, diversion, and education. | ★ Part-time quality group care is difficult to find, especially in rural areas, and may be rather expensive on a per-hour basis.
★ Most programs are designed for children grade 3 and below. (Programs are needed for children to age 14.)
★ Some children do not like a structured program after attending school all day.
★ Tutoring may or may not be available. |

23-2 (Continued.)

for by a relative. A little less than half of this relative care is done in the child's home. Only a small percentage of children have care provided by nonrelatives in the home. Three types of caregivers who provide in-home child care are *housekeepers, au pairs,* and *nannies.* Housekeepers are often employed on an hourly basis and take care of the children and clean the house. Au pairs and nannies are mainly hired to care for children.

Au pairs provide child care for a host family as part of a cultural exchange program. This exchange program might last from six months to a year. In addition to child care, au pairs also do light housekeeping. For their services, au pairs receive room, board, and transportation from the host family. Most au pairs are young, single women without children. They often have limited child care knowledge and experience. Although au pairs work for families, they are live-in guests of host families. Au pairs should be treated as members of families and should not be expected to work "around the clock." Host families are expected to provide cultural experiences and free time for au pairs.

Nannies are professionals who contract with a family to provide in-home child care. They typically care for children from birth to age 10 or 12. Like au pairs, most nannies are young, single women. However, nannies are not cultural exchange persons. They may live in the home or come to the home daily. Nannies do not do housework beyond preparing meals for the children. They have set responsibilities and hours even if they live with the family. Nannies often have training beyond high school in child care, health and safety, and nutrition. Some have a college degree and are certified. (These nannies are called: *Certified Household Managers, Certified Professional Nannies,* or *Certified Professional Governesses.*) Because of their training, nannies often earn more than housekeepers, au pairs, or babysitters. While some nannies stay with the same family for years, many see their jobs as short-term. These nannies often complete their schooling and then direct child care centers or teach in group programs.

Family Child Care

Family child care is care provided by a person for a small number of children in his or her own home. Some family child care homes are run much like child care centers. For example, these homes might offer a structured schedule, meals and snacks, and activities. Other family child care homes are run by a parent of young children. This parent stays home with his or her own children and provides care for other children, too. About 13 percent of children under age five with working parents attend family child care programs.

Many parents need family child care for various reasons, 23-3. These families might need more flexible hours than often provided by large group programs. Other families need family child care because larger group programs may not be available in their locale. Furthermore, many parents want family child care because they see it as similar to the type of care they would provide if not employed. Many family child care homes follow less of a schedule than child care centers. Children in family child care may do many homelike activities.

Advantages of Family Child Care Placements for Some Children

Children	Advantages of Family Child Care
Infants and toddlers	Using family child care for infants and toddlers is often much less expensive than using child care centers. Also, infants and toddlers need much individual attention, which may be available in a family child care home.
Children who are prone to mild illnesses, such as colds, sore throats, and ear infections	Pediatricians often advise parents of these children to limit the children's contact with large groups of children. Because family child care homes have fewer children, these may be a better choice than child care centers.
Children who need part-time care	Part-time care is more often available in family child care homes than in child care centers. Centers try to maximize their profits by filling as many placements as they can with children who need full-time care. Some centers charge the same rate for part- and full-time care, while many family child care providers charge a reduced rate for part-time care.
School-age children	Most center-based child care programs are designed for young children. These programs may not meet the needs of children who are school-age. Furthermore, most older children need only part-time care.
Children who live in rural areas	Many rural areas do not have much selection in center-based care. In these areas, many more children attend family child care homes than centers.

23-3 Quality family child care may be the best child care option for many families.

They may "help" the provider do housekeeping tasks, visit with friends who come to the home, and even go on shopping trips. Due to the many advantages of family child care, the military and some large corporations are seeking ways to increase the number of regulated family child care homes for their employees' children.

Child care laws vary among the states. All state laws limit the total number of children family child care homes can serve. Often this is six or seven children, including the caregiver's own children. If the children are all under two years of age, the total number is often four or five children.

Many family child care homes do not report their business to the state; thus, they do not have a state license or certificate of registration to operate. If the state is unaware of a family child care home, it cannot regulate the care provided there. Some of these non-regulated homes have too many children or do not provide safe care. Caregivers have not had a criminal background check. Thus, parents cannot be certain of the care provided in unlicensed homes.

Parents should instead seek a family child care home that is licensed or registered. Programs using government subsidies are licensed. In this type of home, parents can be assured of at least a minimum standard of quality. Still, parents must keep a watchful eye on their child's care.

Center-Based Child Care

Center-based child care is a large group program in which child care is provided in a center (not a home). Center-based child care is planned for children whose parents are full-time employees. Sometimes, these centers are called *preschools* because they serve preschool-age children. (In this text we will use the term *preschool program* to refer to another type of program.) About 29 percent of all children under age five with working parents attend center-based child care programs.

Centers differ in the number of children they serve. Many centers serve 20 or fewer children who are cared for in a building with one or two large rooms. Others enroll several hundred children who are placed in age-related groups and cared for in a multi-room building that resembles a school setting. State licensing laws set the standards for all aspects of center-based child care programs (building requirements, staff, and program).

Most center-based child care programs are **for-profit programs**.

Child Care Center Director

Child care center directors oversee the daily operations of child care facilities to ensure proper care and education of children. They prepare budgets, authorize purchase of instructional materials, and interview and hire teaching and service staff. Child care directors also confer with parents regarding facility activities, policies, and enrollment procedures.

Education: Some child care center directors have an associate's degree in early childhood education. However, a bachelor's degree in early childhood education or a related field is preferred.

Job Outlook: Employment of child care center directors is projected to increase rapidly.

This means they are set up to make money. Individuals or family corporations own them as a business. A few for-profit center programs have grown into national chains. Other center-based child care programs are **not-for-profit programs** (also called *non-profit*) although they need a profit to cover costs and to stay in operation. These not-for-profit centers may be funded by parents as cooperatives or by religious or service groups. Others are sponsored by businesses, hospitals, branches of the armed services, and colleges. Programs sponsored by businesses for their employees' children are often called **work-related child care programs**. Parents usually pay lower fees for a not-for-profit program than for a for-profit program.

School-Age Child Care

School-age child care (SACC) programs provide child care for 5- to 14-year-olds when school is not in session. This includes before and after school, on school holidays or vacations, and during the summer. (SACC programs are also called *before- and after-school programs* and *out-of-school programs*.) SACC programs are needed today because the majority of households with school-age children have working parents. Although schools provide care for children much of the day, the school day is shorter than the standard workday. Self-care is not a good choice for most families, so quality SACC programs are definitely needed. Part-time care is difficult to find in other child care programs because these are mainly designed for the full-time care of younger children.

The majority of SACC programs are affiliated with schools or agencies that serve youth. In the schools, space is often provided to non-school sponsors, such as the YMCA, to operate these programs. Other groups that operate SACC programs are religious groups, park and recreation facilities, housing authorities, military bases, family child care homes, child care centers, and companies. In some SACC programs called *clubs*, parents choose from a menu of activities for their children.

The basic goals of SACC programs are the following:
* care (protection, shelter, food, and guidance)
* recreation (supervised play or specific skill development, such as dance, ball games, or swimming)
* diversion (crafts, drama, or field trips), 23-4
* education (help with homework or lessons in music or dance)

As is true of all types of child care, parents may have trouble finding quality SACC programs and affording the costs for quality. For providers, the main challenges are finding suitable housing for a part-time program and planning details if space must be shared.

Trends in Child Care Programs

Several trends are seen in today's child care programs. These include the following:
* More infant and toddler care. The need is great because the majority of women return to their jobs within the child's first year. Programs for the

23-4 Some school-age child care programs provide materials for children to do craft projects.

youngest children are still most difficult to find. Quality infant and toddler programs are really scarce for they are very expensive and thus not affordable for many families.

★ Growth in SACC programs. Most SACC programs are in urban and suburban areas and serve children grade three and below. More programs are needed, especially those whose activities interest older children.

★ Growth in work-related child care programs. Some businesses, especially those employing many women and the military, are providing

work-related child care programs for their employees. Many other businesses are promoting the growth of child care programs within their communities and paying some of the costs of child care.

★ Growth in **child care resource and referral (CCR&R) agencies**. These agencies promote local child care programs and help parents find child care. They are funded by the state or by community business and civic groups. In CCR&R agencies, experts research the need for and availability of local child care. Information is given to providers and would-be providers to help them know what type of care is most needed and how to provide quality care. Although CCR&R staff members do not recommend a given program to parents, they share listings of local providers and information on the programs and current openings. They also help parents learn how to select quality programs.

Child Development Laboratories

Child development laboratories, formerly called *nursery schools*, provide education and physical care for children under age five. Besides these services, these programs serve as research sites for child development experts. They also offer training opportunities for students, teachers, and caregivers. Parents sign releases that allow for the study of their children and adult training in the classroom. All observing and reporting should follow ethical guidelines. Parents often get detailed reports on their child's development.

Nursery schools began in England in the early 1900s to help needy children. When nursery schools started in the United States, child development was becoming a science. The schools opened as laboratory schools directed by staff members of research and teaching hospitals and colleges. The schools studied children. They also trained mothers and teachers to care for and teach children.

Today, many child development laboratories are still part of research and teaching universities. These programs operate in some high schools, too. These high-quality programs are directed by child development experts who oversee adults' research and teaching. These experts also plan children's activities, which ideally build on life within the family. Thus, most activities are firsthand experiences. Children play in a setting that is rich with materials, equipment, other children, and teachers who are caring and well trained. (Child development laboratories should not be confused with campus child care programs which are operated for the benefit of college students needing child care. These programs are child care centers.)

Head Start

In the 1960s, Americans became concerned with the effects of poverty. Studies showed how important the early years were to a child's development. **Head Start** was launched in 1965 as a federal program for three- and four-year-old children from low-income families. These children needed food and medical care, as well as help in learning important concepts and language skills, 23-5. Head Start researchers realized that quality programs for infant and toddler development is critical for all later development. Thus, in 1995, the Early Head Start program was launched to serve children from birth through 35 months.

The Office of Head Start provides grants to local public and private not-for-profit agencies to provide educational, health, nutritional, social, and other services to children and their families who

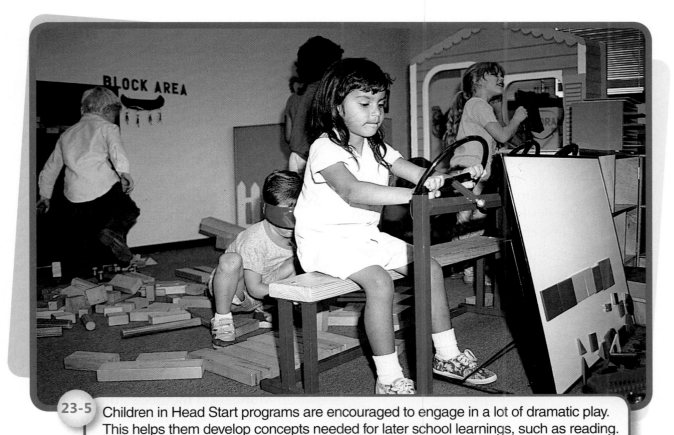

23-5 Children in Head Start programs are encouraged to engage in a lot of dramatic play. This helps them develop concepts needed for later school learnings, such as reading.

Photo © Nancy P. Alexander

are low income. Parents and families are a key part of planning and operating local Head Start programs. Head Start involves parents in their children's learning. The program also helps parents progress toward their own educational, literacy, and employment goals.

When program quality was good and home and school follow-through on basic goals occurred, research studies showed long-term benefits for children. Overall, these children have greater school achievement and higher high school graduation rates than their peers from similar backgrounds. Compared with these same peers, Head Start graduates also show better social behaviors as adults— more responsible in family, work,

and community settings. Experience with Head Start has also helped researchers know more about how to meet the needs of children from low-income families. This research is being applied to new Head Start goals, such as getting fathers involved, and to other early childhood programs, such as preschool programs.

Preschool Programs

Preschool programs, also called *pre-kindergartens*, usually refer to state-financed programs for three- and four-year-olds from families of low-income. Some states are already offering *universal preschools* (for children of all income levels) and others will soon follow. The majority of children in preschools are in public school settings, but some attend Head Start. A few children in these programs are in not-for-profit child care settings.

Some preschool programs use the Head Start program's learning standards, but offer fewer supportive services (medical and social) than Head Start. Other preschool programs offer specific learning curricula developed for the needs of these children, such as High Scope®, Reggio Emilia, and Montessori.

Montessori Schools

Another type of group program is a Montessori school. **Montessori schools** encourage young children to learn independently through the use of highly specialized materials rather than direct input from teachers. Children usually enter Montessori schools between ages 30 to 36 months. Montessori classrooms are formed from a group of children within a three-year age span. Children in this group are not separated by age, grade, or level. They are free to move about the classroom, work with other children, and use any materials they understand.

Sensory learnings that involve specialized materials are a major focus of the program. Activities center on what children learn to see, hear, touch, taste, and smell in the world around them. Self-help activities, such as preparing food and washing hands, are also a big part of the program. Cooking and other household-type tasks and gardening are ways children get physical activity while working. Materials are designed to teach math and language concepts, too.

Many specialized *self-correcting materials*, such as puzzles that work only one way, aid children's independent work. Teachers trained in Montessori methods guide the children's use of materials. However, they do not use direct teaching. In this way, Montessori schools strive to put each child more in charge of his or her own learnings. Montessori schools also emphasize work for works sake rather than play. For example, children really prepare foods rather than do pretend eating.

Learn More About...
Montessori Schools

Named for their founder, Maria Montessori, the first Montessori schools opened in Rome, Italy, in the early 1900s. Montessori was a medical doctor who had worked quite successfully with children with mental disabilities. This success led her to plan an all-day program for poor children between ages 30 months and 7 years. She named her school the *Casa dei Bambini*, which means *Children's House*.

Montessori schools opened in the United States in the 1950s. Soon, some of these Montessori schools began adding various activities found in American early childhood programs to the Montessori curriculum. These included creative art, dramatic play, science activities, and gross-motor play using playground equipment. Other Montessori schools, however, continued to follow the more traditional Montessori approach.

Montessori felt children can absorb and learn from their world as they work at tasks.

Kindergartens

Kindergartens are educational programs for four- and five-year-old children. In the United States, kindergartens are part of each state's public education system. Private schools sometimes offer kindergarten, too. Kindergarten serves as an entrance to school education and gives children the chance to play and develop through various activities.

Kindergarten is a German word meaning *children's garden.* The kindergarten was named by its founder, Friedrich Froebel, who thought children need nurturing like plants. He founded kindergartens as private programs in Germany. (**Private programs** are programs owned by individuals, churches, or other nongovernment groups.) The programs enrolled children from ages three to seven years and provided teaching suggestions for mothers with younger children.

Froebel felt a school for young children should be different from a school for older children. He planned many of the activities that occur in kindergartens and other programs for young children today. Examples include activities with building blocks, beads, art materials, sand, math concepts, animals, plants, stories, and music. Another example is **fingerplays**, or poems and rhymes that are acted out with the hands. These activities were unlike the drill methods used in other schools of Froebel's time. In fact, Froebel's statement that "play is the highest level of child development" was scorned by many of his time.

Primary School Programs

Because the early childhood years do not end until children are nine years of age, *primary school programs* are an important part of the education setting for young children. The United States has long mandated school attendance for primary grade children. These children may attend private schools, which include parochial or religious schools, or public schools.

Although each state sets its own learning standards, these standards

Focus on Social Studies

Kindergartens

Kindergartens came to the United States with German immigrants in the mid-1800s. Soon, English-speaking groups began to adopt the concept of *kindergarten*. People began to see the good effects of kindergarten on the lives of young children. Public schools began to include kindergarten as part of their public school system. States now mandate kindergarten attendance. Over the years, kindergartens have changed. Many are teaching beginning reading, math, and other abstract concepts. Many teachers and parents feel this causes too much stress on children. The challenge of kindergartens is to fit the needs of children today and slowly lead toward children's next years in school. What differences might a kindergarten teacher see in students who have been in preschool programs and students who have not, especially during the first few weeks of school?

are rather consistent throughout the nation. Children in all primary school programs learn the 3Rs (reading, 'riting, and 'rithmetic) as well as concepts in science and social studies. Many primary schools offer music, art, computer literacy, and physical education as part of their programs, too.

Choosing a Group Program

Group programs cannot replace the teachings of home life. However, when quality group life is used to support and enrich home life, children can grow in many ways. Children learn values away from home as well as in the home. Adults need to look for programs that promote their beliefs and priorities.

Parents should choose programs that meet the needs of their family. The needs of families differ, and not all programs will meet each family's needs equally well. To get a good fit, all families should consider a few basic guidelines when choosing a group program for children.

Regulations

Regulations are standards that govern a group program. Regulations cover housing, equipment, staff, children's services, and business operations. Some regulations, such as fire safety, apply to all programs. Other regulations apply only to private programs. Still other regulations apply only to public programs. **Public programs** are those funded by local, state, or federal government. Examples of public

programs are public schools and Head Start programs.

Parents must be sure the program they choose meets all applicable regulations. Even then, high-quality may be lacking for these three reasons. First, regulations are minimum standards. Compare this idea to passing a test. Some students pass with high grades, others barely pass, and many others fall between these groups. In the same way, even though a program meets regulations, it may still be of rather poor quality. The one exception to minimum standards is accredited programs. *Accredited programs* are not only licensed, but have met even higher standards of quality set forth by a professional organization. Thus, accredited programs are like high achievers on tests.

Second, some regulations are easier to check than others. If a fence is required around the outside play area, this is easy to see. On the other hand, evaluating the warmth and nurturance provided by a staff member is much more difficult to check. Third, some regulations are simply on record with little or no enforcement. For example, many regulations cover family child care, but due to the number of homes, they are seldom checked.

Housing and Equipment

The type of housing and equipment varies with a program's goals. For example, a family child care home, kindergarten, and Montessori program have different housing and equipment because they have different goals and activities. Furniture, equipment, and materials should meet the needs of the children in the program. No matter what type of housing and equipment are provided, these should be safe and meet health standards. The conditions must be sanitary. Adequate space for comfort and activities is a must. The housing and equipment should convey the message "It's nice here!"

Staff

Children have many needs and must have plenty of adult help and supervision. Staffing regulations assure that the number of children in one room and the number of adults who work with them are appropriate. The numbers vary from state to state. However, all states base their numbers on professional recommendations.

Group size should be kept small with adequate adult coverage. *Group size* refers to the number of children in one room who will interact with each other throughout the day, 23-6. Younger children and children with special needs must have the most physical care and supervision. Therefore, their groups must be very small. Older children require less physical care; thus they can be cared for in groups that are somewhat larger.

Regulations also state how many adults must be on duty in each child care program. The **adult-child ratio** (read as *adult to child ratio*) is the number of adults per number of children. An adult-child ratio of 1:10 (read as *adult to child ratio of 1 to 10*) means 1 adult per 10 children. This ratio can be reversed by saying child-adult ratio is 10:1 (read as *child to adult ratio is 10 to 1*). This means

exactly the same thing—there are 10 children for each adult. Similar to group size, programs enrolling the youngest children and children with special needs have better adult-child ratios. (See 23-6 again.)

Adults should ask about group size and adult-child ratios when choosing a program. After enrolling their child, they should spot check on these numbers at different times of the day. (Some directors enroll the maximum number of children and then allow drop-in children to attend, which increases the number beyond legal limits.)

In addition to teachers or caregivers, group programs need other staff members to direct the center, prepare meals, clean, and perform other special duties. These people, as well as regular volunteers, are called *support staff*.

Recommended Group Sizes and Adult-Child Ratios

Age of Children	Group Size*	Adult-Child Ratio*
0 to 1 year	6	1:3
1 to 2 years	8	1:4
2 to 3 years	12	1:6
3 to 6 years (excluding first grade)	18	1:9

* Numbers for group size and children per adult should be reduced if children with special needs are included.

23-6 For safety and quality programming, group programs for young children should adhere to recommended group size and adult-child ratios.

Support staff are vital to quality programs, but are not counted when the adult-child ratio is calculated.

Children need adults who are in good physical and mental health. Children must feel secure, loved, and wanted. To feel loved, children must know they matter to others. They need to have adults who hug, comfort, listen to, and talk with them. Children even need adults to say *no* and correct them when needed.

Adults must also guide children in their care. Children need adults to help them develop during their early years. In order to meet children's needs, adults must apply their knowledge of child development at each stage. For example, adults who care for infants must cuddle them and accept their dependency. Caregivers of toddlers must encourage them to explore and learn. Adults who serve preschool children must welcome their curiosity, questions, and energy.

Staff members must also work well with adults. They must be able to work together as a team. Staff members must also be able to communicate well with parents. They must be sensitive to parents' concerns and convey needed information about each child to his or her parents.

Parent Communication and Participation

In high-quality programs, staff members promote parent involvement. When parents and teachers work together, it is best for children's development. For better communication and participation, teachers or caregivers need to do the following:

★ Convey the importance of parents. Parents need to know they play the most important role in their child's life. They need to feel respected by the staff as the child's first teacher. Studies show the parent-child relationship influences the child's development more than any other aspect of a child's life.

★ Know about each family they serve. Part of knowing includes understanding how a family's culture might influence parenting practices and child development. Culture also influences how parents view behavior because cultures differ in their priorities and beliefs. Thus, those who work with young children need to understand culture and how it affects families. Even within the same culture, however, not everyone sees the "ideal child" in the same way. Thus, the teacher must get to know each child's family.

★ Find ways to work with parents as a team. To do this, the teacher must know a great deal about child development and understand and be open to a parent's specific goals for a child. The teacher must also examine his or her own beliefs, attitudes, and goals. If the goals of the teacher and parent differ, the teacher should find ways to meet both sets of goals, 23-7, except when parent wishes violate program policy or professional ethics.

Combining Parent and Teacher Goals

Goal area: Discipline

Teacher's goal and reason: Children should begin to learn self-control. Through learning self-control, children use problem-solving skills to resolve conflicts and gain self-esteem.

Parents' goal and reason: Children should respect authority. Children have to respect parents, just as adults have to respect the authority of their employers.

Using both goals: After discussing both goals, the teacher may suggest how both can be met. For example, children will be asked to resolve some of their conflicts with the teacher's help. They will also be expected to follow rules and show respect for other people and property. In some situations (such as safety issues), children will be expected to comply immediately with what the teacher says.

23-7 Teachers and parents should work as a team in setting goals for children in a group program.

★ Know the ways in which parents prefer to communicate with and participate in their children's group program. Parents have the right to refuse all communication and involvement. Teachers must accept this choice, but leave the door open for them to change their minds. For the parents who will participate, teachers need to offer some options, 23-8.

Program Activities

Program activities vary with the goals of early childhood programs. Goals should be determined in keeping with **developmentally appropriate practices (DAPs)**. A program with DAPs is one that uses knowledge about the following:
★ child development
★ the strengths, needs, and interests of each child within the group

★ the social and cultural contexts in which children in a given program live

The opposite of DAPs are **developmentally inappropriate practices (DIPs)**. A program with many DIPs is not a desirable environment for young children. Parents should avoid placing their child in this type of program.

It can be somewhat difficult to determine whether a program has DAPs or DIPs. To judge whether a certain practice is developmentally appropriate or inappropriate, you would have to consider the development of the children and the circumstances surrounding the practice. For example, asking two-year-olds to sit still for a 15-minute story would likely be considered as a DIP. However, this same activity would be a DAP for five-year-olds. (Sitting still this long might still be a DIP for a given five-year-old with a short attention span.)

Communicating and Involving Families

Family Communication

Parent room or reception area
★ Photos and stories of program activities are displayed on a bulletin board.
★ Materials including videos on child development and the group program are available for parents to read and view.
★ Handouts for parents are available.
★ Informal networks often form among parents.

Group meetings and workshops
★ Orientation meetings are helpful for parents and children.
★ Discussion groups on child development, program activities or policies, or community concerns can be planned as needed.
★ Make-and-take workshops are popular with parents. (Parents, who are provided materials and directions, make a take-home learning game for their child.)

Open house
★ Parents see facilities and view displayed materials, such as children's drawings and stories.
★ Parents may participate in some of the children's activities.
★ Parents and extended family members meet staff members and other families.

Individual conferences
★ Teachers and parents set goals for child in the group program.
★ Teachers and parents review child's work, accomplishments, strengths, and needs.

Home visits
★ Teachers see child and family in home setting.
★ Parents share some of the child's home life.
★ Children bond with their teachers.

Parent visits to the program
★ Parents see their child in the program.
★ Parents learn more about the program's goals and activities.

Newsletters
★ Parents receive descriptions of current program activities, suggestions for home learning and fun activities, and information on new books, Web sites, TV shows, or community events.
★ Parents receive newsletters weekly or monthly. Some programs also post newsletters on the program's Web site.

Informal notes to family members
★ Parents learn about a child's activity or achievement.
★ Staff members recognize each family's special events (new baby, new job) and show concern for family problems (illness, death).

23-8 Teachers can find a variety of ways to communicate with parents and invite their participation in the group program.

(Continued.)

Family Participation

Member of an advisory board

★ Parents help plan activities for program.

★ Parents can advise director or administration on desired program goals, such as services needed for children or families.

★ Parents can discuss general concerns.

Volunteer in the program

★ Parents can be regular volunteers either assisting in program activities or making learning materials for the children's use.

★ Parents can serve as occasional volunteers by helping teachers during children's outings or special activities in which extra adult help is needed; helping with fundraising activities; sharing talents, hobbies, or work roles with children; or helping with special cleaning, painting, or repair jobs at the program site.

23-8 *(Continued.)*

In choosing the right group program, parents should know the major DAPs that make for high-quality early childhood programs, 23-9.

Generally, a program that uses DAPs promotes all areas of development. This type of program builds confidence and gives children the feeling they can handle tasks themselves.

Programs with DAPs use day-to-day routines to help children learn. In these programs, eating serves more purposes than curbing hunger. Snacks and meals offer a time to learn about foods and styles of eating. Eating also offers the chance to practice table manners and talk with others. Self-care is also part of daily routines. Children want to become independent by learning to take care of themselves. Many programs encourage self-help skills.

In programs with DAPs, activities are often planned as ways to help children develop. These program activities often include

★ language learnings. Language skills are improved by talking, listening, and reading (or looking at) good books.

★ math learnings. Math skills are developed by counting, matching shapes in puzzles, and seeing who is taller.

★ social learnings. Social learnings increase as children try new home and world of work roles and help each other. Holidays and birthdays are fun social events, too.

★ science learnings. Learning about living and nonliving worlds is most exciting for young children. Children learn through activities with pets, plants, foods, water, sand, and many other things.

★ creative fun. Children enjoy expressing themselves through art, dramatic play, music, and storytelling.

Contrasting Developmentally Appropriate and Inappropriate Practices

	DAP	DIP
Program goals	Goals are planned for physical, mental, and social development. Children are seen as individuals who differ developmentally and will grow and change at their own rates. Children are also seen as having their own unique styles of learning, their own interests, and cultural understandings.	Goals are mainly planned for mental development. Although children may differ developmentally at time of program entrance, they should achieve age-norms by the end of the program. Children's unique styles of learning, interests, and cultural understandings are not seen as important; children must conform to group instruction.
Housing and materials	Room is arranged with several learning or activity centers (art, book, science, manipulative, blockbuilding). Materials are mainly for play. Most materials have no right or wrong answers (dramatic play props, art materials, sand, and water). Many materials invite children to play together in small groups.	Room is often arranged with tables with an assigned place for each child facing the teacher's desk. Materials are often workbooks or duplicated sheets for teaching beginning reading and arithmetic. Drill software is often used on computers.
Curriculum content	Children's activities help them develop gross- and fine-motor skills, literacy skills, social and scientific concepts, and creative abilities.	Children's learnings are mainly focused on developing reading and arithmetic skills. All other activities are not seen as important.
Assessment	Teachers assess children mainly through observations and note what they observe about each child in anecdotal records, check sheets, etc. Teachers also collect samples of children's work (artwork, photos of children's block structures, and videos of children in many types of activities). Often a *portfolio* (much like a scrapbook) is kept, which includes the teacher's observations of a child and samples of the child's work. This portfolio is shared with the parents.	Teachers give "paper and pencil" tests and even end-of-the-year standardized tests. Scores that compare each child with the norms (how the typical child does) are shared with the child's parent(s).

23-9 Programs with DAPs are based on child development, the strengths, needs, and interests of each child, and the child's social and cultural context. In contrast, programs with DIPs are based on teacher expectations for the group of children, and these expectations are often directed mainly toward early academic achievement.

(Continued.)

Teaching methods	Teachers permit children to work on their own or in small groups as much as possible. Through the teacher's constant observations, he or she decides when the children need a little help or when the housing or materials need changing.	Teachers do a great deal of group "telling." Drill methods are often used for learning (such as colors, letters, and numbers).
Guidance of children	For a given child, teachers encourage self-control based on his or her stage of development. Teachers help children achieve self-control through simple explanations ("Hitting hurts."), modeling the desired behavior, and redirecting ("Chairs are for sitting. You may climb on the _____.") Teachers use positive comments when children use self-control.	Teachers expect all children to sit still and listen most of the day. When they do not conform, they are often punished (time-out chair, etc.). Treats are sometimes given as a bribe to keep children doing what teachers expect.

23-9 *(Continued.)*

★ motor skills. Gross-motor skills are developed through active play, especially outdoor play. Fine-motor skills are improved as children manipulate materials, such as art materials, puzzles, and building materials.

Many good programs invite adults who are not on staff to share their special skills with children. These volunteers (including parents) can teach the children and be role models for them. When a parent shares skills, this builds the self-esteems of both the parent and child.

To provide firsthand learnings, teachers can plan **field trips** (outings) that take children to places off the program's property. Field trips are a fun way to teach children about their community. For example, a field trip to the fire station helps children learn about the firefighters who protect their community. This field trip can help children experience firefighting in a way they cannot through regular classroom activities and materials.

Cultural Diversity in Group Programs

Children in group programs reflect the great cultural diversity of society. They are members of families that differ in language, social customs, beliefs, and goals for their children. Some children entering group programs may experience **culture shock**, an uncomfortable response to an unfamiliar culture. Children may also sometimes encounter **bias**, a belief or feeling that results in unfair treatment of another person or makes such treatment seem right.

As young children work to develop self-awareness, they notice differences between themselves and others, too. In a carefully planned program, children have the chance to build self-identity, respect diversity, and develop anti-bias attitudes. In such a program, adults

★ affirm each child's identity. Adults should learn how to pronounce each child's name and say useful words in the child's language. They should help children learn to describe themselves and their activities. They should respond to children's questions and comments about culture in positive ways.

★ respect diversity by making the program culturally rich. Children need to live in a classroom that represents people from many cultures. Characteristics of a culturally rich program can be noted in materials, activities, and people, 23-10.

★ help children learn that biased behaviors hurt. Adults might read books on feelings

Characteristics of a Culturally Rich Program

Materials

★ Books about all types of children and families, books that show positive roles, and books that celebrate various cultural activities and customs
★ Housekeeping centers filled with dolls of both genders and various cultural and ethnic groups; tools, play foods, and cooking utensils from various cultures
★ Puzzles, pictures, and posters depicting families from various cultures
★ Crayons, paints, and paper to represent all skin tones
★ Musical instruments and recordings from various cultures
★ Toys and games from around the world
★ Photos and posters of multicultural activities shared in the program

Activities

★ Reading stories, singing songs, learning poems, cooking foods, or playing games that have their origins in various cultures
★ Learning words, phrases, songs, or rhymes in various languages
★ Using art materials to depict oneself and others, various celebrations, and multicultural program activities
★ Sharing an object from home or telling and showing photos about a family activity
★ Attending parades and festivals in the community
★ Making a book of multicultural activities using photos, children's artwork, and child-dictated stories of these activities

People

★ Welcoming volunteers of all cultural and ethnic groups and generational groups
★ Having parents from various cultures share activities involving favorite foods, songs, stories, and games
★ Seeing people of various cultures and both genders engaged in their work roles

23-10 The ideal multicultural community begins in group programs for young children.

and describe feelings when hurtful things are said and done. Adults can also help children find ways to include others during play and avoid competitive situations, such as "boys versus girls" or games with winners and losers.

Providing Child Care and Education for Children with Special Needs

More and more children with special needs are enrolling in child care and education programs. To meet the needs of all children, many group programs for young children practice *inclusion*. This means placing of children with special needs and other children in the same group, while providing special help for the children who need it.

Inclusion seems very natural in programs for young children. In these programs, diversity of all kinds is seen as positive. Furthermore, teachers and caregivers in programs often work in teams. Thus, it seems natural for a teacher or caregiver to work with other adults who provide help for children with special needs.

In inclusionary programs, the room must be arranged with children's special needs in mind, 23-11. For example, space must be provided for the ease of movement of children with wheelchairs and walkers. Teachers and caregivers also learn how to help the children with this equipment.

Planning activities requires teamwork. All children work on many of the same concepts and skills.

23-11 Group programs need to meet the special needs of children, as well as including them in class activities.
Photo courtesy of RIFTON for People with Disabilities

However, some activities must be adapted for children with special needs. Activities are easiest to modify when they involve a single child. For example, a child with disabilities could enjoy puzzle time with other children by using a puzzle with fewer pieces or larger knobs. This accommodation is easy to make.

The learning needs of all children can be met in group activities, too. For example, a teacher may include squatting and singing in a beanbag toss game. Many children could do all parts of the activity, while children with special needs could enjoy at least parts of the activity. The nature of each child's needs determines what he or she can do. A child with physical disabilities might not be able to squat or toss the beanbag, but could learn the song.

A child with hearing loss can enjoy squatting and tossing the beanbag, even if he or she cannot hear the song. Thus, teachers can plan activities that meet the goals of all children and truly include children with special needs.

Other Considerations

Some families need child care programs that offer some special services. These services might include transportation to and from the program, child care for the mildly ill, or extended-hour care. Programs with these services are not always conveniently located. If several families need the same services, they may be able to persuade programs to add these services. Work-related child care programs are good examples of how businesses have met the special child care needs of their employees. For example, some hospital child care programs are open 24 hours a day to serve employees' children.

Good programs for young children cost money. Costs of programs are rising due to increased costs of staff salaries, buildings, equipment, food, and supplies. Costs of programs vary with the type of program, days and hours of care, age-group served, and location.

Families may or may not have to pay all program costs. For-profit programs earn most, if not all, of their income by charging fees (also called *tuition*). These programs cost families the most money. Not-for-profit programs are often funded mainly by nonfamily sources, such as the state and federal government or service groups. Often families either pay

little or none of the costs for these programs. Not-for-profit programs that are operated as *cooperatives* (co-ops) are funded by families. In co-ops, parents offer their time and services to help keep costs low. Work-related child care programs are usually funded by both the business and through parent fees.

Families must decide what they can afford and seek the best program for their money. Often families spend 10 percent or more of their total gross income to meet child care costs. Besides the direct costs, families need to look at the costs in terms of **hidden added costs**. These are costs that add to the direct costs. Examples are costs of transportation, supplies, and disposable diapers (if cloth diapers would have otherwise been used). Services or items donated to a child care program are hidden added costs, too. Families must also consider **hidden cost credits**. These are credits that lower direct costs of child care. They include money earned from a second income. They also include money saved in the cost of utilities, food for at-home care, and child-care tax credits.

Quality of Group Programs

Only high-quality programs can have good effects on children. However, parents cannot judge a program by simply meeting the staff members or checking the indoor and outdoor areas. Also, they cannot judge a program by noting the papers that say the program meets state standards. The only way to be sure of a program's quality is to observe the day-to-day activities.

Families need to quickly recognize programs that are unsafe for children. The following are signs of low-quality programs:

★ parents cannot visit without asking in advance (Programs should welcome parents' visits at any time.)

★ staff members are not trained to work with young children

★ the program does not take special interest in children's needs (Programs with large groups of children and few adults are more likely to have this problem.)

★ adults push children to perform above their abilities, causing them stress

Adults need to remember that children are defenseless clients of programs they attend. That is, young children cannot measure the quality of a program for themselves or take action if the quality is poor. Children depend on their parents to find quality programs for them.

See 23-12 for a checklist to use when evaluating a child care facility. As many children often spend a great deal of their early life in child care, parents must make sure the program meets the needs and priorities of their family.

Effects of Group Care on Children

Families are concerned with the effects group care has on their children. They want to do what is best for their children. Experts have studied the effects of group care on children's health, mental development, and social development.

Effects on Health

There has been some concern over the health of young children enrolled in group programs. Studies do not agree on the number of common illnesses in enrolled children versus children not enrolled. Centers that enroll 50 or more children seem to have a higher rate of illness as compared to programs with lower enrollments. However, there seems to be no increase in serious illness in children who attend programs that follow good health practices. Families should consult their doctors about what is best for their children. For some children with chronic illnesses, pediatricians may advise less exposure to others through in-home child care or family child care programs.

Effects on Mental Development

Group programs do not seem to have either a positive or negative effect on the mental development of children from middle-class homes. As a whole, group programs offer more activities in certain areas than do most homes. Programs such as Head Start and preschools can help the mental development of children from low-income families. If gains from such programs are to remain stable, however, home and school follow-up is needed for many years.

Effects on Social Development

Since the early 1900s, experts have been concerned that group programs might weaken bonds between children and families.

Child Care Program Checklist

Overall Evaluation

_____ Does the program meet regulations?

    _____ Is the child care center licensed?

    _____ Is the family child care home licensed or registered?

    _____ Is the licensed center or family child care home also accredited?

Health and Safety

_____ Does the inside and outside appear clean, orderly, and safe?

    _____ Is the outside area fenced?

    _____ Are both the inside and outside areas childproofed?

    _____ Are equipment and materials in good condition?

_____ Do staff members follow good health and sanitation practices?

_____ Is at least one staff member trained in first aid?

_____ Are parents required to complete health records and emergency forms?

_____ Has the facility been inspected by the fire department and health department?

_____ Are disaster emergency plans posted and practiced?

Equipment and Materials

_____ Is the equipment the right size for children?

_____ Is the furniture the right size for children?

_____ Are the equipment and materials right for the children's ages and special needs?

_____ Is there a variety of equipment and materials available?

_____ Is there enough equipment and materials for all children in the program?

_____ Do the materials invite a child to play?

_____ Are there shelves for the equipment and materials when they are not in use?

_____ Is there enough space for children to play?

Group Size and Number of Staff

_____ Are different age groups of children cared for separately or are mixed-age groups developmentally compatible?

_____ Does the adult-child ratio for each age group meet state laws and guidelines?

_____ Is there an adequate number of staff members with children at all times?

_____ Does the group size meet state laws and guidelines?

_____ Does the program employ additional staff to cook and clean?

_____ Are volunteers available to help with special activities, such as field trips?

Staff

_____ Are all staff members warm and loving with the children?

    _____ Do staff members kneel or sit at children's eye-level to speak with them?

    _____ Do staff members look at children when they speak with them?

    _____ Do staff members smile often?

    _____ Do staff members use pleasant voices and words?

    _____ Do staff members seem calm and unhurried?

_____ Do staff members provide appropriate activities for physical, mental, and social development?

23-12 Parents need to assess prospective programs for children with care.

(Continued.)

Staff (Continued.)

_____   Do staff members welcome parents at any time?

_____   Do staff members talk with each parent every day at pick-up and drop-off times?

_____   Do staff members handle behavioral problems and separation anxiety in appropriate ways?

_____   Are routines (eating, toileting, napping, and putting on outside clothes) handled pleasantly?

_____   Is self-care encouraged when appropriate?

_____   Are some special activities planned each day?

_____   Have staff members passed criminal background checks?

Special Services

_____   Is transportation provided, especially for SACC programs?

_____   Can parents arrange for extended care?

_____   Does the program enroll children with special needs?

_____   Does the program have ways to serve children who are mildly ill?

Costs

_____   Is the cost reasonable as compared with programs offering similar services?

_____   Are there hidden costs, such as an extra charge for supplies?

_____   Can the program costs be reduced for low-income families, families with several children enrolled, or parents who can provide services, such as volunteering?

_____   Is the payment plan workable?

23-12   (Continued.)

Many recent studies do not find the child-family bond damaged because of care in group programs. One example is a recent two-year study of children between 3½ months and 2½ years. The study found that constant, daylong separation of children from families did not change the importance of family in the child's life.

Some studies do show children are more aggressive as a result of group programs. Contact with peers tends to increase aggression in children because they must stand up for themselves. How teachers handle this aggression seems to affect how much children continue to express it. When children are enrolled in group programs, parents can help by reducing other possible aggression-promoting influences. One way to do this is to limit children's exposure to media portrayals of aggression. On the positive side, children in group programs have the opportunity to learn needed social skills that will help them in the future, 23-13.

Helping Children Adjust to Group Care

The change from home care to group care is a time of adjustment for children who are six months of age and older. These children often have separation anxiety. Even school-age children may feel a bit uneasy for the first few days away from home. (Young infants—those between six weeks and six months—are usually not distressed by receiving care from someone else.)

Adults need to make the adjustment seem casual. They can make a child anxious by talking too much about the change. Parents may be anxious, too, but must do their best to stay calm and confident. Parents' demeanor should show they are sure of the child's ability to adjust. The adult may say, "I know there are many new boys and girls, but you will make new friends. Everyone is new for a while."

About a month before enrolling a child in a group program, the parent should explain what the program is like. He or she may explain there will be other children, toys, and activities. The parent and child should also visit the program, if possible.

Some children do not adjust well to group care, even after a few weeks. In these cases, parents should investigate the cause. Unannounced visits to the program might reveal problems. Parents should also ask the teachers what problems they have noted and what efforts are being made to help the child adjust. Children should be encouraged to share with parents why the program makes them uncomfortable. Parents should take their answers seriously.

Suppose parents find no problems with the care, but the child still has adjustment problems. In this case, parents should find other ways to help the child adjust.

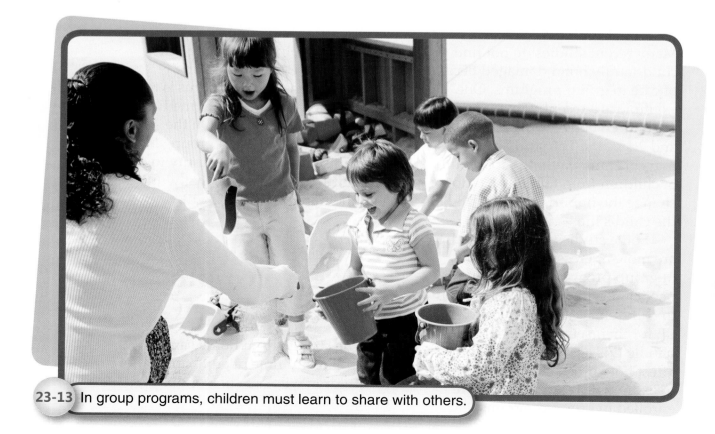

23-13 In group programs, children must learn to share with others.

They might offer the child more chances to play with other children. They could ask their child's doctor for advice.

If parents find problems with the care their child is receiving, they should immediately start to look for a new placement. Parents should monitor the situation closely until a new program can be found. Their children's safety and well-being should be the primary concern. The child should receive extra love and support as parents search for a more acceptable group program. Once a new program is selected, parents may want to begin care gradually, if at all possible.

Summary

Parents have several options when it comes to child care and education for their young children. Parents can choose in-home child care, family child care homes, child care centers, or school-age child care programs.

Parents can also look for programs that provide more direct educational activities for their children. Some of these programs are child development laboratories, Head Start, preschools, Montessori schools, and kindergartens. Young school-age children attend primary schools. All of these have a history of meeting particular needs of children and families.

Because many children spend a great portion of their life in group programs, parents must choose these programs carefully. By learning about the key factors on which they should focus, parents can increase the chance they will find a quality program that is a good match for the child and the family. Getting involved in programs also helps parents find out whether they are of high quality.

Studies show that children in group programs do not seem to have any more serious illnesses than those not attending programs. The mental development of children from middle-class families does not seem to be positively or negatively affected by group programs. On the other hand, many group programs offer activities that provide needed skills and concepts for children from low-income families and for children with special needs. According to many studies, being in a group program does not change the importance of the family in the child's life. Although the interactions with others may make children somewhat more aggressive, they often learn self-control. Learning to get along with others is a worthwhile coping skill for their future.

Parents need to help children adjust to group care. Visits to the program by the parents and child are recommended. If children are not adjusting easily to group care, adults might try other programs. Parents may shorten the time children spend in group care. Having others play with children in their own homes or in the home of a friend is helpful, too. If the program is not suitable, parents should find a new one as soon as possible.

Companion Web Site

Interactive Activity

Review vocabulary terms and key concepts for Chapter 23 at **g-wlearning.com**.

Review and Reflect

Write your answers to the following questions on a separate sheet of paper.

1. Group programs for children are growing both in _____ and _____.

2. The types of nonrelative caregivers who provide in-home child care are _____, _____, and _____.

3. List the four main types of child care that parents use and briefly describe each.

4. True or false. Child care laboratories provide education and physical care for children over age five.

5. _____ is a federal program for three- and four-year-old children from low-income families.

6. _____ schools encourage young children to learn independently through the use of highly specialized materials rather than direct input from teachers.

7. True or false. The adult-child ratio pertains to the number of children housed together.

8. List four criteria for making program activities DAPs.

9. Cultural diversity in child care and education programs for young children can be reflected through the chosen _____, _____, and _____.

10. True or false. Inclusion is the placement of children with special needs in regular classrooms.

11. Name one hidden added cost and one hidden cost credit in enrolling a child in a group program.

12. List five guidelines for choosing a quality child care program.

13. True or false. Children in group care are at a higher health risk for serious illnesses than children who stay at home.

14. Suggest three ways families can help their young children adjust to group care.

Cross-Curricular Link

15. **Career Study.** Interview a nanny, au pair, or other in-home child care provider. What does he or she see as the challenges and rewards of this job? How is the person compensated, and what duties are expected of him or her?

16. **Speech.** Work with a partner to brainstorm activities and services that might be needed in a school-age child care program. Share your ideas in a class discussion.

17. **Social Studies, Writing.** Use Internet or print sources to learn about regulations in your state for licensing of center-based and family child care programs. Based on what you have

learned, how easy do you think it is for child care programs to be licensed? What changes do you think should be made in the current requirements? Compose a brief paper summarizing your findings and your reactions. Check your paper for correct spelling, grammar, and punctuation.

18. **Financial Literacy.** Shop online or in stores or catalogs for materials, equipment, and toys for child care programs. What items are culturally rich? What items have been adapted for children with various special needs? Share your findings with the class.

19. **Social Studies, Writing.** Work with your classmates to compile a directory of local child care programs. The directory can include the program's name, owner, address, phone number, admission requirements, hours operated, and comments on special services or indicators of quality (licensing and accreditation). Be sure to include programs of all types mentioned in the chapter, if possible.

Making Observations

20. Observe activities in two types of group programs for children. How were the programs similar? What differences did you note?

21. After carefully studying Chart 23-12, observe a child care program. Use the checklist to rate the program. Explain why you would or would not enroll a child in this program based on your observation.

Thinking Critically

22. Today, there are many types of early childhood programs. What factors should parents consider in choosing a program? Which factor or factors do you consider most important? Why?

23. Visit two different types of child care and education programs for young children in your area. Discuss in class your findings about how these programs differ in terms of their goals and services.

24. Suppose you or a friend were the parent of a preschooler and were deciding whether to return to the work-world or stay at home with your child. What factors should enter into the decision-making process? Be specific. What is the most important factor to consider? Why?

24 Children with Special Needs

After studying this chapter, you will be able to

★ **define** the term *children with special needs*.

★ **explain** why children with and without special needs are more alike than different.

★ **describe** some of the common forms of special needs in children.

★ **outline** steps people can take to help children with special needs.

Terms to Know

child with special needs
borderline
profound
chronic
correctable
hearing impaired
IQ tests
gifted and talented
physical disability
visually impaired
legally blind
speech impaired
aphasia
mental disability

learning disabilities
spatial orientation
developmental dyslexia
developmental dyscalculia
behavior disorders
aggressive behavior
withdrawn behavior
attention-deficit hyperactivity
    disorder (ADHD)
attention-deficit disorder (ADD)
hyperactivity
Individualized Family Service
    Plan (IFSP)
Individualized Education Plan
    (IEP)

Reading Advantage

Predict what you think will be covered in this chapter. Make a list of your predictions. After reading the chapter, decide if your predictions were correct.

Companion Web Site

Interactive Activity

Learn more about how to help children with behavior disorders by completing the *Read, Discuss, and Analyze* Activity for Chapter 24 at **g-wlearning.com**.

Each person is unique. Most children, however, differ only somewhat in their growth and development. Through research, child development experts have learned which developmental milestones most children generally attain within each stage. A child whose development follows these patterns exhibits *typical development*. What makes these developments *typical* is that most children attain them within the same stage. See Appendix A, *Developmental Milestones*, for a list of typical developmental milestones of children through age 12.

How does a child with special needs differ? The development of a **child with special needs** differs from that of the development typical for most children who are his or her age in one or more ways. Because the development is different, they have special needs beyond the basic needs of all children.

Children with special needs may have abilities that differ from most children in thinking, seeing, hearing, motor skills, speech and language, learning, and social behaviors. As with all children, each child with special needs is unique. Special needs can vary widely. As a general rule, however, developmental differences are seen between children with special needs and other children in one or more of the following ways:

★ First, a child can have special needs in one area or more than one area. For example, one child may differ from typical development in language only. Another may differ from typical development in both language *and* social interactions.

★ Second, skills may not follow the typical pattern of development or may be accelerated or delayed in rate of appearance. For example, some children with special needs develop far ahead of most other children in one or more areas. Other children with special needs develop behind most other children in one or more ways. These delays are often caused by a disability or disorder.

★ Third, observations and tests are used to identify both talents and problems. For example, a doctor might test a child's hearing and score his or her abilities. The test results show the degree of a talent or of a problem. Words such as *borderline* and *profound* can be used to describe either a child's strengths or problems. **Borderline** means a talent is just above average or a problem is mild. **Profound** describes a talent as extreme or a problem as severe.

★ Fourth, a problem (not a strength) may be described as *chronic* or *correctable*. **Chronic** means the problem may exist for a long time, perhaps a lifetime. (Down syndrome presents a chronic, lifelong problem.) Some problems may be **correctable**, which means they can be overcome with the appropriate support. (Speech problems are thought of as correctable if a child can overcome them with therapy.)

Children Are More Alike Than Different

Children with special needs and other children are more alike than they are different. All children have the same basic needs. They need physical care, adults to rely on, and love, 24-1. In addition, however, children with special needs require care that differs or exceeds the care required by most other children.

Children with special needs and other children are also alike in many other ways. They like to learn and achieve. Almost all children like to spend time playing with friends and enjoying themselves. Children with special needs and other children are also more alike than different because of the following reasons:

★ Most children follow the same *patterns of development* (developmental milestones). Three percent of children do not reach developmental milestones on time. Only one-fifth of these children follow a different pattern and sequence of development than other children. Some of these children may even lose skills they once attained, such as language skills. However, the vast majority of children with special needs are like typically developing children in their pattern of development.

★ Many children with special needs reach developmental milestones, but they do so at different *rates* (speeds). For example, children with a slight hearing loss often learn to talk the same way most other children do, except they learn more slowly.

24-1 All children need safe playthings, a stimulating environment, and nurturing adults.
Photo courtesy of Landscape Structures, Inc.

★ Children with special needs and other children develop abilities in the same areas— motor skills, thinking abilities, and social-emotional skills. However, children with special needs almost always show differences in the *degree* of development (strength or force of the skill). For example, a child who is highly gifted will likely reach higher levels of abstract thinking than most adults do.

★ Children with special needs differ from other children only in the area or areas (physical, mental, or social-emotional) affected by the special need. For example, a child who is unable to walk may perform on the same academic level as most other children his or her age. In addition, a child may have a disability in one area, but is gifted in another. For example, a child who is **hearing impaired** (has a hearing loss) may excel in sports.

Children with Special Needs

How are children with special needs described or defined? Some children develop faster or achieve higher degrees of development than most other children. These children are often described as *gifted* or *talented*. Developmental delays, differences in patterns of development, and lower degrees of development are called *impairments*, *disabilities*, and *disorders*.

Observations and tests are used to identify children with special needs. Some special needs are noted at birth, such as visible physical disabilities. Most special needs are not apparent right away, however. In many cases, parents or teachers may question some of the child's behaviors. Parents should bring these behaviors to the attention of the child's doctor. The doctor can examine the child and decide whether further testing is needed. In many cases, certain tests can be done to determine the type and degree of the special need. For a few children, the special need may be difficult to identify.

One test that is frequently used for measuring mental ability is the IQ test. *IQ* stands for *intelligence quotient*. **IQ tests** measure how quickly a person can learn and how able a person is to reason using words, numbers, and spatial concepts. IQ tests also measure how easily a person can find solutions to problems. Thus, IQ tests measure what is called *intelligence*.

Intelligence tests are more accurate when given to only one person at a time. Although intelligence tests can be given to preschool children, the results are more accurate when given in middle childhood and later. Intelligence tests for infants and toddlers are not accurate. These very young children cannot sit still to take the test. They also do not have the skills needed to understand what to do or how to respond to the tester. An IQ score is more accurate when children have the ability to remember, reason, comprehend, respond verbally, make patterns, and work puzzles.

Children with Gifts and Talents

Almost every child has a talent he or she can do better than most other children. A child might read, swim, or jump rope better than other children. Because all children have strengths, the words *gifted* and *talented* are difficult to define. Children who are **gifted and talented** are defined as children who show high performance in one or more of the following areas:

★ general mental ability (the child shows above average intelligence)

★ specific academic aptitude (the child excels in one or more subject areas)

* creative or productive thinking (the child writes or invents)

* leadership ability (the child plans or organizes)

* high skill in visual or performing arts (the child excels in art, music, or dance)

* high psychomotor ability (the child excels in sports)

Some children seem to be gifted or talented in almost all areas. Others are talented in only one or two areas, 24-2.

Statistics on children with gifts and talents show about 16 out of every 100 children are above average. About 3 children of these 16 are *gifted* (have an IQ of 130 or higher). About 2 to 5 percent of all school-age children qualify for special school programs for gifted and talented children (called *GT programs*).

Why are some children gifted and talented? These strengths seem to be partly due to genes. Giftedness and talents seem to run in families. For example, musical ability ran in the Mozart family. Giftedness and talents are also due to an environment that encourages a child to pursue his or her strengths. Wolfgang Amadeus Mozart had a father who encouraged him to play music at a young age.

Just as all children are unique, so are children with gifts and talents. However, these children often have some shared traits that set them apart from their peers, 24-3. Experts use test scores; art products; or judged performances in music, dance, or sports to see if a child is gifted and talented.

24-2 This young boy is talented in music. Giving children extra attention in their talent areas helps them advance.

Common Traits of a Child with Gifts and Talents

Traits	Examples
The child uses advanced vocabulary at an early age.	At age two years, a child says, "I see a kitten in the backyard, and he's climbing our fence," instead of just saying, "I see a kitten."
At age two or three years, a child may learn to read on his or her own.	Most gifted children do not read at an early age. This may be because they see no need to read. However, those who do read learn on their own.
The child is quite observant and curious.	As a toddler, the child remembers where all the toys are stored on the shelf. At age two and three years, the child begins to ask many questions that begin with *what*, *where*, *how*, and *why*. They may ask, "How does the water get out of the bathtub?" "Where does the water go?" "Why does water go down?"
The child remembers many details.	The child can recall many past experiences with details that adults may have forgotten.
The child has a long attention span.	At one year of age, the child may look at a book for five minutes. Other children may just glance at the book. By the school-age years, the child may spend hours on a project and even be totally unaware of other events.
The child understands complex ideas.	A child who is gifted wants to learn so much that topics of interest often change.
The child develops critical thinking skills and makes careful judgments.	A child who is gifted notes when something seems illogical. For example, seeing water drops form on the outside of a glass, the child may ask, "How does the water get there? It did not rain on the glass." A child who is gifted is also more self-critical. The child may say, "I should have done better. That was a silly mistake."
The child shows talents early.	A child who is talented in the visual arts may draw facial expressions, such as sadness or surprise, at a young age. At this same time, friends are drawing circles for the eyes and nose and a curved line for the mouth.
The child does not like repetition.	A child who is gifted likes the new and unsolved. The child may become bored when asked to do 50 basic math problems.

24-3 Each child with gifts and talents is unique, but may share some common traits with other children who are also gifted and talented.

Children with Physical Disabilities

There are many types of physical disabilities. A **physical disability** is a limitation of a person's body or its function. Examples of physical disabilities include having limited mobility (ability to move about); missing limbs; bone, joint, and muscle diseases; and damage to the brain or nervous system, such as cerebral palsy. Any of these problems cause delays in gross-motor development. Children with these types of physical disabilities may need special aids, such as artificial limbs, walkers, crutches, braces, or wheelchairs, to participate fully in daily life.

Two other areas of physical disability are vision and hearing problems. As with other disabilities, these can range from mild to profound. Children with vision or hearing loss may need special supports.

Children who are **visually impaired** have problems seeing. Signs of possible vision loss include squinting, holding objects close to the face, and rubbing the eyes often. Poor distance judgment (missing steps and bumping into objects) may also be a sign. Some vision problems can be corrected with eyeglasses. A few require a special reader that magnifies and lights print. Some people may only see light, colors, shadow forms, or large pictures. Other problems are so severe they make a person unable to see. A person who is **legally blind** has a level of vision loss that makes him or her eligible to receive certain services. (A person is often designated as *legally blind* if his or her best eye has a corrected visual acuity of 20/200. The same designation is used if the person's visual field is 20 degrees or less in the better eye.) Children who are legally blind might learn to use the Braille system of raised dots to help them read.

People who are hearing impaired may have a hearing loss that ranges from mild to profound (deafness). Hearing aids may help a child with hearing loss learn to hear and communicate. In severe cases, hearing aids cannot help. Sign language can be a very useful way for these children to communicate with others.

Signs of possible hearing loss are being unresponsive to sounds, making speech sounds incorrectly, or major delays in talking. Many children who are hearing impaired use their sense of touch more than other children. They also watch other peoples' faces and mouths closely.

Children with Speech and Language Disorders

Some children differ from most other children in the sound of their speech. Children who are **speech impaired** speak in ways that draw attention, are not easily understood, or cause the speaker to have a poor self-concept. Children who are speech impaired can have problems in one or more of the following three areas:

★ articulation. Children may use one sound for another, distort sounds, or leave out or add sounds in words.

★ voice problems. Children's voices may be too high or too low in pitch, too loud or too quiet, nasal, or husky.

★ rhythm problems. Children may repeat sounds, including words, or may be unable to get speech out (called *stuttering*, also known as *stammering*). Children may also speak too fast, stumble on words or phrases, and double back trying to impart meaning (called *cluttering*).

Profound problems in speech are very noticeable, but smaller differences are more difficult to detect. Parents may not hear these differences because they are used to their child's speech. In other cases, parents have the same speech problem as the child, which the child learned through imitating their speech. Doctors and teachers are often better able to hear consistent irregularities in a child's speech. Children with suspected speech problems need to be evaluated by a speech therapist (also called a *speech pathologist*). This professional is trained to evaluate and treat speech problems.

The most serious language problem of childhood is called *acquired childhood aphasia*. **Aphasia** is the partial or total loss of the ability to understand words and use language. It is called *acquired* because it happens after the child has developed some language skills. Aphasia is due to a brain injury. The injury may be caused by a head trauma, a brain infection, a brain tumor, a stroke, or other brain disorders. Recovery depends on the severity of the damage. The child works with a speech therapist who tries to find ways to make up for the lost skills.

Children with Mental Disabilities

A **mental disability** is often defined as having intellectual abilities that, when compared with others of the same age, are a year or more delayed. Mental disabilities vary from mild to profound. Causes include gene disorders, prenatal and birth problems, and injuries to or infections of the brain after birth. A lack of basic experiences in the environment may also cause mental delays. There is a wide variance among children with mental disabilities, but many share the following signs:

★ delays in motor skills

★ smaller vocabulary and shorter sentence length

Focus on Science
Brain Development

Because the brain is involved in all aspects of development, children with mental disabilities need to be diagnosed and treated early in life. The windows of opportunity for brain wiring close rather early in life. Children with mental disabilities need the help of highly specialized teachers. Working with children with mental disabilities is not simply a matter of teaching skills more slowly. These teachers must often use innovative methods to break skills down into steps the children can practice.

Interview a parent whose child has a mental disability. Find out when and how the child's special need was diagnosed. How does this special need change parenting duties? What methods are used to help the child learn new skills? What community resources can the family access for support?

★ a grasp of simple, but not highly complex ideas

★ avoidance of difficult tasks

★ short attention spans

★ more-than-average fondness for repetition

★ difficulty making choices

Children with Autism Spectrum Disorders (ASDs)

Autism is the third most common developmental disability in the United States. It affects one in every 150 babies. Boys are four times more likely than girls to have ASDs.

ASD is a broad term. It includes autistic-like forms which vary along a continuum from very severe (*classical autism*) to very mild (*Asperger's syndrome)* problems. ASD symptoms within a child may vary in intensity, too. For example, a child might show mild problems in the use of language, but severe problems in social behaviors.

ASDs are usually diagnosed by a developmental pediatrician or a team of specialists. Parents, however, should also be aware of certain signs. In general, children with ASDs often have sensory problems, communication problems, mental disabilities, social relationship problems, and even seizures.

The causes of ASDs are unknown. Something interferes with normal brain development before or after birth. Faulty genes appear to be involved because ASDs are more common in identical twins than fraternal twins. Something in the environment, such as a virus, may cause faulty genes to produce a full-blown problem. At this time there is no cure. However, diagnosing and

Learn More About...
Signs of Autism Spectrum Disorders

Although autism spectrum disorders are usually diagnosed by a specialist, parents should also be aware of certain signs. Following is a list of some recognizable signs of ASDs:

★ Has small head at birth followed by abnormal growth (too fast or a sudden decrease in rate of growth).

★ Does not make, or makes little, eye contact.

★ Does not smile.

★ Has severe language delays (no babbling or gesturing by one year; unable to use single words by 16 months and two-word phrases by 24 months).

★ Shows no response to name.

★ Uses repetitive motor actions (hand flapping or object twirling).

★ Fixates (stares) at parts of objects and cannot be distracted.

★ Repeatedly lines up toys and other objects, including food, without a useful need to do this.

★ Lacks interest in pretend play.

★ Lacks interest in peers.

★ Has loss of skills (motor, toilet learning, language, play, problem-solving, and social) over a few months between ages three and four.

treating autism at the earliest possible age can sometimes lessen symptoms. The training and supervision of children especially helps those with milder cases.

Children with Learning Disabilities

Learning disabilities are defined as problems in one or more areas of spoken or written language, math, and spatial orientation. (**Spatial orientation** is the ability to see relationships between objects in space.) Some learning disabilities include *developmental dyslexia* and *dyscalculia*. Children with learning disabilities may have average or above-average intelligence. However, they may perform at lower levels due to their disabilities.

Developmental dyslexia is a disability that affects a child's ability to read. Children with dyslexia also have problems writing and spelling. They may find it difficult to connect words with their written forms. These children may reverse words and letters when they read or write them. They may confuse the order of letters in words or read words backward. More boys than girls have dyslexia.

Developmental dyscalculia is a learning disability that affects a child's math abilities. This problem is similar to dyslexia except that it involves math skills rather than reading skills. For example, the child may reverse numerals. He or she may not develop a mental number line necessary for calculating. Unlike dyslexia, dyscalculia is equally common in girls and boys.

Causes of Learning Disabilities

What causes a child to have a learning disability? Studies show learning disabilities are not caused because parents do not help children learn. Studies also show these disabilities are not caused because children are spoiled, lazy, or stubborn, or have a mental disability. Learning disabilities seem to result from physical problems. For example, imaging shows the misfiring of electrical charges in the brain of these children. The type of learning disability depends on what part of the brain is affected. What causes these misfirings is unknown. It may be prenatal problems, such as lack of oxygen for the fetus. Problems during birth itself may also cause learning disabilities. Other possible causes are accidents, high fevers, and breathing or nutritional problems after birth.

In the past, learning disabilities were rarely noted before the school years. This is because a disability often shows up when formal learning begins. Some children can hide their disability, even in the lower grades. They may memorize words in a reading text rather than really reading them. The signs shown in 24-4 seem to be common for many children. However, the difference is that a child with a learning disability thinks in a disordered way. This happens at the same time his or her peers without learning disabilities are correcting their earlier mistakes, such as reversing letters or numerals. Learning problems are part of the everyday life of a child with a learning disability.

Basic Traits of Children with Learning Disabilities or Disorders

Traits	Examples
Brain messages are jumbled even though the sense organs are normal	★ Reverses letters when reading, writing, or speaking. For example, may read *on* as *no*, write *24* for *42*, or say *aminal* for *animal*. ★ Confuses related words, such as saying *breakfast* instead of *lunch*. ★ Stops often in mid-sentence and starts a new idea. ★ May have trouble identifying the question asked, such as confusing the questions, "How are you?" and "How old are you?"
Poor spatial orientation	★ Has problems doing tasks that involve spatial concepts, such as *up*, *down*, *left*, *right*, *top*, *bottom*, *above*, and *below*. ★ Does not see items that are within the line of vision. ★ Has trouble judging distances. ★ Gets lost often. ★ Has problems writing on a line. ★ Has problems with jigsaw puzzles.
Seems awkward or clumsy	★ Has trouble tying shoes or buttoning small buttons. ★ Is poor at sports. ★ Trips or loses balance because of misjudging distance. ★ Has poor timing. ★ Cannot coordinate several tasks at one time.
Has a short attention span	★ Cannot listen to a story or finish a project.
Is overactive	★ Is always moving, to the point of bothering others. ★ Fidgets constantly through quiet activities.
Acts disorderly	★ Needs more attention than most children of the same age and seeks this attention by misbehaving. ★ May misbehave (often clowning) to convince others that he or she is "bad" rather than struggling with learning tasks.
Is inflexible	★ Becomes upset when any routine changes. ★ Becomes anxious in new places or around new people. ★ Rejects objects that are different (for example, refuses a cracker that is broken). ★ Demands that others cater to his or her needs, even when it is not possible.

24-4 In general, children with learning disabilities face more problems in learning than do other children because they do not think in the same way as other children do.

Greater awareness of learning disabilities has made better help available. Also, the increased number of children in early childhood education programs makes it possible to detect learning disabilities at earlier ages. More widespread use of testing programs has also contributed to diagnosis of these disabilities.

Children with Behavior Disorders

Behavior disorders are patterns of problems that surface in a person's behavior. (Behavior disorders are also called *conduct* or *disruptive disorders*.) Such disorders are often marked by extremes of behaviors. As with other special needs, behavior disorders vary in terms of severity. The causes of a disorder are often a puzzle. In some cases, severe and constant stress seems to be the cause. Brain injuries and other physical causes sometimes exist. Experts are in the early stages of solving the puzzle of behavior disorders. There are several common behavior disorders.

Aggressive behavior is an outward (disruptive) behavior disorder. For example, children with *oppositional defiant disorder (ODD)* name-call, fight, and bully without being provoked into such actions. They cannot seem to control these behaviors.

Withdrawn behavior occurs when children do not relate well with others. They may resist change and panic when changes occur. They often have poor self-concepts and do not always think realistically. These behaviors are called *anxiety disorders*.

Two related behavior disorders have to do with the ability to pay attention. People must use attention and memory to learn, retain information, and solve problems. To pay attention, a person has to focus one or more of the senses on a certain aspect of the environment (listen to a recording) and ignore irrelevant information (a humming fan).

Although all people sometimes become distracted, some people are highly distractible. The two disorders that involve attention are **attention-deficit hyperactivity disorder (ADHD)** and **attention-deficit disorder (ADD)**. ADHD involves the lack of attention and **hyperactivity** (behavior that is extremely active beyond a child's normal energy level). Some children with ADHD are also impulsive in their behaviors. ADD involves the lack of attention, but does not include hyperactive behaviors, 24-5. For this reason, ADD is sometimes called *hypoactivity disorder*.

ADHD and ADD are difficult to diagnose. In children, diagnosis is based on observation rather than medical tests. Similar symptoms appear in childhood anxiety and depression. Although lack of attention and learning disabilities are different, they often occur in the same children.

Some researchers state that 10 percent of all children have either ADHD or ADD. Others claim the numbers are much lower. Hyperactivity is often misdiagnosed. Some experts say only one to three percent of children who are labeled hyperactive are truly hyperactive in a medical sense. Hyperactivity is present, however, in 75 percent of the cases involving attention disorders. Attention disorders affect boys four to five times more often than girls.

Common Traits of Children with Attention Disorders

Attention-Deficit Hyperactivity Disorder

★ Are inattentive; easily distracted; forgetful
★ Act as if "driven"
★ Are fidgety (may constantly run, climb, or move in other ways; get out of their chairs or their places in group settings)
★ Constantly change activities often without completing anything
★ Do sloppy and incomplete work
★ Blurt out in class
★ Will not wait for their turns
★ Have frequent and intense emotional outbursts (fight, have self-imposed isolation, defiant, cannot take criticism)
★ Are clumsy and accident-prone
★ Have excessive activity in sleep

Attention-Deficit Disorder

★ Are inattentive; easily distracted; forgetful
★ Act disinterested ("tune-out") or daydream
★ Fail to finish a task or play activity
★ Appear not to listen
★ Cannot organize work

24-5 Children who cannot pay attention are often diagnosed with attention disorders. Most are also hyperactive.

Several techniques are being tried to help children with attention disorders. These include the following:

★ restricting stimuli (having fewer items to see and hear, at the same time)

★ establishing and adhering to a routine

★ giving short, clear instructions

★ using praise and rewards

★ providing experiences that are challenging, but manageable, 24-6

★ offering physical activities while curtailing over-excitement

★ watching diet, especially food coloring

24-6 Special programs that meet the needs of children, especially those with disabilities, are available through public funds.

Photo © John Shaw

★ giving medications to calm hyperactivity

When carefully monitored by doctors, some children's behaviors improve with medications. Giving medication without careful observations has been criticized for several reasons, however. First, it is often the first treatment tried. Second, these medications have side effects, such as slowing children's appetite and growth and causing sleeplessness, listlessness, and a stupor-like state. Third, frustrated adults may view these drugs as a way to control children who have high energy levels, but do not actually need the medication.

Help for Children with Special Needs

All children with special needs should have special help. The first step in providing this help is to identify children with special needs. Family members are often shocked when they first learn their child has special needs. Giftedness or talent shocks parents because the active minds or special talents of these children often baffle adults. It may take parents some time to adjust to this news and learn how to meet their child's special needs. This news is even more shocking when the special need is a disability. Sometimes families face this adjustment when a child is born. Other times, the problem may not be noticed until the school-age years when the child seems to fall behind or differ from peers. For still other parents, an accident or illness disables a child.

How Many Children Have Special Needs?

An estimated one out of every 10 children has special needs. Some special needs are more common than others, however. For example, about 3.5 percent of all children have speech disorders, but deafness affects far fewer children (about .075 percent of all children).

Anywhere from 3 to 45 percent of all children have learning disabilities, depending on the way the term *learning disabilities* is defined. This definition may differ from one professional to another. State laws also vary in the definitions used to determine which students have special needs and are therefore eligible for a free public education. (Laws require that all children with special needs receive a free and appropriate public education.)

School Bus Driver

School bus drivers take children to and from schools and related events. They must maintain order on their buses and enforce school safety standards and rules. Many drivers transport students with physical disabilities or behavior disorders. These drivers must know how to accommodate these children's special needs.

Education: Most school bus drivers are high school graduates. State and federal governments have established bus driver qualifications and standards, which include a commercial driver's license (CDL) with the proper endorsements.

Job Outlook: Employment of school bus drivers is expected to grow.

What Kinds of Help Are Needed?

Children with special needs require extra help or help that differs from that of most other children. According to brain development research, intensive help is needed and should begin early for the assistance to be most effective.

Parents generally start to seek help through a pediatrician. The doctor can refer the child for needed tests, 24-7. Once testing is complete, doctors can explain the child's condition to parents and discuss ways to help the child.

The *Individuals with Disabilities Education Act* (IDEA), a federal law, governs the education of children with disabilities. IDEA guarantees the rights of children with disabilities (not gifts and talents) to receive a free and appropriate public education. IDEA outlines ways to help children with special needs and their families.

IDEA provides two written documents that outline the required services. The first document is the **Individualized Family Service Plan (IFSP)**. This plan guarantees families can get

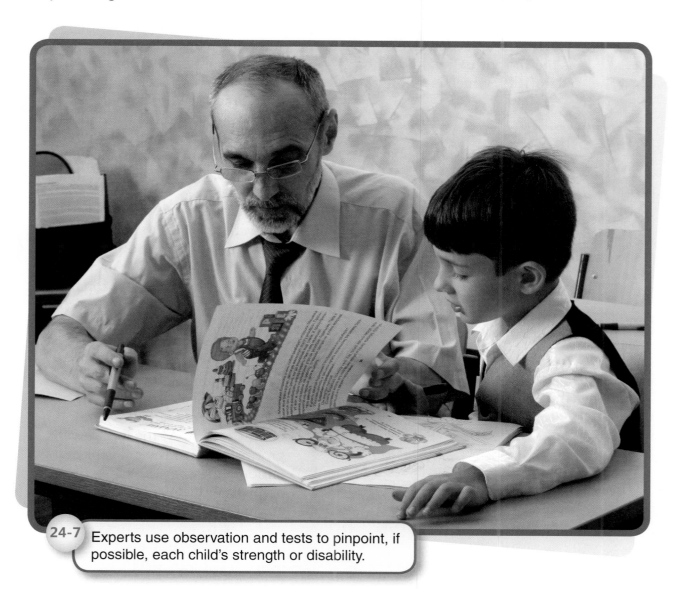

24-7 Experts use observation and tests to pinpoint, if possible, each child's strength or disability.

needed help between the birth of their child with disabilities until the child is age 3. The IFSP focuses on the entire family's needs. A team is composed of parents and experts from various agencies, such as schools and social service agencies. One of the experts serves as a coordinator who makes sure the child and parents get all the services they need. Services take place near the home of the parents. The ISFP encourages families to learn the special parenting skills they need for their child.

IDEA also states that all children with disabilities between the ages of 3 and 21 are eligible to receive appropriate educational services. The second document is the **Individualized Education Plan (IEP)**, which is tailored to the child's specific educational needs. It includes goals for the child and a placement agreement. The most common placement is *inclusion* (full-time placement in a regular classroom) rather than *mainstreaming* (an older term for placing the child in the classroom only part of the day).

Parents, teachers, and school administrators design the IEP together and agree to carry it out. Parents also meet with their child's teachers on a regular basis. The child is retested on a regular basis, and the plan is adjusted as needed to fit the child's changing educational needs and goals.

Unless children with gifts and talents also have disabilities, they do not qualify for help under IDEA. State and local funds are sometimes used to help these children develop their gifts and talents. On the whole, however, it is up to parents to find and finance any services that may meet their child's needs.

Members of families who have children with special needs often join support groups. Many of these groups are national with local chapters. At the national level, these groups provide family members with the latest information on children with special needs. National groups also seek money for research and assistance for families of children who need costly training or equipment. At the local level, groups support the goals of the national groups. They also provide helpful contacts and services among those with similar needs.

Human Services

Social Service Coordinator

Social service coordinators make sure families of children with special needs receive the services they need through a variety of social service programs. They perform a basic assessment and planning for required services. Social service coordinators also establish eligibility for specific programs or services and determine how to meet client needs.

Education: Although a bachelor's degree in social work (BSW) is sufficient for entry into the field, a master's degree has become the standard for many positions. All states have licensing, certification, or registration requirements regarding social work practice.

Job Outlook: Employment for social workers is expected to grow much faster than the average for all occupations.

Summary

Children whose development differs in pattern, rate, or degree have special needs. These needs can occur in the areas of thinking, seeing, hearing, motor skills, speech and language, learning, or social behaviors.

Children with special needs and other children are more alike than different. All children have the same basic needs, although children with special needs do need extra help in certain areas.

Children who are gifted and talented show high performance in one or more areas. These areas include mental ability, specific academic aptitude, and creative or productive thinking. Other areas of high performance may be in leadership, visual or performing arts, or psychomotor abilities. Gifted children tend to show their talents early and share some common traits, such as an early use of vocabulary and a memory for details. Gifts and talents may be due to both heredity and the environment.

Developmental problems are sometimes called *disabilities*, *impairments*, or *disorders*. The most common types of developmental delays include physical disabilities, speech and language disorders, mental disabilities, autism spectrum disorders, learning disabilities, and behavior disorders.

Tests can help identify how to best help a child with special needs. Federal funds are available for the education of children with disabilities. When problems are indicated, the family and child qualify for help under IDEA's two documents—the Individualized Family Service Plan and the Individualized Education Plan. Both plans set up services, including education, that will best meet the child's special needs. Although children with gifts and talents do not receive aid under IDEA, local and state school funding may provide some needed services. Parents, however, carry the responsibility to find and finance most of the services needed by children with gifts and talents.

It can be challenging to parent a child with special needs. Learning how to meet the child's special needs is important. Support groups help, too, because they provide contact with others in similar circumstances.

Companion Web Site

Interactive Activity

Review vocabulary terms and key concepts for Chapter 24 at **g-wlearning.com**.

Review and Reflect

Write your answers to the following questions on a separate sheet of paper.

1. Special needs _____ (are, are not) seen in degrees and may or may not last a lifetime.

2. Delays have to do with the _____ (rate, pattern, degree) involved in reaching developmental milestones.

3. True or false. Some forms of special needs are difficult to identify.

4. Name three areas in which children may have gifts and talents.

5. Define the term *aphasia*.

6. List three signs of a possible mental disability in children.

7. True or false. Girls are four times more likely than boys to have ASDs.

8. Name three signs of a possible learning disability in children.

9. Name two disorders that involve attention.

10. IDEA guarantees the rights of children with _____ (disabilities, gifts and talents) to receive a free and appropriate public education.

11. Order from 1 to 5 the steps for helping a child with special needs.

    _____ testing

    _____ writing an IEP

    _____ referral for testing

    _____ finding a suitable program to help the child

    _____ retesting and writing a new IEP from time to time

Cross-Curricular Link

12. **Reading, Speech.** Read the biography or autobiography of a famous person who is gifted or talented. Prepare an oral report to present to the class on the person's accomplishments and struggles.

13. **Reading, Writing.** Read the biography or autobiography of a famous person with disabilities. (An excellent book from which to get names is Deborah Kent's *Extraordinary People with Disabilities*.) Write a brief report on the person's accomplishments and struggles. Check your report for correct spelling, grammar, and punctuation.

14. **Social Studies.** Use Internet or print sources to find toys and play equipment designed for children with physical disabilities. What features of these items make them easier to use by a person with a physical disability?

15. **Technology.** Use the Internet to research the most current technological devices used to help children with hearing

and speech impairments. For example, children with hearing impairments may use speech amplification equipment or visual signaling systems. Children with limited mobility or hand use may use a "sip-and-puff" keyboard. Share your findings with the class.

16. **Health, Writing.** Use Internet or print sources to learn more about ADHD or ADD. Write a short report describing recent advances that have been made in diagnosing or treating these disorders. Check your report for correct spelling, grammar, and punctuation.

17. **Social Studies, Writing.** Work in a small group to investigate the resources available in your community for the families of children with special needs. Create a directory of all the resources you locate, including name, address, contact person, phone number, and a brief description of services offered.

Making Observations

18. Observe a special needs classroom or an inclusionary classroom. Note ways in which children with special needs and other children are alike.

19. Observe children with special needs in a group setting. List all the instances you observe of the children receiving special help.

20. Observe a program that serves children with special needs. How does the program differ from other classrooms in terms of housing and equipment, class size, staff to child ratio, subjects taught, teaching methods, and other factors? How is it the same as other classrooms?

Thinking Critically

21. Do you know children with any special needs? What special needs do they have?

22. What types of problems do families face when they have children with special needs?

23. What is the overall goal of the special help given to children with special needs? Does this differ from the overall goal for meeting the needs of most other children?

25 Concerns of Children and Families

After studying this chapter, you will be able to

- ★ describe four sibling relationships and explain how a child's birth order affects development.
- ★ describe how parental employment affects children.
- ★ explain how stress from family moves can hurt children and how to lessen these effects.
- ★ describe ways parents can help children handle death, divorce, and remarriage.
- ★ point out problems single parents and teen parents face.
- ★ describe ways to protect children from neglect and abuse.
- ★ list resources available for helping children in crises.

Terms to Know

singletons	physical neglect
separate identities	educational neglect
role strain	medical neglect
role guilt	moral neglect
quality time	emotional neglect
children in self-care	child abuse
child support order	physical abuse
social isolation	sexual abuse
mortality rate	emotional and verbal abuse
abstinence	Shaken Baby Syndrome (SBS)
child neglect	mandated reporters

Reading Advantage

After reading each section, answer this question: If you explained the information to a friend who is not taking this class, what would you tell him or her?

Companion Web Site

Interactive Activity

Learn more about how to help children cope with crises by completing the *Read, Discuss, and Analyze* Activity for Chapter 25 at **g-wlearning.com**.

The relationships children have with family members play an important role in their development. Sibling relationships are especially important. Children learn a lot by playing and living with brothers and sisters.

Family life is complex these days. Some parents must balance family and work issues. Sometimes other stressful events occur that cause tensions and problems that affect family life. In turn, these problems affect children.

Children need to grow up in a strong family. When the family must relocate, adults must reassure children they will soon feel secure in their new environment. When death, divorce, or remarriage upsets the family, adults need to help children cope. Single and teen parents face additional challenges when raising and supporting their children.

Child neglect and abuse cause serious physical, mental, and emotional scars for children. Many carry the problems with them all their life. Adults must protect children from abuse.

Sibling Relationships

In most families, children grow up with siblings. This means most children interact with at least one brother or sister. In some families, children have several siblings.

Sibling Interactions

Siblings influence each other's lives in many ways. Sibling interactions influence mental development as children play roles of teachers and learners. By being both protectors and rivals, children experience social give-and-take.

Playmates

Brothers and sisters are built-in playmates for each other. In play, siblings learn to set goals and cooperate. Siblings also share hours of fun, 25-1. Brothers and

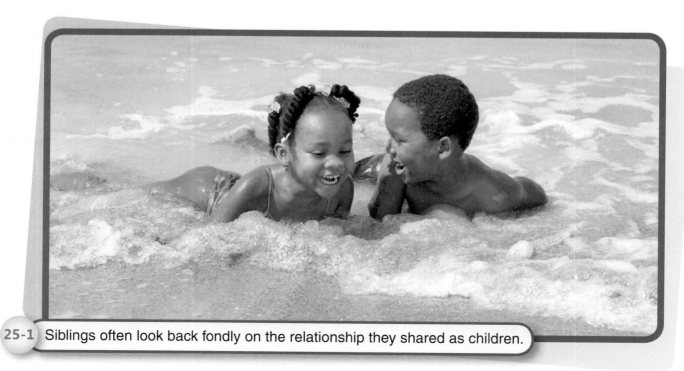

25-1   Siblings often look back fondly on the relationship they shared as children.

sisters remember these fun times throughout their adult years.

Teachers and Learners

Older children often act like teachers while younger siblings play the part of eager learners. As teachers, siblings explain, define, describe, show, and offer examples. Most brothers and sisters show interest in their younger sibling's efforts. They help them reach their goals as well.

Older siblings also model social skills. These social skills include learning gender roles. Younger siblings learn gender roles faster than firstborns and only children. Having a sibling also helps children learn the difference between acceptable and unacceptable social behaviors. From a child's point of view, a sibling shows acceptable social behavior if he or she plays nicely, helps with chores, and does not tattle.

Protectors

If you have ever seen an older child run to a younger sibling's defense, you know that siblings protect each other. Siblings protect each other most often when

★ siblings have an age gap of three or more years

★ siblings come from large families

★ children are unsupervised outside, on the way to and from school, or with a babysitter

★ peers attack a younger sibling in a physical or verbal way

Older children can help adults watch younger brothers and sisters (although adults should never leave children alone). As a bonus, older children who help parents care for siblings are better prepared for parenthood and child-related careers.

Rivals

Two or more children in a family will often compete with one another in both physical and verbal ways. Why does rivalry occur? Children may compete for the love and attention of parents and friends for several reasons. They may be jealous of siblings who seem more capable than they are. They also may not be able to see a situation from another's point of view. To young children, *fair* means *equal*.

Adults cannot prevent rivalry, but they can lessen it by giving each child lots of love. Each child needs positive feedback. Parents must not compare one child with another. Children are different, and comparing them usually makes one child resent the other and feel angry toward parents.

Space

Parents need to control the space children use. Each child needs space for his or her belongings. For example, high shelves keep toddlers away from older children's toys and books. Adults should teach children to share, but they should not expect them to share all the time. Children should share in the same ways adults share—sometimes, but not in all cases. Also, children should have some time to play without siblings. Playing alone and with friends is healthy. Siblings, especially younger ones, can pester children when they are always around.

Fights

Parents should ignore small squabbles unless children are in physical danger or property may be damaged. If adults settle each dispute, children may feel rewarded with the parents' attention. If the fight must be stopped, parents should tell children to stop without adding a threat. If children do not obey this command, parents should physically separate the children.

Family Togetherness

Parents should stress the importance of family togetherness and support. Families should take part in some activities everyone enjoys. Parents must teach children to take pleasure in another's good fortune. Parents should explain that family members love one another although they sometimes get angry at each other. Above all, parents should praise loving behavior, 25-2.

Birth Order and Development

To some degree, the birth order of children affects their social roles and personalities. Alfred Adler (1870–1937), an Austrian psychologist, developed the theory of birth order in the early 1900s. Kevin Leman, the first American psychologist to popularize Adler's birth order theory, has observed the effects of birth order since the 1960s. Leman believes that differences in siblings are due to the ways parents relate to the child in his or her birth-order position. Leman's ideas have been supported by some research. His ideas have long been promoted by other popular psychologists.

Facts about birth order cannot be applied to all children, however. More recent research is calling some of these ideas into question. For example, intelligence is determined

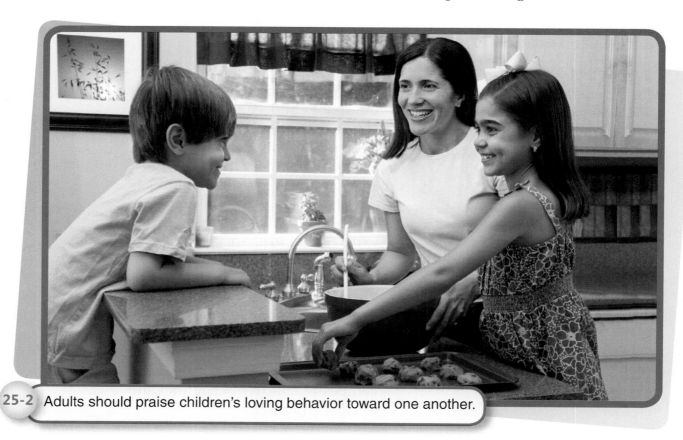

25-2　Adults should praise children's loving behavior toward one another.

to a large extent by one's genes, not by birth order. Personality traits depend on many things. For example, the gender of the children, the number of older and younger siblings, and a family's culture, including where they live.

The attention a child gets or does not get may be the most important determiner of personality. This was recognized by Leman who felt only children and first born children receive the most attention. Would this always be true? The age of the parents and their knowledge of child development and parenting could make a major difference. The number of children and spacing also affects attention given to children. (Generally, multiples have been excluded from studies of birth order.) Greater age gaps between a child and the next older sibling reduce the effects of birth order on development. Long hours spent in child care settings also has its effects on the amount of attention a child receives.

Only Children

The number of children being raised as "only children" is growing. Reasons for this include women in the workforce, delayed childbearing, and the cost of childrearing.

Many myths surround only children. Some believe only children are lonely, spoiled, selfish, and more dependent on parents. Only children seldom live up to these ideas.

Like all children, only children are distinct persons with their own personalities. They are usually not lonely if playmates are a part of their lives. In fact, they learn to spend time alone as well as with others. Only children are often less selfish or jealous than other children. They are not threatened by the loss of family attention or of possessions by siblings. In order to keep friends, they quickly learn social give-and-take, too. See 25-3 for a list of some common traits of only children.

Firstborn Children

You will see in 25-3 that firstborns have many of the same traits as only children. This is partly because most firstborns are only children for a little while (except siblings from a multiple birth). Firstborns are often high achievers in the areas of family values. Their skills are often bettered through the teaching of younger siblings.

Some parents call their firstborns *experimental children* because the parents must try untested ideas on them. This means they are not treated the same as later children in the family. Firstborns are often disciplined in inconsistent ways as parents try to find their parenting style. Many firstborns report their parents were stricter with them than with their siblings.

Compared with their younger siblings, firstborns may be less popular with peers. They tend to use high-power social tactics, such as bossing, threats, and physical force, used in sibling rivalry with their peers. These tactics do not make them popular with peers. However, they are often chosen by their peers for leadership positions due to their achievements and drive.

Middle Children

The term *middle children* refers to the second child in a family of three siblings. It also refers to both the second and third children in families of four siblings. Findings on middle children, shown in 25-3, do not fit

Traits Commonly Associated with Birth Order

Only Children
Achievers (in areas of family values)
Perfectionists
High level of self-esteem
Relaxed
Not jealous
Unselfish
Socially outgoing
Leaders as adults

Firstborns
Achievers (in areas of family values)
Creative
Zealous and driven
Ambitious
Anxious
Conservative
Mature
Conformists
Company seekers in times of stress
Angry and irritable at times
Less popular
Leaders as adults

Middle Children
Less highly driven to achieve
Attracted to nonacademic areas, such as
    sports or the arts
Cheerful
Easygoing
Relaxed
Patient
Adaptable
Gentle
Tactful
Outgoing
Popular
Charming
Less skillful than older siblings (in their own eyes)
Lost in the middle at times (in their own view)

Youngest Children
Underachievers unless motivated
Dependent if "babied"
Pleasure seekers
Relaxed
Secure
Calm
Kindhearted
Popular
Negotiators
Good companions
Prone as adults to feel a need to be loved and
    cherished

25-3　Birth order can affect a child's mental and social-emotional development.

large families (five or more siblings) or families with multiples.

When children are spaced closer than three years, adults tend to spend less time with middle children. Thus, they may not be as high of achievers as their older siblings. They may excel in areas of interest, however, because they do not feel as driven to achieve in all areas.

Socially, middle children seem to adjust easily to new situations. When other children are born, middle children do not feel as displaced as firstborns. This may be because they have always shared their parents. They have even shared hand-me-down clothes and toys. On the negative side, they may feel caught in the middle. Some middle children feel they must constantly compete with older siblings. A middle child may also feel a younger child steals attention as the family baby.

Youngest Children

As shown in 25-3, youngest children do better socially than in achievement. This may be due to the fact that they rarely play the role of teacher with their older siblings. They may also feel less need to achieve.

Youngest children are often relaxed and cheerful. Parents usually are comfortable with their parenting skills by the time this child is born. Youngest children deal with more personalities from the time they are infants than do older siblings. Plus, they are used to receiving attention and care from older siblings, 25-4.

On the negative side, parents may treat the youngest child more like a baby because they know he or she is their last child. Siblings tend to take care of the youngest child, too. These factors may cause the youngest to be more dependent and less mature. Youngest children are more likely to resort to sulking, tattling, teasing, and fighting.

A Child's Identity

The treatment a child receives affects achievement and personality. Thus, birth order does not need to affect a child's later success. Parents can avoid the pitfalls of birth order by focusing on the child, not the child's place in the family.

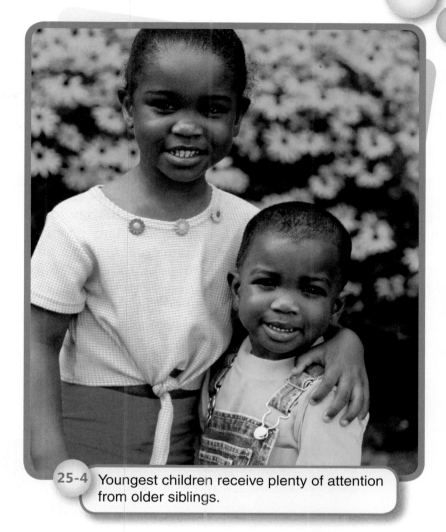

25-4 Youngest children receive plenty of attention from older siblings.

Parents need to avoid making comments to their children that reference birth order. For example, parents can cause stress in a firstborn by saying, "You are the oldest so you should know better." Commenting in front of the youngest that he or she is "just a baby" will create more dependency.

Parents need to treat each child fairly. Unfair treatment includes showing favoritism and forgetting to praise all children. Spoiling the youngest and expecting too much from firstborns and only children are also unfair treatments. Parents need to promote their children's best traits. They also need to help children overcome the negative effects of birth order. If parents treat children as individuals, children will develop their own identities.

Children of Multiple Births

As you read in Chapter 4, the number of multiple births has grown since the early 1990s. Many people ask whether parenting multiple-birth children is different from **singletons** (children born one at a time). In many ways it is. Parents must meet more sets of needs at once. In meeting these needs, tasks, time, and costs often multiply. Most parents soon realize they need extra help, especially right after birth.

Multiple birth children react to the world differently than singletons. This is because they spend a lot of time with each other, go through school together, and may look alike. For these reasons, children of multiple births share perhaps the closest of all human relationships. Their relationship may even be closer than that of parent and child, 25-5. These siblings have few problems remaining close. Instead, they may have problems developing **separate identities** (feelings of being distinct people rather than a unit). Those who have the most problems with this are identical children and same-gender, look-alike fraternal children. Treating multiple-birth siblings as distinct children, rather

25-5 Twins and other multiple-birth children often have very close relationships.

than as a single unit, will help each child form a separate identity.

When fostering these separate identities, parents need to preserve the siblings' special bond. Identical children share more than the same birthday—they share a common genetic makeup. Stories and research abound concerning identical children with similar health problems, interests, and traits, even when raised thousands of miles apart. Being more alike than different is often normal for them. Parents should allow children to choose how much alike or different they wish to be. In this way, multiple-birth children will work out separateness and closeness just as other siblings do.

Parental Employment

Today, almost all families with children have one or both parents employed. Some nuclear families need or want two incomes. Many single parents, whether mothers or fathers, are forced to work in order to support their children. Changes in welfare laws have caused many parents to look for work. Many parents see careers outside the home as rewarding.

Not all parents work outside the home. Some have family businesses, such as farms and stores. More and more people are working from home. Many home-based workers have computers, cell phones, modems, video teleconferencing, and faxes in their home offices. This equipment allows them to conduct business without leaving home. When families are involved, working at home takes special planning. Parents must set aside time and space to complete work tasks in an efficient way.

Effects on Children

How does a parent's job affect a child's development? Research shows that babies have fewer separation anxieties if mothers return to work before they are three months old or after age two. Babies develop strong attachments to their caregivers between 3 and 24 months. Another awkward time to enter the workforce is when children are ages 11 through 13. At this time, children are coping with many changes in their life. Having a parent return to work may be too much.

Some studies show today's children receive as much attention from their working parents as yesterday's children did from their full-time mothers. This may be true. Today's working parents use more timesaving home appliances, so keeping a home does not require as much of their time. Working parents use conveniences, such as eating out, more often than other parents. They may also try to make up for the hours away from home by spending meaningful time with their children each day.

Children of working parents enjoy some advantages over children with at least one parent who stays home. Children with working parents tend to miss fewer days of school. They usually enjoy meaningful and well-planned free time with parents. They also help with household chores and learn home-care skills. These children may live in homes with more structured times and more clearly stated rules.

In this environment, children often show more confidence. Another advantage of working parents is that children interact more with others and spend more time with other adults and children.

When both parents work, children think in broader terms about gender roles. Children who grow up in these homes do not think of women only as homemakers and men only as wage earners. They see their mother arrive home from a day at work and help their father prepare dinner.

Effects on Parents

Finding a balance between work and family is sometimes difficult. Working does affect the emotional state of parents. Sometimes, working brings happiness. Often it brings **role strain**, a feeling of having too many tasks to do at one time. Working may also cause a parent to feel *role guilt*. **Role guilt** is a feeling of not doing the best job at work or at home because of role strain. When parents are happy with either working full-time or staying home, then children seem to adjust well, 25-6. However, if either parent is unhappy, it creates family stress.

Most parents do have some problems as a result of their work. They cannot always find time to relax. They may have trouble with child care arrangements. Some parents end up spoiling children as they try to make up for time away from home. Parents often feel guilty for not being able to attend some school functions that occur during work hours.

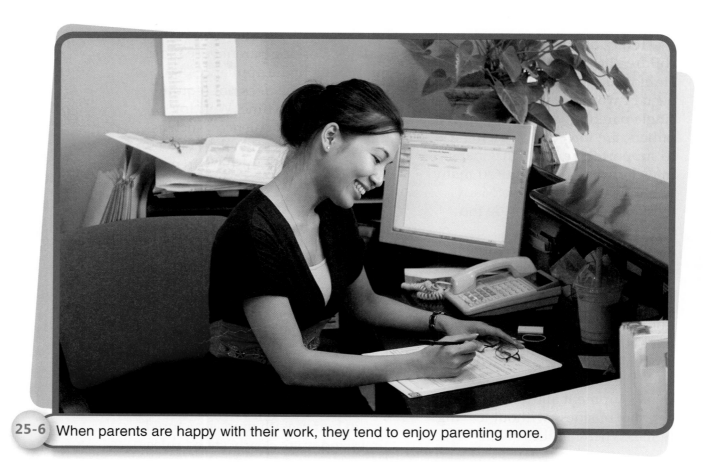

25-6 When parents are happy with their work, they tend to enjoy parenting more.

Balancing Family and Work

By planning carefully, parents can lessen the stress of parenting while holding a job. Working parents need to budget their time carefully. Letting some minor tasks slide may be necessary. They should plan family time, which is essential, in their daily schedules. Parents need to give their children some **quality time** (time when parents are totally attentive to their children) each day. Also, parents should check on the next day's clothes, lunch, and homework before children go to bed. This helps avoid morning panic.

What do working parents do if a child is sick, the caregiver is ill, or the child care center is closed? Parents must think about this in advance. If an older child must stay home alone after school, parents must talk about safety measures before problems occur.

Working parents should meet and talk with teachers. They should attend as many of their children's school-related events as possible. Likewise, parents should include their children in their work life. They can set up a visit to their worksites, explain their jobs, and share stories about their day at work.

Working parents still need to set limits for their children. Parents cannot make up for time away from the family by letting children do what they want to do. As with other children, children of working parents want and need guidance.

Parents who return to work after a time spent with children need to recognize and accept the feelings of their children. Children show feelings in many ways. Two-through four-year-olds may *regress* (act less mature than before) for a few weeks after the parent returns to work. During the early evening hours, when everyone is tired and hungry, children usually express their feelings. At this time, children often want to reconnect and share the entire day's events. However, parents may need to relax for a few minutes after long hours at work. After spending a few quiet minutes, parents can devote their complete attention to the family.

Children in Self-Care

In the 1800s, the problems of the children of working parents began to surface. These children wore their house keys around their necks. They stayed home alone for a portion of a day and cared for themselves until a parent returned from work. During World War II, they were called *latchkey children*. Today, they are called **children in self-care**.

Many children under age 13 are in self-care. When teens are included in this number, it increases greatly. The number of children in self-care continues to increase for the following reasons:

★ more dual-career and working single-parent households

★ decrease in the number of extended families in which other adults are in the home

★ high costs of child care

★ lack of quality before- and after-school programs designed for the school-age child

Children, their parents, and the community are all affected by self-care. Some of these effects are positive and others are negative, as shown in 25-7. There are ways parents can decrease risks and increase the positive effects.

Effects of Self-Care

Positive Effects for Children

★ Children can show initiative and industry. (This is especially true for 8- through 13-year-old children. These children are old enough to understand rules and are less prone to peer pressure than teens.)

★ Children may develop more self-esteem.

Negative Effects for Children

★ Minor emergencies can become life threatening. For example, a young child may open a window "to let the fire out."

★ Children are at greater risk for sexual abuse from older siblings and adults.

★ Children may have increased feelings of being separated from or rejected by parents (who are at work) and friends (with whom they cannot play). This may lead to emotional or social problems.

★ Eight- through 13-year-old children, who fear burglaries, may develop especially strong feelings of anxiety.

★ Children may be overexposed to television and computer content and have no guidance while parents are working.

★ Children may make poor food choices and thus have improper nutrition due to the lack of parental guidance.

★ Children's academic achievement may drop due to excessive television viewing and computer use. Parents may not be able to help children with homework until they return from work when both children and parents are tired.

★ Children may have increased risks of exposure to alcohol and other drugs.

Positive Effects for Parents

★ Child care costs are reduced.

★ With careful planning for the self-care situation, the parent-child relationship may be close, and children may quickly learn self-care and how to be more responsible.

Negative Effects for Parents

★ Parents have many feelings of guilt and concern.

★ Loss of work productivity occurs for parents while checking on or refereeing children over the telephone. This is especially true during after-school hours.

Positive Effects for the Community

★ Community leaders may challenge people to consider the needs of children and their families, such as low-cost child care and after-school programs.

★ Others see the need to provide training for parents and children who must rely on self-care.

Negative Effects for the Community

★ A greater risk of accidents, including home fires, exists.

★ Rates of vandalism, arson, shoplifting, and vagrancy may rise during hours when children are in self-care.

25-7 Self-care has both positive and negative effects.

First, and foremost, parents should plan for self-care by deciding carefully whether their child can handle being in self-care. Parents must check state laws about the age at which children can legally be left at home. (State laws vary, but the legal age is often around 12 years.) They should learn whether the laws set different legal ages for self-care and caring for younger siblings. The care of younger siblings takes even more maturity, and may be legal only at an older age as set by the state.

If the child is of legal age to provide self-care, parents should consider the following when deciding about self-care:

★ **How mature is the child?** Around 12 or 13 years of age, many children are legally able to stay home alone, but developmental maturity is the key factor. Is the child afraid of staying home alone? Can the child handle unexpected situations without panicking? Has the child shown responsible behavior in other situations?

★ **How safe is the home?** Any object in your home that requires adult supervision during use is dangerous for older children. Most injury-related deaths occur when children are out of school and unsupervised.

★ **How safe is the neighborhood?** An unsafe neighborhood can result in fears, injury or death, and involvement in illegal actions. (Rate of juvenile violence is highest in the afternoon between 3 and 7 p.m.)

★ **How do children feel about self-care?** Do they feel prepared and confident to provide this care? Are they concerned or afraid? What do children think would make them safer or less safe during self-care? What can parents do to help?

Once parents have chosen self-care for their children, they need to teach their children the skills needed to provide self-care. As a part of this process, parents and children should do the following:

★ Make sure the child learns safety rules, 25-8.

★ Work out a way for the parent to know the answers to the three *ws*: *where* are the children? *what* are they doing? *who* are they with?

Rules for Safe Self-Care

★ Keep house keys with you at all times.
★ If walking home from school, walk with friends; come straight home unless other plans are first approved by parent.
★ Call parent upon your arrival.
★ Do not enter the house if things do not look right.
★ Tell parents if anything or anyone frightens you.
★ Call 911 in case of *emergency* (know how to define an emergency) and know how to give address and directions to your house.
★ Upon entering the house, use locks and set alarm system if you have one.
★ Never open the door at home, but instead talk through the door.
★ Answer phone calls (it may be a parent calling).
★ Never tell people at the door or over the phone you are home alone.
★ Arrange an emergency evacuation plan.

25-8 If children will be in self-care, parents must make sure the children understand these important safety rules.

★ Set rules about using appliances, TV, computer, stereo, phone, and other equipment; having friends over; and leaving the house.

★ Establish a routine for children to follow.

★ Begin self-care gradually, if possible. Start with a short period when the parent does a quick, nearby errand or visits briefly with a neighbor. As the child shows confidence, parents can gradually increase the time to cover the amount of time between school and their arrival home. (The average weekly home-alone time is 6 hours.) In the beginning, parents should call to check on children more often, too.

Parents need to understand that self-care is *always* more risky than adult supervision. For this reason, parents should advocate for quality school-age child care (SACC) programs in their area. A parent may find other community-based youth programs suitable for older school-age children. If a SACC program or youth program is not available, parents can join a McGruff House or another block-parent program that helps children in self-care during emergencies or if they become frightened. Parents can also help establish a homework help line.

Coping with Family Moves

Today, the United States is a *mobile society*, which means people move from place to place. Earlier in history, more people lived in

Learn More About...
Reducing the Stress of Moving for Children

Parents can reduce the stress of moving for children. Pointing out the positive reasons for moving is a good start. For example, parents may let children know whether the family will have more income or the children will go to better schools. Moving can enable children to widen their interests, make more friends, and learn more about other people. However, parents need to be honest about the move. They need to mention the bad as well as the good. For example, the family will miss old friends and their house. Parents should also explain each step that will happen as they move. Children will ask many questions. They may even want to act out certain events.

If possible, parents should take children with them to see the new home and school before the move. Otherwise, a few pictures of the new area may help make the change easier.

Children should help with packing. It is often best to pack young children's items last. A few favorite toys should be placed in the car or in luggage carried with the family.

Parents need to plan more time to be with children both before and after the move. Parents have a lot to do to prepare for a move and get settled in a new place. Therefore, it can be challenging for parents to find extra time to set aside for their children. This is important, though, because children need special family times to help them feel secure at this stressful time.

extended families in one locale. Today, many people move several times in their lifetime.

Although some people enjoy moving, most feel some stress. Usually the stress lasts only a few weeks or months. However, for others, it may last a couple of years. Stress lessens when the following are true:

★ moves do not occur too often

★ no added stress is present, such as death of a family member or divorce

★ parents are pleased about the move

★ children have siblings who can act as playmates until they make new friends

★ school-age children move at the beginning or end of a school term

★ school-age children have good grades and do well in school

★ children have special skills or interests (such as sports or hobbies) that help provide some stability

Stress occurs because moving is a change. People need time to adjust to a new community, city, school, job, and people. Moving can cause loneliness. Children may feel less certain about the past if they move often. They may ask, "Did I know this person when we lived in our old town?" "Where was my bedroom when we lived in our old house?"

Coping with Death

Death is a basic part of life, and even young children need to learn to come to terms with it. Some children may lose a parent before they finish elementary school. Many more may face the death of a close friend, relative, or even a pet during childhood.

Children gradually begin to understand death. Around six or seven months of age, the baby notices separations from caring adults. These separations, most of which are brief, are the earliest times of loss in a child's life. Early separation may set the stage for later responses to separation, loss, and even death. Until age three or four, children have little, if any, understanding of death. Preschool children's concepts of death are still limited. They try to learn the physical facts of death. They find many facts difficult to believe, and thus, they question the facts. Some concepts that give children trouble include the following:

★ Life can stop.

★ Death is forever.

★ People and pets cannot come back to life, even if children really want them to.

Young preschool children may not react at all to a death. Even older preschoolers find it hard to understand their family's beliefs about death. However, they may repeat statements they have heard others say.

When a Death Occurs

Usually, parents do not talk about death with children unless a person or pet dies. If a child asks about death, parents should answer all questions honestly. Many books suggest ways to explain death to a child. Parents need to help children understand and deal with death and grief.

If a family member or close friend is terminally ill, parents should prepare the child for the upcoming death. Simple, truthful statements are best. A parent may say, "You know Grandma is very sick. The nurses and doctors are trying to help, but Grandma is getting sicker. She may die soon." Parents should not tell children a terminally ill person is on vacation.

When death occurs, parents should explain at the child's level what has happened. They should say what they believe to be true about death. Children become worried if they feel parents are keeping facts from them or avoiding their questions. Parents should explain death well enough so children do not expect the person (or pet) to return. A parent may say, "Uncle Bill is dead. This means he doesn't move or breathe any more." Parents should not tell children a deceased person is sleeping. They should also simply explain religious beliefs. Children need to know they have not caused the death. (For example, they may think they have caused the death by having a fight with the person.)

Parents should be prepared to answer questions and repeat facts for a long time after a death. At first, for example, a child may seem to understand the death. However, a week later the child may again ask about the death.

As children begin to understand death, they may become afraid a parent will die. Parents can reassure their children they will probably live a long time. However, they should never promise children they will not die. If a parent does die after such a promise, the child might feel betrayed and develop a lack of trust in others.

Parents need to decide whether the child should be included in rituals, such as funerals. The decision largely depends on the child's age and maturity, the child's wishes, and the family's beliefs. Some feel that seeing the open coffin makes death more real. Others feel this is too traumatic for a child. If the child will be participating in any rituals, a parent should provide these cultural teachings in advance so the child will know what to expect.

Helping Children Cope with Grief

Once a child understands and reacts to death, parents can help their child cope. Experts say that, when it comes to death, the feelings of preschool children and adults are much alike. Both feel anger, protest, sadness, and loneliness. Both parents and children need close contact with others. Even in their own time of grief, parents should comfort and reassure their child.

Toddlers and preschool children may act in what may seem to be an improper way to a death or to its rituals. Thus, cultural teachings should help children learn to express their grief, 25-9. Parents should set an example by not trying to mask their own sadness, although they should not overburden the child. They should let their child know it is all right to be sad and cry. They need to allow their child to talk about death and grieve in their own developmental ways, such as through pretend play or by carrying photos of a loved one. In time the child will come to terms with the loss and the stress will lessen. Through these experiences the child learns more about death and grief.

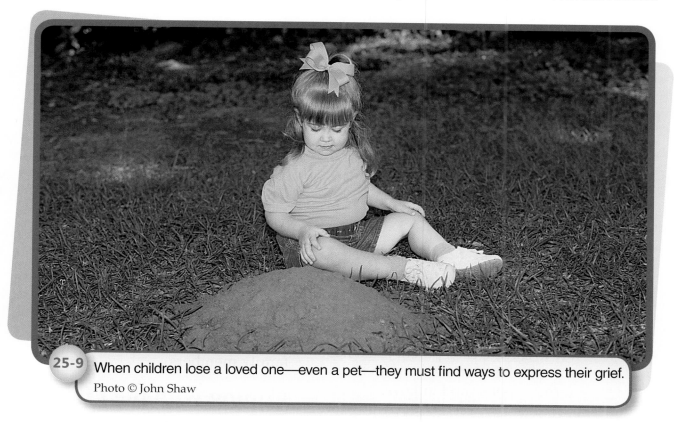

25-9 When children lose a loved one—even a pet—they must find ways to express their grief.
Photo © John Shaw

Coping with Divorce

In the United States, many couples divorce. The divorce rate for teens is especially high. Divorce statistics are not a reliable indicator of the breakup of families. First, many couples separate although they are still legally married. It is not known how many couples are in this category. Next, the number of unmarried couples living together has greatly increased. Many of these couples have children. Because unmarried partners do not file legal paperwork when they separate, the exact number of separations among these families is not known. However, research indicates that unmarried-partner households do have a much higher rate of breakup than married-partner households.

Causes of Divorce

Why do so many people divorce? Many factors contribute to the high rate of divorce. Today's more mobile society brings people of differing backgrounds to meet and marry. Some of these couples find their differences are too great for them to get along well as marriage partners. Being pregnant before marriage, as well as marrying as a teen, also increases the risk of divorce. Studies show living together prior to marriage does not reduce a couple's chance of divorce.

Marital problems often result from financial strain. Other stresses are related to family or work demands. These stresses can build and affect the marriage. When one spouse is unfaithful, violent, or addicted to drugs or alcohol, the other spouse may seek divorce as a way to regain a healthy home life.

Society also contributes to divorce by emphasizing personal happiness. Some spouses may seek divorce as a way to escape an unhappy situation rather than staying married and trying to solve problems. Society also places less stigma on divorce today than in the past.

Effects of Divorce

Divorce affects both parents and children. Parents have to overcome their negative feelings and adjust to a new lifestyle. When children are involved, each parent often has a continual relationship with the former spouse and in-laws.

Children are affected during the separation process and often for years following the divorce. Even children who were infants when their parents divorced deal with these issues in their school-age years.

It is difficult to predict how divorce will affect a particular child.

Age and gender tend to affect how children cope, 25-10. Divorce usually confuses young children. They do not understand the divorce process, but they know one parent is not living with the family. A child's personality affects how he or she will cope, too. Some children are more positive than others and have fewer coping problems.

The family's standard of living often changes after a divorce. The income of single mothers drops a great deal, but the income of single fathers rises. Most children live with their divorced mother, which often means their standard of living drops. This affects all family members.

Coping with the Effects

Parents seeking to divorce may find professional counseling helpful. Counselors or members of support groups can discuss the effects of divorce on parents and children. Parents may need help coping with their personal feelings and meeting their children's new needs. Both parents may have new stresses, such as changes in residence, jobs, income, or roles.

Parents should not discuss problems of the marriage or divorce with children. Children cannot understand these complex issues. Because they cannot help solve the problems of marriage, they should not be burdened with them. However, parents should give children honest answers. They may say something, such as "Your dad (or mom) and I once were happy together. We no longer are happy living together, so we have decided never to live together again. We both love you,

Child Support Officer

Child support officers examine court decree requirements, interview claimants, and contact absent parents. They collect child support by enforcing court orders. They work to help children and families become financially secure.

Education: Child support officers must usually have at least a high school education. Many have college training in police science or military police experience.

Job Outlook: Employment for child support officers is expected to grow.

Reactions to Loss of a Parent Through Death or Divorce

Two- and Three-Year-Olds

Whine, cry, and cling
Act fretful
Have sleep and appetite problems
May regress (This occurs most often at a time of day when the absent parent was usually with the child.)

Four-Year-Olds

Whine and cry
Hit or bite others
Feel they caused the death or divorce

Five-Year-Olds

Feel anxious
Seem moody and restless
Act aggressively
Want physical contact with others
Deny the loss and even pretend parents will be together again
Have problems in creative play

School-Age Children

Daydream more and worry more about the future
Deny the loss
Feel angry and bitter (blame the parent whom they think is responsible)
Feel lonely, abandoned, and rejected by the absent parent
Show antisocial behavior, such as lying or stealing

Have more headaches and stomachaches
Have school problems, such as not being able to pay attention
Show premature detachment, rejecting the parent who is gone and the qualities shared with this absent parent (For example, if the parent had athletic ability, the child may reject sports.)
Become the confidant of the remaining parent and thus have too much adult-like pressure

Common Behaviors and Feelings: Boys

Act oblivious and inattentive
Have a drop in school achievement
Act more aggressively
Have more problems during the divorce process and for the first two years after the divorce
Do better if they have a positive relationship with the absent parent

Common Behaviors and Feelings: Girls

Feel grief and frustration
Cry
Withdraw
Blame themselves
Are more troubled a year after the divorce than at the time of the divorce

25-10 How a child is affected by the loss of a parent through death or divorce depends on the child's age and gender.

and we will always love you. We will always take care of you." Parents may need to repeat this message many times. They should not explain why they are unhappy. It is more important to reassure children that both parents will continue to love and care for them.

When children are in their late teen years, parents may explain more about the marriage failure. Even then, it is best for parents to state their feelings rather than discuss the flaws of the other parent. A parent might say, "I was very hurt," or, "I felt misunderstood."

Once custody plans are firm, parents should tell children about them (if they are old enough to understand). Custody battles can hurt children. For this reason, parents should shelter children from the details of custody decisions. Parents can explain the custody plan in terms of living and visiting arrangements and that both parents feel this plan is best for the family. They should not discuss other details with children.

Family Members Need Support

Children also need neutral people to support them. These people can help children express their sadness or anger in acceptable ways. Support people can also help children cope with loneliness and a new lifestyle. They can serve as role models, too.

Both parents and children may need a support system for many years. Long-term effects occur more often if there are prolonged tensions in the relationships or other major problems. Children have more problems if they are girls, if their parents divorce during their school-age years, or if their parents suffer role strain. Mothers often experience more role strain because they usually have primary custody in addition to less income. This leads to more conflicts with their children. An equal percentage of divorced fathers report a better relationship. Role strain can be reduced with understanding of causes, with support when needed, and with some loving apologies for unnecessary conflicts.

Each parent should be careful not to express hostile feelings about the other parent to children or in their presence. A parent should never ask children to choose sides or relay messages to the other parent.

Children need to know their parents still love them. Both parents should explain the divorce is not the child's fault. They should not expect children to handle the divorce in an adult way. Children may feel stress if they are expected to act too maturely for their age. On the other hand, these children still need consistent, firm discipline.

When the family structure changes, parents should alert teachers and other adults who work with children. These adults can help children cope if they are aware of the home situation.

Single Parenting

At any given time in the United States, about a third of all families are headed by single parents. Mothers head many more of these households than fathers. The number of single-father families is rising, 25-11.

How do single-parent families form? In some cases, single parenting is caused by death of a spouse, separation and divorce, or a breakup of never-married parents. These circumstances change a nuclear family to a single-parent family. While some single-parent families are formed in this way, many are also formed by parents who have never been married. Because these families start with just one parent, they may have somewhat different concerns than other single-parent families.

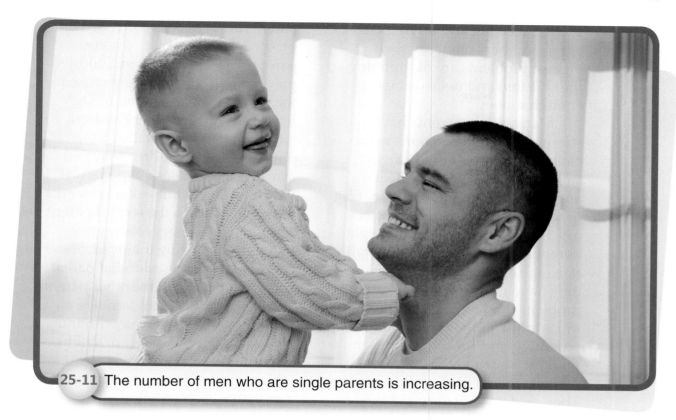

25-11 The number of men who are single parents is increasing.

Problems Single Parents Face

Single-parent families face many of the same problems as other families. Families with one parent may experience some of these same problems in different ways from other families. In addition, they experience some problems that are unique to their family structure.

Financial problems are often the greatest problems single parents face. This is because the parent who heads the household is often the only parent who pays the children's expenses. Although both parents have a legal responsibility to contribute financially, few parents who live separately from their children actually do. In some cases, the matter is never taken before the court, so a child support order is never issued. A **child support order** is a judgment of the court that states how much the parent who does not live with the children must pay toward the children's expenses. Even when a child support order is issued, however, it can be difficult to enforce if the parent does not willingly pay. For these reasons, many single-parent families have incomes below the poverty level. This is especially true of single parents who are younger, have never been married, are less educated, or have more than one child to support. Families with more than one of these risk factors are even more likely to live in poverty.

Men and women who are single parents report different types of problems. Single fathers often report problems with housework and the physical aspects of child care, such as cooking and buying clothes. Single mothers often say their biggest problems are disciplining the children and not earning enough money.

Many single parents have strong emotional reactions to the circumstances that made them single parents. They may feel anger, resentment, depression, fear, or sadness at having to carry so much responsibility alone. Single parents report more **social isolation** (feelings of being alone). They may have no one to talk to about problems and feelings. Because they must fulfill all the responsibilities of parenting and running a household without a partner, single parents often have less time of their own. They are less able to spend time with friends or in activities they enjoy. In cases in which nuclear families lose a parent through death or divorce, family life is disrupted. Feelings of grief and confusion may also be present.

Helping Children Cope

Besides coping with their own feelings, single parents must help their children cope. Parents are the base from which children grow. When death or divorce ends a nuclear family, children feel the loss of a relationship and role model. In these families, children's daily routines change as one parent takes over the duties two parents once shared. The way a child reacts to these changes depends on his or her age and personality. Most of these homes become stable within two years of a death or divorce.

In never-married families, children may have other issues with which they must cope. If both parents are actively involved, these problems are lessened. When one parent is absent, however, children may wonder whether they caused the parent to abandon them. They may wonder why other children have two parents and they have only one. These children may feel a lasting sense of loss, especially if they have never known or no longer have contact with the second parent. They may feel angry toward this parent for not being involved. Some children blame the custodial parent for not staying with the other parent.

In all single parent families, a few long-term effects may continue. In homes where fathers are absent, boys may rebel or do poorly in school. Teen girls may become overly aggressive or shy around boys.

Single parents need support. They may need outside help with problems such as finances, child care, and housework. Parents may need to talk about their feelings with other adults. Some single parents find support or social groups, such as Parents Without Partners®, are helpful. In any event, parents should not rely on their children as a sole source of friendship. This is unfair to the children and unhealthy for the parent-child relationship.

Children in single-parent families also need extra support. They need time to work out their feelings. Adults should allow children to express their feelings through actions and words. Books on the topic may be helpful. Children in single-parent families need adult role models of both genders. These can be relatives, friends, neighbors, or adults from an organization such as Big Brothers

Big Sisters. Forming relationships with other children in single-parent families can help, too.

Remarriage and Stepparenting

Many divorced people remarry within a few years of being divorced. Many widowed parents remarry, and parents who have not been married may marry, too.

The younger people are at the time of becoming single parents, the more likely they are to remarry. Other factors that influence the potential for remarriage include how long the first marriage lasted and whether the divorced person has children. Women under age 30 who have young children are the most likely to marry a new partner.

In most cases, one stepparent enters a single-parent family. (In more than half of cases, stepfathers join a single-parent family headed by the mother.) A new living arrangement changes daily living patterns. Single parents are often proud they can run a household by themselves. After remarriage, they may have problems sharing the parenting roles with a spouse.

Preparing for Family Changes

Before single parents begin a new stepfamily, they should speak to family counselors. Social workers or religious leaders may conduct such sessions. Older children may want to take part in some of the sessions.

All children beyond infancy need to be prepared for the new marriage and family life. Each remarrying parent should share with his or her children that he or she loves the new spouse and wants the marriage to work well for everyone. Telling children the new marriage will last, be better, or be fun is not an honest approach.

Children also need to know they are not the only ones who live in stepfamilies. Many stepchildren face the same issues. They may not know what to call the stepparent. They may worry about whom to invite to school or other special functions. Books on stepfamilies may help children adjust, 25-12.

Perhaps one of the most difficult tasks for a stepparent is to know how much to discipline stepchildren. It is more difficult to discipline stepchildren than biological children. Stepparents are often afraid to correct their stepchildren for fear the children will not like them.

It is usually difficult for children to adjust to a new family structure.

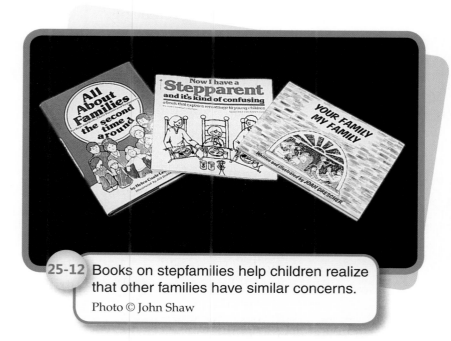

25-12 Books on stepfamilies help children realize that other families have similar concerns.

Photo © John Shaw

The adjustment is even more difficult if the new stepparent has children of his or her own that will join the household, too. However, both parents can help the children adjust over time. When these new family relationships work, the added family ties are worth the effort.

Teens as Parents

Many teen girls become pregnant in the United States every year. Teen parenting, however, is a major social concern and a risk. Becoming a parent in the teen years has no advantages over having children between the ages 20 and 34 years. The risks of teen pregnancy and parenting affect many aspects of the teens' lives, and it is impossible to reverse the consequences. See Chart 25-13 for the consequences of teen parenting. Many of these problems relate to health, financial concerns, and lifestyle changes. Most teens who choose to parent their babies become single mothers. Being a single, never-married parent results in the highest risk for the child's overall well-being.

Health Risks for the Teen Mother and Her Baby

Teens' bodies are still growing and developing—only babies in the womb and infants develop more quickly. Because of all these physical changes, proper nutrition is crucial for a teen. When a teen is pregnant, the baby depends on the mother for nutrition. This depletes her body of nutrients. Poor nutrition before or during pregnancy puts the mother and her baby at risk.

The lack of medical care is another health risk for teen mothers. All mothers-to-be need early and continuous prenatal care. They also need medical care for about two months after delivery. Although the rate of prenatal care has increased, some teens still do not receive care they need early in pregnancy. Reasons for this risk are that teen mothers-to-be:

★ may think they are not pregnant

★ feel their parents will be upset

★ are afraid the relationship with the baby's father will end

★ lack money for medical care or do not know where to go for help

★ cannot find transportation to a medical facility

★ do not know that medical care is necessary

★ are afraid of medical procedures

Both mother and baby are affected by these risks. Even with good health care, teen mothers experience other health risks. These include longer labors and thus a great many C-section deliveries. Compared to all mothers, teen mothers are at the highest risk of postpartum depression (PPD), too. Thus, postpartum care is needed to protect both physical and mental health.

The **mortality rate** (rate of death) for the babies of teen mothers is high. Many of the babies who survive have low birthweights. These small babies have higher rates of SIDS and grow slowly throughout childhood. Studies show they have more learning problems in school and more social problems with peers.

Consequences of Teen Parenting

For teen mothers

★ Health risks are greater for younger teen mothers and for all teen mothers who do not receive quality prenatal and postnatal care.

★ The majority of teen mothers never complete high school.

★ Teen mothers lack entry-level skills for the job market. Their income is usually much below that of mothers who have their first child after the teen years.

★ Teen parents who marry are at high risk for divorce. The divorce rate increases between the first- and sixth-year after marriage.

★ Married teen mothers report major marital problems. These problems include the following:
—more sexual activity than they desire
—loneliness (Many times a teen husband maintains his social life while the wife assumes more child care responsibility. Also, most teen wives tend to lose touch with girlfriends.)
—lack of support (Many times, older men who father many babies are not interested in marriage or parenting. The teen mother may not receive companionship, parenting support, or child support.)

For teen fathers

★ Teen fathers have poor school performance and many times drop out of high school.

★ Teen fathers often lack education and training. For these reasons, they usually cannot earn adequate incomes to support their family.

★ Unmarried teen fathers report not being able to see their babies when they wish. Married teen fathers report problems with the child's maternal grandparents.

★ Teen fathers show less self-esteem than other teens because of less education and more financial problems.

For children of teen parents

★ The mortality rate is high for babies of mothers who are age 15 years or younger. This death rate is twice as high as that for babies of mothers between ages 20 and 34 years.

★ Babies of teen parents are a greater risk for congenital problems.

★ Children of teens have lower achievement in school because of
—having birth defects
—being born too soon or too small
—having less family income

★ Children of teens are at a higher risk of being abused because of
—having birth defects
—being born too soon or too small
—having parents who do not know when a child is ready to do or learn a task (A study shows that a group of teen parents thought babies could use the toilet at six months of age.)
—crying when parents want to sleep, study, or socialize or when parents are depressed

For society

★ Often extra child care tasks and the need for more income burdens the grandparents of the teen's child.

★ Teen parents lose productive income because of their lower-income jobs or unemployment.

★ Society pays the costs of assistance programs to teen parents.

★ Society pays for assistance to children and loss of productive income in the next generation if children do not overcome their problems.

★ Societies may be more violent if children are abused.

★ The numbers and problems faced by single-parent, divorced, and remarried families may increase.

25-13 The risks of teen parenting affect parents, children, and society in general.

As discussed in earlier chapters, health risks increase even more for both mother and baby if the mother smokes, drinks alcohol, or has an STI that is untreated. Health risks also increase for both mother and baby if the teen mother is younger than 15 years or has had more than one pregnancy in the teen years. Many teens have a repeat pregnancy before 20 years of age.

Financial Concerns

Prenatal care and delivery are expensive. Most teens are not covered by insurance. Even if they are covered by their parents' policies, the costs of pregnancy and childbirth may not be covered. Health problems add to the costs for mother and baby. The added expense of a baby is a real burden for teens, most of whom are financially strapped. Parents must pay for a baby's food, clothing, equipment, and perhaps child care. These costs increase as babies grow.

Some teens turn to their parents for help. This is usually stressful both for them and for their parents. Some teen parents require public assistance in the form of Medicaid; Temporary Assistance to Needy Families (TANF); Women, Infants, and Children (WIC); food stamps; and housing subsidy. Recent changes in welfare laws will make assistance more difficult to receive on a long-term basis.

Sadly, these financial problems can continue into adulthood. Studies show teens who become parents usually have financial problems all their lives. Over half of all teen mothers never finish high school. Teen fathers may drop out of school to get a job. Because they have not completed their education, teens do not have entry-level job skills. This means they usually qualify for only low-paying jobs. Even teens who finish high school rarely complete college, which also keeps them from earning adequate pay. College graduates earn almost twice as much in income over the course of their lifetimes as high school graduates.

Teen parents find completing their education difficult or impossible for the following reasons:

★ Adequate child care is unaffordable.

★ Teen parents feel out of place in a traditional program because they are older than other students.

★ The need for a job, even a low-paying one, may keep teen parents out of school.

★ Teen parents' time to study is limited because of their parenting responsibilities, 25-14.

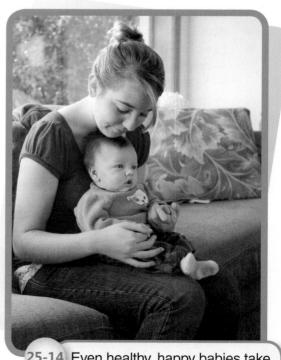

25-14 Even healthy, happy babies take so much care that teen mothers find little time to study.

Many teen-parent families live in poverty. Living in poverty causes problems that adversely affect the lives of teen parents and their children.

Lifestyle Changes

When teens become parents, their lives change in dramatic ways. Those who marry because of a pregnancy may find themselves in unhappy marriages. They may encounter problems living with their baby in their parents' home. Most have financial pressures. Many also socialize less often with friends because they have more responsibility. Teen parents usually lead stressful lives.

Life with Mom and Dad

Teen parents who continue to live with their own parents report additional friction at home. A teen's parents may have a difficult time adjusting to their teen's early parenthood. They may be disappointed and concerned. They may insist the baby's other parent stay out of the baby's life. Grandparents of the baby often feel the most stress because they are juggling child care, work, and other family obligations.

Social Life Changes

Before pregnancy, a teen's life focuses on school, social activities, and family, 25-15. Once a teen becomes a parent, life changes. Now the teen focuses on the medical aspects of pregnancy, the costs of a baby, and ways to meet the baby's needs. Teen parents have little time to study or spend with friends because baby care takes too much time. Baby expenses leave little or no money to spend on nonessential items.

Many teen mothers say they feel isolated. Although friends usually stand by teen mothers, they may not maintain the same social contact. This often happens during the pregnancy and after the baby is born. This leads to depression and frustration for the teen parent.

Family Violence

Teen frustrations may initiate family violence. Spouse abuse may occur in unhappy marriages. Children of teens are at high risk for abuse. Teens' needs do not mesh with their children's needs. Teen parents rarely have enough support in parenting tasks. They seldom know about child development and may expect their children to reach unreasonable goals. The parents' frustration with a child's "lack of progress" often leads to child abuse.

Although teen parents face challenges, many overcome them and have positive experiences as young parents. However, this happens only

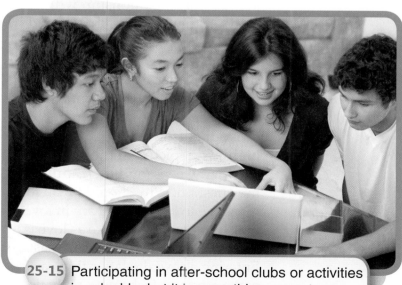

25-15 Participating in after-school clubs or activities is valuable, but it is something many teen parents do not have the time to do.

through hard work. Each parent must be determined to do all he or she can to help the baby and family. Teen parents also need people they can turn to for help. They need emotional, practical, and financial support to overcome the obstacles they face. Today, more community programs are available to help teens finish school and learn to become successful parents and wage earners.

Why Wait?

From the time of birth, human beings want acceptance, loving relationships, and deep intimacy. Although human beings have a strong sexual aspect to their nature, sex cannot by itself satisfy their desires to become truly social beings. A relationship built on sex is very unstable. Sex does not create intimacy—rather sex is one expression of an intimacy that already exists.

Furthermore, some people desire sex for reasons that are not even related to intimacy. For example, some people use sex to avoid a close relationship with their partners; that is, they spend less time in other aspects of the relationship or use sex to end conflicts rather than engage in problem solving. Others may use sex to get back at their parents, prove themselves, or get the "sexual high" as depicted in the media.

Many teens (and even adults) ask the question: Why should I wait for marriage to have sex if I am in love? First, what many mistake as love is a passing feeling that does not last. Entering a sexual relationship can make a person feel emotionally tied to the other person. Imagine how painful this would make a breakup.

The results of a sexual relationship can be life-altering and permanent. Two of the most troubling risks are unplanned pregnancy and STIs. (For example, the majority of all STIs occur in people younger than 25 years of age. Among teens, the number of AIDS cases is very high.) Many birth control methods are available, but the idea of "completely safe sex" is a myth. The only guaranteed way to avoid unwanted pregnancies and STIs is **abstinence**. This choice involves postponing a sexual relationship until marriage. More people realize they have the right to say no to the following:

★ unwanted pregnancies that will forever change their lives

★ STIs that may result in sterility, health problems, or death

★ emotional scars that may follow a broken relationship

★ conflicts with parents and other adults who care for them

★ conflicts with their own consciences, goals, and values

Child Neglect and Abuse

Even the thought of neglect or abuse of children evokes emotion in almost everyone. Some people feel outraged. Others are confused by the problems involved in preventing neglect and abuse. Those who work in child protection agencies are frustrated in trying to fight these crimes.

Neglect and abuse threaten children's health and welfare. Adults who neglect or abuse children cause them physical, mental, or emotional harm. Many children die from these adult actions.

Untold numbers of children suffer neglect and abuse by parents, friends, relatives, or child care workers. Statistics never tell the whole story. Many cases are never reported. Some reported cases are not investigated due to heavy caseloads of social workers. Still other cases are never confirmed (cannot be proven). Thus, the number of cases is higher than data indicate. Furthermore, cases are confirmed based on legal definitions of neglect and abuse as given in a state's child protection laws. Some experts believe these legal definitions should be expanded to include more cases.

Child neglect and abuse are very serious problems. About one-fourth of all children suffer more than one type of neglect or abuse. Of the children who die from neglect and abuse, the majority are younger than age five. Of these very young children, almost half are under age one.

Most neglect and abuse occurs in the home and is done by a person the child knows and trusts. Of reported cases, the vast majority involve at least one parent. About one case in ten involves a relative other than parents. Very few cases involve adults working in child care or foster care settings, and even fewer cases involve strangers. (Stranger abuse is reported most often.)

What Are Child Neglect and Abuse?

Child neglect refers to harm or endangerment of a child caused by an adult's failure to do something legally expected of him or her. States' legal definitions of *neglect* vary. Most, however, focus on the failure of adults to provide for the child's needs. This includes giving a proper level of care with respect to food, clothing, shelter, hygiene, medical attention, or supervision. There are several types of neglect, which include the following:

* **Physical neglect** refers to endangering a child's health or safety by failing to provide supervision and basic survival needs, such as clothing, food, and shelter. (As you read in Chapter 8, a particular kind of physical neglect involving failure to feed a baby or small child sufficiently is called "failure to thrive" syndrome.)

* **Educational neglect** is failure to conform to state legal requirements regarding school attendance.

 Law, Public Safety, Corrections & Security

Family Court Judge

Family court judges are in charge of trials and hearings. They hear cases related to families, such as child neglect and abuse, adoption, custody, and visitation. They resolve differences. To make their decisions, judges research legal issues. Judges also write about their decisions and legal opinions.

Education: A graduate college degree in law, the passing of the state's bar exam, and work experience are the requirements to be a judge.

Job Outlook: Employment of judges is expected to grow more slowly than the average for all occupations due to limited funding at all levels of government.

★ **Medical neglect** is harm or endangerment of a child caused by failure to seek treatment for health problems or accidents.

★ **Moral neglect** is failure to teach the child right from wrong in terms of general social expectations, such as stealing is wrong.

★ **Emotional neglect** is inadequate care and attention, violence or drug use in the home, or failure to meet the child's emotional needs at each stage of development.

In contrast to neglect, **child abuse** refers to an intentional act committed by an adult that harms or threatens to harm a child's well-being. Specific definitions of the types of child abuse follow.

★ **Physical abuse** (even when done in the name of *discipline*) is violence that results in pain, injuries, or both to a child.

★ **Sexual abuse** is any act of a sexual nature that involves an adult and a child. Some states define *sexual abuse* as any act of a sexual nature between a child and someone who is at least five years older than the child. Chart 25-16 explains some of the myths and realities related to sexual abuse.

★ **Emotional and verbal abuse** is any act in which an adult makes excessive demands, harasses, belittles, or verbally threatens the child. Emotional and verbal abuse lowers a child's self-esteem.

Myths and Realities of Sexual Abuse

Myth: Sexual abuse is rare.
Reality: Sexual abuse occurs frequently and takes many forms, such as pornography and incest.

Myth: The offender is an unknown, dangerous person.
Reality: In the vast majority of cases, the offender is a known person, such as a relative or friend.

Myth: The incident occurs suddenly, such as when an adult is momentarily out of the room.
Reality: The abuse is usually repeated over and over again and may occur for several years.

Myth: Child sexual abuse is usually a violent attack.
Reality: More often, child sexual abuse is subtle "force." The offender may call it a "new game."

Myth: Children often make up stories of sexual abuse.
Reality: Children rarely make up stories of sexual abuse. In fact, they are often reluctant to tell about sexual abuse because they fear the offender or feel guilty for being involved.

Myth: Children who recant stories of sexual abuse were lying about the first report.
Reality: Abusers may have pressured children to change their stories.

25-16 Adults need to know the realities of sexual abuse in order to help children and prevent and treat this serious problem.

What Happens to the Victims?

Although some children who suffer neglect and abuse are resilient, most are left with deep and long-lasting scars. These scars affect every aspect of development. In many cases, the idea that "time heals all wounds" does not seem to apply to those who have been neglected or abused as children.

Physical Scars

Many neglected children lack adequate food, clothing, or housing. Poor hygiene and other unsafe living conditions exist. Many babies fail to thrive.

Abused children are often beaten, bruised, burned, and cut. Their bones and teeth may be broken. Even without physical marks, they suffer pain from slapping and other physical attacks. People who are sexually abused suffer internal and external injuries, may contract STIs, and may become pregnant.

The statistics show the youngest children are most prone to die from physical neglect and abuse. For example, death can occur due to **Shaken Baby Syndrome (SBS)**, a condition in which a baby or young child has been violently shaken. Shaking a baby causes a "whiplash" motion in which the brain hits the skull repeatedly. These hits cause veins in the brain to break, filling the area around the brain with blood. This blood collects around the brain in the skull and causes swelling. This swelling damages brain cells and puts pressure on the brain stem, which controls breathing and heartbeat. Many shaken babies develop cerebral palsy, paralysis, brain seizures, blindness, deafness, and learning and behavior problems. Between 15 and 30 percent of children with SBS will die from their injuries.

Mental Scars

Mental scars are common when children are neglected and abused. Some mental problems come from brain injuries. Many others result from educational neglect and the inability to concentrate during learning tasks due to abuse. Lack of brain stimulation during the windows of opportunity can also have a negative effect. Studies indicate that about 30 percent of abused children have some type of language or learning problem. In addition, over half of all abused children have difficulty in school.

Emotional Scars

Emotional scars occur when children are neglected and abused. Children often lack self-esteem, and have feelings of anger, anxiety, shame, guilt, or depression due to the neglect or abuse. Over half of neglected or abused children have social and emotional problems.

Dr. Bruce Perry, a pediatric psychiatrist, works with the Child Trauma Academy in Houston, Texas. He believes there are six core personality strengths: attachment, self-regulation, affiliation, awareness (of how we are alike and different), tolerance, and respect. Children need nurturing and supportive parents to develop these core strengths. Neglected and abused children would need extensive treatment to overcome their past or ongoing traumas and develop these core strengths.

Focus on Science

Brain Development

The brains of infants and toddlers are forever altered by abuse. Physically abused babies have brains that are tuned to track nonverbal cues that may signal the next abusive attack. Abused children closely track the "ups and downs" of adults' emotional states. Brain-stress hormones, such as *cortisol*, prune the brain wiring. By age three, the regions of the brain responsible for emotions are 20 to 30 percent smaller for abused children than for other children. Abused children have less brain development in the brain center for joy and other light-hearted emotions. In these children, the slightest stress results in hyperactivity, anxiety, impulsive behavior, and difficulties in paying attention and using self-control.

Use Internet or print sources to further research the effects of child neglect and abuse on the brain. Share your findings with the class.

Treatment for Victims

When a case of neglect or abuse is confirmed, children can begin to receive help and treatment. This is the first step toward being a neglect or abuse survivor rather than remaining a victim.

Physical treatment for the neglected or abused child is the first priority. As a doctor examines and treats the child, he or she will take a history (from the child, an older sibling, or parents) and document the examination. Records will include the doctor's observations, lab reports, and photographs or drawings.

Caseworkers or advocates from a child abuse prevention agency may also be involved in helping the child. These professionals make decisions about the child's welfare and advocate on his or her behalf.

As caseworkers make decisions about the children, they keep the following questions in mind:

★ What is the relationship of the child to the abuser?

★ What risks are present for further abuse?

★ What role, if any, should the courts have in this case?

★ Should the child remain with the family?

★ What support services could help both the child and family?

The services recommended will depend on the particulars of the case and the age of the child. Foster care, residential treatment facilities, child advocacy centers, counseling, Head Start programs, group therapy, family intervention therapy, and individual therapy are examples of support services that are often used.

In working with adults, courts and caseworkers consider the severity of the neglect or abuse, the adult's relationship to the child, and any past history of neglectful or abusive behaviors. Adults may be restricted from seeing the child or have their parental rights ended. They may also be convicted of a crime or ordered to receive therapy. This therapy could include treatment for mental illness or substance abuse, individual or group counseling, or attendance in classes for neglectful and abusive adults. The reason behind these treatments is to deter the adult from choosing further neglectful or abusive actions.

What Are the Causes of Neglect and Abuse?

Why would an adult neglect or hurt a child? There is no simple cause-effect explanation. *Very different reasons cause the same results.* For example, neglect may occur when parents cannot afford to meet a child's needs or when parents think only about their own needs. Sometimes neglect occurs when parents do not know how to provide proper care for children.

Neglectful and abusive parents come from all levels of income, intelligence, and education. Generally, abusive parents do not have obvious signs of problems that others can see. Abusive parents may seem nice, quiet, and kind when they are at work or around friends.

Risk factors do exist for neglect and abuse. Experts who study neglect and abuse believe it is important to look at the entire family system for answers, 25-17. Although experts cannot weigh the degree of risk for each factor, studies show that drug and alcohol abuse is present in about two-fifths of reported neglect and abuse cases.

Furthermore, *experts cannot always predict from the risk factors what form the abuse will take.* Two exceptions are the following: a parent who physically abuses a spouse is likely to physically abuse a child, and a person who has a history of sexual abuse is more likely to sexually abuse others.

Risk Factors for Neglect and Abuse

Society
★ Poverty
★ Overcrowding
★ Illegal drug culture
★ High crime area
★ High unemployment rate
★ Few social services
★ Unaffordable health care

Parent and family
★ Unwanted pregnancy
★ Single parent
★ Teen parent
★ Physical, sexual, or emotional abuse as a child
★ Emotional neglect as a child
★ Use of violence to express anger
★ Lack of self-esteem
★ Emotional immaturity
★ Poor coping skills
★ Alcohol or illegal drug abuse
★ Marriage problems
★ Financial stress
★ Recent stressful events (divorce, recent move, death in family)

★ Illness (physical or mental health, especially depression)
★ Lack of parenting skills including no preparation for the extreme stress of a new baby
★ Lack of knowledge of child development leading to unrealistic expectations for the child
★ Heavy parenting responsibility (multiple births or single children less than 18 months apart in age)
★ Weak bonding or attachment to a child (often due to child's care in ICU after birth)
★ Use of physical punishment (called *corporal punishment*)
★ Isolation (lack of family or friend support)

Child
★ Under the age of five, especially under age one
★ Low birthweight or premature
★ Looks like or has traits like a disliked relative
★ Irritable or cries a great deal (colic; ADHD)
★ Disobeys parents or argues a great deal (older child)

25-17 Certain risk factors are commonly found in cases of child neglect and abuse.

Abuse is a complex, interactive process. For this reason, some parents may abuse only one child in the family or may abuse a child only during times of high parental stress. An example of an interactive process is: An unplanned pregnancy leads to more financial stress for a family who already lives near the poverty level. To save costs, the mother does not get prenatal care. Her baby is born at a low birthweight. The tiny baby has feeding problems that cause him or her to cry for hours at a time. The parent, who already has problems in coping, abuses the infant "to stop the crying." This does not, however, mean the child is to blame for the abuse. Abusers are *always* responsible for their actions.

How Can Neglect and Abuse Be Prevented?

Neglect and abuse have many causes. These complex problems do not have a single, quick solution. Work must be done on many fronts to put an end to them. Preventing neglect and abuse will take the efforts of individuals, families, communities, and society at large. Each person's involvement counts in the fight against these crimes.

Public Awareness

First, people need to be more aware of neglect and abuse. They need to understand which behaviors are neglectful or abusive. They need to learn more about how these problems threaten children and affect families' lives. People also need to be aware of the legal consequences of neglect and abuse. They need to be informed about how they can help in the fight against these crimes.

Many organizations are leading the way to increased public awareness about child neglect and abuse. These organizations provide a variety of information on prevention and support services. Some of these agencies host Web sites at which people can learn more about neglect and abuse, 25-18.

Social Changes

Neglect and abuse are more likely in a society in which people feel undervalued, financial problems abound, and violence is condoned. To effectively prevent abuse, some of these societal problems must be addressed. Needed changes include the following:

★ societal rejections of violence and aggression

★ better economic security for families

★ reduction in the numbers of mothers who do not receive adequate prenatal care

★ provision for high-quality child care facilities, including crisis child care programs that provide respite for parents through child care

★ increased emphasis on respecting children, their needs, and their rights

Being active in groups that work for any of these changes can help prevent abuse. Making elected officials aware of needed changes is important, too.

Professional Support

Doctors and other professionals who come into contact with families need to be aware of risk factors that lead to neglect or abuse. They

Web Sites for Information on Child Neglect and Abuse

AVANCE Family Support and Education Program	**www.national.avanceinc.org**
Child Abuse Prevention Network	**www.childabuse.com**
ChildHelp	**www.childhelp.org**
Family Life Development Center	**www.human.cornell.edu/che/fldc/ progrmas/Child-Abuse.cfm**
Parents as Teachers National Center	**www.parentsasteachers.org**
National Exchange Club Foundation	**www.preventchildabuse.com**
Prevent Child Abuse America	**www.preventchildabuse.org**

25-18 These Web sites provide valuable information regarding child neglect and abuse.

should note any risk factors they observe in specific families and connect high-risk families to the appropriate social programs.

For example, during a prenatal visit, a doctor might ask about how the pregnancy affects others in the family. This helps the doctor determine whether there are other problems the family is facing. The doctor could make referrals for the family to seek other needed support services and social programs.

During well-child checkups, doctors can talk with parents about child development. They can answer questions and offer advice about expected behaviors and issues such as toilet learning, teething, crying, and sleep or eating problems. Understanding child development can help parents form more realistic expectations of their children. When parent expectations exceed children's abilities, it can lead to frustration. This is a problem because frustrated parents are more likely to lash out at their children with abusive behaviors.

Appropriate expectations of the child can reduce this frustration and prevent some abusive outbursts.

Doctors can also assess a child's home life by asking simple questions, such as the following:

★ What is it like for you taking care of your child?

★ Do you get time for yourself?

★ Do you get any help with your children from family or friends?

★ Do you think your baby cries too much?

★ How do you deal with your child's behavior problems?

It is not enough just to assess, however. Support services must be available in the community. One type of support program is home visitation. In *home visitation*, a professional comes to the home to monitor the health of mother and infant, provide one-on-one parent education, and suggest other helpful community programs parents can access.

Education

Adults need to continue to learn more about children and their care. This education should include life skills training for children, teens, and young adults and education in child development and parenting. Learning more about healthy relationships, communication, stress and anger management, and coping skills will also help people prepare themselves to work with or care for children.

In addition, parents can also benefit from learning parenting techniques from such parent-education programs as Parent Effectiveness Training (PET), Nurturing Parent Programs® (NPPs), and Systematic Training for Effective Parenting (STEP).

Recognizing and Reporting Neglect and Abuse

To end neglect and abuse, people must recognize and report it. Knowing what behaviors are neglectful or abusive is the first step. As a citizen, however, the responsibility does not stop there.

Adults should be alert to signs that neglect and abuse may be occurring. Some common signs children exhibit are listed in 25-19. When adults notice these signs and suspect neglect or abuse, they should report this to an agency that can help. The local or state departments of human services are a good place to start. Adults can also call child abuse hot lines to report suspected abuse. The numbers for these hot lines are listed in local phone books as well as in national directories of toll-free numbers.

Some professionals who work with children are known as **mandated reporters** of child abuse. These professionals are legally bound to report any known or suspected cases of neglect or abuse. Mandated reporters include health care workers, teachers, counselors, social service workers, and child care providers. In many states, mandated reporters can be charged with a criminal offense if they fail to report known or suspected cases of neglect or abuse.

Depending on state laws, other adults may not be mandated to report neglect or abuse. However, these adults should still feel compelled to make a report. Reporting neglect and abuse is the only way these adults can help protect the child from further mistreatment. They must remember that children are defenseless victims in these cases. In most cases, the name and information of someone who makes a report remains confidential.

When a report is made, the appropriate state agency will document the facts. If there is enough evidence, a caseworker will investigate the case. He or she will make a visit to the home and talk to all the family members. If the case is confirmed, steps will be taken to help the child and work with the adult to end the cycle of abuse.

Even in cases where enough evidence is not presented, the report will still be kept on file. It is still important to make the report because this helps to build a case. Over time, if more reports are made about the same abuser, the case will be more likely to be investigated and confirmed.

Stopping abusive cycles is equally important. Children must not be allowed to go through life being neglected, abused, or both. Children need to receive help as soon as possible in order to end the harm and heal the wounds they have already received. Healing lessens children's chances of repeating these behaviors.

Signs of Child Neglect and Abuse

Anyone who suspects child neglect or abuse should report it to proper authorities so the child can receive help. In fact, the law in most states requires certain people to report suspected neglect or abuse. The following signs will help you identify children who need help.

Neglect

A child may be physically neglected when he or she

- ★ is malnourished
- ★ fails to receive needed health care without a parental objection, such as for religious reasons
- ★ fails to receive proper hygiene (is not washed or bathed; has poor oral hygiene; has ungroomed skin, nails, and hair)
- ★ has insufficient clothing or clothing that is dirty, tattered, or inappropriate for the weather
- ★ lives in filthy conditions or inadequate shelter

A child may suffer mental or educational neglect when he or she

- ★ lacks moral training
- ★ lacks constructive discipline
- ★ fails to receive positive examples from adults
- ★ fails to have adequate supervision
- ★ is left alone for hours
- ★ fails to attend school regularly because of parents
- ★ fails to receive parent stimulation toward learning or education suited to his or her ability
- ★ is not allowed to take part in wholesome recreational activities

A child may be emotionally neglected if he or she

- ★ experiences constant friction in the home
- ★ is denied normal experiences that produce feelings of being wanted, loved, and protected
- ★ is rejected through indifference
- ★ is overly rejected, such as through abandonment

Abuse

A child may be physically abused if he or she

- ★ seems fearful or quiet around parents, but has no close feeling for them
- ★ is wary of physical contact initiated by an adult
- ★ has little or no reaction to pain and seems much less afraid than most children the same age
- ★ has unexplained injuries or shows evidence of repeated injuries, such as having bruises in various stages of healing or repeated fractures
- ★ is dressed inappropriately, such as an injured child dressed in pajamas who was reportedly injured on a bicycle or a child dressed in a turtleneck in the summer to cover bruises
- ★ when x-rayed, shows a history of past injuries to the long bones
- ★ has injuries not reported on previous health records
- ★ has parents who have taken the child to many hospitals and doctors without appropriate explanation
- ★ has parents who refuse further diagnostic studies of their child's injuries
- ★ has parents who show detachment or see the child as bad or "different" during medical treatment
- ★ has parents who give too many minute details about the cause of injury
- ★ tries to protect parents when they are questioned about the child's injuries

25-19 People must know the signs of neglect and abuse so they can help children with these problems.

(Continued.)

Abuse *(Continued.)*

A child may suffer verbal abuse if he or she

★   lacks self-esteem
★   is either too quiet and polite or uses harsh and improper language when dealing with others, especially those who are smaller or younger
★   expresses long-term feelings of damage and isolation

A child may be sexually abused if he or she

★   has extreme and sudden changes in behavior, such as loss of appetite or sudden drop in grades
★   has nightmares and other sleep problems
★   regresses to previous behaviors, such as renewed thumb sucking
★   has torn or stained underwear
★   has infections (with symptoms like bleeding or other discharges and itching) or swollen genitals
★   fears a person or shows an intense dislike of being left alone with that person
★   has an STI or is pregnant
★   has unusual interest in or knowledge of sexual matters for his or her age

25-19   *(Continued.)*

Another important piece of the puzzle lies with the abusers themselves. These adults play perhaps the biggest role in stopping abuse. They need to recognize that what they are doing is wrong and find help to stop. When abusers sincerely want to change their behavior, the chances for success are much higher. If parents feel out of control and think they may abuse a child, they can call a national organization called *Parents Anonymous*®. Members of this group form local chapters, and they can provide support services any time. Parents can also call a crisis hot line to ask for help.

Resources for Children in Crises

Many resources are available to help children in crises. Some of the resources directly assist children and their families. Others provide information, registries, referrals to local support groups, or counseling.

Some of these resources are departments and agencies of federal, state, or local government. Other resources are national private agencies funded by membership dues and contributions. Still other resources are the work of religious groups, hospitals and medical associations, mental health centers, crises intervention centers, law enforcement agencies, legal associations, counseling services, schools, and civic or volunteer organizations.

Many agencies have online bookstores for purchasing books and other materials designed for aiding children and families facing different problems. When searching for items on a specific topic of interest, a bookstore might also offer resources for parents, children, or families. Other book titles and materials can be located through online publishers and libraries. The telephone book, library, or the Internet are other means of finding good resources.

Summary

Children's lives are influenced by their siblings. They learn by interacting with them. Children's birth order tends to affect their social roles and personalities. Multiple-birth children strive to develop their separate identities.

When both parents work outside the home, all family members must cooperate to care for the home and plan time to spend together. How children adjust depends on how much time the parents spend with their children each day, when they enter the workforce again, and how they feel about working.

The numbers of children in self-care are increasing. Self-care has many negative effects and may be illegal for children younger than 12 or 13 years. If self-care is a must for older children, parents must teach them how to safely care for themselves when the parents will be away for short periods.

Families in the United States tend to move a great deal. Moves can be less stressful for children if parents feel positive about the moves and help their children get used to the new place.

It is difficult for children to understand the concept of death and to deal with grief. Adults should answer children's questions truthfully and at the child's level of understanding. They need to understand that children grieve losses, too.

Divorce can have many causes, and its effects can be lasting. Parents need to help their children who are faced with these new stresses. When the family structure changes, such as through divorce or remarriage, families must adapt to these changes. Single-parent families have challenges that are unique in addition to the ordinary problems all families face. Children need to be prepared for a new marriage and the changes this will create.

Pregnant and parenting teens face many additional risks and problems, too. Because of the high-risk nature of teen relationships, many marriages end in divorce. Some teen family structures survive through dedicated work and much effort.

Neglect and abuse are major problems that threaten children's health and well-being. Some social changes have been suggested to help protect children from neglect and abuse. Many signs of child neglect and abuse are observable, but others are not as easily observed. When people report suspected cases of neglect and abuse, the children and adults involved can get the help they need. Treatments are available both for the children and the adult.

Companion Web Site

Interactive Activity

Review vocabulary terms and key concepts for Chapter 25 at **g-wlearning.com**.

Review and Reflect

Write your answers to the following questions on a separate sheet of paper.

1. List the four main types of sibling interactions.

2. True or false. Birth order almost totally determines personality.

3. True or false. A parent should not allow multiple-birth children to wear identical outfits, even if the children want to wear these outfits.

4. Name four possible advantages that children whose parents work outside the home have over those whose parents do not.

5. Name two positive effects and two negative effects self-care may have on children.

6. True or false. Most children readily adapt and look forward to family moves.

7. List the three physical concepts about death that children must learn.

8. True or false. Most teen parents stay together for the sake of the baby and work out their financial problems.

9. True or false. Parents should give children a detailed explanation about why their marriage has failed so they can better accept it.

10. Explain the difference between child neglect and child abuse.

11. True or false. An abusive parent often acts mentally ill outside the home.

12. True or false. In an abusive family, certain children are more likely to be abused than others.

Cross-Curricular Link

13. **Writing.** Write a fiction story on the joys and trials of being an only child, the oldest child, a middle child, a youngest child, or a multiple-birth child. Check your story for correct spelling, grammar, and punctuation.

14. **Social Studies.** Design a pamphlet for parents featuring tips for preparing a child for self-care. As part of the pamphlet, encourage parents to find or initiate school-age child care programs.

15. **Reading, Writing, Technology.** Use Internet or print sources to locate articles about children in self-care. Read the articles and write a report on what you have read. Check your report for correct spelling, grammar, and punctuation.

16. **Speech.** In a small group, list some statements you have heard people make about death. Find the word *euphemism* in the dictionary. Are any of the statements on your list euphemisms? Why or why not? Why do you think these statements are used? Discuss how you think young

children might respond to these statements.

17. **Reading, Writing.** Ask an elementary school librarian for children's books on one of the following topics: family moves, death, divorce, single parenting, and stepfamilies. For each book, give the bibliographical information, the age for which the book was written, and a few statements giving the main content.

18. **Social Studies, Speech.** Interview a resource person from a local social service agency. Ask this person about specific services of the agency as they pertain to children and families.

Making Observations

19. Observe older siblings with their younger siblings. In what ways, either directly or indirectly, do older siblings influence their younger brothers and sisters?

20. Observe a family in which the parent or parents work outside the home. What advantages do you see for the child or children? What disadvantages do you see? Do you feel the parent or parents show any role strain? Explain.

21. Observe a child who has recently experienced the stress of a move, death, or a family divorce. What seems to be the child's greatest stressor? How is the child coping? How are parents, teachers, family friends, peers, and others helping the child cope?

Thinking Critically

22. A young couple is trying to decide whether to have another child as a companion to their only child. They do not really want another child, but they have heard that only children are often spoiled and friendless. What do child development experts recommend? What do you think might happen to a child who was wanted only as a companion for an older child?

23. Do you think role strain is solely caused by demands in a person's life or also by personality? Explain. What are some specific ways parents can lessen role strain?

24. In general, why are family moves, deaths, and divorces all difficult for children? What factors can affect children's adjustment to these situations?

26 Making Career Decisions

After studying this chapter, you will be able to

★ **identify** steps in self-assessment.

★ **explain** how to research careers and develop a career plan.

★ **describe** how to find a job.

★ **describe** careers in child-related fields.

★ **explain** how personal and professional qualifications affect your career choice.

★ **identify** skills needed for job success.

Terms to Know

lifestyle
self-assessment
values
aptitudes
abilities
career clusters
personal plan of study
career plan
goals
resources
networking
résumé
cover letter
references

portfolio
direct intervention
consultants
licensing personnel
entrepreneur
personal qualifications
career burnout
leader
professional qualifications
work ethic
codes of professional ethics
formal leadership
informal leaders

Reading Advantage

As you read the chapter, write a letter to yourself. Imagine that you will receive this letter in a few years when you are working at your future job. What would you like to remember from this chapter? In the letter, list key points from the chapter that will be useful in your future career.

Companion Web Site

Interactive Activity

Learn more about preparing for a career by completing the *Read, Discuss, and Analyze* Activity for Chapter 26 at **g-wlearning.com**.

A career is more than just a job title. A *career* is a progression of related jobs that result in employment and personal growth. Choosing a career will affect many factors in your **lifestyle**, or typical way of life. Your career choices will likely influence where you live, what skills you must develop, with whom you will associate, what free time you will have, and what your financial picture will be.

You live in a world of change. No one can be sure of all the changes people will face in coming years. However, today's trends can guide you to explore promising career options. For example, most careers today involve knowledge-based work as opposed to work with one's hands. In general, the information-age economy needs a new type of employee. This employee is one who

★ adapts and copes with the stress of change

★ learns quickly and is willing to learn new skills continuously

★ possesses skills from more than one field that can be useful in a career

Additionally, career success today is thought of more in terms of the career skills gained, not in keeping one job until retirement. Today, success also means finding work that is rewarding and fulfilling. Making career decisions is a lifelong process of living and learning.

Many people who are interested in children and their development will seek a child-related career, 26-1.

26-1 An interest in helping children learn and develop musical skills led this man to start a business instructing children on the piano.

Other people will seek careers in other areas. No matter which career field you choose, you will need to develop many skills that are important for all careers. These skills include human relations, communication, teamwork, leadership, and role-management skills. People should start developing these skills in childhood and continue building them throughout life.

In addition, the boundaries between work and personal life sometimes blur. This blurring goes beyond being "plugged in" to work during nonworking hours through communication devices, such as cell phones and e-mail. Workers often find it challenging to balance their many work and personal roles. As you prepare for the world of work, it is good to learn more about how to balance multiple roles.

Heading Toward a Career

Your life is an expression of what you are now and can become in the future. The decisions you make about how and with whom to spend time are personal statements about what you feel life is and can be. Some of the most important choices you will make in your life will be related to your chosen work.

People constantly face choices. For the most part, these choices do not seem like choices or at least important ones. Most people simply do what they think is expected. Sometimes choices are made from very limited alternatives. Thus, people often act in rather unthinking ways.

In life, however, some choices are crucial and require much careful thought. Career decisions fall into this category. When career decisions are made without much thought, people are likely to be unproductive and unhappy. Career decisions are also important because they influence many other choices. These include making choices about education and training, considering the timing of marriage and parenthood, and deciding about other major purchases.

Identifying Your Interests, Aptitudes, and Abilities

The most difficult and important step in career planning is identifying your interests, aptitudes, and abilities. Another name for this step is **self-assessment**. By doing self-assessment, you learn more about who you are as a person and what type of job would suit you well. It is worth the effort because self-assessment often leads to finding a career that is personally fulfilling. Without this step, some people pursue a career that turns out to be unsatisfying.

Interests

What do you care about? What are you proud of? What challenges you? In answering these questions, you are talking about your *interests*. Some of your deeper interests are called **values**. These are ideas, beliefs, and objects that are important and meaningful to you. Your family, culture, and experiences have helped to shape your values. Your personality traits also play a large role.

You might wonder how interests relate to the world of work. Try to view yourself in a particular career. How do you see yourself? What feelings do you think you would have about doing this type of work? Talk with people in a given career who are passionate about what they do, 26-2. What brings them satisfaction in their work? Do you think you would feel a similar satisfaction and fulfillment from such work? The answers to these questions will teach you much about yourself.

Many people seek and stay in careers that align with their values and interests. Being interested in your work is only one factor, however. Not all interests will lead to a promising career. Some interests are best pursued as hobbies or volunteer opportunities.

Aptitudes

Aptitudes are natural talents. People are born with aptitudes—these are a part of their heredity. Think of the talents you have that seem to come naturally to you. Some of your aptitudes will be quite obvious to you. However, you may even have some aptitudes of which you are not aware. Suppose you have a natural talent for nurturing children. This aptitude might go unnoticed unless you have an opportunity to interact with children.

Most people enjoy doing things that come naturally, so a person's aptitudes often become interests. Aptitudes and interests can differ, however. You might not have an interest in a certain area even if you are talented in that area. Likewise, you might be

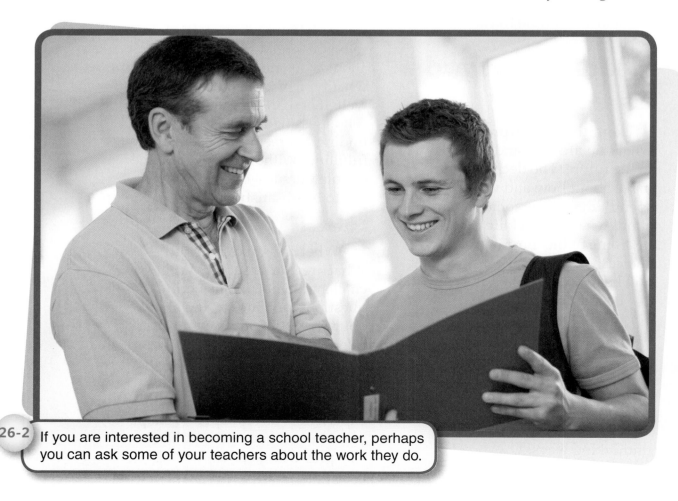

26-2 If you are interested in becoming a school teacher, perhaps you can ask some of your teachers about the work they do.

interested in many areas in which you have no natural talents.

When it comes to careers, aptitudes do have an influence. To do well in a career, you will need to develop certain skills. These skills will enable you to perform the tasks of your chosen career. You will likely develop career skills most quickly and easily in areas in which you have natural talents.

For this reason, consider your aptitudes when choosing a career field. Otherwise, it may be difficult or even impossible to develop the needed skills. Even if you select a career that draws upon your aptitudes, you will still need training and practice to develop all the career skills you will need.

A guidance counselor can give you an aptitude test. Aptitude tests are also available online. Your answers to any aptitude test will identify the areas in which you seem to have aptitudes. The test may also reveal some career areas that might suit you well.

Abilities

Abilities are skills that have been learned or developed. People are not born with abilities. Instead, abilities are acquired through effort and practice. Abilities can be developed to help a person use an aptitude. For example, if you have an aptitude for leading others, you can develop leadership abilities to help you succeed. Abilities can also be developed in place of aptitude. Even a person who is not naturally inclined to teach children can learn ways to interact well with them.

In careers, two types of abilities are needed. The first set includes rather general skills desired of all employees. For example, communication skills are needed in all jobs. The second kind of abilities is career specific. For example, if you are going to illustrate children's books, you need to develop abilities in drawing and graphic design.

For the most part, you will develop career-specific skills only after choosing a career path. People gain career-specific abilities in colleges, universities, training schools, and on-the-job programs. For entry into some careers, certain tests are also required after training is complete. These tests measure a person's career-specific abilities.

Skill development is a life-long learning process. Most workers are expected to continue to develop skills as they work. Many workplaces continue teaching new skills to their employees. Continued learning enhances a person's abilities on the job.

Career Counselor

Career counselors focus on helping people with career decisions. They explore and evaluate their clients' education, training, work history, interests, skills, and personality traits. Career counselors also work with clients to develop job-search skills and assist them in locating and applying for jobs. In addition, career counselors provide support to people experiencing job loss, job stress, or other career transition issues.

Education: Education requirements vary based on occupational specialty. However, a master's degree is usually required to be a counselor. In addition, many states require licensure and certification.

Job Outlook: Employment for counselors is expected to grow much faster than the average.

Learning About Careers

Once you choose a career field of interest, it is time to find out more about this field. As you learn more, you will form a more realistic picture of what it is like to work in the field. You will also find out about future opportunities that might exist in this career field. From this information, you can decide whether this field is truly a fit for you. You can learn more by using career clusters, getting a market overview, researching the education and training you would need, and taking an inside view at the career field.

Use Career Clusters

Using the *career clusters model* is a good way to begin exploring careers. The **career clusters** are 16 broad groupings of occupational and career specialties, 26-3. Each career cluster contains *career pathways*, or subgroups of occupations, that require common knowledge and skills. Occupations in a pathway range from entry-level to those requiring advanced skills.

Begin by identifying the cluster and pathways that fit your career interests. With the help of your teachers and counselors, develop a **personal plan of study**. This plan identifies the core courses and other learning experiences you must complete to meet your educational and career goals. You will have greater flexibility when job hunting if you design a plan that leads to several related occupations.

Sixteen Career Clusters

 Agriculture, Food & Natural Resources
 Architecture & Construction
 Arts, A/V Technology & Communications
 Business, Management & Administration

 Education & Training
 Finance
 Government & Public Administration
 Health Science

 Hospitality & Tourism
 Human Services
 Information Technology
 Law, Public Safety, Corrections & Security

 Manufacturing
 Marketing
 Science, Technology, Engineering & Mathematics
 Transportation, Distribution & Logistics

The Career Clusters icons are being used with permission of the States' Career Clusters Initiative
www.careerclusters.org

26-3 The career clusters help students identify the knowledge and skills needed for specific careers.

Analyze the Market

The next step in learning about careers is analyzing the labor market for career opportunities. Learning about the entire field is a good idea in case a specific career is becoming *obsolete* (no longer useful). You do not want to waste time and money preparing for a career in which jobs will soon cease to be available. Instead, you should try to enter a field that is growing or at least holding steady. When researching the outlook for a career area, look for the following information:

★ current and expected employment opportunities for specific occupations

★ working conditions and environment

★ typical work hours

★ salaries for entry-level and experienced positions

Many resources related to careers are readily available online, 26-4. You can also keep up with the labor market by reading national and local newspapers and business magazines. Trade or professional journals published within a certain career field can also give you an idea about employment trends in the field.

Web Sites for Researching Careers

Source	Internet Address
USAJOBS, the official job site of the U.S. Federal Government	www.usajobs.gov
Occupational Outlook Quarterly, U.S. Department of Labor	www.bls.gov/opub/ooq/ooqhome.htm
Occupational Outlook Handbook, U.S. Department of Labor	www.bls.gov/oco
Career Guide to Industries, U.S. Department of Labor	www.bls.gov/oco/cg/cgjobout.htm
U.S. Department of Labor Employment and Training Administration	www.doleta.gov
The Occupational Information Network (O*NET™)	www.onetcenter.org
Career Voyages	www.careervoyages.gov
CareerOneStop	www.careeronestop.org
Mapping Your Future	www.mappingyourfuture.org
Career Resource Center	www.careers.org

Note: Internet addresses and content are subject to change without notice.

26-4 Making a wise career choice means getting the facts about a career.

Determine Education and Training

Before you can enter your chosen career field, you will first need the required education and training. If you know what career pathway you would like to pursue, you can find out exactly what the requirements are. Some training programs have entry-level requirements. If you are aware of these requirements while you are still in high school, you can begin to work toward them. Taking this step-by-step approach will help you enter the career field as soon as possible.

When you know what education or training you need, you can search for the best place to acquire it. Your guidance counselor can help you with this search. Most colleges and other training programs have online information and toll-free phone lines. You might also wish to meet with faculty at colleges or other training programs. After reviewing the requirements for your chosen career, you can make your career plan more final.

Get an Inside View

Getting an inside view is the best way to learn about a particular career. An inside view is the best test for comparing career expectations with your interests, aptitudes, and abilities. There are a few ways you can get an inside view of various careers.

Talk to People in the Career Field

Talk to employers and business owners about the career you are considering. Get as many perspectives as possible. Ask each employer what qualities he or she desires in new employees. Perhaps you can talk with a person who is working in your career of interest. Find out what the person likes most and what is most challenging for him or her.

You may also want to learn more about the job duties and typical job demands. Your high school may have programs in which students learn about a career of interest through job shadowing. *Job shadowing* is going through a workday or days as a "shadow" to a competent worker. By job shadowing, you can see the work environment, the career skills in practice, and the value of training. You may also ask questions and get advice about preparing to enter this career.

Professional organizations offer another opportunity to meet people working in your desired career field. Members of such organizations can provide advice as you prepare to enter a career. For example, if you are interested in a child-related career, you may want to contact a local chapter of the National Association for the Education of Young Children (NAEYC) or the Association for Childhood Education International (ACEI).

Gain Related Experiences

Another way to get an inside look at careers you are considering is to get involved. Your experiences will help you learn more about children and decide whether a child-related career is right for you. For example, if you are interested in a child-related career, you might consider taking a babysitting class. Your babysitting experiences will teach you about providing care for young children, 26-5. Another way to gain experience is to work as a volunteer in a child care center, children's program, or summer camp.

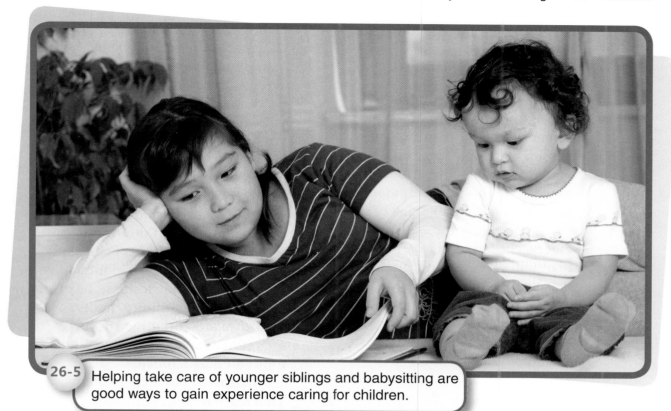

26-5 Helping take care of younger siblings and babysitting are good ways to gain experience caring for children.

Work-based learning programs are school programs that aid students in getting quality experiences in the world of work. In these programs, students take classes and are placed at a work site. A school program coordinator works with both the student and the work-site mentors to make the student's learning meaningful. Work-based programs can take on one of the following forms:

★ *Cooperative education.* Students enroll in a cooperative education class to learn more about careers and develop needed general skills. Students receive paid, on-the-job training through part-time work.

★ *Apprenticeships.* Students take a specific career class, such as child care, and then apply what they learn in class by working under the supervision of a highly skilled tradesperson. This is not the same as a *registered apprenticeship*, which is an advanced training program that usually lasts for several years. A registered apprenticeship program operates under standards set forth by a division of the U.S. Department of Labor called the *Office of Apprenticeship*. You can learn more about registered apprenticeships by visiting the Office of Apprenticeship Web site at **www.doleta.gov/OA/**.

★ *Internships.* Students have paid and unpaid supervised work experiences. Some students may be able to earn academic credits for internships.

All of these programs provide valuable learning experiences. In some cases, students may find entry-level positions with the employer who supervised their work-based learning.

Develop a Career Plan

After you have done a self-assessment, learned about careers using the career clusters, and chosen a possible career pathway, you are ready to "tie it all together." You can do this by creating a **career plan**. This is a detailed list of steps a person must complete in order to enter a chosen career path. A career plan will serve as your guide. It will help you identify your **goals**, what you want to achieve or obtain, as you pursue your chosen career.

As you develop your career plan, you will set short- and long-term goals. *Short-term goals* are achievements you desire in the near future. When planning for a career, short-term goals are the many steps you will need to take as you work toward entry in your career field of choice. Short-term goals help you focus on what you need to attain now and help you keep track of your progress.

Long-term goals are the major achievements toward which you strive. Long-term goals take much more time to achieve than short-term goals. These goals often take a year or more to complete. Long-term goals will keep you focused on the needed abilities, experience, and credentials for a career. *Credentials* are proof of having certain skills, such as a college degree, license, certificate, or designation. In addition, long-term goals also serve as a guide to planning short-term goals. For example, a long-term goal might be to earn a college degree. Suppose the college of choice had a minimum high school grade point

average for admission. A logical short-term goal would be to attain a grade point average that meets or exceeds this minimum.

You will also need to identify your **resources**, which are tools you can use in achieving your goals. Your goals and resources should be realistic. You will want to be challenged, but not feel overwhelmed. Perhaps your goal seems realistic, but the resources seem unrealistic. If this is the case, talk with your guidance counselor and the admissions office at colleges or training schools. Financial aid and other resources are often available to those who are motivated to achieve.

Keep a log of achievements. This log will help you track your progress and motivate you to accomplish other goals. Reviewing your log can also help you prepare materials for job searches.

Job Search Skills

Being qualified is one part of finding a child-related career. Another part is looking for and securing a job. Finding the job you want takes effort. There are many steps involved. Knowing what to expect and how to handle yourself at each stage will increase your chances of job-search success.

Searching for Jobs

Job leads may be found on the Internet, on bulletin boards located in shopping areas and recreational centers, at employment agencies, and through networking. **Networking** is making professional contacts with family, friends, and other people you know for job information or referrals.

To search for a job as a camp counselor, for example, you might look at job listings online. You may also call local park districts, schools, or houses of worship to ask whether they offer camp programs. You might also talk to relatives or friends who have children that attend camps. Once you find out where the camps are located, you can call each camp to ask who handles hiring counselors and how to apply.

Applying for Jobs

To apply for jobs, you need a résumé. A **résumé** is a short, written history of your education, work experience, and other qualifications for employment, 26-6. Prospective employers will look at your résumé

Mia Holtz

1603 Green Street

Southland Township, Wisconsin 66732

(262) 555-7472

miaholtz@provider.com

Objective	Seeking a summer camp aide position.
Education	Southland High School, Southland Township, Wisconsin, 20XX to present
	Focus on human services, with an emphasis in child development courses. Computer skills include keyboarding and Microsoft Word, Excel, and PowerPoint. Graduating in June 20XX.
Experience	Volunteer, Southland High School-Age Child Care Program, 20XX to present
	Responsible for caring for children, planning lessons and activities, and preparing snacks.
	Babysitter, 20XX to present
	Provide quality child care for five families with children ages 10 months to 12 years.
Honors and Activities	Southland High Honor Roll, 20XX
	Member, Family, Career and Community Leaders of America (FCCLA), Southland High Chapter, 20XX to present
	Member, Southland High Writing Club, 20XX to present
	Team Captain, Southland High Volleyball Team, 20XX

26-6 An organized, well-written résumé makes a positive impression on employers.

to understand more about your experiences. Your résumé will help them decide whether you are qualified for a job. Some employers and Internet job boards require the use of an *electronic résumé*, a text-only file without any special formatting.

When applying for some jobs, you may need to submit a cover letter with your résumé, 26-7. A **cover letter** is addressed to the appropriate contact person and introduces your résumé. It may also highlight some of your job-related skills and qualifications.

1603 Green Street
Southland Township, Wisconsin 66732
April 15, 20XX

Ms. Anna Martinez
Program Director
Big Lake Day Camp
Rural Route 3
Southland Township, Wisconsin 66732

Dear Ms. Martinez:

I am interested in working as a counselor-in-training at Big Lake this summer. My guidance counselor at Southland High School, Mr. O'Brien, suggested I write you.

This job would be a good learning experience for me. I also have much to offer you as an employee. I have taken three child development classes in high school. Two of the classes included working eight hours per week in the school child care center. My duties involved planning a variety of activities for children, such as puppet shows, crafts, games, and snacks. I enjoy being with children and helping them learn. My long-term career goal is to open my own child care center when I graduate from college.

My résumé is enclosed. I would appreciate the opportunity to meet for an interview. I will call your office next week to see whether we can schedule an appointment. If you would like to speak with me sooner or have any questions, please contact me at 555-7472 or at miaholtz@provider.com. Thank you for your time and consideration.

Sincerely,

Mia Holtz

Mia Holtz

26-7 Job seekers often use cover letters to introduce a résumé and highlight specific skills.

Prospective employers may ask you to complete a *job application*. The application asks for information such as your name, address, Social Security number, educational background, and work history. It often asks for references, too. **References** are people who know you well enough to discuss your qualifications for a job. Employers may call references to find out more about you before making a hiring decision. You should not list relatives as references. However, you can ask past employers, teachers, and other adults you know well if they will serve as references for you. Application information and your résumé information should match.

Preparing a Portfolio

Many job seekers prepare a portfolio to show when interviewing with prospective employers. A **portfolio** is an organized collection of materials that supports your job qualifications. A portfolio should reflect your work, academic, and personal experiences. Some of the items you might want to include in a portfolio are

★ a résumé

★ work samples demonstrating specific skills

★ letters of recommendation documenting work-related skills

★ honors and awards

★ summaries of volunteer work

★ certifications or licenses

★ a list of references

Accumulate items for your portfolio over time and assemble them in an organized format, such as a three-ring binder. Some portfolios may be Web-based. Update your portfolio on a regular basis to reflect new skills and qualifications.

If you are unsure what to showcase in a portfolio, consider your career plan. For example, if you are seeking an entry-level job upon graduation, showcase both general skills needed for all jobs as well as career-specific ones. For example, for child-related careers, experience working with children and families is most important. If you are college-bound, match your portfolio to admission and scholarship requirements. Student portfolios will contain samples of your academic and extra-curricular experiences.

Interviewing for a Job

At the interview, you need to put your best foot forward. Your personal appearance should be neat. As a rule, jeans do not make a good impression at an interview. Clean, neat dress pants, dresses, or suits are

Focus on Speech
Interviewing

You may want to rehearse for an interview with someone before you go. This will help you prepare answers to some of the questions interviewers often ask. In addition to the questions listed below, what other questions might you be expected to answer in an interview? Add five questions to this list. Sequence the eight questions for the interview. Then, work with a partner to conduct a mock interview. Take turns being the interviewer and the prospective employee.

★ Why are you interested in this job?

★ Where do you see yourself professionally in five years?

★ What are your strengths and weaknesses?

appropriate (depending on the type of job you want). Good posture, a pleasant smile, and eye contact are also important during an interview.

Be sure to speak clearly and be yourself. It is also a good idea for you to prepare some questions for the interviewer. These questions should focus on information about the business, agency, or program seeking job applicants and on the work duties required for the job position. Asking these questions shows you are interested in the job and the employer. Avoid asking any questions about pay, vacation time, or other benefits until you have been offered the job.

After the interview, you might be offered the job. However, employers often have other applicants to interview before making hiring decisions. If there are many applicants, you might be asked to interview a second or third time before the employer makes a decision.

Awaiting a Response

Unless you are told differently, the employer will probably contact you within two weeks. If the employer offers you a job, respond promptly and politely as to whether you will accept or decline. If you decline the job or you are not offered the position, it is still important to be polite and friendly. The employer may consider you for a future position.

Careers in Child-Related Fields

If you are interested in children and their development, then a career in a child-related field might be for you. Many opportunities exist for working in a career that involves children in some way. Child-related careers are constantly growing. The widespread effort to improve children's quality of life is one trend that makes child-related work a good career choice. Many of today's parents work outside the home, which puts child care workers and early childhood teachers in high demand. In addition, consumers expect more goods and services tailored to children's needs. This increases the demand for workers who create and provide these goods and services.

Learning more about the many types of careers that relate to children can help you decide whether this field is right for you. To be successful in child-related careers, workers also need certain personal and professional qualifications.

Types of Careers

One way to describe child-related careers is in terms of the amount of contact with children. In some careers, adults work with children directly, which is **direct intervention**, 26-8. People in such careers include teachers and pediatricians.

In other child-related careers, adults work on behalf of children, but not directly with children. For example, **consultants** share their knowledge about children with other adults. College child development professors may serve as consultants to teachers of young children. In other careers, professionals develop and sell products for children. These adults use their knowledge of children to design and sell toys, clothing, furniture, and educational products.

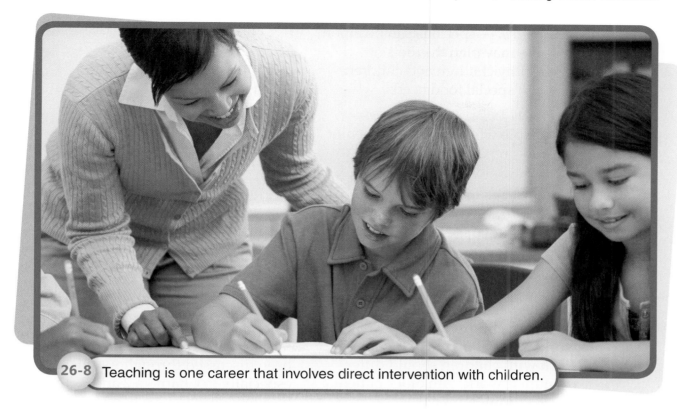

26-8 Teaching is one career that involves direct intervention with children.

Regardless of the amount of child contact, all adults in child-related careers need to understand children and their needs in order to do their jobs well.

Careers in child-related fields can be grouped into seven areas. These are health and protective services; care and education; entertainment; design; advertising, marketing, and management; research, consulting, and advocacy; and entrepreneurship.

Health and Protective Services

It takes many health care professionals to keep children healthy. Demand for workers in children's physical and mental health services has increased. Adults in these services have the knowledge and skills needed to provide quality health care. They also understand children's health needs. Careers in children's health care include the following:

★ *pediatricians*—doctors who specialize in the care of children

★ *pediatric dentists*—dentists who specialize in the care of children

★ *pediatric and school nurses*—nurses who specialize in the care of children

★ *clinical child psychologists*—professionals who specialize in the emotional and mental health of children

★ *counseling psychologists*—professionals who help people cope with life challenges

★ *school psychologists*—professionals who help with child and teen educational decisions

★ *developmental psychologists*—professionals who assess children's developmental status and make recommendations

★ *dietitians*—specialists in nutrition who may plan the diets of healthy children and children with special food needs

★ *school food service personnel*—people who plan school menus and prepare and serve food to meet children's needs

Other health professionals, such as eye doctors, speech therapists, hearing specialists, sports medicine doctors, physical therapists, occupational therapists, play therapists, emergency room and hospital personnel, and pharmacists also serve children regularly. These workers need to know how their work with children should differ from their work with older patients. Special training may be needed.

Adults with careers in protective services work to find injustices to children and to correct problem situations. Careers in protective services are increasing as society becomes more concerned about the rights and needs of children. Some positions include the following:

★ *child, family, and school social workers*—professionals who assist children and families in crisis, place foster children, arrange adoptions, and serve as a link between students' families and the schools

★ *medical and public health social workers*—professionals who help children and their families cope with chronic and terminal illnesses and help plan for the child's needs after hospital discharge

★ *mental health and substance abuse social workers*—professionals who provide individual

and group therapy, crisis intervention, and other supportive interventions

★ **licensing personnel**—professionals who check the quality of services for children, such as the quality of child care centers

★ *juvenile officers and family court judges*—professionals who make legal decisions about children and their family's rights and responsibilities

Care and Education

Parenting is a demanding career in care and education. Parenting has been discussed throughout this text, especially in Chapters 2 and 3. To be effective, parents need to apply what is known about children and to seek assistance of professionals who work in child-related careers when the need arises.

More young children are enrolled in group settings than ever before. Private programs are growing in number. Government agencies on both federal and state levels are committed to children's education, 26-9. Thus, there has been an increasing growth in public preschool programs.

The following care and education careers can be found in both public and private settings:

★ *child care providers*—people who care for infants, toddlers, preschool children, and school-age children (when school is not in session)

★ *teachers and teachers' assistants*—people trained to teach or assist teachers in public and private school programs

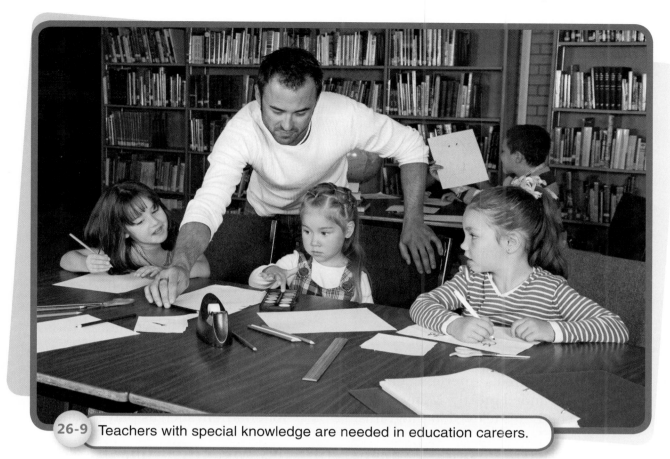

26-9 Teachers with special knowledge are needed in education careers.

★ *special education teachers*—teachers who work with children who have special needs

★ *leaders, managers, and administrators*—directors of child care and education programs as well as principals and supervisors of school programs

★ *parent educators*—people who teach parents about child development and parenting

★ *family life educators*—people who provide direct services to children and families or train professionals in providing services for children and families

★ *family life coordinators*—people who connect and coordinate support, services, and resources for children and their families

★ *children's librarians*—librarians trained to work in school libraries or in children's sections of other libraries

★ *high school teachers and college professors*—teachers who instruct high school or college students in child-related courses, such as health, education, development, and parenting

★ *child and youth leaders*—people plan, organize, and work with children and their instructors in religious programs or youth organizations, such as scouting groups, recreational programs, and camps

★ *recreational instructors*—people who guide or teach children in areas, such as music, art, sports, and hobbies

Career opportunities in child care and education are increasing rapidly. In some areas of the country, demand for workers in this field even surpasses the number of workers available. More quality child care and education programs are needed. As these programs are created, more people will be needed to staff them. Child care workers and teachers will likely remain in high demand in the future. Demand for professionals with special skills will be even higher. Examples are teachers of children with special needs and computer teachers.

Entertainment

In recent years, the business of children's entertainment has expanded greatly. Many new children's television programs, movies, and live programs have been produced. A wider variety of children's books and games (including video and computer games) are available. People in entertainment careers include producers, directors, technicians, writers, and performers.

Design

Because children differ from adults, they need items designed especially for them. These items should be designed to meet children's physical, intellectual, and social-emotional needs. Items designed for children include clothing, personal care items, dishes and flatware, furniture, books, and toys, 26-10. Designers plan indoor and outdoor spaces for children, such as playgrounds

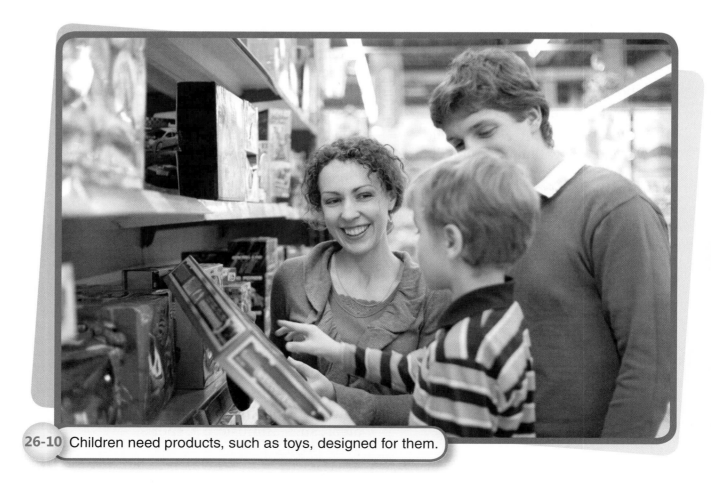

26-10 Children need products, such as toys, designed for them.

and child care centers. Designers may also work in the entertainment industry, such as in set design. People who design child-related products and spaces must understand child development. They also need creative skills and an understanding of design principles.

Advertising, Marketing, and Management

As more children's products are produced, businesses need many employees who understand children's needs. These businesses need people who are trained to advertise and market the children's products they produce. Another growing career choice is managing the businesses that produce and sell children's products. Positions for advertising, marketing, and managing can be found in corporations, agencies, firms, and small businesses.

Research, Consulting, and Advocacy

Many fields, such as health, education, entertainment, design, and business, conduct research on children and their needs. Research studies provide knowledge that allows people to serve children well. The field of research is growing so quickly that a massive amount of information is now available. Thousands of research studies on children and parents are published each year.

Consultants work on behalf of children. They serve as a link between researchers and others in child-related careers. Consultants relay information to those in direct intervention, product development, and sales. Some adults consult on

a daily basis. Child development experts who provide state and federal lawmakers with information are an example. Other adults work as consultants when called upon for written or oral input. With research continuing to increase, consultants will continue to be in demand.

Child advocates are professionals who focus on research addressing mental health, education, and legal or medical issues that affect children. Most advocates specialize in one issue, such as child support, substance abuse, delinquency, or housing. Advocates work in the judicial and legislative branches of government and through professional associations. They conduct and compile research on an issue, witness about the issue, seek support for needed changes, and keep others informed on the status of the issue.

Entrepreneurship

Many child-related careers offer chances for self-employment. A person who creates and owns a business is called an **entrepreneur**. Family child care homes are the most common child-related businesses started by entrepreneurs. However, some people own and operate child care centers as well. Entrepreneurs can also start many other types of businesses. Examples are child photography, recreational instruction, private medical practice, children's clothing and toy stores, and writing for and about children.

Entrepreneurs need many skills other than those directly related to their specialties. For example, a person who owns and operates a child care center must know much more than how to teach and care for children. This entrepreneur must be able to manage money, including handling budgets and fees, paying expenses, and making purchasing decisions. This professional would also advertise, hire staff, oversee enrollment, know and follow laws and regulations, maintain the facilities, communicate with parents, and supervise the staff.

Many people find owning a business rewarding, 26-11. They like having the freedom to run their businesses in their own ways. They also like the variety of being able to fill different roles, such as teacher, manager, and budget director. There are drawbacks, however. Entrepreneurs may have to use their personal money for starting costs or if the business goes into debt. They must make key decisions about the business and live with their choices. Another drawback is that many owners work longer hours and have fewer vacations than they would if they were employed by others.

If you have the skills, knowledge, and energy, you might enjoy starting a business of your own. Entrepreneurship in a child-related field can be satisfying and rewarding. Creativity, knowledge, and hard work can make your business profitable, too.

Personal Qualifications for a Child-Related Career

Personal qualifications are all the traits you possess that cannot be learned in career training. Personal traits are harder to define and measure than learnings that result from career training. For this reason, little research has been done on personal qualifications. Thus, only general traits are discussed.

Concern for Children

For a person in a child-related career, the most important personal qualification is a deep concern for children. Sometimes, in the effort to perform well, people lose sight of the most important concern of all—the children. If you work directly or indirectly with children, you must always make decisions based on what is best for them.

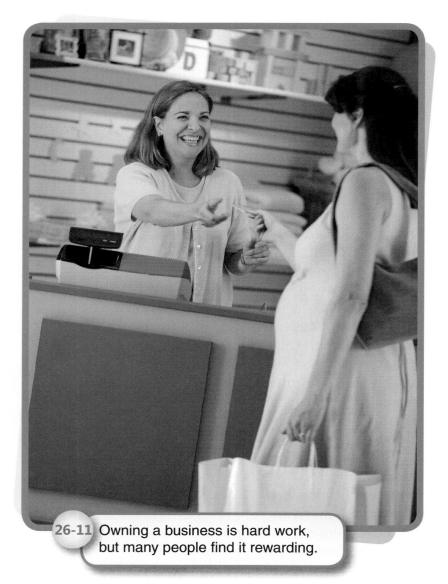

26-11 Owning a business is hard work, but many people find it rewarding.

When working directly with children, your concern is expressed as a genuine liking for children. How do adults show that they like children? Liking is seen in their behaviors as shown in 26-12.

Flexibility

In working with children, it is important to remain open to new ideas. Flexibility is important, too, because children can be unpredictable. Research shows the constant changes required in working with children often cause people to have career burnout. **Career burnout** is a state in which a person becomes emotionally tired of a career. It may even lead to health problems from stress. A person who is *flexible* (adapts to change) will be less likely to have career burnout. He or she will adapt more easily to change.

Leadership

Being able to lead others is very important when working in a child-related career. A **leader** is a person who influences or motivates the thoughts, feelings, or actions of others. Children see adults and teens as leaders. A leader should be self-confident, which helps children feel secure. A leader provides clear instructions for the group or individual child. A leader sets limits and is firm with children when needed. Self-discipline has to be taught. Being able to listen patiently is important, too. For example, children may need to try several times before they say something in ways adults understand. Leadership skills are also needed in working with adults, such as other staff members or the children's parents.

Behaviors of Adults Who Like Children

★ Respect the uniqueness of each child
★ Are kind and patient with children and families
★ Tolerate noise and physical activity
★ Enjoy the child's world—games, songs, stories, concepts, play, and humor
★ Feel comfortable helping young children with physical needs—dressing, toileting, and caring for scrapes, bruises, and sick tummies
★ Accept physical closeness—the child's touching of your hair, clothing, and jewelry; hugging; wet-cheek kisses; and clinging when hurt or distraught

26-12 Adults express their liking of children in various ways.

Professional Qualifications for a Child-Related Career

Professional qualifications are the physical, intellectual, and social-emotional skills you need to perform in a career. People most often learn these skills from training or entry-level work experience. Training might include classes in high school or college as well as on-the-job training. For example, if you want to become a pediatrician, you need a college degree in certain areas (often premedicine). After graduating, you need to score at a certain level on tests that measure your knowledge. You might also need to submit references, interview with faculty at medical school, and pass physical examinations. After completing years of medical school, you may then go through an internship to become a pediatrician.

You will be 30 or more years of age before you achieve your professional qualifications for this career.

Child development is the science of understanding children. If you want to have a career in a child-related field, you must know and use child development concepts. Because physical, intellectual, and social-emotional development are related, you study all aspects of child development. However, professional training for a career often stresses one aspect of development more than others. Pediatricians deal more with physical aspects of development. They must be aware of how other aspects of development affect a child's health, however.

In addition to learning about child development, you will become specialized in your career area. For example, teachers must have specialized knowledge in the following, as well as other areas:

★ how children learn

★ what to teach and in what order to teach certain facts and skills

★ the best methods and materials for teaching the facts and skills

★ how to assess children's knowledge

For some careers, people must learn specialties within a specialty. Specialties require in-depth learnings. *Pediatric ophthalmologists* are children's eye doctors. These adults learn general medicine and then learn to treat diseases of the eye. Finally, they learn to care for children's eye problems. Because so few adults have specialties within specialties, these adults often serve as researchers or consultants. They may directly handle only the most difficult cases.

The level of a job determines the amount of training needed. There are many levels of positions within the field of child care. The career ladder in 26-13 shows some of these levels. Teachers' assistants and some associate teachers do not need college degrees. They may have had some training in high school, vocational classes, community college, or college. Supervisors generally have at least bachelor's degrees in child development, early childhood education, or related areas. Many supervisors and most directors have a master's degree in a specialized area of child development. Consultants may have more than one master's degree or a doctoral degree.

Job Training

The amount of training a job requires depends on the level of responsibility it demands. Teachers have greater professional responsibilities than teachers' assistants. Some careers require study in schools and colleges and supervised work in the career field. People may earn professional qualifications for other careers, such as entertainment, through on-the-job training, rather than through schools and colleges.

In addition to basic career training, adults in child-related careers are expected to keep up with the latest knowledge and practices in their field. Keeping up in a child-related career may require more classroom study, seminar attendance, or independent study. It may also involve on-the-job training in a different setting. In addition, it

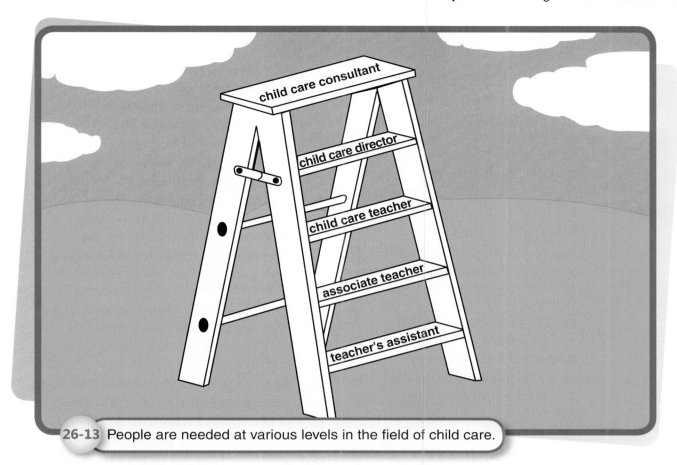

26-13 People are needed at various levels in the field of child care.

may involve exchanging knowledge and practices among those working in the many child-related careers. This type of exchange often occurs at professional meetings.

Skills for Job Success

At this point in your life, you may not know exactly what type of career you want. You still have time to make this decision. However, you need to start today to develop some skills all employers seek in job candidates. It takes time and experience to develop these skills. If you begin now, you will be much more prepared when it is time to enter the job market.

Human Relations Skills

Human relations skills include good attitudes toward others, work ethic, and manners. These skills are perhaps the most important you will develop both personally and professionally. Human relations skills affect how you get along with other people. These skills often determine whether you will get a desired job, keep your job, or be promoted. People also damage relationships with family and friends due to the lack of human relations skills. For these reasons, it is important to build your skills in relating to others.

Positive Attitudes Toward Others

Although a person's basic temperament is largely determined by genes, basic attitudes begin to develop early in life. Their development is influenced by role models, such as family members, friends, and others, as well as by the media. Parents, teachers, and youth leaders often encourage children to develop positive attitudes. For example, they teach children to show respect and solve conflicts peacefully. Positive attitudes are closely tied to self-esteem.

As adults, people are responsible for their own attitudes. To a great extent, work performance is linked to attitude. Employers need employees with positive attitudes. These people are friendly, cheerful, and considerate of others in the workplace. In turn, they are liked and respected. Respecting differences is a key part of a positive attitude. Getting along with coworkers, supervisors, and clients or customers is essential, 26-14.

Employees with negative attitudes complain about everything and everyone. They often argue with coworkers, superiors, and clients or customers. Others with negative attitudes are sullen and withdrawn. These negative attitudes result in reduced job performance for everyone involved.

Work Ethic

Work ethic refers to a standard of conduct and values for job performance. A good employee is said to have a *strong work ethic*. This person understands what behaviors are appropriate for the workplace. He or she is honest, hardworking, and dependable. A dependable employee shows up for work, comes to work on time, and works steadily through the workday except for normal breaks.

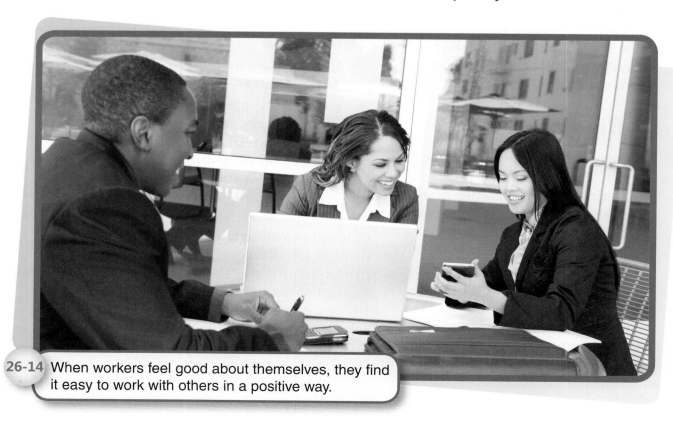

26-14 When workers feel good about themselves, they find it easy to work with others in a positive way.

He or she does more than what is asked by the employer. An employee with a strong work ethic strives to get along with others. He or she does the best work possible and cares about the quality of work. This employee works independently. Employers want employees who have a strong work ethic.

Other employees do not have a strong work ethic. These employees are less likely to succeed. Employers seek to avoid hiring workers who lack a strong work ethic. These employees are also subject to being fired because they cost the company through their poor work behavior.

In addition to personal work ethic, many professions have written standards of conduct for workers in a certain career field. These standards are called **codes of professional ethics**. An employee is expected to follow any code of professional ethics that apply to his or her profession. In some careers, violating the code of professional ethics can result in suspension or termination.

Manners

Manners are about comfort. You want to be comfortable around others, and you want others to be comfortable around you. Employers must trust you will not embarrass them in any situation. Furthermore, good manners help others take you seriously. The following basics should always be practiced:

★ consider people's feelings

★ use manners in meetings, telephone conversations, e-mail messages, and memos

★ apologize if you must interrupt a meeting, conversation, or someone's concentration on a task

★ keep any conflicts situation-related rather than attacking a person

★ keep your voice moderated in loudness and pitch

★ talk and visit with everyone

★ be thoughtful to coworkers and clients

Communication Skills

Many executives of the nation's largest corporations say their employees must have good communication skills. However, many companies identify writing skills as their organization's greatest weakness. In general, communication skills are listed as the scarcest skills in the workforce.

Employers expect employees to do the following:

★ have good listening skills

★ be good readers

★ communication in both speaking and writing situations using standard English grammar, capitalization, punctuation, and spelling

★ have needed computer and other technological skills

Although the specific skills will vary some with the career, some commonly needed skills are given in 26-15. Which communication skills have you mastered, and which do you have yet to develop? If you can boost your communications skills, you can greatly increase your chances of job success in your chosen career. On the other hand, if your communication skills are weak, no matter the extent of your career-specific abilities, you will lose credibility.

Commonly Needed Communication Skills

Listening skills
★ Following directions
★ Grasping information
★ Clarifying information
★ Asking questions

Speaking skills
★ Giving instructions
★ Responding to phone calls, voice mail, and personal conversations
★ Participating in meetings and conferences
★ Making presentations

Reading skills
★ Understanding office signs and maps, such as evacuation plans
★ Grasping office memos, letters, and manuals
★ Comprehending business reports; mastering specialized vocabulary, codes, and labels; interpreting statistical data; and understanding graphs and diagrams

Writing skills
★ Writing messages and memos
★ Making records
★ Composing business letters
★ Drafting business reports

Computer-based skills
★ Organizing work tasks
★ Writing e-mail messages for business purposes
★ Using the Internet for gathering work-related information
★ Using word processing software
★ Making spreadsheets
★ Creating databases
★ Preparing materials through desktop publishing
★ Creating drawings and images (computer graphics)
★ Preparing multimedia presentations

26-15 Many communication and computer skills are needed for today's workplace.

Nonverbal communication can have positive or negative effects on others, too. Appearing to be alert and interested, focusing on the speaker, smiling, and greeting others with a friendly voice and firm handshake tells others you think they are important. Falling asleep, yawning, slouching, looking away, or getting into someone's physical space convey negative impressions.

Being a Team Player

For many years, the American economy encouraged and rewarded individual effort. The information-age economy has resulted in a more group-oriented workplace. Workplace teams are now pooling their knowledge, making group decisions, and reaching team goals. Most careers involve some team efforts. Child-related careers are very much a team effort.

Developing teamwork skills takes time and should begin in the early years of schooling. Working on group projects is the best way to learn to be a team player. These projects may be assigned as part of a class. Teamwork skills can also be built in clubs, organizations, youth groups, and volunteer activities.

Good team players are people who get along well with others. Team members work to develop problem-solving and decision-making skills. They learn to brainstorm, compromise, build consensus for ideas, and evaluate results of decisions. They also develop the following skills:

★ being respectful of others' ideas

★ taking responsibility for certain tasks and being accountable to team as well as self

★ being adaptable and open to new ideas

★ sharing roles with team members

★ dealing with personality clashes and managing conflicts over ideas

Team members must participate by listening and speaking. They also take different roles, such as the following:

★ presenting agenda

★ keeping the team focused on goals

★ encouraging every member to participate

★ analyzing ideas presented

★ keeping records of ideas and decisions

Leadership Skills

No matter what career you choose, at some time you will need to be a leader. Sometimes people take formal leadership roles. Your community's mayor and a store manager practice **formal leadership**. These people are chosen by others to lead a group. At other times, people take informal leadership roles. **Informal leaders** lead or guide others even though they are not officially chosen to lead. People may be informal leaders within an organized group as well as outside of one.

Leadership skills have their roots in the early years of life. As children, future leaders often receive *unconditional love* (love without strings attached) from their parents and other adults. They are given many chances to develop autonomy and responsibility. This type of upbringing fosters feelings of self-confidence even in the face of risks. Young leaders-to-be often have leadership role models in their lives, too. Thus, they learn by imitating others' actions.

Most effective leaders are also good team players. They have what it takes to get along with others and work together. In addition, effective leaders have many other qualities in common, 26-16.

Like other personal qualities, leadership qualities are a part of your whole life, not just your working hours. For some people, leadership is an aptitude. These people seem to have more natural leadership talent than others.

Qualities of Effective Leadership

Effective leaders often fit the following descriptions:

★ Have a positive outlook and motivate others; they excite people about possibilities
★ Handle responsibility by following through to complete tasks, accepting blame for mistakes, and keeping promises
★ Are honest; followers trust them because they do not take advantage of others
★ Show acceptance of others; they are flexible and open to others' ideas
★ Are aware of differing points of view and work to resolve conflicts
★ Share reasons and explain their positions
★ Seek good group interaction through open and ongoing communication
★ Listen to get other people's perspectives and seek common ground
★ Know how to set and articulate goals to help the team achieve its purpose
★ Assign responsibilities to others
★ Develop team support by getting all members to participate
★ Make sound decisions and are confident in their choices

26-16 Which of these effective leadership skills do you possess? Are there others you could develop?

If leadership is not one of your aptitudes, you can improve your ability to lead through practice. Babysitting or providing child care could give you practice at making decisions and being responsible.

You can also gain leadership skills by joining a school organization. You might even run for office and serve as a leader. Career and technical student organizations, such as Family, Career and Community Leaders of America (FCCLA), also offer leadership opportunities. You can learn more about FCCLA by visiting their Web site at **www.fcclainc.org**.

Managing Multiple Roles

Most adults have more than one role. Many are workers, spouses, family members, parents, consumers, and community members. Some adults have even more roles that include their membership in organizations and other groups. Each role comes with expectations. A person who is a parent, for example, is expected to provide care for his or her children. Workers are expected to perform their job tasks.

Conflict can occur between these many roles and their demands. For emotional and physical health, a person must achieve a sense of balance between his or her roles. When roles do not balance well, role strain can occur. (Refer to Chapter 25 to review this concept.) People who face role strain are often stressed, guilty, and unhappy. Stress comes from an overload of tasks and responsibilities. Stress can also occur because of conflict among these due to time limits. Guilt results when one tries to do it all, but is unable to achieve everything. Stress and guilt often create more problems. The most common problem is a *spillover* from one role to another, 26-17.

Signs of a Spillover

Signs of spillover from job

★ Worrying about work while away from work

★ Being too tired to enjoy family life or to do household tasks

★ Not having time for leisure activities or not enjoying them

★ Bringing work home

★ Receiving complaints from family and friends about long work hours

★ Being irritable over little things

Signs of spillover from personal life

★ Being sleepy at work

★ Thinking about other things while at work

★ Feeling your employer expects too much of you

★ Being late for or absent from work; spending time on the job dealing with family or other personal matters; and asking to leave early to deal with nonwork matters

★ Making lots of careless mistakes

★ Reacting in overly sensitive ways to others and hurting other people's feelings

26-17 Spillovers between work and other aspects of life will always occur to some extent because everyone is human. Frequent negative spillovers are damaging both to work and to other aspects of life.

Learn More About...
Managing Multiple Roles

How does one achieve a well-balanced life? Suggestions include the following:

★ Get in touch with your values. Knowing your values allows you to be intentional about choices rather than just letting things happen.

★ Rank your values. When two roles conflict, use ranking to select which one to meet first. Use remaining resources to meet other demands.

★ Relax your standards where possible. For example, choose to let some household tasks go longer than you would like. In some cases, your work load, but not standards, may be reduced by asking for a new job description.

★ Get organized. A written schedule helps you think about tasks in advance, make time available for special events, and plan ahead.

★ Establish daily routines. Routines make the day go more smoothly.

★ Take time to mentally shift gears. Have a few minutes of down time before the workday begins and again before beginning evening tasks.

★ Ask for help. Having help when needed makes it possible to manage multiple roles without undue strain.

★ Combine activities. For example, quality family time may be combined with "fitness time," meal preparation and eating, and household chores.

★ Communicate with others. Just talking to empathetic listeners may help relieve role strain. Sometimes others can offer helpful ideas to better manage role demands.

★ Take care of yourself at work. Organize your tasks and focus for effectiveness and efficiency. Relax on breaks by eating, exercising, or socializing. Do your work, but do not allow others to give you their work.

★ Reconsider role requirements. If the role expectations are still too great, seek help.

Leaving a Job

Few people stay in the same workplace for a career lifetime. People change jobs for many reasons. Sometimes people discover after working in a certain career that it is not a good match for them. Others "outgrow" their jobs due to more education and learning. Some people find their present work is more than they expected or can do. Many job changes occur when a family moves due to one spouse being transferred. Some people are laid off due to business problems. A few people are fired or asked to resign.

If you plan to voluntarily leave a job, it is best if you already have found another job. You should not use your work time at the current job to search for another job. However, you can look for another job in your nonworking hours. In most cases, quitting your current job without another job is less responsible than securing another job first.

Even when leaving your current job, you have an obligation to treat your employer fairly. See 26-18 for guidelines to follow when you wish to leave a job.

Regardless of why you are leaving, you should strive to end the job on a positive note. Leaving in this way will help others remember you in a good light. In the future, you might need a reference or recommendation from your employer or coworkers. Tips for leaving on a positive note include the following:

★ Leave when the business is less busy, if possible. For example, an accounting firm would not want to lose employees during income tax season.

Obligations When Leaving a Job

Before leaving your current job, you should do the following:

★ Consult your employee handbook or personnel policies to learn the correct procedure for terminating (ending) employment. Adhere to this procedure as you notify the employer you wish to leave the job.

★ Check on the status of your 401K or other work-related retirement funds and insurance.

★ Provide ample notice so the employer can find a suitable replacement. The personnel policy may address the required time of notice. If it does not, you will need to decide how much notice to give. An acceptable amount of notice depends on the level of skills required in the job. Employers often need more time to fill a high-skill job than an entry-level job. Two weeks' notice is generally the minimum for an entry-level job.

★ Complete a letter of resignation and any other termination forms, if required by the employer. You should address your notice to your direct supervisor. You may also have an exit interview. In this interview, employers may ask questions, such as "Why are you leaving?" or "What do you expect to find in another job?" Be honest, but remain professional and respectful.

★ Try to complete all current tasks. Employers expect and are paying for your work through the final day. You may be expected to help train the employee who will take your place.

26-18 To leave a job in the most professional way, an employee should follow these tips.

★ Avoid bragging about your new job. Your employer and coworkers do not want to hear all the wonderful things about your new position. You might instead point out what you will miss about your current job, supervisor, and coworkers.

★ Show appreciation to your supervisor and coworkers for helping you to learn needed skills or for being positive role models.

Employees and their employers do have certain rights that are protected by law. If you are fired or laid off, you will need to learn about these rights. In these cases, it might be wise for you to seek legal advice. Some Web sites and other publications provide information about the legal rights that apply to the termination of a job.

Summary

Choosing a career is a crucial decision that affects your lifestyle. Therefore, you need to begin making career decisions early. To make a wise choice, you should begin with self-assessment. After learning about careers, you should be able to find one or more matches between your interests, aptitudes, and abilities and the requirements for a career. From this information, you can design a career plan.

Careers in child-related fields continue to grow. Adults can work in a number of child-related career areas. These include health and protective services; care and education; entertainment; design; advertising, marketing, and management; research, consulting, and advocacy; and entrepreneurial services.

To work well with children, people need a basic knowledge of their development. Personal

and professional qualifications are required to enter a child-related field. After becoming qualified for a child-related job, you must use organized, efficient job search skills to find a job.

No matter what career you choose, it is important to develop some general skills that are needed in every field. These include human relations, communication, teamwork, leadership, and role-management skills. Developing these skills is a lifelong process. Leaving a job the right way is also important for career success.

Interactive Activity

Review vocabulary terms and key concepts for Chapter 26 at **g-wlearning.com**.

Review and Reflect

Write your answers to the following questions on a separate sheet of paper.

1. Self-assessment involves identifying your _____, _____, and _____.

2. Career plans have _____ goals and _____ goals.

3. In general, careers in child-related fields are _____ (increasing, decreasing) in number.

4. Use two phrases for describing two types of child-related careers in terms of contact with children.

5. For each of the following career areas, list two specific careers within that area: health and protective services; care and education; entertainment; design; advertising, marketing, and management; research, consulting, and advocacy; and entrepreneurship.

6. List three personal qualities needed by adults working directly with children.

7. Professional qualifications are mainly (taught, not taught).

8. All adults involved in child-related careers must have a basic knowledge of _____ in order to be effective.

9. True or false. Some job skills are used for success in many careers.

10. What three skills are part of human relations?

11. True or false. Employers feel that most of their employees have adequate communication skills.

12. Describe three responsibilities workers have when leaving a job.

Cross-Curricular Link

13. **Writing, Career Study.** As an individual project, list some of your interests, aptitudes, and abilities. For each item, ask yourself how your traits match the desired personal and professional qualifications of those entering careers in child-related fields.

14. **Technology, Career Study.** Choose a career within one of the seven child-related career areas described in the chapter. Use the Internet to find information regarding this career. Based on your findings, prepare a chart listing the occupation, as well as the personal and professional qualifications needed by people wishing to enter this career.

15. **Writing, Speech, Career Study.** Design a sample career plan for a career in a child-related career. This does not necessarily need to reflect the career you will pursue. Write three long-term goals and

five short-term goals a person might set to prepare to enter this career field. Present your career plan to the class. Share feedback with other students about the career plans they have designed.

16. **Speech, Career Study.** Work with a partner to role-play several interview situations. Conduct yourselves as you would during an interview. Take turns being the interviewer and the person being interviewed. After your role-plays, form a small group and discuss insights you gained while doing the role-play.

17. **Writing, Technology, Career Study.** Explore the FCCLA Web site at **www.fcclainc.org**. How could membership in a local FCCLA chapter aid the development of leadership skills needed for job success? Write a brief report of your findings. Check your paper for correct spelling, grammar, and punctuation.

18. **Writing.** Compose a hypothetical letter of resignation following the guidelines described in the chapter. Check your letter for correct spelling, grammar, and punctuation.

Making Observations

19. Observe people working in child-related careers. What skills do they use? What aspects of the child's development (physical, intellectual, and social-emotional) do they especially need to know for this career?

20. Observe your friends as they become involved with children in different settings. What skills are they developing? Would these skills be helpful in parenting?

21. Observe a national, state, or local leader. List the leadership skills you have observed. Give example(s) of each skill.

Thinking Critically

22. Why would it be good to take one or more courses in child development regardless of career choice?

23. If you wanted to inquire about particular careers in child-related fields, how would you proceed? What questions would you need answered?

24. Why is it wise to get involved in child-related fields before completing high school? How can early involvement help you after you complete your training or education for the career?

Developmental Milestones Q and A

Q: Will the developmental milestones listed and the ages given vary somewhat from source to source?

A: Yes. Authors list milestones to fit the content of their writing. Ages differ even for the same milestones because researchers interpret the milestones differently. (For example, *walking* may be taking a couple of unsure steps or toddling across a room.) Depending on the researcher, the age norms may be based on the age in which 50%, 67%, or 75% of children reach the milestone; this makes for reported differences in the typical age. Thus, *developmental milestones are only a general idea of the timing of certain changes.*

Q: Do developmental milestones "fit" premature babies?

A: They do fit if you adjust the baby's age to his or her due date. For example, if a baby is born two months early, the baby will likely achieve milestones two months later during the first two years.

Q: When are developmental milestones the most precise?

A: These charts are rough guidelines for the first year and even less precise in the following years due to differences in children's environments.

Q: Do developmental milestones remain the same from generation to generation?

A: Some milestones have remained somewhat the same for many years. However, the environment can cause changes. For example, putting babies to sleep on their backs (a SIDS preventive) has caused babies to roll over about a month later than when tummy sleeping was common. Also, due to more learning materials (games, books, media) and preschool programs, many more young children are learning colors, letters, and numbers before the kindergarten year than in the past.

Q: Is the accomplishment of the milestone or the age the most important to development?

A: The accomplishment of the milestone, regardless of age, is by far the most important factor. For example, think about this question: Among your friends can you tell who walked earlier and who walked later as a baby?

Q: Why are ages given?

A: Ages help parents discuss any possible delays with their child's doctor. Doctors usually watch a child for a few weeks or months before drawing a conclusion. If a doctor notes *significant delays*, he or she may refer the child to a specialist for further testing.

Q: If the child is ahead of the norms, does it mean he or she is gifted?

A: A gifted child continues to accelerate over the course of several years. Many children with more average intelligence learn some skills early due to an early exposure to that skill. With the exception of children who are profoundly gifted, giftedness is not usually confirmed until age nine or even later.

Q: Will the child maintain the same pace of development; that is continue to be slow, average, or above average in reaching each milestone?

A: Because development in one area reinforces and enhances development in other areas, children do not maintain a steady pace in reaching milestones. Development is a journey without a cruise control.

Q: Is regression in skills a cause for concern?

A: Some brief regressions are due to an illness or to a change in the child's environment, such as a move, a change in child care and education programs, or even a change in family make-up (a new baby, a divorce, death). Regression that continues, worsens, or spreads to several developmental areas may be a symptom of a serious developmental problem. *Parents should always discuss developmental regression with their child's doctor.*

Developmental Milestones of Children Through Age 12

Newborn Milestones

Physical

1 Month	Has reflexive movements. Startles easily (Moro reflex). Roots for breast. Stares at objects, but does not try to grasp. Attempts to lift head when on tummy.
2 Months	Has more voluntary actions. Cycles arms and legs. Holds head up when on stomach at 45-degree above surface. Uses a reflexive grasp. Holds objects placed in hands for a few seconds.
3 Months	Leans on elbows and holds chest up and head erect for 10 seconds. Moves arm and leg on each side of the body in unison. Holds hands open. May swipe at dangling objects. Explores face with hands.
4 Months	Rolls from stomach to side. Holds head steady for a short time. Turns head in all directions. Splashes and kicks in bath. Sits with support of cushions for a short time. Touches objects close to hand and may bat objects. Pulls objects placed in hand toward mouth.

Physical *(Continued.)*	
5 Months	Rolls from stomach to back.
	Holds head erect when supported in a sitting position.
	Lies on stomach and makes body into an airplane.
	Moves by rocking, rolling, and twisting.
	Kicks while on back and may move by pushing feet against the wall or footboard of a crib.
	Aims well when trying to grasp.
	Grasps a dangling, large ring.
	Puts hand(s) on bottle held by parent or caregiver.
	Shakes rattle placed in hand.
6 Months	Rolls from back to stomach.
	Sits upright in high chair if secured with belts.
	Bounces when held in standing position.
	Makes crawling motions with arms and legs.
	Explores objects.
	Grasps small objects with palm.
	Scratches at tiny objects.
	May hold a bottle.
7 Months	Sits without support for a few minutes.
	Crawls.
	Holds objects in both hands; bangs objects together.
	Brings fingers to mouth.
8 Months	Sits without support for a few minutes.
	Pushes up on knees and rocks back and forth on knees.
	Stands if helped.
	Puts feet in mouth.
	Transfers toys from hand to hand.
9 Months	May creep a few feet.
	Pulls self up using people or furniture for support.
	Stands holding with one hand while leaning on something.
	Claps and waves hands.
	Tastes everything.
	Pokes at objects with forefinger.
10 Months	Creeps.
	Rocks and bounces to music when held.
	Sits without support indefinitely.
	Has superior palm grasp.
	Carries two objects in one hand.

Physical *(Continued.)*	
11 Months	Walks when led. Turns around while creeping. May stand a few seconds without support. Lowers body from standing position without falling or sitting hard. Lifts lid from box. Puts objects into containers. Begins pincer grasp. Brings spoon to mouth. Eats finger foods.
Intellectual	
1 Month	Remembers objects if they reappear in a couple of seconds. Recognizes mother's voice and smell. Cries for assistance. Is alert for more time than at birth.
2 Months	"Sees" connections within his or her own body (uses mouth and thumb to suck). Has no understanding of object permanence ("out of sight" is "out of mind"). Follows slow movement of objects with eyes (called *tracking*). Discriminates among voices, people, tastes, and objects. Attends and responds to voices. Cries and coos some.
3 Months	Looks for a few seconds where object or person was last seen (beginning of object permanence). Studies own hands. Seeks sources of sound by turning head and neck. Cries less; gurgles and coos.
4 Months	Notices response of an object to his or her action; repeats action to get same response. Remembers object for 5 to 7 seconds. Likes detail in objects. Recognizes specific characteristics of some things in the environment (bottle, family dog, a toy). Makes new sounds. Vocalizes to social stimulation.
5 Months	Learns new actions to repeat. Looks around when in new places. Wants to explore objects. Utters a few consonants. Babbles one syllable repeatedly *(ba ba ba)*. Squeals and grunts. Imitates sounds and gestures with model present.

Intellectual *(Continued.)*	
6 Months	Inspects objects for a long time. Looks at objects upside down to create a new perspective. Compares two objects. Connects own actions to environmental response (shaking rattle causes the sound). Utters more and more consonants. Babbles two different syllables in close sequence *(ba da)*.
7 Months	Discriminates between familiar and unfamiliar adults. Searches for an object partially hidden (object permanence is well underway). Discriminates between angry and friendly tones. Recognizes self in mirror or photo. Picks out his or her name in a conversation. Makes more consonant-vowel combinations. Babbles two syllables by repeating the first syllable *(ma ma)*.
8 Months	Begins to have goals and combines actions to achieve goals (pushes a pillow away to reach a block). Imitates somewhat new actions and makes some effort to improve imitation. Babbles by repeating one syllable many times close together *(dadadada)*; may use inflections.
9 Months	Actively tries to recover a totally hidden toy where last seen (object permanence rather mature). Remembers games played on previous day. Follows simple directions. Understands and uses gestures (shaking head and waving). Responds to the word *no*. Imitates coughs and tongue clicks.
10 Months	Tries to fit things together. Responds to commands. Understands idea of verbal labeling (people and things have names).
11 Months	Imitates inflections and speech rhythms. Begins to understand some labels (words) for people and things. Says first words.
Social-Emotional	
1 Month	Is quiet and still when looking at a face within 12-inches. "Molds" to adult's body when held. Responds to human voices by moving.

Social-Emotional *(Continued.)*	
2 Months	Can be soothed by being held or rocked. Soothes self by sucking.
3 Months	Shows excitement when people are nearby. Smiles when stimulated by a face. Tries to attract people's attention. Shows delight and distress.
4 Months	Smiles broadly and laughs. Vocalizes to initiate socializing. Cries if play is disrupted. Easily excited or upset.
5 Months	Imitates facial expressions. Distinguishes strangers from family members. Recognizes voices of family members. Responds to name.
6 Months	Turns when name is said. Disturbed by the presence of strangers. Vocalizes pleasure and displeasure. Protests if toys are taken.
7 Months	Pats mirror image. Wants to be included in group. Understands "no" by tone of adult voice. Shows humor.
8 Months	Pats, smiles, and kisses mirror image. Shouts for attention. Pushes away undesirable objects. Becomes "angry" during confinement.
9 Months	Performs for others. Shows attachment to parents. Initiates play. Shows intense stranger anxiety.
10 Months	Seeks social approval. Enjoys games, such as "peek-a-boo." Displays affection and anger.
11 Months	Shows or offers toys to others. Sometimes uncooperative during daily routines. Becomes angry when enjoyable play is stopped. Has separation anxiety.

Toddler Milestones

Physical

12 to 18 Months	Takes a step or two without support (12 months).
	Walks without assistance (13 to 14 months).
	Walks sideways (16 months) and backwards (17 months).
	Creeps up and downstairs (14 months) and walks up and downstairs with help (16 months).
	Squats or stoops without losing balance.
	Throws ball while sitting.
	Pushes, pulls, and dumps objects while sitting.
	Uses cup and holds spoon in palm and attempts to feed self (messy).
	Picks up small objects with thumb and index finger.
	Makes a few marks on paper.
	Turns two or three book pages at one time.
	Builds a crooked tower of two or three blocks.
	Inserts large objects into holes.
	Removes hat, shoes, socks, and mittens.
18 to 24 Months	Pushes and pulls objects while walking.
	Does a hurried walk that resembles a run (feet do *not* leave surface).
	Steps off of low objects (first stage in jumping).
	Stands on one foot unsteadily.
	Seats self in child-size chair.
	Climbs on furniture.
	Walks stairs without adult help but needs hand railing; does *not* alternate feet.
	Throws ball while standing.
	Squats or bends to "catch" a ball.
	Moves against a ball with foot (*not* a real kick).
	Turns door knobs (23 months).
	Turns pages in a book one at a time.
	Strings large beads on a cord.
	Helps wash hands.
	Scribbles.

Physical *(Continued.)*	
2 to 3 Years	Runs awkwardly, but cannot stop or change directions easily.
	Jumps down with both feet (24 months); jumps up with both feet (28 months).
	Kicks ball with legs straight and little body involvement.
	Climbs on play equipment.
	Rides push and pedal toys.
	"Catches" a ball by bending at the waist to pick it up or by responding to an aerial ball with delayed arm action.
	Begins to show hand preference.
	Has better grip on crayons and pencils.
	Draws or copies vertical lines.
	Drinks from a straw; feeds self with a spoon (less messy).
	Builds a somewhat straighter tower of several blocks.
	Hits pegs with hammer.
	Is ready to start potty training.
Intellectual	
12 to 18 Months	Varies actions on objects to receive many results.
	Notices attributes of objects.
	Uses physical trial and error to solve problems.
	Imitates others—coughing, sneezing, and making animal sounds.
	Looks for hidden objects in last place seen (*rather* mature object permanence).
	Points and vocalizes wants.
	Points to named objects and animals in books.
	Says 3 words (12 months) to 15 or more words (17 months).
	Gestures when talking.
	Uses one-word "sentences."
	Follows one-step directions.
18 to 24 Months	Thinks how to solve some problems without using physical actions.
	Solves simple problems requiring two or three steps.
	Begins deferred imitation.
	Hunts objects in all possible places (object permanence).
	Pictures objects mentally.
	Realizes words have referential meaning (refer to something).
	Says 200 words.
	Uses two- and three-word sentences.
	Enjoys "singing" a few songs.
	Understands questions, such as "Can you show me your eyes?"
	Names pictures in a book.
	Repeats others (20 to 21 months).

Intellectual *(Continued.)*	
2 to 3 Years	Begins to use a few symbols in pretend play, such as a doll for a baby.
	Has many jumbled ideas (preconcepts).
	Says up to 500 words which include names of toys, a color or two, and a few prepositions (*in, under*).
	Uses three- or more-word sentences.
	Laughs at silly labels ("Duck goes *quack, quack*").
	Enjoys some books over and over.
	Repeats a few rhymes.
	Asks for information ("What's dat?") and starts asking "why."
	Watches and listens to stories and other activities on a computer screen.
Social-Emotional	
12 to 18 Months	Seeks attention.
	Shows affection.
	Protests when frustrated.
	Shows intense separation anxiety.
	Resists napping and bedtime even when tired and sleepy.
	Plays alone on floor with toys for a few minutes.
	Looks at the person who is talking to him or her.
18 to 24 Months	Directs another's attention to an object.
	Uses *hi, bye,* and *please* (if reminded).
	Shows some separation anxiety.
	Is shy around strangers.
	Wants things now.
	May be aggressive when frustrated.
	Often responds with *no.*
	Uses possessive words (*me, mine*).
	Shows attachment to a toy or blanket.
	Responds to simple requests.
2 to 3 Years	Verbalizes feelings.
	Shows love to non-caregiving adults, children, and pets.
	Begins to interact more with children.
	Is possessive about toys.
	Fears more real and imaginary things.
	Begins having nightmares.
	Is persistent and demanding.
	Has tantrums.
	Is curious about self (wants to know names of body parts).

Preschool Milestones

Physical

3 Years	Walks with arms swinging alternately. Walks a straight line heel-to-toe. Walks on tiptoes. Runs with some arm movement. Walks upstairs with alternating feet. Stands on preferred foot for a second or two. Hops one to three steps on preferred foot (3½ years). Turns body slightly when throwing a ball. Catches a ball by trapping ball in arms. Pedals a tricycle. Draws lines and encloses space (a crude circle or oval). Manipulates Play-Doh™ and finger paints. Stacks blocks up to about a nine-block tower (somewhat crooked). Works a 20-piece jigsaw puzzle. Handles large interlocking blocks. Buttons and unbuttons clothing; pulls up zipper if started. Draws face with dots for eyes, nose, and mouth.
4 Years	Walks in a line around the periphery of a circle heel-to-toe. Walks a balance beam. Runs with great reciprocal arm action (4½ years). Runs with ability to start, stop, and turn as needed. Walks downstairs with alternating feet. Stands on preferred foot for up to five seconds. Hops four to six steps on preferred foot. Jumps with forward arm motion. Gallops. Pedals and steers tricycle skillfully. Throws ball with a slight weight shift from back to front foot when thrown. Catches a bounced ball with rather stiff, outstretched hands (4 years) and with arms to the side (4½ years) Draws a cross (+). Copies a few capital letters (T, E, F, H). Draws human figure by adding arms and legs extending from face. Uses table flatware. Cuts on a straight line with scissors. Builds a straight tower with blocks. Works a 40-piece jigsaw puzzle. Toilet learning is nearing completion. Dresses and undresses with assistance needed for tying shoes and working difficult fasteners.

Physical *(Continued.)*

5 Years	Runs with good speed. Jumps rope. Ascends and descends slide ladders and play structures with alternating feet. Stands on preferred foot for 10 seconds or longer. Hops eight to 10 steps on preferred foot. Does rhythmic and precision hopping. Skips. Throws ball with definite weight shift. Likes doing physical stunts. Rides bicycle with training wheels. Copies squares and triangles and traces (sometimes copies) diamonds. Copies most letters and writes first name from memory. Colors within lines. Draws human figure with neck, torso, arms and legs extending from torso, and details on face. Cuts and pastes simple shapes. Folds paper horizontally, vertically, and diagonally. Builds with smaller interlocking blocks. Builds taller towers and other structures (bridges, buildings) with blocks. Works a 50-piece jigsaw puzzle. Strings smaller beads on a cord and laces lacing cards. Dresses and undresses without much assistance, including tying shoes.

Intellectual

3 Years	Expresses thinking through pretend play, drawings, and language. Gives illogical "reasons" (relies on appearance of things, confuses cause and effect, and has fantasy ideas about natural events). Matches attributes of objects. Sorts by shape and color. Matches real objects with pictures. Rationally counts two or three objects and rote counts further. Knows about 900 words. Articulates with about 75 percent understandable. Uses four- to five-word sentences. Knows some rules of grammar (*s* sound for plurals; *ed* sound for past tense) but over generalizes rules to include irregular forms (says *singed* instead of *sang*). Understands a few prepositions (*on, in, under*) and a few time words (*now, soon, later*). Says full name, age, and gender. Repeats common rhymes. Tells a simple story often with some incorrect facts and/or incorrect sequence of events. Learns to operate a mouse or trackball; understands what is done with the mouse or keyboard makes things happen on the computer screen; can control the direction of the cursor; and uses a few software programs.

Intellectual *(Continued.)*	
4 Years	Solves some problems correctly through intuition (not true reasoning).
	Enjoys pretending and has a vivid imagination.
	Sorts by shape, color, and size.
	Begins classifying by one attribute (but often changes attributes in mid-stream).
	Rationally counts seven to 10 objects, rote counts further, and recognizes a few numerals.
	Arranges by size (with the help of a base line).
	Knows most basic colors by name.
	Knows some opposites.
	Has some sense of time (but says *yesterday* for the past and *tomorrow* for the future).
	Knows about 1500 words.
	Uses five- to six-word sentences.
	Uses compound and "run on" sentences (by using the word *and*).
	Has trouble with the word order of questions and the use of negatives.
	Names some letters, especially those in his or her name.
	Recognizes a few written words (name, STOP sign, and EXIT sign).
	Understands math words *(more, less, bigger, smaller)*.
	Understands more prepositions *(behind, in front of)*.
	Follows a three-part command.
	Recalls parts of a story and can play a role in a simple story.
	Experiments on the computer with interactive stories and play rooms; dabbles with paint programs; and enjoys sing-a-longs and finding games.
5 Years	Likes pretend play with themes (play house, fire station, zoo, grocery store) and uses props.
	Has better attention span.
	Has better problem-solving skills, but still uses intuition.
	Draws pictures that represent real things (called *representational art*).
	Names basic colors and knows names of some additional colors *(pink, grey, white)*.
	Rationally counts 10 or more objects and may rote count to 100.
	Extends or makes patterns with beads or blocks.
	Knows address, phone number, and parents' names.
	Knows 2000 to 2200 words.
	Articulates most sounds with 90 to 95 percent understandability.
	Uses complex sentences.
	Speaks using present, past, and future tense.
	Recognizes several words in books.
	Sees connection between speaking, writing, and reading.
	Understands books are read from left to right and from top to bottom.
	Enjoys language humor (Dr. Seuss books).
	Identifies the basic components of a computer; uses software programs to reinforce kindergarten learnings (colors, shapes, letters and numbers, sight words, logos, labels, and signs); enjoys more advanced levels of interactive stories, games, and creativity software programs; and begins to use *smart toys*.

Social-Emotional	
3 Years	Seeks attention and approval of adults. Shows affection for special friends. Comforts hurt children. Enjoys helping parents with household tasks. Understands *mine* and *his* or *hers*. Shares toys at times (but may be possessive). Plays "solo roles" rather than "team roles" in pretend play (housekeeping area may have five "mothers"). Expresses a wide range of emotions. Fears the unknown, imagined, and dark; fears pain. Feels jealousy. Displays less aggression when angry (if taught to "use his or her words"). Has less separation anxiety.
4 Years	Is more independent. Seeks attention from friends more than from adults. Plays "team roles" in pretend play. Takes turns, shares, and cooperates (as long as things go his or her way). Is sometimes stubborn and quarrelsome. Resents adult directions and limits and challenges authority. Is boastful at times. Lies to protect himself or herself. Tattles. Uses "shock" words. Fears monsters. Expresses anger by yelling; sometimes regresses to physical expressions of anger. Begins to see self as a whole (body, mind, and feelings).
5 Years	Wants to please adults. Accepts directions and limits and asks permission. Desires friendships. Conforms to his or her friends' dress style and interests. Plays with two or three best friends and excludes others. Protects younger children. Is sensitive to the feelings of other children. Begins to follow rules and plays fairly. Distinguishes right from wrong (but does not recognize intent). Organizes children for pretend play. Shows emotional dependency on parents and teachers. Begins to distinguish fantasy from reality (less fearful of imaginary monsters and events). Argues, but can negotiate solutions to conflicts. Has a gender-role concept.

School-Age Milestones

Physical

6–7 Years	Is constantly active. May fidget. Can skate and jump rope with ease. Has a better sense of balance and timing (seven years). Copies or draws complex shapes. Ties own shoelaces. Uses self-care tools (comb, brush, toothbrush, flatware). Has improved eye-hand coordination.
8–9 Years	Is in rather constant motion—jumps, climbs, and chases. Kicks, throws, catches, and hits balls with growing skill. Has smooth and quick large-motor skills. Enjoys organized games. Dresses self completely. Is skillful with hands; uses tools, does handicrafts, plays musical instruments; writes and draws with control.
10–12 Years	Shows greater strength and endurance. Engages in sports and games. Applies large-motor skills to sports and games. May feel awkward during growth spurt (girls). Has excellent fine-motor coordination.

Intellectual

6–7 Years	Is eager to learn. Begins to rely on reason, rather than perception, in problem-solving. Sees others point of view. Begins to note several aspects of a situation at one time. Begins to note transformations, understand reversibility, and conserve number, continuous quantities, liquid, mass, and length. Wants detailed explanations of some complex "why" and "how" questions. Begins to read (but not expressively), write (with phonetic spellings, such as *kat* for *cat*), and do some arithmetic (six years). Reads more fluently (and with expression) and writes with more correct spellings (seven years). Can do multiple classifications (seven years). Knows day segments—morning, afternoon, and night (six years). Reads clock-time on the hour and half hour (six years). Reads clock-time and calendars fluently (seven years). Uses math in recipes and for counting money (seven years). Uses descriptive phrases in talking. Expresses needs by "begging." Is confused by irrelevant information, complex sentence construction (passive voice), and implied word meanings. Appreciates humor in language. Locates letters, numbers, and special keys on the computer keyboard; begins learning a word processing program; uses subject-specific software programs to reinforce school subjects.

Intellectual *(Continued.)*

8–9 Years	Likes mental competition. Knows days of week, months of year, and day's date. Conserves area. Draws 3-D figures. Knows left and right. Describes objects in detail. Has vocabulary over 5000 words. Is a more proficient reader; enjoys recreational reading. Becomes more advanced in keyboarding and using word processing programs; uses computer peripherals (printers and scanners); uses more sophisticated creativity programs to make slide shows and animations; uses search engines on the Internet to locate information for school assignments; uses skills to do school assignments.
10–12 Years	Likes cooperative (group) learning projects in school and youth groups. Applies math and science concepts to daily activities. Conserves weight and volume. Expresses needs and verbally tries to justify needs. Has a vocabulary of 7200 words. Reads for information and recreation. Can keep information details straight. Writes notes and letters. Learns computer-use ethics; uses digital cameras; begins to use spreadsheets and database software; learns basics of one multimedia software program (HyperStudio); uses computer for school assignments and hobbies and for socializing; uses other high-tech equipment.

Social-Emotional

6–7 Years	Shows industry. May have tantrums (six years). May be boastful. Enjoys peers. Plays with same-sex peers. Can spend time alone. May be afraid of monsters and the dark and may have nightmares (six years). Tattles to check sense of right and wrong (six years). Wants to be right and win in arguments (six years). May be moody (seven years). Wants approval from adults and peers (seven years).

Social-Emotional *(Continued.)*	
8–9 Years	Is sensitive to what others think. Wants to look and act like peers. Is more self-critical. Wants more independence from parents. Has preference for certain friends. Is anxious about school failure. Enjoys group activities. Competes in games. Worries a great deal.
10–12 Years	Shows growing independence. Builds self-image as a worker and can take some responsibilities (household tasks, school and youth projects, homework, and a pet). Cooperates with adults and shows attachment to parents, teachers, and youth leaders. Enjoys family times (extended family gatherings, outings, and vacations). Enjoys talking with peers. Likes to plan with a group. Enjoys youth groups. Is friend-focused. Talks about friends constantly. Shows more loyalty to a best friend than to an adult. Has some interest in boy-girl relationships. Conforms to peer groups. Is self-conscious about appearance, possessions, school work, and activities that lead to self-esteem. Has reality-based fears (the unknown, failure, rejection, and death). Can show tact with others, especially with young children and older adults. Gets feelings hurt easily. Can endure some frustrations, but may be aggressive at times and may complain. Often shows emotional turmoil as body changes (girls).

Recommended Childhood Immunizations

Recommended Immunization Schedule for Ages 0 Through 6
—United States • 2009

For those who fall behind or start late, see the catch-up schedule

Vaccine▼ Age ►	Birth	1 month	2 months	4 months	6 months	12 months	15 months	18 months	19–23 months	2–3 Years	4–6 Years
Hepatitis B	HepB	HepB				HepB					
Rotavirus			RV	RV	RV						
Diphtheria, Tetanus, Pertussis[1]			DTaP	DTaP	DTaP		DTaP				DTaP
Haemophilus influenzae type b			Hib	Hib	Hib	Hib					
Pneumococcal			PCV	PCV	PCV	PCV				PPSV	
Inactivated Poliovirus			IPV	IPV		IPV				IPV	
Influenza						Influena (Yearly)					
Measles, Mumps, Rubella						MMR					MMR
Varicella[2]						Varicella					Varicella
Hepatitis A						HepA (2 doses)				HepA Series	
Meningococcal										MCV	

▮ Range of recommended ages   ▮ Certain high-risk groups

[1.] Pertussis — whooping cough

[2.] Varicella — chicken pox

[3.] Human Papillomavirus — virus that can cause cervical cancer and genital warts (STD); vaccination given to females.

Note: Recommendations are reviewed and updated regularly. Check for updates at the American Academy of Pediatrics (http://www.aap.org).

Recommended Immunization Schedule for Ages 7 Through 18
—United States • 2009
For those who fall behind or start late, see the catch-up schedule

Vaccine▼ Age ►	7–10 Years	11–12 Years	13–18 Years
Diphtheria, Tetanus, Pertussis[1]		DTaP	DTaP
Human Papillomavirus[3]		HPV (3 doses)	HPV Series
Meningococcal	MCV	MCV	MCV
Influenza	Influenza (Yearly)		
Pneumococcal	PPSV		
Hepatitis A	HepA Series		
Hepatitis B	HepB Series		
Inactivated Poliovirus	IPV Series		
Measles, Mumps, Rubella	MMR Series		
Varicella[2]	Varicella Series		

Range of recommended ages   Certain high-risk groups   Catch-up immunization

[1.] Pertussis — whooping cough

[2.] Varicella — chicken pox

[3.] Human Papillomavirus — virus that can cause cervical cancer and genital warts (STI); vaccination given to females.

Note: Recommendations are reviewed and updated regularly. Check for updates at the American Academy of Pediatrics (http://www.aap.org).

Indoor Dangers

Environment

Carbon monoxide (A colorless, odorless toxic gas.)

Possible causes

★ Wood-burning, coal, gas, kerosene, and propane heating devices emit more carbon monoxide than electric heating.

★ Homes with attached garages are at higher risk because vehicles emit carbon monoxide as waste.

★ Cooking on a barbeque grill nearby the house increases risk because carbon monoxide is released in the smoke.

Childproofing measures

★ Maintain fireplaces and heating system.

★ Keep home well ventilated.

★ Keep grill farther from the home. Close doors and windows when using the grill.

★ Install a carbon monoxide detector on each floor in the home. Replace or repair as needed.

★ Learn the warning signs of carbon monoxide poisoning. Seek help at once if these are noted.

Fire

Possible causes

★ Problems with household wiring, electrical appliances, chimney fires, and space heaters are main causes of fires.

★ Accidents with matches, lighters, cigarettes, and candles often lead to fires.

★ Cooking accidents can cause fires.

Childproofing measures

★ Install smoke detectors in every bedroom and near the kitchen. Check monthly and install new batteries twice yearly.

★ Have working fire extinguishers near kitchen and fireplaces.

★ Keep matches, lighters, cigarettes, and candles out of the reach of children.

★ Do *not* leave lit candles or food cooking on the stovetop unattended.

★ Plan escape routes from various rooms of the house. Teach fire safety and escape routes to even very young children.

Lead paint (Used in buildings built before 1978.)

Possible cause

★ Lead poisoning comes from breathing lead dust or fumes or eating paint chips. (Lead causes brain damage.)

Environment *(Continued.)*

Childproofing measure

★ Lead paint must be removed by a professional or covered with an approved sealant.
For more information, check the EPA or CPSC Web sites (search *removing lead paint*).

Inhalants (Substances breathed into the lungs.)

Possible cause

★ Accidental or willful sniffing or "huffing" of glue, paint, felt-tip markers, hair spray, air freshener, etc.

Childproofing measures

★ Keep away from younger children.
★ Talk to school-age children about the danger.
For more information, check the National Inhalant Prevention Coalition Web site.

Structure

Doors, sliding glass

Possible causes

★ Children may walk into or through glass.
★ Fingers can be pinched.

Childproofing measures

★ Block off door, if seldom used, but be sure door can be used in case of an emergency.
★ Put colorful decals on glass at children's eye level.
★ Use doorstop high on doorjamb.

Doors, hinged

Possible causes

★ Fingers can be pinched.
★ Children may lock themselves in the room.
★ Inside doors can lead to unsafe places.
★ Inside doors can lead to outside.

Childproofing measures

★ Use doorstops and door holders to protect fingers.
★ Keep unlocking tools handy and learn how to unlock. Consider removing doorknob locks and install hook-and-eye locks if needed.
★ Use high hook-and-eye locks on outside of door when *not* in room or storage area.
★ Utilize safety gates.
★ Use door monitor that sounds an alarm. Keep doors to the outside locked, but keep keys nearby and out of children's reach.

Electrical outlets

Possible cause

★ Children can be electrocuted by putting fingers or objects in outlets.

Structure *(Continued.)*

Childproofing measures

★   Use outlet safety devices. The best are outlet covers that replace existing plates. When unplugged, a sliding cover snaps into place over outlets.
★   Use power strip covers.
★   Outlets can be sealed with electrical tape.
★   Use devices that replace outlet covers that keep cords plugged in for freezer, television, washer, dryer, and refrigerator.
★   If safe, place heavy furniture in front of outlets that are never or seldom used.

Fireplaces

Possible causes

★   Children can be burned or cause fire in the fireplace to spread throughout the house.
★   Children can be injured in falls against hearth.

Childproofing measures

★   Install a fireplace grill and keep it in place.
★   Keep keys for gas fireplace out of reach.
★   Keep fireplace logs, tools, and matches out of children's reach.
★   Cover sharp corners of hearth.

Heaters and radiators

Possible cause

★   Children can be burned.

Childproofing measure

★   Keep guards around open heaters, radiators, and floor furnaces.

Stairs

Possible causes

★   Children can be injured in falls.
★   Children can be trapped or fall through openings in stair railings.

Childproofing measures

★   Move furniture away from staircases.
★   Install a hardware-mounted safety gate at the top of stairs and three steps from the bottom of stairs. Gate should carry the seal of the Juvenile Products Manufacturers Association.
★   Attach safety netting against railings.

Windows

Possible cause

★   Children can fall through or out of windows.

Childproofing measures

★   Never put furniture or other climbable objects in front of windows.
★   Do *not* depend on locked screens to prevent falls.
★   Open casement windows from the top. Open low windows no more than 4 inches. Use window stops to prevent wider openings.
★   Install window guards with approved release mechanisms for all upper-floor windows and first-floor windows that open onto unsafe surfaces. (For secure mounting, window frame must be in good condition.)
★   Plant shrubs or use soft edging, such as wood chips, under windows.

Furnishings

Appliances, small

Possible causes

★ Appliances can fall on children if dangling cord is pulled.
★ Dangling cords can strangle children.
★ Children can be electrocuted by playing with cord near socket or water.

Childproofing measures

★ Drape cords behind appliances while in use.
★ Put cords out of reach when appliances are *not* in use.
★ Store appliances out of children's reach.

Blinds

Possible causes

★ Double cords on Venetian blinds and continuous-looping drapery cords can loop around neck, causing strangulation.
★ Venetian blinds bought before September 2000 have inner cords that can form loops when *not* locked into position.

Childproofing measures

★ Cut cords and install safety "break-away tassels."
★ Place cords on hooks called *cleats* to keep them out of reach.
★ Continuous-looping drapery cords should be anchored near the floor to keep the cord taut.
★ Keep cribs, playyards, and other furniture away from windows. (Deaths can occur when children play with cords or crawl on furniture and jump or fall off with the cords around them.)
★ Use cordless blinds with a spring-loaded system.

   For additional descriptions and photos of how to make cords safe, see **www.windowcoverings.org**. This site also supplies free repair kits for older blinds.

Curtains

Possible cause

★ Suffocation can occur if curtain is wrapped around head.

Childproofing measures

★ Keep babies and young children away from curtains.
★ Move cribs and playyards out of reach of curtains.
★ If purchasing new curtains, consider buying short ones.

Fans

Possible causes

★ Fingers can be cut by twirling fan blades.
★ Injury can result if fan falls on children.

Childproofing measures

★ Place window screening between fan blades and grills.
★ Keep fans out of children's reach.

Furnishings *(Continued.)*

Floor lamps

Possible cause

★   Injury can result if children pull lamps over.

Childproofing measures

★   Place floor lamps behind sturdy furniture.
★   If buying new, consider smaller table lamps or overhead lighting.

Rugs, area and throw

Possible cause

★   Children can slip or trip over loose rugs.

Childproofing measures

★   Use nonskid pads under rugs or buy rugs with nonslip backing.
★   Tape loose edges of rug to the floor.

Wastebaskets

Possible cause

★   Children can find many harmful objects inside.

Childproofing measures

★   Never place anything in a wastebasket that could harm children. Dispose of medications appropriately. Take unsafe items directly to an outside garbage can. Tie knots in plastic can liners.
★   Use child-resistant covers on all outdoor garbage cans.

Room Dangers

Bathroom

Possible causes

★   Children can drown in toilet.
★   Children can bump into hardware.
★   Children can be burned by hot water or hot hardware in the bathtub.
★   Children can fall or drown in the bathtub.
★   Children can be electrocuted by nearby electric devices when using tub or sink.
★   Children can be poisoned or harmed by personal care items, medicines, and cleaning products.

Childproofing measures

★   Install a toilet lid lock.
★   Install a safety cover on the doorknob or a hook-and-eye lock near top of door outside the bathroom door to prevent children from entering without an adult's knowledge.
★   Put a rubber-covered guard over tub faucet and knobs.
★   Use a nonslip mat in the tub.
★   Have children sit in the tub.
★   Supervise children at all times when they are bathing.
★   Set water heater below 120°F.
★   Run cold water after bath water briefly to cool faucet.
★   Paint hot water faucet with red fingernail polish to help your children remember which faucet is hot.
★   Use only 2 to 3 inches of water when bathing children. Empty tub immediately after bath.
★   Keep personal care products (including baby wash and baby shampoo), medicines, and cleaning products out of the reach of children. Lock these away when *not* in use. Keep them from children's reach when in use, and put them away promptly after use.
★   Unplug bathroom appliances when *not* in use. Never store these plugged in near a bathtub or sink.

Room Dangers *(Continued.)*

Kitchen

Possible causes

★ Sharp utensils or glass items (if broken) can cut children.
★ Doors on large appliances can pinch fingers. Children can crawl inside large appliances and be trapped.
★ Children can be burned with hot beverages, foods, or appliances.
★ Children can be poisoned.
★ Children can fall from high chairs.

Childproofing measures

★ Use safety locks to keep cabinet doors locked. Use plastic safety latches on drawers.
★ Store sharp utensils or glass items in highest and hardest-to-reach places.
★ Set aside one cabinet as a safe place for toddlers to play. Store safe and interesting objects in this cabinet.
★ Use appliance latches and keep these latched when appliances are *not* in use.
★ Use a safety gate to keep children out of the kitchen unless supervised by an adult. Other options are to place children in a playyard nearby or strap children into high chairs and offer safe toys for play.
★ Use heat-resistant stove guard to block access to burners. Cover stove knobs with guards. Use back burners instead of front burners when possible and turn handles of pots and pans toward the center of the stove.
★ Never carry children while cooking or carrying hot items.
★ Keep cleaning products and chemicals locked in high cabinets.
★ Avoid using a tablecloth. (Children can use this to pull hot foods on face or head.)
★ Use high chair straps when securing children in their seat. Keep high chairs away from cabinets or table legs. (Children can push on these with feet and tip a high chair.) Do *not* allow children to "rock" a high chair.

Living room, den, family room, and bedrooms

Possible causes

★ Unstable furniture can fall on children.
★ Furniture with sharp edges or glass components can cause scrapes and cuts.

Childproofing measures

★ Remove unsteady items, such as end tables and plant stands, when possible.
★ Anchor heavy bookcases, shelves, and entertainment centers to the wall with nylon straps screwed into wall studs. Use kits that are made to bolt a TV to your stand.
★ Pad sharp edges of furniture.
★ Remove furniture with glass components. Large glass-front cabinets can be turned toward the wall.
★ Place furniture away from windows and stairs.

Nursery

See Figure 22-12 "Safety Standards for Baby and Toddler Items."

Other Items

Beverages

Possible causes

★ Hot beverages can burn children.
★ Consuming alcoholic beverages can harm children.

Childproofing measures

★ Keep hot beverages out of children's reach.
★ Do *not* carry hot beverages around children or leave these sitting unattended.
★ Keep bottles of alcoholic beverages locked out of the reach of children.

Tools

Possible cause

★ Many tools are heavy or sharp and can cause injuries if used improperly.

Childproofing measures

★ Lock dangerous tools out of children's reach.
★ If children show interest in tools, buy play tool sets or tool sets made for children.

Insects, spiders, and rodents

Possible causes

★ Insects, spiders, and rodents can bite and spread disease.
★ Repellents can be poisonous.
★ Rodent traps can injure children.

Childproofing measures

★ Exterminate for pests.
★ Be careful *not* to allow children into exterminated areas until sprays have been cleaned off surfaces.
★ Keep traps out of children's reach.

Houseplants

Possible cause

★ Many houseplants are poisonous.

Childproofing measures

★ Ask your local extension agency or plant nursery to identify safe plants for houses with young children.
★ Keep all houseplants out of reach of children and teach children *not* to touch or eat the plants.

Glossary

A

abilities. Skills a person has learned or developed. (26)

abstinence. Choice to postpone a sexual relationship until marriage. (25)

abstract. Anything that stands for, but is detached from, the real object, such as words. (17)

acquired immunodeficiency syndrome (AIDS). Disease caused by the human immunodeficiency virus (HIV), which attacks the body's immune system. (5)

active immunity. Immunity in which a person's body produces antibodies to a disease. (22)

active-physical play. Play that uses gross-motor skills. (21)

active vocabulary. Words a person uses in talking or writing. (9)

adoption. Process by which a child of one pair of parents legally becomes the child of other parents (or parent). (2)

adoption agency. State-funded or private agency licensed by the state to handle adoptions. (2)

adult-child ratio. Number of adults per number of children in a group setting. (23)

age-appropriate behaviors. Proper or expected ways to express emotions at certain ages. (10)

age norm. Typical time when a developmental milestone, such as walking or talking, occurs; an age norm can be expressed as an average age or an age range. (8)

age of viability. Age at which most babies could survive if they were born (28th week of pregnancy). (4)

aggression. Attempt to hurt or an act of hurting someone. (19)

aggressive behavior. Outward behavior disorder in which people name-call, fight, or bully without being provoked into such actions. (24)

allergen. Substance that causes an allergic reaction. (22)

allergy. Condition that results when a person's immune system is very sensitive to a particular allergen and reacts negatively when exposed to it. (22)

altruistic behavior. Actions that show concern for others. (19)

amniocentesis. Prenatal test in which a needle is inserted through the woman's abdomen into the amniotic sac and a sample of the fluid is removed for cell study. (5)

amnion. Fluid-filled sac that surrounds the baby in the uterus. (4)

anemia. Condition that occurs when the level of healthy red blood cells, which carry oxygen to all parts of the body, becomes too low. (7)

anger. Feeling caused by frustration. (19)

antibodies. Proteins in the blood that fight disease. (22)

antigens. Substances made in a laboratory and transferred to people in the form of an injection (shot) to help their bodies form antibodies against a disease. (22)

anxiety. Fear of a possible future event. (10)

Apgar test. Test that checks the baby's chance of survival. (7)

aphasia. Partial or total loss of the ability to understand words and use language. (24)

aptitudes. Natural talents. (26)

articulation. Making the sounds of a language. (13)

artificial insemination. Assisted reproductive technology (ART) procedure that involves introducing sperm into the vagina or uterus by a medical procedure rather than by sexual relations. (3)

artificially acquired immunities. Immunities formed as a reaction to antibodies or an antigen received through medical care; also called *acquired immunities*. (22)

assertive. Act of speaking out, standing up for one's rights, and defending oneself. (19)

assisted reproductive technologies (ARTs). Methods infertile couples can use to help them conceive. (3)

attachment. Closeness between people that remains over time. (10)

attachment behaviors. Actions one person demonstrates to another person to show closeness to that person. (10)

attention-deficit disorder (ADD). Disorder that involves the lack of attention, but does not include hyperactive behaviors. (24)

attention-deficit hyperactivity disorder (ADHD). Disorder that involves the lack of attention and extremely active behavior that exceeds a typical high energy level. (24)

attributes. Distinctive characteristics of an object, such as size, shape, color, and texture. (13)

auditory. Term used to refer to the sense of hearing. (20)

au pairs. Professionals who provide child care for host families as part of a cultural exchange program. (23)

authoritarian. Parenting style in which the main objective is to make children completely obedient. (2)

autonomy. Form of self-control in which a person seeks to do his or her will. (14)

axons. Long, thick cables that transmit all the signals from a neuron to other neurons. (1)

B

babble. Making a series of vowel sounds with consonant sounds slowly added to form syllables. (9)

baby blues. Mild postpartum mood disorder that goes away on its own. (6)

behavior disorders. Patterns of problems that surface in a person's behavior. (24)

bias. Belief or feeling that results in unfair treatment of another person or makes such treatment seem right. (23)

binocular vision. Type of vision that involves fusing an image so it appears as one image using both eyes. (9)

birth control methods. Methods couples use to prevent conception. (3)

body proportions. Relative size of body parts. (8)

body rotation. Action of turning the trunk of the body to one side when the hand of the other side is used to throw. (16)

bonding. Developing a feeling of affection. (6)

borderline. Term used to identify a talent as just above average or a problem as mild. (24)

Brazelton scale. Test used to determine whether a baby has problems interacting with the environment, handling motor processes, controlling his or her physical state, or responding to stress. (7)

breech birth position. Buttocks-first position in which some babies enter the birth canal. (6)

C

career burnout. State in which a person becomes emotionally tired of a career. (26)

career clusters. Model of 16 broad groupings of occupational and career specialties. (26)

career plan. Detailed list of steps a person must complete in order to enter a chosen career path. (26)

cartilage. Soft, elastic, flexible tissue that provides structure for the body. (4)

cell. Smallest unit of life that is able to reproduce itself. (4)

center-based child care. Large group program in which child care is provided in a center rather than in a home. (23)

certified child safety seats. Restraint systems for infants and young children that have been tested and approved by federal agencies; also known as *car seats*. (22)

certified nurse midwives (CNMs). Nurses who have special training in delivering babies during normal pregnancies. (6)

cesarean section. Delivery method in which the mother's abdomen and uterus are surgically opened and the baby is removed. (6)

character. Principles and beliefs that guide one's conduct and define one's personality and behavior. (1)

child abuse. Intentional act committed by an adult that harms or threatens to harm a child's well-being. (25)

child care programs. Programs that operate to care for children for extended hours (usually between 9 and 12 hours a day). (23)

child care resource and referral (CCR&R) agencies. Agencies that promote local child care programs and help parents find child care. (23)

child-centered society. Society that sees children as important, cares about their well-being, and works to meet their needs. (1)

child development. Scientific study of children from conception to adolescence. (1)

child development laboratories. Child care programs for children under age five that serve as research sites for child development experts. (23)

child neglect. Harm to or endangerment of a child caused by an adult's failure to do something legally expected of him or her. (25)

child passenger seat (CPS) technician. Professional who provides information on child safety seats and inspects them after installation. (22)

childproofing. Process of moving unsafe objects out of a child's reach or preventing dangerous situations. (22)

children in self-care. Children who are at home alone after school or for a portion of the day and must care for themselves during that time. (25)

child support order. Judgment of the court that states how much the parent who does not live with the children must pay toward the children's expenses. (25)

child with special needs. Child whose development differs from that of the development that is typical for most children of the same age. (24)

chorion. Membrane that surrounds the baby in the uterus. (4)

chorionic villus sampling (CVS). Prenatal procedure for finding abnormalities in the unborn by testing a small sample of the chorion. (5)

chromosomes. Threadlike structures that carry genes in living cells. (4)

chronic. Term used to indicate that a problem will be long-lasting and perhaps lifelong. (24)

class. Group of items that have an attribute in common. (19)

class complement. Term used in classifying to describe any groups of objects that do not belong within the class being considered. (19)

classifying. Ability to choose an attribute and group all the objects from a set (either physically or mentally) that possess that attribute. (17)

closed adoption. Adoption in which the identity of the birthparents and adopting family are not revealed. (2)

codes of professional ethics. Sets of standards created by various professions to govern the conduct of employees in these careers. (26)

cognition. Act or process of knowing or understanding. (9)

colic. Condition in which a baby has intense abdominal pain and cries inconsolably. (7)

collective monologue. Talking to another person, but not listening to what the other person has said. (17)

communication. Skill needed to understand others and to be understood by them. (13)

compare. To see how objects and people are alike. (19)

concept. Idea formed by combining what is known about a person, object, place, quality, or event. (9)

conception. Union of the ovum and sperm cells. (4)

concrete operational stage. Piaget's third stage of mental development, in which children begin to think logically, but base their logic on past experiences. (20)

congenital problem. Physical or biochemical problem that is present at birth and may be caused by genetic or environmental factors. (5)

conservation. Concept that changing an object's shape, direction, or position does not alter the quantities of the object. (20)

consultants. Professionals who share their knowledge, such as knowledge about children, with other adults. (26)

contagious disease. Disease that can be caught from another person. (22)

contrariness. Tendency to oppose almost everything others do or say. (15)

contrast. To see how objects and people are different. (19)

convergent thinking. Coming up with only one right answer or way to do a task. (19)

coo. Light, happy sound babies begin to use to communicate between six and eight weeks after birth. (9)

cooperation. Joint effort; getting along with others and considering their goals. (19)

coordination. Working together of muscles to form movements. (11)

correctable. Term used to indicate that a problem can likely be overcome with the appropriate support. (24)

cover letter. Correspondence sent with a résumé to introduce the accompanying material. (26)

crawl. Moving by pulling with the arms, but not lifting the abdomen from the floor. (8)

creeping. Moving by using the hands and knees or the hands and feet with the abdomen off the floor. (8)

cruising. Walking by holding something for support. (8)

cultural diversity. Having more than one culture represented. (2)

culture. Way of life within a group that includes language, beliefs, attitudes, values, rituals, and skills. (1)

culture shock. Uncomfortable response to an unfamiliar culture. (23)

D

deciduous teeth. First set of teeth, which will later be replaced by permanent teeth; also called *nonpermanent* or *baby teeth*. (8)

deductive reasoning. Reasoning from the general to the specific. (20)

deferred imitation. Ability to recall and later imitate someone's behavior. (13)

democratic. Parenting style in which parents set some rules, but allow children some freedom; also called *authoritative*. (2)

dendrites. Short, bushy cables that allow each neuron to receive signals sent by other neurons. (1)

dental caries. Decayed places in teeth. (22)

dependence. Reliance of one person on another to meet his or her needs. (10)

depressants. Substances that slow the functions of organs and the nervous system. (11)

depth perception. Ability to tell how far away something is. (9)

development. Gradual process of growth through many stages, such as before birth, infancy, childhood, adolescence, and adulthood. (1)

developmental acceleration. When a child performs like an older child. (1)

developmental delay. When a child performs like a younger child. (1)

developmental dyscalculia. Learning disability that affects a child's mathematical abilities. (24)

developmental dyslexia. Learning disability that affects a person's ability to read, write, and spell. (24)

developmentally appropriate practices (DAPs). Child care and education that uses knowledge about child development and considers each child's strengths, needs, interests, and culture. (23)

developmentally inappropriate practices (DIPs). Child care and education that do not use knowledge about child development and focus mainly on the group instead of each child. (23)

developmental tasks. Skills that should be mastered at a certain stage in life. (1)

diabetes. Disorder caused by the body's inability to use sugar properly. (5)

diagnosis. Identifying the cause of a person's illness. (22)

dilation. First stage of labor during which the cervix opens. (6)

direct intervention. Term used to describe a child-related career in which a person works in close contact with children. (26)

direct observation. Watching children in their natural environments. (1)

discipline. Use of methods and techniques to teach children self-control. (2)

disposition. General mood of a person. (10)

divergent thinking. Coming up with different possible ideas. (19)

dominant traits. Traits that always show in a person even if only one gene of the pair is inherited for that trait. (4)

dynamic balance. Balance maintained while moving. (16)

E

educational neglect. Failure to conform to state legal requirements regarding school attendance. (25)

egocentrism. Child's belief that everyone thinks in the same way and has the same ideas as he or she does. (17)

embryo. Medical term used to describe the unborn baby in the embryonic stage of development (week 3 through 8 of pregnancy). (4)

embryonic stage. Second stage of prenatal development, lasting about six weeks. (4)

emotional and verbal abuse. Any act in which an adult makes excessive demands, harasses, belittles, or verbally threatens the child. (25)

emotional dependency. Act of seeking attention, approval, comfort, and contact. (18)

emotional neglect. Inadequate care and attention, violence or drug use in the home, or failure to meet the child's emotional needs at each stage of development. (25)

emotions. Thoughts that lead to feelings and cause changes in the body. (10)

enriched environment. Environment that offers a person many chances to learn. (11)

entrepreneur. Person who creates and owns a business. (26)

enuresis. Any instance of involuntary (accidental) urination by a child over three years of age. (19)

environment. Sum of all the conditions and situations that surround and affect a child's growth and development. (1)

environmental factors. Those factors caused by a person's surroundings. (5)

episiotomy. Incision made to widen the birth canal and prevent tearing. (6)

extended family. Family in which several generations live together. (2)

eye-hand coordination. Ability to coordinate what a person sees with the way the person moves his or her hands. (12)

F

failure to thrive. Condition in which a child fails to grow at a healthy rate. (8)

fallopian tubes. Two hollow tubes that connect to the uterus and have fingerlike projections that reach toward each ovary. (4)

Family and Medical Leave Act. Law that protects the rights of the workers of large companies to take up to 12 weeks of unpaid leave per year for various family-related reasons. (3)

family child care. Care provided by a person for a small number of children in his or her own home. (23)

family life cycle. Series of six stages that many families go through over the years. (2)

family planning. Decisions couples make about the desired number and spacing of future children. (3)

fertility counseling. Medical evaluation that seeks to determine the reasons for fertility problems and explore available treatment options. (3)

fetal alcohol syndrome (FAS). Group of symptoms that appears in infants whose mothers drank during pregnancy. (5)

fetal stage. Third stage of pregnancy, lasting from about nine weeks after conception until birth. (4)

fetus. Medical term used to describe the unborn baby in the fetal stage of development (week 9 until the end of pregnancy). (4)

field trips. Outings that take children to places away from a child care program's property. (23)

filtering program. Program that prevents a child from accessing inappropriate material on the Internet. (22)

fine-motor skills. Being able to use and control the small muscles, especially those in the fingers and hands. (8)

finger foods. Foods a baby can self-feed using the fingers. (11)

fingerplays. Poems and rhymes that are acted out with the hands. (23)

first aid. Emergency treatment for an illness or accident that is given before professional medical help arrives. (22)

flexibility. Ability to move, bend, and stretch easily. (20)

food allergy. Abnormal response to a food triggered by the body's immune system. (15)

forceps. Curved instrument that fits around the sides of a baby's head and is used to help the doctor ease the baby down the birth canal during a contraction. (6)

foregone income. Potential income given up by a parent who leaves the workforce and stays home to raise a child. (3)

formal leadership. People chosen by others to lead a group, such as elected or appointed officials and managers in organized groups. (26)

formal operational stage. Piaget's final stage of mental development, in which a person can reason abstractly. (20)

for-profit programs. Programs set up to make money. (23)

foster families. Families in which adults provide temporary homes for children who cannot live with their birthparents. (2)

fraternal. Term used to describe children from multiple pregnancies who develop from two or more fertilized ova and differ in genetic makeup. (4)

G

gamete intrafallopian transfer (GIFT). Assisted reproductive technology (ART) procedure in which a mixture of sperm and eggs is placed in the woman's fallopian tubes, where fertilization can occur. (3)

gender-role learning. Learning what behavior is expected of males and females. (18)

genes. Sections of the DNA molecule found in a person's cells that determine the individual traits the person will have. (1)

genetic factors. Traits that are passed through the genes. (4)

genetics. Study of the factors involved in the passing of traits from one generation of living beings to the next. (1)

germinal stage. First stage of prenatal development, lasting about two weeks after conception. (4)

gifted and talented. Children who can or who do show high performance in one or more of six key areas. (24)

goals. Things a person wants to achieve or obtain. (26)

grammar. Study of the preferred word usage and order in a given language. (13)

gross-motor skills. Being able to use the large muscles to roll over, sit, crawl, stand, and walk. (8)

growth pains. Muscle aches that occur when the muscles grow rapidly to catch up with increasing skeletal size. (20)

growth spurt. Period of rapid growth. (20)

guardian. Person often chosen by a child's biological parents to take responsibility for the child in the event of the birthparents' death or extended absence. (2)

guidance. Words and actions parents use to influence their children's behavior. (2)

guilt. Blaming oneself for something done wrong. (18)

H

Head Start. Federally sponsored program that was launched to meet the needs of children from low-income families. (23)

hearing impaired. Term used to indicate that a person has hearing loss. (24)

heredity. Sum of all the traits that are passed to a child from blood relatives. (1)

hidden added costs. Costs of child care that add to the direct costs. (23)

hidden cost credits. Credits that lower the direct costs of child care. (23)

hierarchical classification. Having classes within other classes. (20)

hyperactivity. Pattern of extremely active behavior in which a person is overactive, restless, and has a short attention span. (24)

I

identical. Term used to describe children from multiple pregnancies who develop from one fertilized ovum and have the same genetic makeup. (4)

illegal market adoption. Adoption in which a child is bought or sold. This is against the law in all states. (2)

imitating. Copying the actions of someone else. (9)

imitative-imaginative play. Play in which children pretend to be persons or objects other than themselves. (21)

immunity. Body's defense against disease. (22)

immunization. Injection of antigens given to a person to provide immunity from a certain disease. (22)

independent. Wanting to do things for oneself. (10)

independent adoption. Adoption in which a person, such as a lawyer or physician, works out the details between the birthparents and adoptive parents. (2)

indirect costs. Resources used to meet child-related costs that could have been used to meet other goals. (3)

indirect observation. Observation done by methods other than watching children, including asking other people questions about the children and observing the products children make. (1)

Individualized Education Plan (IEP). Educational plan that is tailored to the specific educational needs of a child with special needs between the ages of 3 and 21 years. (24)

Individualized Family Service Plan (IFSP). Plan that focuses on the needs of a family with a child younger than three years of age who has been identified as having special needs. (24)

individual life cycle. Description of the stages of change people experience throughout life. (1)

induction. Technique in which parents discipline by reasoning and explaining. (2)

inductive reasoning. Reasoning from specific facts to general conclusions. (20)

industry. Sense of joining others in striving to become a competent member of society. (20)

inferiority. Feeling that one is incompetent and less valuable as a member of society. (20)

infertile. Term used to refer to a person who is unable to conceive after a year of trying. (3)

inflections. Changes of pitch. (9)

informal leaders. People who lead or guide others even though they are not officially chosen to lead. (26)

in-home child care. Child care that takes place in the child's own home. (23)

initiative. Ability to think or act without being urged. (18)

intellectual development. How people learn, what they learn, and how they express what they know through language. (9)

intensive care nursery (ICN). Special nursery that can provide immediate intensive care just after birth for babies who need it. (7)

internalized. Something that is only thought about and not shared with others. (17)

internal organs. Parts inside of the body, such as the heart, lungs, and liver. (16)

intolerance. Negative physical reaction caused by eating a food. (11)

intuitive substage. Substage of the preoperational stage in which children can solve many problems correctly by imagining how they would act out the solution instead of using logic. (17)

in vitro fertilization (IVF). Assisted reproductive technology (ART) procedure in which some of the mother's eggs are surgically removed, fertilized with sperm in a laboratory dish, and then implanted in the mother's uterus. (3)

IQ tests. Tests that measure how quickly a person can learn, how able a person is to reason using words and numbers, and how easily a person can find solutions to problems. (24)

J

jaundice. Liver condition that can make the skin, tissues, and body fluids look yellow. (7)

joint custody. Term used to describe the shared legal right of parents who are not married to provide care and make decisions about their children's lives. (2)

K

kindergartens. Programs publicly and privately operated for four- and five-year-old children; serve as an entrance to school education. (23)

L

labor. Process that moves the baby out of the mother's body. (6)

Lamaze method. Delivery method in which the pregnant woman is trained to use breathing patterns to keep her mind off pain. (6)

language. Symbol system in which words are used as labels for people, objects, and ideas. (13)

language-logic play. Form of mental play common in school-age children that involves words and logical concepts. (21)

large-muscle development. Development of the trunk and arm and leg muscles. (12)

LATCH system. Attachment installed in new motor vehicles to make child safety seats safer and easier to use. (22)

leader. Person who influences or motivates the thoughts, feelings, or actions of others. (26)

learning disabilities. Problems in one or more areas of spoken or written language, mathematics, and spatial orientation. (24)

legally blind. Person with a level of vision loss that makes him or her eligible to receive certain services. (24)

licensing personnel. Professionals who check the quality of services provided for children, such as the quality of child care centers. (26)

lifestyle. Typical way of life for a person, group, or culture. (26)

lightening. Change in the baby's position in which the uterus settles downward and forward, and the baby descends lower into the pelvis. (6)

logical thinking concepts. Concepts that are not directly experienced through the senses, but are developed through thought. (17)

love withdrawal. Discipline techniques in which parents threaten children with being unloved or suggest some form of parent/child separation. (2)

low birthweight. Term used to describe babies who weigh less than 5½ pounds at birth. (5)

M

mandated reporters. Professionals who are legally bound to report any known or suspected cases of neglect or abuse. (25)

manipulate. To work with an object by using the hands. (16)

manipulative-constructive play. Play that uses fine-motor skills. (21)

manipulative stage. First stage in children's visual-arts development in which they play with art materials rather than use them to create artwork. (21)

maternity leave. Time a woman takes off from work for the birth or adoption of a child. (3)

medical neglect. Harm or endangerment of a child caused by failure to seek treatment for health problems or accidents. (25)

melody percussion instruments. Instruments that produce various pitches when certain bars are struck, such as xylophones. (21)

mental disability. When a person has intellectual abilities that are a year or more delayed when compared with the abilities of other people of the same age. (24)

mental images. Symbols of objects and past experiences that are stored in the mind. (17)

middle childhood. Period of development from 6 to 12 years of age; also called *school-age years*. (20)

miscarriage. Expulsion of a baby from the mother's body before week 20 of pregnancy. (5)

mistrust. Most serious form of not trusting, which includes a lack of trust and feelings of suspicion. (10)

monologue. Talking to oneself as though thinking aloud. (17)

monotone. Sounds all in a single pitch. (9)

Montessori schools. Schools that encourage children to learn independently through the use of highly specialized materials. (23)

moral neglect. Failure to teach the child right from wrong in terms of general social expectations. (25)

mortality rate. Rate of death. (25)

motor development. Use and control of muscles that direct body movements. (8)

multicultural families. Families with members from two or more cultural groups. (2)

multiple pregnancy. Pregnancy in which two or more babies develop. (4)

muscle development. Lengthening and thickening of muscles. (12)

MyPyramid. Food guidance system developed by the USDA to help people make more healthful food and physical activity choices. (15)

N

nannies. Professionals who contract with a family to provide in-home child care. (23)

natural childbirth. Delivery method in which the pregnant woman learns about the birth process and uses breathing and relaxation techniques to reduce fear and pain. (6)

naturally acquired immunities. Immunities that are developed after direct contact with infection or by receiving antibodies from the mother during pregnancy or breast-feeding; also called *natural immunities*. (22)

neonatal intensive care units (NICUs). Heated, completely enclosed beds for newborns who need intensive care. (7)

neonate. Medical term used to describe the baby from birth to one month of age. (7)

neonatology. Branch of medicine concerned with the care, development, and diseases of newborns. (7)

networking. Term used for making professional contacts with family, friends, and other people for job information or referrals. (26)

neurons. Brain cells that send and receive electrical impulses amongst each other to direct the various tasks of the brain. (1)

not-for-profit programs. Child care programs in which income only covers costs. (23)

nuclear family. Family consisting of a father, a mother, and their biological child or children who live together. (2)

nurturance. Providing all aspects of care for a child, which includes meeting physical, mental, and social-emotional needs. (2)

nutrients. Substances in food that give people energy and help them grow. (11)

O

obedience. Acting within the limits set by others. (15)

object concept. Ability to understand that an object, person, or event is separate from one's interaction with it. (9)

object constancy. Ability to understand that objects remain the same even if they appear different. (9)

object identity. Ability to understand that an object stays the same from one time to the next. (9)

object permanence. Ability to understand that people, objects, and places still exist even when they are no longer seen, felt, or heard. (9)

obstetricians. Doctors who specialize in pregnancy and birth. (5)

open adoption. Adoption that involves some degree of communication between the birthparent(s) and adoptive family. (2)

orthodontist. Dentist who specializes in correcting irregular teeth. (22)

orthopedic problems. Problems relating to the bones and muscles. (20)

ossification. Hardening of bones caused by the depositing of the minerals calcium and phosphorus. (8)

ovum. Female sex cell; also called the *egg*. (4)

P

parentese. High-pitched style in which parents speak to their children. (13)

passive immunity. Immunity in which a person obtains antibodies formed by another person's body. (22)

passive observing. Watching another's actions without responding. (19)

passive vocabulary. Words a person understands, but does not say or write. (9)

paternity leave. Time a man takes off from work (usually without pay) for a set period after a child's birth or adoption. (3)

pediatrician. Doctor who cares for infants and children until adulthood (age 21 or 22) when physical growth is complete. (7)

peers. Unrelated children who are near the same age. (18)

perception. Organizing information that comes through the senses. (9)

perceptual learning. Term used to describe the process of developing mental images. (9)

percussion instruments. Musical instruments that produce a tone when struck. (21)

permanent teeth. Set of teeth that begins to come in during the school-age years and is meant to last a lifetime. (20)

permissive. Parenting style in which parents give children almost no guidelines or rules. (2)

personal plan of study. Plan that identifies the core courses and other learning experiences a person must complete to meet his or her educational and career goals. (26)

personal qualifications. All the traits a person has that cannot be learned in career training. (26)

phenylketonuria (PKU). Disease that can cause mental retardation if left untreated by diet. (7)

physical abuse. Violence that results in pain, injuries, or both to a child. (25)

physical disability. Limitation of a person's body or its function. (24)

physical neglect. Endangering a child's health or safety by failing to provide supervision and basic survival needs, such as clothing, food, and shelter. (25)

placenta. Organ filled with blood vessels that nourish the baby in the uterus. (4)

plasticity. Ability of the brain to be shaped and reshaped, which is greatest early in life. (1)

play therapy. Use of play between a child and a trained counselor to help the child resolve certain problems. (21)

portfolio. Organized collection of materials that supports a person's job qualifications. (26)

postpartum care. Care the mother receives during the six to eight weeks following the birth of her baby. (6)

postpartum depression (PPD). Less frequent, but serious form of depression that may occur after giving birth. (6)

postpartum psychosis (PPP). Rare and extremely severe mental illness that may result after giving birth. (6)

power assertion. Discipline technique in which parents use or threaten to use some form of physical punishment. (2)

precision. Ability to perform motor skills accurately. (20)

preconceptual substage. Substage of the preoperational stage in which children ages two to four years are developing some concepts. (17)

pregnancy-induced hypertension (PIH). Name for high blood pressure caused by pregnancy. (5)

premature. Term used to describe babies who are born too soon. (5)

prenatal development. Development that takes place between conception and birth. (4)

preoperational stage. Second of Piaget's developmental stages in which children have begun to do some mental thinking rather than solving all problems with their physical actions. (17)

preschool children. Children between the ages of three and five years. (16)

pre-term birth. Delivery that occurs before 37 weeks of pregnancy. (5)

principles of growth and development. Statements of the general patterns in which growth and development take place in people. (1)

private programs. Programs owned by individuals, churches, or other nongovernment groups. (23)

problem solving. Noting a problem, observing and questioning what you see, and solving the problem. (19)

professional qualifications. Physical, intellectual, and social-emotional skills a person needs to perform well in a career. (26)

profound. Term used to identify a talent as extreme or a problem as severe. (24)

prop box. Container that holds a set of realistic objects related to a certain role for children's use in play. (21)

pruning. Process of weeding out underused or weak pathways between neurons. (1)

psychological security. Feeling that someone cares and will help when needed. (20)

public programs. Child care programs funded by local, state, or federal monies. (23)

Q

quality time. Time when parents are totally attentive to their children. (25)

quickening. Movements of the fetus that can be felt by the mother. (4)

R

reaction time. Time required to respond to a sight, sound, or other stimuli. (16)

recessive traits. Traits that typically do not show in a person unless both genes for the trait are inherited. (4)

reduplication babbling. Repeating the same syllable over and over again. (9)

references. People who know a person well enough to discuss his or her qualifications for a job. (26)

reflexes. Automatic, unlearned behaviors. (7)

registered dietitians. People who have special training in nutrition and diet and meet the qualifications of the American Dietetic Association. (15)

regression. Going back to an earlier stage of development. (15)

regulations. Standards that govern a group program. (23)

representation stage. Second stage in children's visual-arts development in which they create symbols to represent objects, experiences, and feelings. (21)

repressed jealousy. Feelings of jealousy not directly expressed and may even be denied. (18)

resources. Tools a person can use in achieving his or her goals. (26)

restraint systems. Car seats, seat belts, and other devices that hold children safely in place while traveling in a motor vehicle. (22)

résumé. Short, written history of a person's education, work experience, and other qualifications for employment. (26)

reversals. Mentally doing and undoing actions. (19)

Rh factor. Protein substance found in the red blood cells of about 85 percent of the population. (5)

rhythm instruments. Percussion instruments without a definite pitch, such as most drums. (21)

ritual. Pattern of activities repeated at a regular time each day, such as a bedtime story. (15)

role guilt. Feeling of not doing the best job at home or work due to role strain. (25)

role strain. Feeling of having too many tasks to do at one time. (25)

rooting reflex. Reflex that helps babies search for food by turning the head and moving the mouth in response to a touch on the cheeks or mouth. (7)

S

safety recall. Issuing of a notice by the product manufacturer stating the product has been found to be unsafe. (22)

scapegoating. Blaming others for one's own mistakes. (20)

school-age child care (SACC) programs. Programs that provide child care for 5- to 14-year-olds when school is not in session. (23)

school-age children. Children between ages 6 and 12 years. (20)

scientific reasoning. Form of logic commonly used by scientists; also called *inductive reasoning*. (20)

scribbling. Second step in the manipulative stage of visual arts development in which writing consists of dots, straight and curved lines, loops, spirals, and imperfect circles. (21)

self-assertion. Doing as one chooses rather than what others want. (15)

self-assessment. Step in career planning that involves a person identifying his or her interests, aptitudes, and abilities. (26)

self-awareness. Understanding a person has of himself or herself as a person. (11)

self-esteem. Feeling good about oneself and what one can do. (14)

self-restraint. Ability to control oneself. (15)

sensorimotor stage. First of Piaget's stages of cognitive (intellectual) development in which children use their senses and motor skills to learn and communicate with others. (9)

sensory stimulation. Using the senses to learn about the environment. (11)

separate identities. Feelings of being distinct people rather than a unit. (25)

separation anxiety. Anxiety common in babies caused by the fear that loved ones who leave them will not return. (10)

sequenced steps. Steps in growth and development that follow one another in a set order. (1)

sex typing. Treating boys and girls differently. (18)

sexual abuse. Any act of a sexual nature that involves an adult and a child. (25)

sexually transmitted infections (STIs). Infectious illnesses that are passed primarily through sexual intercourse. (5)

sexual stereotyping. Statement or hint that men and women always do or should do certain tasks. (18)

Shaken Baby Syndrome (SBS). Condition in which a baby or young child has injuries as a result of being violently shaken. (25)

shortcomings. Areas in which a person wants or needs to improve. (20)

siblings. Brothers and sisters. (10)

single-parent families. Families headed by one adult. (2)

singletons. Children born one at a time, as opposed to children of multiple births. (25)

six-year molars. First permanent teeth, which grow in behind the second set of deciduous molars. (20)

skeletal system. Body system that includes the bones and teeth. (8)

small-muscle development. Development of small muscles, especially those in the hands and fingers. (12)

social-emotional development. Type of development involving a person's disposition, interaction with people and social groups, and emotions. (10)

social isolation. Feelings of being alone. (25)

socialize. To train a child to live as part of a group, such as the family, culture, or society. (1)

solids. Semi-liquid and mushy foods fed to an infant by spoon. (11)

spatial. Term pertaining to space. (15)

spatial orientation. Ability to see the relationship between objects in space. (24)

speech impaired. Term used to indicate that a person has speech problems. (24)

sperm. Male sex cell. (4)

static balance. Balance maintained while being still. (16)

stepfamilies. Families formed when a single parent marries another person. (2)

sterile. Condition of being permanently unable to conceive or carry fully biological children. (3)

stillbirth. Loss of a fetus after 20 weeks of pregnancy. (5)

stimulants. Substances that speed up the functions of organs, such as the heart and nervous system. (11)

stimuli. Changes in the environment, such as sound or light, that affect the sensory organs causing the person to react. (9)

stressors. Situations that cause stress. (18)

sudden infant death syndrome (SIDS). Syndrome in which a baby dies without warning in his or her sleep. (7)

surrogate mother. Woman who bears (sometimes both conceives and bears) a child for a couple. (3)

symptoms. Evidence of an illness or injury. (22)

synapse. Tiny gap between a dendrite of one neuron and the axon of another across which electrical impulses can be transmitted. (1)

T

teachable moment. Time when a person can learn a new task because the body is physically ready, caregivers encourage and support, and the child feels a strong desire to learn. (1)

temperament. Tendency to react in a certain way to events. (10)

temper tantrum. Sudden emotional outburst of anger commonly displayed by a toddler. (14)

terminally ill. Having a disease that will result in death. (22)

toilet learning. Process by which adults help children learn to use the toilet to manage their elimination needs. (15)

training pants. Special underpants or pants made of disposable diaper material that help lessen the mess of accidents during toilet learning. (15)

transformation. Sequence of changes by which one state is changed to another. (19)

transitional stage. Stage of development in which a person is passing from one stage to another. (15)

transparencies. Pictures that show the inside and outside of an object at the same time, much like an X-ray. (21)

U

ultrasound. Prenatal test in which sound waves bounce off the fetus to produce an image of the fetus inside the womb. (5)

umbilical cord. Cord that connects the baby to the placenta. (4)

uterus. Organ in which the baby develops and is protected until birth. (4)

V

vacuum extraction. Technique that uses suction to help the doctor move the baby down the birth canal as the mother pushes. (6)

values. Ideas, beliefs, and objects that are important and meaningful to a person. (26)

visual. Referring to the sense of sight. (20)

visual arts. Forms of art that create products that appeal to the sense of sight. (21)

visually impaired. Term used to indicate that a person has vision problems or vision loss. (24)

vocabulary. Words a person understands and uses. (9)

voluntary grasping. Intentional grasping of objects. (8)

W

weaning. Gradual process of taking a baby off the bottle or breast. (11)

weight shift. Change of weight from the back foot to the front foot. (16)

well-baby checkup. Routine medical visit in which the doctor examines a baby for signs of good health and proper growth. (7)

window of opportunity. Prime period in a child's life for developing a particular skill if given the opportunity. (1)

wiring. Network of fibers that carry brain signals between neurons. (1)

withdrawn behavior. Behaviors that show a separation from the rest of society, such as not relating well to other people, not wanting changes to occur, and lacking self-esteem. (24)

work ethic. Term used to refer to a standard of conduct and values for job performance. (26)

work-related child care programs. Child care programs funded by businesses for their employees' children. (23)

Z

zygote. Single cell formed at conception; also called a *fertilized egg*. (4)

Index